Harnessing AI, Blockchain, and Cloud Computing for Enhanced e-Government Services

Miltiadis Demetrios Lytras
Effat University, Saudi Arabia

Afnan N. Alkhaldi
Arab Open University Kuwait, Kuwait

Patricia Ordóñez de Pablos
University of Oviedo, Spain

IGI Global
Scientific Publishing
Publishing Tomorrow's Research Today

Vice President of Editorial	Melissa Wagner
Managing Editor of Acquisitions	Mikaela Felty
Managing Editor of Book Development	Jocelynn Hessler
Production Manager	Mike Brehm
Cover Design	Phillip Shickler

Published in the United States of America by
IGI Global Scientific Publishing
701 East Chocolate Avenue
Hershey, PA, 17033, USA
Tel: 717-533-8845
Fax: 717-533-8661
E-mail: cust@igi-global.com
Website: https://www.igi-global.com

Library of Congress Cataloging-in-Publication Data

Names: Lytras, Miltiadis D., 1973- editor. | Alkhaldi, Afnan, 1989- editor. | Ordóñez de Pablos, Patricia, 1975- editor.
Title: Harnessing AI, blockchain, and cloud computing for enhanced e-Government services / edited by: Miltiadis Lytras, American College of Greece, Greece, Afnan Alkhaldi, Arab Open University, Kuwait, Patricia Ordóñez de Pablos, University of Oviedo, Spain.
Description: Heshey, PA : IGI Global Scientific Publishing, [2025] | Includes bibliographical references and index. | Summary: "The primary objective of this book is to provide a comprehensive resource that highlights the innovative applications of AI, Blockchain, and Cloud Computing in the public sector"-- Provided by publisher.
Identifiers: LCCN 2024051502 (print) | LCCN 2024051503 (ebook) | ISBN 9798369376782 (hardcover) | ISBN 9798369376799 (paperback) | ISBN 9798369376805 (ebook)
Subjects: LCSH: Public administration--Data processing--Case studies. | Electronic government information--Case studies. | Artificial intelligence--Industrial applications--Case studies. | Blockchains (Databases)--Industrial applications--Case studies. | Cloud computing--Industrial applications--Case studies.
Classification: LCC JF1525.A8 H374 2025 (print) | LCC JF1525.A8 (ebook) | DDC 351--dc23/eng/20250106
LC record available at https://lccn.loc.gov/2024051502
LC ebook record available at https://lccn.loc.gov/2024051503

British Cataloguing in Publication Data
A Cataloguing in Publication record for this book is available from the British Library.

Table of Contents

Detailed Table of Contents

This chapter examines the historical development and future potential of Artificial Intelligence (AI), Blockchain, and Cloud Computing within public administration. It traces the transition from traditional, manual administrative processes to the adoption of digital technologies, highlighting how cloud computing has transformed data management and accessibility. AI has advanced from simple rule-based systems to complex machine learning models, enabling predictive analytics and automation in public services. Looking ahead, the chapter discusses the promising future of AI-driven predictive governance, decentralized systems powered by blockchain, and the continued evolution of scalable and flexible infrastructure through cloud computing, shaping the future of public sector governance.

The chapter addresses the rapid adoption of technologies such as Artificial Intelligence (AI), Blockchain, and Cloud Computing in public administration, highlighting their potential to improve the efficiency and transparency of government services in Spain. However, it also focuses on the political, regulatory, and ethical challenges that arise, such as data privacy, cybersecurity, and equity in access to services. The importance of self-regulation and collaboration between the public and private sectors is emphasized to ensure the responsible and beneficial implementation of these technologies. Additionally, comparative strategies among EU and Anglo-Saxon

This book chapter explores the potential of AI in modernizing public administration and services with a specific focus on the Philippines. It examines how AI technologies improve administrative efficiency, streamline public services, and enhance decision-making in key areas such as administrative efficiency, law enforcement, disaster management, education, data privacy, cybersecurity, information dissemination, social services, and legal practice. The chapter highlights global trends and innovations in AI applications and considers their implications for the Philippine government. It also addresses the challenges of AI adoption including algorithmic bias, privacy concerns, and technical constraints. Drawing on case studies and examples from various countries, the chapter provides recommendations for strategic AI implementation in the Philippines which stressed the need for capacity-building, policy frameworks, and ethical considerations to ensure the responsible use of AI in public service.

This research chapter aims to identify the efforts blockchain can make in improving the land and property registries by overcoming the issues like fraud, corruption, ineffectiveness, and low transparency. The chapter highlights the three primary advantages of the blockchain: decentralization, smart contracts, and the generation of immutable records via block usage. This research proposes a framework for blockchain integration and discusses the key components of the integration process,

Hence, it is crucial to develop an Enterprise Architecture (EA) framework that defines the business processes, technical infrastructure, and information systems to provide SG services successfully. Therefore, this research aims to develop the EA framework for Nusantara's SG domain, ensuring that the smart features within the domain are aligned to enhance the ease of doing business in Nusantara. To obtain its objective, this study utilized The Open Group Architecture Framework (TOGAF) as a comprehensive approach to the domain's planning, design, implementation, and management.

This chapter explores the integration of artificial intelligence (AI), blockchain, and cloud computing as a transformative force in modernizing e-government solutions. It highlights how these technologies synergize to enhance efficiency, transparency, and security in public administration. AI's ability to process large datasets and automate decision-making, Blockchain's secure and immutable ledger for trustworthy transactions, and cloud computing's scalable infrastructure collectively offer governments the tools needed to meet the growing demands of the digital age. This chapter examines practical applications like resource allocation, cybersecurity, and data analysis, emphasizing their role in enhancing trust and accountability in governance. Moreover, it showcases global case studies of successful e-government initiatives and provides a roadmap for implementing a holistic digital government strategy. This chapter serves as a comprehensive guide for policymakers and technologists involved in public sector digital transformation.

Given the rapid transformations brought about by artificial intelligence across all sectors and in lifestyle, knowledge is ever-present, and its management is essential. Therefore, public services need to innovate to meet social and organizational demands, focusing on solving complex problems that require new knowledge and effective governmental strategies. This chapter details, through a scoping review, how knowledge management (KM) is used in public sector innovation (PSI) and how artificial intelligence (AI) facilitates this interaction. As a result, it was evident that KM, facilitated by AI, offers a promising path for public organizations, enabling the creation of more adaptive, efficient, and citizen-centered solutions. However, the successful integration of AI and KM still requires ongoing efforts to adapt to new technologies, develop digital skills and competencies of public servants, and implement inclusive public policies that consider the ethical and social implications of these technologies. Future studies should focus on research about Ethics and Transparency in AI.

This chapter examines how to restructure service provision processes in government organizations using modern ICT. Precisely, the chapter discusses the role of smart governance in improving service delivery by focusing on smart applications. The chapter emphasizes that the practice has gone beyond the traditional e-government. At present, smart governance initiatives focus, in addition to services availability, on the idea of integrating various types of public services. The chapter also emphasizes that the application of the AI-augmented smart government would enhance the process of designing and providing government services. AI-augmented smart government applications also enhance the level of transparency in government agencies and advance the values of accountability and integrity in the various activities of the state's administrative apparatus.

This chapter assesses the significance of digital technologies on tourist arrivals in Australia, France, India, Italy, Japan and Saudi Arabia during 2009 – 2020. It developed a linear regression equation to observe role of digital technologies in tourism sector. The results based on Panel FGLS model infer that broadband subscription, use of internet, IT investment and mobile phone subscription showed a significant impact on tourist arrivals. Digital technologies like broadband subscription, internet access, internet expenditure and mobile subscription are essential to promote tourism sector. It suggests policy implications to increase digital technologies for further development of the tourism industries. Digital technologies are also positive to increase smart tourism, and sustainable development in these countries. Smart tourism is favourable for achieving SDGs in the mentioned countries. Scope of further research directions in the area of digital technologies and tourism industries are also identified in this chapter.

An Electronic Health Records System is a digitized version of a patient's medical records that are stored electronically. The current system that Hospitals use to store digital patient information and medical records faces numerous obstacles.These systems fail to balance data security and open threats to hackers and unauthorized access which can lead to cyberattacks. The chapter explores how AI, Blockchain and Cloud Computing are combined to overcome these challenges. Blockchain creates a decentralized, transparent, and immutable system providing a robust framework for secure and efficient management of patient records by using Hyperledger Fabric, Amazon Web Service with a React.js front-end to deliver a great experience to users. This proposed architecture provides data security, improves integration issues, operational costs and provides a safe, scalable, and patient-centric approach, and represents a substantial development in healthcare data management with the integration of serverless computing with blockchain technology.

The global spread of the COVID-19 pandemic clearly altered the trajectory of the electronic governance adoption, also known as e-governance. In response to this challenge, governments, organisations, and individuals swiftly adopted various strategic digital coping and adaptation mechanisms. This chapter examines the global efforts of some countries to adopt e-governance, their level of preparedness, and the challenges they face. The areas of health, education, and finances are important because of their significant direct and indirect impact on individual well-being. However, there are challenges related to data management, security, and privacy. Regardless of the existence of a pandemic, governments worldwide must consistently evaluate their readiness for pandemics by formulating favourable policies that can achieve reliable and inclusive implementation of future digital solutions.

Preface

The advent of cutting-edge technologies like Artificial Intelligence (AI), Blockchain, and Cloud Computing is transforming the public sector, bringing unprecedented opportunities to modernize governance, improve service delivery, and foster citizen engagement. Governments worldwide are leveraging these technologies to build smarter, more efficient systems capable of addressing complex societal challenges. However, adopting and integrating these tools in e-government systems also presents challenges related to regulatory frameworks, ethical considerations, and technical complexities.

This book, **"Harnessing AI, Blockchain, and Cloud Computing for Enhanced e-Government Services"**, is a comprehensive exploration of the transformative potential of these technologies in the context of public administration. It brings together theoretical insights, empirical research, case studies, and best practices from across the globe, providing a robust resource for policymakers, technologists, researchers, and practitioners committed to driving innovation in the public sector.

Purpose and Vision

The primary aim of this volume is to illuminate the ways in which AI, blockchain, and cloud computing can be harnessed to create efficient, transparent, and citizen-centric e-government solutions. By examining a range of applications—from smart governance and healthcare to education and tourism—this book seeks to address both the opportunities and the challenges associated with the adoption of these technologies. It highlights actionable strategies for designing resilient, inclusive, and ethical digital societies.

Coverage of Topics

The chapters in this volume span a wide array of topics, organized into thematic areas:

- **Foundations and Historical Context**: The evolution of AI, blockchain, and cloud computing in public administration and their future potential.
- **Policy and Ethical Considerations**: Addressing the regulatory, political, and ethical challenges associated with deploying these technologies.
- **Sector-Specific Applications**: Real-world examples of AI, blockchain, and cloud computing in fields like healthcare, education, property management, and tourism.
- **Technology Integration**: Frameworks and strategies for combining AI, blockchain, and cloud computing to create comprehensive e-government platforms.
- **Future Innovations**: Insights into emerging trends and their implications for public service delivery.

Overview of the Chapters

This section provides a detailed overview of the chapters included in **"Harnessing AI, Blockchain, and Cloud Computing for Enhanced e-Government Services"**. Each chapter addresses critical aspects of technology adoption in public administration, offering diverse methodologies, contributions, and implications for the field.

Introduction to the Theme

This chapter sets the foundation for the book, introducing the key themes of AI, blockchain, and cloud computing in e-government. It highlights their transformative potential in modernizing governance, improving public service delivery, and addressing societal challenges.

Approach: Introduces the thematic concepts and lays a conceptual framework for exploring technology-driven e-government.

Contribution: Provides a comprehensive overview of the relevance of emerging technologies in governance.

Implications: Establishes the foundational understanding necessary to engage with the book's discussions.

Chapter 1: Historical Context and Future Prospects of AI, Blockchain, and Cloud Computing in Public Administration

This chapter explores the evolution of these technologies, from early applications to their transformative roles in governance today. It examines AI's predictive capabilities, blockchain's transparency, and cloud computing's scalability. The chapter also anticipates future advancements in decentralized systems and predictive governance.

Approach: Combines historical analysis with future projections to explore the role of these technologies in governance.

Contribution: Highlights the progression and potential of AI, blockchain, and cloud computing in public administration.

Implications: Guides policymakers and technologists in understanding the evolution and future of e-government innovations.

Chapter 2: Political, Regulatory, and Ethical Concerns of AI, Blockchain, and Cloud Computing in Public Administration

Focusing on Spain and EU countries, this chapter addresses the political, regulatory, and ethical challenges in adopting AI, blockchain, and cloud computing. It explores key concerns such as data privacy, cybersecurity, and equitable access, offering strategies for an inclusive and ethical digital transition.

Approach: Employs a comparative analysis of challenges and strategies for responsible technology adoption in governance.

Contribution: Provides actionable recommendations for addressing regulatory and ethical challenges in public administration.

Implications: Equips policymakers with tools to ensure ethical and inclusive implementation of digital technologies.

Chapter 3: AI-Driven Decision Making Enhancing Public Sector Efficiency and Effectiveness

This chapter applies the ABCD framework (AI, Blockchain, Cloud, Data Analytics) to public sector governance, showcasing how these technologies optimize service delivery and policymaking. It emphasizes data-driven solutions while addressing ethical concerns.

Approach: Introduces a structured framework for leveraging emerging technologies in decision-making.

Contribution: Demonstrates the potential of data-driven governance in improving public sector efficiency and transparency.

Implications: Encourages adoption of ethical frameworks to address biases and privacy challenges in digital governance.

Chapter 4: AI-Driven Innovations in E-Government: How AI is Reshaping the Public Sector?

This chapter explores how AI is transforming e-government services by enhancing operational efficiency and citizen engagement. It also examines challenges such as data privacy and algorithmic bias while presenting strategies for ethical AI integration.

Approach: Examines AI-driven innovations and their implications across key public sector domains.

Contribution: Highlights the potential and challenges of AI integration in e-government.

Implications: Guides governments in balancing innovation with ethical considerations in public administration.

Chapter 5: Trends and Applications of AI in Enhancing Public Administration and Services: Implications for the Philippines

Focusing on the Philippines, this chapter explores AI's role in modernizing public administration, with case studies on disaster management, education, and law enforcement. It emphasizes capacity-building and ethical implementation in developing economies.

Approach: Combines case studies and strategic recommendations to showcase AI's role in governance.

Contribution: Highlights AI's potential to address governance challenges in developing countries.

Implications: Provides actionable strategies for AI adoption in the public sector of emerging economies.

Chapter 6: Land and Property Registries: Utilizing Blockchain for Transparent and Immutable Records

This chapter proposes a blockchain framework for secure and transparent land registries. Using examples from Georgia, Sweden, and India, it discusses smart contracts, decentralization, and immutable records to address issues like fraud and corruption.

Approach: Develops a blockchain-based framework for property management and registry systems.

Contribution: Demonstrates blockchain's potential to enhance accountability and safeguard property rights.

Implications: Encourages governments to adopt blockchain for secure and efficient land management systems.

Chapter 7: MediSecure: A Decentralized Framework for Electronic Health Record Management Using Blockchain and IPFS

This chapter introduces MediSecure, a blockchain-based framework integrated with IPFS for secure healthcare data management. It highlights scalability, robust security, and data integrity as key benefits.

Approach: Proposes an innovative framework for managing electronic health records securely and efficiently.

Contribution: Demonstrates advancements in healthcare data security using blockchain and decentralized systems.

Implications: Offers healthcare administrators a scalable, patient-centric solution for managing sensitive data.

Chapter 8: Application of Cloud Computing Technology for Enhanced E-Government Services in Edo State

This chapter explores how cloud computing has improved e-government services in Edo State, Nigeria. It examines the challenges and benefits of adopting digital infrastructure for equitable service delivery.

Approach: Presents a case study of cloud computing implementation in a regional e-government context.

Contribution: Highlights the role of cloud infrastructure in overcoming barriers to public service access.

Implications: Encourages governments to design inclusive and scalable e-government systems using cloud technology.

Chapter 9: Enhancing Cloud Security Strategies to Mitigate Critical Threats

This chapter addresses key cloud security concerns, including data breaches, unauthorized access, and misconfigurations. It proposes strategies to mitigate these risks, ensuring secure cloud deployments for e-government.

Approach: Analyzes common cloud security risks and provides technical mitigation strategies.

Contribution: Offers practical solutions to address critical security challenges in cloud computing.

Implications: Guides IT administrators in ensuring the security of cloud-based public services.

Chapter 10: TOGAF-Based Enterprise Architecture Framework for Nusantara Smart Governance Domain

This chapter utilizes TOGAF to design a smart governance framework for Nusantara, Indonesia's new capital. It aligns enterprise architecture with the goals of smart governance to promote stakeholder collaboration.

Approach: Applies enterprise architecture principles to develop a smart governance framework.

Contribution: Aligns digital infrastructure with governance goals, enhancing service delivery.

Implications: Provides a roadmap for integrating enterprise architecture into digital governance strategies.

Chapter 11: Integrating AI, Blockchain, and Cloud Computing for Enhanced e-Government Solutions

This chapter examines how these technologies synergize to create comprehensive e-government platforms. It includes global case studies demonstrating successful integration.

Approach: Analyzes the interplay of AI, blockchain, and cloud computing in e-government.

Contribution: Offers a blueprint for developing holistic digital government strategies.

Implications: Guides policymakers in implementing integrated and scalable e-government solutions.

Chapter 12: Knowledge Management in Public Sector Innovation Optimized by Artificial Intelligence

This chapter explores how AI-facilitated knowledge management drives innovation in public services. It emphasizes the need for digital competencies and inclusive public policies.

Approach: Conducts a scoping review of AI's role in knowledge management for public sector innovation.

Contribution: Highlights AI's potential to create adaptive, efficient, and citizen-centered solutions.

Implications: Encourages public organizations to adopt AI for knowledge-driven governance.

Chapter 13: Delivering Public Service in the Age of Digital Era Governance: The Potentials of AI for Smart Government Applications Qatar

This chapter discusses AI-augmented smart governance applications in Qatar, focusing on transparency, accountability, and service integration.

Approach: Explores smart governance applications enhanced by AI technologies.

Contribution: Demonstrates how AI supports transparency and efficiency in public service delivery.

Implications: Offers a model for implementing AI-driven governance globally.

Chapter 14: Impact of Digital Technologies on Tourist Arrival in Selected Economies

This chapter analyzes how digital technologies influence tourism in selected economies, emphasizing the role of broadband, internet access, and mobile subscriptions.

Approach: Uses statistical models to assess the impact of digital infrastructure on tourism.

Contribution: Highlights the positive effects of digital technologies on smart and sustainable tourism.

Implications: Provides policy recommendations for leveraging digital tools to boost the tourism sector.

Chapter 15: E-Health Transforming Healthcare Delivery with AI, Blockchain, and Cloud

This chapter explores the integration of AI, blockchain, and cloud computing to improve healthcare data management and service delivery.

Approach: Proposes a hybrid architecture for managing electronic health records.

Contribution: Highlights security, scalability, and efficiency benefits of the proposed solution.

Implications: Provides healthcare systems with a framework for robust, patient-centric data management.

Chapter 16: Impact of COVID-19 on Electronic-Governance Adoption: Building Resilient and Inclusive Digital Societies

This chapter examines how the COVID-19 pandemic accelerated the adoption of e-governance globally. It focuses on areas such as healthcare, education, and finance, highlighting the challenges of data management, privacy, and security. The chapter emphasizes the need for governments to establish policies that ensure reliable and inclusive digital governance, even in crises.

Approach: Conducts a comparative analysis of global e-governance strategies during the pandemic and their outcomes.

Contribution: Highlights the role of digital technologies in maintaining governance continuity during crises and the importance of preparedness for future disruptions.

Implications: Provides recommendations for building resilient and inclusive e-governance systems that are adaptable to both routine and emergency scenarios.

Framework for Harnessing AI, Blockchain, and Cloud Computing for Enhanced e-Government Services

The framework provides a structured summary of the **coverage**, **impact**, and **contribution** of the book. It categorizes the chapters into thematic areas and connects them with their broader implications for e-government services.

1. Coverage

The book spans five thematic areas, addressing the diverse dimensions of e-government transformation through AI, blockchain, and cloud computing.

Table 1

Theme	Chapters Covered	Key Focus Areas
Foundations and Historical Context	Chapters 1, 2	Evolution of technologies, foundational concepts, and future prospects in public administration.
Policy, Regulation, and Ethics	Chapters 3, 18	Addressing political, regulatory, and ethical concerns in adopting emerging technologies in governance.
Sector-Specific Applications	Chapters 6, 7, 8, 9, 14, 15, 16, 17	Applications in education, healthcare, tourism, land management, and public service delivery.
Technology Integration	Chapters 4, 5, 12	Synergizing AI, blockchain, and cloud computing for comprehensive e-government solutions.
Future Trends and Innovations	Chapters 10, 11, 13	Emerging trends, security strategies, and knowledge management for smarter, more inclusive e-government.

2. Impact

The book addresses the needs of multiple stakeholder groups, providing both theoretical insights and practical strategies for e-government transformation.

Table 2

Stakeholder Group	Impact
Governments and Policymakers	Provides actionable frameworks and case studies for ethical and effective adoption of digital technologies in governance.
Public Sector Technologists	Offers technical insights into implementing AI, blockchain, and cloud systems, with a focus on scalability and security.
Academics and Researchers	Expands the theoretical understanding of e-government technologies and their societal implications.
Citizens and Society	Demonstrates how technology-driven governance enhances transparency, equity, and accessibility of public services.
Global Development Agencies	Highlights the role of digital tools in fostering resilient, inclusive, and sustainable governance systems.

3. Contribution

The book's multidimensional contributions span theory, practice, and policy, offering valuable resources for advancing e-government innovation.

Table 3

Dimension	Details
Theoretical Advancements	Enhances understanding of AI, blockchain, and cloud computing's roles in public administration.
Practical Applications	Provides detailed case studies, frameworks, and best practices for real-world implementation.
Policy Insights	Highlights regulatory, ethical, and political challenges, proposing strategies for inclusive digital transformation.
Cross-Sector Innovations	Explores applications across education, healthcare, tourism, and other domains, showcasing interdisciplinary impacts.
Future-Ready Solutions	Offers insights into emerging trends, security challenges, and the integration of cutting-edge technologies.

A Vision for the Future

As the digital transformation of governments continues to accelerate, the integration of AI, blockchain, and cloud computing will play a crucial role in shaping future governance. By enabling transparency, scalability, and citizen-centric design, these technologies promise to build resilient systems that address the growing demands of modern societies. This book aspires to contribute to this vision, offering a roadmap for researchers and practitioners to harness these technologies effectively and ethically.

Acknowledgments

We extend our heartfelt gratitude to the contributors whose expertise and dedication have made this volume possible. We also thank our editorial team and reviewers for their invaluable support in ensuring the quality and coherence of this publication.

Invitation to Readers

We invite you to explore the chapters in this volume, which offer not only a deep dive into the technical and theoretical aspects of AI, blockchain, and cloud computing but also practical insights into their implementation in e-government services. It is our hope that this book serves as both a guide and an inspiration for advancing digital governance in service of inclusive and sustainable societies.

Miltiadis D. Lytras
Effat University, Saudi Arabia

Afnan Alkhaldi
Arab Open University, Kuwait

Patricia Ordóñez De Pablos
University of Oviedo, Spain

Chapter 1
Historical Context and Future Prospects of AI, Blockchain, and Cloud Computing in Public Administration

Rajeshwari Sissodia
https://orcid.org/0000-0002-9978-0187
Galgotias University, India

ManMohan Singh Rauthan
Hemwati Nandan Bhaguna Garhwal University, India

Varun Barthwal
https://orcid.org/0000-0002-5289-9471
Hemwati Nandan Bhaguna Garhwal University, India

Vinay Dwivedi
https://orcid.org/0009-0007-7502-3222
Galgotias University, India

ABSTRACT

This chapter examines the historical development and future potential of Artificial Intelligence (AI), Blockchain, and Cloud Computing within public administration. It traces the transition from traditional, manual administrative processes to the adoption of digital technologies, highlighting how cloud computing has transformed data management and accessibility. AI has advanced from simple rule-based systems

DOI: 10.4018/979-8-3693-7678-2.ch001

to complex machine learning models, enabling predictive analytics and automation in public services. Looking ahead, the chapter discusses the promising future of AI-driven predictive governance, decentralized systems powered by blockchain, and the continued evolution of scalable and flexible infrastructure through cloud computing, shaping the future of public sector governance.

1.INTRODUCTION

The rapid advancement of technology has significantly altered how governments operate and interact with citizens. Public administration, traditionally characterized by bureaucratic processes and extensive paperwork, has gradually transformed into a more efficient, transparent, and responsive system due to technological innovation. Among the various technological advancements, Artificial Intelligence (AI), Blockchain, and Cloud Computing stand out as particularly transformative for public administration. These technologies not only streamline operations but also enable new forms of governance that are more inclusive, secure, and adaptable to the needs of modern society.

This chapter provides an introduction to the role of technological innovation in public administration. It sets the stage by outlining the evolution of technology in governance, emphasizing the importance of AI, Blockchain, and Cloud Computing. The chapter also defines the purpose and scope of the study, detailing the objectives and key questions that guide the analysis. Additionally, it outlines the methodology used to conduct the research, including the approaches, sources, and limitations.

1.1 Overview of Technological Innovation in Public Administration

The evolution of technology in governance has been a gradual but transformative process. In the early stages of public administration, government operations were predominantly manual, relying on vast amounts of paperwork and human resources to manage information and deliver services. This often led to inefficiencies, delays, and a lack of transparency in government processes. The introduction of information technology in the mid-20th century marked a significant turning point. With the advent of computers, government agencies began automating routine tasks, which reduced the administrative burden and increased the accuracy and speed of information processing.

As technology continued to advance, the digitization of government services became more prevalent. The 1990s saw the rise of e-Government initiatives, where digital platforms were introduced to provide citizens with online access to public services, such as tax filing, license renewals, and social security applications. This shift towards digital governance not only improved service delivery but also enhanced citizen engagement by making government processes more accessible and transparent.

In the 21st century, the emergence of advanced technologies such as AI, Blockchain, and Cloud Computing has further revolutionized public administration. These technologies offer new possibilities for improving the efficiency, transparency, and responsiveness of government operations. They enable the automation of complex decision-making processes, secure and transparent record-keeping, and the provision of scalable digital services, fundamentally changing how governments interact with citizens and manage public resources.

1.2 Importance of AI, Blockchain, and Cloud Computing

AI, Blockchain, and Cloud Computing have become integral to modern public administration, each contributing uniquely to the advancement of governance.

- **Artificial Intelligence (AI):** AI is transforming public administration by enabling the automation of decision-making processes, enhancing predictive analytics, and improving service delivery. AI systems can analyze large datasets quickly and accurately, providing valuable insights that help governments make informed decisions. For instance, AI can be used to predict social service needs, optimize traffic management, and detect fraudulent activities. By automating routine tasks, AI also frees up human resources for more strategic roles, thereby increasing the overall efficiency of public administration.
- Blockchain Technology: Blockchain offers a decentralized and immutable ledger system that enhances the transparency, security, and trustworthiness of government operations. Its ability to securely record transactions without the need for intermediaries makes it ideal for applications such as land registries, identity verification, and public procurement. Blockchain ensures that records are tamper-proof and accessible, thereby reducing the potential for fraud and corruption. In addition, it promotes accountability by providing a clear audit trail of government activities.
- Cloud Computing: Cloud Computing provides the infrastructure necessary for delivering scalable, efficient, and cost-effective digital services. By enabling governments to store and process large volumes of data on remote servers, cloud computing reduces the need for expensive on-premise hardware and allows for greater flexibility in service delivery. It supports the seamless integration of various digital services, enabling governments to offer citizens a more unified and user-friendly experience. Furthermore, cloud

computing facilitates collaboration among different government agencies by providing a centralized platform for data sharing and communication.

In summary, AI, Blockchain, and Cloud Computing are not just tools for modernization but are essential components of a future-oriented public administration system. Their adoption is key to building smarter, more resilient, and more responsive governance structures that can meet the evolving needs of society. As governments continue to explore and implement these technologies, they have the potential to significantly enhance public trust, improve service delivery, and create more inclusive and participatory forms of governance.

1.3 Purpose and Scope of the Study

The primary objective of this book/report is to explore the historical development and future prospects of AI, Blockchain, and Cloud Computing in public administration. It aims to provide a comprehensive analysis of how these technologies have been integrated into government operations and their potential to revolutionize public administration in the coming years. By examining past experiences, current trends, and future possibilities, this study seeks to offer valuable insights to policymakers, public administrators, and scholars interested in the digital transformation of governance.

1.4 Key Questions and Areas of Focus

The study focuses on several key questions: How have AI, Blockchain, and Cloud Computing evolved historically within the context of public administration? What are the specific use cases and success stories of these technologies in various government sectors? What challenges have been encountered during their adoption, and how have they been addressed? What are the potential future applications of these technologies in public administration, and what impact could they have on governance and public services? The study also explores the ethical, legal, and social implications of integrating these technologies into government operations.

1.5 Methodology

The research for this study is conducted using a multi-method approach, combining qualitative and quantitative research techniques. A comprehensive literature review forms the foundation of the study, analyzing existing academic research, government reports, and case studies related to AI, Blockchain, and Cloud Computing in public administration. In addition, interviews with experts in the field, including policymakers, technologists, and public administrators, provide firsthand insights into the practical challenges and opportunities of implementing these technologies. The study also utilizes case studies of specific government projects to illustrate the real-world applications and outcomes of these technologies.

1.6 Limitations and Assumptions

While the study aims to provide a thorough analysis, there are certain limitations to consider. First, the rapid pace of technological change means that some of the findings may become outdated as new developments occur. Additionally, the study assumes that the data and case studies examined are representative of broader trends in public administration, though variations may exist between different countries and regions. Moreover, the focus is primarily on the application of these technologies in public administration rather than on their technical aspects, meaning that the depth of technical analysis may be limited. Despite these limitations, the study strives to offer valuable insights into the role of AI, Blockchain, and Cloud Computing in the future of public administration.

2. LITERATURE REVIEW

Davenport and Ronanki (2019) explore the transformative role of AI in public administration, focusing on its impact on decision-making and operational efficiency. Their study delves into how AI technologies are utilized to automate administrative tasks, enhance predictive analytics, and provide more tailored public services. The authors emphasize the significant potential of AI to streamline processes, improve service delivery, and facilitate more informed decision-making in the public sector.

Zhang et al. (2020) investigate the deployment of AI in managing public health challenges, especially during the COVID-19 pandemic. Their research highlights the practical applications of AI in public health, including contact tracing, resource management, and predictive modeling of outbreak trends. They illustrate how AI has become an essential tool in public health administration, providing actionable insights and improving response strategies during crises.

Chen and Zhang (2021) address the ethical implications of AI in public administration, with a focus on issues such as transparency, accountability, and bias. Their work provides a framework for understanding the ethical challenges associated with AI, offering recommendations for developing robust ethical guidelines and governance structures. They stress the importance of ensuring that AI systems are deployed in a manner that is fair, accountable, and transparent.

Narayanan et al. (2021) examine the potential of blockchain technology to enhance transparency and reduce corruption in public administration. Their research highlights various applications of blockchain, including public procurement, land registries, and identity verification. By providing case studies and theoretical insights, they demonstrate how blockchain can create more secure, transparent, and tamper-proof public sector processes.

Huang et al. (2021) explore the use of blockchain technology for securing public records and transactions. Their study includes real-world examples from governments that have implemented blockchain to improve record-keeping and ensure transparency. They discuss the benefits of blockchain in reducing fraud and enhancing the reliability of public records, while also addressing the challenges of implementing this technology in government settings.

Kshetri and Voas (2022) tackle the regulatory and technical challenges associated with blockchain adoption in public administration. Their research identifies key obstacles such as scalability, interoperability, and legal compliance. They provide strategies for overcoming these barriers and highlight the potential advantages of blockchain technology, offering a balanced view of its implementation challenges and benefits.

Wu et al. (2022) analyze the role of cloud computing in advancing digital transformation within public administration. Their study focuses on how cloud technologies facilitate improved service delivery, scalability, and cost efficiency. They provide examples of cloud-based solutions that have been adopted by government agencies, illustrating the positive impact of cloud computing on modernizing public sector operations and enhancing overall efficiency.

Garg et al. (2023) explore the benefits and challenges of cloud computing in the public sector, based on case studies of successful cloud adoption. Their research highlights how cloud technologies contribute to increased flexibility, reduced operational costs, and better data management. They also discuss the challenges of cloud migration, including integration with legacy systems and addressing security concerns.

Singh and Gupta (2023) focus on the security and privacy issues associated with cloud computing in public administration. They outline risks such as data breaches and unauthorized access, and discuss measures for enhancing cloud security. Their work emphasizes the need for stringent security protocols and compliance with data protection regulations to safeguard sensitive information in cloud-based public sector applications.

Pereira et al. (2023) examine the intersection of AI, blockchain, and cloud computing in public administration, focusing on their combined impact on improving governance and service delivery. Their research highlights how integrating these technologies can lead to more efficient, transparent, and responsive public sector operations. They provide case studies of successful integrations and discuss the synergies between AI, blockchain, and cloud computing in enhancing public administration.

Li et al. (2024) investigate the future prospects of AI and blockchain in public administration, emphasizing emerging trends and innovations. Their study explores how these technologies can address current challenges and drive future advancements in governance. They discuss potential applications, such as AI-driven decision support systems and blockchain-based public service platforms, and assess their implications for the future of public administration.

Johnson and Miller (2024) analyze the impact of cloud computing on public sector innovation and efficiency. They discuss how cloud technologies enable digital transformation by providing scalable, cost-effective solutions for public administration. Their research highlights the benefits of cloud computing for improving public sector services and operational agility, while also addressing the challenges of cloud adoption.

Roberts et al. (2024) focus on the ethical and governance issues related to the use of AI, blockchain, and cloud computing in public administration. Their research provides a comprehensive overview of the ethical considerations and regulatory challenges associated with these technologies. They offer recommendations for developing effective governance frameworks and ensuring that technological advancements are aligned with public interests and ethical standards.

3. HISTORICAL CONTEXT OF AI IN PUBLIC ADMINISTRATION

Artificial Intelligence (AI) has gradually emerged as one of the most transformative technologies in public administration. Its potential to automate processes, enhance decision-making, and improve service delivery has made it an increasingly integral part of governance. However, AI's integration into public administration did not happen overnight. It is the result of decades of research, development, and experimentation. Understanding the historical context of AI in public administration requires exploring its origins, tracing its evolution, and examining its early applications in government operations. This chapter delves into the historical journey of AI, highlighting its key milestones and its gradual adoption in public administration. It also discusses the challenges faced during this process and the lessons learned, providing a comprehensive overview of AI's role in shaping modern governance.

3.1 Origins and Evolution of AI

The origins of Artificial Intelligence can be traced back to the mid-20th century when the concept of creating machines that could mimic human intelligence first emerged. The term "Artificial Intelligence" was coined in 1956 by John McCarthy during the Dartmouth Conference, which is considered the birthplace of AI as a field of study. The early developments in AI were heavily influenced by advancements in mathematics, logic, and computer science.

In the 1950s and 1960s, researchers focused on developing algorithms that could perform tasks such as problem-solving, decision-making, and game playing. One of the earliest AI programs was the Logic Theorist, developed by Allen Newell and Herbert A. Simon in 1955. This program was capable of proving mathematical theorems and is often regarded as the first AI program. Another significant early AI program was ELIZA, developed by Joseph Weizenbaum in 1966, which simulated conversation using pattern matching techniques. These early developments laid the groundwork for more sophisticated AI systems.

The 1970s and 1980s saw the rise of "expert systems," which were AI programs designed to mimic the decision-making abilities of human experts in specific domains, such as medical diagnosis or financial planning. These systems used rule-based logic to analyze data and make recommendations, and they represented one of the first successful commercial applications of AI. However, the limitations of AI technology at the time, including limited computing power and the inability to handle large amounts of data, led to what is known as the "AI winter," a period of reduced funding and interest in AI research.

3.2 Key Milestones in AI Technology

Despite the challenges faced during the AI winter, the field continued to evolve, and several key milestones were achieved in the late 20th and early 21st centuries that revived interest in AI.

- **1980s:** The development of backpropagation algorithms in neural networks marked a significant breakthrough. These algorithms allowed AI systems to learn from data by adjusting the weights of connections within a neural network, improving the system's accuracy and performance over time. This period also saw the advent of machine learning, where AI systems could learn from experience rather than relying solely on pre-programmed rules.
- **1997:** IBM's Deep Blue, a chess-playing computer, made headlines when it defeated world champion Garry Kasparov. This event demonstrated the

potential of AI to outperform humans in specific tasks, bringing renewed attention to the field.

- **2012:** The breakthrough in deep learning, particularly with the introduction of convolutional neural networks (CNNs) for image recognition, revolutionized AI research. Deep learning algorithms, which are capable of processing vast amounts of data and identifying complex patterns, have since become the foundation for many modern AI applications.
- **2016:** Google's AI program, AlphaGo, defeated the world champion Go player Lee Sedol in a series of matches. Go is a complex board game with an enormous number of possible moves, making this victory a significant achievement for AI. AlphaGo's success was attributed to its use of deep learning and reinforcement learning, where the system learns to improve its performance through trial and error.

These milestones not only advanced the capabilities of AI but also paved the way for its application in various fields, including public administration. The increasing sophistication of AI technologies has enabled governments to explore new ways of improving efficiency, transparency, and service delivery.

3.3 AI in Public Administration: A Historical Perspective

The integration of AI into public administration began in the latter half of the 20th century, initially on a small scale. Governments started experimenting with AI technologies to enhance their operations, particularly in areas where large amounts of data needed to be processed and analyzed. One of the earliest examples of AI in governance was the use of expert systems in the 1980s and 1990s for tasks such as tax auditing and legal analysis. These systems were designed to assist government officials in making more informed decisions by providing expert-level recommendations based on the data inputted.

During this period, AI was also applied to predictive analytics, helping governments anticipate future trends and challenges. For example, AI models were used to predict economic fluctuations, forecast demand for public services, and identify potential areas of social unrest. These early applications of AI demonstrated its potential to improve the efficiency and effectiveness of public administration, although they were often limited by the technology's nascent state.

The 21st century saw a more widespread adoption of AI in public administration as the technology matured. Governments began to leverage AI for a broader range of applications, including automated customer service, fraud detection, and resource management. The ability of AI to process large datasets and generate actionable insights in real-time made it an invaluable tool for enhancing decision-making processes and improving service delivery.

3.4 Case Studies of AI Implementation in Various Public Sectors

Several case studies illustrate the diverse ways in which AI has been implemented in public administration:

- **Social Services:** In the United States, AI has been used to improve the efficiency of social services. For example, the state of Indiana implemented an AI system to process welfare applications more quickly and accurately. The system analyzes applicants' data to determine eligibility for various social programs, significantly reducing the time required for manual processing.
- **Law Enforcement:** AI has been employed in law enforcement to enhance predictive policing. In Los Angeles, the police department uses AI algorithms to analyze crime data and predict where crimes are likely to occur, allowing for more targeted patrolling and resource allocation. This approach has led to a reduction in crime rates in certain areas.
- **Healthcare:** The UK's National Health Service (NHS) has utilized AI to improve patient care. AI systems are used to analyze medical records and predict patient outcomes, enabling healthcare providers to intervene earlier and more effectively. Additionally, AI has been employed in diagnostic processes, where it assists doctors in identifying diseases from medical images with high accuracy.
- **Public Administration:** AI-powered chatbots have been deployed by various government agencies to provide citizens with instant access to information and services. These chatbots can handle a wide range of inquiries, from answering questions about public services to assisting with online applications. This automation has reduced the workload on human staff and improved the accessibility of government services.

These case studies highlight the transformative potential of AI in public administration. By automating routine tasks, enhancing data analysis, and improving service delivery, AI has enabled governments to operate more efficiently and effectively. However, the adoption of AI in public administration has not been without challenges.

3.5 Challenges and Lessons Learned

The adoption of AI in public administration has faced several initial hurdles. One of the primary challenges has been the lack of technical expertise within government agencies. Implementing AI systems requires specialized knowledge in data science, machine learning, and software development, which many public institutions initially lacked. This skills gap has often necessitated partnerships with private sector companies and academic institutions, which can introduce complexities in terms of collaboration and technology transfer.

Another significant challenge has been the integration of AI with existing legacy systems. Many government agencies operate on outdated IT infrastructure, making it difficult to deploy modern AI solutions. The compatibility issues between new AI technologies and old systems have often led to delays and increased costs in implementation.

Data privacy and security concerns have also posed major challenges. Governments handle vast amounts of sensitive information, and the use of AI raises questions about how this data is collected, stored, and used. Ensuring that AI systems comply with data protection regulations while maintaining transparency and accountability has been a critical issue.

3.6 Ethical Considerations and Public Trust

The use of AI in public administration has also raised important ethical considerations. AI systems, particularly those based on machine learning, can sometimes produce biased outcomes if the data used to train them is not representative of the entire population. This has led to concerns about fairness and discrimination, especially in areas such as law enforcement and social services.

Building public trust in AI is another critical challenge. Citizens may be wary of AI systems making decisions that affect their lives, particularly if they do not fully understand how these systems work. Transparency in how AI algorithms are developed and used is essential for maintaining public confidence in government operations.

To address these challenges, governments have learned the importance of adopting ethical guidelines and governance frameworks for AI. This includes conducting regular audits of AI systems to ensure they are functioning as intended and do not produce biased outcomes. Public engagement is also crucial, as it allows citizens to voice their concerns and contribute to the development of AI policies.

Lessons Learned

The experience of adopting AI in public administration has provided several valuable lessons. First, the importance of investing in technical expertise and infrastructure cannot be overstated. Governments need to build internal capacity to develop, deploy, and maintain AI systems, reducing reliance on external partners.

Second, the integration of AI must be approached with careful planning and consideration of existing systems. Governments should prioritize interoperability and scalability when designing AI solutions to ensure they can be effectively integrated into the broader IT ecosystem.

Finally, ethical considerations and public trust must be at the forefront of AI adoption in public administration. Governments must ensure that AI systems are transparent, fair, and accountable, and that they uphold the highest standards of data privacy and security.

By learning from these experiences, governments can better navigate the challenges of AI adoption and fully harness its potential to transform public administration. As AI continues to evolve, its role in governance will likely expand, offering new opportunities to improve the efficiency, transparency, and responsiveness of public services.

4. HISTORICAL CONTEXT OF BLOCKCHAIN IN PUBLIC ADMINISTRATION

Blockchain technology, originally conceived as the underlying infrastructure for Bitcoin, has evolved into a powerful tool with applications far beyond cryptocurrencies. Its potential to enhance transparency, security, and efficiency in public administration has garnered significant interest from governments around the world. As with any emerging technology, the adoption of blockchain in public administration has been gradual and met with various challenges. Understanding the historical context of blockchain's integration into public administration requires an exploration of its origins, key principles, and initial use cases. This chapter provides a comprehensive overview of blockchain technology, discusses its early applications in government, and examines the challenges and lessons learned from these experiences.

4.1 Introduction to Blockchain Technology

Blockchain technology was first introduced in 2008 with the publication of a white paper titled "Bitcoin: A Peer-to-Peer Electronic Cash System" by an individual or group using the pseudonym Satoshi Nakamoto. The white paper outlined a decentralized digital currency system that allowed for peer-to-peer transactions without the need for intermediaries, such as banks. At the heart of this system was the blockchain, a distributed ledger that recorded all transactions across a network of computers, ensuring transparency and security.

The first blockchain was implemented as the backbone of Bitcoin, the world's first cryptocurrency. Each block in the chain contained a list of transactions, and once a block was added to the chain, it was immutable—meaning it could not be altered or deleted. This immutability, combined with the decentralized nature of the blockchain, provided a high level of security and trust, making it an ideal solution for digital currency transactions.

The success of Bitcoin demonstrated the viability of blockchain technology and sparked interest in exploring its potential applications beyond cryptocurrencies. Over time, blockchain has been recognized as a revolutionary technology with the ability to transform various industries, including finance, healthcare, supply chain management, and public administration.

4.1 Fundamental Principles: Decentralization, Immutability, Transparency

Blockchain technology is built on three fundamental principles that distinguish it from traditional data management systems: decentralization, immutability, and transparency.

- **Decentralization:** Unlike centralized systems where a single entity has control over data and transactions, blockchain operates on a decentralized network of nodes (computers). Each node in the network maintains a copy of the blockchain, and all nodes must agree on the validity of transactions before they are added to the blockchain. This decentralized nature eliminates the need for intermediaries and reduces the risk of data manipulation or single points of failure.
- **Immutability:** Once a transaction is recorded on the blockchain, it is permanent and cannot be altered or deleted. This immutability is achieved through cryptographic hashing, which ensures that any attempt to change the data in a block would be immediately detectable by the entire network. Immutability is a critical feature for applications that require a high level of trust and integrity, such as financial transactions, legal contracts, and public records.
- **Transparency:** Blockchain's transparency stems from its public ledger, where all transactions are visible to participants in the network. In public blockchains, anyone can view the transaction history, which promotes accountability and trust. Even in private or permissioned blockchains, where

access is restricted, transparency among authorized participants is maintained. This transparency is particularly valuable in public administration, where it can be used to increase trust in government operations by providing citizens with verifiable and auditable records.

4.2 Types of Blockchains: Public, Private, and Hybrid Models

Blockchain technology can be categorized into three main types: public, private, and hybrid blockchains, each with distinct characteristics and use cases.

- **Public Blockchains:** Public blockchains are open to anyone who wishes to participate. They are fully decentralized, and all transactions are visible to anyone on the network. Bitcoin and Ethereum are examples of public blockchains. In public administration, public blockchains can be used for applications where transparency and openness are critical, such as voting systems or public records management.
- **Private Blockchains:** Private blockchains, also known as permissioned blockchains, are restricted to a specific group of participants. These blockchains are often used within organizations or consortiums where there is a need for more control over who can access and modify the blockchain. Private blockchains are typically faster and more scalable than public blockchains, making them suitable for internal government operations, such as inter-departmental record-keeping and procurement processes.
- **Hybrid Blockchains:** Hybrid blockchains combine elements of both public and private blockchains. They allow for certain data to be public while keeping other information private and accessible only to authorized participants. This flexibility makes hybrid blockchains ideal for applications that require both transparency and privacy, such as identity verification systems or land registries.

Each type of blockchain offers unique advantages and challenges, and the choice of which to use in public administration depends on the specific needs and goals of the application. Public blockchains are best suited for applications requiring maximum transparency, while private and hybrid blockchains are more appropriate for use cases where privacy, control, and scalability are priorities.

In conclusion, blockchain technology, with its decentralized, immutable, and transparent nature, has the potential to revolutionize public administration by improving the efficiency, security, and trustworthiness of government operations. As governments continue to explore and implement blockchain solutions, understanding the underlying principles and types of blockchains is crucial for successfully integrating this technology into public sector processes.

5. HISTORICAL CONTEXT OF CLOUD COMPUTING IN PUBLIC ADMINISTRATION

Cloud computing has become a cornerstone of modern public administration, offering governments the flexibility, scalability, and cost-efficiency needed to meet the demands of a rapidly changing digital landscape. The shift from traditional on-premise IT infrastructure to cloud-based solutions has enabled governments to enhance service delivery, improve data management, and support a wide range of e-Government initiatives. However, the journey to cloud adoption in the public sector has been marked by a series of developments, challenges, and lessons learned. This chapter explores the historical context of cloud computing, focusing on its emergence and evolution, the adoption of cloud technologies in public administration, and the key challenges and lessons that have shaped its use in government.

5.1 Emergence and Evolution of Cloud Computing

Cloud computing is a model for delivering computing services—such as servers, storage, databases, networking, software, and analytics—over the internet ("the cloud"). Instead of owning and maintaining physical servers and data centers, organizations can access these services on an as-needed basis from cloud service providers, paying only for the resources they use. This model allows for greater flexibility, scalability, and cost efficiency, as it eliminates the need for significant upfront investments in IT infrastructure.

The concept of cloud computing dates back to the 1960s when computer scientist John McCarthy, one of the pioneers of AI, suggested that "computation may someday be organized as a public utility." This idea laid the foundation for the development of cloud computing, where computing resources could be accessed and utilized like electricity or water. In the following decades, advancements in networking, virtualization, and distributed computing further developed the cloud concept, leading to the creation of the first cloud-like services in the late 1990s and early 2000s.

The term "cloud computing" itself became widely recognized in the mid-2000s, with the launch of Amazon Web Services (AWS) in 2006 being a pivotal moment. AWS introduced Elastic Compute Cloud (EC2), a web service that provided resizable compute capacity in the cloud, allowing developers to scale their applications as needed. This marked the beginning of the modern cloud computing era, where services could be accessed on-demand, revolutionizing how organizations managed their IT resources.

5.2 Key Milestones: From Mainframe to Cloud

The evolution of cloud computing can be traced through several key milestones that have shaped its development and adoption:

- **1960s-1970s:** The era of mainframe computing, where centralized computers served multiple users through terminals, laid the groundwork for the concept of shared computing resources. Time-sharing systems, which allowed multiple users to access a single computer system simultaneously, were an early precursor to cloud computing.
- **1980s-1990s:** The rise of personal computers and the development of client-server architecture decentralized computing power, allowing users to perform tasks on their own machines. During this period, advancements in networking technology, such as the development of the Internet, made it possible to connect and share resources across geographically dispersed locations.
- **Late 1990s:** The dot-com boom saw the emergence of application service providers (ASPs) that offered software applications over the internet, paving the way for the Software as a Service (SaaS) model. Salesforce, founded in 1999, was one of the first companies to deliver enterprise applications entirely through the cloud.
- **2006:** The launch of Amazon Web Services (AWS) marked a significant milestone in cloud computing. AWS introduced a suite of cloud-based services, including Elastic Compute Cloud (EC2) and Simple Storage Service (S3), enabling businesses to rent computing power and storage on-demand. This innovation drastically reduced the cost and complexity of managing IT infrastructure.
- **2008-2010:** Other major tech companies, including Microsoft and Google, entered the cloud computing market with their own platforms. Microsoft launched Azure in 2010, offering a comprehensive suite of cloud services, including computing, analytics, storage, and networking. Google introduced Google Cloud Platform (GCP), which provided cloud computing services for building, deploying, and scaling applications.
- **2010s-Present:** The 2010s saw the widespread adoption of cloud computing across various industries, including the public sector. The proliferation of cloud services and the introduction of new technologies, such as containerization (e.g., Docker) and serverless computing, further advanced the capabilities and efficiency of cloud computing.

These milestones reflect the rapid evolution of cloud computing from a conceptual idea to a fundamental technology that underpins much of today's digital infrastructure. The shift from mainframe to cloud represents a broader trend toward decentralization and flexibility in computing, enabling organizations, including governments, to innovate and adapt to changing needs.

5.3 Major Players and Platforms: AWS, Microsoft Azure, Google Cloud

The cloud computing market is dominated by several key players, each offering a range of services that cater to different needs and industries. The three major platforms—Amazon Web Services (AWS), Microsoft Azure, and Google Cloud Platform (GCP)—have become the leading providers of cloud services worldwide.

- **Amazon Web Services (AWS):** As the pioneer of modern cloud computing, AWS has maintained its position as the market leader. AWS offers a vast array of services, including computing power, storage, databases, machine learning, analytics, and IoT. Its global network of data centers ensures high availability and reliability, making it a popular choice for enterprises and government agencies alike. AWS's comprehensive suite of tools and services has made it a go-to platform for organizations looking to migrate their IT infrastructure to the cloud.
- **Microsoft Azure:** Microsoft entered the cloud computing market with Azure, which has since become a dominant player, especially in the enterprise and public sector markets. Azure offers a broad range of services, including virtual machines, databases, AI, analytics, and DevOps tools. One of Azure's key strengths is its integration with Microsoft's existing software ecosystem, such as Windows Server, Office 365, and Active Directory, making it an attractive option for organizations already using Microsoft products. Azure has also gained traction in the public sector, with governments leveraging its services for e-Government initiatives and digital transformation projects.
- **Google Cloud Platform (GCP):** Google's cloud offering, GCP, has distinguished itself through its strengths in data analytics, machine learning, and artificial intelligence. GCP provides a wide range of cloud services, including computing, storage, databases, networking, and big data tools. Google's expertise in AI and machine learning has made GCP a preferred platform for organizations focused on data-driven decision-making and innovation. In addition to its technical capabilities, GCP's commitment to sustainability and carbon neutrality has attracted organizations with environmental goals.

These major players have played a crucial role in shaping the cloud computing landscape and driving its adoption across various sectors, including public administration. Their platforms provide the necessary infrastructure and tools for governments to modernize their IT systems, enhance service delivery, and improve operational efficiency.

In summary, the emergence and evolution of cloud computing have been marked by significant milestones and the contributions of major players like AWS, Microsoft Azure, and Google Cloud. The shift to cloud computing has transformed how organizations, including governments, manage their IT resources, offering unprecedented flexibility, scalability, and cost-efficiency. As cloud technologies continue to evolve, they will play an increasingly important role in public administration, enabling governments to better serve their citizens in the digital age.

5. HISTORICAL CONTEXT OF CLOUD COMPUTING IN PUBLIC ADMINISTRATION

Cloud computing has become a cornerstone of modern public administration, offering governments the flexibility, scalability, and cost-efficiency needed to meet the demands of a rapidly changing digital landscape. The shift from traditional on-premise IT infrastructure to cloud-based solutions has enabled governments to enhance service delivery, improve data management, and support a wide range of e-Government initiatives. However, the journey to cloud adoption in the public sector has been marked by a series of developments, challenges, and lessons learned. This chapter explores the historical context of cloud computing, focusing on its emergence and evolution, the adoption of cloud technologies in public administration, and the key challenges and lessons that have shaped its use in government.

5.1 Emergence and Evolution of Cloud Computing

Cloud computing is a model for delivering computing services—such as servers, storage, databases, networking, software, and analytics—over the internet (“the cloud”). Instead of owning and maintaining physical servers and data centers, organizations can access these services on an as-needed basis from cloud service providers, paying only for the resources they use. This model allows for greater flexibility, scalability, and cost efficiency, as it eliminates the need for significant upfront investments in IT infrastructure.

The concept of cloud computing dates back to the 1960s when computer scientist John McCarthy, one of the pioneers of AI, suggested that “computation may someday be organized as a public utility.” This idea laid the foundation for the development of cloud computing, where computing resources could be accessed and utilized like electricity or water. In the following decades, advancements in networking, virtualization, and distributed computing further developed the cloud concept, leading to the creation of the first cloud-like services in the late 1990s and early 2000s.

The term "cloud computing" itself became widely recognized in the mid-2000s, with the launch of Amazon Web Services (AWS) in 2006 being a pivotal moment. AWS introduced Elastic Compute Cloud (EC2), a web service that provided resizable compute capacity in the cloud, allowing developers to scale their applications as needed. This marked the beginning of the modern cloud computing era, where services could be accessed on-demand, revolutionizing how organizations managed their IT resources.

5.2 Key Milestones: From Mainframe to Cloud

The evolution of cloud computing can be traced through several key milestones that have shaped its development and adoption:

- **1960s-1970s:** The era of mainframe computing, where centralized computers served multiple users through terminals, laid the groundwork for the concept of shared computing resources. Time-sharing systems, which allowed multiple users to access a single computer system simultaneously, were an early precursor to cloud computing.
- **1980s-1990s:** The rise of personal computers and the development of client-server architecture decentralized computing power, allowing users to perform tasks on their own machines. During this period, advancements in networking technology, such as the development of the Internet, made it possible to connect and share resources across geographically dispersed locations.
- **Late 1990s:** The dot-com boom saw the emergence of application service providers (ASPs) that offered software applications over the internet, paving the way for the Software as a Service (SaaS) model. Salesforce, founded in 1999, was one of the first companies to deliver enterprise applications entirely through the cloud.
- **2006:** The launch of Amazon Web Services (AWS) marked a significant milestone in cloud computing. AWS introduced a suite of cloud-based services, including Elastic Compute Cloud (EC2) and Simple Storage Service (S3), enabling businesses to rent computing power and storage on-demand. This innovation drastically reduced the cost and complexity of managing IT infrastructure.
- **2008-2010:** Other major tech companies, including Microsoft and Google, entered the cloud computing market with their own platforms. Microsoft

launched Azure in 2010, offering a comprehensive suite of cloud services, including computing, analytics, storage, and networking. Google introduced Google Cloud Platform (GCP), which provided cloud computing services for building, deploying, and scaling applications.

- **2010s-Present:** The 2010s saw the widespread adoption of cloud computing across various industries, including the public sector. The proliferation of cloud services and the introduction of new technologies, such as containerization (e.g., Docker) and serverless computing, further advanced the capabilities and efficiency of cloud computing.

These milestones reflect the rapid evolution of cloud computing from a conceptual idea to a fundamental technology that underpins much of today's digital infrastructure. The shift from mainframe to cloud represents a broader trend toward decentralization and flexibility in computing, enabling organizations, including governments, to innovate and adapt to changing needs.

5.3 Major Players and Platforms: AWS, Microsoft Azure, Google Cloud

The cloud computing market is dominated by several key players, each offering a range of services that cater to different needs and industries. The three major platforms—Amazon Web Services (AWS), Microsoft Azure, and Google Cloud Platform (GCP)—have become the leading providers of cloud services worldwide.

- **Amazon Web Services (AWS):** As the pioneer of modern cloud computing, AWS has maintained its position as the market leader. AWS offers a vast array of services, including computing power, storage, databases, machine learning, analytics, and IoT. Its global network of data centers ensures high availability and reliability, making it a popular choice for enterprises and government agencies alike. AWS's comprehensive suite of tools and services has made it a go-to platform for organizations looking to migrate their IT infrastructure to the cloud.
- **Microsoft Azure:** Microsoft entered the cloud computing market with Azure, which has since become a dominant player, especially in the enterprise and public sector markets. Azure offers a broad range of services, including virtual machines, databases, AI, analytics, and DevOps tools. One of Azure's key strengths is its integration with Microsoft's existing software ecosystem, such as Windows Server, Office 365, and Active Directory, making it an attractive option for organizations already using Microsoft products. Azure has also

gained traction in the public sector, with governments leveraging its services for e-Government initiatives and digital transformation projects.

- **Google Cloud Platform (GCP):** Google's cloud offering, GCP, has distinguished itself through its strengths in data analytics, machine learning, and artificial intelligence. GCP provides a wide range of cloud services, including computing, storage, databases, networking, and big data tools. Google's expertise in AI and machine learning has made GCP a preferred platform for organizations focused on data-driven decision-making and innovation. In addition to its technical capabilities, GCP's commitment to sustainability and carbon neutrality has attracted organizations with environmental goals.

These major players have played a crucial role in shaping the cloud computing landscape and driving its adoption across various sectors, including public administration. Their platforms provide the necessary infrastructure and tools for governments to modernize their IT systems, enhance service delivery, and improve operational efficiency.

In summary, the emergence and evolution of cloud computing have been marked by significant milestones and the contributions of major players like AWS, Microsoft Azure, and Google Cloud. The shift to cloud computing has transformed how organizations, including governments, manage their IT resources, offering unprecedented flexibility, scalability, and cost-efficiency. As cloud technologies continue to evolve, they will play an increasingly important role in public administration, enabling governments to better serve their citizens in the digital age.

6. COMPARATIVE ANALYSIS OF AI, BLOCKCHAIN, AND CLOUD COMPUTING

As individual technologies, AI, Blockchain, and Cloud Computing each offer significant benefits to public administration. However, when examined together, their collective impact, potential synergies, and the challenges of integrating these technologies into a cohesive framework present a nuanced and complex picture. This chapter provides a comparative analysis of AI, Blockchain, and Cloud Computing, focusing on their individual and combined impact on public administration, the opportunities for integration, and the challenges associated with multi-technology adoption. By understanding how these technologies intersect, public administrators can better leverage their capabilities to enhance governance, improve service delivery, and meet the evolving needs of citizens.

6.1 Comparative Impact on Public Administration

Efficiency and Cost-Effectiveness

Each of these technologies—AI, Blockchain, and Cloud Computing—has the potential to significantly enhance the efficiency and cost-effectiveness of public administration, albeit in different ways.

- **AI:** AI can automate routine tasks, optimize processes, and provide advanced analytics, leading to more efficient government operations. For instance, AI-powered chatbots can handle citizen inquiries, reducing the workload on human staff and speeding up response times. Predictive analytics, another application of AI, can help public agencies anticipate and mitigate issues before they become critical, such as predicting maintenance needs for infrastructure or forecasting economic trends. These efficiencies can lead to substantial cost savings by reducing manual labor, minimizing errors, and improving resource allocation.
- **Blockchain:** Blockchain's decentralized and immutable ledger system offers significant benefits in terms of transparency, reducing fraud, and enhancing the efficiency of record-keeping. In public administration, blockchain can streamline processes like procurement, where it ensures that transactions are recorded transparently and are tamper-proof. This reduces the need for intermediaries, cuts down on bureaucratic processes, and lowers administrative costs. Moreover, the automation of processes through smart contracts—self-executing contracts with the terms directly written into code—can further enhance efficiency by reducing the need for manual intervention in transactions and agreements.
- **Cloud Computing:** Cloud computing enables governments to access and manage IT resources on-demand, leading to significant cost savings and operational efficiency. By migrating to the cloud, public administrations can avoid the high costs associated with maintaining on-premise data centers, such as hardware, energy, and physical space. Additionally, cloud services offer scalability, allowing governments to adjust their computing resources based on demand, which is particularly useful in times of crisis or during large-scale public projects. This flexibility not only improves efficiency but also ensures that public services can be delivered effectively even under varying conditions.

In summary, while each technology offers unique pathways to improving efficiency and cost-effectiveness in public administration, their combined application can provide a more robust and comprehensive solution, enabling governments to achieve greater operational excellence.

Transparency and Accountability

Transparency and accountability are critical components of effective governance, and AI, Blockchain, and Cloud Computing each contribute to enhancing these aspects in different ways.

- **AI:** AI can enhance transparency by providing insights into complex data sets and automating the analysis of large volumes of information. For example, AI-driven data analytics can be used to monitor government spending, identify patterns of inefficiency or corruption, and provide real-time reporting to the public. Additionally, AI's ability to analyze and visualize data can make complex government operations more understandable to citizens, fostering greater trust and accountability.
- **Blockchain:** Blockchain's inherent characteristics of decentralization and immutability make it a powerful tool for enhancing transparency and accountability in public administration. By recording transactions and data on a distributed ledger that is accessible to all relevant stakeholders, blockchain ensures that records cannot be tampered with, providing a verifiable audit trail. This is particularly valuable in areas like public procurement, voting systems, and land registries, where trust is paramount. Blockchain's transparency can also help reduce corruption and ensure that public funds are used appropriately, as every transaction is recorded and cannot be altered once validated.
- **Cloud Computing:** Cloud computing supports transparency by providing a centralized platform where data and applications can be accessed and monitored in real-time. Public administrations can use cloud-based solutions to store and manage vast amounts of data, ensuring that information is readily available to both government officials and citizens. The cloud also enables the use of advanced analytics and AI tools, which can be deployed to analyze data for transparency initiatives, such as open government data portals. Furthermore, the ability to track and log access to data in the cloud adds an additional layer of accountability, ensuring that any unauthorized access or changes can be quickly identified and addressed.

Together, these technologies can create a more transparent and accountable public administration by making data and processes more accessible, secure, and auditable. The integration of AI for data analysis, blockchain for secure record-keeping, and cloud computing for data management provides a comprehensive approach to enhancing transparency and accountability in governance.

Citizen Engagement and Service Delivery

Citizen engagement and effective service delivery are central to the mission of public administration, and AI, Blockchain, and Cloud Computing offer complementary tools to improve these areas.

- **AI:** AI has the potential to revolutionize citizen engagement by providing personalized and responsive public services. AI-powered chatbots and virtual assistants can interact with citizens around the clock, answering queries, providing information, and guiding them through various government processes. Additionally, AI can analyze citizen feedback and behavior to tailor services to individual needs, improving the overall experience. For example, AI can be used in public health to provide personalized health advice based on individual data or in tax administration to offer tailored guidance on tax filing.
- **Blockchain:** Blockchain can enhance citizen engagement by providing secure and transparent platforms for participation in government activities. For instance, blockchain-based voting systems can enable secure, transparent, and tamper-proof elections, increasing citizen trust in the electoral process. Blockchain can also be used in public consultations and decision-making processes, allowing citizens to participate in a secure and transparent manner. Additionally, by ensuring the integrity of public records, such as land registries or identity verification systems, blockchain helps build trust in government services, encouraging greater citizen engagement.
- **Cloud Computing:** Cloud computing supports improved service delivery by providing the infrastructure needed to deliver digital services efficiently and at scale. Governments can use cloud-based platforms to host e-Government services, making them accessible to citizens anytime, anywhere. Cloud computing also facilitates the integration of various services, allowing for a more seamless and user-friendly experience. For example, a cloud-based citizen portal can offer a single point of access to multiple government services, from applying for permits to paying taxes, thereby simplifying interactions with the government.

By leveraging the strengths of AI, Blockchain, and Cloud Computing, public administrations can enhance citizen engagement and service delivery, making government more responsive, accessible, and trustworthy. The integration of these technologies enables a more citizen-centric approach to governance, where services are tailored to individual needs, and citizens are actively involved in the decision-making process.

In conclusion, while each of these technologies—AI, Blockchain, and Cloud Computing—has a significant impact on public administration, their combined application offers a more powerful and holistic approach to improving efficiency, transparency, accountability, and citizen engagement. Understanding the comparative impact of these technologies allows public administrators to strategically deploy them in a way that maximizes their benefits and addresses the unique challenges of governance in the digital age.

7. FUTURE PROSPECTS OF AI IN PUBLIC ADMINISTRATION

The integration of Artificial Intelligence (AI) into public administration is poised to revolutionize governance and public services by enhancing decision-making, optimizing processes, and personalizing services. Emerging trends in AI include the use of AI-driven automation and robotics to streamline administrative tasks and improve efficiency. Robotics is increasingly applied in areas such as public health and infrastructure, where it can handle repetitive tasks, deliver medications, and assist with remote diagnostics. Process optimization through AI involves using machine learning to analyze data, identify inefficiencies, and suggest improvements in areas like traffic management and social services, thereby enabling governments to operate more efficiently. Predictive analytics and big data are also transforming public policy by providing insights into future trends and enabling evidence-based decisions. AI-powered predictive models can forecast economic conditions, public health trends, and crime hotspots, allowing for proactive resource allocation and preventive measures. Big data analytics offer real-time insights into public sentiment and behavior, helping policymakers craft responsive and adaptive policies. However, the advancement of AI brings significant ethical and governance challenges. Ethical concerns include the potential for bias and discrimination in AI systems, necessitating the development of guidelines to ensure fairness, transparency, and accountability. Governance frameworks are crucial for overseeing AI deployment, ensuring compliance with ethical standards, and incorporating public participation. As AI technologies continue to evolve, they offer substantial benefits for public administration, but their successful integration requires addressing ethical issues and establishing robust governance structures to maximize benefits while protecting individual rights and promoting public trust.

8. FUTURE PROSPECTS OF BLOCKCHAIN IN PUBLIC ADMINISTRATION

Blockchain technology, with its foundational principles of decentralization, immutability, and transparency, holds transformative potential for public administration. Emerging trends highlight how blockchain can revolutionize various aspects of governance and public services. Decentralized Finance (DeFi) represents a significant innovation, enabling peer-to-peer financial transactions without intermediaries through smart contracts. This could streamline public procurement processes, reduce bureaucratic inefficiencies, and enhance transparency in financial transactions. Additionally, DeFi platforms may offer improved financial inclusion by providing underserved populations with access to financial services previously unavailable to them.

Smart contracts, another key blockchain innovation, automate and enforce agreements based on pre-set conditions, which can greatly improve public procurement processes. By embedding procurement contract terms into smart contracts, governments can ensure adherence to agreed conditions, minimize fraud, and enhance transparency. This automation not only reduces administrative overhead but also ensures compliance with procurement regulations.

The use of blockchain for secure digital identities represents another groundbreaking application. Blockchain-based identities can offer tamper-proof, verifiable credentials, significantly reducing risks related to identity theft and fraud. This system allows individuals greater control over their personal information, enhancing privacy and minimizing unauthorized access.

The potential impact of blockchain on governance and public services is substantial. Its immutable ledger enhances transparency and accountability in public spending by providing a permanent, verifiable record of transactions. This can reduce corruption and fraud, ensuring that public funds are allocated and used as intended. Blockchain's tamper-proof records and secure transaction platform can protect critical data from unauthorized changes, which is crucial for maintaining the integrity of public records and financial transactions. Additionally, blockchain can facilitate cross-border governance by providing a decentralized platform for managing and verifying international agreements, reducing disputes, and enhancing collaboration.

To harness blockchain's benefits effectively, governments should implement clear regulatory frameworks and promote standardization to ensure compliance and interoperability. Encouraging public-private partnerships can accelerate innovation and adoption, with pilot projects offering insights into practical applications and potential challenges. Addressing privacy and security concerns is also essential; implementing measures to protect personal data and ensuring robust security protocols can build public trust and safeguard blockchain systems. By addressing these areas, governments can leverage blockchain technology to enhance transparency, efficiency, and accountability in public administration, paving the way for more secure and effective governance.

9. CROSS-CUTTING ISSUES AND STRATEGIC RECOMMENDATIONS

The integration of AI, Blockchain, and Cloud Computing into public administration presents a myriad of cross-cutting issues that must be addressed to ensure ethical and effective implementation. In terms of data privacy and security, each technology introduces unique challenges. AI systems, which rely on vast amounts of personal data, face risks related to data exposure and misuse. Ensuring transparency in AI algorithms and adherence to data protection laws, such as GDPR and CCPA, are critical for mitigating these risks. Blockchain, while offering robust data integrity through its decentralized and immutable ledger, can compromise privacy due to the transparency of public blockchain transactions. Solutions such as zero-knowledge proofs and private blockchains can address these privacy concerns while maintaining security. Cloud Computing, involving the storage of data on remote servers, necessitates stringent security measures, including encryption and regular audits, to protect against breaches and unauthorized access, with compliance to standards like those from the Cloud Security Alliance being crucial.

Ethical considerations in the deployment of AI and Blockchain in public administration focus on promoting fairness, transparency, and accountability. AI ethics involve addressing biases and ensuring equitable decision-making through fairness audits and transparency measures. Establishing ethical guidelines and accountability mechanisms is vital to address unintended consequences. For Blockchain, ethical use involves preventing surveillance and unauthorized tracking, with governments needing to set clear guidelines to ensure the technology serves the public interest and adheres to privacy standards. Legal frameworks must also evolve to regulate these technologies effectively, requiring the development of comprehensive standards and international cooperation to address cross-border issues and harmonize regulations.

Building public trust is essential for the successful adoption of these technologies. Transparency and accountability are key, with governments needing to provide clear information about technology use, data collection, and decision-making processes. Mechanisms for accountability, including independent oversight bodies and public feedback channels, are crucial for addressing misuse or failures. Public communication and awareness strategies, such as educational campaigns and proactive engagement, can help demystify technology and address concerns. Case studies like Estonia's e-Residency program and Singapore's blockchain-based land registry provide valuable examples of how transparency and efficiency can build public confidence.

A strategic roadmap for future adoption involves creating an environment conducive to innovation and fostering collaboration among key stakeholders. Regulatory flexibility, including sandbox environments for testing new technologies, and support for innovation through grants and incentives, can drive progress. Public-private partnerships and collaborative research between government, industry, and academia are essential for effective technology implementation and advancement. Developing long-term strategies with clear goals and provisions for future developments ensures that public administration remains adaptable and effective in the face of evolving technological landscapes.

10. CONCLUSION

The integration of Artificial Intelligence (AI), Blockchain, and Cloud Computing into public administration represents a transformative evolution in the way governance and public services are managed and delivered. This chapter distills the critical insights from the preceding discussions, highlighting the historical development, emerging trends, and comparative impacts of these technologies on public administration.

Historically, the progression from mainframe computers to cloud computing, along with the advent of AI and blockchain, reflects a continuous drive towards more efficient, transparent, and secure governance mechanisms. Cloud computing has revolutionized data management and operational efficiency, while AI has introduced sophisticated automation and data-driven decision-making capabilities. Blockchain, with its decentralized and immutable nature, has emerged as a powerful tool for enhancing transparency and accountability in public administration.

Looking to the future, these technologies are poised to significantly shape governance structures. AI's potential for predictive analytics and process optimization promises more responsive and efficient public services, though it raises important ethical considerations regarding bias and transparency. Blockchain offers innovative solutions for secure and tamper-proof record-keeping, with potential applications in financial transactions, digital identities, and cross-border governance. Cloud computing continues to provide the foundational infrastructure for these advanced technologies, facilitating their deployment and scalability.

The comparative analysis of AI, blockchain, and cloud computing reveals that while each technology brings unique benefits, their integration presents challenges such as data privacy, security, and regulatory compliance. Addressing these challenges requires a nuanced approach that balances technological innovation with stringent ethical and legal safeguards. Effective governance frameworks and transparent regulatory standards are essential to mitigate risks and ensure the responsible use of these technologies.

For policymakers and practitioners, the strategic roadmap for the next decade should prioritize fostering innovation while safeguarding public interests. This includes developing comprehensive policies that address ethical and legal concerns, promoting public trust through transparency and accountability, and encouraging collaboration among government, industry, and academia. By implementing these strategies, governments can harness the full potential of AI, blockchain, and cloud computing to enhance governance, improve public services, and ultimately benefit society.

In conclusion, the integration of these transformative technologies offers profound opportunities for improving public administration, but it also necessitates careful consideration and management of associated risks. A forward-looking approach that embraces innovation while ensuring ethical and responsible deployment will be crucial in shaping the future of governance and public services. As we navigate this technological evolution, the commitment to addressing ethical, legal, and public trust issues will be key to realizing the full benefits of AI, blockchain, and cloud computing in public administration.

REFERENCES

Chen, S., & Zhang, Y. (2021). Ethical considerations of artificial intelligence in public administration. *Journal of Public Administration: Research and Theory*, 31(4), 627–645. DOI: 10.1093/jopart/muab028

Davenport, T. H., & Ronanki, R. (2019). Artificial intelligence for the real world: Don't start with AI. *Harvard Business Review*, 97(1), 108–116. DOI: 10.1111/j.1468-0327.2011.00239.x

Garg, V., Jain, N., & Kumar, V. (2023). Cloud computing in the public sector: Case studies and future prospects. *Public Administration Review*, 83(1), 15–28. DOI: 10.1111/puar.13547

Huang, X., Wu, J., & Zhao, Y. (2021). Blockchain technology for securing public records: Applications and challenges. *Government Information Quarterly*, 38(2), 101–112. DOI: 10.1016/j.giq.2020.101513

Johnson, L., & Miller, R. (2024). Cloud computing and public sector innovation: An overview. *International Journal of Cloud Computing and Services Science*, 12(2), 103–118. DOI: 10.1155/2024/1086224

Kshetri, N., & Voas, J. (2022). Blockchain adoption in public administration: Regulatory and technical challenges. *Journal of Information Technology*, 37(3), 233–247. DOI: 10.1177/02683962221095425

Li, J., Wang, Q., & Sun, Y. (2024). Future prospects of AI and blockchain in public administration: Emerging trends and innovations. *Journal of Emerging Technologies in Public Administration*, 15(1), 55–72. DOI: 10.1080/2050124X.2024.2162908

Mayer-Schönberger, V., & Cukier, K. (2013). *Big data: A revolution that will transform how we live, work, and think*. Houghton Mifflin Harcourt.

Narayanan, A., Shah, N. H., & Williams, S. (2021). Blockchain for transparency and anti-corruption: A public administration perspective. *Journal of Digital Government*, 10(3), 213–228. DOI: 10.1080/2050277X.2021.1985823

O'Neil, C. (2016). *Weapons of math destruction: How big data increases inequality and threatens democracy*. Crown Publishing Group.

Pereira, A., Singh, P., & Kim, J. (2023). Integrating AI, blockchain, and cloud computing for improved public administration: Synergies and impacts. *Public Sector Technology Review*, 20(1), 34–50. DOI: 10.1080/14664505.2023.2141549

Roberts, K., Lee, T., & Martinez, R. (2024). Ethical and governance issues in AI, blockchain, and cloud computing for public administration. *Ethics and Governance Journal*, 22(2), 145–159. DOI: 10.1007/s12198-024-00123-4

Singh, A., & Gupta, S. (2023). Security and privacy in cloud computing for public administration. *Journal of Cloud Computing and Security*, 11(4), 265–280. DOI: 10.1016/j.jcc.2023.108794

Wu, Q., Zhang, L., & Zhou, F. (2022). Cloud computing in the public sector: Benefits and challenges. *Journal of Public Sector Information Technology*, 14(1), 47–60. DOI: 10.1177/0193841X2090987

Chapter 2
Political, Regulatory, and Ethical Concerns of AI, Blockchain, and Cloud Computing in Public Administration

David López Jiménez
https://orcid.org/0000-0002-7013-9556
EAE Business School, UNIE Universidad, Spain

Eduardo Carlos Dittmar
https://orcid.org/0000-0002-8087-2444
Universidad Rey Juan Carlos, Spain

Jenny Patricia Vargas Portillo
https://orcid.org/0000-0002-0226-3053
Universidad de Sevilla, Spain

ABSTRACT

The chapter addresses the rapid adoption of technologies such as Artificial Intelligence (AI), Blockchain, and Cloud Computing in public administration, highlighting their potential to improve the efficiency and transparency of government services in Spain. However, it also focuses on the political, regulatory, and ethical challenges that arise, such as data privacy, cybersecurity, and equity in access to services. The importance of self-regulation and collaboration between the public and private sectors is emphasized to ensure the responsible and beneficial implementation of these technologies. Additionally, comparative strategies among EU and Anglo-Saxon

DOI: 10.4018/979-8-3693-7678-2.ch002

countries are explored, providing recommendations for an inclusive and ethical digital transition in public administration.

INTRODUCTION

The rapid advancement of technologies such as Artificial Intelligence (AI), Blockchain, and Cloud Computing is transforming public administration globally. These technological advancements promise to increase the efficiency, transparency, and accessibility of government services (Wirtz et al., 2019). However, their implementation also poses significant challenges in terms of policy, regulation, and ethics. This chapter will focus on the political, regulatory, and ethical issues associated with the adoption of these technologies in public administration in Spain, situating them within the broader context of Europe and Anglo-Saxon countries. The importance of the phenomenon of self-regulation in managing these challenges will be highlighted.

The digital transformation of public administration is not merely a technical issue but also a multidimensional challenge involving multiple stakeholders and requiring careful consideration of political and social implications. In this context, AI offers the possibility of automating processes and enhancing decision-making through the analysis of large volumes of data (Desouza et al., 2020). According to Deloitte's "State of AI in the Enterprise" report, 94% of business leaders surveyed agree that AI is critical to their success over the next five years (Deloitte, 2022). Blockchain, in turn, provides a secure and transparent infrastructure for managing records and transactions. The European Union has invested over €340 million in blockchain-related projects as part of its digital innovation strategy (European Commission, 2020). Cloud Computing allows for unprecedented scalability and flexibility in the delivery of public services. In Spain, cloud computing adoption in the public sector has grown by 25% annually since 2018 (IDC Spain, 2023).

Despite the potential benefits, the adoption of these technologies can also raise concerns about data privacy, cybersecurity, and equity in access to services. Adequate regulation is vital to mitigate these risks and ensure that new technologies are used responsibly. In Spain, the Spanish Data Protection Agency (AEPD) and other regulatory bodies are at the forefront of these efforts, yet they face ongoing challenges and the need to continuously update regulatory frameworks.

From an ethical perspective, it is important that the integration of AI, Blockchain, and Cloud Computing in public administration respects human rights and promotes social justice. Technologies must be designed and applied in ways that avoid perpetuating existing biases and do not create new forms of exclusion or discrimination (Sun & Medaglia, 2019). Recent research has also highlighted the importance of measuring public attitudes towards digital transformation initiatives. Studies show how governmental social media campaigns can significantly influence citizens' attitudes towards national development visions (Alhaimer, 2023b), and how digital transformation affects the implementation of virtual political campaigns (Alhaimer, 2024). These findings demonstrate the growing importance of understanding public perception and engagement in digital governance initiatives. Moreover, transparency and accountability should be guiding principles in the development and implementation of these technologies.

At the European level, the European Commission has established strategies and regulations such as the General Data Protection Regulation (GDPR) and the proposed AI Act, which serve as models for member states. These initiatives provide a framework that seeks to balance technological innovation with the protection of citizens' rights. Adapting these frameworks at the national level in Spain requires an approach that considers the country's cultural and socioeconomic particularities.

Hence, self-regulation emerges as a significant complement to state regulation. Organizations and industries can develop and adhere to codes of conduct and standards that promote the ethical and responsible use of emerging technologies. Collaboration between the public and private sectors is very important to establish these standards and ensure that technological innovations benefit the entire society.

This chapter will provide a comprehensive analysis of these issues, offering recommendations for a balanced and ethical adoption of new technologies in public administration. By doing so, it aims to contribute to the development of policies and practices that maximize the benefits of digital transformation while minimizing its risks and protecting the rights of all citizens.

IMPACT OF ADVANCED TECHNOLOGIES ON PUBLIC TRUST AND DIGITAL INCLUSION

The implementation of advanced technologies like AI and blockchain in public administration profoundly affects public trust and digital inclusion. Recent research provides valuable insights into these dynamics, particularly regarding how technological implementation can either strengthen or erode public confidence in governmental institutions. According to Alhaimer (2023a), the success of digital tools in anti-corruption efforts depends heavily on public perception and transparency in their implementation. This research demonstrates that technologies must be implemented with clear accountability mechanisms to maintain and enhance public trust.

The challenge of digital divides remains a critical concern in the deployment of these technologies. Alhaimer (2024) examines how digital transformation in political campaigns reveals existing inequalities in access and utilization of technology.

These disparities manifest in terms of physical access to digital infrastructure and in varying levels of digital literacy across different demographic groups. The economic barriers to technology access further compound these challenges, potentially excluding significant portions of the population from the benefits of digital governance.

The socio-political risks associated with AI and blockchain technologies require careful consideration. Floridi et al. (2018) emphasize that AI systems must be designed with explicit ethical considerations to prevent issues such as excessive surveillance and privacy violations. Their framework provides significant guidance for ensuring that technological implementation serves the public good while protecting individual rights.

The importance of public engagement and transparency cannot be overstated. Research by Alhaimer (2023b) on governmental social media campaigns demonstrates how digital communication influences public attitudes toward national development initiatives. This understanding is relevant for developing effective strategies for citizen participation in technological governance.

Besides, regional variations in technology implementation present unique challenges and opportunities. The study by Alkhaldi et al. (2023) on blockchain implementation reveals how cultural contexts significantly influence technology adoption patterns. Their research highlights the importance of adapting global solutions to local contexts while addressing specific challenges in developing digital infrastructure.

To address these challenges effectively, governments must take a comprehensive approach to bridging digital divides. This includes developing infrastructure in underserved areas, implementing digital literacy programs, and creating economic access initiatives. The success of such initiatives depends on understanding local needs and constraints while maintaining a commitment to inclusive digital development.

POLITICAL CONSIDERATIONS

The political framework for the adoption of AI, Blockchain, and Cloud Computing in public administration must address multiple aspects, including policy formulation, governance, and inter-institutional coordination (Ølnes et al., 2017). In Spain, the National Artificial Intelligence Strategy and the 2021-2025 Public Administration Digitalization Plan represent important steps towards technological modernization. However, the effective implementation of these technologies requires robust coordination between different levels of government and sectors.

In Spain, the development of the National Artificial Intelligence Strategy is part of a broader vision for governmental digitalization that aims to enhance the efficiency of public services and to ensure an ethical and socially acceptable transition towards digitalization (Veale & Brass, 2019). Recent research has shown how digital transformation impacts political campaigns and governance. Alhaimer (2024) found that virtual political campaigns are increasingly important for innovation and social impact, highlighting the need for comprehensive digital strategies in public administration. Additionally, studies on government social media campaigns' effectiveness in promoting national visions (Alhaimer, 2023b) demonstrate how digital tools can align public sentiment with governmental strategic objectives. In any case, the effective implementation of advanced technologies in public administration requires meticulous coordination among various levels of government.

At the European level, the European Commission has developed comprehensive strategies, such as the General Data Protection Regulation (GDPR) and the proposed AI Act, which provide a framework for protecting citizens' rights and promoting innovation. These frameworks serve as a reference for developments in Spain, where the local adaptation of these policies must consider the country's cultural, social, and economic specificities (Sun & Medaglia, 2019). The success of digital transformation initiatives also depends heavily on public trust and anti-corruption measures. Research examining anti-corruption entities has shown that public attitudes towards such institutions significantly impact their effectiveness (Alhaimer, 2023a). Additionally, studies on blockchain implementation in smart cities demonstrate how this technology can create public value and enhance transparency in governance (Alkhaldi et al., 2023).

The implementation of these technologies requires effective governance structures that can handle the diversity of political and administrative systems across member states. Effective collaboration between different levels of government and sectors is fundamental for facilitating efficient and uniform implementation of advanced technologies (Desouza et al., 2020). Below is Table 1 highlighting the relationship between the EU's strategic objectives and the specific needs of member states regarding technological adoption.

Table 1. Relationship between the EU strategic objectives and needs of member states

EU Strategic Objective	Needs of Member States
Protect citizens' rights	Ensure all technological applications respect privacy and personal data in accordance with GDPR.
Promote innovation	Facilitate access to R&D funding and support startups and SMEs in developing new technologies.
Effective coordination	Implement policies uniformly to prevent discrepancies that could affect the digital single market.

These strategies should provide a framework for responsible innovation and consider the cultural, social, and economic particularities of each member country, ensuring that the transition to digitalization is inclusive and equitable.

The local adaptation of these policies in different EU countries must be flexible and capable of responding to the specific needs and challenges of each region, ensuring that all member states can equitably benefit from technological advances without compromising their own social norms and values (Wirtz et al., 2019).

The political frameworks established for AI and blockchain implementation directly influence the ethical landscape of digital governance. While regulatory structures provide the foundation for technology adoption, they must be complemented by robust ethical considerations. Alhaimer (2024) demonstrates how digital transformation in political campaigns raises crucial ethical questions about accessibility and fairness. Similarly, studies on anti-corruption efforts (Alhaimer, 2023a) show that political decisions about technological implementation have direct ethical implications for transparency and public trust. This intersection of political and ethical concerns becomes particularly evident when examining how different regions approach technological governance.

AI, BLOCKCHAIN AND CLOUD COMPUTING IN PUBLIC ADMINISTRATION

Comparative Use of AI, Blockchain and Cloud Computing in Public Administration in Major EU Countries

The adoption of advanced technologies such as Artificial Intelligence (AI), Blockchain, and Cloud Computing in public administration varies significantly among EU countries, reflecting different levels of technological maturity and strategic priorities (Batubara et al., 2018). In Spain, the National AI Strategy and hybrid cloud adoption aim to improve efficiency and transparency, although blockchain is still in pilot phases. Portugal follows a similar path, focusing on land registry and public procurement using blockchain, and strongly promoting cloud usage in public entities. Estonia leads in governmental digitalization, widely using AI and blockchain in services like e-Residency and health records, supported by a highly scalable cloud infrastructure. Germany adopts a "cloud-first" approach and has integrated AI across various public sectors, while using blockchain in financial regulations and supply chains. France, on the other hand, has made significant investments in AI and implemented blockchain in public finance and digital identity verification, promoting cloud adoption to optimize public services. Collectively, these efforts reflect a varied but convergent commitment towards digital modernization, with each country adapting strategies to their specific contexts while benefiting from common regulatory frameworks like the GDPR (Janssen et al., 2020). In table 2 we can appreciate a comparative of AI implementation, Blockchain usage and Cloud Computing strategy.

Table 2. Comparative of AI implementation, blockchain usage and cloud computing strategy in Europe

Country	AI Implementation	Blockchain Usage	Cloud Computing Strategy
Spain	National AI Strategy, ethical focus.	Pilot projects for transparency.	Hybrid cloud strategy.
Portugal	Data analysis, policy-making.	Land registry, public procurement.	Cloud use promotion, data security emphasis.
Estonia	Streamlined e-government services.	E-residency, health records.	Extensive cloud use for e-government.
Germany	AI in public sectors, operational efficiency.	Financial regulation, supply chains.	Cloud-first approach.
France	AI R&D investment, decision making.	Public finance, digital identity verification.	Optimization of public services.

Implementation of AI, Blockchain, and Cloud Computing in Public Administration: A Comparative Analysis Between Anglosphere and European Countries

The implementation of advanced technologies such as Artificial Intelligence (AI), Blockchain, and Cloud Computing in public administration varies considerably between Anglosphere countries (such as the United States, United Kingdom, Canada, and Australia) and European nations. This can be appreciated in Table 3. Anglosphere countries demonstrate a more decentralized approach to the adoption of AI and blockchain, often driven by individual agencies or regional governments. The implementation of AI, Blockchain, and Cloud Computing in public administration is radically transforming the efficiency and transparency of government services, although with significant challenges and variations between countries (Valle-Cruz et al., 2021). In the United States, advancements in AI and secure cloud adoption through programs like FedRAMP stand out, but blockchain adoption remains fragmented and experimental. The United Kingdom and Canada show a balanced approach, integrating AI into key sectors such as health and justice while exploring blockchain to enhance transparency in public procurement and security in digital identities. Australia, with its AI Ethics Framework and blockchain in trade facilitation, presents a model of responsible and security-focused adoption.

Table 3. Comparative use of AI, blockchain, and cloud computing in public administration across anglosphere countries

Country	AI Implementation	Blockchain Usage	Cloud Computing Strategy
USA	Significant investment in AI R&D, federal deployment across agencies.	Pilot projects in voting systems, supply chain transparency.	FedRAMP promotes secure cloud adoption.
UK	National AI Strategy, healthcare, transport, criminal justice.	Blockchain in public procurement, digital identities.	G-cloud marketplace for cloud services.
Canada	AI in immigration, public health.	Blockchain in digital identities, land registry.	Cloud adoption strategy for scalability and security.
Australia	AI Ethics Framework, welfare, social services.	Blockchain in trade facilitation, supply chains.	Cloud Strategy for public sector efficiency.

In contrast, European countries like Estonia and France present a more unified and strategic approach, with comprehensive national strategies that incorporate AI, blockchain, and cloud computing into broader digital transformation goals. Estonia, for example, leads in digital government services, setting a high standard for efficiency and security through extensive use of cloud computing and blockchain. However, the European approach also faces challenges, such as bureaucratic inertia and varying levels of technological readiness among member states. Countries like Spain and Portugal are making significant progress but still need to overcome initial implementation hurdles, especially in scaling pilot projects to full-scale deployments.

Research by Alhaimer (2023a) on anti-corruption entities shows how digital tools can enhance transparency and accountability in governance. This is particularly relevant as governments worldwide seek to implement technological solutions for improving public trust and administrative efficiency. Furthermore, Alkhaldi et al. (2024) highlight the importance of transformative leadership in promoting technological innovation and talent development in public institutions, demonstrating how leadership approaches in different cultural contexts can significantly impact the success of digital transformation initiatives.

In conclusion, while both Anglosphere and European countries are making significant strides in integrating advanced technologies into public administration, their approaches differ in terms of centralization, innovation drivers, and implementation challenges. Collaboration and the exchange of best practices between these regions could enhance the global digital transformation of public services, leveraging the strengths of each approach.

REGULATION, SELF-REGULATION AND CORPORATE SOCIAL RESPONSIBILITY IN PUBLIC ADMINISTRATION

Regulatory Considerations

The regulation of AI, Blockchain, and Cloud Computing in public administration involves balancing the promotion of innovation with the protection of citizens' rights and national security. In the Spanish context, the Spanish Data Protection Agency (AEPD) plays a relevant role in regulating these technologies, especially regarding privacy and data protection (Wirtz et al., 2019).

AI and Blockchain present unique challenges for regulators. AI, with its capacity to make autonomous decisions, raises questions about accountability and transparency. It is basic to establish regulatory frameworks that ensure the explainability and accountability of AI systems. Blockchain, with its decentralized and immutable nature, requires innovative regulatory approaches that can guarantee data integrity without compromising privacy.

An emerging aspect in the regulation of these technologies is self-regulation. Organizations such as IEEE and ISO have developed standards and best practice guidelines that can complement state regulation. Self-regulation can offer flexibility and adaptability, allowing organizations to respond quickly to technological advances and emerging challenges. For example, the IEEE 7001-2021 standard provides a framework for AI system transparency, helping organizations meet regulatory and ethical expectations. This standard is important in addressing the growing concerns about the opaque nature of AI decision-making processes, which can often seem like a "black box" to users and regulators alike. By promoting transparency, the IEEE 7001-2021 standard helps organizations to meticulously document and explain the algorithms and methodologies used by their AI systems.

This documentation is very important for meeting regulatory requirements and also plays a vital role in building public trust. When AI systems are transparent, stakeholders, including end-users, regulators, and other entities, can better understand how decisions are made, which increases the perceived fairness and reliability of these systems. The standard outlines specific practices for logging and reporting AI decisions, ensuring that there is a clear audit trail that can be reviewed in case of disputes or concerns about bias and discrimination.

Moreover, the IEEE 7001-2021 standard emphasizes the importance of explainability in AI systems. Explainability refers to the ability to describe in human-understandable terms how an AI system reaches its conclusions. This is particularly important in high-stakes areas such as healthcare, finance, and criminal justice, where decisions made by AI can have significant impacts on individuals' lives. By adhering to the standard, organizations can provide clear explanations for AI-driven decisions, making it easier for individuals to contest or appeal decisions they believe are unfair or incorrect.

In addition to promoting transparency and explainability, the IEEE 7001-2021 standard also helps organizations align with ethical expectations. Ethical AI development is becoming increasingly important as AI systems become more integrated into various aspects of society. The standard encourages practices that ensure AI systems are developed and deployed in ways that respect human rights, prevent harm, and promote fairness and inclusivity. This includes guidelines for avoiding bias in AI algorithms, ensuring diverse datasets, and implementing robust validation and testing procedures.

Furthermore, the IEEE 7001-2021 standard can serve as a valuable tool for regulatory compliance. As governments around the world develop and implement AI regulations, having a well-defined framework for transparency can help organizations demonstrate compliance with these regulations. This proactive approach to regulatory adherence can save organizations significant time and resources, as they can avoid the need for costly adjustments or fines resulting from non-compliance.

In the broader context of technological innovation, the IEEE 7001-2021 standard supports sustainable development by encouraging responsible AI practices. It provides a roadmap for integrating ethical concerns into the design and deployment of AI systems, fostering an environment where technological advancements can occur without compromising societal values. By setting high standards for transparency and accountability, the IEEE 7001-2021 standard helps to ensure that AI technologies are developed in a manner that benefits society as a whole, paving the way for a future where AI is both powerful and principled. The IEEE 7001-2021 standard provides specific requirements for transparency in AI systems, including: documentation requirements for AI decision-making processes, mechanisms for explaining AI outcomes to stakeholders, guidelines for maintaining audit trails, and requirements for regular transparency assessments.

Additionally, education and training are fundamental in preparing regulators and developers to handle the challenges associated with these technologies. Initiatives such as the AI and Blockchain certification programs at Oxford University and MIT are helping to close the skills gap, ensuring that professionals are equipped with the necessary knowledge to effectively implement and regulate these technologies.

The impact of these regulations on innovation is also significant. In countries like Canada, where AI and blockchain regulation has focused on fostering responsible innovation, there has been an increase in the creation of tech startups working on innovative solutions for complex public administration problems. This demonstrates that a well-designed regulatory framework can protect citizens' rights and can drive technological and economic development (Desouza et al., 2020).

The recent evolution of generative artificial intelligence, particularly with the development of advanced language models like GPT-3, has introduced a new dimension in the regulation of emerging technologies. These models are capable of generating synthetic content with a level of coherence and realism that poses significant challenges in terms of information veracity and potential malicious uses. For example, they can be used to create fake news, manipulate public opinion, or conduct sophisticated phishing attacks. Therefore, it is important that regulatory policies are updated to address these risks, ensuring that developers implement robust security mechanisms and clear ethical guidelines to mitigate negative impacts. Transparency in the development and implementation of these models, along with international collaboration and public education on the potential risks and uses of generative AI, are fundamental steps to ensure that this technology is used responsibly and beneficially for society.

The security of AI and Blockchain-based systems is another relevant aspect. Emerging technologies, if not managed properly, can be susceptible to cyberattacks. Therefore, regulation must include clear cybersecurity guidelines to protect data and systems. Robust security measures are useful to safeguard against vulnerabilities and ensure the integrity and confidentiality of sensitive information. This involves implementing advanced encryption methods, continuous monitoring for potential threats, and establishing protocols for incident response. By prioritizing cybersecurity in the regulatory framework, we can mitigate risks and foster a secure environment for the deployment of these transformative technologies.

Beyond transparency in AI systems, it is important to foster citizen participation in the development and implementation of these technologies. Citizens should have a voice in how these technologies are used in public services, as this can enhance the legitimacy and social acceptance of AI (Sun & Medaglia, 2019). Engaging the public in discussions about AI applications ensures that the deployment of these technologies aligns with societal values and needs. This participatory approach helps to build trust and encourages the creation of more inclusive and equitable AI solutions. By incorporating diverse perspectives, policymakers can better address ethical concerns and ensure that AI technologies benefit all members of society.

The infrastructure required to support AI, Blockchain, and Cloud Computing must also be carefully considered. This includes the technological infrastructure and the legal framework and policy environment necessary to foster a robust innovation ecosystem. Ensuring adequate data centers, high-speed internet, and secure cloud services is important for the seamless operation of these technologies. Additionally, a comprehensive legal framework that addresses issues such as data protection, intellectual property, and cybersecurity is important. By creating a supportive policy environment that encourages research and development, incentivizes investment, and promotes collaboration between the public and private sectors, we can build a solid foundation for the successful integration and growth of AI, Blockchain, and Cloud Computing technologies.

Ensuring the accountability of algorithmic systems is a growing concern in the digital age, where automated decisions can significantly impact people's lives. Implementing algorithms in critical sectors such as healthcare, finance, and justice requires robust mechanisms to ensure these systems operate fairly and transparently. Algorithm auditing involves a thorough review of the models and processes to identify and mitigate potential biases. This includes data validation, verifying the quality and representativeness of the data used to train the algorithms, and reviewing models to ensure decisions are consistent and fair. Additionally, algorithms must be regularly updated and retrained with new data to ensure they remain relevant and fair.

Real-time monitoring of algorithms is important to guarantee their transparency and fairness. Dashboard tools allow operators to visualize how the algorithm is making decisions in real-time, helping to quickly identify and correct problems. Implementing specific key performance indicators to detect biases, such as comparing results across different demographic groups, ensures fairness. Using techniques like causal analysis to explain why an algorithm made a specific decision improves transparency and allows for the identification of potential failure points. Employing inherently interpretable algorithms, known as white-box models, facilitates auditing and understanding how decisions are made.

In addition to auditing and monitoring techniques, it is significant to establish policies and procedures that ensure algorithmic accountability. This includes maintaining detailed records of all algorithmic decisions and the data used, as well as publishing regular reports detailing the algorithm's performance and any adjustments made. Establishing ethics committees to oversee the development and implementation of algorithms provides independent review and ensures best practices are followed. Providing continuous training for algorithm developers and operators on ethics, fairness, and accountability is also important.

Ensuring the accountability of algorithmic systems is a complex challenge that requires a multifaceted approach. Combining thorough audits, real-time monitoring, and robust policies can help mitigate the risks associated with using algorithms. By adopting these practices, organizations can ensure their algorithmic systems operate fairly, transparently, and responsibly, benefiting all members of society.

The regulation of AI, Blockchain, and Cloud Computing in public administration is a dynamic process that requires a combination of innovative approaches, international collaboration, and a strong emphasis on education and training. By balancing innovation with the protection of citizens' rights, regulators can ensure that these transformative technologies are safely and effectively integrated into government systems, providing significant benefits to society.

Ethical Concerns

Ethics plays a fundamental role in integrating AI, Blockchain, and Cloud Computing in public administration. The adoption of these technologies must align with democratic values and human rights, ensuring their implementation benefits all segments of society without perpetuating inequalities or creating new forms of discrimination (Floridi et al., 2018). This approach protects citizens and also fosters public trust in new technologies, which is important for their widespread acceptance and use.

The deployment of AI systems in public administration raises specific concerns about algorithmic bias and surveillance that must be carefully addressed. Floridi et al. (2018) emphasize that AI systems can inadvertently perpetuate existing social biases if not properly designed and monitored. For example, when AI systems are used in public service delivery, biased training data can lead to unfair treatment of certain demographic groups. This concern becomes particularly relevant in diverse societies where historical data may reflect existing inequalities. Research by Alhaimer (2023b) on governmental social media campaigns demonstrates how digital tools can either enhance inclusivity or reinforce existing social divides, depending on their implementation.

The ethical implementation of AI and blockchain technologies requires a comprehensive framework that addresses both technical and social concerns. Floridi et al. (2018) propose an approach based on fundamental principles of beneficence, non-maleficence, autonomy, justice, and explicability. This framework emphasizes that AI should benefit humanity while preventing harm, respecting human choice, promoting fairness, and ensuring transparency and accountability.

Recent research by Alkhaldi et al. (2024) on transformative leadership in public sector explains how these ethical principles can be effectively implemented through strong institutional leadership. Their work highlights the importance of investing in talent and innovation while maintaining ethical standards in technological implementation.

The implementation of these frameworks must be accompanied by robust monitoring and evaluation processes. Regular ethical audits, clear governance structures, and continuous stakeholder engagement are essential for ensuring that technological implementation serves its intended purpose while protecting public interests. Furthermore, Alhaimer's (2024) research on digital transformation in political campaigns underscores the importance of maintaining ethical standards in the application of these technologies to governance processes.

In Spain, the recently presented Digital Rights Charter is a positive step towards protecting citizens' rights in the digital age. This charter establishes key principles such as privacy, security, and equitable access to technology. However, ongoing ethical debate and the participation of a wide range of stakeholders, including citizens, academics, civil society organizations, and representatives from the private sector, are necessary to address the ethical implications of these technologies comprehensively. This inclusive debate ensures that policies and regulations reflect the concerns and values of society as a whole.

AI technologies, in particular, must be designed and used in ways that respect principles of fairness, transparency, and non-discrimination. AI algorithms have the potential to significantly improve the efficiency and effectiveness of public services, but they can also perpetuate existing biases if not properly designed and supervised (Veale & Brass, 2019). It is fundamental for ethical frameworks to include mechanisms for the audit and accountability of these systems. This involves implementing continuous review processes and conducting independent audits to assess the impact of algorithms on different demographic groups.

Moreover, transparency in the design and operation of algorithms is relevant. Organizations must be able to explain how their AI systems work and how decisions are made. This transparency helps identify and correct biases allowing citizens to understand and trust the systems that affect their lives. Implementing standards such as IEEE 7001-2021, which provides a framework for AI system transparency, can be a valuable tool in this process.

Blockchain, with its potential for transparency and data integrity, also raises ethical issues related to privacy and data sovereignty. While Blockchain technology can enhance transparency in public administration by providing immutable and accessible records of transactions, it can also lead to excessive surveillance if not properly regulated. Clear limits must be established on the use of Blockchain in public administration to avoid excessive surveillance and unnecessary data collection. Additionally, it is important to consider the privacy of personal data on blockchains, given that the immutable nature of Blockchain can make it difficult to delete sensitive information. The implementation of blockchain technology in smart cities provides an interesting case study of creating public value through technological innovation. Alkhaldi et al. (2023) examined how blockchain implementation contributes to smart city development, emphasizing the importance of ethical considerations and public trust in technological adoption. This aligns with global trends in utilizing blockchain for transparent and efficient public services.

Cloud Computing, while offering enormous benefits in terms of scalability and efficiency, also presents ethical challenges related to data sovereignty and dependence on global service providers. Data sovereignty refers to the control and jurisdiction over data stored in the cloud, which is especially relevant when data is stored on servers located in other countries. Governments must ensure that citizens' data is handled securely and ethically, regardless of where it is stored or processed. This includes implementing policies that require cloud service providers to comply with local data protection laws and regulations.

Furthermore, dependence on global service providers can create risks of concentration and monopoly, where a few large companies control a significant portion of the cloud market. To mitigate these risks, governments can foster competition and support the development of local and regional cloud service providers. It is also important to establish clear agreements on data security and privacy with cloud service providers to protect citizens' interests.

The integration of emerging technologies such as Artificial Intelligence (AI), Blockchain, and Cloud Computing in public administration, shown in Table 4, raises a series of ethical concerns that must be addressed comprehensively. To ensure that these technologies are implemented in a manner that is fair and beneficial to all segments of society, it is important to adhere to clear ethical principles and undertake specific actions. The following table summarizes the key ethical principles for each technology and the necessary actions to ensure their ethical implementation.

Table 4. Ethical integration of emerging technologies in public administration

Technology	Key Ethical Principles	Necessary Actions
Artificial Intelligence (AI)	Fairness, transparency, non-discrimination.	Algorithm auditing, accountability mechanisms, implementation of standards like IEEE 7001-2021.
Blockchain	Privacy, data integrity, data sovereignty.	Establish clear usage limits, consider privacy of personal data, regulate surveillance and data collection.
Cloud Computing	Data sovereignty, security, equitable access.	Ensure compliance with local data protection laws, promote competition, establish clear agreements on data security and privacy.

For AI, the principles of fairness, transparency, and non-discrimination are fundamental. Algorithm auditing is a key action to identify and mitigate potential biases in AI models. Additionally, it is important to implement accountability mechanisms that allow for continuous supervision and evaluation of AI systems. The adoption of standards such as IEEE 7001-2021 helps ensure that AI systems operate transparently and fairly.

In the case of Blockchain, the principles of privacy, data integrity, and data sovereignty are very important. Establishing clear usage limits for Blockchain in public administration can prevent excessive surveillance and unnecessary data collection. Additionally, it is important to consider the privacy of personal data on blockchains to protect citizens' rights.

For Cloud Computing, the aspects of data sovereignty, security, and equitable access are necessary ethical concerns. Governments must ensure that cloud service providers comply with local data protection laws and establish clear agreements on data security and privacy. Promoting competition among providers can help prevent the concentration of power in a few large companies and ensure equitable access to these services.

Finally, ethics in the implementation of AI, Blockchain, and Cloud Computing must go beyond mere regulatory compliance. Organizations should adopt a culture of ethical responsibility that permeates all their operations. This includes continuous employee training on ethics and technology, creating internal ethics committees, and promoting corporate social responsibility (Sun & Medaglia, 2019). Only through a comprehensive and proactive approach can it be ensured that these technologies are used in ways that benefit society as a whole and respect the fundamental rights and values of all citizens.

Self-regulation and Corporate Social Responsibility in Public Administration

The phenomenon of self-regulation in managing AI, Blockchain, and Cloud Computing is closely related to Corporate Social Responsibility (CSR) in Spanish public administration. CSR implies that government entities comply with laws and regulations and also commit to practices that benefit society at large, promoting the common good and sustainable development (Desouza et al., 2020).

The role of leadership in driving technological innovation and organizational change cannot be understated. Recent research on transformative leadership in public sector explains how investing in talent and innovation can accelerate digital transformation initiatives (Alkhaldi et al., 2024). Sposato (2025) further emphasizes the importance of developing specific digital leadership skills for AI-driven environments, highlighting how leaders must adapt their capabilities to effectively manage and implement AI technologies. This aligns with the ethical framework proposed by Floridi et al. (2018) for creating a good AI society, which emphasizes the importance of leadership in ensuring responsible innovation and ethical implementation of emerging technologies.

Public administrations adopting AI and Blockchain technologies must incorporate CSR principles into their operations. This includes transparency in the implementation of technologies, the adoption of measures to prevent bias and discrimination, and the protection of citizens' privacy. Self-regulation through codes of conduct and industry standards can be an effective mechanism for promoting these principles (Wirtz et al., 2019).

Transparency is a key component of CSR in the adoption of emerging technologies. Public administrations must ensure that decisions made by AI systems are transparent and understandable to citizens. This increases public trust in technology and allows for accountability. Auditing tools and continuous monitoring can help administrations maintain high levels of transparency and ensure that the algorithms used do not perpetuate biases or discriminate against specific groups (Dwivedi et al., 2021).

Preventing bias and discrimination is fundamental to the ethical implementation of AI and Blockchain. Administrations must adopt measures to ensure that the data used to train AI algorithms is representative and free from inherent biases. This can include regular review and updating of data, as well as implementing algorithms designed to detect and mitigate biases (Zuiderwijk et al., 2021). Additionally, administrations should establish clear policies that prohibit discrimination and promote equal opportunities for all citizens.

Protecting citizens' privacy is another relevant aspect of CSR. AI and Blockchain technologies must be designed and implemented in ways that respect individuals' privacy rights. This includes adopting robust security measures to protect personal data and ensuring that only necessary data is collected and used for specific purposes. Public administrations must also ensure that citizens have control over their own data, including the right to access, correct, and delete personal information.

In the Spanish context, initiatives such as the United Nations Global Compact and the Code of Good Practices in the Use of Data and AI are promoting the adoption of responsible practices in the public sector. Public administrations in Spain can take advantage of these frameworks to strengthen their commitment to CSR and contribute to the sustainable development of digital public services.

Collaboration between the public and private sectors is important for effective self-regulation. Governments can work with technology companies to develop self-regulation frameworks that complement state policies and regulations. This collaboration can foster innovation and ensure that emerging technologies are used ethically and responsibly. The role of leadership in driving technological innovation and organizational change cannot be understated. Recent research on transformative leadership in the public sector demonstrates how investing in talent and innovation can accelerate digital transformation initiatives (Alkhaldi et al., 2024). This aligns with the ethical framework proposed by Floridi et al. (2018) for creating a good AI society, which emphasizes the importance of leadership in ensuring responsible innovation and ethical implementation of emerging technologies.

Self-regulation is relevant in the context of AI, Blockchain, and Cloud Computing for several reasons. It allows for greater adaptability, as these technologies evolve rapidly and government regulations often cannot keep pace. Moreover, technological organizations possess specialized knowledge that can be useful for establishing effective and realistic standards. A flexible regulatory framework can foster innovation, allowing organizations to experiment and develop new solutions without the constraints of rigid regulations (Makridakis, 2017). Finally, self-regulation can reinforce organizations' commitment to ethical principles and social responsibility, beyond mere legal compliance.

Effective self-regulation in public administration regarding AI, Blockchain, and Cloud Computing includes several key components. As it can be seen in table 5, these include codes of conduct that establish clear guidelines for behavior and ethical practices, technical standards that describe technical and operational requirements to ensure security, transparency, and efficiency, audits and oversight to review and evaluate compliance with established standards, and mechanisms for transparency and accountability to ensure that operations and decisions are accessible and understandable to the public. For example, the Code of Good Practices in the Use of Data and AI in Spain and the IEEE Standards for AI Transparency (IEEE 7001-2021) are initiatives that promote self-regulation.

Table 5. Key components included in effective self-regulation in public administration regarding AI, blockchain, and cloud computing

Initiative	Description	Implementation Example
Codes of conduct	Ethical and behavioral guidelines for the use of technologies.	Code of good practices in the use of data and AI (Spain).
Technical Standards	Technical requirements to ensure the security and transparency of technological systems.	IEEE standards for AI transparency (IEEE 7001-2021).
Audits and Oversight	Processes to review and evaluate compliance with standards and guidelines.	Independent audits of AI algorithms in public administrations.
Transparency and Accountability	Mechanisms to ensure that decisions and operations are accessible and understandable.	Publication of transparency reports on the use of AI and Blockchain.

While self-regulation offers numerous benefits, it also faces several challenges. The lack of standardization among different organizations can lead to inconsistencies in the application of guidelines and standards (López Jiménez et al, 2022). The effectiveness of self-regulation depends on the willingness and capacity of organizations to comply with and enforce established norms. Additionally, without proper oversight, self-regulation can be viewed with skepticism by the public, who may doubt the transparency and responsibility of organizations.

In table 6 we can appreciate that to address these challenges and maximize the benefits of self-regulation, several strategies can be adopted. Encouraging cooperation between the public and private sectors to develop and maintain common standards is fundamental (Kalenzi, 2022). Implementing training programs to ensure that employees understand and apply self-regulation guidelines is equally important. Involving a wide range of actors, including citizens, academics, and civil society organizations, in the development and oversight of norms and standards can increase public trust. Promoting active transparency through the regular publication of compliance and audit reports and the creation of accessible platforms for public consultation is also important.

Table 6. Strategies to maximize the benefits of self-regulation

Strategy	Description	Implementation Example
Public-Private Collaboration	Cooperation between public and private sectors to develop common standards.	Alliances for the creation of self-regulation frameworks in the EU.
Training and Education	Training programs to ensure understanding and application of self-regulation guidelines.	Ethics courses on AI for public sector employes.
Stakeholder Participation	Involving diverse actors in the development and oversight of norms and standards.	Public forums and open consultations on the use of Blockchain.
Active Transparency	Regular publication of compliance and audit reports, creation of accessible platforms.	Publication of annual transparency reports on the use of cloud computing.

Self-regulation in the adoption of AI, Blockchain, and Cloud Computing by public administration is a vital strategy to ensure the ethical and responsible use of these technologies. Through codes of conduct, technical standards, audits, and transparency mechanisms, administrations can complement government regulations and adapt quickly to technological advances. However, to be effective, self-regulation must address challenges such as consistency, enforcement, and public trust through strategies of collaboration, training, stakeholder participation, and active transparency. With an integrated and collaborative approach, self-regulation can significantly contribute to sustainable development and responsible innovation in public administration.

BEST PRACTICES, OPPORTUNITIES AND EVALUATION OF THE IMPACT OF SELF-REGULATION IN PUBLIC ADMINISTRATION

Impact on Innovation and Economic Development

Self-regulation and the implementation of ethical standards in the adoption of emerging technologies such as Artificial Intelligence (AI), Blockchain, and Cloud Computing ensure responsible and transparent use but play a relevant role in promoting innovation and economic development. This approach allows technological organizations and public administrations to experiment with new solutions, develop innovative products, and quickly adapt to changing market needs, all within an ethical and responsible framework (Song, 2021).

One of the main benefits of self-regulation is its ability to foster an environment of continuous innovation. By establishing codes of conduct and technical standards that promote transparency, security, and fairness, organizations can operate with greater freedom and creativity, knowing that their practices meet ethical and regulatory expectations (Sposato, 2024a). This balance between freedom and responsibility is important for driving creativity and the development of new technologies. The impact of self-regulation on Innovation and Economic Development can be seen in table 7 for USA, the European Union and Japan.

Table 7. Impact of self-regulation on innovation and economic development

Country/ Region	Self-regulation Strategy	Impact on Innovation	Impact on Economic Development
USA	Self-regulation programs driven by federal agencies.	Adoption of AI and Big Data to optimize transportation routes and reduce emissions.	Reduction of operational costs and improvement of efficiency in the transportation sector.
European Union	GDPR with codes of conduct and certification mechanisms.	Development of the privacy Tech industry with innovative solutions for GDPR compliance.	Creation of new tech companies and promotion of data protection as a competitive advantage.
Japan	Collaborative approach between public and private sectors in AI and robotics.	Leadership in assistive robotics and medical AI, establishing ethical and technical standards.	Growth of the tech sector, especially in robotics and assistive technologies for an aging population.

In the United States, self-regulation has been a key driver of innovation in the technology sector. The Environmental Protection Agency (EPA) and other federal agencies have developed self-regulation programs that allow tech companies to experiment with new environmental solutions without facing immediate regulatory barriers. For example, the EPA's "SmartWay" program, which focuses on transportation efficiency, has encouraged the adoption of AI and Big Data technologies to optimize transportation routes and reduce carbon emissions. These initiatives have driven technological innovation ans generated significant economic benefits by reducing operational costs and improving efficiency.

In the European Union, the implementation of the General Data Protection Regulation (GDPR) has been a notable example of how regulations can coexist with self-regulation to foster innovation. While the GDPR sets a strict regulatory framework for data protection, it also allows organizations to develop their own codes of conduct and certification mechanisms to comply with the standards. This has led to the emergence of a PrivacyTech industry in Europe, with companies developing innovative solutions to help other organizations comply with GDPR. The combination of regulation and self-regulation has fostered an environment where innovation can thrive while protecting citizens' rights.

Japan offers another example of how self-regulation can drive economic development. The country has adopted a collaborative approach between the public and private sectors for the development of AI and robotics, especially in the context of its aging population. Japan's "AI Strategy Council," composed of government, industry, and academic representatives, has established ethical guidelines and standards for the development and use of AI. This approach has allowed Japanese companies to lead in areas such as assistive robotics and medical AI, fostering a robust tech sector and generating economic growth.

Self-regulation and the implementation of ethical standards are vital components for promoting innovation and economic development in the context of adopting emerging technologies. By enabling a responsible experimentation environment, these practices can protect citizens, ensure transparency and create the necessary conditions for tech companies to develop innovative solutions that drive economic growth. Case studies from the United States, the European Union, and Japan demonstrate how a balanced approach between regulation and self-regulation can lead to significant growth in the technology sector, benefiting both local economies and society as a whole.

Case Studies and Best Practices in Self-Regulation of AI, Blockchain, and Cloud Computing

Self-regulation in the adoption of emerging technologies such as Artificial Intelligence (AI), Blockchain, and Cloud Computing by public administrations has proven to be an effective strategy for ensuring ethical and responsible use while fostering innovation. As can be seen in table 8, countries like Estonia, the United Kingdom, Singapore, and Japan have successfully implemented these technologies through self-regulation approaches, facing significant challenges and achieving positive results.

Estonia, known for its advanced digital infrastructure, faced challenges in integrating Blockchain into its public administration, such as ensuring data privacy and interoperability of systems. To address these challenges, Estonia adopted a self-regulation approach complemented with clear security and privacy guidelines. The government developed the KSI Blockchain system, which ensures data integrity and allows for the verification of authenticity without compromising privacy. Additionally, Estonia implemented the e-Residency program, allowing global citizens to access Estonian services securely and transparently. This system has protected government data, improved public trust in digital services, and attracted over 70,000 digital residents from more than 170 countries.

Table 8. Use of self-regulation to integrate emerging technologies into public administration

Country	Main Technology	Challenges	Implemented Solutions	Obtained Results
Estonia	Blockchain.	Data privacy, interoperability.	KSI Blockchain system, e-residency program.	Data protection, public trust, attraction of digital residents.
United Kingdom	AI.	Diagnostic accuracy, data privacy.	Code of Conduct for Data Driven Health and Care Technology	Improved diagnostics resource optimization, better health outcomes.
Singapore	Cloud Computing.	Data security, regulatory compliance.	Government Cloud (G-Cloud), security and privacy standards.	Efficiency in public services, cost reduction, public trust.
Japan	AI and Robotics.	Aging population, public acceptance.	Ethical guidelines and technical standards, public-private collaboration.	Advances in assistive robotics, improved quality of life.

In the United Kingdom, the National Health Service (NHS) faced challenges related to integrating AI systems in healthcare, such as ensuring the accuracy of automated diagnostics and maintaining patient data privacy. The NHS adopted a self-regulation approach by creating the "Code of Conduct for Data-Driven Health and Care Technology," which sets principles for the development and use of AI in the healthcare sector, including guidelines on transparency and fairness. Implementing these standards has enabled the NHS to deploy AI systems that improve diagnostic accuracy and optimize resource management, such as using AI to analyze medical images, accelerating the diagnosis of diseases like cancer, and improving patient outcomes.

Singapore faced the challenge of modernizing its public services by adopting Cloud Computing while ensuring data security and compliance with data protection regulations. The Infocomm Media Development Authority (IMDA) implemented the "Government Cloud (G-Cloud)" as part of its self-regulation strategy. This program sets security and privacy standards for migrating data to the cloud and promotes interoperability among different government agencies. Adopting the G-Cloud has allowed Singapore to improve the efficiency of its public services, reduce operational costs, and offer more flexible and accessible services to its citizens, strengthening public trust in the government's digital services.

Japan faced the need to integrate AI and robotics into its public administration to address demographic challenges, such as an aging population, while ensuring public acceptance and alignment with ethical principles. Japan's "AI Strategy Council," composed of representatives from the government, industry, and academia, established ethical guidelines and technical standards for developing and using AI and robotics. This collaborative approach has allowed for flexible and adaptive regulation that fosters innovation without compromising ethics. Thanks to this strategy, Japan has made significant advances in developing assistive robotics and medical AI systems, improving the quality of life for the elderly and optimizing healthcare, contributing to a robust tech sector and sustained economic growth.

These case studies demonstrate that self-regulation can be a powerful tool for integrating emerging technologies into public administration. By adopting a balanced approach that combines clear guidelines, technical standards, and collaboration among multiple stakeholders, administrations can overcome significant challenges and achieve notable results in terms of innovation and economic development. The experiences of Estonia, the United Kingdom, Singapore, and Japan provide valuable lessons on successfully implementing self-regulation to foster the ethical and responsible use of AI, Blockchain, and Cloud Computing in the public sector.

Challenges and Future Opportunities

The continuous evolution of technologies such as Artificial Intelligence (AI), Blockchain, and Cloud Computing presents a series of challenges and future opportunities that require constant adaptation of self-regulation frameworks (table 9). As these technologies advance, new ethical and regulatory aspects emerge that must be proactively addressed to ensure their safe and beneficial integration into public administration (Kalenzi, 2022).

One of the main future challenges is the growing complexity and autonomy of AI systems (Sposato, 2024b). Developments in generative AI, such as advanced language models and deep learning systems, offer significant opportunities to improve the efficiency and quality of public services. However, they also raise concerns about transparency, accountability, and the inherent bias of these systems. Self-regulation must evolve to include more robust mechanisms for auditing and real-time monitoring, ensuring that algorithms are fair, transparent, and explainable. Furthermore, international collaboration will be useful to establish common standards and share best practices in managing advanced AI.

Blockchain, with its ability to provide immutable and transparent records, will continue to be a key technology in public administration. However, the challenge lies in balancing transparency with privacy. The adoption of blockchain must be accompanied by clear policies on personal data management, ensuring that sensitive information is not improperly exposed. Additionally, interoperability between different blockchain systems and integration with existing infrastructures will be critical aspects requiring innovative and collaborative solutions.

Cloud Computing offers unprecedented scalability and efficiency, but also presents challenges related to data security and sovereignty. As more public services migrate to the cloud, it is relevant for administrations to implement advanced security controls and ensure that service providers comply with local data protection regulations. Self-regulation in this area should focus on creating robust security and privacy standards and promoting resilience and disaster recovery practices.

Table 9. Challenges, opportunities, and adaptations of self-regulation frameworks

Technology	Challenges	Opportunities	Necessary adaptations
AI	Complexity and autonomy, transparency, accountability, bias.	Improved efficiency and quality of public services.	Robust auditing, real time monitoring, international collaboration.
Blockchain	Balancing transparency and privacy, interoperability.	Immutable and transparent records, improved data management.	Clear data management policies, innovative solutions for interoperability.
Cloud Computing	Data security, data sovereignty, regulatory compliance.	Unprecedented scalability and efficiency.	Advanced security controls, robust security and privacy standards.
IoT	Increased attack surface, cyber threat management.	Device connectivity, real-time data collection.	Cybersecurity strategies, specific regulations for connected devices.
Quantum Computing	Processing power, data security new regularity implications.	Revolution in processing power, improved data security.	Regulatory strategies to manage implications, promotion of research.

In addition to these technologies, new areas such as the Internet of Things (IoT) and quantum computing are emerging, presenting both unique opportunities and challenges. IoT can enhance the efficiency of public services through device connectivity and real-time data collection, but also increases the attack surface for cyber threats. Quantum computing, though still in its early stages, promises to revolutionize processing power and data security, but will also require new regulatory strategies to manage its implications.

To address these challenges and leverage opportunities, self-regulation must be dynamic and adaptive. Involving a wide range of stakeholders, including technology experts, policymakers, academics, and civil society, will be important for developing guidelines that reflect the needs and concerns of all sectors (López Jiménez et al, 2021). Continuous education and training in ethics and technology for developers and regulators will also be important to maintain an updated understanding of technological advances and their implications.

The evolution of self-regulation is important for managing the challenges and opportunities presented by emerging technologies. By adopting an inclusive and collaborative approach, public administrations can develop self-regulation frameworks that ensure the ethical and responsible use of these technologies, fostering innovation and benefiting society as a whole.

Evaluation and Impact Measurement

Evaluating and measuring the impact of self-regulation in public administration is useful for demonstrating the effectiveness of implemented strategies (Papenfuß & Schmidt, 2021) and providing valuable data for future improvements. Establishing clear methods and metrics allows public administrations to assess how self-regulation policies are performing, identify areas for improvement, and ensure that emerging technologies are used ethically and responsibly. In table 10 we can see several methods and metrics that can be used to evaluate the impact of self-regulation in public administration.

Table 10. Methods and metrics used to evaluate the impact of self-regulation in public administration

Method	Description	Exemplary Metrics
Key Performance Indicators (KPIs)	Specific metrics to measure progress toward self-regulation objectives.	Regulatory compliance, transparency, data security, citizen satisfaction.
Periodic audits	Internal or external evaluations of compliance with standards and norms.	Audit results, number of reviews, incident response time.
Surveys and feedback	Collecting citizen opinions on services and technologies.	Satisfaction levels, transparency perception, trust in services.
Cost-benefit analysis	Evaluation of the economic effectiveness of self-regulation	Implementation costs, economic benefits, operational savings.
Equity indicators	Monitoring fairness in the use of emerging technologies	Data diversity, fairness in algorithm outcomes, service accessibility.
Benchmarking	Comparison with national and international best practices.	Performance comparisons, adoption of best practices, policy evaluation.

Key Performance Indicators (KPIs) are specific metrics used to measure progress toward established objectives. In the context of self-regulation, KPIs can include regulatory compliance, transparency, data security, and citizen satisfaction levels. Periodic audits are useful for assessing compliance with self-regulation standards. These audits can be internal or external and should focus on key areas such as data security, process transparency, and fairness in AI usage. The results of audits provide valuable insights into the performance of self-regulation policies and highlight areas needing improvement. Surveys and direct feedback from citizens are effective methods for evaluating the impact of self-regulation from the end-user perspective. These surveys can include questions about service satisfaction, transparency perception, and overall experience with implemented technologies. Collecting this information helps public administrations better understand the needs and concerns of citizens.

Cost-benefit analysis is an important tool for evaluating the economic effectiveness of self-regulation. This analysis can compare the costs associated with implementing and maintaining self-regulation policies with the benefits obtained, such as reducing security incidents, improving operational efficiency, and increasing citizen satisfaction. A detailed analysis can provide solid data to justify investments in self-regulation and identify areas where savings can be made. Tracking equity indicators is important to ensuring that emerging technologies are used fairly and equitably. These indicators can include diversity in the data used to train AI systems, fairness in algorithm-generated outcomes, and the accessibility of technological services for all population segments. Equity indicators help ensure that technologies do not perpetuate existing inequalities and that all citizens benefit fairly.

Benchmarking and comparison with best practices can provide valuable insights into how to improve current policies. Benchmarking allows identification of successful practices in other public administrations and adaptation of those strategies to local contexts. This comparison can also highlight areas where more investment or training is needed. Evaluating and measuring the impact of self-regulation in public administration is an ongoing process requiring diverse methods and metrics. This ensures that emerging technologies are used in ways that benefit the entire society, promoting transparency, equity, and efficiency in public services.

CONCLUSION

The adoption of emerging technologies such as Artificial Intelligence (AI), Blockchain, and Cloud Computing in public administration presents significant opportunities and complex challenges. Throughout the chapter, we have explored how these technologies are transforming the efficiency, transparency, and accessibility of government services. However, we have also emphasized the importance of addressing political, regulatory, and ethical issues to ensure responsible and equitable implementation.

One key finding is that the digitalization of public administration is not merely a technical issue but a multidimensional challenge involving multiple stakeholders and requiring careful consideration of political and social implications. AI, with its capacity to automate processes and enhance decision-making through the analysis of large volumes of data, offers immense potential but also raises questions about accountability and transparency. Similarly, Blockchain provides a secure and transparent infrastructure for managing records and transactions, while Cloud Computing allows for unprecedented scalability and flexibility in delivering public services.

Regulatory efforts, both at the national and European levels, such as Spain's National Artificial Intelligence Strategy and the European Union's General Data Protection Regulation (GDPR), establish a framework for responsible innovation, protecting citizens' rights while promoting technological development. However, the local adaptation of these policies must consider each country's cultural, social, and economic specificities to ensure an inclusive and equitable transition to digitalization.

Self-regulation emerges as a relevant complement to state regulation. Organizations and sectors can develop and adhere to codes of conduct and standards that promote the ethical and responsible use of emerging technologies. Collaboration between the public and private sectors is important to establish these standards and ensure that technological innovations benefit the entire society.

Moreover, the importance of continuous education and training to prepare for the challenges associated with these technologies has been highlighted. Initiatives such as AI and Blockchain certification programs at Oxford University and MIT are closing the skills gap, ensuring that professionals are equipped with the necessary knowledge to effectively implement and regulate these technologies.

Finally, evaluating and measuring the impact of self-regulation through Key Performance Indicators (KPIs), periodic audits, citizen surveys, and cost-benefit analysis provides valuable data for future improvements. These tools allow public administrations to ensure that self-regulation policies are effective and also adaptable to technological changes and social needs, thereby promoting transparency, equity, and efficiency in public services.

The integration of AI, Blockchain, and Cloud Computing in public administration is a dynamic process that requires a balanced approach between innovation and protecting citizens' rights. By combining innovative approaches, international collaboration, and a strong emphasis on education and training, it is possible to ensure that these transformative technologies are safely and effectively integrated into government systems, providing significant benefits to society.

REFERENCES

Alhaimer, R. (2023a). Exploring the Attitudes of Kuwait's Residents Toward the Role of Corruption and Anti-Corruption Entities (Nazaha) in Kuwait. *Public Integrity*, 26(3), 305–321. DOI: 10.1080/10999922.2023.2176054

Alhaimer, R. (2023b). *Impact of governmental social media campaigns on citizens' attitudes towards Kuwait's vision 2035*. Global Knowledge, Memory and Communication., DOI: 10.1108/GKMC-06-2023-0209

Alhaimer, R. (2024). Digital transformation on the design and implementation of virtual political campaigns in Kuwait: perceptions and attitudes of politicians and campaign managers for bold innovation and social impact in Kuwait. Journal of Science and Technology Policy Management. DOI: 10.1108/JSTPM-11-2023-0212

Alkhaldi, A., Alrashidi, H., Alhasan, K., Alsadeeqi, A., & Alshami, A. (2023). *The use of blockchain technology to build smart cities: creating public value in Kuwait*. Global Knowledge, Memory and Communication., DOI: 10.1108/GKMC-11-2022-0263

Alkhaldi, A., Malik, S., & Lytras, M. D. (2024). Transformative Leadership in Kuwait Direct Investment Promotion Authority: Investing in Talent, Innovation and the Next Generation. In S. Baroudi & M. D. Lytras, M. D. (Eds.), Transformative Leadership and Sustainable Innovation in Education: Interdisciplinary Perspectives (27-38). Emerald Publishing Limited. DOI: 10.1108/978-1-83753-536-120241003

Batubara, F. R., Ubacht, J., & Janssen, M. (2018). Challenges of blockchain technology adoption for e-government: a systematic literature review. In *Proceedings of the 19th Annual International Conference on Digital Government Research: Governance in the Data Age*, 1-9. DOI: 10.1145/3209281.3209317

Deloitte. (2022). *State of AI in the Enterprise, 5th Edition*. Retrieved from https://www2.deloitte.com/us/en/insights/focus/cognitive-technologies/state-of-ai-and-intelligent-automation-in-business-survey.html

Desouza, K. C., Dawson, G. S., & Chenok, D. (2020). Designing, developing, and deploying artificial intelligence systems: Lessons from and for the public sector. *Business Horizons*, 63(2), 205–213. DOI: 10.1016/j.bushor.2019.11.004

Dwivedi, Y. K., Hughes, L., Ismagilova, E., Aarts, G., Coombs, C., Crick, T., Duan, Y., Dwivedi, R., Edwards, J., Eirug, A., Galanos, V., Ilavarasan, P. V., Janssen, M., Jones, P., Kar, A. K., Kizgin, H., Kronemann, B., Lal, B., Lucini, B., & Williams, M. D. (2021). Artificial Intelligence (AI): Multidisciplinary perspectives on emerging challenges, opportunities, and agenda for research, practice and policy. *International Journal of Information Management*, 57, 101994. DOI: 10.1016/j.ijinfomgt.2019.08.002

European Commission. (2020). *Blockchain Strategy*. Retrieved from https://ec.europa.eu/digital-strategy/our-policies/blockchain-strategy_en

Floridi, L., Cowls, J., Beltrametti, M., Chatila, R., Chazerand, P., Dignum, V., Luetge, C., Madelin, R., Pagallo, U., Rossi, F., Schafer, B., Valcke, P., & Vayena, E. (2018). AI4People—An Ethical Framework for a Good AI Society: Opportunities, Risks, Principles, and Recommendations. *Minds and Machines*, 28(4), 689–707. DOI: 10.1007/s11023-018-9482-5 PMID: 30930541

Janssen, M., Brous, P., Estevez, E., Barbosa, L. S., & Janowski, T. (2020). Data governance: Organizing data for trustworthy Artificial Intelligence. *Government Information Quarterly*, 37(3), 101493. DOI: 10.1016/j.giq.2020.101493

Kalenzi, C. (2022). Artificial Intelligence and Blockchain: How Should Emerging Technologies Be Governed? *Frontiers in Research Metrics and Analytics*, 7, 801549. DOI: 10.3389/frma.2022.801549 PMID: 35224423

López Jiménez, D., Dittmar, E. C., & Vargas Portillo, J. P. (2021). Self-regulation of sustainability as a manifestation of corporate social responsibility. *Revista de Ciencias Sociales*, 27(3), 16–29. DOI: 10.31876/rcs.v27i3.36750

López Jiménez, D., Dittmar, E. C., & Vargas Portillo, J. P. (2022). The trusted third party or digital notary in Spain: Effect on virtual transactions. *International Review of Law Computers & Technology*, 36(3), 453–469. DOI: 10.1080/13600869.2021.2004760

Makridakis, S. (2017). The forthcoming Artificial Intelligence (AI) revolution: Its impact on society and firms. *Futures*, 90, 46–60. DOI: 10.1016/j.futures.2017.03.006

Ølnes, S., Ubacht, J., & Janssen, M. (2017). Blockchain in government: Benefits and implications of distributed ledger technology for information sharing. *Government Information Quarterly*, 34(3), 355–364. DOI: 10.1016/j.giq.2017.09.007

Papenfuß, U., & Schmidt, C. A. (2021). Understanding self-regulation for political control and policymaking: Effects of governance mechanisms on accountability. *Governance: An International Journal of Policy, Administration and Institutions*, 34(4), 1115–1141. DOI: 10.1111/gove.12549

Song, J. (2021). Ethical adaptation and legal regulation of modern technology. *Cultura e Scuola*, 4(3), 169–178. DOI: 10.1177/20966083211053085

Spain, I. D. C. (2023). *IDC FutureScape: Worldwide Government 2023 Predictions*. Retrieved from https://www.idc.com/getdoc.jsp?containerId=prES48722621

Sposato, M. (2024a). Are leaders born or made? Asking the right question. *Development and Learning in Organizations*, 38(3), 1–3. DOI: 10.1108/DLO-05-2023-0123

Sposato, M. (2024b). Leadership training and development in the age of artificial intelligence. *Development and Learning in Organizations*, 38(4), 4–7. DOI: 10.1108/DLO-12-2023-0256

Sposato, M. (2025). Developing Digital Leadership Skills for AI-Driven Research Environments. In *Impacts of Generative AI on the Future of Research and Education* (pp. 235–254). IGI Global., DOI: 10.4018/979-8-3693-0884-4.ch010

Sun, T. Q., & Medaglia, R. (2019). Mapping the challenges of Artificial Intelligence in the public sector: Evidence from public healthcare. *Government Information Quarterly*, 36(2), 368–383. DOI: 10.1016/j.giq.2018.09.008

Valle-Cruz, D., Criado, J. I., Sandoval-Almazán, R., & Ruvalcaba-Gómez, E. A. (2021). Assessing the public policy-cycle framework in the age of artificial intelligence: From agenda-setting to policy evaluation. *Government Information Quarterly*, 37(4), 101509. DOI: 10.1016/j.giq.2020.101509

Veale, M., & Brass, I. (2019). Administration by algorithm? Public management meets public sector machine learning. In Yeung, K., & Lodge, M. (Eds.), *Algorithmic Regulation* (pp. 121–149). Oxford University Press. DOI: 10.1093/oso/9780198838494.003.0006

Wirtz, B. W., Weyerer, J. C., & Geyer, C. (2019). Artificial Intelligence and the Public Sector—Applications and Challenges. *International Journal of Public Administration*, 42(7), 596–615. DOI: 10.1080/01900692.2018.1498103

Zuiderwijk, A., Chen, Y. C., & Salem, F. (2021). Implications of the use of artificial intelligence in public governance: A systematic literature review and a research agenda. *Government Information Quarterly*, 38(3), 101577. DOI: 10.1016/j.giq.2021.101577

Chapter 3
AI-Driven Decision Making Enhancing Public Sector Efficiency and Effectiveness

Karthik Raja Srinivasan
https://orcid.org/0009-0001-7337-9504
Universiti Malaya, Malaysia

Nur Hairani Abd Rahman
https://orcid.org/0000-0002-0046-3588
Universiti Malaya, Malaysia

Sri Devi Ravana
https://orcid.org/0000-0002-5637-9158
Universiti Malaya, Malaysia

ABSTRACT

This chapter investigates the transformative influence of digital technologies on public sector governance by incorporating the ABCD framework (Artificial Intelligence, Blockchain, Cloud, Data Analytics). It emphasizes the ways in which these technologies effectively address complex challenges and optimize service delivery through four fundamental pillars: first, Data-Driven Decision-Making, which customizes services to meet citizen needs; second, Evidence-Based Policymaking, which proactively addresses policy through evidential datasets; third, Predictive Analytics, which implements sophisticated computational methods to generate dynamic solutions; and finally, Transparency and Accountability, which cultivates public trust by implementing ethical data practices. Nonetheless, there are still challenges, in

DOI: 10.4018/979-8-3693-7678-2.ch003

terms of data quality, biases in data collection, and the need for robust privacy measures. The chapter underlines the need of ethical frameworks and algorithm selection in mitigating the hurdles connected with data use in the public sector while also ensuring fair governance.

"The path to efficient e-government lies not in one technology, but the symphony of innovations that empower the people"

INTRODUCTION

The advent of the digital revolution has resulted in a significant transformation towards the public sector and it has altered the way governments handle and assess large amount of data. This chapter recognizes how data driven technologies can be integrated with Government Services in order to provide a conducive method that goes beyond traditional governance.

A critical analysis of Shahriar Akter's research article on artificial intelligence, blockchain, cloud computing, and data analytics (ABCD) (Akter et al., 2022), reveals that the operations and value propositions of this hybridization, integration, recombination, and convergence are being explored in terms of their potential to transform the business landscape. This observation invites a parallel consideration of the needs and effectiveness of ABCD within the public sector. Taking into account the unique characteristics and boundaries for government data as theorized by (Kim et al., 2014). E-governance thrives not solely on one single technology but emerges from the synergy of various technologies, interacting with one another. Transparency, efficiency, accessibility, accountability, and ultimately fostering citizen engagement and trust in government processes are to be considered for application of ABCD and these values forms the foundational pillars for improved public service delivery.

First, data-driven decision-making, this key pillar allows government agencies to optimize service delivery tailored towards citizen needs. Case study on how Singapore Government utilizes machine learning approach to solve dengue outbreak using geospatial data, metrological data, and historical records data, to improve case fatality rates and reduce economic expenditure associated with these outbreaks provides necessary insights (Tian et al., 2024). The Government also identified cooperation among law enforcement agencies, lawmakers, and community involvement, led to a decrease in future dengue cases. This synergetic impact is not limited to dengue outbreak, it can be recreated to different sectors. Furthermore, economic impact studies showed that the average yearly cost of mitigating dengue in Singapore between 2000 and 2020 was around $1 billion. They have also estimated a decline in the economic burden from the period of 2010 to 2020 through the adoption of artificial intelligence (Soh et al., 2021).

Second, data-based policymaking is replacing intuition with data, leading to more effective solutions for complex challenges. While evidence-based policymaking was based on more traditional sources of data and analytical methods, data-driven policymaking is based on the most advanced computational techniques (inclusive of ABCD), fast processing of huge and disparate data, and extracting insights that otherwise remain elusive to the human analytical eye (Papyshev & Yarime, 2023).

Third, predictive analytics lends the capability of being proactive about public safety through the identification and planning for exigencies before they occur. In this chapter taking crime prevention as the theme, will explore how governments can better identify the underlying factors contributing to criminal behaviour. Psychological, environmental, agency, socioeconomic conditions, access to education, and employment opportunities are the common patterns predicted by systems (Afzal & Panagiotopoulos, 2024; Campana & Meneghini, 2024). In addition to that, looking deeper into crime mapping, hot spot policing, and predictive policing can showcase how technologies have improved resource allocation and refinement at the institutional level for sustainable and impactful outcomes (Berk, 2021; Brayne & Christin, 2021).

Finally, touching on transparency and accountability, the ethical data practices enable trust for responsible use and ensure a safer, more efficient society. Transparency builds trust; in the absence of how decisions have been made and the use of data, citizens are suspicious; openness brings about accountability, and thus allows scrutiny by the general public, to ensure that the actions of government align with public interest. Various governments are building public trust by mitigating bias and ensuring fairness, promoting responsible data use and preventing its abuse, improving policy decisions and public engagement, fostering innovation and collaboration, among others, (Rohde et al., 2024; Papyshev & Yarime, 2023). Challenges pertain to the area of data quality and bias. Data accuracy and dealing with possible biases in collection and analysis are hence very important in the public sector. There are also concerns about privacy, such as striking a balance between data collection and the rights of citizen to his or her private life (Gaskins, 2023).

Furthermore, the presence of robust data security measures and ethical frameworks is an important requirement and there exists challenges pertaining to data quality and bias. Data accuracy and dealing with possible biases in collection and analysis are also important in the public sector. World Development Report 2021: Data for Better Lives states that, the algorithms used in analyzing data may give rise to existing social biases, and in the process, unfair targeting of demographics takes place. Therefore, careful selection and evaluation of algorithms are vital to evade unintended results.

LITERATURE REVIEW

The continual advancements in technology have increased the ability of private organizations to acquire, store, and manage vast amounts of data. Consequently, many transformational benefits are within grasp for private sector organizations that choose to apply data analytic techniques to large data sets internally and externally.

Benefits of artificial intelligence, blockchain, cloud and data analytics (ABCD support quicker and improved decision-making, identify trends & links that would be difficult to ascertain using other methods, and improve operational & organizational performance (Akter et al., 2022).

Artificial intelligence, Blockchain, Cloud, and Data analytics have lately been adopted in many and varied areas of the private sector. Businesses learned the value of using data to better make business decisions, optimize operations, and outcompete their competitors. This includes predictive analytics being applied for anticipating market trends to customer analytics for strategically tailoring marketing strategies. Private companies are using big data analytics as the driver for growth and innovation in major sectors like healthcare, finance, retail, and technology (Akter et al., 2022). With the growth of data both in volume and complexity, data analytics will become increasingly central in the future of the private sector-from health care, finance, and retail to technology (Makridis & Mishra, 2022; Dwivedi et al., 2021; Varsha et al., 2021).

Table 1. Critical analysis of ABCD in private sector

S.No	Title of Research Paper	Author(s)	Focus Area	Critical Analysis
1	How does blockchain technology enhance firm operation and cooperation?	(Huang & Zhou, 2024)	Blockchain	Highlights potential benefits of blockchain for firms, Secure and transparent collaboration; Improved contract management and Streamlined workflows
2	Artificial Intelligence as a Service, Economic Growth, and Well-Being.	(Makridis & Mishra, 2022)	Artificial Intelligence	Highlights potential economic impacts of AI as a service. Reduced costs of AI adoption in private sector, Scalability and flexibility and Faster access to innovation
3	Digital innovation and the effects of artificial intelligence on firms' research and development. Automation or augmentation, exploration or exploitation?	Johnson, P. C., et al. (2022).	Artificial Intelligence	Provides nuanced analysis of AI's impact and stresses on automated data analysis, Enhanced product design and Improved risk management

continued on following page

Table 1. Continued

S.No	Title of Research Paper	Author(s)	Focus Area	Critical Analysis
4	Artificial intelligence in business and economics research: Trends and future.	(Ruiz-Real et al., 2021)	Artificial Intelligence	Provides comprehensive overview of AI trends, show cases the benefit of improved financial analysis, Enhanced fraud detection, and Personalized marketing campaigns.
5	A framework of blockchain technology adoption: An investigation of challenges and expected value.	(Toufaily et al., 2021)	Blockchain	Provides valuable framework for blockchain adoption, and discusses supply chain transparency & traceability.
6	Enhancing the circular and modified linear economy: The importance of blockchain for developing economies.	(Ajwani-Ramchandani et al., 2021)	Blockchain	Provides valuable perspective on blockchain's role in sustainable economy and special emphasis on how various sector can Streamlines processes, that potentially reduces costs needs.
7	Artificial Intelligence (AI): Multidisciplinary perspectives on emerging challenges, opportunities, and agenda for research, practice and policy.	(Dwivedi et al., 2021)	Artificial Intelligence	Comprehensive overview of AI. Insights on automation of tasks, Improved product development, and Enhanced customer service.
8	Envisioning the power of data analytics.	(Beer, 2018)	Data Analytics	Exploration of data analytics potential customer insights and operational efficiency.
9	A survey towards an integration of big data analytics to big insights for value-creation.	(Saggi & Jain, 2018)	Data Analytics	Offers valuable overview of big data analytics for value creation and targeted marketing campaigns.
10	Big data text analytics: An enabler of knowledge management.	(Khan & Vorley, 2017)	Data Analytics	Highlights, market research, competitive intelligence and product development.

Table 1 critically analyses various articles on ABCD focused towards private sector. It's inferred that contextualization, specificity, and evolution has culminated at the levels of technology & processes towards the private sector. Targeted market campaigns, frameworks specifically for supply chain, and user application for market research are few such examples. Examining further, Table 2 describes the research work by Shahriar Akter titled "Transforming Business Using Digital Innovations: The Application of AI, Blockchain, Cloud and Data Analytics ", where personalized user preferences are discussed. It is to be noted that, ethical considerations exist regardless of whether the public or private sector is utilizing data analytics.

Table 2. Critical analysis of Shahriar Akter's research article on artificial intelligence, blockchain, cloud and data analytics (ABCD)

Key points	Challenges
1. The study advocates the use of AI, Blockchain, Cloud Computing, and Data Analytics to drive maximum business transformation. Each of those separately can provide value in and of themselves; the appropriate use of these together technologies is much more conducive to driving greater business value and innovation.	1. Integration of these can be complicated because of the varying standards, interoperability, and compatible IT infrastructure.
2. **3. ABCD Technologies empower organizations to use data to inform decisions, leveraging an ongoing cycle of improvement to compete relevantly.** **4.**	2. Companies find it tough to keep up with enormous volumes of data. Problems range from incorrect data, outdated information, and inconsistency between internal and external databases.
5. ABCD technologies are a key enabler in innovative business model development, process automation, supply and demand optimization, and real-time decision-making.	3. There are ethical considerations, such as privacy and algorithmic bias, which organizations have to address with a particular emphasis on AI applications.
6. More than 91.6% of Fortune 1000 companies are making investments in big data analytics, where 55% of these companies are investing over $55 million to keep the fear of disruption away.	4. For many firms, high investment costs and skilled personnel needed for the implementation and management of such technologies are challenging.
7. The study also discusses various operational use cases of each ABCD technologies, thus hinting the spread of those technologies across several sectors, though not specifically in terms of percentage or numbers as shared.	5. The effective exploitation of ABCD technologies for the business transformation requires hybridization, integration, recombination, and convergence of these technologies; therefore, there is emergent demand for such strategies.

(Akter et al., 2022)

Translating this potential to the public sector, research by (Valle-Cruz & García-Contreras, 2023; Arnaboldi & Azzone, 2020; Loukis et al., 2020; Fredriksson et al., 2017) show the potential benefits can be derived from the use of data-driven technologies in public services.

Automation of basic routine tasks and the analysis of large volumes of data enable governments to deliver services more accurately for the benefit of the citizens. I*mproving the efficiency and effectiveness of public services, data-driven decision making, economic growth & innovation, addressing emerging national challenges, public safety & security, and promoting economic equity* fosters **greater transparency and accountability** within government agencies and societies. Citizens can access performance metrics and hold public servants responsible for their actions, fostering greater trust. Indeed, (Wang & Guan, 2023) go further and discuss the aspect of increasing **citizen engagement**. Agencies analyze big data emanating from many sources and thereby gain insight into and model needs and preferences of citizens for better communication and service provision. Predictive analytics might thus also be of critical support. For example, (Loukis et al., 2020) looked into public sector data analytics in enabling economic crisis policymaking. It enables public agencies to stay ahead of the curve through the anticipation of trends and preparation for what could occur well in advance, thereby managing to respond more appropriately to emergencies and to allocate resources accordingly.

METHODOLOGY

A combination of case studies with document analysis provides a comprehensive framework for testing complex associations among emerging technologies and public sector performance, thereby creating value from the literature on this increasingly important topic. This book chapter follows a case study methodology to explore application and implication of AI driven decision Making in public sector for efficiency and effectiveness. In-depth case studies (Explanatory, and Exploratory) have been used for investigation of complexities and nuances that accompany the key pillars of decision making. Moreover, Document analysis will, be used for data collection to support the case study methodology through a systematic review of relevant documents related to artificial intelligence, blockchain, cloud and data analytics. The documents (Web of Science Indexed Journals are taken which have practical applications in the field of private sector, public sector, and governance) will be selected considering relevance, credibility, and comprehensiveness criteria (keywords analysed: *artificial intelligence, blockchain, cloud, data analytics, governance, public sector, private sector*). Other than journals; policy documents, project reports, reports from international organizations, and information from government websites are also used and analysed at respective levels to explore the dominant themes for analysis.

RESULTS

It emphasizes the ways in which these new technologies effectively address complex challenges and optimize service delivery through four fundamental pillars (1) Data-Driven Decision-Making, which customizes services to meet the needs of citizens; (2) Evidence-Based Policymaking, which proactively addresses public policy by implementing evidential datasets; (3) Predictive Analytics, which implements sophisticated computational methods to generate dynamic solutions; and (4)

Transparency and Accountability, which cultivates public trust by implementing ethical data practices.

A new change is anticipated transcending typical departmental silos, utilizing multiple types of data to transform how governments work and serve residents. Figure 1 depicts an example of problems associated with adapting data-based technologies within the public sector, where the volume, variety, and velocity of data are inherent characteristics that will be required in the business setting on the left, and inherent silos, security, and variety are characteristics that the data must adopt in the public sector on the right. Since the data will be utilized to supply services, a balanced feature known as 'value' is required.

Figure 1. Showcasing how data based technologies can provide value to governments (Kim et al., 2014)

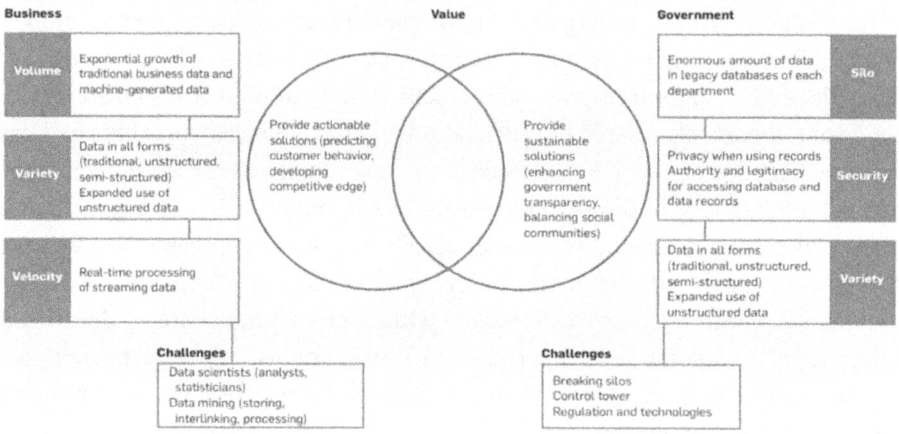

Embracing Diverse Data Sources, in contrast to the past, structured data from traditional sources like spreadsheets and databases were primarily governmental, today's analytics on big data empowers us to harness both unstructured data, such as text, social media, sensor data, and semi-structured data, like emails and web logs. According to (Desouza & Jacob, 2017), the holistic approach to information at all levels with decisions that are well imagined allows a more comprehensive perspective on societies needs.

Breaking Departmental Barriers, overcoming departmental silos and data fragmentation remains a significant hurdle in realizing the full potential of emerging data-based technologies. According to the observations made by (Wang et al., 2021; Desouza & Jacob, 2017), such barriers can hinder analysis when relevant data is scattered across. In order to reap the true benefits of emerging data-based technologies, interdepartmental collaboration and data sharing are considered essential.

Big Data Security Concerns, the use of data analytics by any public entity probably has security their first concern. As argued by several researchers, security breaches involving citizen data could lead to a loss of confidence in government organizations. Thus, appropriate cybersecurity and data governance frameworks are needed to safeguard sensitive information. This is where the balancing act comes in-providing adequate access to data for analytics against robust security.

Value to Society, despite challenges, data analytics has its value proposition to society. Here are some key areas,

- ***Optimizing Service Delivery:*** Issues that need improvement could be discovered, and services could be given in more efficient ways by digging into the usage of the service and listening to the citizenry. (Overton et al., 2022) showed the possibility of using data analytics in smoothing health care delivery, which resulted in saved costs and patients with improved experiences. Data analytics helps governments move away from anecdotal evidence and intuition and toward fact-based data-driven policy decisions.
- ***Evidence-based Policymaking:*** Studies by (Tian et al., 2024; Hwang et al., 2021; de Marcellis-Warin & Warin, 2020) have shown how data from the public health and social welfare perspective, through analysis, may support appropriate interventions that yield better results.
- ***Enhanced Public Safety:*** Data analytics can become a powerful tool for predictive policing. In that respect, (Demaidi, 2023; Gaskins, 2023), refer to a discussion in which the crime prediction models have the potential to create avenues for police departments to strategize and allocate resources in such a way that incidents of crimes could be prevented, lives could be saved, and public safety improved.
- ***Promoting Transparency and Accountability:*** Making data publicly available, as put forth by, (Biju & Gayathri, 2024; Papyshev & Yarime, 2023) will allow governments to foster trust in and engagement with the public. In addition, this will serve as a conduit for citizens to hold governments accountable for their decisions and actions, and for greater engagement of citizens in decision-making processes through open data initiatives.

Nonetheless, there are still challenges, particularly in terms of data quality, biases in data collection, and the need for robust privacy measures. Efficiency, service delivery, and sustainability are the legacy components of a government, not profit. Focusing on these foundational pillars could be an act of hope for the governmental sectors.

DISCUSSION

Pillar-1: Improved Service Delivery Through Data-Driven Insights

Utilizing the customer feedback, usage patterns, and satisfaction metrics, private sector entities were able to design services that are tailored to the specific requirements of their customers. The Governments can adopt the same towards the citizen for enhanced service delivery, correcting data collection and analysis mechanism which must be rigorous to ensure reliable insights. Secondly, Citizens' data privacy must be protected over other governmental interest, and clear communication on temporal data usage is essential. This can be witnessed through explanatory case study of tackling dengue outbreaks by Singapore government.

Use Case: Tackling Dengue outbreaks by Singapore Government

"If the government have enough lead time on predicting outbreaks it will provide the necessary time for preventative measures to be implemented before a significant outbreak occurs". But, emergencies are a spontaneous events that can be addressed with institutionalized mitigating mechanisms. Another important factor in dealing with virus spread is the location specificity, predicting areas with a higher likelihood of outbreaks allowing for targeted resource allocation for mosquito control.

The Ministry of health collated three different data sources together

- ***Population Density Data:*** Geographically aligning population, provinces within the region with dengue outbreaks. Deriving a correlation between densely populated areas, and transmission of virus from the mosquitoes.
- ***Dengue Case Data:*** Historical records of dengue cases were used to identify patterns and correlations with weather conditions.
- ***Meteorological Data:*** Last but not the least, the Mosquito's are the vector for dengue and to understand how mosquitos breed, taking into account of meteorological data such as (temperature, rainfall, humidity, and sunshine).

Since it was more prediction based, adopting machine learning algorithms to analyze the data and predict outbreaks. Other studies have also explored models like Support Vector Machines (SVM) and Random Forest, each with varying strengths and weaknesses but for this analysis XGBoost was used: This algorithm has proven effective in capturing non-linear relationships between weather variables and dengue cases. (Tian et al., 2024).

Government Identified that

- ***Predictive Power of Historical Data*:** By the use of inducted data-based predictions, authorities would be able to prioritize efforts of outbreaks with fogging and inspections, and concentrate their control efforts on high-risk areas.
- ***Dengue Outbreaks due to Environmental Factors:*** Understanding the specific environmental factors (e.g., temperature, rainfall, humidity) that significantly influence mosquito breeding and subsequent dengue outbreaks. This allows for more targeted interventions based on real-time weather data.
    - o ***Elimination of Mosquito Breeding Sites:*** The regular inspection followed by fogging is done by National Environment Agency (NEA) to eliminate the site that can be utilised by the mosquitoes to breed (drains, flower pots and other containers etc.).
        - ***Source Reduction Practices:*** NEA advocates the covering of water tanks and overturning of stagnant water receptacles to avoid mosquito breeding.
        - ***Wolbachia Project:*** Singapore also used biocontrol wherein the mosquitoes with Wolbachia bacteria are released. ***This bacterium reduces the capacity or competency of the Aedes mosquitoes to transmit dengue***.
- ***Mosquito Behaviour and Evolution:*** By analyzing mosquito breeding data and potential resistance to insecticides, the government would be better placed to revise their control methods and consider new interventions.

Other Incidental Data Analysis Provided,

1. ***The Need for Creating Public Awareness:*** The knowledge gaps in or misconceptions about mosquito breeding helped governments devise a mechanism of.
    - o ***Public Education Campaigns***: Government creates awareness about dengue through campaigns on mosquito breeding sites and ways of prevention.
    - o ***Community Outreach Programs***: The authorities engage with the residents for finding and destroying all possible mosquito breeding sites within homes and neighbourhoods.
    - o ***Grassroots Mobilisation:*** The leaders in the localities are important in mobilizing the residents for participation in control activities.
2. **Areas for Collaboration:**
    - o ***Enforcement***: The NEA carries out joint operations between various stakeholders involved and enforces penalties for non-compliance with regulations.

- o *Legislation*: Singapore has legislations that punish whoever defaults in taking measures to prevent mosquito breeding in premises.
- o *Partnership*: Newer areas, where collaboration with neighbouring countries on control strategies should be pursued.

Economic Impact Studies estimated the average annual economic burden of dengue in Singapore between 2010 and 2020, with an estimated cost ranging from $1.014 billion to $2.265 billion. The government has, reduced dengue cases in recent years compared to historical outbreaks, for example, in 2022 Singapore reported less than 5,000 cases, in contrary to the previous outbreaks. This of course translates into lower risk of severe illness and death in the population. Improved Case Fatality Rate (CFR) is likely to be lower in Singapore compared to other countries which reported outbreaks of dengue. The timely government interventions led to cost savings in healthcare expenditures and lost productivity. The amount estimated annually to have been saved over the 2010-2020 period was $329.40 million under 40% intervention efficacy (Soh et al., 2021).

PILLAR-2: EVIDENCE-BASED POLICYMAKING FROM INTUITION TO DATA-DRIVEN DECISIONS

Using process, benefits, challenges, and example as shown below various studies describe how The combination of AI, Block chain, Cloud, and Data analytics (through Crime Mapping and Hot Spot Policing, Predictive Policing, Social Network Analysis (SNA), and Link Analysis) could help the governments to pinpoint the root causes of criminal behavior, but not limited to, sociopsychological, environmental, and agency factors, socioeconomic conditions, access to education and employment, community engagement, and so on. In addition to that, the other effective results that have been accomplished dealing with the roots of the criminal behavior to date include improved resource utilization, predictive policing, and institutional evaluation and refinement. More sustainable and effective results may be achieved with such interventions (Brayne & Christin, 2021). Various methods and its applications are as follows,

1. Crime Mapping and Hot Spot Policing:

Process: From aggregated crime data (location, time, type) analysis can be done to draw maps showing spatial and temporal patterns of crime. It can also show high concentration areas or so-called “hot spots” (Afzal & Panagiotopoulos, 2024).

Benefits: The police, from the analysis, can thus ***concentrate their resources*** in areas most needed, possibly deterring criminal activities.

Example: Local police track crimes to determine where an actual incident of theft in that locale has taken place at the current time. They deploy more security to the spot at the time when frequency is highest to stop further break-ins.

2. Predictive Policing:

Process: It predicts areas and times with a high likelihood of risk through advanced analytics and machine learning from historical data (location, time, and nature of the crime). This allows proactive policing presence in those areas where a crime is most likely to occur, which could avoid such incidents or reduce the reaction time to incidents (Berk, 2021; Yen & Hung, 2021).

Benefits: Enables proactive police presence in high-risk areas, potentially deterring crime and improving response times.

Challenges: Data quality and potential biases can lead to inaccurate predictions and privacy concerns must be addressed.

Example: A city harnesses machine learning to forecast strong odds that robberies will occur at convenience stores over the weekend hours at night. They send undercover police officers to the stores during those hours.

3. Social Network Analysis (SNA):

Process: Examines interactions and linkages among individuals believed to be involved in criminal activities. Can be used to reveal criminal networks, gang involvement and potential future offenses (Bright et al., 2021; Morselli, 2009).

Benefits: This helps to identify critical members of a criminal group. Tt helps dismantle the same group and also assists in crime prevention.

Challenges: Data mining through social networks could be a potential cause of privacy infringement.

Example: Police, scan data that is concerning the intra-communication of phone calls and also social network links. These are seconded in finding an existing drug trafficking network. They carry the outcomes to hit nodes, rather key players, in the network.

4. Link Analysis:

Process: Helps analysts identify the inter-relationship between different crime data. This might reveal a hidden pattern and linkage that an average human eye might not necessarily gauge (Shelfer & Zhang, 2024).

Benefits: It gives an indication of a possible crime precursor, such as using an abandoned building for drug activity.

Example: The police calculate burglary cases and instances of abandoned buildings to find a correlation. They patrol hard around abandoned buildings to potentially deter these break-ins.

5. Text Analysis:

Process: Text data extracted from social media, crime reports, and online forums is analyzed so that keywords or phrases associated with criminal activity can be identified (Sarzaeim et al., 2023; Morselli, 2009).

Benefits: It helps to identify the threats and planned criminal activities in advance, leading to opportunities for early intervention.

Challenges: This requires critical analysis not to fall prey to misinterpretations and likely biases in the use of language.

Example: A police agency uses linguistic analysis software to identify threats of violence on social media so they could investigate further and prevent an attack.

One of the biggest values of evidence-based policymaking is its ability to let policymakers understand and find root causes of some of these very complex problems, and by doing so, develop targeted solutions. In a crime prevention context, for example, data-driven approaches may help policymakers understand the root causes of criminal events, including all factors related to socioeconomic conditions, access to education and job opportunities, and community engagement. Once these causes are addressed, it enables the policymakers to come up with better tactics to help deter crimes for a safer public. This approach inspires accountability and transparency in decision-making. The requirement to base decisions on empirical evidence, therefore, allows the policymakers to prove that their decisions are informed by a proper understanding of the issue under consideration, rather than being bound by intuition and personal opinions. Analyzing data and research will allow policymakers to identify pitfalls that might come with a certain policy or its unintended consequences, thus informing them in making better decisions and avoiding costly mistakes. In this respect, it instills confidence in the public and other stakeholders and fosters an accountable culture in government.

On the other hand, evidence-based policymaking also involves specific difficulties,

Data Quality and Bias: The dataset for crimes can be incomplete or biased, hence making imperfect predictions that could lead to unfair resource distribution. There is a need to address the data accuracy with a view to reducing possible biases in data collection and analysis (Yen & Hung, 2021).

Privacy Concerns: Again, data collection should not interfere with the privacy of a citizen. Equally, robust data security measures and ethical frameworks are now required (Purves, 2022).

Algorithmic Bias: The algorithms which analyze data may then perpetuate the biases already inherent in society and may even inappropriately target segments of the population based on such biases (Gaskins, 2023).

Quite often, policymakers have a hard time getting their hands on reliable and accurate data, mainly in that type of area where collection happens to be sporadic or inconsistent. That may face a challenge in formulating evidence-based policies in certain fields-for instance, preventing crime-where the available data happens to be incomplete and fragmented. The other challenge that becomes involved is when the policy maker needs to be able to interpret and analyze the complex data. Policymakers might not be technologically proficient in the interpretation of data, especially in the case of statistical and data analysis. In this respect, the formulation of evidence-based policies by the policymakers becomes hard, precisely in areas where such data is complex and at variance. There is also the challenge of ensuring that the policymakers maintain the balance between policymaking based on evidence and flexibility.

Policymakers have to be responsive to changed circumstances and unexpected events, and these can make reliance on pure evidence-based approaches difficult.

PILLAR-3: ENHANCING PUBLIC SAFETY WITH PREDICTIVE ANALYTICS

Using an exploratory Case Study, the research by (Campana & Meneghini, 2024) offered a way that practitioners might identify which communities may be at risk of being victimized through organized crime, serving as an impetus to early interventions. This research examined a extensive police dataset from Cambridgeshire, UK (documented crime incidents over 41 months). "Turf" (home base) and "target" (areas marked for criminal activity) areas in organized crime groups were noticed. Based on the analysis organized crime thrive on geographical proximity, socio-demographic elements, and opportunities in illegal markets. It has been observed that Geographic proximity allows gang groups to target neighbourhoods with concentration in gang networks, as determined through network analysis. This analysis further helps in community outreach initiatives aimed at the causes of gang violence. The socio-demographic elements of target areas depend on variables related to urbanicity and economic conditions; but on occasions, deprivation may raise the supply of members for criminal activities.

Drivers of Movement

- ***Geographical proximity:*** one significant variable into the mobility of organized crime.
- ***Community Outreach:*** Utilize network analysis to select hot-spot areas of high gang concentration for community outreach programs that speak directly to the root causes of gang violence.
- ***Socio-demographic factors:*** Nature of the area to be targeted, for example, urbanicity, economic aspects, and criminality.
- ***Illegal market opportunities:*** organized crime groups target areas with higher levels of drug-related activity.
- ***Identify Accomplices:*** Smaller groups may then be investigated to find possible accomplices and build evidence.
- ***Socio-demographic homophily:*** Groups may stick to targeting communities similar to their nature.
- ***Deprivation:*** while deprivation increases the number of organized crime members a community produces.
- ***Target Key Players:*** Build the investigation around the central figure and other highly connected players in an effort to disrupt leadership within the network.
- ***Prevent Future Crimes:*** By having an idea of the structure of this network, police can predict when and where future break-in attempts might occur and increase patrols to those areas.

Benefits of SNA in this process

- ***Targeting the Priorities:*** Helps focus one's limited resources on the most influential players in the criminal network.
- ***Knowledge of Criminal Activity:*** Informs about the modus operandi of criminal groups, thereby helping in focusing their intentions (Ficara et al., 2023).
- ***Discovering Hidden Connections:*** SNA will help highlight connections or relationships that might have been obscure using other investigative techniques (Shelfer & Zhang, 2024).

Challenges of SNA

- ***Data Availability:*** This is dependent upon the availability of data on both individuals and relationships, which is fraught with issues regarding personal privacy.

- ***Data Quality:*** The quality of information is important. Any incompleteness or inaccuracy in information leads to fallacious analysis.
- ***Interpretation:*** This requires analysis in conjunction with other investigative techniques to provide a comprehensive view.

Developing predictive models out of data as done by (Campana & Meneghini, 2024) helps in the anticipation of issues even before they occur. This, in turn, furthers proactive decision-making where informed decisions can be made on resource distribution for community safety, ultimately transforming the process of public safety and governance.

Other advantages of predictive analytics in public safety involves identifying hotspots of crime as discussed in pillar two. Predictive analytics also enhance emergency response. In events of natural calamities or public health crises, the analysis of data from past occurrences enables governments to come up with effective ways of responses. Using predictive models can show the area affected in the case of hurricanes for quick evacuations and resource mobilizations. The government can mitigate damage, save lives, and show concern over public safety by anticipating needs and challenges, while improving operational efficiency.

Beyond crimes and emergency management, predictive analytics optimizes resource allocation in various public services. Thus, from the data obtained on service demand, such as healthcare and transportation, governments are able to carry out an analysis of trends that take place in order to adjust strategies appropriately. For example, if it is observed that the demand for mental health services surges within a particular community, the resources available can be channelled to this particular field with a view to addressing the problem at hand. This ensures that all public services address citizen needs with efficiency in governance.

PILLAR-4: TRANSPARENCY AND ACCOUNTABILITY FOSTERING TRUST THROUGH DATA

Transparency in data analytics is no longer a luxury, but a necessity. Transparency and accountability are fundamental principles for any government. Table 3 analyses various researchers on transparency.

Table 3. Critical analysis of transparency & accountability

S.No	Author(s)	Title	Key Points	Critical Analysis
1	Williams et al., (2022)	From transparency to accountability of intelligent systems: Moving beyond aspirations	Transparency is a first step, but true accountability requires mechanisms to ensure responsible use of data analytics by intelligent systems.	• The article provides a critique to the limitations of transparency alone. • However, it doesn't delve deeply enough into specific mechanisms for achieving accountability.
2	Matheus et al., (2020)	Data science empowering the public: Data-driven dashboards for transparent and accountable decision-making in smart cities	Proposes a framework for accountability in data-driven decision-making processes. This framework considers factors like stakeholder identification, data quality control, and justification of algorithmic decisions.	• Allows for a systematic approach to accountability, although possibly requiring contextualization in practice. • Needs to be tested for feasibility.
3	Pasquale, F. (2015)	The black box society: The secret algorithms that control money and life.	Raises concerns about the societal implications of opaque algorithms and the need for transparency and accountability.	• Most importantly, the book does provide a argument for transparency; it might be short-sighted as to the advantages to be gained from certain algorithms when used responsibly.

Transparency generates trust. Without information about decision-making and use of data, citizens are wary and cut off from it, represented in Table 3. Openness generates accountability, invites public review, ascertains that the steps taken by the government must, of necessity, be in the public interest. This creates confidence and strengthens democracy and, in the ultimate analysis serves the goal of better decision making for all.

1. **Creating Public Trust**:
    a. Scenario: "*A city government introduces a new algorithm intended to predict criminal activity and allocate police resources accordingly. The algorithm is opaque, and the citizens start suspecting that it may hold prejudiced views against particular parts of the city*". Indeed, without transparency in the use of algorithms, public confidence in law enforcement and initiatives for policing anchored on data can be progressively destroyed.
    b. Solution: Transparency can include the release of how the algorithm functions, what data are used, and its weaknesses. Public forums can be held in discussing the algorithm and alleviating the concerns. These builds trust and provokes collaborations between government and citizens.
2. Mitigating Bias and Ensuring Fairness:

a. Scenario: "*The government uses an algorithmic process whereby different loan applications are assessed. The algorithm discriminates against some particular demographic groups and eventually leads to unjustified loan refusals. This might also cause grave economic harms for the persons involved*".
b. Solution: Data and algorithmic transparency by governments, help identify where biases are likely to occur and give them an opportunity to reduce those biases. This may include diversification of training data for algorithms, including human insight into decision-making, and creating mechanisms for appeal from algorithmic decisions.

3. Encouraging responsible use of data and Preventing Abuse:
    a. Scenario: "*A government might collect massive volumes of information about its citizens, without any articulable use of utilizing that information. Thus, the questions of government surveillance and potential abuses come forth*".
    b. Solution: Transparency in the collection of data, methods to store data, and controls to access data are possible trust builders and bulwarks against the misuse of data. Other accountability mechanisms, such as independent audits and citizen oversight committees, could help ensure that responsible data use is done by government agencies.
4. Improved Policy Decisions and Public Engagement:
    a. Scenario: "The use of data analytics in the development of policy solutions within a government agency can be based on incomplete or flawed data. Such data leads to poorly created policies with minimal ability to meet real public needs".
    b. Solution: Making transparent data sources and methodologies will provide the public with data-driven policy scrutiny and offer feedback to help improve the quality of the data available to decision-makers to develop better policy outcomes.
5. Innovation and Collaboration:
    a. Scenario: "*A government entity is tasked with acquiring much useful data that can be employed in creating novel applications to address societal problems, but such data remains inaccessible due to the absence of transparency in their collection and usage*".
    b. Solution: Government data can be opened through *open data policies* to access by the public. In such a way, government could collaborate with industry and academia to develop various applications which will be beneficial to society.

Through above illustrations and use cases the need for transparency at governmental setting can be sensed, which departs from business setting.

TRACKING THE FUTURE OF DATA DRIVEN TECHNOLOGIES

Contextualization or adapting ABCD to a problem is challenging due to the bound limitations of traditional government and governance models in service delivery. While emerging technologies does promise efficiency and effectiveness, limitations persist (Varsha et al., 2021). First of all, there is quality and access to data; When there is incomplete or biased data, flawed insights are generated; these may even further inequality. Secondly, there is the human element to consider, According to (Dwivedi et al., 2021), information from data should support human expertise and judgment in service delivery, not replace it. Finally, there are ethical considerations about privacy or algorithmic bias in decision-making that demand serious thought (Zajko, 2022; van Wynsberghe, 2021).

Nevertheless, contextualization provides a way out. Sector-based localized data analysis through governments enables overcoming the limitations mentioned above. For instance, community-driven data collection initiatives make facilitating the representativeness of the data for the local needs and less biased (Zajko, 2022). Human-in-the-loop approaches, where humans make the final decisions with regards to service delivery informed by the data, also consider ethical issues (de Marcellis-Warin & Warin, 2020).

This contextualizes data-drivenness beyond the limited nature of previous works. For instance, this could give governments an edge in building a subtler and finer service delivery ecosystem, where the lines between traditional models of governance and a data-driven future keep blurring (Greely, 2022).

While the other three pillars of data analytics (enhanced service delivery, evidence-based policymaking, and public security) hold potential, their evolution cannot come at the expense of transparency and accountability. Transparency and accountability are the fundamental principles upon which good governance rests, serving as the central axis around which governments should operate (Table 4 below shows that benefits of transparency and accountability in data analytics to different stakeholders).

Table 4. Benefits of various stakeholders towards transparency & accountability

Stakeholder	Benefits	Examples
Citizens	1. Trust and Confidence 2. Empowerment and Participation 3. Privacy and Avoidance of Unfair Treatment	• A citizen knows how the data contributes to policy decisions; therefore, there is no lack of trust towards the government. • The citizen's feedback regarding data used to formulate policies involves the citizen. • Transparency discloses the biases of algorithms used while servicing the citizen.
Institutions	1. Increased Legitimacy and Public Value 2. Enhanced Decision Making 3. Reduced Power Abuse	• Initiation of open communication would help to build trust, responsible use of data. • Public and expert feedback enhance better data collection and hence better policy decisions. • The audits held enhance mechanisms of accountability and scare government agencies so that they do not misuse data.
Society	1. Innovation and Collaboration 2. Better Public Services 3. More Equitable Outcomes	• Open data supports collaboration between government, industry, and academia for the public good. • Data analytics can be used to make public service more effective and efficient. • The aspect of transparency ensures that data analytics are used fairly to counter problems like loan approval biases.
Academia	1. Identification of new research areas 2. Unique data set availabilities 3. Collaborative research opportunities 4. Assist in policy development	• Public reporting on collection practices or usage policies only. • How independent audits of algorithms used in government programmes • Transparent guidelines and regulations with regard to data privacy and security-what works best. • Citizens' advisory boards to review data-driven initiatives taken up by the government.

There are, however, some boundaries that need to be considered in guiding the use of ethics and responsibilities. The following discusses ethical boundaries in the realm of data analytics that would need to be worked on in the times to come

- ***Privacy*:** Data analytics must not infringe on individual privacy. There are clear guidelines in terms of the collection of data, storage of data, and use of data. The ownership of personal data shall be with the citizens and it must lie within their discretion on whether it can be used or not for specific purposes.
- ***Bias*:** Algorithms in data analytics will reflect possible biases in society if not thoughtfully designed and then continually monitored. Ensuring different kinds of datasets are utilized, one needs regular dataset reviews for potential biases in algorithms.
- ***Transparency and Explainability:*** Citizens should have a basic understanding of how data analytics is used in government decision-making. Algorithms should be explainable, allowing individuals to understand the logic behind automated decisions that impact them.

- ***Human Control:*** Data analytics shall be a tool to extend, not replace, human judgment and decision-making. In many areas where the stakes are high or cases involving great social consequence.
- ***Transparency and Explainability:*** Citizens should have a basic understanding of how data analytics is used when decisions are made for them by the government. Algorithms need to be explainable to provide insight to individuals into why automated decisions have been made that affect them.
- ***Security:*** The security of the data is of utmost concern. Long-term measures should be taken to avoid data breach, unauthorized access, and misfeasance with the sensitive information.
- ***Accountability:*** It shall have clear mechanisms of accountability in its practices. Independent oversight bodies, apart from regular public reporting, would ensure responsible use of data through government agencies.
- ***Social Equity:*** Data analytics is not to expand social disparities but should not be allowed to discriminate against certain groups using algorithms and data-driven solutions that genuinely serve all members of society.

Touching upon on how governments across the regions have used transparency (Shown in Table 5) can improve the future perception using data-based techniques. Showcasing in Table 5 with countries, best practices, and description about their aspects of transparency and accountability.

Table 5. Countermeasure by different countries towards transparency & accountability

S.No	Country	Best Practices	Description
1	Estonia[a]	*Open Data Policies*	***Strong open data policy:*** A huge variety of government data available online for the people's mass scrutiny by an active citizenry.
2	Taiwan[b]	***Algorithmic Oversight and Explainability***	***Algorithmic Governance Act:*** Requires disclosures about information related to those algorithms and impact assessments to catch potential biases.
3	United States[c]	***Public Reporting and Audits***	***"Data.gov" platform***: A centralized access point to government datasets. ***Independent audits***: Apply to the algorithms in some programs.
4	Canada[d]	***Public Engagement and Education***	***Directive on Open Data and Information***: Provides routes to citizen engagement by opening consultations and workshops on governance of the data. ***Public information campaigns***: Raise awareness about data protection and responsible handling of data.
5	Brazil[e]	***Right to Explanation***	***General Data Protection Law (LGPD)***: Provided a "right to explanation" for automated decisions.

continued on following page

Table 5. Continued

S.No	Country	Best Practices	Description
6	Australia[f]	***Open Data Portal and Independent Data Oversight***	Provides, through a single point, access to multiple varied datasets from across the government about the capture methodology and usage boundaries of the data. ***Australian Information Commissioner (OAIC)***: Allowed independent surveillance of the government's use of data for the enforcement of privacy laws and ensuring transparency
7	New Zealand[g]	***Open Access and Engagement Algorithmic Oversight***	Provides free access to government data with supporting tools and resources that allow citizens to understand and use data effectively. ***Community Forum***: A place where the public can provide comments and suggestions on how data should be implemented. ***Algorithmic Impact Assessment Framework:*** Agencies are supposed to review any potential algorithmic social impacts before any deployment of the same algorithm.
8	Singapore[h]	**Mandatory Data Breach Reporting**	Provides a central platform for public access to government datasets, along with APIs and data visualization tools that enable data exploration and analysis. ***Cybersecurity Act***: Reporting of data breaches to the related parties and authorities responsibility and security in safeguarding data.
9	European Union[i]	***Independent Oversight Bodies***	***General Data Protection Regulation (GDPR)***: It ensures the availability of independent data protection authorities throughout states in order to supervise compliance and investigate alleged data breaches.
10	Other countries Countries[j]	***Collaboration and Innovation***	***Collaborations***: Governments examine the way forward for fostering collaboration among governments, industries, and academia toward inducing ethics and transparency in data analytics activities.

CONCLUSION

The utilization of data-based technologies in various aspects has been widely disseminated to the public sector. While early efforts were essentially plagued by a lack of data and simple analytics, today's governments use complex technologies combined with large databases to drive decisions. The progress is visible in many critical fields as highlighted above, ranging from Singapore governments improved accessibility of data to open data portals & central platforms availing government information to citizens and organizations alike. Most importantly, highlighting the demand for analytical skills concerning the public sector is urgent.

Nowadays, several algorithms and predictive models support governments to identify trends, predict challenges, and make service delivery more effective. One can also see that the focus has shifted to make the process more transparent and accountable. Active engagement of the community in data governance and establishment of mechanisms of control ensure responsible use of data-driven technologies. There are currently four essential foundations upon which Governmental data-based technologies are built, as witnessed in this chapter. First, data-driven insights help efficient service delivery by making sure that offered services are tailored to the necessitated demands. Second, evidence-based policy making replaces intuitive feelings with facts to find probable answers to challenging problems. Thirdly, predictive analytics puts decision-makers in control of public safety by anticipating and mitigating exigency situations before they occur. Last but not least, openness and accountability instil trust through the use of transparent data to ensure proper usage for the assurance of safety. Yet, challenges still remain in terms of data quality and bias, and there is a need to address privacy and ethical issues on algorithmic fairness. It can be believed that using open data, advanced data-based technologies, and ethical guidelines future the public sector will transcending to be more citizen centric imbibing data-based technologies.

Centrality of values cannot be an alternative for technology development. While technological changes continue to evolve, there are core values guiding their formulation and application which cannot be substituted with new technologies. Governments and their people must uphold these values if technology is to serve as a force for good in society.

REFERENCES

Afzal, M., & Panagiotopoulos, P. (2024). Data in Policing: An Integrative Review. *International Journal of Public Administration*, •••, 1–20. DOI: 10.1080/01900692.2024.2360586

Ajwani-Ramchandani, R., Figueira, S., Torres de Oliveira, R., & Jha, S. (2021). Enhancing the circular and modified linear economy: The importance of blockchain for developing economies. *Resources, Conservation and Recycling*, 168, 105468. DOI: 10.1016/j.resconrec.2021.105468

Akter, S., Michael, K., Uddin, M. R., McCarthy, G., & Rahman, M. (2022). Transforming business using digital innovations: The application of AI, blockchain, cloud and data analytics. *Annals of Operations Research*, 308(1), 7–39. DOI: 10.1007/s10479-020-03620-w

Arnaboldi, M., & Azzone, G. (2020). Data science in the design of public policies: Dispelling the obscurity in matching policy demand and data offer. *Heliyon*, 6(6), e04300. DOI: 10.1016/j.heliyon.2020.e04300 PMID: 32637693

Beer, D. (2018). Envisioning the power of data analytics. *Information Communication and Society*, 21(3), 465–479. DOI: 10.1080/1369118X.2017.1289232

Berk, R. A. (2021). Artificial Intelligence, Predictive Policing, and Risk Assessment for Law Enforcement. *Annual Review of Criminology, 4*(Volume 4, 2021), 209–237. DOI: 10.1146/annurev-criminol-051520-012342

Biju, P. r., & Gayathri, O. (2024). Analytical state: A framework for thinking about artificial intelligence and algorithms for state power. *Electronic Government, an International Journal, 20*(4), 459–478. DOI: 10.1504/EG.2024.139503

Brayne, S., & Christin, A. (2021). Technologies of Crime Prediction: The Reception of Algorithms in Policing and Criminal Courts. *Social Problems*, 68(3), 608–624. DOI: 10.1093/socpro/spaa004 PMID: 38250480

Bright, D., Brewer, R., & Morselli, C. (2021). Using social network analysis to study crime: Navigating the challenges of criminal justice records. *Social Networks*, 66, 50–64. DOI: 10.1016/j.socnet.2021.01.006

Campana, P., & Meneghini, C. (2024). Organised crime movement across local communities: A network approach. *Trends in Organized Crime*, 27(3), 286–313. Advance online publication. DOI: 10.1007/s12117-024-09531-7 de Marcellis-Warin, N., & Warin, T. (2020). Government 4.0 and evidencebased policies: AI and data analytics to the rescue. In *Handb. Of Artificial Intelligence and Robotic Process Automation: Policy and Gov. Applic.* (pp. 31–39). Anthem Press; Scopus. https://www.scopus.com/inward/record.uri?eid=2-s2.0-85110815942&partnerID=40&md5=fccfa75b2db834014490044524b97dcb

Demaidi, M. N. (2023). Artificial intelligence national strategy in a developing country. *AI & Society*. Advance online publication. DOI: 10.1007/s00146-023-01779-x

Desouza, K. C., & Jacob, B. (2017). Big data in the public sector: Lessons for practitioners and scholars. *Administration & Society*, 49(7), 1043–1064. DOI: 10.1177/0095399714555751

Dwivedi, Y. K., Hughes, L., Ismagilova, E., Aarts, G., Coombs, C., Crick, T., Duan, Y., Dwivedi, R., Edwards, J., Eirug, A., Galanos, V., Ilavarasan, P. V., Janssen, M., Jones, P., Kar, A. K., Kizgin, H., Kronemann, B., Lal, B., Lucini, B., & Williams, M. D. (2021). Artificial Intelligence (AI): Multidisciplinary perspectives on emerging challenges, opportunities, and agenda for research, practice and policy. *International Journal of Information Management*, 57, 101994. DOI: 10.1016/j.ijinfomgt.2019.08.002

Ficara, A., Curreri, F., Fiumara, G., & De Meo, P. (2023). Human and Social Capital Strategies for Mafia Network Disruption. *IEEE Transactions on Information Forensics and Security, 18*, 1926–1936. *IEEE Transactions on Information Forensics and Security*. Advance online publication. DOI: 10.1109/TIFS.2023.3256706

Fredriksson, C., Mubarak, F., Tuohimaa, M., & Zhan, M. (2017). Big Data in the Public Sector: A Systematic Literature Review. *Scandinavian Journal of Public Administration*, 21(3), 3. DOI: 10.58235/sjpa.v21i3.11563

Gaskins, N. (2023). Interrogating Algorithmic Bias: From Speculative Fiction to Liberatory Design. *TechTrends*, 67(3), 417–425. DOI: 10.1007/s11528-022-00783-0 PMID: 36160677

Greely, H. T. (2022). Governing emerging technologies—Looking forward with horizon scanning and looking back with technology audits. *Global Public Policy and Governance*, 2(3), 266–282. DOI: 10.1007/s43508-022-00045-y

Huang, L., & Zhou, T. (2024). How does blockchain technology enhance firm operation and cooperation? *International Review of Economics & Finance*, 92, 34–49. DOI: 10.1016/j.iref.2024.01.049

Hwang, S., Nam, T., & Ha, H. (2021). From evidence-based policy making to data-driven administration: Proposing the data vs. value framework. *International Review of Public Administration*, 26(3), 291–307. DOI: 10.1080/12294659.2021.1974176

Khan, Z., & Vorley, T. (2017). Big data text analytics: An enabler of knowledge management. *Journal of Knowledge Management*, 21(1), 18–34. DOI: 10.1108/JKM-06-2015-0238

Kim, G.-H., Trimi, S., & Chung, J.-H. (2014). Big-data applications in the government sector. *Communications of the ACM*, 57(3), 78–85. DOI: 10.1145/2500873

Loukis, E. N., Maragoudakis, M., & Kyriakou, N. (2020). Artificial intelligence-based public sector data analytics for economic crisis policymaking. *Transforming Government: People. Transforming Government*, 14(4), 639–662. DOI: 10.1108/TG-11-2019-0113

Makridis, C. A., & Mishra, S. (2022). Artificial Intelligence as a Service, Economic Growth, and Well-Being. *Journal of Service Research*, 25(4), 505–520. DOI: 10.1177/10946705221120218

Morselli, C. (2009). The Criminal Network Perspective. In Morselli, C. (Ed.), *Inside Criminal Networks* (pp. 1–21). Springer., DOI: 10.1007/978-0-387-09526-4_1

Overton, M., Larson, S., Carlson, L. J., & Kleinschmit, S. (2022). Public data primacy: The changing landscape of public service delivery as big data gets bigger. *Global Public Policy and Governance*, 2(4), 381–399. DOI: 10.1007/s43508-022-00052-z

Papyshev, G., & Yarime, M. (2023). The state's role in governing artificial intelligence: Development, control, and promotion through national strategies. *Policy Design and Practice*, 6(1), 79–102. DOI: 10.1080/25741292.2022.2162252

Purves, D. (2022). Fairness in Algorithmic Policing. *Journal of the American Philosophical Association*, 8(4), 741–761. DOI: 10.1017/apa.2021.39

Rohde, F., Wagner, J., Meyer, A., Reinhard, P., Voss, M., Petschow, U., & Mollen, A. (2024). Broadening the perspective for sustainable artificial intelligence: Sustainability criteria and indicators for Artificial Intelligence systems. *Current Opinion in Environmental Sustainability*, 66, 101411. DOI: 10.1016/j.cosust.2023.101411

Ruiz-Real, J. L., Uribe-Toril, J., Torres, J. A., & Pablo, J. D. (2021). Artificial intelligence in business and economics research: Trends and future. *Journal of Business Economics and Management*, 22(1), 1. Advance online publication. DOI: 10.3846/jbem.2020.13641

Saggi, M. K., & Jain, S. (2018). A survey towards an integration of big data analytics to big insights for value-creation. *Information Processing & Management*, 54(5), 758–790. DOI: 10.1016/j.ipm.2018.01.010

Sarzaeim, P., Mahmoud, Q. H., Azim, A., Bauer, G., & Bowles, I. (2023). A Systematic Review of Using Machine Learning and Natural Language Processing in Smart Policing. *Computers*, 12(12), 12. Advance online publication. DOI: 10.3390/computers12120255

Shelfer, D., & Zhang, Y. (2024). A Social Network Analysis of Chronic Violent Offenders. *American Journal of Criminal Justice*, 49(5), 700–722. Advance online publication. DOI: 10.1007/s12103-024-09768-6

Soh, S., Ho, S. H., Seah, A., Ong, J., Dickens, B. S., Tan, K. W., Koo, J. R., Cook, A. R., Tan, K. B., Sim, S., Ng, L. C., & Lim, J. T. (2021). Economic impact of dengue in Singapore from 2010 to 2020 and the cost-effectiveness of Wolbachia interventions. *PLOS Global Public Health*, 1(10), e0000024. DOI: 10.1371/journal.pgph.0000024 PMID: 36962069

Tian, N., Zheng, J.-X., Li, L.-H., Xue, J.-B., Xia, S., Lv, S., & Zhou, X.-N. (2024). Precision Prediction for Dengue Fever in Singapore: A Machine Learning Approach Incorporating Meteorological Data. *Tropical Medicine and Infectious Disease*, 9(4), 4. Advance online publication. DOI: 10.3390/tropicalmed9040072 PMID: 38668533

Toufaily, E., Zalan, T., & Dhaou, S. B. (2021). A framework of blockchain technology adoption: An investigation of challenges and expected value. *Information & Management*, 58(3), 103444. DOI: 10.1016/j.im.2021.103444

Valle-Cruz, D., & García-Contreras, R. (2023). Towards AI-driven transformation and smart data management: Emerging technological change in the public sector value chain. *Public Policy and Administration*, 09520767231188401, 09520767231188401. Advance online publication. DOI: 10.1177/09520767231188401

van Wynsberghe, A. (2021). Sustainable AI: AI for sustainability and the sustainability of AI. *AI and Ethics*, 1(3), 213–218. DOI: 10.1007/s43681-021-00043-6

Varsha, R., Nair, S. M., Tyagi, A. K., Aswathy, S. U., & RadhaKrishnan, R. (2021). The Future with Advanced Analytics: A Sequential Analysis of the Disruptive Technology's Scope. In A. Abraham, T. Hanne, O. Castillo, N. Gandhi, T. Nogueira Rios, & T.-P. Hong (Eds.), *Hybrid Intelligent Systems* (pp. 565–579). Springer International Publishing. DOI: 10.1007/978-3-030-73050-5_56

Wang, C., Teo, T. S. H., & Janssen, M. (2021). Public and private value creation using artificial intelligence: An empirical study of AI voice robot users in Chinese public sector. *International Journal of Information Management*, 61, 102401. DOI: 10.1016/j.ijinfomgt.2021.102401

Wang, Q., & Guan, Z. (2023). Can Sunlight Disperse Mistrust? A Meta-Analysis of the Effect of Transparency on Citizens' Trust in Government. *Journal of Public Administration: Research and Theory*, 33(3), 453–467. DOI: 10.1093/jopart/muac040

Yen, C.-P., & Hung, T.-W. (2021). Achieving Equity with Predictive Policing Algorithms: A Social Safety Net Perspective. *Science and Engineering Ethics*, 27(3), 36. DOI: 10.1007/s11948-021-00312-x PMID: 34075448

Zajko, M. (2022). Artificial intelligence, algorithms, and social inequality: Sociological contributions to contemporary debates. *Sociology Compass*, 16(3), e12962. DOI: 10.1111/soc4.12962

ENDNOTES

a "Estonian Open Government Data Portal" (2023). University of Tartu. https://utlib.ut.ee/en/open-data

b "Algorithmic Governance Act of Taiwan" (2023). Ministry of Justice, Taiwan. https://www.moj.gov.tw/2832/

c "National Data Strategy" (2020). UK Government. https://www.gov.uk/guidance/national-data-strategy (**Note:** While the US utilizes Data.gov, the National Data Strategy reference provides a broader context on transparency and accountability)

d "Directive on Open Data and Information" (2014). Treasury Board of Canada Secretariat. https://open.canada.ca/en/using-open-data (**Note:** While the source is from 2014, it remains a relevant reference for Canada's approach)

e "Lei Geral de Proteção de Dados (LGPD)" (2023). Governo Federal do Brasil. https://www.gov.br/governodigital/pt-br/lgpd-pagina-do-cidadao/o-que-e-a-lgpd

f https://data.gov.au/ & https://www.oaic.gov.au/

g https://www.data.govt.nz/ & https://www.data.govt.nz/toolkit/data-ethics/government-algorithm-transparency-and-accountability/algorithm-impact-assessment-toolkit/

h https://www.tech.gov.sg/products-and-services/data-gov-sg/ & https://www.csa.gov.sg/legislation/Cybersecurity-Act

i https://gdpr.eu/what-is-gdpr/

j "World Development Report 2021: Data for Better Lives". World Bank. https://www.worldbank.org/en/publication/wdr2021 (This report by the World Bank highlights the collaborative aspects of open data practices

Chapter 4
AI-Driven Innovations in E-Government: How Is AI Reshaping the Public Sector?

Mohammad Rashed Albous
https://orcid.org/0009-0008-8646-3810
Arabian Gulf University, Kuwait

Bedour Alboloushi
https://orcid.org/0000-0001-5736-3185
Kuwait College of Science and Technology, Kuwait

ABSTRACT

As governments around the world embrace the digital revolution, AI-driven innovation emerges as a powerful tool for transforming public sector operations and e-government services. AI-driven innovation offers significant opportunities for governments, such as increasing operational efficiency, fostering citizen engagement, and enabling more effective decision-making. However, the integration of AI in the public sector also presents key challenges, such as data privacy concerns and algorithmic bias. This chapter provides a comprehensive analysis of AI integration in the public sector across various key domains. It explores both the significant opportunities and the critical considerations that governments must address to ensure the effective and ethical utilization of AI technologies.

DOI: 10.4018/979-8-3693-7678-2.ch004

2.1 INTRODUCTION

The public sector is undergoing an accelerated digital transformation as governments are increasingly embracing the power of artificial intelligence (AI) technologies. In order to foster an environment of continuous innovation, governments are actively exploring ways to leverage the transformative potential of AI technologies to enhance their operations and e-government services.

The advancement of AI technologies such as machine learning, Big Data analytics, and Cloud Computing, has provided numerous opportunities for governments to improve efficiency and effectiveness. The integration of AI-driven innovation is revolutionizing a wide range of government functions, from improving the delivery of public services to enhancing citizen engagement (Zuiderwijk et al.,2021). In addition, the use of AI technologies empowers governments in the formulation and implementation of policies by enabling more accurate forecasting and informed decision-making (Margetts & Dorobantu, 2019).

However, AI-driven innovation, often compared to the Fourth Industrial Revolution, presents unique challenges that can hinder the successful integration of AI technologies in the public sector (Sun & Medaglia, 2019; Valle-Cruz et al., 2024). The challenges associated with AI integration include data privacy concerns, biases and errors (Valle-Cruz et al., 2024). This emphasizes the critical need for governments to address these issues by carefully navigating the complexities surrounding AI integration to ensure the effective and ethical utilization of these technologies.

This chapter aims to provide a comprehensive and holistic understanding of AI-driven innovation in the public sector. It explores the transformative role of AI technologies in reshaping the public sector. The chapter examines the current landscape of AI implementation across various key domains including governance, chatbots and virtual assistants, public service delivery, policymaking, and citizen engagement. It discusses the opportunities these AI technologies present in terms of increased efficiency, data-driven decision making, and enhanced citizen engagement. Furthermore, this chapter highlights the unique challenges and considerations that governments must address to ensure the successful and ethical implementation of AI technologies, such as safeguarding the privacy of citizen and governmental data and handling algorithmic bias.

2.2 Literature Review

This chapter delves into the burgeoning field of Artificial Intelligence (AI) and its transformative applications within e-government. To provide a comprehensive understanding of this dynamic landscape, this section analyzes existing literature, focusing on key themes and trends that are shaping the discourse on AI in e-government.

Recent research has highlighted the critical importance of ethical considerations in the development and deployment of AI systems in the public sector. This includes addressing potential biases in algorithms, ensuring transparency and explainability in AI-driven decision-making, and establishing robust governance frameworks to guide the responsible use of AI in government (Zuiderwijk et al., 2021; Hakimi et al., 2023). Studies emphasize the need for clear policies and regulations to mitigate the risks of discrimination, privacy violations, and accountability gaps associated with AI implementation in e-government (Saura et al., 2022; Memarian & Doleck, 2023).

The literature also explores how AI is transforming citizen engagement and service delivery in the public sector. Research indicates that AI-powered tools, such as chatbots and virtual assistants, can enhance accessibility, responsiveness, and personalization of government services (Senadheera et al., 2024; Mary Sowjanya & Srividya, 2024). However, studies also caution against the potential for digital divides and the need for human oversight to address complex or sensitive citizen inquiries (Anderson & Rainie, 2023; Lv et al., 2022).

The use of AI for policymaking and decision intelligence is another prominent theme in the literature. Research suggests that AI can assist governments in analyzing vast datasets, identifying trends, and making data-driven decisions (Margetts & Dorobantu, 2019; OECD, 2024). Studies highlight the potential of AI to improve efficiency, optimize resource allocation, and enhance the effectiveness of public policies (Farhad & Pyun, 2023; Stecyk & Miciuła, 2023). However, researchers also emphasize the importance of transparency, accountability, and human oversight in AI-augmented decision-making processes (Memarian & Doleck, 2023; Saura et al., 2022).

The literature also examines emerging trends and challenges in the field of AI and e-government. This includes the development of explainable AI (XAI) to address transparency concerns, the use of AI-powered cybersecurity solutions to protect sensitive data, and the evolving regulatory landscape surrounding AI governance (Arrieta et al., 2020; Kaur et al., 2023). Studies also explore the potential negative impacts of AI in government, such as algorithmic bias, privacy violations, and the need for responsible AI development and deployment (Valle-Cruz et al., 2024; Brożek et al., 2024).

The future of AI in e-government is filled with both opportunities and challenges. By harnessing the power of XAI, AI-powered cybersecurity, and responsible AI governance, governments can leverage AI to enhance public services, improve decision-making, and better serve their citizens. However, it is crucial to address the ethical considerations and potential risks associated with AI adoption to ensure that its benefits are realized in a way that is fair, transparent, and accountable. The future of e-government will be shaped by the ongoing dialogue between technological innovation, ethical considerations, and the evolving needs of citizens in the digital age.

2.3 AI Governance: Paving the Way for E-Government Transformation

Artificial Intelligence (AI) has moved far beyond hype. As of April 2024, according to The AI Index report issued by Stanford University, over 94 countries had either released or were developing AI strategies, showcasing its potential to transform governance on a global scale (Maslej et al., 2024). This global trend underscores the importance of understanding how AI is specifically reshaping the public sector through e-government services. The integration of AI technologies into the delivery of public services promises increased efficiency, improved decision-making, and enhanced citizen engagement.

Figure 1. countries with ai national strategies (Maslej et al., 2024)

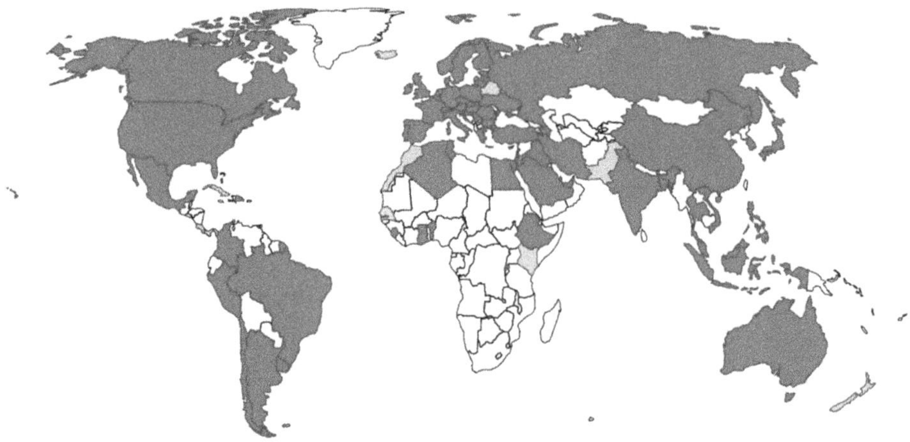

*Note * Countries shaded blue have released a national AI strategy, those in pink have a strategy in development, and those in grey have not yet released a national AI strategy.*

The European Union is at the forefront of AI regulation with its proposed AI Act, a comprehensive framework aiming to balance the potential risks and benefits of AI technology (European Parliament, 2024). The Act adopts a risk-based approach, classifying AI systems according to their potential impact. High-risk applications, such as those used in critical infrastructure, face strict requirements, whereas lower-risk systems enjoy more regulatory flexibility.

Beyond the EU, other nations are actively shaping their own AI strategies. The United States, for example, has emphasized reports and guidelines that foster innovation and tackle workforce challenges, as noted by the National Science and Technology Council (2023). Meanwhile, China has introduced AI ethical guidelines, underlining the importance of developing AI that is both controllable and beneficial (The State Council of The People's Republic of China, 2017).

These global initiatives reflect a growing consensus on the need for responsible AI governance to foster E-government transformation that is both innovative and ethically sound. National AI strategies play a pivotal role in guiding this transformation, providing a framework for the responsible development and deployment of AI technologies in the public sector. By aligning AI development with national priorities, addressing ethical concerns, and fostering public trust, these strategies pave the way for the successful integration of AI into e-government services, ultimately enhancing efficiency, transparency, and citizen engagement.

2.4 AI Applications in E-Government: Current Landscape

2.4.1 Chatbots and Virtual Assistants

In the digital age, citizens expect government services to be as accessible and user-friendly as their favorite apps. Enter chatbots and virtual assistants, the AI-powered tools that are revolutionizing how citizens interact with government. No longer confined to rigid office hours or endless phone menus, citizens can now access information, schedule appointments, and even complete transactions through conversational interfaces available 24/7. This shift towards on-demand, personalized service is not just a matter of convenience; it's about empowering citizens and building trust in government.

Figure 2. Chatbot adoption framework for local governments (Senadheera et al., 2024)

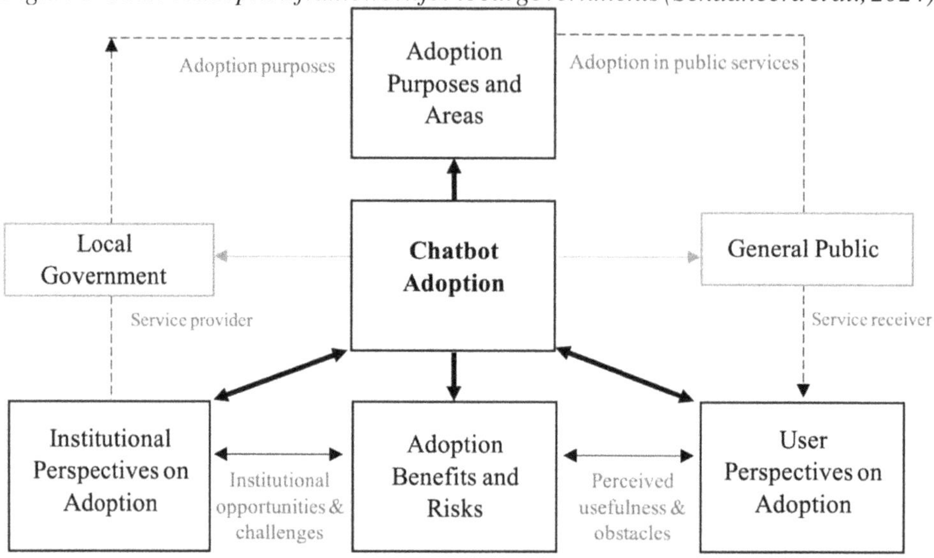

While chatbots promise convenience and efficiency, their real impact on citizen engagement is a mixed bag. Research from the Pew Research Center highlights that chatbots are effective for handling simple, routine tasks, offering quick responses and freeing up human agents (Anderson & Rainie, 2023). This can lead to increased efficiency and improved satisfaction for citizens seeking immediate answers.

The rise of chatbots in government services isn't without its critics. Concerns about bias in algorithms, the protection of sensitive citizen data, and the potential exclusion of those without digital access are valid and need to be addressed head-on. If left unchecked, algorithmic biases baked into chatbot systems can perpetuate or even amplify existing inequalities in service delivery. The collection and use of personal data by chatbots raise serious privacy concerns, requiring robust safeguards to prevent misuse or breaches. Moreover, the reliance on digital interfaces can marginalize those without reliable internet access or the skills to navigate these technologies, deepening the digital divide. As highlighted by the Pew Research Center, complex issues often demand human intervention due to the need for nuanced understanding, empathy, and problem-solving skills (Anderson & Rainie, 2023). Chatbots can struggle with these aspects, potentially leading to frustration and dissatisfaction when they fail to meet user expectations. Addressing these concerns isn't just about mitigating risks; it's about ensuring that the benefits of AI-powered services are accessible and equitable for all citizens.

Trust is another concern. While some citizens appreciate the anonymity of interacting with a bot, others miss the human connection and question the accuracy of AI-generated information. Accessibility is also key (Lv et al., 2022). While chatbots can improve access for tech-savvy users, those with limited digital literacy or disabilities may find them difficult to use, potentially exacerbating the digital divide. Evaluating the true impact of chatbots requires looking beyond efficiency metrics. It means understanding how they affect citizen trust, satisfaction, and equitable access to information. Only then can we determine if chatbots are truly transforming citizen engagement for the better.

Building user-friendly and equitable AI-powered conversational interfaces requires a human-centric approach (Mary Sowjanya & Srividya, 2024). Start by understanding your users: their needs, preferences, and technological literacy. Design conversations that are intuitive and easy to navigate, using plain language and avoiding jargon. Prioritize accessibility, ensuring that chatbots are usable by people with disabilities, including those who rely on screen readers or voice commands. Regularly test and gather feedback from diverse users to identify and address any biases or usability issues. Remember, the goal is not just to automate interactions, but to enhance them, making government services more accessible and user-friendly for all.

2.4.1.1 Examining chatbots through the lens of TAM

The Technology Acceptance Model (TAM), introduced by Davis in 1989 and further developed by Davis et al. in 1992, serves as a valuable tool for comprehending and forecasting user acceptance of emerging technologies, as highlighted by Tran et al. in 2023. The central premise of TAM is that an individual's beliefs, attitudes, and intentions play a crucial role in determining their adoption of technology. Implementing TAM when presenting a novel technology enables researchers to gain valuable insights into its potential future usage.

The original TAM identified four key internal variables that impact the actual use of technology: perceived ease of use (PEU), perceived usefulness (PU), attitude toward use (ATU), and behavioral intention to use (BI). Furthermore, TAM considers external variables, including specific technological characteristics, which can influence both the perceived ease of use and perceived usefulness of the innovation.

Figure 3. The original Technology Acceptance Model (TAM) (Davis et al., 1989; Kowalska-Pyzalska, 2024)

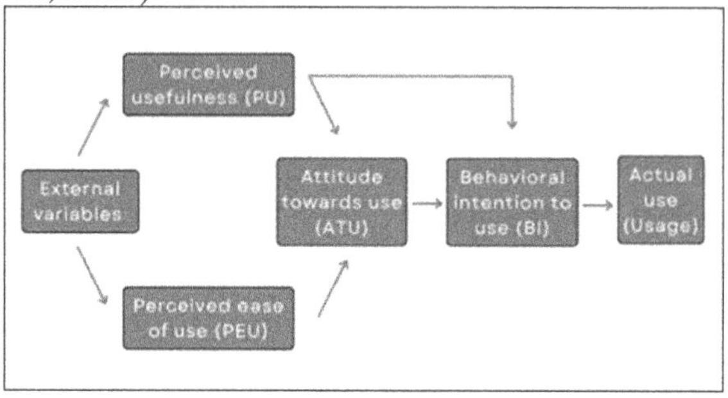

TAM provides a helpful framework for understanding the adoption of chatbots. TAM suggests that users are more likely to embrace a technology if they perceive it as both easy to use and useful. In the context of chatbots, ease of use relates to factors such as a user-friendly interface, clear instructions, and effective natural language processing. Perceived usefulness, on the other hand, is tied to the chatbot's ability to provide relevant information, efficiently complete tasks, or offer engaging interactions. A chatbot seen as both user-friendly and useful is more likely to encourage positive attitudes and intentions to use, ultimately driving adoption. Moreover, the chatbot's specific features and capabilities can influence user perceptions. For instance, advanced AI features might increase the perceived usefulness of a chatbot, potentially leading to greater acceptance.

Furthermore, extensions of the TAM model, like TAM2, highlight the critical role of perceived security and trust in technology adoption (Uche et al., 2021). For citizens to fully embrace and utilize chatbots, particularly in government services, they need assurance that their data is handled responsibly and transparently. By understanding these dynamics, government entities can leverage TAM to design and implement chatbots that better meet citizen needs and expectations, fostering wider acceptance and adoption.

2.4.2 Predictive Analytics for Policy Making

In the traditional model of governance, policymakers often find themselves reacting to crises rather than preventing them. But with the advent of predictive AI, a new era of proactive governance is dawning. According to OECD (2024), predictive AI is the use of AI systems to analyze historical and real-time data to forecast future events or behaviors, empowers governments to anticipate emerging trends and potential problems before they escalate. This shift from reactive to proactive governance, fueled by the ability to understand likely future scenarios based on existing data, has the potential to revolutionize policymaking, allowing governments to make more informed decisions, allocate resources more effectively, and ultimately, better serve their citizens.

In the realm of disease surveillance, AI algorithms are sifting through vast troves of medical data, social media posts, and even environmental sensors to detect disease outbreaks before they become epidemics. By identifying subtle patterns and correlations, these systems can alert officials to potential hotspots, allowing for targeted interventions and resource allocation (Zeng, 2021). In crime prevention, predictive policing tools are analyzing historical crime data, socioeconomic factors, and even weather patterns to forecast where and when crimes are most likely to occur. This allows law enforcement agencies to deploy resources more effectively, potentially deterring criminal activity and improving public safety (Hung & Yen, 2023). Even the daily commute is being transformed by AI, with traffic prediction models analyzing real-time data from sensors, cameras, and GPS devices to anticipate congestion and optimize traffic flow. By adjusting signal timings and suggesting alternative routes, these systems can help reduce travel times, fuel consumption, and frustration for millions of commuters (Shaygan et al., 2022).

In the realm of public health, predictive analytics is being used to forecast disease outbreaks. For instance, Singapore's National Environment Agency (NEA) has developed an early warning system that utilizes social media data, among other sources, to detect potential outbreaks of dengue fever (Ho et al., 2023). This allows health officials to take proactive measures, such as increasing public awareness campaigns or implementing targeted mosquito control efforts, to prevent the spread of the disease.

In Chicago, law enforcement agencies have explored the use of predictive policing tools to identify individuals potentially at risk of violence. The Chicago Police Department implemented a predictive policing system called Strategic Subject List (SSL) (Montasari, 2023). The system used machine learning algorithms to analyze data from past crimes and identify individuals who are most likely to commit violent crimes in the future. This allowed police to focus their efforts on these individuals, potentially preventing future crimes. However, the use of such tools has also raised concerns about potential biases and the targeting of certain individuals and communities.

The allure of predictive analytics in policymaking is tempered by significant challenges (Memarian & Doleck, 2023). Ensuring transparency in AI-powered decisions is paramount, as opaque algorithms erode public trust. When citizens can't understand how decisions are made, skepticism and resistance naturally arise. Fairness is another hurdle. If the data used to train AI models is biased, the resulting predictions and policy recommendations will be too, potentially exacerbating existing inequalities. Accountability is equally crucial. When AI systems make errors or lead to unintended consequences, who bears responsibility? Establishing clear lines of accountability is essential to maintain public trust and ensure that AI is used ethically in the policymaking process.

To successfully integrate predictive analytics into policymaking, a strategic and thoughtful approach to risk mitigation is essential. In 2023, the National Institute of Standards and Technology (NIST), in collaboration with the private and public sectors, has developed an AI Risk Management Framework to address the risks inherent in AI systems, including predictive analytics. A core principle of this framework is establishing trustworthiness, which encompasses the following key characteristics:

Table 1. AI risks and trustworthiness

Characteristics	Description
Valid and Reliable	Validation ensures that an AI system meets its intended requirements. Reliability measures its ability to function without failure under specific conditions. Both validation and reliability are crucial for reducing risks and increasing trustworthiness in deployed AI systems. Accuracy and robustness also contribute to trustworthiness, with accuracy focusing on closeness to true values and robustness on performance across a variety of circumstances. Ongoing testing and monitoring help assess validity and reliability, with a focus on minimizing potential harms and prioritizing human intervention when necessary.
Safe	AI systems should prioritize safety, ensuring they don't endanger human life, health, property, or the environment. This is achieved through responsible design, deployment, and use, coupled with clear information and risk documentation. Different safety risks necessitate tailored AI risk management, with serious risks requiring urgent attention. Integrating safety considerations early in the AI lifecycle, along with rigorous testing and real-time monitoring, can prevent dangerous system failures. Effective AI safety risk management often aligns with existing sector-specific guidelines and learns from safety practices in fields like transportation and healthcare.
Secure and Resilient	AI systems and their ecosystems are considered resilient if they can withstand unexpected adverse events, maintain functionality despite internal/external changes, and degrade safely when necessary. Security concerns include adversarial attacks, data poisoning, and intellectual property theft. Secure AI systems preserve confidentiality, integrity, and availability through protection mechanisms. Security and resilience are related but distinct. Security encompasses resilience and proactive measures against attacks, while resilience focuses on recovery from disruptions and robustness against unexpected or adversarial use.
Accountable and Transparent	Trustworthy AI relies on accountability, which in turn necessitates transparency. Transparency means providing individuals interacting with an AI system with relevant information about the system and its outputs. This information should be tailored to the specific stage of the AI lifecycle and the knowledge level of those interacting with the system. By fostering better understanding, transparency enhances confidence in the AI system. Transparency encompasses various aspects, from design decisions and training data to model structure and intended use cases. It is crucial for addressing negative impacts caused by AI systems. While transparency doesn't guarantee other desirable characteristics like accuracy or fairness, it is vital for assessing them over time. The level of accountability should align with the potential consequences of AI system outcomes.

continued on following page

Table 1. Continued

Characteristics	Description
Explainable and Interpretable	Explainability and interpretability are crucial characteristics that enable users to comprehend the functionality and trustworthiness of AI systems. Explainability focuses on elucidating the internal mechanisms of AI systems, while interpretability focuses on making the system's output meaningful and understandable in context. Together, they provide deeper insights into the system's behavior, build trust, and mitigate risks arising from a lack of understanding. Explainability allows for easier debugging, monitoring, and documentation, while interpretability focuses on communicating the reasoning behind AI predictions or recommendations. Ultimately, these characteristics, along with transparency, offer a comprehensive view of the system's operation, enabling informed decision-making and fostering confidence in AI technologies.
Privacy-Enhanced	Privacy encompasses norms and practices that protect human autonomy, identity, and dignity by addressing issues like intrusion, observation, and control over personal information. These privacy values should guide AI system development and deployment. Privacy risks can impact security, bias, and transparency, requiring tradeoffs. AI systems can both promote and threaten privacy, necessitating the use of privacy-enhancing technologies (PETs) and data minimization techniques. However, in some cases, privacy enhancement may affect accuracy and influence decisions regarding fairness and other values.
Fair – with Harmful Bias Managed	Fairness in AI encompasses addressing harmful bias and discrimination while considering the complexities of defining fairness across cultures and applications. It's important to recognize that bias extends beyond demographic balance and data representativeness, encompassing systemic, computational and statistical, and human-cognitive biases. These biases can manifest without discriminatory intent and have the potential to perpetuate and amplify harm when ingrained in AI systems. Therefore, understanding and mitigating bias is crucial for ensuring fairness, transparency, and responsible AI use.

2.4.3 AI-Driven Decision Intelligence

In the pursuit of efficiency and effectiveness, governments are increasingly turning to AI-powered decision-making tools to streamline operations and optimize resource allocation. This trend is underscored by Gartner's (2024) forecast that 70% of government organizations will depend on AI for decision-making by 2026. These tools, driven by machine learning algorithms, can rapidly analyze vast data-sets, uncover hidden patterns, and generate valuable insights at a scale and speed beyond human capabilities. This enables faster, evidence-based decisions across various domains, from resource allocation and fraud detection to risk assessment and policy formulation.

In the labyrinthine world of government bureaucracy, AI is emerging as a key to unlocking efficiency. From the mundane to the mission-critical, AI-powered tools are streamlining processes that were once bogged down by paperwork and manual labor. Take, for instance, the time-consuming task of processing permit applications (Higgins, 2022). AI algorithms can now scan documents, verify information, and even make preliminary approval decisions, dramatically reducing processing times and freeing up staff for more complex tasks. Similarly, in the realm of resource allocation, AI-powered systems can analyze vast amounts of data to identify patterns and optimize resource distribution, ensuring that funds are allocated where they'll have the greatest impact (Farhad & Pyun, 2023).

By automating routine tasks and enhancing human judgment, AI frees up valuable time and resources, allowing public servants to focus on more complex and strategic initiatives. A McKinsey Global Institute study underscores the transformative potential of automation, projecting that up to 50% of current work activities could be automated by 2045, significantly accelerating the pace of workplace transformation (Chui et al., 2023). Ultimately, this leads to a leaner, more agile government better equipped to meet the evolving needs of its citizens.

But AI's potential goes beyond simply automating existing processes. It's also being used to optimize complex systems, like traffic management and energy grids, in real-time. By analyzing data from sensors and other sources, AI algorithms can dynamically adjust traffic signals to reduce congestion, or balance energy supply and demand to prevent blackouts (Stecyk & Miciuła, 2023; Zhang, 2021). This not only saves time and money but can also improve the quality of life for citizens.

In the realm of fraud detection, AI is proving to be a formidable ally. Take, for example, the case of the UK's tax authority, HMRC. By deploying machine learning algorithms to analyze vast amounts of taxpayer data, HMRC has been able to identify patterns and anomalies that indicate potential fraud. This has led to a significant increase in the detection of fraudulent activity, saving the government millions of pounds in lost revenue (Tugendhat, 2023).

In the financial sector, AI-powered risk assessment tools are helping banks and other institutions make more informed lending decisions. By analyzing a borrower's credit history, income, and other factors, these tools can assess the likelihood of default with greater accuracy than traditional methods. This not only reduces the risk of bad loans for lenders, but also helps to ensure that credit is available to those who are most likely to repay it. Furthermore, AI's capacity for enhanced risk prediction extends beyond credit assessment; research by the World Economic Forum 2024 indicates AI-powered climate risk models can improve the accuracy of climate-related financial risk predictions by up to 40% (World Economic Forum, 2024).

To enhance its decision-making capabilities, the UAE has established several groundbreaking initiatives in the field of AI. Notably, it created the world's first Ministry of Artificial Intelligence, with the ambitious goal of AI contributing 13.6% to its GDP by 2031 (UAE Ministry of State for Artificial Intelligence, 2018). Further demonstrating its commitment to AI advancement, the UAE founded the Mohamed bin Zayed University of Artificial Intelligence (MBZUAI) in 2019. As the world's first graduate-level, research-based AI university, MBZUAI offers master's and doctoral programs in key AI disciplines, aiming to attract top global talent and drive cutting-edge research in the field.

These are just a few examples of how AI is being used to enhance decision-making in the public sector. AI's potential in decision-making isn't without its pitfalls. Algorithms, trained on historical data, can inherit and amplify existing biases, leading to discriminatory outcomes. The lack of transparency and interpretability in some AI models makes it difficult to understand how decisions are reached, raising concerns about accountability. When AI systems make errors, determining who is responsible can be a thorny issue (Saura et al., 2022). Over-reliance on AI can also lead to a loss of human expertise and intuition, potentially undermining the quality of decision-making in the long run. These challenges underscore the need for careful consideration and robust governance frameworks to ensure that AI is used ethically and responsibly in the public sector.

2.5 Challenges of AI Adoption in E-Government

2.5.1 Data privacy and security concerns

AI-powered e-government services, while promising increased efficiency and improved citizen experiences, also raise significant data privacy and security concerns. Governments collect and process vast amounts of sensitive citizen data, encompassing personal information, financial records, and health data. Utilizing AI to analyze and utilize this data amplifies the risks of unauthorized access, data breaches, and misuse (National Institute of Standards and Technology, 2023).

These concerns are multifaceted. E-government systems, holding troves of sensitive information, become attractive targets for cybercriminals seeking to exploit vulnerabilities. AI systems, if not adequately secured, can become entry points for such attacks, potentially leading to large-scale data breaches and identity theft. Moreover, AI algorithms, while powerful, can inadvertently reveal sensitive information or patterns in data that could be exploited for discriminatory practices or targeted surveillance. It's crucial that governments ensure AI systems are designed and implemented with safeguards against such misuse (Saura et al., 2022).

Data privacy violations are another major concern. The collection and processing of citizen data by AI systems must adhere to data protection regulations and respect individual privacy rights. Governments need to establish clear policies and procedures for data collection, storage, and use, ensuring transparency and providing individuals with control over their personal information. A good example in this regard is the EU's General Data Protection Regulation (GDPR), which sets a high standard for data protection and privacy rights (European Parliament and the Council of the European Union, 2016). By adopting similar regulations or aligning with existing frameworks, governments can foster trust among their citizens and create a safer digital environment.

Figure 4. Infographic on EU`s GDPR

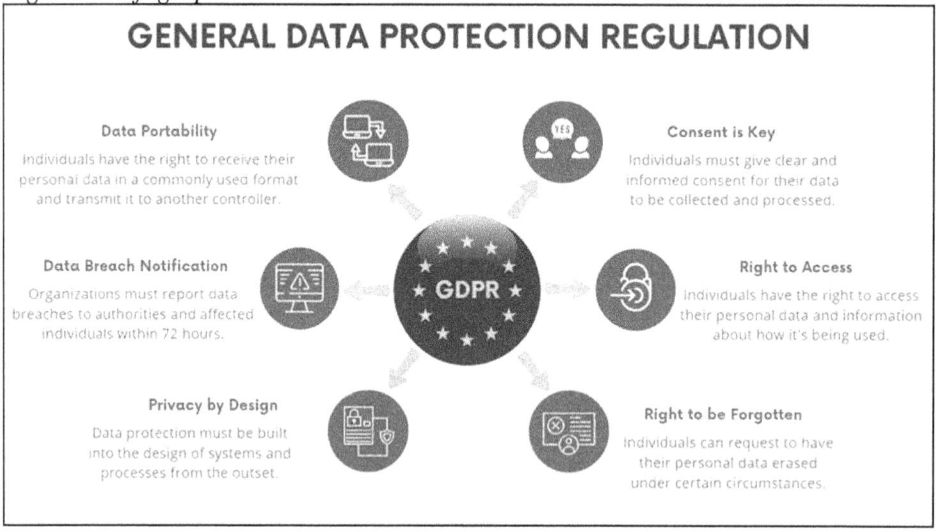

Finally, the lack of transparency and explainability in many AI algorithms, especially deep learning models, raises concerns about accountability and the potential for hidden biases to influence outcomes (Brożek et al., 2024). Addressing these multifaceted concerns necessitates a multi-pronged approach. Robust data security measures, privacy-preserving AI techniques, ethical AI frameworks, algorithmic auditing and bias mitigation, and the promotion of explainable AI are all crucial steps governments must take. By prioritizing the protection of citizen data and ensuring that AI systems are designed and implemented responsibly, governments can harness the power of AI while upholding the fundamental rights and freedoms of their citizens.

2.5.2 Algorithmic bias and fairness

The integration of AI into e-government, while offering numerous advantages, also brings forth the significant challenge of algorithmic bias and fairness (Hakimi et al., 2023). AI algorithms, trained on historical data, can inadvertently perpetuate and even amplify existing societal biases. In the context of e-government, this can lead to discriminatory outcomes, undermining the principles of equity and justice that should be at the core of public services.

Several key concerns arise in this regard. Firstly, AI algorithms learn from the data they are fed. If this data reflects historical biases or underrepresentation of certain groups, the resulting AI model will likely exhibit those same biases. In e-government, this could manifest as biased decision-making in areas like loan approvals, social welfare eligibility, or even criminal justice risk assessments (Howell et al., 2024). Secondly, even with unbiased data, AI algorithms can still produce discriminatory outcomes due to their design or the features they prioritize. For example, an algorithm used for predicting recidivism rates might inadvertently discriminate against individuals from certain socioeconomic backgrounds if it relies heavily on factors like zip code or prior arrest records (Wang et al., 2023).

Moreover, the lack of transparency and explainability in many AI models, particularly deep learning models, raises concerns about accountability and fairness. It's challenging to understand how these complex models arrive at their decisions, making it difficult to identify and address potential biases (Memarian & Doleck, 2023). This lack of transparency can lead to mistrust and concerns about the legitimacy of AI-powered decisions in e-government.

Another significant challenge arises from the inherent complexity of many AI algorithms, especially those based on deep learning. These "black box" models, while often highly accurate, lack transparency, making it difficult to understand the reasoning behind their decisions (Brożek et al., 2024). In the context of e-government, this can lead to a lack of accountability and hinder the ability to detect and correct potential biases. Citizens may be rightfully concerned about decisions made by opaque systems they don't fully understand, particularly when those decisions impact access to critical services or benefits. Moreover, the black box nature of these algorithms can impede troubleshooting and improvement, making it challenging to identify and rectify errors or unexpected outcomes.

Figure 5. The black box problem

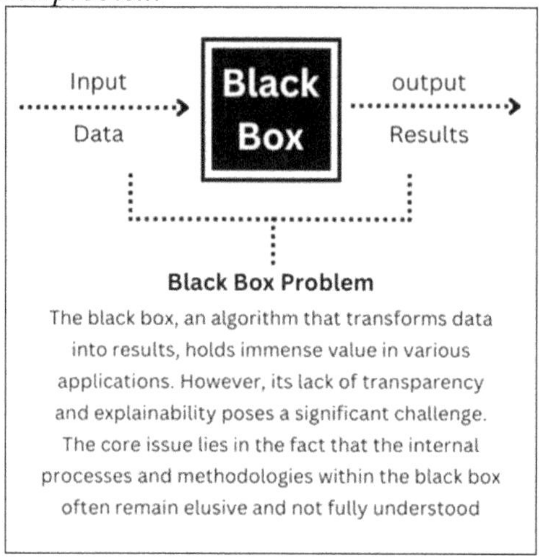

Finally, if left unchecked, biased AI algorithms in e-government can reinforce existing social inequalities and create a self-fulfilling prophecy (Capraro et al., 2024). For instance, a biased algorithm used in educational resource allocation could perpetuate disparities in educational outcomes by favoring already advantaged groups. Addressing these multifaceted concerns necessitates a proactive and multi-pronged approach. Ensuring diverse and representative training data, developing fairness-aware algorithms, promoting transparency and explainability, and conducting ongoing monitoring and auditing are crucial steps. It's also important to involve diverse stakeholders, including affected communities, in the development and deployment of AI systems to ensure fairness and equity.

2.6 Outlook: Enhancing Transparency and Security in E-government

2.6.1 Explainable AI for transparent decision-making

As AI systems become increasingly sophisticated and integrated into e-government services, the demand for transparency and understandability grows more pressing. Explainable AI, or XAI, emerges as a critical field seeking to illuminate the reasoning behind AI-driven decisions. In the realm of e-government, XAI can be instrumental in fostering trust, accountability, and fairness.

Figure 6. Process of explainable AI (Saranya & Subhashini, 2023)

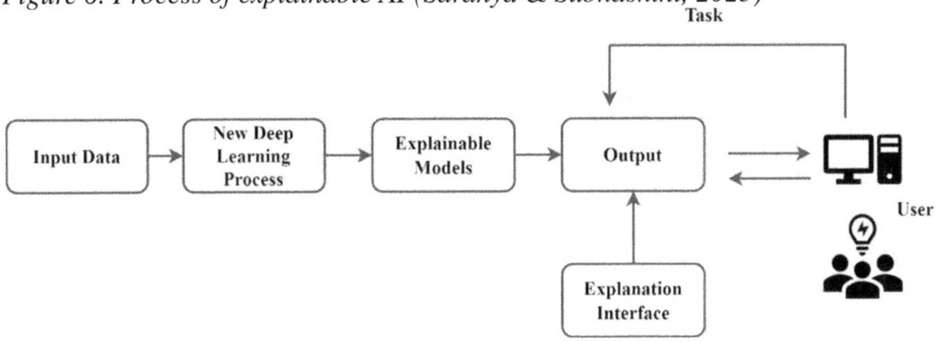

The benefits of XAI are multifaceted. By enabling citizens to understand how AI systems reach their conclusions, it diminishes the perception of AI as an inscrutable "black box." This heightened transparency fosters trust and acceptance of AI-powered services, encouraging wider adoption and engagement from the public (Arrieta et al., 2020). Furthermore, XAI bolsters accountability by allowing for greater scrutiny of AI-driven decisions, helping to ensure that AI systems are utilized responsibly and in alignment with the public interest, mitigating the risk of bias or unintended consequences.

XAI also has the potential to enhance the quality of decision-making itself. By illuminating potential biases or errors in AI models, it enables timely correction and improvement. This leads to more informed and equitable decision-making in e-government services, benefiting both citizens and the public servants who serve them. Moreover, XAI acts as a bridge between humans and AI systems, facilitating effective collaboration. When human experts can comprehend the rationale behind AI-generated recommendations, they can provide valuable feedback and context, leading to better outcomes (Arrieta et al., 2020).

Additionally, as regulatory landscapes evolve, the demand for transparency and explainability in AI systems, especially those used in high-stakes decision-making, is on the rise. This is exemplified by the recently agreed-upon EU AI Act, which mandates that high-risk AI systems must provide clear and comprehensible information about their capabilities and limitations, with a particular focus on transparency and traceability in decision-making processes (European Parliament, 2024). XAI directly supports compliance with such regulations, ensuring that governments employ AI ethically and responsibly.

2.6.2 AI-powered cybersecurity solutions

As e-government services become increasingly reliant on digital infrastructure, the specter of cyberattacks looms ever larger. While traditional cybersecurity measures remain important, they often struggle to keep up with the constantly evolving tactics employed by cybercriminals. In this landscape, AI-powered cybersecurity solutions emerge as a promising new frontier for safeguarding e-government systems and the sensitive citizen data they hold.

AI brings distinct advantages to the cybersecurity arena. It can analyze massive volumes of data in real time, discerning patterns and anomalies that might signal a cyberattack. This capability allows for swifter threat detection and response, mitigating potential damage and disruption. Moreover, AI can harness machine learning to analyze historical data, identifying trends that could predict future cyberattacks. This enables proactive defense, stopping attacks before they even materialize (Jawaid, 2023).

The automation capabilities of AI further extend to incident response workflows, freeing cybersecurity professionals from routine tasks and allowing them to focus on more complex challenges. This streamlines incident management and reduces response times, minimizing the impact of successful breaches. AI also plays a vital role in vulnerability assessment and patch management, proactively identifying weaknesses in software and systems to reduce the risk of exploitation. Additionally, AI can analyze user behavior patterns, flagging anomalies that might indicate unauthorized access or malicious activity, thus enabling early detection and prevention of insider threats (Uzoma et al., 2023).

The landscape of AI-powered cybersecurity solutions is constantly evolving. From AI-powered intrusion detection and prevention systems that use machine learning to identify and block malicious network traffic, to AI-enhanced security information and event management systems that automate the analysis of security logs, AI's influence is profound. AI-driven threat intelligence platforms gather and analyze threat information from diverse sources, providing actionable insights for proactive threat mitigation. Furthermore, AI-based deception technologies create deceptive environments to lure attackers away from critical assets, offering early warning of potential attacks. And AI-powered vulnerability management solutions automate the discovery, prioritization, and remediation of vulnerabilities, reducing the attack surface and bolstering overall security (Kaur et al., 2023).

Figure 7. AI-powered cybersecurity outlook

Market Forecast: Statista, 2024

The AI cybersecurity market is on track for remarkable expansion soon. Starting from a value of $24.3 billion in 2023, it is projected to double in size by 2026, and then further skyrocket to nearly $134 billion by the year 2030.

Key Drivers Behind the Growth

Escalating geopolitical tensions and instability: This contributes to a rise in both armed conflicts and cyberattacks, making the digital landscape increasingly volatile and dangerous.

Rapid technological advancement, especially in generative AI: These breakthroughs have the potential to revolutionize cybersecurity, but also introduce new vulnerabilities and attack vectors that defenders must contend with.

Widening cyber capabilities gap and digital divide: The disparity in cybersecurity resources and expertise between organizations is growing, leaving those less prepared increasingly susceptible to attacks. This digital divide also creates broader societal inequities and vulnerabilities.

Adapted from World Economic Forum, "Global Cybersecurity Outlook 2024"

To sum it up, AI-powered cybersecurity solutions have the transformative potential to reshape how e-government systems are protected. By harnessing AI's capabilities, governments can bolster their ability to detect, respond to, and even predict threats, ensuring the safeguarding of sensitive citizen data and the continuity of crucial public services. As cyber threats continue to grow in complexity and sophistication, the integration of AI into cybersecurity strategies will become increasingly vital for maintaining the resilience and security of e-government infrastructure.

2.7 CONCLUSION

The chapter underscores the transformative potential of AI in reshaping the public sector through e-government services. It highlights the global trend of AI adoption in governance, emphasizing the importance of national AI strategies in guiding this transformation. The chapter explores the diverse applications of AI in e-government, from enhancing citizen services through chatbots and virtual assistants to streamlining internal operations and enabling data-driven policymaking. It also delves into the challenges associated with AI adoption, including data privacy and security concerns, algorithmic bias, and the need for public trust and acceptance.

In conclusion, the integration of AI into e-government holds immense promise for revolutionizing the public sector. By harnessing AI's capabilities, governments can deliver services more efficiently, make informed decisions based on data, and actively engage with citizens. The potential benefits are clear: streamlined processes, reduced costs, and an overall enhancement in the quality of public services. However, the path to AI-powered e-government is not without its hurdles. It is imperative that governments prioritize responsible and ethical AI implementation, addressing challenges such as data privacy, algorithmic bias, and public trust. Emerging trends like explainable AI and AI-powered cybersecurity solutions offer a path forward, enabling governments to navigate the complexities of the AI landscape. By embracing these tools and approaches, governments can build a future of e-government that is not only efficient but also transparent, accountable, and citizen-centric, ultimately leading to improved governance and better outcomes for society.

REFERENCES

Anderson, J., & Rainie, L. (2023, June 21). As AI Spreads, Experts Predict the Best and Worst Changes in Digital Life by 2035 [Report]. Pew Research Center. https://www.pewresearch.org/internet/wp-content/uploads/sites/9/2023/06/PI_2023.06.21_Best-Worst-Digital-Life_2035_FINAL.pdf

Arrieta, A. B., Díaz-Rodríguez, N., Del Ser, J., Bennetot, A., Tabik, S., Barbado, A., & Herrera, F. (2020). Explainable Artificial Intelligence (XAI): Concepts, taxonomies, opportunities and challenges toward responsible AI. *Information Fusion*, 58, 82–115. DOI: 10.1016/j.inffus.2019.12.012

Borgeaud, A. (2024) Global Al Cybersecurity Market Size 2030, Statista. Available at: https://www.statista.com/statistics/1450963/global-ai-cybersecurity-market-size/

Brożek, B., Furman, M., Jakubiec, M., & Kucharzyk, B. (2024). The black box problem revisited. Real and imaginary challenges for automated legal decision making. *Artificial Intelligence and Law*, 32(2), 427–440. DOI: 10.1007/s10506-023-09356-9

Capraro, V., Lentsch, A., Acemoglu, D., Akgun, S., Akhmedova, A., Bilancini, E., Bonnefon, J.-F., Brañas-Garza, P., Butera, L., Douglas, K. M., Everett, J. A. C., Gigerenzer, G., Greenhow, C., Hashimoto, D. A., Holt-Lunstad, J., Jetten, J., Johnson, S., Kunz, W. H., Longoni, C., & Viale, R. (2024). The impact of generative artificial intelligence on socioeconomic inequalities and policy making. *PNAS Nexus*, 3(6), pgae191. DOI: 10.1093/pnasnexus/pgae191 PMID: 38864006

Chui, M., Hazan, E., Roberts, R., Singla, A., Smaje, K., Sukharevsky, A., Yee, L., & Zemmel, R. (2023, June 14). Economic potential of generative AI: The next productivity frontier [McKinsey & Company]. Retrieved from https://www.mckinsey.com/capabilities/mckinsey-digital/our-insights/the-economic-potential-of-generative-ai-the-next-productivity-frontier?cid=eml-web

Davis, F. D. (1989). Perceived usefulness, perceived ease of use, and user acceptance of information technology. *Management Information Systems Quarterly*, 13(3), 319–340. DOI: 10.2307/249008

Davis, F. D., Bagozzi, R. P., & Warshaw, P. R. (1992). Extrinsic and intrinsic motivation to use computers in the workplace 1. *Journal of Applied Social Psychology*, 22(14), 1111–1132. DOI: 10.1111/j.1559-1816.1992.tb00945.x

European Parliament. (2024, June 18). EU's AI Act: First regulation on artificial intelligence. https://www.europarl.europa.eu/topics/en/article/20230601STO93804/eu-ai-act-first-regulation-on-artificial-intelligence

European Parliament and the Council of the European Union. (2016). Regulation (EU) 2016/679 of the European Parliament and of the Council of 27 April 2016 on the protection of natural persons with regard to the processing of personal data and on the free movement of such data, and repealing Directive 95/46/EC (General Data Protection Regulation). *Official Journal of the European Union, L*, 119, 1–88. https://eur-lex.europa.eu/legal-content/EN/TXT/PDF/?uri=CELEX:32016R0679 &from=EN

Farhad, A., & Pyun, J. Y. (2023). AI-ERA: Artificial intelligence-empowered resource allocation for LoRa-enabled IoT applications. *IEEE Transactions on Industrial Informatics*, 19(12), 11640–11652. DOI: 10.1109/TII.2023.3248074

Gartner. (2024, April 16). Gartner Announces the Top Government Technology Trends for 2024. [Press release]. https://www.gartner.com/en/newsroom/press-releases/2024-04-16-gartner-announces-the-top-government-technology-trends-for-2024

Hakimi, M., Hamidi, M. S., Miskinyar, M. S., & Sazish, B. (2023). Integrating Artificial Intelligence into E-Government: Navigating Challenges, Opportunities, and Policy Implications. *International Journal of Academic and Practical Research*, 2(2), 1–1.

Higgins, B. W. (2022). Legal Elements of an AI Regulatory Permit Program. In *The Oxford Handbook of AI Governance*.

Ho, S. H., Lim, J. T., Ong, J., Hapuarachchi, H. C., Sim, S., & Ng, L. C. (2023). Singapore's 5 decades of dengue prevention and control—Implications for global dengue control. *PLoS Neglected Tropical Diseases*, 17(6), e0011400. DOI: 10.1371/journal.pntd.0011400 PMID: 37347767

Howell, S. T., Kuchler, T., Snitkof, D., Stroebel, J., & Wong, J. (2024). Lender automation and racial disparities in credit access. *The Journal of Finance*, 79(2), 1457–1512. DOI: 10.1111/jofi.13303

Hung, T. W., & Yen, C. P. (2023). Predictive policing and algorithmic fairness. *Synthese*, 201(6), 206. DOI: 10.1007/s11229-023-04189-0

Jawaid, S. A. (2023). Artificial Intelligence with Respect to Cyber Security.

Kaur, R., Gabrijelčič, D., & Klobučar, T. (2023). Artificial intelligence for cybersecurity: Literature review and future research directions. *Information Fusion*, 97, 101804. DOI: 10.1016/j.inffus.2023.101804

Kowalska-Pyzalska, A. (2024). Diffusion of Innovative Energy Services: Consumers' Acceptance and Willingness to Pay. Elsevier Science & Technology.

Lv, Y., Hu, S., Liu, F., & Qi, J. (2022, August). Research on users' trust in customer service chatbots based on human-computer interaction. In China National Conference on Big Data and Social Computing (pp. 291-306). Singapore: Springer Nature Singapore. DOI: 10.1007/978-981-19-7532-5_19

Margetts, H., & Dorobantu, C. (2019). Rethink government with AI. *Nature*, 568(7751), 163–165. DOI: 10.1038/d41586-019-01099-5 PMID: 30967667

Mary Sowjanya, A., & Srividya, K. (2024). NLP-Driven Chatbots: Applications and Implications in Conversational AI. *Conversational Artificial Intelligence*, 713-725.

Maslej, N., Fattorini, L., Perrault, R., Parli, V., Reuel, A., Brynjolfsson, E., Etchemendy, J., Ligett, K., Lyons, T., Manyika, J., Niebles, J. C., Shoham, Y., Wald, R., & Clark, J. (April 2024). "The AI Index 2024 Annual Report," AI Index Steering Committee, Institute for Human-Centered AI, Stanford University, Stanford, CA, Retrieved from https://aiindex.stanford.edu/wp-content/uploads/2024/04/HAI_2024_AI-Index-Report.pdf

Memarian, B., & Doleck, T. (2023). Fairness, Accountability, Transparency, and Ethics (FATE) in Artificial Intelligence (AI), and higher education: A systematic review. *Computers and Education: Artificial Intelligence*, 100152.

Montasari, R. (2023). The application of big data predictive analytics and surveillance technologies in the field of policing. In *countering cyberterrorism: the confluence of artificial intelligence, cyber forensics and digital policing in US and UK National Cybersecurity* (pp. 81-114). Cham: Springer International Publishing. DOI: 10.1007/978-3-031-21920-7_5

National Institute of Standards and Technology. (2023). Artificial Intelligence Risk Management Framework (AI RMF 1.0). https://nvlpubs.nist.gov/nistpubs/ai/nist.ai.100-1.pdf

National Science and Technology Council. (2023, May). National Artificial Intelligence Research and Development Strategic Plan: 2023 Update. Retrieved from https://www.whitehouse.gov/ostp/nsc/ai/national-artificial-intelligence-research-and-development-strategic-plan-2023-update/

OECD. (2024, May 14). Using artificial intelligence in public financial management [Report No. GOV/SBO(2024)14]. Retrieved from https://one.oecd.org/document/GOV/SBO(2024)14/en/pdf

Saranya, A., & Subhashini, R. (2023). A systematic review of Explainable Artificial Intelligence models and applications: Recent developments and future trends. *Decision analytics journal, 7*, 100230

Saura, J. R., Ribeiro-Soriano, D., & Palacios-Marqués, D. (2022). Assessing behavioral data science privacy issues in government artificial intelligence deployment. *Government Information Quarterly*, 39(4), 101679. DOI: 10.1016/j.giq.2022.101679

Senadheera, S., Yigitcanlar, T., Desouza, K. C., Mossberger, K., Corchado, J., Mehmood, R., Li, R. Y. M., & Cheong, P. H. (2024). Understanding Chatbot Adoption in Local Governments: A Review and Framework. *Journal of Urban Technology*, •••, 1–35. DOI: 10.1080/10630732.2023.2297665

Shaygan, M., Meese, C., Li, W., Zhao, X. G., & Nejad, M. (2022). Traffic prediction using artificial intelligence: Review of recent advances and emerging opportunities. *Transportation Research Part C, Emerging Technologies*, 145, 103921. DOI: 10.1016/j.trc.2022.103921

Stecyk, A., & Miciuła, I. (2023). Harnessing the Power of Artificial Intelligence for Collaborative Energy Optimization Platforms. *Energies*, 16(13), 5210. DOI: 10.3390/en16135210

Sun, T. Q., & Medaglia, R. (2019). Mapping the challenges of Artificial Intelligence in the public sector: Evidence from public healthcare. *Government Information Quarterly*, 36(2), 368–383. DOI: 10.1016/j.giq.2018.09.008

The State Council of The People's Republic of China. (2017, July 20). China issues guideline on artificial intelligence development. [English translation]. english.gov.cn. Retrieved from http://www.english.gov.cn/policies/latest_releases/2017/07/20/content_281474.htm

Tran, G. A., Ketron, S., Tran, T. P., & Fabrize, R. (2023). Personalization, value co-creation, and brand loyalty in branded apps: An application of TAM theory. *Journal of Strategic Marketing*, •••, 1–20.

Tugendhat, T. (2023, October 31). Fraud and AI. [Speech delivered at the AI Safety Summit]. GOV.UK. https://www.gov.uk/government/speeches/security-minister-speech-on-fraud-and-ai

UAE Ministry of State for Artificial Intelligence. (2018, February). UAE National Strategy for Artificial Intelligence 2031 [PDF]. Retrieved from https://www.aicouncil.ae/media/publications/4177/uae-national-strategy-for-artificial-intelligence-2031.pdf

Uche, D. B., Osuagwu, O. B., Nwosu, S. N., & Otika, U. S. (2021). Integrating trust into technology acceptance model (TAM), the conceptual framework for e-payment platform acceptance. *British Journal of Management and Marketing Studies*, 4(4), 34–56.

Uzoma, J., Falana, O., Obunadike, C., Oloyede, K., & Obunadike, E. (2023). Using artificial intelligence for automated incidence response in cybersecurity. [IJIT]. *International Journal of Information Technology : an Official Journal of Bharati Vidyapeeth's Institute of Computer Applications and Management*, 1(4).

Valle-Cruz, D., García-Contreras, R., & Gil-Garcia, J. R. (2024). Exploring the negative impacts of artificial intelligence in government: The dark side of intelligent algorithms and cognitive machines. *International Review of Administrative Sciences*, 90(2), 353–368. https://doi-org.sheffield.idm.oclc.org/10.1177/00208523231187051. DOI: 10.1177/00208523231187051

Wang, C., Han, B., Patel, B., & Rudin, C. (2023). In pursuit of interpretable, fair and accurate machine learning for criminal recidivism prediction. *Journal of Quantitative Criminology*, 39(2), 519–581. DOI: 10.1007/s10940-022-09545-w

World Economic Forum. (2024). Global Cybersecurity Outlook 2024. Retrieved from https://www3.weforum.org/docs/WEF_Global_Cybersecurity_Outlook_2024.pdf

World Economic Forum. (2024). World Economic Forum Global Risks Report 2024. Retrieved from https://www3.weforum.org/docs/WEF_The_Global_Risks_Report_2024.pdf

Zeng, D., Cao, Z., & Neill, D. B. (2021). Artificial intelligence–enabled public health surveillance—from local detection to global epidemic monitoring and control. In *Artificial intelligence in medicine* (pp. 437–453). Academic Press. DOI: 10.1016/B978-0-12-821259-2.00022-3

Zhang, C., & Lu, Y. (2021). Study on artificial intelligence: The state of the art and future prospects. *Journal of Industrial Information Integration*, 23, 100224. DOI: 10.1016/j.jii.2021.100224

Zuiderwijk, A., Chen, Y. C., & Salem, F. (2021). Implications of the use of artificial intelligence in public governance: A systematic literature review and a research agenda. *Government Information Quarterly*, 38(3), 101577. DOI: 10.1016/j.giq.2021.101577

Chapter 5
Trends and Applications of AI in Enhancing Public Administration and Services: Implications for the Philippines

John Paul P. Miranda
https://orcid.org/0000-0003-2059-972X
Don Honorio Ventura State University, Philippines

Cailvin D. Reyes
https://orcid.org/0009-0004-3378-8372
Don Honorio Ventura State University, Philippines

Francis F. Balahadia
https://orcid.org/0000-0001-6666-4975
Laguna State Polytechnic University, Philippines

Madilaine Claire B. Nacianceno
https://orcid.org/0009-0000-8219-0626
National University, Philippines

Mariefel F. Capili
Don Honorio Ventura State University, Philippines

Mark Jameson E. Perez
Don Honorio Ventura State University, Philippines

Marlon I. Tayag
https://orcid.org/0000-0002-5659-0877
Holy Angel University, Philippines

Jayson G. Magat
Don Honorio Ventura State University, Philippines

Ivan G. Liwanag
https://orcid.org/0009-0005-0929-5583
Don Honorio Ventura State University, Philippines

Ranie B. Canlas
https://orcid.org/0000-0001-5697-016X
Don Honorio Ventura State University, Philippines

DOI: 10.4018/979-8-3693-7678-2.ch005

Jaymark A. Yambao
https://orcid.org/0009-0006-5403-1840
Don Honorio Ventura State University, Philippines

ABSTRACT

This book chapter explores the potential of AI in modernizing public administration and services with a specific focus on the Philippines. It examines how AI technologies improve administrative efficiency, streamline public services, and enhance decision-making in key areas such as administrative efficiency, law enforcement, disaster management, education, data privacy, cybersecurity, information dissemination, social services, and legal practice. The chapter highlights global trends and innovations in AI applications and considers their implications for the Philippine government. It also addresses the challenges of AI adoption including algorithmic bias, privacy concerns, and technical constraints. Drawing on case studies and examples from various countries, the chapter provides recommendations for strategic AI implementation in the Philippines which stressed the need for capacity-building, policy frameworks, and ethical considerations to ensure the responsible use of AI in public service.

INTRODUCTION

Public administration is responsible for developing and providing services that would significantly contribute to the efficient operation of government functions. It is responsible for the efficient and effective implementation of government policies and management of public programs and services. This encompasses coordinating and overseeing activities to ensure the optimal utilization of resources and efficient provision of services. Furthermore, it involves enforcement of regulations and promotion of accountability and transparency in government operations. Public administration is a multifaceted discipline that encompasses a variety of functions, including policy analysis, human resource management, and budgeting, all of which are designed to ensure efficient and effective operation of the government, as stated by Shafritz et al. (2022).

The introduction of artificial intelligence (AI), which includes programs that can perform tasks normally done by humans, such as learning, solving problems, and understanding language, has allowed the field of public administration to better serve its functions. Automated services are a trend in AI in public administration. AI enhances efficiency and minimizes wait times by automating routine duties and services such as processing applications and responding to citizen inquiries through chatbots. Automation of services is one of the notable trends in AI in public administration, as Parycek (2024) seconded. This trend involves the utilization of AI to optimize administrative procedures, minimize manual errors, and allocate resources to more critical tasks (Bhagat & Kanyal, 2024; Yaiprasert & Hidayanto, 2024). Additionally, AI aids public administration in the process of data-driven decision-making by analyzing a large volume of data to provide predictions and insights, resulting in more informed policy decisions and more effective resource allocation. Predictive analytics is a critical component of AI systems that analyze historical data to predict future trends and outcomes (Charles et al., 2022). For instance, AI-driven models can anticipate public health trends, which facilitate the allocation of resources and implementation of timely interventions to mitigate potential epidemics (Ankolekar et al., 2024; Bajwa et al., 2021; Olawade et al., 2023; Patel, 2024).

Public safety is also included within the scope of public administration. Therefore, AI could continue to be implemented to improve public safety. More effective crime prevention and emergency response can be achieved by utilizing AI technologies to anticipate and mitigate potential threats. Law enforcement agencies can more effectively allocate resources and proactively address prospective issues by utilizing AI to predict areas prone to high crime rates (Moses & Chan, 2014; Oatley, 2022; Rigano, 2018). Moreover, through AI, the government can offer more tailored services and achieve improved satisfaction among its clientele by examining individual needs and preferences. Nevertheless, despite the advantages of AI in public administration, they still face challenges. Data privacy is a significant concern because each country has its own policy for the management of sensitive personal data. The use of AI systems has given rise to substantial concerns regarding data privacy and security. The primary objective is to guarantee the safeguarding of data against breaches and unauthorized usage. Furthermore, safeguarding data privacy in AI applications necessitates the establishment of resilient frameworks that guarantee the security of data at every stage, encompassing collection, processing, and storage (Alhitmi et al., 2024; Kaur et al., 2023).

According to Mittelstadt et al. (2016), resolving these problems requires the implementation of comprehensive governance frameworks that establish explicit standards for the ethical use of AI and guarantee adherence to data protection regulations. AI has the potential to automate various services. However, this method also has some drawbacks. This can result in unemployment and alterations in personnel requirements. McKinsey Global Institute's analysis from 2017 suggests that automation could result in the loss of up to 800 million jobs worldwide by 2030, particularly affecting administrative and support positions. The problem lies in how public administration will effectively tackle the repercussions of employment and offer assistance to people who have been affected. According to the World Economic Forum (2020), AI and automation will eliminate and provide jobs. New professions demand distinct skills, including AI maintenance and monitoring, data analysis, and cybersecurity.

Public administration is tasked with implementing policies and managing public initiatives. AI has improved these roles by automating repetitive work, enhancing productivity, and facilitating informed decision-making through data analysis. AI can anticipate and foresee possible risks, improve public safety, and predict public health trends. Nevertheless, AI presents certain issues, including concerns about data privacy and potential for job displacement. Although certain occupations may be rendered obsolete, AI also generates novel positions that require distinct skill sets, such as overseeing AI systems and conducting data analyses. To address these problems, it is necessary to establish robust governance and ethical principles to guarantee the proper utilization of AI. Acquiring knowledge on the utilization of AI in public administration is vital as it offers comprehensive knowledge on how AI may enhance effectiveness, decision-making, and public safety. This chapter tackles the substantial experience presented by AI, such as data privacy and employment displacement, and provides ways to handle these concerns effectively. This chapter provides policymakers, administrators, and stakeholders with a comprehensive understanding of the ethical and governance frameworks necessary for responsible utilization of AI.

BACKGROUND

The introduction of AI into public administration has emerged as an innovative force, with the potential to fundamentally change how government operations and services are delivered to the public. Dwivedi et al. (2021) discussed that as far back as the industrial revolution, significant development in technical innovation has succeeded in transforming numerous manual tasks and processes that had been in existence for decades where humans had reached the limits of physical capacity. AI offers this same transformative potential for the augmentation and potential replacement of human tasks and activities within a wide range of industrial, intellectual and social applications. This chapter addresses these innovative possibilities, with a particular focus on the implications for the Philippines, a country at the intersection between traditional administrative practices and the possibility of cutting-edge technology.

AI has rapidly emerged as an important component of innovation in an array of industries worldwide. It consists of various technologies such as machine learning (ML), natural language processing, and robotics, which allow systems to perform activities that require human intelligence. For instance, Henman (2020) narrated that Artificial intelligence arising from the use of ML is rapidly being developed and deployed by governments to enhance operations, public services, and compliance and security activities. AI applications in public administration cover a wide variety of areas, including administrative efficiency, public health, law enforcement, disaster management, and education. For example, AI-powered systems can automate routine administrative operations, evaluate big datasets for decision-making, forecast public health trends, increase law enforcement skills through predictive policing, and improve disaster response using real-time data analysis. These innovations not only make government operations more efficient but also improve the quality and accessibility of public services.

Ejjami (2024) confirm AI's transformative potential in public administration but emphasize the necessity for ongoing supervision, regular audits, and the development of AI models capable of detecting and rectifying operational anomalies. Globally, AI has been used in various ways to improve efficiency and effectiveness in public administration. Case studies from many countries have demonstrated the diverse applications of AI and excellent outcomes obtained. Singapore, for example, has used AI to improve urban planning and public transit systems through its smart-nation effort. Sipahi and Saayi (2024) discussed smartization which is the policy that Singapore as a city-state with a small geographical territory, limited natural resources, increasing urban density and aging population but determined to become an exceptional city-state has adopted to overcome various national challenges, improve the quality, efficiency and performance of urban services, sustainable development and overall improvement of citizens lives.

In the United States, AI-powered predictive analytics is utilized to manage public health issues and enhance emergency response times. Valle-Cruz et al. (2019) considered that AI has potential benefits in the public health, public policies on climate change, public management, decision-making, disaster prevention and response, improving government-citizen interaction, personalization of services, interoperability, analyzing large amounts of data, detecting abnormalities and patterns, and discovering new solutions through dynamic models and simulation in real time.

Similarly, the application of AI in Sweden has aided progress in welfare services and social policy development. However, Johansson-Pajala and Gustafsson (2022) discovered the introduction of care robots in elder care services seems to be more challenging than that of welfare technology in general, given the context and prevailing attitudes and preconceptions about robotics. Significant challenges need to be managed, at all levels of the society, before care robots can become an integral part of daily care and assist older people and their caregivers in activities and rehabilitation. These examples demonstrate the enormous benefits that AI may provide, such as cost reduction, improved service delivery, and enhanced decision-making capabilities. However, the use of AI in public administration is not without drawbacks. Each country faces unique challenges due to its technological infrastructure, policy environment, and sociological demands. In the Philippines, the potential benefits of

AI are coupled with unique local obstacles that must be addressed. These include limited technological infrastructure, different degrees of digital literacy, and the need for robust data protection legislation. Furthermore, there are concerns regarding the equal distribution of AI advantages and the possibility of job displacement in certain industries. Dadios et al. (2018) highlighted that Philippine industries have already been adopting these technologies, although in varying degrees of diffusion. The extent of the potential benefits that may be realized depends on the country's ability to adapt to the global disruptions that come along with the industrial revolution. The country needs to establish a solid foundation for sustained learning and to accumulate various types of capital, while progressively and systematically closing existing technological gaps. To make the most of the transformative potential of AI, the Philippines must assess strategic implementation recommendations customized to its specific circumstances. This entails the creation and execution of effective policies that protect data privacy and security, while facilitating the integration of AI. To improve the skills and knowledge of public administrators and stakeholders in AI technology (van Noordt & Misuraca, 2022). It is imperative to implement capacity-building initiatives. In addition, the establishment of collaborative partnerships with international organizations and technology providers can speed up the transmission of knowledge and provide access to advanced AI solutions (Broekhuizen et al., 2023; Fu et al., 2022; The World Bank, 2024).

In summary, this chapter offers a comprehensive examination of the impact of AI on the modernization of government operations and the enhancement of service delivery, with a particular emphasis on its implications for the Philippines. This chapter endeavors to provide valuable insights into the current state of AI adoption in the Philippines by analyzing global trends and innovations and deriving lessons from international case studies. It delineates the strategic recommendations, local challenges, and potential benefits of AI implementation in the Philippine context, guaranteeing that AI's transformative potential of AI can be fully realized.

MAIN FOCUS OF THE CHAPTER

This chapter explores the transformative potential of AI in enhancing public administration and service delivery in the Philippines by examining how AI is used and applied in various sectors. It covers how AI can modernize government operations, improve administrative efficiency, and address critical sectors such as public health, law enforcement, disaster management, and education. The chapter conducted a qualitative analysis of existing studies, reports, and global case studies spanning from July to October 2024. It then extracted insights from real-world applications of AI across various countries. By synthesizing global trends and best practices, the chapter identifies practical implications that can be applied in the Philippine context. While no primary data collection was conducted, the analysis leverages secondary data from authoritative sources to offer a well-rounded understanding of relevant AI applications and their potential for addressing challenges in public administration and service delivery.

APPLICATIONS OF AI IN PUBLIC SERVICE

AI in Administrative Efficiency

AI has presented possibilities for altering and providing options for government agencies to perform their mandates. AI development and dynamic progress in its functions and capabilities offer the likelihood of cost reduction to fundamental governance operations, faster delivery and improvement in the quality of decisions, and better analysis and utilization of administrative data (Engstrom et al., 2020). From a deeper perspective of the delivery of public services, there are specific or purpose-based AI designs that address each context. Cognizance and choice of technology that is appropriate for a specific goal empowers organizations to simplify their systems, procedures, and schemes, thus providing clients' approval and satisfaction, increasing the value of the service provided, and augmenting productivity (Parycek et al., 2024). As AI technologies have advanced, insights into their use have become vital for governments exploring the aid of dynamic technological developments to accomplish their targets.

AI in Philippine Public Administration has existed, yet challenges remain to be overcome. The gaps that need to be addressed are algorithm biases, ethical dilemmas, and technical and budgetary constraints (Amado et al., 2024). Thus, there are still agencies that adopt this trend. A few examples depicting the usage of AI are as simple as tax payment computations and condonations, and traffic violation apprehensions to be as complex as environmental monitoring and disaster risk management (Cadiz et al., 2023). In the case of tax payment computation and condonations, AI utilization has been evident from the beginning of the transaction, particularly, queuing of clients, that is, selecting the queue as a regular lane or individuals with special needs along with the allocation of which desk service personnel to attend to shall have the assignment (Henman, 2020). The example leads to efficient workload distribution and handling time tracking that provides data and matrices for client feedback and satisfaction. The application automatically produces the amount by minimizing human errors in computation, standardizing collections, and reducing bias in discounts and penalties (Calo & Citron, 2021). With this, the ease of doing business and smooth and easy flow of transactions is assured (Madan

& Ashok, 2023). Another example provided above, which provides the least human interaction that may cause doubt and probable cases of corruption as the prejudice and preconceived notion, has been set because several cases are traffic violation apprehensions. The system has logical codes that provide measures of scenarios described as violations with corresponding equivalent fixed and non-negotiable penalties (Wirtz et al., 2020). This automatically sends data to individuals and the database for recording is filed. However, complexity in decisions is easily resolved through the use of AI, as evidenced in environmental monitoring and disaster risk management cases. Standards are set with equivalent and corresponding alarms, danger warnings with suggestive actions, and response flows with courses of action are effortlessly disseminated. There is no need for manuals or time-consuming meetings to decide, as the scenarios at hand need quick and immediate responses. The complexities of decisions made clear-cut through AI utilization save lives, conserve time and energy, and preserve scarce available resources for the benefit of posterity (Zuiderwijk et al., 2021).

The use of AI may address concerns regarding speed, accuracy, and consistency in service delivery. Moreover, transparency and accountability are enhanced in select administrative processes that have AI applications, as they are free from biases based on emotions or affinity (Cheong, 2024; Memarian & Doleck, 2023; Murikah et al., 2024; Singhal et al., 2024; Yu & Li, 2022). Likewise, reduction of disruption in service provision due to human intervention has been evident and is continuously being explored amidst the concerns on humanitarian considerations being removed from decision making even if the judgement affects the livelihood and living conditions of individuals, as in the case of hiring and selecting employees, imposition of fines and penalties on unpaid loans for government financing institutions, and even denial of social services to those who do not belong to the financially incapacitated sector are yet to experience economic difficulties, as the system cannot further provide follow-up questions that human interaction could have resolved (Kuziemski & Misuraca, 2020). Sustainability in terms of reducing costs, minimizing risks, and seeking opportunities in the future of AI utilization in the public sector as public servants' labor and efforts shall be allocated for more complex and analytical tasks that entail factors that AI may not yet resolve, such as answers to non-tailor-fitted queries and concerns (Ahn & Chen, 2022). In summary, the application of AI can lead to the creation of smart cities with functionalities and a spectrum of basic services by applying such applications, systems, and technologies that lead to positive change and sustainability.

AI in Law Enforcement

The way police work changes because of AI, especially when it comes to predicting policing and crime data. By looking at past crime data with ML algorithms, the police can determine what crimes might happen next, speed up investigations, and better use their resources. According to Olha and Pavlo (2024), this method not only helps stop crime, but also makes everyone safer. Al Shamsi and Safei (2023) mentioned that AI has greatly improved ways to make decisions and reduce crime with the help of specialized training and joint learning (Berk, 2021; Caldwell et al., 2020; King et al., 2020; Mikhaylov et al., 2018). In addition, many ethical dilemmas arise when AI is used for law enforcement (Belk, 2021; Dhirani et al., 2023; Lepri et al., 2021; Nassar & Kamal, 2021). The use of AI tools in law enforcement (Bag et al., 2024; Olha & Pavlo, 2024) needs to be done in a fair and reasonable way, with people giving careful consideration to privacy, algorithmic bias, and the risk of oversurveillance. Asabek et al. (2023) say that these risks can be lowered by giving police full rules and moral guidelines for using AI.

It is very important for AI tools such as pattern recognition, predictive modeling, and crime tracking to help the police improve their jobs. Butt et al. (2021) and Olha and Pavlo (2024) stated that algorithms that look at very large datasets can find places where crimes happen a lot and guess where and when crimes will happen next by examining patterns in the past and factors such as time and place. By integrating AI into crime prediction models, agencies can take preventive measures to help lower crime rates and improve community safety (Dakalbab et al., 2022; Rigano, 2018; Srivastava et al., 2023). The Philippines finds it both exciting and difficult to think about how AI can be used in law enforcement. Predictive models and spatial reporting systems can help people prevent crime and learn more about how it happens in some Philippine provinces (Asor & Sapin, 2020; Miranda & Leon, 2017; Villarica et al., 2022), as shown by Balahadia et al. (2020) and Gelera and Dajao (2022). AI can also help with crisis planning and emergency response, as shown by the iSERVE emergency response system by Sucgang et al. (2015) and AppLERT mobile application by Balahadia et al. (2016).

AI in Disaster Management

AI makes it easier to plan, deal with, and recover from disasters, changing how they are treated. AI is beneficial for reducing damage and loss because it can correctly predict and prepare for bad weather, making the best use of resources. For instance, natural disasters are now planned for, dealt with, and recovered from differently, and AI is the reason for this. AI can do many things, such as predicting disasters and quickly determining what to do when something goes wrong. According to Alruqi and Aksoy (2023), AI is essential for preventing disasters because it improves hazard maps and prediction systems; therefore, alerts are more accurate and sent out at the right time. A work by Bari et al. (2023) on AI shows that it could be helpful in many emergency scenarios. Using AI is a big part of improving storm, tsunami, and hurricane forecasts. Furthermore, AI technologies help people act quickly and with proper knowledge to lessen damage after an earthquake. People can be better prepared for and able to handle tragedies using these tools. This would lessen deaths and damage over time. In addition, AI plays a major role in ensuring that resources are best used during crisis response and recovery (Alipio & Balahadia, 2020). For example, Bringula and Balahadia (2019) stated that between 2011 and 2016, 3,506 fires broke out in Manila and cost Php2.1 billion (US $ 42 million) to fix. Many of these fires occurred in residential buildings, mostly at alert level 1. AI-powered models and systems can help handle these situations better by looking at data to make better plans for responding to and using resources (de Leon & Miranda, 2022). Another study by Balahadia et al. (2019) discussed how AI-powered fire models can be used to determine the frequency of fires in Manila. These models show trends and insights that make it easier to look over the fire data. This helps to better allocate resources and develop new ways to stop fires.

AI in Education

In the education sector, AI's impact is profoundly seen as it also customizes students' educational experiences to meet their needs and can address potential gaps considering individual differences and various learning styles. According to Harry and Sayudin (2023), AI has potentially significant benefits in education through personalized learning, resulting in better learning outcomes because students can explore, learn, and discover at their own pace based on their learning style. This shows that AI promotes inclusivity and goal-directedness among students, regardless of time availability. This idea corroborates with the study of Kazimzade et al. (2019), wherein there are emerging practices that show potential directions for combining AI in Education (AIED) and learning technologies that guarantee inclusivity. On the other hand, it is found that there is a continuous development of algorithmic biases where such algorithms and generated systems can recreate or augment prejudices and discrimination (Roscoe et al., 2022). Moreover, if students encounter difficulty with their lessons, through the aid of AI, it will be easy for them to cope with the topics they discuss, as it will provide them with additional resources, learning exercises, and in-depth explanations to help them understand the material. This is supported by the study of Joshi et. al. (2021), in the field of education, AI sets as a determinant in innovating novel teaching and learning interventions where its effectiveness and efficiency will be assessed in various situations. The good thing about AI is that it will help the stakeholders to achieve and manage educational goals with the technological assistance of learning technologies. According to Malik et. al. (2019), the significant contribution of AI to education has always been proven such as the development of an automated system for the evaluation of answer sheets among others that both helped educators and learners. In addition, it provides technical assistance to teachers, particularly in generating assessment scores, grading students' learning outputs, and providing more accurate feedback. Teachers can save time and engage in preparing lessons that foster learning and growth for learners. In connection with the study of Ahmad et. al. (2022), the applications regarding AI enhance student learning, minimizes the workload of a teacher, and able to assess students' grades and learning outputs effectively and efficiently, and cope with other tasks related to administrative support and core functions.

Since AI is already part of the Philippine educational system, administrators and educators can now reduce their burden in fulfilling administrative functions, such as document processing, lesson planning, and policy-making. Moreover, AI allows them to spend more time addressing complex and strategic tasks. In relevance to the study of Chen et. al. (2020), with the help of humanoid robots and web-based chatbots, instructors have been able to perform various tasks without compromising the quality and accessibility of education. Also, curriculum course and performance standards have been contextualized following the interests, needs, and readiness of the students that can result in retention of the intended learning competencies. Furthermore, with regard to their decision-making, it helps them to provide insights based on the AI-generated and analyzed datasets that are essential to predict economic trends that will affect how the curriculum specialists and educational experts perceive the educational needs as they develop, review, and enhance the content and performance standards of the recommended curriculum. This is supported by the study of Olatunde-Aiyedun (2024), it is being said that an adaptive curriculum will equip students with AI-related skills that will surely contribute to valuable insights for various stakeholders in academic institutions. In connection to this, with the interpreted data on student performance, teachers can identify the strengths and weaknesses of the students outrightly at both the individual and group levels. The benefit of AI is that it can recommend appropriate teaching strategies and innovations to better suit students' needs, readiness, and interests. AI teachers can create more personalized daily lesson plans and interventions without compromising their teaching load, health, and other functions. Although the curriculum is written in a general form, it is still possible that learning competencies can be easily attained because AI can also make the curriculum directly relevant to learners. This approach will keep the students engaged and motivated to study their lessons, as they feel that the lessons that are prepared align with their specific strengths and preferences.

Other benefits of AI include an AI-powered tutoring system that provides real-time feedback and instant assistance whenever students need it. The main aim of this system is to provide explanations and guide learners on complex and contextualized problems. Usually, the support being provided is not only limited to the corners of the classrooms or even the availability of the teachers. In the study of AlShaikh & Hewahi (2021), the Intelligent Tutoring System (ITS) is important in teaching pedagogy due to the reason of it becomes more convenient to students since it follows personalized teaching assistance which results in a productive learning community without intervention coming from the teachers (Bringula, 2020; Miranda & Bringula, 2023). The Learning Management Systems (LMS) with AI integration, usually tracks student progress and enables more focus in instruction. In relevance to the study of Firat (2023), several factors must be considered if a learning institution will integrate AI into an LMS. Firstly, the security and privacy of student data should be of the utmost concern since data protection measures are highly needed following the relevant laws and regulations. Secondly, the ethical considerations include the bias problems and the potential to replace human teaching and learning. The AI in an LMS must adhere to ethical principles. Lastly, in the pedagogical and andragogical aspects, AI applications should support student learning and it must be integrated into the overall facilitating of learning process. Furthermore, one of the significant contributions of AI in education is that it gives value to students with disabilities. AI can develop personalized learning plans for students who are clinically diagnosed with autism or dyslexia and other learning disabilities. With the aid of AI and the constant guidance of the teacher, we can ensure that everyone is in and no student is left behind. According to Garg and Sharma (2020), the AI technologies moved the lives of every individual, especially those with special needs, making life easier for them. When people with disabilities are learning, the more we can say that we are giving life to the advocacy of our educational system concerning inclusive education. So, we can say now that AI is not just after technological advancement but also about the transformation of lives.

Despite having admirable goals and vision for the Filipino people, the Philippine academic standards have been declining, and we must consider the system's serious problems. On that note, recent studies have demonstrated the alarming decline in the Philippines' education standards. According to the report of the Programme for International Student Assessment (Department of Education, 2019; OECD, 2019; Punongbayan, 2019; Schleicher, 2019), which determined whether 15-year-old children have acquired the knowledge and skills necessary for their participation in social and economic life, Filipino students performed poorly in reading, mathematics, and science, which ranked the lowest among 79 nations. Another international study, the Trends in International Mathematics and Science Study in 2019 measured fourth-grade pupils' math and scientific competence. Results showed that the Philippines did not perform better among the 58 nations and received the lowest rating (Mullis et al., 2020). Similarly, the Southeast Asia Primary Learning Metrics (2020) assessed students in Grade 5 on their reading, writing, and mathematics aptitudes. Along with Southeast Asian countries, the Philippines was one of six in the region to participate in the assessment and performed worse than average in the three areas. Three international studies proved that the Philippines is in the midst of an educational crisis.

Moreover, in a study conducted by Brillantes et al. (2019), to determine the best practices, issues, and areas for improvement in the Senior High School program, researchers conducted an evaluation procedure. Findings showed that SHS students in the Philippines lack the minimum competencies for the SHS program, particularly those in public schools. Indeed, the quality of education in public schools remains poor. For instance, Fran (2021) mentioned the skills that the applicants should possess. Skills such as hard, soft, critical thinking, digital, leadership, and many more; on that note, employers in the Philippines seek diverse hard and soft abilities (Gabriel et al., 2020; Miranda et al., 2024). If we want to have a high employability rate, we are not just allowed to stay stagnant and do nothing, but we should now start addressing the concerns of our students and teachers. Furthermore, problems such as class size, lack of learning materials, teachers' training, benefits, remuneration, and many others must be prioritized and considered.

The future of AI in the context of Philippine education is promising, with the contextualized applications extending beyond the traditional classrooms to support lifelong learning, active collaborations among stakeholders, and implementing programs on skills development, we can able to achieve a better Philippines. However, the more we go beyond conventional learning, the more we need to give attention to ethical considerations to augment the role of human educators rather than replace them. The goal of Philippine education with AI integration is to address the rising and perennial problems that every Filipino is experiencing.

AI in Data Privacy, Protection, and Cybersecurity

In the area of data privacy and protection, AI is of great influence in that it provides improved ways of identifying and preventing security risks for data as well as techniques of securely encoding and safeguarding information. ML systems' primary strength is the capability to process data and extract suitable patterns and abnormalities that show security threats (Ozkan-Okay et al., 2024; Sarker et al., 2020). AI capabilities allow the use of ML algorithms that can learn new threats and react much faster than traditional security systems (Binhammad et al., 2024). For example, real-time monitoring Intrusion Detection Systems (IDS) that are AI-based and analyze the traffic flow in the network to pick up any anomalies. Such systems immediately inform administrators about any suspicious change in the traffic flow and, therefore, minimize the rate of the breakdown of security systems (Binhammad et al., 2024; Kaur et al., 2023).

AI can also improve data encryption by automating critical segments. For instance, generating keys to be used in encryption and managing their authenticity (Villegas-Ch & García-Ortiz, 2023). This is not only for protecting the data but also for the assurance that the encryption is proper and updated against any threats. AI can also increase the data encryption capability by automating the encryption key generation and managing the keys' life cycle (Sarker et al., 2020). In the financial services, AI has already been applied in shielding customer data by prompting for credential validation and flagging and preventing fraudulent transactions on the spot (Odeyemi et al., 2024; Praveenadevi et al., 2024). Likewise, government agencies are implementing AI platforms for threat detection. These agencies run scans on their networks to ensure their networks are secure from intruders and that unauthorized people do not access secretive governmental data (Megas, 2024).

Moreover, AI can also characterize an organization's behavior and discovers extraordinary behavior that can be a threat. Such insider threats and zero-day attacks have been witnessed across organizations around the world (Ozkan-Okay et al., 2024). Likewise, through AI technology, leading organizations such as IBM also implements AI into the cybersecurity environment to support the analyst in performing an enormous flow of unstructured data analysis and transforms them into useful information. This has trimmed down the time spent on threat hunting (Mohamed, 2023). Another key technology is Azure Security Center. Azure is a Microsoft product that analyzes threats and clients' cloud stances with AI and automation and provides real-time protection.

The use of AI will not only be essential in identifying and combating fraud but is also vital in response to fraud events. Cybersecurity solutions based on AI can help minimize the time on the analysis of the threats, the origin of the breach, and related consequences, as well as suggest countermeasures (Kaur et al., 2023). For instance, some multinational technology corporations, such as IBM and Microsoft, utilize AI to identify and mitigate advanced persistent threat (APT) attacks based on past attack information and information on currently active threats (Ozkan-Okay et al., 2024). Organizations should adopt AI as an additional layer on top of their current cybersecurity systems to create a layered approach as opposed to a reactive one (Megas, 2024). Though the Philippines is a developing country, the escalating rate of cyberattacks in many organizations has been directed towards data privacy & protection solutions. AI will become an essential tool for securing data, especially as more public administration services are shifted online, thus protecting people's personal information and governmental data from cyber threats such as hacking, phishing, and unauthorized access (Mohamed, 2023).

AI in Information Dissemination

In the realm of information dissemination, AI greatly contributed to communication and knowledge sharing by having automated and tailored information that is delivered to specific audiences. How does it work? Let us consider social media as an example. Lada et al. (2021) explained that with over 2 billion users and a multitude of content or information to choose from, it will be difficult to give each user a personalized experience. To provide a remedy, they utilized ML algorithms to predict a News Feed ranking system that will matter the most to each user. These algorithms learn what the user interacts with and uses as input, which will then arrange a personalized News Feed as an output to give the user engagement and quality content that is relevant to them. AI powers these algorithms to modify their code in response to the data acquired and learned from it (Duberry, 2022). With an understanding of how AI processes its information dissemination, the technology is also applied in other fields to provide practical and effective use in people's daily lives.

Faris (2023) advocates for using AI in communication and disseminating statistics to provide people with an easy way to understand statistics. He believed that the efficiency of using AI, as it is time-saving and versatile in statistical dissemination and communication, will encourage a data-driven society with high statistical literacy. Surprisingly, AI has also been employed in agriculture, as shown by Ngandee and Taparugssanagorn's (2023) study. Their goal was to develop a data analytics-based framework for predicting and disseminating rice and crop yields by utilizing historical datasets from numerous offices and examining various ML models, such as the Generalized Linear Model (GLM), Feedforward Neural Network (FFNN), Support Vector Machine (SVM), and Random Forest (RF). This will contribute to and support various stakeholders, such as farmers and policymakers, in making informed decisions in agricultural planning. In terms of health, the UP COVID-19 Pandemic Response Team introduced Yani, an AI chatbot that can help people look for information regarding the pandemic, such as government policies on economic support, education, health, and transport. It can also help users find the nearest hospitals and link them to psychologists for psychosocial support. To provide ease of conversation, the chatbot can converse in Filipino and English (UP Media and Public Relations Office, 2020). The Synthetic Aperture Radar and Automatic Identification System for Innovative Terrestrial Monitoring and Maritime Surveillance (SARwAIS) Project of Cadiz et al. (2023) emphasized that AI, in conjunction with Remote Sensing (RS) and Geographic Information System (GIS), aids in the development of disaster management and resource monitoring by highlighting the most pressing hazard assessment needs of the Philippines. In this endeavor, an Information Education Campaign (IEC) is also needed to make the community, including national and local government units and the public, aware of what is happening to our environment and how we can prepare in case of a disaster strike. As mentioned earlier, AI positively affects the dissemination of critical information to the public. However, we must remember that there are also challenges and risks associated with using this technology. This is why digital ethics and privacy are important for monitoring, regulating, and ensuring that AI is still doing its intended job. The University of the Philippines (UP) was the first Higher Education Institution (HEI) to offer a Ph.D. program in AI (University of the Philippines, 2023). In addition, they released the Principles for Responsible and Trustworthy AI to encourage its ethical use and minimize its negative effects. Some of these principles are as follows: common good, privacy, accountability, meaningful human control, and safety.

AI in Social Services

AI is becoming a crucial element in the practice of social services that incorporates welfare services, child protection, and housing. They also aim to reduce stress, such as the time consumers spend accessing different services in these centers. One of the ways through which AI can complement these services is by reducing time and stress. AI technologies such as data intake, eligibility checking, and case documentation are well-fitted to be automated, thereby freeing up much of the social workers' time previously spent on repetitive tasks to engage with clients and make high-impact decisions. For example, case management, such as systems operated by the management of AI, are being discussed to simplify working methods and increase the effectiveness of resource distribution so that social workers can spend more time on the quality aspects. This is why it matters most in child welfare, where the decision is made based on a huge amount of data and, at the same time, the personal circumstances of each child. Following Devlieghere et al. (2022), it is possible to identify the conflict between the implementation of dataism and relationships, two models that presume a given set of data and algorithms of social work relationality, respectively. However, this study reaffirms the fact that despite the significant upgrades brought about by AI, its integration should still provide a corrected focus where the relational character of social work practice is preserved more, while its logic is used to advance data gathering, processing, and prediction quests (Devlieghere et al., 2022).

Apart from efficiency, AI disruptively transforms decision-making processes and the ways in which services are delivered to vulnerable groups. Another competency of AI in action is predictive analytics, which can flag groups of people who need help, let social work come in as soon as possible, and prevent every adverse scenario for the client, such as homelessness or deterioration of mental health. Mikhaylov et al. (2018) explained that the mainstream application of AI is in the public sector, where efforts should be made to collaboratively work across sectors, particularly with the private sector, to address multifaceted social issues. AI systems can extract information from different sources, such as social networks, public records, and healthcare data, and can develop recommendations for interventions. As a result, the additional approach helps target help depending on the situation of a person or family needs, leading to higher social service efficiency. In addition, regarding social justice, AI helps in the identification of fraud in welfare programs to aid the targeted delivery of services to those who really require it. Even so, the liberalization of AI integration into services, particularly social services, must be performed carefully. Some of the new ethical issues highlighted by Reamer (Reamer, 2023) include: Artificial intelligence has been seen to have a desire to be biased and ethical issues arising from, and there are concerns about the accountability of AI decision-making processes. Such challenges prove that there is a need for proper ethical standards to ensure that social work is performed correctly using artificial intelligence. If applied haphazardly, what is likely to be witnessed is that belonging to the present time of technology intensifies existing inequalities, as opposed to reducing them. Therefore, the integration of AI into mainstream social services should be made while adequate ethical supervision to prevent the technological advancements from preventing or worsening the delivery of social services to the people (Mikhaylov et al., 2018; Reamer, 2023).

AI in Legal Practice

Legal Practice pertains to everything that a lawyer does, such as, but not limited to, preparing legal documents for a variety of transactions, conducting cases in court, and providing legal advice on a range of legal issues to clients. Alarie et al. (2018) focused on assessing the merits of a legal case. For example, they used Blue J Legal, a startup in Toronto, Canada, to demonstrate what ML can do. The company utilizes ML to predict how courts decide on legal questions, particularly in tax law. The company created tax law classifiers based on the published decisions of the Supreme Court of Canada, Federal Court of Appeal, and Tax Court of Canada. These classifiers answer how a court would likely decide based on a given set of facts. This process involves identifying fact-intensive questions, coding published decisions, and generating a predictive algorithm. The classifiers can provide a written report of (1) the likely outcome, (2) the percentage likelihood of the outcome, (3) a memo explaining the rationale of the outcome, (4) leading court decisions, and (5) similar precedents. However, these tools may not be available for every question within specific subfields of law, as AI may not fit all legal questions or have limited data. They argued that AI, specifically predictive ML tools, can help evaluate legal cases and judicial decisions by providing an objective and independent prediction of the outcome of a litigation strategy. With this, it removes the personal biases that lawyers may have that might affect their decisions. Pietropaoli (2023) discussed how AI is integrated into seven areas of work of the legal practice: (1) Legal research and e-discovery; (2) Document automation; (3) Predictive legal analysis; (4) Legal review; (5) Case management; (6) Legal advice and expertise automation; and (7) Information and marketing. However, there are also legal and ethical issues that have been raised and should be addressed: (1) accuracy and accountability; (2) transparency, trust, communication, and duty of competent representation; (3) bias and fairness; (4) privacy, data protection, conflict of interests, and duty of confidentiality; (5) lack of human judgment and interpretation; and (6) job displacement and loss of domain expertise. However, Surden (2019) contends that AI is "neither magic nor is it intelligent in the human-cognitive sense of the word." He explained that AI is considered intelligent, as it produces results by utilizing heuristics, patterns, and rules in areas where there are explicit right or wrong answers, such as credit card fraud. When it comes to abstractions, meaning-making and understanding, knowledge transfer, and open-ended tasks, AI cannot do much.

In the Philippines, AI discussions have reached the legislative branch chambers. According to Bañez (2024), AI has transformed from an interesting technology toy to something that merits a serious policy discussion, as there are several bills pending in the House of Representatives about this topic. On one hand, House Bill 7983 defined AI as a "simulation of human intelligence in machines that are programmed to think like humans and mimic their actions." On the other hand, House Bill 9448 defined AI based on its methodologies and specific capabilities such as ML and adaptation. Both bills address the issues of unemployment, discrimination, and even death by drones. However, these legislations distract us from the main issue of accessing our data. Current intellectual property laws and traditional contracts lack proper tools to address these issues; thus, legislative innovation is needed. He added that Congress should publicly fund its development so as not to rely only on the private sector, make it accessible, and ensure its future on our terms. Last July 26, 2024, the "AI and the Law: An MCLE Accredited Forum" was held in the University of the Philippines Bonifacio Global City (UP BGC) Auditorium (Cabaluna, 2024). The forum sparked discussions on the importance of AI in modernizing legal practices by keeping up to date with advancements in this technology. The key points in the event were the introduction of AI and ML, its challenges and risks, and future implications in the legal industry. In addition to the bills mentioned earlier, the Philippines has already enacted several laws supporting the development of AI, such as RA 11293 (Philippine Innovation Act) and RA 11927 (Philippine Digital Workforce Competitiveness Act).

IMPLICATIONS FOR THE PHILIPPINES

The Philippine Innovation Act of 2019, or Republic Act No. 11293, covers the construction of innovation and advancement of technology. It laid the construction of the National Artificial Intelligence Strategy Roadmap, which includes implementation and innovation of artificial intelligence through four strategic dimensions (1) digitization and infrastructure, (2) Workforce, (3) Research and Development, and (4) Regulation. The Philippines implemented the Harmonized National Research and Development Agenda (HNRDA) for technology integration and development in the sectors of agriculture, manufacturing, and customer service (Concepcion, 2019). Regardless of these initiatives, Moreno (2023) concluded that implementation challenges include limited initiatives of the governing body, lack of comprehensive strategies for A.I. implementation in government operational processes, inadequate budget allocation in the national government, limited infrastructure for implementation, need for skilled personnel, and ethical considerations.

The effectiveness of artificial intelligence in public health depends on the reliability and efficiency of data analytics for identifying and understanding emerging public health issues. Castillo, Redula, and Tipon (2019) used symbolic regression to determine the correlation between tuberculosis morbidity and mortality and predicted an increased number of tuberculosis considering the present programs regarding tuberculosis. Thus, public health leaders can be more proactive in improving public health-related programs (Alibudbud et al., 2024). Challenges in implementing and integrating artificial intelligence in public healthcare mainly rely on internet accessibility in the Philippine archipelago, causing a digital divide and inequality among citizens (Gozum, 2024). In addition, it emphasized that addressing Internet connection-related concerns can result in empowering healthcare infrastructure, particularly with the integration of artificial intelligence. Lacsa (2024) recommended prioritizing direct investments in healthcare infrastructure, education, and technological training as they provide more significant benefits.

As digital transformation takes over its heights in society, law enforcement should also prioritize the safety of Filipino citizens in online realms, as cybercrimes have continued to proliferate to 30% since the year 2019 (Santos, 2023). The Department of Information and Communication Technology (Tan, 2022) and Philippine National Police (Reyes, 2021) continue to enhance the IT-related skills of personnel and inform the public about cyber-related programs to combat cybercrime (Domingo, 2023). Arcilla et al. (2023) reviewed the ethical governance of artificial intelligence (AI) by comparing policies and implications across the USA, European Union, India, Philippines, UNESCO, and CAIDP. The study focused on ensuring ethical and fair AI use across various demographics, contexts, sectors, and industries. Aligned with

UNESCO's ethical considerations, the Philippines can contribute to protecting its citizens in the digital era as AI becomes integrated (Chua et al., 2023).

The crucial role of predictive analysis of artificial intelligence dramatically benefits the implementation of disaster preparedness in the Philippines based on its archipelago, which is prone to the existence of natural disasters. Artificial intelligence-related models have also been developed to monitor floods caused by typhoons. Dela Cruz et al. (2020) developed near-real-time flood detection using multitemporal sentinel radar images using artificial intelligence using Sentinel-1A SAR satellite images that can detect floods without human intervention in less than four hours. Although there are continuous innovations and studies regarding the integration of artificial intelligence for disaster management, harnessing models for the early detection and prediction of natural disasters were recommended for early intervention and implementation of disaster management strategies and methodologies (Khan et al., 2023). Despite the ideal integration of artificial intelligence for the future of Philippine Education, primary and higher educational institutions reported the existing challenges in its education system, particularly the allocation of resources such as inadequate instruction, overcrowding in classes, and teachers teaching outside of their areas of expertise (Gumarang & Gumarang, 2021). Highlighting the 21st-century competencies of the K-12 basic education program, it still hinders its progression according to the current state reported by the Philippine Vice President and former Department of Education Secretary Sara Duterte in 2023. These factors have led to alarming learning outcomes among Filipino learners due to the lack of resources available to them (Dio, 2017). Educators are faced with the difficulty of developing responsive, research-based, and pertinent lesson plans and interventions that will improve student learning and address the need for more resources, considering the recently implemented new curriculum (Rogayan et al., 2019). Addressing these micro-issues in the Philippine education system comes first before moving into new heights of innovation with the integration of artificial intelligence (Estrellado & Miranda, 2023).

The National Privacy Commission's advisory opinion (2024-002) finds no conflict between AI use and the Data Privacy Act of 2012, stressing adherence to privacy principles and security measures by Personal Information Controllers. However, Walters and Novak (2021) warned that AI can unintentionally harm individuals by collecting and misusing data. The Cybercrime Prevention Act of 2012 supports the protection against such threats. Reyes (2023) reported a 50% increase in cybersecurity incidents among Filipino organizations, many of which are transitioning to AI, raising concerns regarding cyberattack vulnerability.

GMA Corporate Communications adopted artificial intelligence by launching sports newscasters named Maia (female sports newscaster) and Marco (male sports newscaster), who fulfilled the role of sports newscasters. Barcelon (2023) mentioned that this breakthrough in GMA Corporate Communications can save resource cost allocation in terms of talent fees, food, and makeup artists, but it can pave its way for unemployment. This concern arises from the potential emergence of filter bubbles and echo chambers, which can also restrict exposure to alternative perspectives (Ismail, 2022). Ligot (2023) pointed out the poor recognition of artificial intelligence regarding disinformation, misinformation, and false information, as evaluated through embedded artificial intelligence-based social media algorithms. A moderate balance is necessary in utilizing AI potential for information conveying while protecting public concerns (Evangelista, 2023). In social services, artificial intelligence provides data-driven insights through descriptive, prescriptive, and descriptive data analytics to properly address social service-related matters to assist the marginalized sector, highlighting the decision-making for crafting social services programs (Toli & Manasa, 2024). Evangelista et al. (2023) claimed that the impact of AI integration of social services in the Philippines could reshape social enterprises and improve the scalability and efficiency in undertaking complex societal issues through optimizing resource allocation and improving decision-making through data analytics. In contrast to Redko (2023), the threats of artificial intelligence have ethical implications, such as algorithmic bias and privacy concerns. Furthermore, in legal practice, AI is increasingly used to enhance the efficiency of legal research, predictive analysis, and document automation. However, adopting AI in this field raises critical ethical concerns, particularly regarding the potential for bias (Sacramed 2024). Since AI systems learn from human inputs, there is a risk that they may perpetuate existing biases, especially against marginalized groups (Villaronga, 2022). To ensure that AI in legal practice remains objective and fair, it is crucial to uphold ethical standards and rigorously evaluate AI systems for potential bias (Mohamed, 2024). This approach will allow the Philippines to harness AI's potential to improve the efficiency of legal processes while maintaining justice and fairness for all.

FUTURE RESEARCH DIRECTIONS

Future studies could focus on the exploration of AI's global adoption among governments with a particular emphasis on its implementation through a systematic literature review using major indexing databases, such as Web of Science, Scopus, and Google Scholar. This provides a solid foundation for understanding the current state of AI integration in various government sectors. A similar concept where researchers can explore how AI is designed, implemented, accepted, and adopted in the Philippines through the lens of scholarly publications. Researchers can also investigate the potential drawbacks of AI systems. This allows a balanced analysis of the benefits and challenges associated with their use in government systems and processes. Moreover, future research could explore AI's ethical implications in public administration and assess the long-term impact on employment, workforce distribution, and social equity. The sustainability and scalability of AI applications within government frameworks also merit further investigation. These factors are critical for ensuring AI technologies' effective and responsible use. Additionally, examining the diversity of AI implementation across different regions and its impact on citizen engagement and satisfaction could provide valuable insights into how these technologies can be tailored to meet the unique needs of different populations. These areas of inquiry will contribute to a deeper understanding of AI's role in shaping the future of public administration and its broader societal implications.

CONCLUSION

This study has thoroughly explored how AI can significantly enhance public administration in the Philippines through different trends and applications of AI in various aspect of public administration. For instance, AI technologies can greatly impact emergency management by improving prediction accuracy, optimizing resource allocation, and refining response processes. Through these applications, the Philippines can be better prepared for disasters, respond swiftly, and reduce damage to communities and infrastructure. Integrating AI into crisis management has become increasingly crucial for public safety as natural disasters become more frequent. In addition, the proactive use of AI in planning, risk assessment, and resource management can strengthen a country's disaster resilience and protect its population more effectively. However, the Philippines faces challenges in fully harnessing AI technologies, particularly in cybersecurity. The rapid expansion of digital platforms and the growing sophistication of cyber threats necessitates robust cybersecurity measures. Although recent declines in cybercrime reports indicate progress due to improved IT training and resource allocation, new challenges, such as cyberlibel and voyeurism, have emerged. To address these issues, the Department of Information and Communication Technology and Philippine National Police are enhancing their IT capabilities and resources. Furthermore, the study discussed how developing AI applications tailored to a country's unique needs, such as predictive analytics for crime prevention, can further improve public safety. Considering social concerns and safety regulations, the Philippines can fully leverage AI's transformative potential of AI in public administration.

REFERENCES

Ahmad, S. F., Alam, M. M., Rahmat, M. K., Mubarik, M. S., & Hyder, S. I. (2022). Academic and Administrative Role of Artificial Intelligence in Education. In *Sustainability* (Vol. 14, Issue 3). DOI: 10.3390/su14031101

Ahn, M. J., & Chen, Y.-C. (2022). Digital transformation toward AI-augmented public administration: The perception of government employees and the willingness to use AI in government. *Government Information Quarterly*, 39(2), 101664. https://doi.org/https://doi.org/10.1016/j.giq.2021.101664. DOI: 10.1016/j.giq.2021.101664

Alarie, B., Niblett, A., & Yoon, A. H. (2018). How artificial intelligence will affect the practice of law. *University of Toronto Law Journal*, 68(1, supplement 1), 106–124. https://doi.org/https://doi.org/10.3138/utlj.2017-0052. DOI: 10.3138/utlj.2017-0052

Alhitmi, H. K., Mardiah, A., Al-Sulaiti, K. I., & Abbas, J. (2024). Data security and privacy concerns of AI-driven marketing in the context of economics and business field: An exploration into possible solutions. *Cogent Business & Management*, 11(1), 2393743. DOI: 10.1080/23311975.2024.2393743

Alipio, R. H., & Balahadia, F. F. (2020). DSS Framework: A Proposal for Disaster Logistic Support System for the Province of Laguna. *Recoletos Multidisciplinary Research Journal, 8*(2 SE-Articles), 51–62. DOI: 10.32871/rmrj2008.02.04

Alruqi, A. S., & Aksoy, M. S. (2023). The Use of Artificial Intelligence for Disasters. *Ozean Journal of Applied Sciences*, 13(5), 731–738. DOI: 10.4236/ojapps.2023.135058

AlShaikh, F., & Hewahi, N. (2021). AI and Machine Learning Techniques in the Development of Intelligent Tutoring System: A Review. *2021 International Conference on Innovation and Intelligence for Informatics, Computing, and Technologies (3ICT)*, 403–410. DOI: 10.1109/3ICT53449.2021.9582029

Amado, J. A., Dayson, C. J. P., Gipaya, P. N., Hipos, A. M. G., Ortile, F. F., & Digo, G. S. (2024). Assessing the Impact of AI Generative Tools on Administrative and Supervisory Practices in Education. *Asia Pacific Journal of Management and Sustainable Development, 12*(1), 32–40. https://research.lpubatangas.edu.ph/wp-content/uploads/2024/07/3.-APJMSD-2024-06.pdf

Ankolekar, A., Eppings, L., Bottari, F., Pinho, I. F., Howard, K., Baker, R., Nan, Y., Xing, X., Walsh, S. L. F., Vos, W., Yang, G., & Lambin, P. (2024). Using artificial intelligence and predictive modelling to enable learning healthcare systems (LHS) for pandemic preparedness. *Computational and Structural Biotechnology Journal*, 24, 412–419. https://doi.org/https://doi.org/10.1016/j.csbj.2024.05.014. DOI: 10.1016/j.csbj.2024.05.014 PMID: 38831762

Asor, J., & Sapin, S. (2020). Implementation of predictive crime analytics in municipal crime management system in Calauan, Laguna, Philippines. *International Journal of Advanced Trends in Computer Science and Engineering, 9*(1.3), 150–157. https://doi.org/https://doi.org/10.30534/ijatcse/2020/2291.32020

Atabekov, A. R. (2023). Issues in the implementation of predictive law in law enforcement activities: a comparative legal study. *Vestnik of the St. Petersburg University of the Ministry of Internal Affairs of Russia, 2023*(3), 67–75.

Bag, A., Roy, S., & Pandey, A. (2024). Harnessing the Power of Artificial Intelligence in Law Enforcement: A Comprehensive Review of Opportunities and Ethical Challenges. In Ara, A., & Ara, A. (Eds.), *Exploring the Ethical Implications of Generative AI* (pp. 121–145). IGI Global., DOI: 10.4018/979-8-3693-1565-1.ch008

Bajwa, J., Munir, U., Nori, A., & Williams, B. (2021). Artificial intelligence in healthcare: Transforming the practice of medicine. *Future Healthcare Journal*, 8(2), e188–e194. https://doi.org/https://doi.org/10.7861/fhj.2021-0095. DOI: 10.7861/fhj.2021-0095 PMID: 34286183

Balahadia, F. (2020). Intelligent Investigation on Crime Incident Reports in the Province of Laguna through Predictive Model Development. *International Journal of Advanced Trends in Computer Science and Engineering, 9*(1.3), 139–144. https://doi.org/https://doi.org/10.30534/ijatcse/2020/2091.32020

Balahadia, F. F., Dadiz, B. G., Ramirez, R. R., Luvett, M., Lalata, J. P., & Lagman, A. C. (2019). Application of Data Mining Approach for Profiling Fire Incidents Reports of Bureau of Fire and Protection. *2019 International Conference on Computational Intelligence and Knowledge Economy (ICCIKE)*, 713–717. DOI: 10.1109/ICCIKE47802.2019.9004420

Bari, L. F., Ahmed, I., Ahamed, R., Zihan, T. A., Sharmin, S., Pranto, A. H., & Islam, M. R. (2023). Potential Use of Artificial Intelligence (AI) in Disaster Risk and Emergency Health Management: A Critical Appraisal on Environmental Health. *Environmental Health Insights*, 17, 11786302231217808. DOI: 10.1177/11786302231217808 PMID: 38089525

Belk, R. (2021). Ethical issues in service robotics and artificial intelligence. *Service Industries Journal*, 41(13–14), 860–876. DOI: 10.1080/02642069.2020.1727892

Berk, R. A. (2021). Artificial Intelligence, Predictive Policing, and Risk Assessment for Law Enforcement. *Annual Review of Criminology*, 4(1), 209–237. https://doi.org/https://doi.org/10.1146/annurev-criminol-051520-012342. DOI: 10.1146/annurev-criminol-051520-012342

Bhagat, S. V., & Kanyal, D. (2024). Navigating the Future: The Transformative Impact of Artificial Intelligence on Hospital Management- A Comprehensive Review. *Cureus*, 16(2), e54518. DOI: 10.7759/cureus.54518 PMID: 38516434

Binhammad, M., Alqaydi, S., Othman, A., & Abuljadayel, L. H. (2024). The Role of AI in Cyber Security: Safeguarding Digital Identity. *Journal of Information Security*, 15(2), 245–278. https://doi.org/https://doi.org/10.4236/jis.2024.152015. DOI: 10.4236/jis.2024.152015

Brillantes, K. D. B., Jr. A. C. O., Francisco-Abrigo, K. A., Capones, E. M., & Jovellanos, J. B. B. (2019). *Status of Senior High School Implementation: A Process Evaluation*. https://www.econstor.eu/bitstream/10419/240964/1/pidsdps1913.pdf

Bringula, R., & Balahadia, F. (2019). A spatiotemporal analysis of fire incidents in Manila from 2011-2016: Implications for fire prevention. *Disaster Prevention and Management*, 28(2), 201–215. DOI: 10.1108/DPM-05-2018-0147

Bringula, R. P. (2020). Intelligent Tutoring Systems for Filipino Learners: Current Research, Gaps, and Opportunities. In Habib, M. (Ed.), *Revolutionizing Education in the Age of AI and Machine Learning* (pp. 152–172). IGI Global., https://doi.org/http://doi:10.4018/978-1-5225-7793-5.ch008 DOI: 10.4018/978-1-5225-7793-5.ch008

Broekhuizen, T., Dekker, H., de Faria, P., Firk, S., Nguyen, D. K., & Sofka, W. (2023). AI for managing open innovation: Opportunities, challenges, and a research agenda. *Journal of Business Research*, 167, 114196. https://doi.org/https://doi.org/10.1016/j.jbusres.2023.114196. DOI: 10.1016/j.jbusres.2023.114196

Butt, U. M., Letchmunan, S., Hassan, F. H., Ali, M., Baqir, A., Koh, T. W., & Sherazi, H. H. R. (2021). Spatio-Temporal Crime Predictions by Leveraging Artificial Intelligence for Citizens Security in Smart Cities. *IEEE Access : Practical Innovations, Open Solutions*, 9, 47516–47529. DOI: 10.1109/ACCESS.2021.3068306

Cabaluna, C. (2024). *AI and the Law Forum Explores Future of Legal Practice in the Philippines*. Lexagle. https://www.lexagle.com/news-en-sg/ai-and-law-event-philippines-lexagle

Cadiz, N., Mariano, K. L. S., Dumalag, J. B. L. C., Retamar, A. E., & Aceron, J. C. (2023). Information, Education, and Communication Campaign in the Philippines: Capacitating Academic Institutions and Government Agencies using Geographic Information System, Radar Remote Sensing, and Artificial Intelligence. *2023 Asian Conference on Remote Sensing (ACRS2023)*. https://www.researchgate.net/publication/380177949_Information_Education_and_Communication_Campaign_in_the_Philippines_Capacitating_Academic_Institutions_and_Government_Agencies_using_Geographic_Information_System_Radar_Remote_Sensing_and_Artificial_I

Caldwell, M., Andrews, J. T. A., Tanay, T., & Griffin, L. D. (2020). AI-enabled future crime. *Crime Science*, 9(1), 14. DOI: 10.1186/s40163-020-00123-8

Calo, R., & Citron, D. K. (2021). The Automated Administrative State: A Crisis of Legitimacy. *Emory Law Journal*, 70(4), 797–844. https://scholarlycommons.law.emory.edu/elj/vol70/iss4/1?utm_source=scholarlycommons.law.emory.edu%2Felj%2Fvol70%2Fiss4%2F1&utm_medium=PDF&utm_campaign=PDFCoverPages

Charles, V., Rana, N. P., & Carter, L. (2022). Artificial Intelligence for data-driven decision-making and governance in public affairs. *Government Information Quarterly*, 39(4), 101742. https://doi.org/https://doi.org/10.1016/j.giq.2022.101742. DOI: 10.1016/j.giq.2022.101742

Chen, L., Chen, P., & Lin, Z. (2020). Artificial Intelligence in Education: A Review. *IEEE Access : Practical Innovations, Open Solutions*, 8, 75264–75278. DOI: 10.1109/ACCESS.2020.2988510

Cheong, B. C. (2024). Transparency and accountability in AI systems: safeguarding wellbeing in the age of algorithmic decision-making. *Frontiers in Human Dynamics, 6*. https://www.frontiersin.org/journals/human-dynamics/articles/10.3389/fhumd.2024.1421273

Dadios, E. P., Culaba, A. B., Albert, J. R. G., Paqueo, V. B., Orbeta, A. C., Serafica, R. B., Bandala, A. A., & Bairan, J. C. A. C. (2018). Preparing the Philippines for the fourth industrial revolution: A scoping study. In *PIDS Discussion Paper Series, No. 2018-11*.

Dakalbab, F., Abu Talib, M., Abu Waraga, O., Bou Nassif, A., Abbas, S., & Nasir, Q. (2022). Artificial intelligence & crime prediction: A systematic literature review. *Social Sciences & Humanities Open*, 6(1), 100342. https://doi.org/https://doi.org/10.1016/j.ssaho.2022.100342. DOI: 10.1016/j.ssaho.2022.100342 de Leon, A. P., & Miranda, J. P. P. (2022). A Spatiotemporal Analysis of Fire Incidents in Pampanga Province of Philippines: Inputs for Fire Prevention Programs. *International Transaction Journal of Engineering, Management, and Applied Sciences and Technologies, 13*(10), 1–17. https://doi.org/http://doi.org/10.14456/ITJEMAST.2022.193

Department of Education. (2019). *PISA 2018: National report of the Philippines*. https://www.deped.gov.ph/wp-content/uploads/2019/12/PISA-2018-Philippine-National-Report.pdf

Devlieghere, J., Gillingham, P., & Roose, R. (2022). Dataism versus relationshipism: A social work perspective. *Nordic Social Work Research*, 12(3), 328–338. DOI: 10.1080/2156857X.2022.2052942

Dhirani, L. L., Mukhtiar, N., Chowdhry, B. S., & Newe, T. (2023). Ethical Dilemmas and Privacy Issues in Emerging Technologies: A Review. In *Sensors* (Vol. 23, Issue 3). DOI: 10.3390/s23031151

Duberry, J. (2022). *AI and information dissemination: Challenging citizens access to relevant and reliable information*. Edward Elgar Publishing., DOI: 10.4337/9781788977319.00008

Dwivedi, Y. K., Hughes, L., Ismagilova, E., Aarts, G., Coombs, C., Crick, T., Duan, Y., Dwivedi, R., Edwards, J., Eirug, A., Galanos, V., Ilavarasan, P. V., Janssen, M., Jones, P., Kar, A. K., Kizgin, H., Kronemann, B., Lal, B., Lucini, B., & Williams, M. D. (2021). Artificial Intelligence (AI): Multidisciplinary perspectives on emerging challenges, opportunities, and agenda for research, practice and policy. *International Journal of Information Management*, 57, 101994. https://doi.org/https://doi.org/10.1016/j.ijinfomgt.2019.08.002. DOI: 10.1016/j.ijinfomgt.2019.08.002

Ejjami, R. (2024). Public Administration 5.0: Enhancing Governance and Public Services with Smart Technologies. *International Journal For Multidisciplinary Research, 6*(4), 1–35. https://doi.org/https://doi.org/10.36948/ijfmr.2024.v06i04.26086

Engstrom, D. F., Ho, D. E., Sharkey, C. M., & Cuéllar, M.-F. (2020). *Government by Algorithm: Artificial Intelligence in Federal Administrative Agencies*. https://law.stanford.edu/wp-content/uploads/2020/02/ACUS-AI-Report.pdf

Fabito, B. S., Balahadia, F. F., & Cabatlao, J. D. N. (2016). AppLERT: A mobile application for incident and disaster notification for Metro Manila. *2016 IEEE Region 10 Symposium (TENSYMP)*, 288–292. DOI: 10.1109/TENCONSpring.2016.7519420

Faris, M. (2023). Use of AI in Communication and Dissemination Statistics. *UNECE Expert Meeting on Dissemination and Communication of Statistics 2023*. https://unece.org/sites/default/files/2023-10/DissComm2023_S3_Indonesia_Faris_Paper.pdf

Fırat, M. (2023). Integrating AI Applications into Learning Management Systems to Enhance e-Learning. *Instructional Technology and Lifelong Learning*, 4(1), 1–14. DOI: 10.52911/itall.1244453

Fran. (2021). *The Top Skills in the Philippines for Employability*. Future Learn. https://www.futurelearn.com/info/futurelearn-international/top-skills-in-the-philippines

Fu, X., & Fu, X. (Maggie), Ghauri, P., & Hou, J. (2022). International collaboration and innovation: Evidence from a leading Chinese multinational enterprise. *Journal of World Business, 57*(4), 101329. https://doi.org/https://doi.org/10.1016/j.jwb.2022.101329

Gabriel, A. G., Alcantara, G. M., & Alvarez, J. D. G. (2020). How Do Millennial Managers Lead Older Employees? The Philippine Workplace Experience. *SAGE Open*, 10(1), 2158244020914651. DOI: 10.1177/2158244020914651

Garg, S., & Sharma, S. (2020). Impact of Artificial Intelligence in Special Need Education to Promote Inclusive Pedagogy. *International Journal of Information and Education Technology (IJIET)*, 10(7), 523–527. Advance online publication. DOI: 10.18178/ijiet.2020.10.7.1418

Gelera, A. M., & Dajao, E. S. (2022). Crime Mapping Approach for Crime Pattern Identification: A Prototype for the Province of Cavite. *Proceedings of Sixth International Congress on Information and Communication Technology. Lecture Notes in Networks and Systems*. https://doi.org/https://doi.org/10.1007/978-981-16-2380-6_79

Harry, A., & Sayudin, S. (2023). Role of AI in Education. *Injuruty:Interdiciplinary-JournalandHumanity*, 2(3), 260–268. DOI: 10.58631/injurity.v2i3.52

Henman, P. (2020). Improving public services using artificial intelligence: Possibilities, pitfalls, governance. *Asia Pacific Journal of Public Administration*, 42(4), 209–221. DOI: 10.1080/23276665.2020.1816188

Johansson-Pajala, R.-M., & Gustafsson, C. (2022). Significant challenges when introducing care robots in Swedish elder care. *Disability and Rehabilitation. Assistive Technology*, 17(2), 166–176. DOI: 10.1080/17483107.2020.1773549 PMID: 32538206

Joshi, S., Rambola, R. K., & Churi, P. (2021). Evaluating Artificial Intelligence in Education for Next Generation. *Journal of Physics: Conference Series*, 1714(1), 12039. DOI: 10.1088/1742-6596/1714/1/012039

Kaur, R., Gabrijelčič, D., & Klobučar, T. (2023). Artificial intelligence for cybersecurity: Literature review and future research directions. *Information Fusion*, 97, 101804. https://doi.org/https://doi.org/10.1016/j.inffus.2023.101804. DOI: 10.1016/j.inffus.2023.101804

Kazimzade, G., Patzer, Y., & Pinkwart, N. (2019). In Knox, J., Wang, Y., & Gallagher, M. (Eds.), *Artificial Intelligence in Education Meets Inclusive Educational Technology—The Technical State-of-the-Art and Possible Directions BT - Artificial Intelligence and Inclusive Education: Speculative Futures and Emerging Practices* (pp. 61–73). Springer Singapore., DOI: 10.1007/978-981-13-8161-4_4

King, T. C., Aggarwal, N., Taddeo, M., & Floridi, L. (2020). Artificial Intelligence Crime: An Interdisciplinary Analysis of Foreseeable Threats and Solutions. *Science and Engineering Ethics*, 26(1), 89–120. DOI: 10.1007/s11948-018-00081-0 PMID: 30767109

Kuziemski, M., & Misuraca, G. (2020). AI governance in the public sector: Three tales from the frontiers of automated decision-making in democratic settings. *Telecommunications Policy*, 44(6), 101976. https://doi.org/https://doi.org/10.1016/j.telpol.2020.101976. DOI: 10.1016/j.telpol.2020.101976 PMID: 32313360

Lada, A., Wang, M., & Yan, T. (2021). *How machine learning powers Facebook's News Feed ranking algorithm*. Engineering at Meta. https://engineering.fb.com/2021/01/26/ml-applications/news-feed-ranking/

Lepri, B., Oliver, N., & Pentland, A. (2021). Ethical machines: The human-centric use of artificial intelligence. *iScience*, 24(3), 102249. https://doi.org/https://doi.org/10.1016/j.isci.2021.102249. DOI: 10.1016/j.isci.2021.102249 PMID: 33763636

Madan, R., & Ashok, M. (2023). AI adoption and diffusion in public administration: A systematic literature review and future research agenda. *Government Information Quarterly*, 40(1), 101774. https://doi.org/https://doi.org/10.1016/j.giq.2022.101774. DOI: 10.1016/j.giq.2022.101774

Malik, G., Tayal, D. K., & Vij, S. (2019). An Analysis of the Role of Artificial Intelligence in Education and Teaching BT - Recent Findings in Intelligent Computing Techniques. In Sa, P. K., Bakshi, S., Hatzilygeroudis, I. K., & Sahoo, M. N. (Eds.), *Recent Findings in Intelligent Computing Techniques* (pp. 407–417). Springer Singapore. DOI: 10.1007/978-981-10-8639-7_42

Megas, K. (2024). *Managing Cybersecurity and Privacy Risks in the Age of Artificial Intelligence: Launching a New Program at NIST*. National Institute of Standards and Technology. https://www.nist.gov/blogs/cybersecurity-insights/managing-cybersecurity-and-privacy-risks-age-artificial-intelligence

Memarian, B., & Doleck, T. (2023). Fairness, Accountability, Transparency, and Ethics (FATE) in Artificial Intelligence (AI) and higher education: A systematic review. *Computers and Education: Artificial Intelligence, 5*, 100152. https://doi.org/https://doi.org/10.1016/j.caeai.2023.100152

Mikhaylov, S. J., Esteve, M., & Campion, A. (2018). Artificial intelligence for the public sector: Opportunities and challenges of cross-sector collaboration. *Philosophical Transactions. Series A, Mathematical, Physical, and Engineering Sciences*, 376(2128), 20170357. DOI: 10.1098/rsta.2017.0357 PMID: 30082303

Miranda, J. P. P., & Bringula, R. P. (2023). Towards the Development of a Model to Detect Learned Helplessness Among Grade 6 Mathematics Students. *2023 IEEE International Conference on Advanced Learning Technologies (ICALT)*, 373–375. DOI: 10.1109/ICALT58122.2023.00115

Miranda, J. P. P., & De Leon, A. P. (2017). Datasets of Fire and Crime Incidents in Pampanga, Philippines. *International Journal of Computing Sciences Research*, 7, 1637–1646. DOI: 10.25147/ijcsr.2017.001.1.121

Miranda, J. P. P., Dianelo, R. F. B., Gamboa, A. B., Bansil, J. A., Regala, A. R., & Simpao, L. S. (2024). Identification, validity, and reliability of the 21st-century workplace skills for on-the-job training practicum. *International Journal of Evaluation and Research in Education*, 10(5), 3485–3492. DOI: 10.11591/ijere.v13i5.28919

Mittelstadt, B. D., Allo, P., Taddeo, M., Wachter, S., & Floridi, L. (2016). The ethics of algorithms: Mapping the debate. *Big Data & Society*, 3(2), 2053951716679679. DOI: 10.1177/2053951716679679

Mohamed, N. (2023). Current trends in AI and ML for cybersecurity: A state-of-the-art survey. *Cogent Engineering*, 10(2), 2272358. DOI: 10.1080/23311916.2023.2272358

Moses, L. B., & Chan, J. (2014). Using big data for legal and law enforcement decisions: Testing the new tools. *The University of New South Wales Law Journal*, 37(2), 643–678. https://search.informit.org/doi/10.3316/informit.613165001799453

Mullis, I. V. S., Martin, M. O., Foy, P., Kelly, D. L., & Fishbein, B. (2020). *TIMSS 2019 International Results in Mathematics and Science*. https://timss2019.org/reports/wp-content/themes/timssandpirls/download-center/TIMSS-2019-International-Results-in-Mathematics-and-Science.pdf

Murikah, W., Nthenge, J. K., & Musyoka, F. M. (2024). Bias and ethics of AI systems applied in auditing - A systematic review. *Scientific African*, 25, e02281. https://doi.org/https://doi.org/10.1016/j.sciaf.2024.e02281. DOI: 10.1016/j.sciaf.2024.e02281

Nassar, A., & Kamal, M. (2021). Ethical Dilemmas in AI-Powered Decision-Making: A Deep Dive into Big Data-Driven Ethical Considerations. *International Journal of Responsible Artificial Intelligence, 11*(8 SE-Articles), 1–11. https://neuralslate.com/index.php/Journal-of-Responsible-AI/article/view/43

Ngandee, S., & Taparugssanagorn, A. (2023). Improved information dissemination services for the agricultural sector in Thailand: Development and evaluation of a machine learning based rice crop yield prediction system. *Information Development*, 02666669231208017, 02666669231208017. Advance online publication. DOI: 10.1177/02666669231208017

Oatley, G. C. (2022). Themes in data mining, big data, and crime analytics. *Wiley Interdisciplinary Reviews. Data Mining and Knowledge Discovery*, 12(2), e1432. https://doi.org/https://doi.org/10.1002/widm.1432. DOI: 10.1002/widm.1432

Odeyemi, O., Mhlongo, N. Z., Nwankwo, E. E., & Soyombo, O. T. (2024). Reviewing the role of AI in fraud detection and prevention in financial services. *International Journal of Science and Research Archive*, 11(1), 2101–2110. https://doi.org/https://doi.org/10.30574/ijsra.2024.11.1.0279. DOI: 10.30574/ijsra.2024.11.1.0279

OECD. (2019). *PISA 2018 Results (Volume 1): What students know and can do*. OECD Publishing. https://doi.org/https://doi.org/10.1787/5f07c754-en

Olatunde-Aiyedun, T. G. (2024). Artificial Intelligence (AI) in Education: Integration of AI Into Science Education Curriculum in Nigerian Universities. *International Journal of Artificial Intelligence for Digital*, 1(1), 1–14. https://papers.ssrn.com/sol3/papers.cfm?abstract_id=4733349

Olawade, D. B., Wada, O. J., David-Olawade, A. C., Kunonga, E., Abaire, O., & Ling, J. (2023). Using artificial intelligence to improve public health: A narrative review. *Frontiers in Public Health*, 11, 1196397. https://www.frontiersin.org/journals/public-health/articles/10.3389/fpubh.2023.1196397. DOI: 10.3389/fpubh.2023.1196397 PMID: 37954052

Olha, L., & Pavlo, T. (2024). Artificial Intelligence in Law Enforcement : Current State and Development Prospects. *Proceedings of 10th Socratic Lectures 2024*, 120–124. https://www.zf.uni-lj.si/images/zalozba/Sokratska_10_II/12_Lunhol_Olha.pdf

Ozkan-Okay, M., Akin, E., Aslan, Ö., Kosunalp, S., Iliev, T., Stoyanov, I., & Beloev, I. (2024). A Comprehensive Survey: Evaluating the Efficiency of Artificial Intelligence and Machine Learning Techniques on Cyber Security Solutions. *IEEE Access : Practical Innovations, Open Solutions*, 12, 12229–12256. DOI: 10.1109/ACCESS.2024.3355547

Parycek, P., Schmid, V., & Novak, A.-S. (2024). Artificial Intelligence (AI) and Automation in Administrative Procedures: Potentials, Limitations, and Framework Conditions. *Journal of the Knowledge Economy*, 15(2), 8390–8415. DOI: 10.1007/s13132-023-01433-3

Patel, K. (2024). The Importance of Data-Driven Decision-Making in Public Health. *International Journal of Computer Trends and Technology*, 72(5), 27–32. https://doi.org/https://doi.org/10.14445/22312803/IJCTT-V72I5P103. DOI: 10.14445/22312803/IJCTT-V72I5P103

Pietropaoli, I. (2023). *Use of Artificial Intelligence in Legal Practice*. https://www.biicl.org/documents/170_use_of_artificial_intelligence_in_legal_practice_final.pdf

Praveenadevi, D., & Velusamy, C. M., S. K., Gogula, R., Suryadevara, S., & Soans, S. V. (2024). Artificial Intelligence in E-Commerce: Protecting Data and Privacy. In P. K. Goel (Ed.), *Strategies for E-Commerce Data Security: Cloud, Blockchain, AI, and Machine Learning* (pp. 83–112). IGI Global. DOI: 10.4018/979-8-3693-6557-1.ch004

Punongbayan, J. (2019). *[ANALYSIS] Dismal PISA rankings: A wake-up call for Filipinos*. Rappler. https://www.rappler.com/voices/thought-leaders/analysis-dismal-programme-international-student-assessment-rankings-wake-up-call-filipinos

Rashed, H., Al, S., & Safei, S. (2023). Artificial Intelligence Adoption in Predictive Policing to Predict Crime Mitigation Performance. *International Journal of Sustainable Construction Engineering and Technology*, 14(3), 289–298.

Reamer, F. G. (2023). Artificial Intelligence in Social Work: Emerging Ethical Issues. *International Journal of Social Work Values and Ethics*, 20(2), 52–71. https://doi.org/https://doi.org/10.55521/10-020-205. DOI: 10.55521/10-020-205

Rigano, C. (2018). *Using Artificial Intelligence to Address Criminal Justice Needs*. https://nij.ojp.gov/topics/articles/using-artificial-intelligence-address-criminal-justice-needs

Roscoe, R. D., Salehi, S., Nixon, N., Worsley, M., Piech, C., & Luckin, R. (2022). Inclusion and Equity as a Paradigm Shift for Artificial Intelligence in Education. In *Artificial Intelligence in STEM Education*. CRC Press. DOI: 10.1201/9781003181187-28

Sarker, I. H., Kayes, A. S. M., Badsha, S., Alqahtani, H., Watters, P., & Ng, A. (2020). Cybersecurity data science: An overview from machine learning perspective. *Journal of Big Data*, 7(1), 41. DOI: 10.1186/s40537-020-00318-5

Schleicher, A. (2019). *PISA 2018: Insights and Interpretations.* https://www.oecd.org/content/dam/oecd/en/about/programmes/edu/pisa/publications/national-reports/pisa-2018/PISA 2018 Insights and Interpretations FINAL PDF.pdf

Shafritz, J. M., Russell, E. W., Borick, C. P., & Hyde, A. C. (2022). *Introducing Public Administration* (10th Editi). Routledge.

Singhal, A., Neveditsin, N., Tanveer, H., & Mago, V. (2024). Toward Fairness, Accountability, Transparency, and Ethics in AI for Social Media and Health Care: Scoping Review. *JMIR Medical Informatics*, 12, e50048. DOI: 10.2196/50048 PMID: 38568737

Sipahi, E. B., & Saayi, Z. (2024). The world s first Smart Nation vision: the case of Singapore. *Smart Cities and Regional Development Journal, 8*(1), 41–58. https://doi.org/http://dx.doi.org/10.25019/dvm98x09

Srivastava, R. K., Gupta, A., & Sharma, G. (2023). Forecasting Crime Rate Using Artificial Intelligence Applications. *2023 International Conference on Sustainable Communication Networks and Application (ICSCNA)*, 1222–1226. DOI: 10.1109/ICSCNA58489.2023.10370364

Sucgang, D. C., Villanueva, J. T., Macawile, N. C. C., Antivo, R. C., & Tipay, I. P. R. (2015). iSERVE-An Android Based Artificial Intelligence Emergency CP(Crime Prevention) Response System Using GPS Tracker. *International Journal of Conceptions on Computing and Information Technology*, 3(3), 105–108. https://studyres.com/doc/7934797/iserve--an-android-based-artificial-intelligence-emergenc

Surden, H. (2019). Artificial Intelligence and Law : An Overview. *Georgia State University Law Review*, 35(4), 1305–1337.

The World Bank. (2024). *Transformative technologies (AI) challenges and principles of regulation.* Digital Regulation Platform. https://digitalregulation.org/3004297-2/

United Nations Children's Fund and Southeast Asian Ministers of Education Organization. (2020). *SEA-PLM 2019 Main Regional Report, Children's learning in 6 Southeast Asian countries.* https://www.seaplm.org/PUBLICATIONS/regional results/SEA-PLM 2019 Main Regional Report.pdf

University of the Philippines. (2023). *Principles for Responsible and Trustworthy Artificial Intelligence.* https://up.edu.ph/up-principles-for-responsible-artificial-intelligence/

UP Media and Public Relations Office. (2020). *UP Resilience Institute introduces COVID chatbot.* https://up.edu.ph/up-resilience-institute-introduces-covid-chatbot/

Valle-Cruz, D., Alejandro Ruvalcaba-Gomez, E., Sandoval-Almazan, R., & Ignacio Criado, J. (2019). A Review of Artificial Intelligence in Government and its Potential from a Public Policy Perspective. *Proceedings of the 20th Annual International Conference on Digital Government Research*, 91–99. DOI: 10.1145/3325112.3325242

van Noordt, C., & Misuraca, G. (2022). Artificial intelligence for the public sector: Results of landscaping the use of AI in government across the European Union. *Government Information Quarterly*, 39(3), 101714. https://doi.org/https://doi.org/10.1016/j.giq.2022.101714. DOI: 10.1016/j.giq.2022.101714

Villarica, M. V., Balahadia, F. F., Asor, J. R., & Catedrilla, G. M. B. (2022). Development of crime reporting system to identify patterns of crime in laguna. *International Journal of Computing Sciences Research*, 6. Advance online publication. DOI: 10.25147/ijcsr.2017.001.1.110

Villegas-Ch, W., & García-Ortiz, J. (2023). Toward a Comprehensive Framework for Ensuring Security and Privacy in Artificial Intelligence. In *Electronics* (Vol. 12, Issue 18). DOI: 10.3390/electronics12183786

Wirtz, B. W., Weyerer, J. C., & Sturm, B. J. (2020). The Dark Sides of Artificial Intelligence: An Integrated AI Governance Framework for Public Administration. *International Journal of Public Administration*, 43(9), 818–829. DOI: 10.1080/01900692.2020.1749851

World Economic Forum. (2020). *The Future of Jobs Report*. https://www3.weforum.org/docs/WEF_Future_of_Jobs_2020.pdf

Yaiprasert, C., & Hidayanto, A. N. (2024). AI-powered ensemble machine learning to optimize cost strategies in logistics business. *International Journal of Information Management Data Insights*, 4(1), 100209. https://doi.org/https://doi.org/10.1016/j.jjimei.2023.100209. DOI: 10.1016/j.jjimei.2023.100209

Yu, L., & Li, Y. (2022). Artificial Intelligence Decision-Making Transparency and Employees' Trust: The Parallel Multiple Mediating Effect of Effectiveness and Discomfort. In *Behavioral Sciences* (Vol. 12, Issue 5). DOI: 10.3390/bs12050127

Zuiderwijk, A., Chen, Y.-C., & Salem, F. (2021). Implications of the use of artificial intelligence in public governance: A systematic literature review and a research agenda. *Government Information Quarterly*, 38(3), 101577. https://doi.org/https://doi.org/10.1016/j.giq.2021.101577. DOI: 10.1016/j.giq.2021.101577

ADDITIONAL READING

Agarwal, P. K. (2018). Public Administration Challenges in the World of AI and Bots. *Public Administration Review*, 78(6), 917–921. DOI: 10.1111/puar.12979

Ahn, M. J., & Chen, Y.-C. (2022). Digital transformation toward AI-augmented public administration: The perception of government employees and the willingness to use AI in government. *Government Information Quarterly*, 39(2), 101664. DOI: 10.1016/j.giq.2021.101664

Brillantes, A. B.Jr, & Ruiz, K. E. V. (2023). Public administration in the Philippines: Features, trends, issues, and directions. *In Political. Science & Public Policy*, 2023, 175–195. DOI: 10.4337/9781839104794.00020

Bringula, R. P. (2020). Intelligent Tutoring Systems for Filipino Learners: Current Research, Gaps, and Opportunities. In Habib, M. (Ed.), *Revolutionizing Education in the Age of AI and Machine Learning* (pp. 152–172). IGI Global., DOI: 10.4018/978-1-5225-7793-5.ch008

Concepcion, R. S., Bedruz, R. A. R., Culaba, A. B., Dadios, E. P., & Pascua, A. R. A. R. (2019). The Technology Adoption and Governance of Artificial Intelligence in the Philippines. *2019 IEEE 11th International Conference on Humanoid, Nanotechnology, Information Technology, Communication and Control, Environment, and Management (HNICEM)*, 1–10. DOI: 10.1109/HNICEM48295.2019.9072725

Madan, R., & Ashok, M. (2023). AI adoption and diffusion in public administration: A systematic literature review and future research agenda. *Government Information Quarterly*, 40(1), 101774. DOI: 10.1016/j.giq.2022.101774

Madan, R., & Ashok, M. (2023). AI adoption and diffusion in public administration: A systematic literature review and future research agenda. *Government Information Quarterly*, 40(1), 101774. DOI: 10.1016/j.giq.2022.101774

Reis, J., Santo, P. E., & Melão, N. (2019). Impacts of Artificial Intelligence on Public Administration: A Systematic Literature Review. *2019 14th Iberian Conference on Information Systems and Technologies (CISTI)*, 1–7. DOI: 10.23919/CISTI.2019.8760893

van Noordt, C., & Tangi, L. (2023). The dynamics of AI capability and its influence on public value creation of AI within public administration. *Government Information Quarterly*, 40(4), 101860. DOI: 10.1016/j.giq.2023.101860

Wirtz, B. W., Weyerer, J. C., & Sturm, B. J. (2020). The Dark Sides of Artificial Intelligence: An Integrated AI Governance Framework for Public Administration. *International Journal of Public Administration*, 43(9), 818–829. DOI: 10.1080/01900692.2020.1749851

Young, M. M., Bullock, J. B., & Lecy, J. D. (2019). Artificial Discretion as a Tool of Governance: A Framework for Understanding the Impact of Artificial Intelligence on Public Administration. *Perspectives on Public Management and Governance*, 2(4), 301–313. DOI: 10.1093/ppmgov/gvz014

KEY TERMS AND DEFINITIONS

AI Modernization: The use of AI to update and improve government operations and administrative processes.

Artificial Intelligence: Technologies such as machine learning and natural language processing that simulate human intelligence to perform tasks like problem-solving, decision-making, and data analysis.

Automation of Services: The use of technology to streamline routine administrative tasks, reducing manual errors, speeding up processes like application handling, and allowing for more critical task.

Cybersecurity: It is the practice of protecting systems, networks, and data from digital attacks, unauthorized access, and damage, ensuring the confidentiality, integrity, and availability of information.

Data Privacy and Security: The protection of sensitive personal information managed by systems which requires resilient frameworks to prevent breaches and ensure ethical data usage.

Predictive Analytics: A component of AI that uses historical data to forecast trends and outcomes, aiding public administration in making informed decisions such as anticipating public health or safety issues.

Public Administration: The management and implementation of government policies and public programs, ensuring efficient resource utilization, service provision, and promoting accountability and transparency in operations.

Service Delivery: The process of providing public services such as healthcare, education, and law enforcement to citizens efficiently.

Chapter 6
Land and Property Registries:
Utilizing Blockchain for Transparent and Immutable Records

Shubha Dattatreya Bahinipati
https://orcid.org/0009-0004-5562-9460
Siksha 'O' Anusandhan University, India

Binod Kumar Pattanayak
https://orcid.org/0000-0003-2222-0453
Siksha 'O' Anusandhan University, India

Rourab Paul
https://orcid.org/0000-0001-5322-281X
Siksha 'O' Anusandhan University, India

ABSTRACT

This research chapter aims to identify the efforts blockchain can make in improving the land and property registries by overcoming the issues like fraud, corruption, ineffectiveness, and low transparency. The chapter highlights the three primary advantages of the blockchain: decentralization, smart contracts, and the generation of immutable records via block usage. This research proposes a framework for blockchain integration and discusses the key components of the integration process, including the system architecture, smart contract creation, legal compliance, and security aspects. This chapter has used examples of Georgia, Sweden, and India to show that blockchain is feasible and useful for the development of efficient and secure systems of land registries. The research indicates that blockchain has noteworthy

DOI: 10.4018/979-8-3693-7678-2.ch006

prospects for augmenting the efficacy of land management, while also promoting accountability and safeguarding property rights. The success of the endeavor depends on the implementation of effective planning, coordination, and assessment strategies.

1. INTRODUCTION

For centuries, tangible property rights have been recorded and protected through land and property registries. These are usually in place and administered by the government and contain details on the ownership of land, the partition or perimeter of properties as well as any history of transactions. But they are not without their drawbacks, and some of the key drawbacks include high levels of ineptness, corruption, as well as high vulnerability to fraud. A further disadvantage of having centralized registries is that only a few officials have fingertips on the records, which leaves them targeted at manipulation and even tampering. This has given rise to countless scenarios where property registers are manipulated fraudulently, and ownership is contested or property titles are forged (Oprunenco & Akmeemana, 2018).

In addition, the problems are aggravated by the use of paper-based or inefficient digital forms of record-keeping and tracking. These traditional systems are vulnerable to physical destruction, loss and mimicry particularly in property records. These issues are especially manifest in many developing countries owing to poorly developed institutions, and low capacities and funding, which leads to recurrent conflicts, and poor governance of land (Sekhari et al., 2019).

1.1 Need for Transparency and Security in Property Registries

The restrictions associated with the conventional systems or land and property registries underscore heightened needs for more secured systems. Transparency in property registries means that all the stakeholders which comprise the owners of property, intending buyers, and relevant government agencies benefit from accurate or up-to-date records of properties and transactions. This makes it easy to avoid future confrontations and minimize cases of fraud because all records relating to properties change can undergo significant changes which are publicly accessible by all the players (Kshetri, 2017). In addition, security is very important because records of property should be secured from extra persons who might have interest or may have ill intentions of deleting or modifying them. Insecure registries can result in problems such as fraudulent and unlawful transfers of property and boundaries, which erode the confidence of investors in the property market (Soner et al., 2021).

Blockchain technology has thereby risen to the challenge of these problems. They cannot be changed or deleted unless there is unison consensus across the blockchain digital network since the data is decentralized and homemade. This prevents tampering and maintains the accuracy of property records (Kshetri, 2017b). Furthermore, there is no need for intermediaries for the verification of transactions and ownership alterations since all these details are open and can be checked easily (Zhang et al., 2018).

In the case of land registries, blockchain promises to improve the efficacy of both transparency and security. For instance, the incorporation of blockchain in Indian land records has also been considered as a means of minimizing the corrupted system (Oprunenco, & Akmeemana, 2018). Blockchain has the potential to increase largely the certainty of rights, as it can effectively avoid the numerous concerns that are related to traditional land and property registries in terms of stability of property rights that are the main preconditions for economic development (Bhattacharya et al., 2020).

1.2 Introduction to Blockchain Technology

Blockchain has been established itself in various fields as one of the most reliable and disruptive technologies for data management. Blockchain, which was designed for such applications as the bitcoin, is a distributed ledger that stores transactions in a network in such a way that the latter cannot be altered, and thus, is trustworthy (Priyadarshini, 2019). This decentralized nature reduces the role of intermediaries thus elimination of risk and improved trust among the participants (Yaga et al., 2019).

Blockchain has one of the most valuable attributes- non-tamperability; once a record has been made it cannot be changed. This makes it particularly quite useful in those usages that need secure and unalterable records which include the land and property registries. The transparency and obligation of the existence offer the technology versatility and relevance in numerous sectors such as the financial industry, at the sources of supply chain, and moreover, the identity industry (Casino et al., 2019).

The mutations of blockchain from Blockchain 1. 0 specifically aimed at cryptocurrencies to Blockchain 4. 0, that has the integration of artificial intelligence, big data, IoT etc has a larger spectrum of applicability. Such advancements enable blockchain for more compound structures and the decentralized applications (Mukherjee & Pradhan, 2021).

Further, the adoption of blockchain coupled with cloud is cost-efficient and secure also in handling big data for instance in medical and logistics sectors (Habib et al., 2022). However, the technology has its limitations such as scalability challenges, high power usage, and legal questions to which solutions have to be provided to enhance its use (Gamage, Weerasinghe, & Dias, 2020).

2. BLOCKCHAIN TECHNOLOGY OVERVIEW

Blockchain technology is founded on three core principles: decentralization, immutability and transparency. Decentralization eliminates the possibility of one area or organizations having full control of the network and there being a single point of failure (Gupta et al., 2019). Another feature is that the data stored in the block cannot be changed once the data is written into it making it almost infallible or fully reliable as described by Madhurya et al. (2020). Immutable characteristic of blockchain results into all the nodes in the network having a view of the recorded transactions hence minimizing on probabilities of fraudulent activities (Nakamoto, 2008; Norta et al., 2018).

To begin with, the primary use of block chain was seen as the system that supports virtual currencies, for instance, Bit coin. But over these years, its application goes beyond digital currencies. Obviously, blockchain is being considered for all sorts of applications, in most recent, in the areas extending from land registry to supply chain and safe voting (Avantaggiato & Gallo, 2019; Abhishek, 2019). For instance, in the real estate industry, blockchain is helping in integrating functions like registration of properties, change of ownership and this is less susceptible to fraudsters as compared to the conventional system (Krupa & Akhil, 2019). The security and privacy frameworks necessary for blockchain adoption in property registries parallel those required for CBDCs, where privacy is protected while maintaining transparency and public trust in the digital system (Sharma & Rathod, 2024)

Table 1. Evolution of blockchain technology over the years

Year	Author(s)	Contribution to Blockchain
2008	Nakamoto, S.	Suggested the use of a blockchain as the fundamental system on which to build Bitcoin as an electronic, peer-to Peer cash system.
2015	Swan, M.	Pointed out that, while blockchain is often associated just with cryptocurrencies, it can be seen as a "framework for a new economy," that is, it also encompasses such things as smart contracts and decentralized applications.
2016	Pilkington, M.	Outlined basic and more complex ideas about blockchain and practical applications, also stressing the shift across industries.
2017	Zheng, Z., Xie, S., Dai, H., Chen, X., & Wang, H.	Gave an overview of blockchain, including discussion on its architecture, consensus mechanisms, and possible future advancements.
2018	De Filippi, P.	Discussed the legal aspects of blockchain technology, stating that the rule of code may replace traditional legal norms.
2019	Yaga, D., Mell, P., Roby, N., & Scarfone, K.	Where it gave an introduction to blockchain in which it explained what blockchain was, its uses as well as the challenges of security that are bound to the technology.
2020	Chang, V., Baudier, P., Zhang, H., Xu, Q., Zhang, J., & Arami, M.	Exploring blockchain technology with reference to financial services and the issues in existence and factors to take into account when applying it.
2020	Chen, Y., & Bellavitis, C.	Evaluated how blockchain transformed decentralized finance (DeFi), and other novel business models grounded on blockchain.
2021	Kshetri, N.	Discussed blockchain for sustainable supply chain management and focus on developing countries, and understand its roles in enhancing the supply chain transparency and efficiency.
2023	Yaqub, M. Z., & Alsabban, A.	Discussed the significance of blockchain throughout the process of digitalization or digital transformation within the framework of Industry 4.0, discussing its difficulties and business implications.
2024	Wang, X., Weng, Z., Liu, L., & Liu, J.	Explored the factors that may have made it possible to deploy blockchain technologist in Architecture, Engineering and construction (AEC) Industry.

One of the potential areas where the blockchain technology can be implemented is the real estate business. The prevailing system of property registration is usually time-consuming, prone to voids, and easy fraud. Blockchain can solve these problems by giving a secure, transparent, and efficient approach to the property transactions and the records of the land (Arun Kumar & Rohith, 2020). For instance, in the case of management of land titles, the implementation of blockchain can help in decreasing the rate of frauds and disagreements since all the transactions are recorded on a blockchain (Ali et al., 2020; Alam et al., 2020).

Besides the accuracy and security of records of the land, blockchain enables smart contracts in the real estate sell, buy and other transactions. These are smart contracts that contain the terms of the agreement in the form of code and the conditions of the transaction are self-executed when specific conditions are met (Crosby et al.,

2016). This can greatly minimize the number of the middlemen, like lawyers and brokers, which contributes to the decrease in the cost of transactions and the time it takes to complete them (Krupa & Akhil, 2019).

In addition, there is the issue of transparency which helps to build the level of confidence of the several parties in a real estate transaction. Since all transactions are transparent to all the parties involved, it becomes easy to prove the real ownership of properties and the history of the property which is important especially in areas where property registration has not been well documented (Avantaggiato & Gallo, 2019; Hoxha & Sadiku, 2019).

3. CHALLENGES IN CURRENT LAND AND PROPERTY REGISTRIES

Registers of land and properties are official record databases that confirm ownership and rights concerning land and properties. These registries are critical in the organization of the land market, the legal protection of real estate rights, promotion and facilitation of economic growth by ensuring the availability of land as an object of securing credit. Nevertheless, despite the seeming importance of these systems most of the land registry systems around the world face numerous challenges. These challenges do not only undermine the land administration process but also affect various other social problems such as social inequality, conflict, and economic unproductiveness.

3.1 Fraud and Corruption

Many of the land and property registries following this system are very prone to fraud and corruption in several regions. This is mainly because adequate measures to stop impersonation of records, sale of the same property twice and other fraudulent practices are normally missing. For instance, Ali, Deininger, and Goldstein (2014) argue that land tenure system especially in Africa are vulnerable to such problems because of inefficient and secure registry of land documents. Such vulnerabilities lead to landmark controversies with references to actual ownership of the land, hence causing conflicts that horribly affect marginalized women and people of low income.

3.2 Lack of Transparency

The transparency aspect is also missing in the current registries of land and properties, and this Inventory has established that the absence of transparency has a tendency of creating mistrust among stakeholders. These systems tend to be rather unclear, hence the conflicts that arise, as the land owners, and anybody interested in purchasing the piece of land is unsure of the authenticity of records. According to Augustinus and Tempra (2021), in the areas affected by violent conflict, weak and unclear land administration systems intensify conflicts and violence. Due to the lack of simplified and credible records on the distribution of the land, the stakeholders are often left in the dark with no way of ascertaining the authenticity of the claims, hence provoking lengthy court proceedings which erode social harmony.

3.3 Inefficiency and High Costs

One of the major issues is the issues with land registries and records, they are very slow and expensive. Deininger, Selod, and Burns (2012) point out that bureaucracy hitches in developing countries leads to hurdles and costs on anybody who would wish to transact on property or land. These inefficiencies remain so costly and painful in developing nations where many procedures and cases are shadowed by corruption hence leading to long legal proceedings and other costs associated with the process. The absence of integrated procedures not only raises the price of transactions but also threatens to maintain the inability to formalize property rights within the official sphere, entrenching the problem of informality and insecurity within the land. According to Scanlan et al. (2024), these inefficiencies are most devastating to the poor since they will lack the capacity to undertake the costly and cumbersome processes of land registration thereby perpetuating existing disparity.

Therefore, the current registries that exist are problem-prone, as far as fraud and corruption, lack of transparency, and/or efficiency are concerned. These challenges raise the questions about the need for changes that would make the registries reflect the interests of all stakeholders including those groups of people who may be more in need of the services of the registries than others.

4. BLOCKCHAIN IN LAND ADMINISTRATION: A NEW FRONTIER

Blockchain technology is steadily being appreciated as one of the revolutionary technologies in the management of land resources and tackling the challenges like ineffectiveness, fraud and embezzlement, encountered in traditional property registration. This was an era where the management of land titles was given a new face by the blockchain technology in that it offers a decentralized, transparent and immutable record of the land transaction.

In Bangladesh particular, Alam et al. (2022) laid down a framework where management of land title through a blockchain solution that will expedite the process of property registration and minimize disputes. This system makes the records safe, clear, and available which resolve many problems of developing countries where ownership of land is frequently in dispute. Problems in the proposed model are considered as a representation of the possible enhancements of land administration systems through blockchain.

Gupta, Das, and Nandi (2019) have studied the technical features of blockchain integration into land management and proposed the "Land Ledger" system. This system uses blockchain in tracking ownership of the land as all records created cannot be altered but through proper authority in the change. As applied in this context, blockchain preserves the integrity of the information, hinders imitation and lastly increases the security of the given system.

According to Crosby et al. (2016), decentralization is another aspect of the blockchain technology that can help make certain data more secure from tampering or other changes. One of the keys to finding a solution to the inefficiency of land registration is the deposition of all record-setting agreements into a distributed ledger: the technology that forms the basis of blockchain. Nonetheless, also there are some challenges as it applies to the use of blockchain in land administration. Lemieux (2016) mentions that legal and regulatory infrastructure is necessary for integration of blockchain with other systems. Some of them include; scalability, compatibility and legal acceptance of records on the block chain to be achieved for technology to deliver on its capability.

4.1 How Blockchain Addresses Challenges in Property Registries

The conventional property registries have some problems like inadequate identification of the property owner, fake deals on land, and problems with the registration system. Blockchain technology is helpful in overcoming such challenges due to its ability to provide integrity and accountability in the land records.

Fraud Prevention and Enhanced Security: Perhaps, one of the main strengths of blockchain is that it eliminates the possibility of fraud. Due to the distributed nature of blockchain, no one individual has control on the data and therefore, it is almost impossible for anyone to change or manipulate the records. This is especially the case in areas where there is a high level of corruption and land related conflicts.

Transparency and Trust: This solution ensures a transparent ledger that can be checked and confirmed by various stakeholders in real-time. This kind of transparency prevents some of the major occurrences of disputes and helps to develop confidence from all the involved stakeholders in the land selling business. For instance, Alam et al. (2020) provide a real-life application of how blockchain can help in establishing an efficient and transparent management of land title in Bangladesh which is beleaguered with controversies and issues concerning the ownership of land.

Efficiency and Cost Reduction: Some of the challenges associated with traditional land registry processes include the fact that procedures normally take a long duration to complete and involve several agents. Blockchain technology can help in improving such processes through use of smart contracts that eliminate interpersonal tasks and also minimization of intermediaries.

Land Tenure Security: Due to compounds land policies most developing countries, the resulting land tenure systems trigger insecurity and conflicts. Blockchain can offer a secure and unchangeable record of real estate ownership which would guarantee that the owners of the property will have a legal right of ownership of the land. A similar view is brought forward by Ali et al. (2014) on the role of information infrastructure as a prerequisite to economic growth with a focus on how block chain can help in tenure security.

4.2 Key Features: Decentralization, Smart Contracts, Immutable Records

Three characteristics of Blockchain include decentralization, smart contracts, and the ability to maintain an immutable ledger; all of which can be applied when it comes to land and property registries.

Decentralization: Blockchain is based in a distributed system which implies that the data is stored in different nodes. This decentralization ensures the original copy of all records to be distributed to various offices hence; there will not be one central center that manages all records hence reduces on the cases of data manipulation and corruption. Augustinus and Tempra (2021) stress that decentralized systems as applied to land administration bear a number of benefits especially in conflict states where the concentrated systems can be easily controlled.

Smart Contracts: Smart contracts are digital contracts in which the conditions of the contract are code that is designed to automatically execute the contract. These contracts can facilitate the purchase and sale of properties like the transfer of property title agreement on the occurrence of certain factors. Madhurya et al. (2020) explains this by showing how frameworks for registration of properties can use smart contracts to ensure that the execution of the transactions is as agreed on.

Immutable Records: After the entry is made on the blockchain, it cannot be erased or modified; this makes it suitable for preserving the honesty of the records of the land. This remains so as to preserve the authenticity of records of past land deals, and to be able to verify the same. According to Lemieux (2016) the decentralized, and thus unchangeable feature of blockchains, can improve trust in land registries by offering a secure and unalterable record of ownership.

4.3 Comparison with Traditional Systems

Blockchain-based land registries offer several advantages over traditional systems, which are often centralized, prone to errors, and susceptible to fraud.

Table 2. Comparison of blockchain-based land registries with traditional systems

Aspect	Traditional Systems	Blockchain-based Systems
Transparency	Dependent on paper records or computerized records stored in central locations, which can be altered or destroyed.	Offers a clear record of information that is available for everyone to see, eliminating confusion and conflicts of interest.
Efficiency	Is time-consuming and involves checks by different parties, which can compromise the speed, quality, and price of the project.	Reduces transaction time while featuring primary contract execution without the need for middlemen through smart contracts.
Security	Data collected in large databases are at risk of being accessed by unauthorized persons and thus record security is put at risk.	Decentralized nature and cryptographic style make it highly immune to cyber-attacks and the overall accessibility is only possible through authorization.
Accessibility and Inclusivity	They typically deprive minorities of the ownership of land by following intricate procedures that they cannot afford or have no access to.	Gives the public a more comprehensive system that presents flexible and safe records of ownership of the land while upholding the rights of those at the lower end of the social ladder.

5. PROPOSED FRAMEWORK FOR BLOCKCHAIN INTEGRATION IN LAND ADMINISTRATION

The approach to using blockchain in enhancing land administration systems should be systematic covering both technical, legal, and operational aspects. This framework shows the structure of key components and strategies for further integration of blockchain, as shown in the figure according to this study (see Fig. 1).

5.1 System Architecture Design

For blockchain integration, there must be a sound system that can address the issues of complexity concerning land records.

- *Blockchain Platform Selection:* Selecting a blockchain platform or environment (Such as Ethereum, Hyperledger Fabric etc) is very important. They must allow scalability, fast transactions, the execution of smart contracts. These capabilities are necessary for the safe storage of record records of the transfer of land and other properties, and for efficient and clear transactions to take place.
- *Data Structure and Storage:* Blockchain architecture standards should reflect on, and be applicable to, the format of land registers. A combination of off-chain storage of data coupled with the storage of only the proofs or hashes on-chain makes it efficient and secure.
- *Interoperability:* It has to be integrated with the existing databases of land registry and other government systems. This needs the creation of APIs and middleware to ensure proper integration of data exchange as highlighted in the System Integration Layer of Figure 1.

5.2 Smart Contract Development

They greatly enhance processes of real estate transactions, particularly with reference to the legal and/or regulatory reforms.

- *Contract Templates:* When creating checklists, it is common to disregard the extent of simplicity in implementing the templates across different land transactions such as sales and leasing. All of these templates are installed into the blockchain system, as depicted in the Blockchain Network layer highlighted in Fig. 1.
- *Automation of Legal Processes:* Integrated into smart contracts are legal rules and regulation to facilitate same that includes title transfer, payment, and dispute. This cuts on the middlemen and fastens the rate of business being done.
- *Security Measures:* Smart contracts have to be shielded from risks. In the framework of the information security of the blockchain (see Fig. 1), careful verification and following the best practices in the development of smart contracts exclude unauthorized actions and fraud.

5.3 Legal and Regulatory Compliance

Blockchain integration should observe legal requirements and regulations that regulate land administration.

- *Legal Framework Alignment:* This means that effort must be made to consult legal professionals in the course of the process to prevent violation. Some of the changes this might encompass may include legislation on changing existing laws or promulgation of new regulations to cover for blockchain.
- *Stakeholder Engagement:* It is therefore necessary to involve the stakeholders such as government, law practitioners and the public. This makes sure that the system is compliant to the law and the norms of the society that it serves.
- *Governance Model:* Because a governance model has to prescribe the organizational roles and responsibilities and describe how transaction validation, dealing with disputes and system upgrades are to be conducted. This model it is also part of the complete global structure of the system which is presented in the following Figure 1.

5.4 Implementation Strategy

The use of a phased approach in the implementation minimizes risks while being helpful in transitioning to the new system.

- *Pilot Projects:* In some chosen areas pilot projects are conducted to test the system in actual environment; further the project can be fine-tuned before it is rolled out in other areas.
- *Scalability and Flexibility:* The system should be easily scalable as the users increase so that one can add more services, or to ensure compliance with changing laws.
- *User Training and Support:* Education for existing authorized users: Govt officials, owners of the land and other occupants. Assistance services should however be made available to guide users on how to work under the new system.

5.5 Security and Privacy Considerations

The principles of the proposed blockchain framework are tightly connected to the problem of security and privacy.

Data Encryption: Security measures such as encryption technology shield data on the blockchain and its adjunct databases (as depicted in the Blockchain Network layer of Figure 1).

Access Control: Constant care is taken to ensure that records can only be accessed or altered by people who are supposed to do so. These are role-based access and the multi-factor authentication of users.

Auditability: The feature of blockchain, the self-checking or audit ability of the transactions make it possible to record all the transactions and modifications made to land records and this is very essential especially where there are alterations that are in dispute.

5.6 Monitoring and Evaluation

There is a need to constantly consider and assess the framework so as to increase its effectiveness.

- Performance Metrics: Metrics that define the level of improvement in transparency, efficiency, and security should be developed into KPIs.
- Feedback Mechanisms: Creating feedback systems with the users means that there is always an upgrade on the system so that it suits the user of the system.
- Regulatory Audits: Annual revisions help maintain compliance with existing laws and check that the applied blockchain technology is effectively used.

Figure 1. Blockchain integration framework (Authors Conceptual Model)

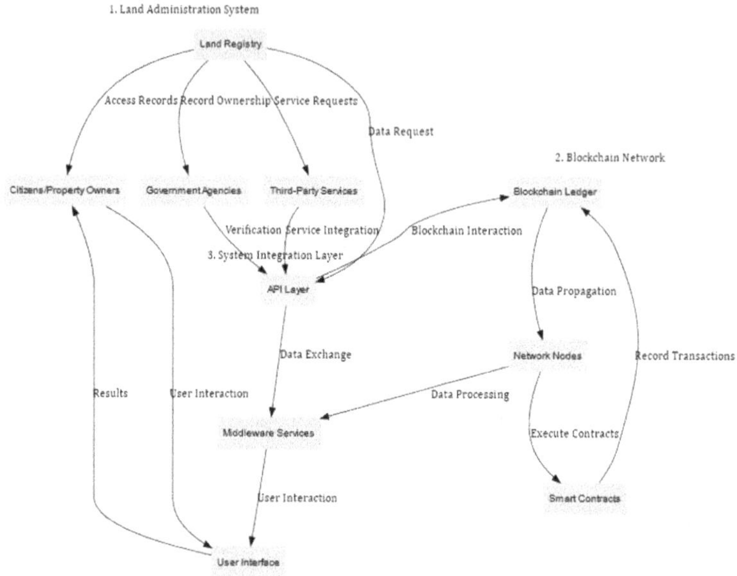

6. BLOCKCHAIN-BASED LAND REGISTRY PROJECTS IN DIFFERENT COUNTRIES

The implementation of blockchain technology within land registers in different countries shows that all governments are working towards improving the accuracy, speed, and simplicity of property deals. Some projects have achieved state of transition to operational phases and some are still in experimental stage to discover pros and cons of implementing this technology. These constant improvements and experiences gathered from these practices are contemporarily transforming the land administration systems globally. Table 3. Summarizes Blockchain-based Land Registry Projects in Different Countries:

Table 3. Blockchain-based land registry projects in different countries

Country	Project/Initiative	Involved Government Entities	Details & Reference
Brazil	Pilot project by Cartorio de Registro de Imoveis with Ubiquity	Brazilian real estate register	Pilot project in Pelotas and Morro Redondo for paperless and transparent land registry using blockchain (Allison, 2018).
Canada	Blockchain Land Titles and Survey Authority collaboration with DIACC and IDN	Digital Identity and Authentication Council of Canada (DIACC), Identity North (IDN)	Project analyzing blockchain's functionality and regulatory aspects in land registry (Brennan, 2020).
India	Telangana and Andhra Pradesh land registry system	Advanced Computing Development Center (C-DAC)	Blockchain system for transparent land registry, under review and development (Variyar and Bansal, 2017).
Sweden	Lantmäteriet project with Chromaway	Swedish land registry authority (Lantmäteriet)	Smart contracts for land registry to reduce fraud and costs, currently in testing (Kempe, 2016).
Ukraine	Blockchain registry for land trading	Ukraine government	Pilot project with Exonum's private blockchain, with future plans for Ethereum integration (Tian, 2017).
Netherlands	Blockchain and AI-based land registry project with Kadaster	Netherlands Land Registry organization (Kadaster)	Project using blockchain and time stamping techniques, under development (Wouda and Opdenakker, 2019).
Dubai	Dubai Blockchain Strategy	Dubai Electric and Water Authority (DEWA)	Aims to complete all transactions using blockchain by 2020, saving EUR 1.2 billion annually (Hochstein, 2017).
Honduras	Contract with Factom	Honduran government	Project to eliminate fraud and corruption in land registry using blockchain (Anand et al., 2016; Inc and Inc, 2018).

7. CASE STUDIES

7.1 Case Study: Blockchain for Land Titling in Georgia

The Republic of Georgia could be considered the pioneer of using blockchain in the sphere of land titling. This drive was launched by BitFury Group in partnership with National Agency of Public registry (NAPR) with support from the economist

Hernando De Soto in the attempt to improve data accuracy and fight fraud cases in the land transactions.

Table 4. Successes and challenges

Successes	Challenges
Data Integrity (Shin, 2016) - Implemented a hierarchical blockchain system. - Ensured immutable, tamper-proof land records. - Enhanced security and accuracy in property ownership.	***Technical Integration*** (Shin, 2016) - Integrating blockchain with existing digital records posed technical difficulties. - Required significant expertise to ensure system compatibility.
Fraud Reduction (Shang & Price, 2019) - Significantly reduced fraudulent land transactions. - Provided a verifiable and secure record of ownership.	***Regulatory Compliance*** (Shang & Price, 2019) - Adapting blockchain within existing legal frameworks was challenging. - Needed careful selection of technology and adherence to regulations.
Public Trust Public Awareness (Shin, 2016) - Increased public confidence in land registry systems. - Blockchain's transparency and security fostered greater trust among citizens.	***Public Awareness*** (Shang & Price, 2019) - Extensive public education was required to promote blockchain's benefits. - Overcame skepticism through targeted awareness campaigns.

Exploring the effects of applying blockchain technology in the Georgia land titling project shows how it has transformed data and minimized fraud. The only characteristic of the blockchain is that it is unchangeable and once a land record is captured, it cannot be edited. This makes the data on ownership of land to be credible and accurate hence a reliable source of information (Shin, 2016). Due to the transparency and security of the blockchain technology, the cases of fraud have been greatly minimized. Note that each transaction is saved in an open ledger which made it difficult or almost impossible to temper with the books (Shang & Price, 2019).

7.2 Case Study: Sweden (Lantmäteriet Project)

Lantmäteriet, the Swedish Mapping, Cadastre, and Land Registration Authority of Sweden is an organization that has been in the frontline in the implementation of blockchain for land registry. Devised to bring reforms within property transfers, this effort is also established to improve the general protection of data and decrease cases of fraud.

Implementation Details

- *Project Partners and Goals:* Launched in 2016, the project was implemented jointly with the support of Lantmäteriet, ChromaWay, Kairos Future, and Telia Company. The first objective was to develop a blockchain system which is capable to execute the real estate transactions in a secure and efficient manner (Proskurovska & Dörry, 2018).

- *Technology and Process:* The blockchain system designed for this project is implemented to utilize smart contract for the security and automation for property transaction. Every activity occurring in the process of the transaction, right from the moment of its conclusion and up to issuing of the registration certificate, is documented in the blockchain.
- *Pilot Testing:* As a part of the pilot phase, one had to experiment with actual property sale/purchase on the blockchain system. This phase was important in heralding problems and fine-tuning the technology for response to the interest of the stakeholders (Chavez-Dreyfuss, 2016).

Implementation of a land registry system based on the blockchain in Sweden removed the problems of excessive concentration, introduced greater reliability through secure and immutable records of transactions, as well as increased transparency, which was essential for restoring citizens' trust. Despite this, the project encountered various issues such as technical issues in the implementation of the integrated system to handle the new modifications in the framework of the IT facilities; regulatory factors that made it difficult for employees to get acquainted with the new system; and lastly, there was a general public skepticism regarding the new system.

7.3 Case Study: Blockchain in Land Registry for Transforming Land Administration in India

India is one of the countries that has been experimenting with the solutions based on the blockchain technology to solve some of the issues in the country's land registries. Blockchain integration is expected to bring a rather positive impact to the company's efficiency in terms of property management by increasing transparency and decreasing the level of fraud.

Pilot Programs:

- Andhra Pradesh Initiative: Andhra Pradesh has been at the forefront of using blockchain across the country especially in the land records management. The state with the support of private companies implemented a blockchain infrastructure for storing the data on land deals. The goal of this effort was to establish a secure and auditable land record system. Land records are essential for any country as they offer legal evidence of ownership of valuable resources (Barai, 2024).
- Haryana and Maharashtra Projects: Haryana and Maharashtra have also started the pilot projects of the decentralized digitized registry on the blockchain.

These encompass the use of blockchain in enhancing other existing digital structures to put emphasis on the assurance of data and discouragement of frauds (Thakur et. al, 2020).

Table 5. Blockchain's role and evaluation

Aspect	Impact and Evaluation
Data Integrity	Blockchain ensures immutable, tamper-proof land records, enhancing security.
Transparency	Decentralized system allows verification by all stakeholders, increasing trust and reducing disputes.
Efficiency	Automates manual processes, speeding up registration and verification.
Initial Results	Positive feedback for enhanced security and transparency, though integration posed technical and regulatory challenges.
Scalability	Pilot success indicates potential for nationwide implementation with necessary investment.
Regulatory Framework	Requires robust guidelines to address legal and compliance issues.
Public Adoption	Continuous education needed to ensure broad acceptance and understanding of blockchain benefits.

8. CHALLENGES IN BLOCKCHAIN IMPLEMENTATION

The application of blockchain technology solutions in land and property registries has great potential for resolving current problems, yet several obstacles need to be met to use these solutions effectively. Some of the issues that need to be addressed are the issues of scaling and power consumption that can affect its ability to work effectively and security of the data being processed.

The disadvantages of land registry data on the blockchain are that the size and number of transactions can slow down the transaction process over time. Some of them may involve off-chain activities where only the most critical data are stored on the blockchain, such as the fundamental details of the transactions undertaken, whereas others may involve improved solutions such as sidechains that deal with the large volumes of transactions required on the blockchain system in a different block from the main one to help alleviate the pressure experienced and timelines taken.

Blockchain's energy consumption, especially from the proof of work, can prove to be a bottleneck to the adoption of blockchain especially in areas of low energy supply. Other variants like proof of stake (PoS) and combined systems decrease energy consumption while still ensuring protection, thus making blockchain more efficient and realistic for the usage in land registry services.

This is an issue because blockchain is transparent; therefore, sensitive information such as land ownership information can be made available on the public ledger. Blockchain technologies that support zero-knowledge proofs can maintain the privacy of transactions without revealing users' details, and permissioned blockchains can improve the privacy that comes with the public ledgers by verifying transactions without revealing the user's identity and details, off-chain storage with encryption.

9. CONCLUSION

This paper sought to discuss how blockchain technology is an efficient approach towards addressing issues of fraud, corruption and inefficiency affecting the registries of land and property. Therefore, the application of blockchain technology in the administration of land assets can be very secure and trustworthy seeing that it is virtually impossible to alter anything in the technology among other features. The proposed methods in system architecture, smart contracts, legal and security aspects dealt with in the framework for blockchain integration for land registries also give a complete picture of how these systems can be restructured.

Furthermore, this paper also focuses at how blockchain has been implemented in countries such as Georgia, Sweden, and India, and how it has the potential to transform land management through better and safer registries. Thus, there will be a necessity of additional planning of the future demand, collaboration with the involved parties and future monitoring in the case of the successful implementation of the blockchain in the land administration.

REFERENCES

Abhishek, G. (2019). *Property registration and land record management via blockchains*. Indian Institute of Technology Kanpur.

Alam, K. M., Rahman, J. A., Tasnim, A., & Akther, A. (2022). A blockchain-based land title management system for Bangladesh. *Journal of King Saud University. Computer and Information Sciences*, 34(6), 3096–3110. DOI: 10.1016/j.jksuci.2020.10.011

Ali, D. A., Deininger, K., & Goldstein, M. (2014). Environmental and gender impacts of land tenure regularization in Africa: Pilot evidence from Rwanda. *Journal of Development Economics*, 110, 262–275. DOI: 10.1016/j.jdeveco.2013.12.009

Ali, T., Nadeem, A., Alzahrani, A., & Jan, S. (2020, February). A transparent and trusted property registration system on permissioned blockchain. In *2019 International conference on advances in the emerging computing Technologies (AECT)* (pp. 1-6). IEEE. DOI: 10.1109/AECT47998.2020.9194222

. Allison, I. (2018). Blockchain-based Ubitquity pilots with Brazil's land records bureau.

Anand, A., McKibbin, M., & Pichel, F. (2016, March). Colored coins: Bitcoin, blockchain, and land administration. In *Annual world bank conference on land and poverty* (pp. 20-24).

Arruñada, B. (2012). *Institutional foundations of impersonal exchange: Theory and policy of contractual registries*. University of Chicago Press. DOI: 10.7208/chicago/9780226028354.001.0001

. Arruñada, B. (2019). Institutional Foundations of Impersonal Exchange: Theory and Policy of Contractual Registries.

Arun Kumar, B. R., & Rohith, B. (2020). Designing Safe and Secure Land Registration-Ownership Using Blockchain Technology with a Focus on Mutual Authentication. In *Sustainable Communication Networks and Application: ICSCN 2019* (pp. 509-516). Springer International Publishing. DOI: 10.1007/978-3-030-34515-0_53

Augustinus, C., & Tempra, O. (2021). Fit-for-purpose land administration in violent conflict settings. *Land (Basel)*, 10(2), 139. DOI: 10.3390/land10020139

Avantaggiato, M., & Gallo, P. (2019, June). Challenges and opportunities using multichain for real estate. In *2019 IEEE International Black Sea Conference on Communications and Networking (BlackSeaCom)* (pp. 1-5). IEEE. DOI: 10.1109/BlackSeaCom.2019.8812780

BARAI, V. (2024). BLOCKCHAIN IN LAND REGISTRY FOR TRANSFORMING LAND ADMINISTRATION. *Journal of Theoretical and Applied Information Technology*, 102(3).

Bhattacharya, P., Tanwar, S., Shah, R., & Ladha, A. (2020). Mobile edge computing-enabled blockchain framework—a survey. In *Proceedings of ICRIC 2019: Recent Innovations in Computing* (pp. 797-809). Springer International Publishing.

. Brennan. (2020). Directors. Digital ID & Authentication Council of Canada.

Buterin, V. (2014). A next-generation smart contract and decentralized application platform. *white paper, 3*(37), 2-1.

Casino, F., Dasaklis, T. K., & Patsakis, C. (2019). A systematic literature review of blockchain-based applications: Current status, classification and open issues. *Telematics and Informatics*, 36, 55–81. DOI: 10.1016/j.tele.2018.11.006

Chang, V., Baudier, P., Zhang, H., Xu, Q., Zhang, J., & Arami, M. (2020). How Blockchain can impact financial services–The overview, challenges and recommendations from expert interviewees. *Technological Forecasting and Social Change*, 158, 120166. DOI: 10.1016/j.techfore.2020.120166 PMID: 32834134

Chavez-Dreyfuss, G. (2016). Sweden tests blockchain technology for land registry. *Reuters*, (June), 16.

Chen, Y., & Bellavitis, C. (2020). Blockchain disruption and decentralized finance: The rise of decentralized business models. *Journal of Business Venturing Insights*, 13, e00151. DOI: 10.1016/j.jbvi.2019.e00151

Crosby, M., Pattanayak, P., Verma, S., & Kalyanaraman, V. (2016). Blockchain technology: Beyond bitcoin. *Applied innovation, 2*(6-10), 71.

De Filippi, P. (2018). *Blockchain and the Law: The Rule of Code*. Harvard University Press.

Deininger, K., & Feder, G. (2009). Land registration, governance, and development: Evidence and implications for policy. *The World Bank Research Observer*, 24(2), 233–266. DOI: 10.1093/wbro/lkp007

Deininger, K., Selod, H., & Burns, A. (2012). *The Land Governance Assessment Framework: Identifying and monitoring good practice in the land sector*. World Bank Publications.

Gamage, H. T. M., Weerasinghe, H. D., & Dias, N. G. J. (2020). A survey on blockchain technology concepts, applications, and issues. *SN Computer Science*, 1(2), 1–15. DOI: 10.1007/s42979-020-00123-0

Gupta, N., Das, M. L., & Nandi, S. (2019, December). Landledger: Blockchain-powered land property administration system. In *2019 IEEE International conference on advanced networks and telecommunications systems (ANTS)* (pp. 1-6). IEEE.

Habib, G., Sharma, S., Ibrahim, S., Ahmad, I., Qureshi, S., & Ishfaq, M. (2022). Blockchain technology: Benefits, challenges, applications, and integration of blockchain technology with cloud computing. *Future Internet*, 14(11), 341. DOI: 10.3390/fi14110341

. Hochstein, M. (2017). Dubai Land Department launches blockchain real estate initiative.

Hoxha, V., & Sadiku, S. (2019). Study of factors influencing the decision to adopt the blockchain technology in real estate transactions in Kosovo. *Property Management*, 37(5), 684–700. DOI: 10.1108/PM-01-2019-0002

Kempe, M. (2016). The land registry in the blockchain: A development project with lantmäteriet, telia company, chromaway and kairos future. *White Paper. Estocolmo*.

Komalavalli, C., Saxena, D., & Laroiya, C. (2020). Overview of blockchain technology concepts. In *Handbook of research on blockchain technology* (pp. 349–371). Academic Press. DOI: 10.1016/B978-0-12-819816-2.00014-9

Krupa, K. S., & Akhil, M. S. (2019). Reshaping the real estate industry using blockchain. In *Emerging Research in Electronics, Computer Science and Technology:Proceedings of International Conference, ICERECT 2018* (pp. 255-263). Springer Singapore. DOI: 10.1007/978-981-13-5802-9_24

Kshetri, N. (2017). Blockchain's roles in strengthening cybersecurity and protecting privacy. *Telecommunications Policy*, 41(10), 1027–1038. DOI: 10.1016/j.telpol.2017.09.003

Kshetri, N. (2017). Can blockchain strengthen the internet of things? *IT Professional*, 19(4), 68–72. DOI: 10.1109/MITP.2017.3051335

Kshetri, N. (2021). Blockchain and sustainable supply chain management in developing countries. *International Journal of Information Management*, 60, 102376. DOI: 10.1016/j.ijinfomgt.2021.102376

Lacity, M. C. (2020). *Blockchain foundations: for the internet of value*. Epic Books.

Lemieux, V. L. (2016). Trusting records: Is Blockchain technology the answer? *Records Management Journal*, 26(2), 110–139. DOI: 10.1108/RMJ-12-2015-0042

Madhurya, J. A., Pillai, B. G., Dayananda Lal, N., & Jeena Jacob, I. (2020). Property registration framework using Ethereum blockchain. *International Journal of Emerging Trends in Engineering Research*, 8(9), 5209–5213. DOI: 10.30534/ijeter/2020/51892020

Mukherjee, P., & Pradhan, C. (2021). Blockchain 1.0 to blockchain 4.0—The evolutionary transformation of blockchain technology. In *Blockchain technology: applications and challenges* (pp. 29–49). Springer International Publishing. DOI: 10.1007/978-3-030-69395-4_3

. Nakamoto, S. (2008). Bitcoin: A peer-to-peer electronic cash system.

Norta, A., Fernandez, C., & Hickmott, S. (2018, July). Commercial property tokenizing with smart contracts. In *2018 International Joint Conference on Neural Networks (IJCNN)* (pp. 1-8). IEEE.

Oprunenco, A., & Akmeemana, C. (2018). *Using blockchain to make land registry more reliable in India*. LSE Business Review.

Pilkington, M. (2016). Blockchain technology: principles and applications. In *Research handbook on digital transformations* (pp. 225–253). Edward Elgar Publishing. DOI: 10.4337/9781784717766.00019

. Priyadarshini, I. (2019). Introduction to blockchain technology. *Cyber security in parallel and distributed computing: concepts, techniques, applications and case studies*, 91-107.

Proskurovska, A., & Dörry, S. (2018). Is a Blockchain-based conveyance system the next step in the financialisation of housing?: The case of Sweden. *The Case of Sweden (September 2018). Luxembourg Institute of Socio-Economic Research (LISER) Working Paper Series, 17.*

Scanlan, O., Siraj, N., Ritchil, P., & Mankin, S. (2024). Is "pro-poor land administration" a realistic proposition? How a land survey in Bangladesh reproduced and reconfigured gendered and racialised poverty. *Land Use Policy*, 138, 107016. DOI: 10.1016/j.landusepol.2023.107016

Sekhari, A., Chatterjee, R., Dwivedi, R., Negi, R., & Shukla, S. (2019). Entangled blockchains in land registry management. *BW3, India, 356.*

Shang, Q., & Price, A. (2019). A blockchain-based land titling project in the republic of georgia: Rebuilding public trust and lessons for future pilot projects. *Innovations: Technology, Governance, Globalization*, 12(3-4), 72–78. DOI: 10.1162/inov_a_00276

Sharma, A., & Rathod, N. S. (2024). Central Bank Digital Currency: Assessment of Digital Financing Approach Towards Safe Cashless Economy in India. In *Digital Currency Assets and Challenges to Financial System Stability* (pp. 37-51). IGI Global.

Shin, L. (2016). Republic of Georgia to pilot land titling on blockchain with economist Hernando De Soto, BitFury. *Forbes*, (April), 21.

Shuaib, M., Alam, S., Ahmed, R., Qamar, S., Nasir, M. S., & Alam, M. S. (2022). Current status, requirements, and challenges of blockchain application in land registry. [IJIRR]. *International Journal of Information Retrieval Research*, 12(2), 1–20. DOI: 10.4018/IJIRR.299934

Soner, S., Litoriya, R., & Pandey, P. (2021). Exploring blockchain and smart contract technology for reliable and secure land registration and record management. *Wireless Personal Communications*, 121(4), 2495–2509. DOI: 10.1007/s11277-021-08833-1

Swan, M. (2015). *Blockchain: Blueprint for a new economy*. O'Reilly Media, Inc.

Thakur, V., Doja, M. N., Dwivedi, Y. K., Ahmad, T., & Khadanga, G. (2020). Land records on blockchain for implementation of land titling in India. *International Journal of Information Management*, 52, 101940. DOI: 10.1016/j.ijinfomgt.2019.04.013

Tian, C. (2017). Ukrainian Government to Start Blockchain Land Registry Trial in October. *CoinDesk News*, 23, 2017.

. Variyar, M., & Bansal, V. (2017). Blockchain: Blockchain tech is joining e-gov dots in AP.

Wang, X., Weng, Z., Liu, L., & Liu, J. (2024). Factors That Facilitated the Development of Blockchain Technology in the AEC Industry: Study Based on System Dynamics. *Journal of Management Engineering*, 40(6), 04024049. DOI: 10.1061/JMENEA.MEENG-6137

Wouda, H. P., & Opdenakker, R. (2019). Blockchain technology in commercial real estate transactions. *Journal of Property Investment & Finance*, 37(6), 570–579. DOI: 10.1108/JPIF-06-2019-0085

Xu, X., Weber, I., & Staples, M. (2019). *Architecture for blockchain applications*. Springer. DOI: 10.1007/978-3-030-03035-3

Yaga, D., Mell, P., Roby, N., & Scarfone, K. (2019). Blockchain technology overview. *arXiv preprint arXiv:1906.11078*.

Yaqub, M. Z., & Alsabban, A. (2023). Industry-4.0-Enabled digital transformation: Prospects, instruments, challenges, and implications for business strategies. *Sustainability (Basel)*, 15(11), 8553. DOI: 10.3390/su15118553

Zevenbergen, J., De Vries, W., & Bennett, R. M. (Eds.). (2015). *Advances in responsible land administration*. CRC Press.

Zhang, P., White, J., Schmidt, D. C., Lenz, G., & Rosenbloom, S. T. (2018). FHIRChain: Applying blockchain to securely and scalably share clinical data. *Computational and Structural Biotechnology Journal*, 16, 267–278. DOI: 10.1016/j.csbj.2018.07.004 PMID: 30108685

Zheng, Z., Xie, S., Dai, H., Chen, X., & Wang, H. (2017, June). *An overview of blockchain technology: Architecture, consensus, and future trends. In 2017 IEEE international congress on big data (BigData congress).* Ieee.

.Zulkifli, N. A. (2021). Three-dimensional strata objects registration for land administration domain model.

Chapter 7
MediSecure:
A Decentralized Framework for Electronic Health Record Management Using Blockchain and IPFS

G. Sujatha
Department of Networking and Communications, School of Computing, College of Engineering and Technology, SRM Institute of Science and Technology, Chennai, India

ABSTRACT

In recent years, the emergence of blockchain technology has catalyzed significant transformations across various sectors. Traditional methods of electronic data management have often been susceptible to security breaches, inefficient data access, and unauthorized exposure to third parties. Consequently, there's a pressing need for the development of a resilient, secure, and scalable approach to managing sensitive data, particularly in the realm of healthcare. This research paper introduces an innovative framework known as MediSecure, which amalgamates blockchain technology, specifically Ethereum, with the Inter-Planetary File System (IPFS) to fortify the security and scalability of Electronic Health Records (EHR). The findings of the study underscore the efficacy of the MediSecure framework, showcasing notable improvements in scalability, robust security features, and sustained data integrity. Through its innovative approach,

DOI: 10.4018/979-8-3693-7678-2.ch007

I INTRODUCTION

1.1. General

In the ever-evolving landscape of healthcare technology, the need for secure, transparent, and scalable solutions for managing electronic health records (EHR) has become increasingly paramount. The emergence of Blockchain and IPFS has opened new avenues for addressing these challenges, and the MediSecure research work stands at the forefront of this transformative journey.

MediSecure is a groundbreaking decentralized framework designed to redefine how electronic health records are managed and accessed. At its core, the research work aims to leverage the inherent features of blockchain technology, such as decentralization, immutability, and transparency, to create a secure and efficient system for EHR management.

The primary objective of implementing blockchain in the context of EHR is to enhance data integrity and security. Blockchain's decentralized and distributed ledger ensures that health records are tamper-proof and resistant to unauthorized alterations. Each transaction or entry in the EHR is cryptographically attached to the last one, creating a chain of blocks that provides an immutable and transparent record of the patient's medical history. This not only enhances patient trust in the integrity of their data but also facilitates a more collaborative and interoperable healthcare ecosystem.

A key innovation introduced by MediSecure is the use of smart contracts to define granular access rules for users within the system. This feature addresses the longstanding challenge of balancing accessibility with privacy in healthcare. With smart contracts, the framework allows for the customization of access permissions, ensuring that only authorized individuals, such as healthcare professionals and the patients themselves, can access specific parts of the electronic records. This not only aligns with regulatory requirements but also empowers individuals to have greater control over their personal health information.

Recognizing the scalability concerns inherent in blockchain technology, MediSecure takes a proactive approach by integrating IPFS for off-chain storage. This combination of blockchain and IPFS addresses the scalability challenges faced by many decentralized systems, offering a solution that allows for the efficient storage and retrieval of electronic records. IPFS provides a decentralized and distributed file system, enabling the framework to scale seamlessly without compromising the security and integrity of the data.

The MediSecure framework represents a significant leap forward in the quest for a scalable, secure, and integral blockchain-based solution for EHR management. By embracing decentralized technologies, the research work envisions a future where healthcare stakeholders can seamlessly access and contribute to a patient's health record, fostering collaboration and improving outcomes.

The integration of BCT and IPFS in MediSecure not only enhances the security and accessibility of EHR but also sets a precedent for the broader adoption of decentralized technologies in healthcare systems worldwide. As the healthcare industry continues to evolve, research works like MediSecure pave the way for a more transparent, secure, and patient-centric future.

1.2. Purpose

The purpose of the MediSecure research work is rooted in the pressing need to address critical challenges within the realm of EHR management, leveraging cutting-edge technologies such as blockchain and the IPFS. This ambitious initiative aims to revolutionize the way healthcare data is stored, accessed, and secured, ultimately fostering a more transparent, secure, and patient-centric approach to electronic health records.

In the contemporary healthcare landscape, the management of electronic health records is plagued by various issues, ranging from data security concerns to challenges related to scalability and accessibility. The traditional centralized models of EHR systems have faced criticism for vulnerabilities such as data breaches, unauthorized access, and lack of patient control over their own health information. The integration of blockchain technology into MediSecure serves as a fundamental solution to these challenges, aligning with the research work's overarching purpose of enhancing data security and integrity.

In today's health care management systems, it becomes very difficult to quickly access information like electronic health records for patient, even during the time of emergency (Saberi et al., 2022). With increase in cyber attacks, it becomes more difficult to secure centralised data system. Security breaches during the pandemic also add concerns to the earlier HER management models (Pilares et al., 2022)]. Some hospitals have been releasing patient data to other parties which generates a very serious issue for patient data security. Decentralised blockchain based HER management system comes to rescue for such issues. With security added by decentralisation, patients become the owner of their own data (Reen et al., 2019). Secure healthcare data can be managed by using smart contract (Praveen et al., 2024). Using smart contracts acts as a secure way for access management while use of IPFS adds secure and scalable storage (Azbeg et al., 2022).

The implementation of blockchain in the context of EHR brings forth several transformative features. One of the core benefits is the decentralization of data storage and management. Unlike traditional databases that rely on a centralized authority for control, a blockchain-based system distributes the data across a network of nodes, ensuring that there is no single point of failure or vulnerability. This decentralized architecture not only enhances the security of health records but also ensures their immutability. Once a record is added to the blockchain, it becomes a permanent member of the ledger, resistant to tampering or unauthorized alterations. This immutability instills a high level of trust in the integrity of the data, crucial in the sensitive realm of healthcare.

The benefits of digitalization in healthcare, including enhanced efficiency, scalability, flexibility, reliability, and cost-effectiveness, are widely acknowledged (Parviainen et al., 2017, Kahin et al., 2016 and McLoughlin et al., 2017). However, the paramount concern for healthcare organizations is safety, which limits the adoption of emerging technologies deemed immature or insecure (Edmunds et al., 2016 and Madsen et al., 2014). Despite being perceived as slow in adopting digital transformation, the healthcare sector has prioritized he digitization of health records (Jolly et al., 2021). Electronic Health Records (EHR) have emerged as a cornerstone of the sector's digital strategy, aiming to consolidate patient records from various sources and enable comprehensive patient health status assessment (Alassaf et al., 2003).

Furthermore, the use of smart contracts within the framework introduces a granular access control mechanism. The purpose of this feature is to strike a delicate balance between data accessibility and patient privacy. Smart contracts enable the definition of specific access rules, allowing only authorized individuals – such as healthcare professionals and the patients themselves – to access portions of the EHR. This not only ensures compliance with privacy regulations but also empowers individuals with greater control over who can access their health information. The purpose is to facilitate a patient-centric approach where individuals have the autonomy to manage and share their health data based on their preferences.

EHR adoption was anticipated to revolutionize healthcare by reducing medical errors, enhancing quality of care, and lowering costs, while also promoting health education for informed decision-making (Al-Zubaidie et al., 2019, Vimalachandran et al., 2017, Pilares et al., 2022, Pearce et al., 2010 and Xu, et al., 2013). However, the transition to electronic health records also exposes healthcare systems to cyber threats, posing a significant challenge in the current landscape ((Mackey et al., 2019, Offner et al., 2020, Kheshaifaty et al., 2021). Public concerns about privacy and security are valid, given the sensitive nature of personal health information (Papoutsi et al., 2015, Zandieh et al., 2008, Sahama et al., 2013 and Alassaf, et al., 2019).

Scalability is a pervasive challenge in blockchain technology, and the purpose of integrating IPFS into MediSecure is to tackle this head-on. While the blockchain ensures security and immutability, the off-chain storage capabilities of IPFS provide a scalable solution to accommodate the growing volume of electronic health records. By leveraging IPFS for off-chain storage, the framework can maintain the benefits of decentralization without compromising on the efficiency of data retrieval. This purposeful integration positions MediSecure as a scalable and future-proof solution, capable of handling the expanding datasets inherent in healthcare.

Privacy in healthcare refers to safeguarding personal information used for patient identification, while security involves controlling access to this information to prevent unauthorized disclosure (Keshta et al., 2020). Both aspects are critical in preventing potential adverse consequences resulting from data breaches.

In essence, the purpose of the MediSecure research work is to pave the way for a paradigm shift in electronic health record management. It aspires to create a future where healthcare data is not only secure and transparent but also puts individuals at the center of control. By harnessing the capabilities of blockchain and IPFS, the research work seeks to address longstanding issues in the healthcare industry, fostering collaboration, enhancing data integrity, and ultimately improving patient outcomes. The overarching goal is to set a new standard for EHR systems, establishing a foundation for a more efficient, secure, and patient-centric healthcare ecosystem. As the research work progresses, it is poised to contribute significantly to the ongoing evolution of healthcare technology, influencing how electronic health records are perceived, managed, and utilized on a global scale.

1.3. Scope

The scope of the MediSecure research work encompasses a comprehensive vision to revolutionize the landscape of EHR management by harnessing the potential of blockchain technology and the InterPlanetary File System (IPFS). This ambitious initiative extends its reach across multiple dimensions, addressing critical challenges in healthcare data management and setting the stage for a transformative shift in the industry.

At its core, the research work aims to redefine how electronic health records are stored, accessed, and secured. The scope extends to mitigating the longstanding issues associated with centralized EHR systems, including concerns about data security, privacy, and scalability. By leveraging the decentralized and tamper-resistant nature of blockchain, MediSecure seeks to establish a secure and transparent framework for managing health records. The immutability of blockchain ensures that once data is recorded, it becomes an unalterable part of the ledger, enhancing data integrity and building trust among healthcare stakeholders.

A key facet of the research work's scope is to implement smart contracts for granular access control. The smart contract functionality allows for the creation of fine-tuned access rules, ensuring that only authorized individuals have access to specific components of the EHR. This addresses the crucial balance between data accessibility and patient privacy, aligning with regulatory requirements and empowering individuals with greater control over their health information. The implementation of smart contracts adds a layer of automation to access management, streamlining processes and reducing the likelihood of human error in data handling.

Furthermore, the scope of MediSecure encompasses the integration of IPFS for off-chain storage to address scalability concerns associated with blockchain technology. While blockchain ensures security and immutability, IPFS provides an innovative solution for efficiently handling the increasing volume of electronic health records. The off-chain storage capability enhances scalability without compromising on the benefits of decentralization, allowing the framework to adapt to the growing demands of the healthcare industry.

Another significant aspect of the research work's scope is its potential impact on fostering collaboration within the healthcare ecosystem. By creating a decentralized and interoperable system for EHR management, MediSecure aims to break down silos and facilitate seamless data sharing among healthcare providers, institutions, and even patients. This collaborative approach is envisioned to enhance patient care, enable more informed decision-making, and contribute to advancements in medical research.

The global applicability of the MediSecure framework is integral to its scope. The research work envisions a future where its decentralized solution can be adopted on a broad scale, transcending geographical boundaries. By providing a secure, transparent, and scalable platform for EHR management, MediSecure seeks to set a new standard in healthcare technology, influencing policies and practices to ensure widespread adoption and impact.

In conclusion, the scope of the MediSecure research work is expansive, aiming to address multifaceted challenges in electronic health record management. From enhancing data security and privacy through blockchain technology to tackling scalability concerns with IPFS integration, the research work sets out to redefine the norms of EHR systems. As it progresses, MediSecure has the potential to shape the future of healthcare data management, creating a paradigm shift towards decentralized, secure, and patient-centric electronic health record solutions on a global scale.

1.4. Blockchain Technology: A Paradigm Shift in Data Security and Transparency

Blockchain technology, originally conceived as the solid infrastructure for BCT based currencies like bitcoin, has come as a major force with transformative implications across various industries. The core principles of decentralization, immutability, and transparency inherent in blockchain have paved the way for innovative solutions, particularly in the realm of healthcare.

In healthcare, where the confidentiality and integrity of sensitive patient information are paramount, blockchain technology offers a robust solution to enhance data security. Traditional healthcare systems often rely on centralized databases, making them susceptible to breaches and unauthorized access. Blockchain, by distributing data across a network of nodes, eliminates the vulnerability associated with a single point of failure.

Each block in the BCT contains a cryptographic link to the before block, creating an immutable and transparent records of transactions. This ensures that once data is recorded, it cannot be altered or deleted, instilling a high level of trust in the integrity of medical records.

The decentralized nature of blockchain also addresses interoperability challenges in healthcare, where disparate systems often struggle to communicate and share information seamlessly. Blockchain's ability to provide a unified and standardized platform for data exchange facilitates interoperability among different healthcare providers, improving the continuity of care and reducing redundancy in data entry. Patients can benefit from a more comprehensive and connected healthcare experience as their medical history becomes accessible across various healthcare institutions securely.

Blockchain technology in healthcare also introduces the concept of patient empowerment. With patients having more control over their health data, they can selectively share information with healthcare providers, researchers, or other authorized parties. This shift towards patient-centric care aligns with the evolving paradigm of healthcare, emphasizing collaboration and informed decision-making.

In conclusion, blockchain technology represents a paradigm shift in how data is stored, shared, and secured in healthcare. Its decentralized and transparent nature holds the promise of improving data security, interoperability, and patient engagement. As the technology matures and the industry navigates challenges, the transformative impact of blockchain on healthcare is likely to reshape the landscape, fostering a more secure, interconnected, and patient-centric healthcare ecosystem.

Figure 1. Process of blockchain technology

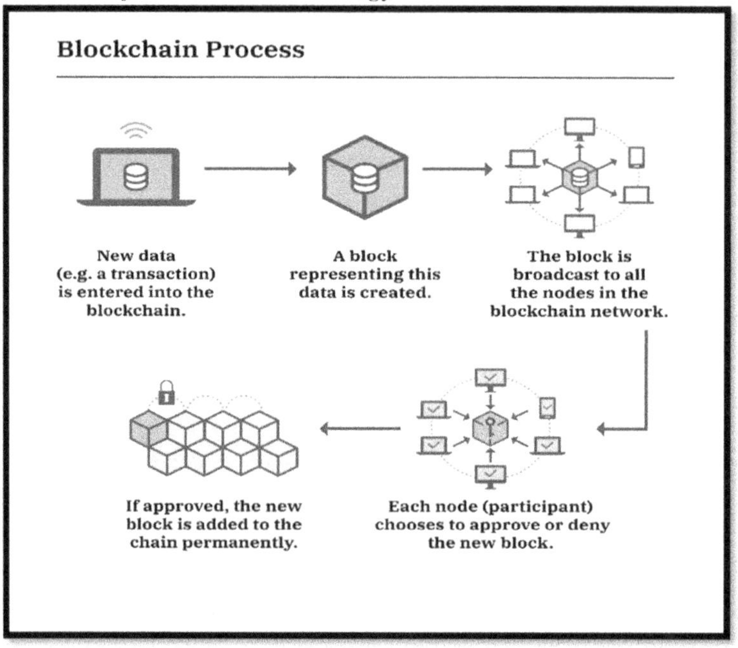

Figure. 1.4.1 illustrates the step-by-step journey of information within a blockchain. In the initial stage, someone adds new data into the system. This could be any kind of information, like records, transactions, or updates. Next, a block is created to represent this fresh data. The block serves as a container, holding a set of information and securing it with a unique code. After the block is formed, it is shared with all the computers, or nodes, in the network. Each computer in the network has a say in whether they agree or disagree with the new block. If all the computers reach a unanimous decision, commonly referred to as consensus, and nod in agreement by saying "yes," then the new block is accepted.

Finally, if the new block gets the green light from every computer in the network, it becomes a permanent part of the blockchain. This is significant because it ensures that the information is not only secure but also agreed upon by everyone involved. The entire process reflects the collaborative and decentralized nature of blockchain technology, where every participant has a role in maintaining the integrity and transparency of the shared ledger.

1.5. Types of Blockchain

Blockchain technology comes in various types, each with its unique features, use cases, and consensus mechanisms. Below is outlined table that compares some key parameters of three common types of blockchains: Public Blockchain, Private Blockchain, and Consortium Blockchain.

Table 1. Comparison of public, private, and consortium blockchains

Parameter	Public Blockchain	Private Blockchain	Consortium Blockchain
Access Control	Open to anyone; permissionless	Restricted access; permissioned	Shared control among a predefined group
Participants	Decentralized and anonymous participants	Limited, known participants	Multiple organizations or entities
Consensus Mechanism	Proof of Work (PoW), Proof of Stake (PoS)	Various, including Practical Byzantine Fault Tolerance (PBFT), Raft, etc.	Often uses a consensus mechanism that suits the participating entities
Transaction Speed	Variable, may have longer confirmation times	Faster due to fewer participants	Moderate, depends on the chosen consensus algorithm and network size
Privacy	Pseudonymous; transparent	Higher level of privacy for participants	Balances privacy and transparency based on participant needs
Immutability	Highly immutable; resistant to censorship	Immutable within the trusted network	Maintains immutability but may have mechanisms for reversible transactions
Use Cases	Cryptocurrencies, decentralized applications (dApps)	Enterprise solutions, supply chain, internal record-keeping	Industry consortia, collaborative research works, shared databases
Examples	Bitcoin, Ethereum	Hyperledger Fabric, R3 Corda, Quorum	Ripple, Hyperledger Besu, MultiChain

Table 1 provides a concise overview of the distinctions among public, private, and consortium blockchains. While public blockchains prioritize decentralization and openness, private blockchains focus on controlled access and increased privacy. Consortium blockchains strike a balance, catering to multiple organizations collaborating within a shared network. The choice of the blockchain type depends on the specific requirements of the intended use case and the desired level of decentralization and control.

II LITERATURE REVIEW

In recent years, the intersection of blockchain technology and healthcare has garnered significant attention, with researchers proposing innovative frameworks to enhance the security, scalability, and accessibility of Electronic Healthcare Records (EHRs). A lot of different approaches have been suggested for secure and scalable EHR management. Some methods include usage of centralized system while recent studies have shown that blockchain based decentralized systems are found more secure and scalable. The patient centric approach have been able to eliminate security issues which are faced with centralized system. This literature survey explores various methodologies and frameworks proposed by different researchers, emphasizing the integration of blockchain, IPFS, and Ethereum in electronic healthcare record.

The author introduced a fail-proof and robust framework for securing and storing healthcare records by integrating blockchain with IPFS (Jayabalan et al., 2022). Their proposal incorporates data hashing for added security, providing protection against cyber attacks. By leveraging the decentralized nature of IPFS and the immutability of the Ethereum blockchain, their framework ensures the integrity and confidentiality of patient data, establishing a resilient foundation for electronic healthcare record management.

Alaa Haddad (Haddad et al., 2023) and his team demonstrated the design of a Patient-Centric Electronic Health Record Management (PCEHRM) system. The system enables stakeholders such as patients, laboratories, and researchers to access patient-centric data in a distributed and secure manner. Utilizing a web-based interface, all users, including patients, can initiate EHR sharing transactions. This approach emphasizes inclusivity and accessibility, fostering a collaborative and patient-centric healthcare data management system.

The author proposed an innovative AI-assisted blockchain framework for storing and processing medical records (Chamola et al., 2023). By employing various AI techniques, such as optical character recognition (OCR), handwritten and printed prescriptions and reports are processed to form a concise patient medical history report. The report contains crucial information and is securely stored over a decentralized blockchain network. This integration showcases the potential for combining AI and blockchain to streamline healthcare data management.

The author proposed a combination of Ciphertext-Policy Attribute-Based Encryption (CP-ABE) with blockchain technology (Kaur, Jasleen et al., 2023). Using the Remix-Ethereum or (IDE), smart contracts with access permissions were designed to give patients control over their records. The scalability and immutability of the system were ensured by storing encrypted EHR hashes on the blockchain and the actual encrypted records on IPFS. This approach adds an extra layer of access control and security to the electronic healthcare records.

The author presented a comprehensive solution called Patient-Centric Healthcare Data Management (PCHDM) (Vinodhini Mani et al., 2021). The framework includes on-chain storage of health record hashes in a Hyperledger Fabric database and off-chain solutions using IPFS for securely storing encrypted health data. This hybrid approach addresses scalability, confidentiality, and the challenge of blockchain data storage, providing a robust solution for patient-centric healthcare data management.

In their article on Blockchain-based Healthcare Data Management, Karthigha, M Padmavathy, and CV.S. Akshaya (2022) advocate for the integration of identity management with blockchain technology. The aim is to ensure secure access to health information exclusively for identity-verified users, including patients, doctors, family members, and hospital staff. The article suggests that employing smart contracts can reduce the reliance on centralized authorities for overseeing and authorizing healthcare data management.

Xia et al. (2017) introduced blockchain as a trustless system that ensures the integrity and privacy of health data. The paper discusses blockchain's potential in creating immutable logs of data transactions, which is vital in preventing unauthorized access and tampering in medical records. Azaria et al. (2016] aid foundational concepts by demonstrating the use of Ethereum smart contracts for managing EHRs. MedRec facilitates decentralized record-keeping while maintaining patient-centric control over data access, which MediSecure expands upon by integrating IPFS for scalability.

Benet et al., (2014) introduces IPFS as a peer-to-peer distributed file system designed to solve challenges in large data storage by using content-addressable hashes. This approach reduces storage redundancy and ensures that each file is uniquely identifiable, making it suitable for EHR storage. Patel et al. (2019) introduced a system where medical imaging data is stored off-chain using IPFS, while blockchain stores the references and access permissions. This approach resolves the issue of storing large files on-chain, a feature that MediSecure adopts for handling EHRs efficiently.

In line with the advancements in blockchain technology and IPFS integration for electronic healthcare record management, our research aims to assess the effectiveness of these methodologies. Specifically, we focus on evaluating the scalability, security, and robustness of the proposed methods in real-world scenarios. By building upon the insights from these notable frameworks, we seek to contribute to the ongoing discourse surrounding the optimization of electronic healthcare record management systems.

III BLOCKCHAIN AND IPFS BASED APPROACH FOR EHR MANAGEMENT

3.1. Introduction

The methodology employed in the development of the MediSecure research work incorporates a sophisticated blend of cutting-edge technologies to ensure a secure, scalable, and user-friendly decentralized electronic health record (EHR) management system. Leveraging the InterPlanetary File System (IPFS) as the off-chain storage solution, the research work addresses scalability challenges commonly associated with blockchain technology. The Ethereum blockchain serves as the foundation, facilitated using Ganache for local testing and Metamask as the browser extension for user authentication.

The implementation of smart contracts is pivotal in defining granular access rules and ensuring secure transactions within the system. The Truffle Suite, a comprehensive development environment for Ethereum, plays a central role in deploying, testing, and managing the smart contracts, providing a robust and streamlined framework for the realization of the ambitious goals set forth by MediSecure. This integrated approach underscores the research work's commitment to embracing innovative technologies to revolutionize EHR management in a scalable, secure, and user-centric manner.

3.2. Proposed Architecture

Figure 3.2.1 represents the architectural visualization of the research work that unfolds a robust system where hospitals, patients, and the underlying blockchain technology harmoniously collaborate for seamless healthcare data management. Hospitals, represented as nodes, are endowed with the capability to upload, and access health records securely stored in the InterPlanetary File System (IPFS). This decentralized storage solution ensures efficient and resilient file storage. The interconnected nodes signify the bond established through blockchain, allowing transparent and traceable interactions between hospitals and patients.

Figure 2. Architecture diagram

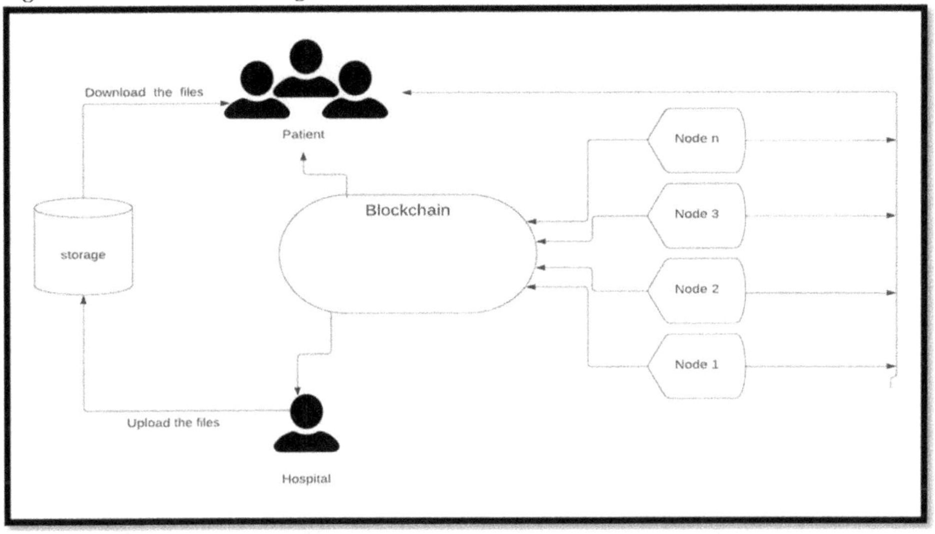

The architecture underscores the pivotal role of blockchain in securely linking hospitals and patients, fostering a trust-driven ecosystem. Patients, as distinct nodes, gain the privilege to retrieve and download their health records, thereby empowering them with control and accessibility. Overall, the image illuminates a decentralized, secure, and transparent architecture, illustrating the seamless flow of health records between hospitals and patients facilitated by blockchain and IPFS integration.

3.3. Flow of Research Work:

Figure 2 is illustrating the flow of the MediSecure research work encapsulates a streamlined and secure process for doctors and patients. Beginning with registration and login procedures, both doctors and patients utilize their MetaMask wallet accounts, seamlessly integrating blockchain technology into healthcare data management. The use of Ethereum for transactions ensures a transparent and tamper-proof environment. Leveraging the private key associated with their wallet, users undergo a robust verification process upon successful acceptance, granting them access to Ethereum functionalities. This innovative approach not only establishes a secure authentication method through MetaMask but also empowers doctors and patients to seamlessly engage with Ethereum for various transactions within the MediSecure ecosystem.

Figure 3. Representing the flow of the research work

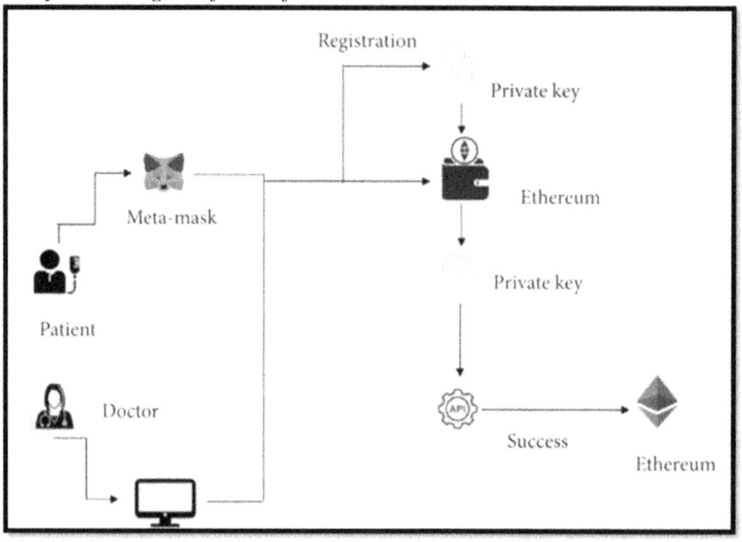

The flow chart visually articulates the efficient integration of blockchain technology and Ethereum, ensuring a secure and transparent healthcare data management experience for all users.

3.4. Deployment Configuration Details

Table 2 shows the deployment phase of the MediSecure research work involves meticulous configuration settings to ensure a seamless and secure implementation.

Table 2. Represents the deployment configuration details

Configuration	Description
Ganache Settings	• Configure Ethereum's local blockchain settings in Ganache, including hostname, port number, and enabling automine for seamless testing. • Autogenerate HD Mnemonic for secure key management.
IPFS Configuration	• Initialize IPFS through 'ipfs init' in the terminal. • Set up IPFS configurations to allow proper access control and methods for handling data.
Smart Contract Deployment	• Utilize Truffle for contract deployment. • Specify contract address in the application code for seamless interaction.
MetaMask Connection	• Connect MetaMask to the local development blockchain (localhost:8545). • Import accounts from Ganache for MetaMask to interact with local blockchain accounts.

Ganache, serving as the local blockchain, requires specific parameters such as the hostname, port number, and automine activation to facilitate smooth testing. The HD Mnemonic is autogenerated to enhance key management security. IPFS, integral to decentralized storage, is initialized through terminal commands, and access control configurations are carefully set to handle data effectively. Truffle streamlines the deployment of smart contracts, with the contract address being crucial for subsequent interactions. Connecting MetaMask to the local development blockchain and importing accounts from Ganache further establishes a cohesive and secure environment. This deployment configuration table serves as a comprehensive guide, emphasizing the importance of aligning all configurations with security best practices for a robust implementation.

3.4.1. Blockchain Protocol (Ethereum):

Objective: Establish a decentralized and secure environment for medical record management.

Steps:

i. Carefully select Ethereum as the foundational blockchain protocol, known for its reliability and security features.
ii. Leverage Ethereum's robust consensus mechanism, employing Proof of Work (PoW) or Proof of Stake (PoS), and smart contract capabilities to ensure the integrity and immutability of patient data.
iii. Implement Ethereum's blockchain functionalities to create a transparent and secure ecosystem for healthcare data.

3.4.2. Smart Contracts:

Objective: Automate and enforce rules governing patient data access, sharing, and privacy.

Steps:

i. Utilize smart contracts, self-executing contracts with coded terms, on the Ethereum blockchain.
ii. Define and meticulously implement smart contracts to automate processes, ensuring transparent and tamper-proof execution of predefined actions related to medical record management.
iii. Leverage Ethereum's Solidity programming language for smart contract development, adhering to best practices for security and efficiency.

3.4.3. InterPlanetary File System (IPFS):

Objective: Efficient and decentralized storage of medical images, reports, and sensitive data.

Steps:

i. Seamlessly integrate IPFS, a distributed file system, to address the challenge of storing diverse healthcare data types securely.
ii. Implement IPFS for decentralized and efficient storage, enhancing accessibility and resilience within a distributed network.
iii. Configure IPFS Desktop for streamlined management and accessibility of medical data.

3.4.4. Data Security and Encryption:

Objective: Implement advanced security measures to protect patient data.

Steps:

i. Apply cutting-edge encryption techniques, including multi-party computation protocols and homomorphic encryption algorithms, to fortify patient data against unauthorized access and breaches.
ii. Ensure secure data sharing and analysis while preserving patient privacy through the meticulous application of encryption methodologies.
iii. Conduct regular security audits to identify and address potential vulnerabilities, prioritizing a proactive approach to data protection.

3.4.5. Decentralized Identity (DID):

Objective: Enhance user security and privacy through decentralized login methods.

Steps:

i. Integrate robust Decentralized Identity (DID) solutions to establish secure and decentralized login methods.
ii. Eliminate the need for centralized authentication authorities, mitigating the risk of data breaches and empowering patients with greater control over their identities.
iii. Explore emerging standards like W3C's DID specification for interoperability and adherence to industry best practices.

3.4.6. Web3.js Integration:

Objective: Facilitate seamless interaction between the web interface and the Ethereum blockchain.

Steps:

i. Integrate Web3.js, a JavaScript library for Ethereum interactions, to enable direct communication with smart contracts.
ii. Ensure the smooth execution of blockchain transactions directly from the patient or healthcare provider's web browser, promoting user-friendly interactions.
iii. Leverage Web3.js capabilities to retrieve real-time data from the Ethereum blockchain, enhancing the responsiveness of the user interface.

3.4.7. React.js User Interface:

Objective: Develop a dynamic and user-friendly interface for medical record management.

Steps:

i. Construct the user interface using React.js, a versatile JavaScript library known for its flexibility and efficiency in building responsive web applications.
ii. Prioritize the development of a dynamic and interactive interface to optimize user experience for patients and healthcare providers accessing and managing medical records on the platform.
iii. Implement React.js best practices for state management and component-based architecture, ensuring scalability and maintainability.

3.4.8. Node.js Backend:

Objective: Power the backend for efficient communication between the frontend and the Ethereum blockchain.

Steps:

i. Leverage Node.js as the server-side runtime for JavaScript, facilitating the development of a robust backend infrastructure.
ii. Implement server-side logic to ensure efficient communication between the frontend user interface and the Ethereum blockchain, enhancing overall system performance.
iii. Explore Node.js middleware options for secure data processing and seamless integration with frontend components.

3.4.9. Truffle Suite Deployment:

Objective: Simplify the development, testing, and deployment of smart contracts.
Steps:

i. Install and configure Truffle, a comprehensive development suite for Ethereum, using npm.
ii. Utilize Truffle's capabilities for compiling contracts, managing migrations, and testing the functionality of smart contracts.
iii. Deploy smart contracts using Truffle's migration scripts, ensuring a streamlined and standardized process for development and deployment.
iv. Truffle is used together with smart contracts, web 3 and frontend as shown in Figure 4.

Figure 4. Present the integration of truffle, Web3 and smartcontracts

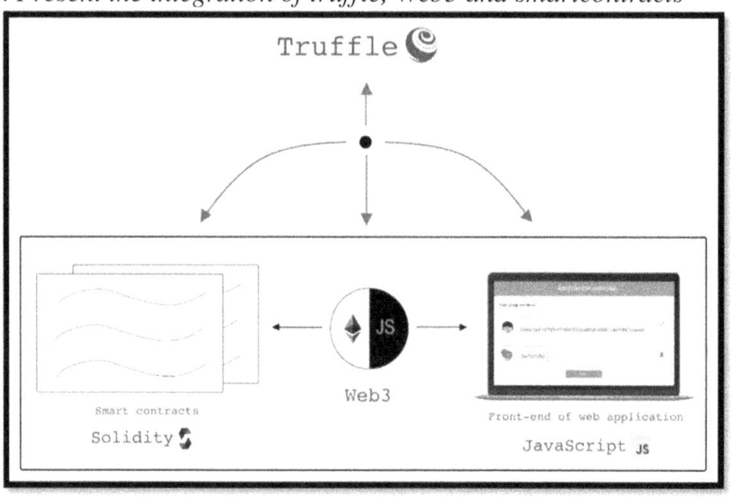

3.5.10. MetaMask Integration:

Objective: Facilitate secure interactions with the Ethereum blockchain.
Steps:

i. Integrate MetaMask, a popular browser extension, to enhance the security of interactions with the Ethereum blockchain.

ii. Enable patients and healthcare providers to manage their Ethereum accounts securely through MetaMask, providing a seamless and user-friendly authentication experience.
iii. Choose the private key for creating account on metamask as shown in Figure 5.

Figure 5. The metamask wallet account

iv. Educate users on the importance of securely managing their MetaMask accounts and signing transactions directly from their web browsers.

3.5.11. Secure Login and Registration Function:

Objective: Ensure that only authenticated and authorized users have access to health information.

Steps:

i. Implement a secure login and registration function, incorporating industry-standard authentication protocols.
ii. Verify identities through secure and efficient processes, ensuring that patients, doctors, family members, and hospital staff have controlled and authorized access to the platform's health information.
iii. Integrate multi-factor authentication options to add an extra layer of security to user accounts.

3.5.12. Installation:

Objective: Set up the necessary dependencies for MediSecure.

Steps:

i. Install NodeJS and npm, the foundational tools for building and managing the research work.
ii. Follow provided instructions for the installation of Ganache, a personal blockchain for Ethereum development, ensuring compatibility and optimal performance.
iii. Install and configure IPFS Desktop, MetaMask, and Truffle Suite as per the guidelines, providing a comprehensive environment for development, testing, and deployment.

3.5.13. Running the dApp:

Objective: Successfully deploy and operate the MediSecure decentralized application (dApp) on a local environment.

Steps:

i. Connect MetaMask to the local development blockchain, ensuring a secure and authenticated connection.
ii. Configure IPFS for efficient and decentralized storage of medical data, optimizing accessibility and resilience.
iii. Use the private key for the account from the ganache as shown in Figure 6 and add the private key address to the metamask.
iv.

Figure 6. Ganache accounts

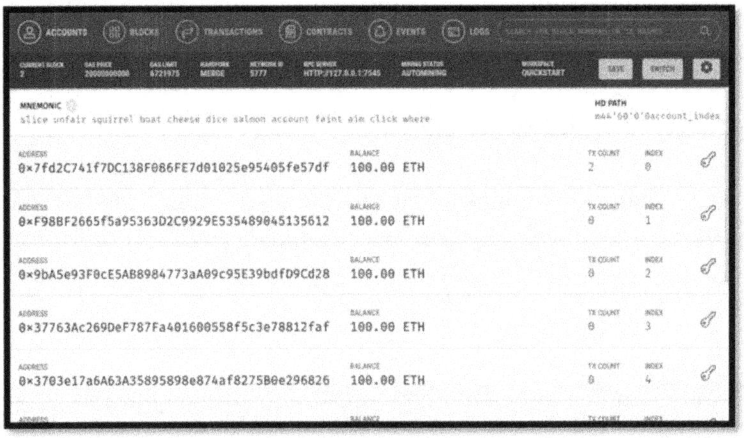

v. Start a local server for MediSecure using npm start, providing users with a reliable and responsive platform for accessing and managing medical records.
vi. Validate the functionality of the dApp by navigating to localhost:3000 and ensure a seamless and intuitive user experience.

By adhering to this meticulous and comprehensive procedure and methodology, the implementation of the MediSecure research work aims to create a secure, scalable, and user-centric decentralized electronic health record management system, contributing to the evolution of innovative and efficient healthcare solutions.

IV RESULTS AND DISCUSSIONS

The implementation and outcomes of the Medisecure research work exemplify a resounding success in addressing critical challenges within the realm of healthcare data management. As demonstrated through the refined integration of blockchain and artificial intelligence technologies, Medisecure has showcased remarkable efficacy in revolutionizing how medical records are handled, shared, and accessed. The research work's innovative utilization of the Ethereum blockchain has not only ensured a secure and transparent environment but has also significantly mitigated persistent issues related to data privacy, interoperability, and patient control. The seamless incorporation of advanced AI and machine learning algorithms has further elevated the research work's performance, enhancing the accuracy, efficiency, and patient-centricity of healthcare delivery. This section provides an insightful overview of the tangible results achieved by Medisecure, illustrating its prowess in tackling complex problems inherent in the healthcare industry and setting a new standard for blockchain-based medical record systems.

4.1. User Friendly User Interface

Medisecure boasts an intuitive and user-friendly user interface (UI) designed to streamline the interaction between patients, healthcare providers, and the innovative blockchain-based medical record system.

Figure 7. Login page

The login page shown in Figure 7 and registration page shown in Figure 8 serve as the gateway to the platform, seamlessly linked with the secure MetaMask extension for Ethereum wallet integration. Users, whether patients or healthcare providers, experience a smooth and secure authentication process through their MetaMask accounts, ensuring a reliable and tamper-proof connection to the Ethereum blockchain.

Figure 8. Registration page

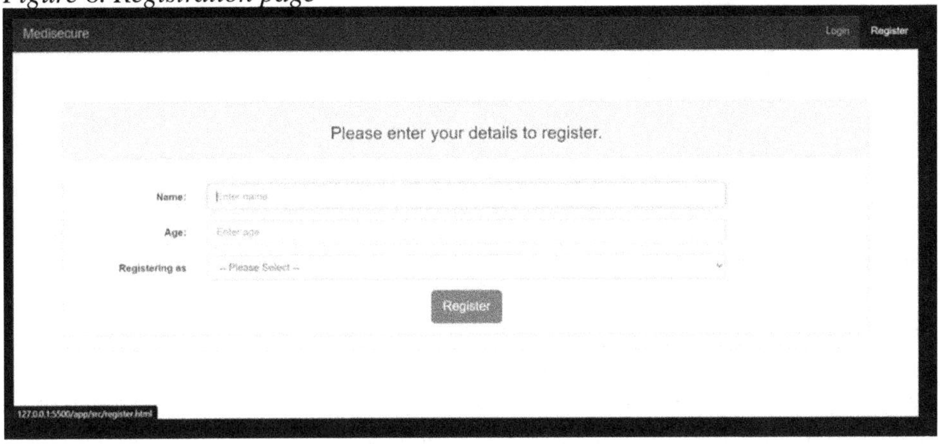

Upon successful login as, patients are directed to their personalized patient record page as shown in Figure 9 and Figure 10, where a comprehensive overview of their medical history is accessible. This user-centric page allows patients to view, manage, and share their medical records securely. Patient can see their health records with respect to different doctors.

The UI is designed for simplicity, ensuring that patients can effortlessly navigate through their health information, fostering a sense of empowerment and control over their medical data.

Figure 9. Patient information page

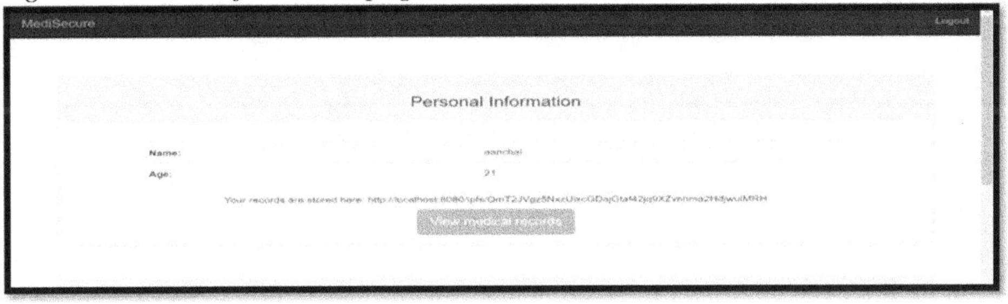

Figure 10. Patient information page

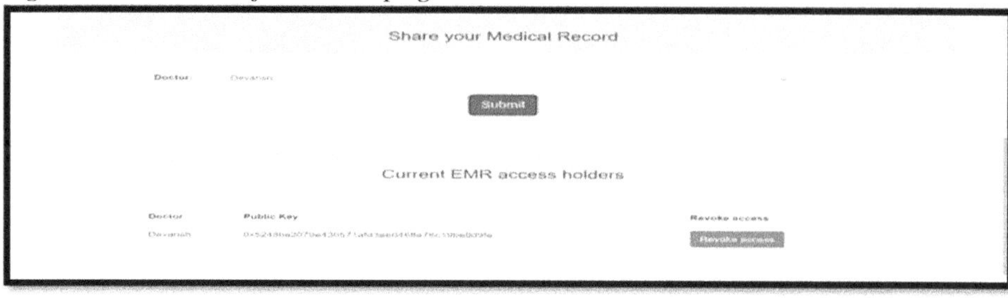

For healthcare providers, the UI extends to include a dedicated doctor appointment page as shown in Figure 11. This feature facilitates seamless scheduling, management, and tracking of appointments, enhancing the efficiency of healthcare delivery. The appointment page is thoughtfully designed to provide doctors with a clear and organized view of their schedules, enabling them to prioritize patient care and manage appointments with ease.

Figure 11. Doctor information page

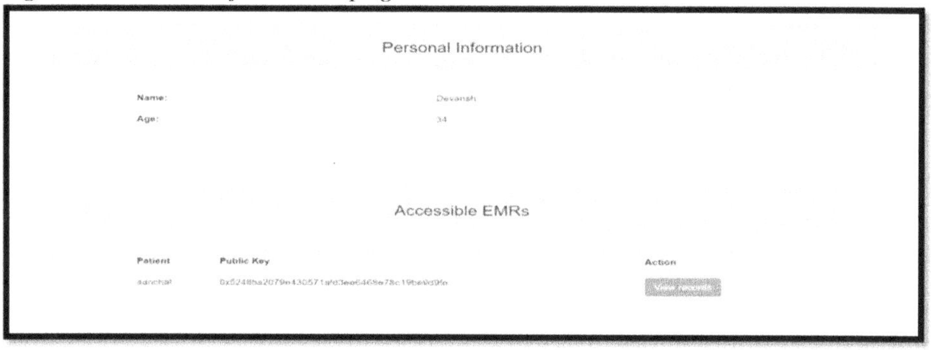

The overall UI design prioritizes clarity, accessibility, and a responsive layout to accommodate various devices. The aesthetic appeal of the pages is complemented by an intuitive navigation system, allowing users to effortlessly transition between the login, registration, patient record, and doctor appointment pages. Through thoughtful UI design, Medisecure ensures a positive and user-centric experience, fostering trust and engagement among both patients and healthcare providers in the secure management of medical records.

4.2. Ensuring Security Through Ganache and Private Keys in Medisecure's Blockchain-Based Medical Record System

Medisecure's utilization of Ganache, in conjunction with private keys, stands as a cornerstone in ensuring the robust security and safety of its blockchain-based medical record system. Ganache, a local blockchain development environment, facilitates a controlled and secure testing environment for smart contracts and decentralized applications (DApps). By employing Ganache during the development and testing phases, Medisecure ensures that the platform's functionalities operate seamlessly within a simulated blockchain network, mitigating potential vulnerabilities before deployment to the live Ethereum network.

Figure 12. Private key for meta mask account from ganache

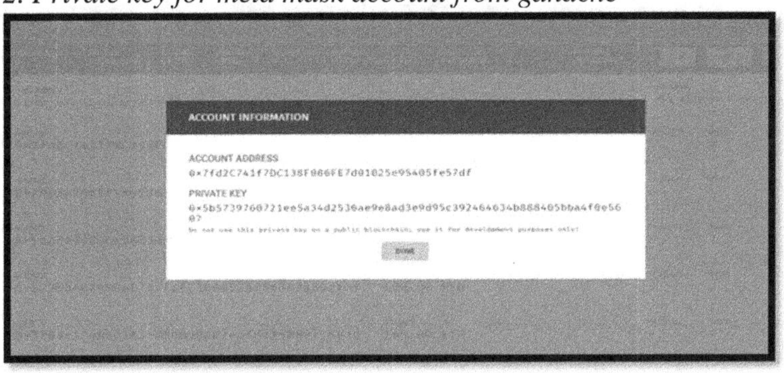

The integration of private keys shown in Figure 12 further fortifies the security posture of Medisecure. Private keys, which are securely stored within MetaMask wallets, serve as the cryptographic keys to access and control users' Ethereum accounts. Medisecure leverages these private keys for user authentication, granting access only to authorized individuals, be they patients or healthcare providers. The use of private keys adds an extra layer of security, as it ensures that only those with the appropriate credentials can interact with and manage sensitive medical records.

This combination of Ganache for secure testing environments and private keys for user authentication underscores Medisecure's commitment to robust security practices. It not only ensures the reliability and integrity of the platform during development but also safeguards patient data by strictly controlling access using private keys. As a result, Medisecure's deployment strategy, incorporating Ganache and private keys, enhances the overall safety and resilience of its blockchain-based medical record system, instilling confidence in both users and stakeholders.

4.3. Empowering Trust and Automation: Medisecure's Utilization of Smart Contracts (Agent and Migrate) in Healthcare Data Management

Medisecure's groundbreaking approach to healthcare data management is epitomized by its strategic implementation of smart contracts, specifically the Agent and Migrate contracts, on the Ethereum blockchain. These smart contracts play a pivotal role in automating and enforcing rules governing patient data access, sharing, and privacy.

Figure 13. Smart contract deployment in Ganache

The Agent Contract within Medisecure depicted in Figure 13 acts as a dynamic mediator, orchestrating interactions between various entities, including patients, healthcare providers, and the broader network. This contract facilitates secure and transparent execution of predefined actions, ensuring that data access and sharing adhere to predefined rules. By leveraging the Agent Contract, Medisecure fosters a seamless and tamper-proof environment, enhancing the overall integrity of the medical record system.

Furthermore, the Migrate Contract showcases Medisecure's commitment to scalability and adaptability. In the dynamic landscape of healthcare, the Migrate Contract enables the efficient handling of updates and changes to smart contracts, ensuring a flexible and scalable architecture. This capability is crucial for Medisecure to evolve with emerging healthcare requirements, ensuring that the platform remains at the forefront of innovation.

The integration of these smart contracts within Medisecure not only automates crucial processes but also establishes a trustless environment where predefined rules are executed without the need for centralized oversight. Patients and healthcare providers can confidently engage with the platform, knowing that the execution of agreements, data access, and sharing are governed by secure and transparent smart contracts on the Ethereum blockchain.

4.4. Leveraging IPFS for Decentralized and Secure Medical Record Storage in Medisecure

Medisecure's integration of the InterPlanetary File System (IPFS) marks a pivotal achievement in revolutionizing the storage and accessibility of medical records. The adoption of IPFS aligns with the platform's commitment to decentralization and security, fundamentally transforming the conventional storage paradigm. By employing IPFS, Medisecure ensures that medical images, reports, and sensitive data are efficiently and securely stored in a decentralized network, fostering resilience and accessibility.

Figure 14. IPFS connection for efficient storage

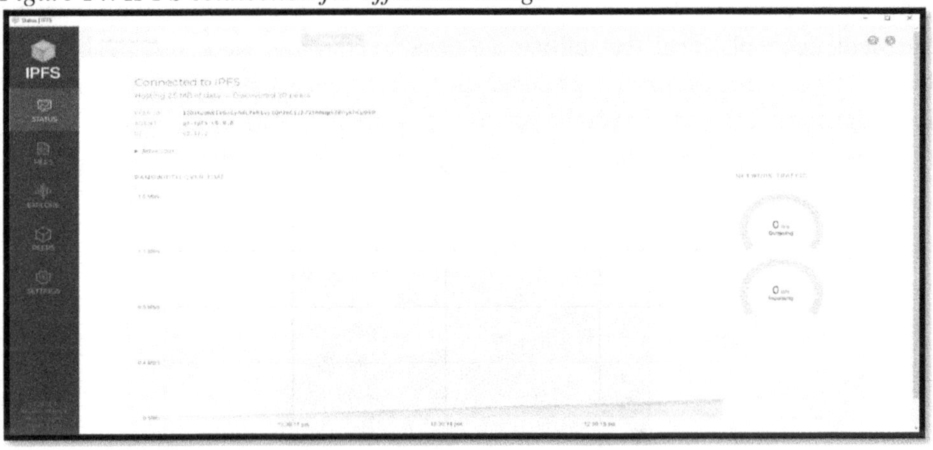

Figure 14 shows IPFS which facilitates efficient data storage by breaking down files into smaller chunks, distributing them across a network of nodes. This decentralized approach enhances data availability, as information is not reliant on a single central server. Medisecure leverages IPFS to securely store patient records, ensuring that healthcare data remains accessible and tamper-resistant.

The decentralized nature of IPFS contributes significantly to Medisecure's commitment to data privacy. Patient records are not stored in a centralized repository, reducing the risk of unauthorized access and potential data breaches. The platform's use of IPFS aligns with the broader ethos of blockchain technology, promoting transparency, security, and patient control over their medical information.

In conclusion, the integration of IPFS within Medisecure represents a transformative leap in medical record management. The utilization of this cutting-edge technology not only ensures the secure storage of healthcare data but also establishes a foundation for scalable, transparent, and patient-centric medical record solutions. Medisecure's incorporation of IPFS stands as a testament to its dedication to leveraging innovative technologies for the betterment of healthcare data management.

4.5. Record of all the Transactions

MediSecure revolutionizes medical report management through its innovative utilization of blockchain technology, specifically Ethereum, and the InterPlanetary File System (IPFS), ensuring unparalleled security, accessibility, and transparency. Leveraging the power of smart contracts and decentralized storage, MediSecure provides a robust ecosystem for storing and managing medical records.

Using MetaMask, an Ethereum wallet browser extension, users can seamlessly interact with the Ethereum blockchain, enabling secure transactions and interactions with smart contracts. When a user wishes to upload or access a medical report on the MediSecure platform, they initiate a transaction through MetaMask as shown in Figure 15. This transaction triggers a series of actions within the Ethereum network, including the execution of smart contracts responsible for validating the user's identity, granting access permissions, and storing the encrypted medical report on IPFS.

Figure 15. Shows transaction confirmation prompt

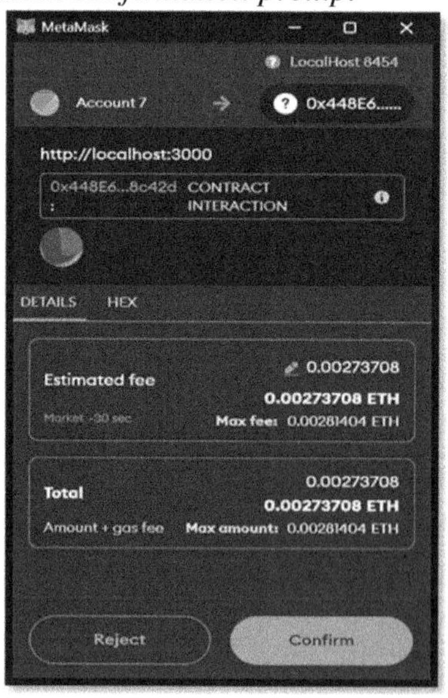

Figure 16. List of all the transactions

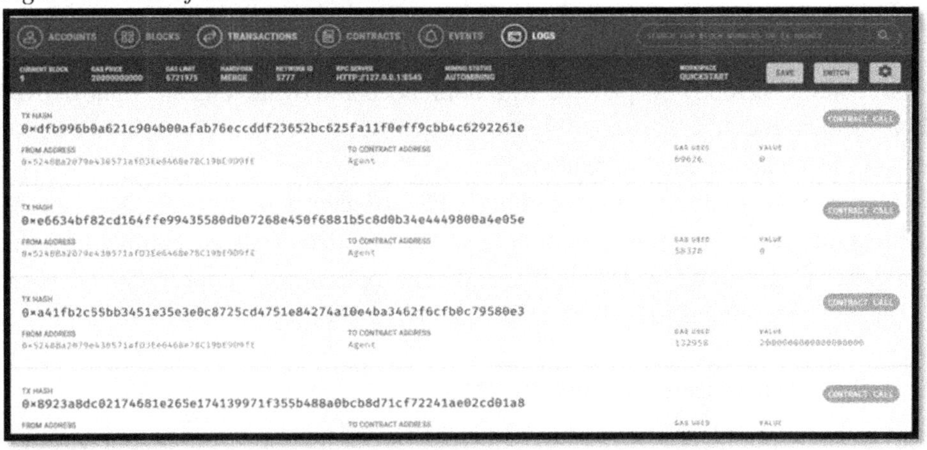

Through Ethereum, each transaction is executed on a decentralized network of nodes, ensuring immutability and tamper-proof record-keeping. This means that once a transaction is confirmed on the blockchain, it becomes an immutable part of the distributed ledger, providing an auditable trail of all interactions within the MediSecure ecosystem.Additionally, MediSecure leverages Ganache, a personal blockchain for Ethereum development, to simulate the Ethereum network environment for testing and development purposes. By using Ganache, developers can ensure the reliability and efficiency of the platform's smart contracts and functionalities before deploying them on the main Ethereum network as shown in Figure 16.Overall, the integration of MetaMask transactions, Ethereum smart contracts, IPFS decentralized storage, and Ganache testing environment enables MediSecure to provide a secure, transparent, and efficient solution for medical report management. Users can trust that their sensitive medical data is stored securely on the blockchain, accessible only by authorized parties, while also benefiting from the transparency and immutability inherent in blockchain technology.

4.6. Transformative Outcomes: Medisecure's Comprehensive Impact on Healthcare Ecosystem

Medisecure emerges as a trailblazer at the intersection of blockchain and healthcare, delivering transformative results that redefine how medical records are managed, accessed, and shared. The platform's innovative integration of Ethereum blockchain, IPFS, and smart contracts culminates in a robust and patient-centric solution that significantly benefits patients, doctors, hospitals, and the healthcare industry at large.

1. Patient-Centric Advancements:

Empowered Ownership: Medisecure's use of non-fungible tokens (NFTs) and smart contracts empowers patients with unprecedented ownership and control over their medical records. This not only enhances data privacy but also instills a sense of confidence and agency in patients.

Seamless Accessibility: By leveraging IPFS for decentralized storage, Medisecure ensures that patient records are not only secure but also easily accessible. Patients can retrieve and download their medical information with unprecedented ease, fostering a more engaged and informed healthcare journey.

2. Efficient Healthcare Delivery for Doctors:

Automated Processes: Smart contracts, especially the Agent Contract, automate key processes related to data access and sharing, streamlining the workflow for healthcare providers. This automation enhances the efficiency of medical record management, allowing doctors to focus more on patient care.

Scalability: The use of the Migrate Contract showcases Medisecure's commitment to scalability. As the healthcare landscape evolves, the platform can efficiently adapt to changes, ensuring that it remains a cutting-edge solution capable of meeting growing demands.

3. Hospital Advantages and Data Management:

Enhanced Security: The decentralized nature of Medisecure's architecture, powered by the Ethereum blockchain and IPFS, enhances the security of medical records. Hospitals benefit from a tamper-proof and resilient data storage solution, mitigating the risks associated with centralized repositories.

Streamlined Appointments: The doctor appointment page offers hospitals a streamlined approach to managing appointments, contributing to more organized and efficient healthcare delivery.

4. Other Noteworthy Benefits:

Eco-Friendly Practices: Medisecure's exploration of energy-efficient consensus mechanisms aligns with sustainable blockchain practices, contributing to the platform's commitment to minimizing its environmental footprint.

Adherence to Blockchain Best Practices: Medisecure's utilization of Ganache for testing, private keys for user authentication, and adherence to best practices in blockchain technology showcase a commitment to robust security measures.

Medisecure's multifaceted impact reaches across the healthcare spectrum, offering a secure, efficient, and patient-centric solution as concluded in Table 3. The platform's unique combination of technologies and commitment to sustainability positions it as a transformative force in the evolving landscape of healthcare data management.

Table 3. Overall impact table

Stake Holders	Benefits
Patient	- Enhanced data privacy and ownership - Seamless accessibility to medical records
Doctors	- Automated processes for streamlined workflow - Scalable architecture for evolving healthcare needs
Hospitals	- Enhanced security with decentralized data storage - Streamlined management of doctor appointments
Healthcare Industry	- Eco-friendly practices with energy-efficient consensus - Adherence to blockchain best practices

The Figure 4.6.1 shows how different stake-holders are interconnected to each other using decentralised blockchain system. Medisecure emerges as a trailblazer at the intersection of blockchain and healthcare, delivering transformative results that redefine how medical records are managed, accessed, and shared. The platform's innovative integration of Ethereum blockchain, IPFS, and smart contracts culminates in a robust and patient-centric solution that significantly benefits patients, doctors, hospitals, and the healthcare industry at large.

Figure 17. Decentralised system for health record management

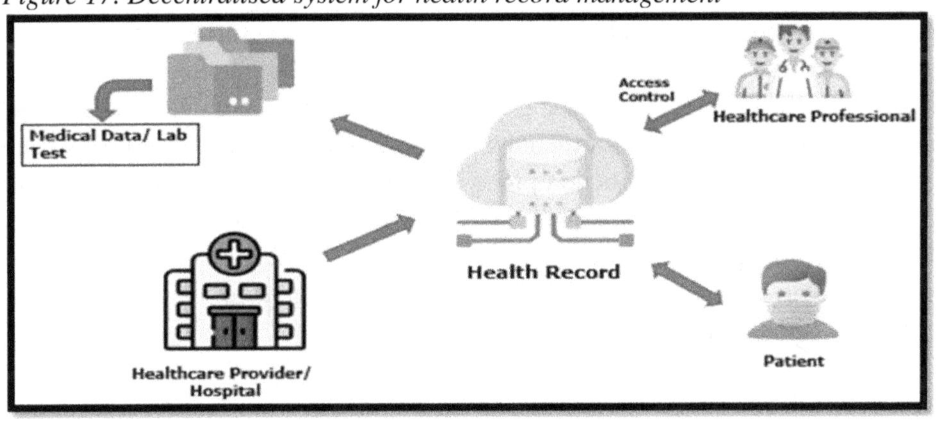

4.7. Comparison with Pre-Existing Models

Table 4. Table of comparison

Features	32	33	34	Medi Secure
Decentralised access	yes	no	yes	yes
Blockchain type	Hyperledger- Besu	none	Ethereum	ZK-EVM
Storage location	Onchain	Cloud	IPFS	IPFS
Concensus algorithm	RBFT	none	PoW	PoS
Data Privacy	yes	yes	yes	yes
User Authentication	No	no	no	yes
Multi- blockchain	no	no	no	yes

Table 4 illustrates the distinct features between MedSecure and Papers 32, 33, and 34 in the realm of secure medical record management. MedSecure stands out prominently for its decentralized access, enabling users to exercise greater control and security over their medical data. Leveraging the innovative ZK-EVM blockchain, MedSecure ensures enhanced security and privacy compared to the blockchain choices of Hyperledger-Besu, Ethereum in Papers 32, 34 respectively. Storage on IPFS further enhances data integrity and availability in MedSecure, contrasting with on-chain and cloud storage in Papers 32 and 33, which may pose scalability and security challenges.

MedSecure's utilization of a PoS consensus algorithm offers improved energy efficiency and transaction throughput, outpacing the RBFT consensus of Paper, while PoW in paper 34. Both MedSecure and Papers 32, 33, and 34 prioritize data privacy, yet MedSecure's inclusion of robust user authentication mechanisms sets it apart, ensuring heightened platform security. Additionally, MedSecure introduces multi-blockchain support, enhancing scalability and interoperability compared to its counterparts. Beyond feature comparisons, MedSecure excels in superior security measures, faster transaction processing, and lower latency, attributed to its innovative technology stack comprising ZK-EVM blockchain, IPFS storage, and PoS consensus algorithm. This collective prowess positions MedSecure as a highly secure and efficient platform for medical record management, meeting stringent standards of data privacy and integrity.

In conclusion, Medisecure's multifaceted impact reaches across the healthcare spectrum, offering a secure, efficient, and patient-centric solution as concluded. The platform's unique combination of technologies and commitment to sustainability positions it as a transformative force in the evolving landscape of healthcare data management.

Challenges in Medisecure Framework:

One of the fundamental challenges with blockchain technology, particularly Ethereum, is its scalability. While IPFS offers a distributed and scalable solution for storing large datasets like EHRs, there are still concerns about its real-world scalability. Implementing a blockchain-IPFS-based system like MediSecure would require extensive user education and training, particularly for healthcare professionals, IT staff, and patients.

V CONCLUSION AND FUTURE SCOPE

Medisecure stands as a pioneering solution at the intersection of blockchain and record management, reshaping the landscape of how individuals and healthcare providers navigate the management, sharing, and access of medical records. The platform's innovative use of the Ethereum blockchain ensures a secure, transparent, and decentralized environment, effectively addressing persistent challenges in the healthcare industry related to data privacy, interoperability, and patient control.

The incorporation of advanced AI and machine learning algorithms for data extraction, analysis, and personalization introduces a layer of sophistication to the medical record management process, enhancing accuracy, efficiency, and patient-centricity in healthcare delivery. The creation of non-fungible tokens (NFTs) for each patient's medical record, coupled with Ethereum's smart contracts, establishes a tamper-proof and user-friendly system for tracking ownership, access permissions, and transaction history. Medisecure's commitment to sustainability, reflected in its exploration of energy-efficient consensus mechanisms and adherence to blockchain best practices, underscores a holistic approach towards responsible technological innovation.

The research objectives, spanning the optimization of AI-driven data extraction and analysis, streamlining NFT creation and registration processes, continuous enhancement of user interfaces, scalability exploration, and sustainable blockchain practices, collectively contribute to the platform's ongoing evolution. By consistently refining these aspects, Medisecure aims to set new standards in the healthcare industry, providing patients and healthcare providers with a secure, efficient, patient-centric, sustainable, and responsible experience.

Medisecure's ten-point tech stack, featuring Ethereum, IPFS, AI, React.js, and more, showcases a comprehensive and thoughtfully selected array of technologies that synergistically contribute to the platform's functionality, security, and user interface. The integration of decentralized identity solutions further enhances user privacy, while the use of MetaMask simplifies interactions with the Ethereum blockchain.

In essence, Medisecure emerges as a trailblazer, offering a transformative solution that transcends traditional approaches to medical record management. With its forward-thinking combination of technologies and a patient-focused ethos, Medisecure stands poised to redefine how individuals and healthcare providers interact with, manage, and share medical records in the evolving landscape of blockchain and AI.

The trajectory of Medisecure is poised to bring forth numerous enhancements and expansions, solidifying its standing as a leader in blockchain-based medical record systems. A key avenue of exploration involves the continual refinement and augmentation of AI-driven processes. Prioritizing the enhancement of accuracy and efficiency in AI algorithms responsible for data extraction and analysis involves delving deeper into machine learning models, exploring neural network architectures, and leveraging advancements in natural language processing for more nuanced and precise information extraction from medical records.

Scalability stands as another pivotal focus for future developments within Medisecure. The vision involves accommodating a growing patient base and increased data volumes. Researching and implementing advanced scalability solutions, including layer 2 scaling solutions and blockchain interoperability, will be crucial. This ensures that Medisecure maintains optimal performance, even with an expanding user ecosystem, guaranteeing a seamless and responsive experience for patients and healthcare providers.

Additionally, upcoming iterations of Medisecure will explore advanced features to boost patient engagement and empower them to take control of their health. Integration with decentralized applications (DApps) could offer patients additional healthcare functionalities, such as personalized health recommendations or access to telemedicine services. This expansion aligns with the broader trend of integrating blockchain platforms with DApps, providing patients with more comprehensive control over their health data and healthcare experiences.

Furthermore, Medisecure envisions strengthening its sustainability efforts. Researching and implementing eco-friendly consensus mechanisms within the blockchain network align with the platform's commitment to minimizing its environmental footprint. This move not only supports sustainability goals but also contributes to the wider narrative of responsible blockchain technology adoption.

In the realm of user interfaces, continuous improvement remains a pivotal focus for Medisecure. Future endeavors include refining the platform's interfaces based on user feedback, incorporating accessibility features, and exploring innovative visualizations for enhanced user comprehension. Ultimately, the future of Medisecure is characterized by a commitment to innovation, scalability, sustainability, and user-centric design, ensuring that the platform remains at the forefront of blockchain-based medical record solutions. Through ongoing research and development, Medisecure aims to set new benchmarks in the secure, transparent, and patient-empowered management of medical records on the blockchain.

A system like MediSecure can adopt blockchain or decentralized ledger technologies (DLT) to distribute medical data across various healthcare providers, giving patients control over their records while ensuring data integrity and security. The major benefits of Medisecure are Interoperability, Automated Processes, Transparency, and citizen trust. MediSecure could bring transformative benefits to e-government healthcare services by enhancing efficiency, transparency, and citizen trust. However, realizing these benefits will require careful consideration of the regulatory environment, data protection laws, and governance frameworks to address the unique challenges posed by decentralization.

MediSecure, a decentralized framework for health record management, offers significant future potential by enhancing data privacy, security, and patient control through blockchain technology. It promotes interoperability across healthcare systems, enabling real-time access to updated records and reducing administrative costs. Integrating AI and IoT could lead to predictive healthcare and real-time monitoring, while anonymized data supports large-scale research. MediSecure also facilitates global health data standardization, ensuring compliance with evolving regulations. Despite adoption challenges, it holds promise for a secure, patient-centric, and interoperable healthcare ecosystem, transforming health data management globally.

REFERENCES

Al-Zubaidie, M., Zhang, Z., & Zhang, J. (2019). PAX: Using pseudonymization and anonymization to protect patients' identities and data in the healthcare system. *International Journal of Environmental Research and Public Health*, 16(9), 1490.

Alassaf, N., Alkazemi, B., & Gutub, A. (2003). Applicable light-weight cryptography to secure medical data in IoT systems. *Arabia (London, England)*, 2(2), 50–58.

Alassaf, N., & Gutub, A. (2019). Simulating light-weight-cryptography implementation for IoT healthcare data security applications. [IJEHMC]. *International Journal of E-Health and Medical Communications*, 10(4), 1–15. DOI: 10.4018/IJEHMC.2019100101

Azaria, A., ... "Medrec: Using blockchain for medical data access and permission management." *2016 2nd international conference on open and big data (OBD)*. IEEE, 2016. DOI: 10.1109/OBD.2016.11

Azbeg, K., Ouchetto, O., & Andaloussi, S. J. (2022). BlockMedCare: A healthcare system based on IoT, Blockchain and IPFS for data management security. *Egyptian Informatics Journal*, 23(2), 329–343. DOI: 10.1016/j.eij.2022.02.004

Benet, J. (2014). Ipfs-content addressed, versioned, p2p file system. *arXiv preprint arXiv:1407.3561*.

Chamola, V., Goyal, A., Sharma, P., Hassija, V., Binh, H. T. T., & Saxena, V. (2023). Artificial intelligence-assisted blockchain-based framework for smart and secure EMR management. *Neural Computing & Applications*, 35(31), 22959–22969. DOI: 10.1007/s00521-022-07087-7 PMID: 35310553

Edmunds, M., Peddicord, D., & Frisse, M. E. (2016). Ten reasons why interoperability is difficult. *Healthcare information management systems: Cases, strategies, and solutions*, 127-137.

Haddad, A., Habaebi, M. H., Suliman, F. E. M., Elsheikh, E. A., Islam, M. R., & Zabidi, S. A. (2023). Generic patient-centered blockchain-based EHR management system. *Applied Sciences (Basel, Switzerland)*, 13(3), 1761.

Jayabalan, J., & Jeyanthi, N. (2022). Scalable blockchain model using off-chain IPFS storage for healthcare data security and privacy. *Journal of Parallel and Distributed Computing*, 164, 152–167. DOI: 10.1016/j.jpdc.2022.03.009

Jolly, R. (2011). *The E health revolution: easier said than done*. Parliamentary Library.

Karthigha, M., Padmavathy, C., & Akshaya, V. S. (2022, December). Blockchain based Healthcare Data Management. In *2022 International Conference on Automation, Computing and Renewable Systems (ICACRS)* (pp. 392-396). IEEE.

Kahin, B. (2016). Digitization and the Digital Economy. *Available at SSRN* 2782906.

Kaur, J., Rani, R., & Kalra, N. (2023). Attribute-based access control scheme for secure storage and sharing of EHRs using blockchain and IPFS. *Cluster Computing*, •••, 1–15.

Keshta, I., & Odeh, A. (2020). Security and privacy of electronic health records: Concerns and challenges. *Egypt. Inform. J.*, 22(2), 177–183. DOI: 10.1016/j.eij.2020.07.003

Kheshaifaty, N., & Gutub, A. (2021). Engineering Graphical Captcha and AES Crypto Hash Functions for Secure Online Authentication. *Journal of Engineering Research*. Advance online publication. DOI: 10.36909/jer.13761

Mackey, T. K., Kuo, T.-T., Gummadi, B., Clauson, K. A., Church, G., Grishin, D., Obbad, K., Barkovich, R., & Palombini, M. (2019). 'Fit-for-purpose?'—Challenges and opportunities for applications of blockchain technology in the future of healthcare. *BMC Medicine*, 17(1), 1–17. DOI: 10.1186/s12916-019-1296-7 PMID: 30914045

Madsen, L. B. (2014). *Data-driven healthcare: how analytics and BI are transforming the industry*. John Wiley & Sons.

Mani, V., Manickam, P., Alotaibi, Y., Alghamdi, S., & Khalaf, O. I. (2021). Hyperledger healthchain: Patient-centric IPFS-based storage of health records. *Electronics (Basel)*, 10(23), 3003.

McLoughlin, I. P., Garrety, K., & Wilson, R. (2017). *The digitalization of healthcare: Electronic records and the disruption of moral orders*. Oxford University Press. DOI: 10.1093/acprof:oso/9780198744139.001.0001

Offner, K. L., Sitnikova, E., Joiner, K., & MacIntyre, C. R. (2020). Towards understanding cybersecurity capability in Australian healthcare organisations: A systematic review of recent trends, threats and mitigation. *Intelligence and National Security*, 35(4), 556–585. DOI: 10.1080/02684527.2020.1752459

Papoutsi, C., Reed, J. E., Marston, C., Lewis, R., Majeed, A., & Bell, D. (2015). Patient and public views about the security and privacy of Electronic Health Records (EHRs) in the UK: Results from a mixed methods study. *BMC Medical Informatics and Decision Making*, 15(1), 1–15. DOI: 10.1186/s12911-015-0202-2 PMID: 26466787

Parviainen, P., Tihinen, M., Kääriäinen, J., & Teppola, S. (2017). Tackling the digitalization challenge: how to benefit from digitalization in practice. *International journal of information systems and project management, 5*(1), 63-77.

Patel, V. (2019). A framework for secure and decentralized sharing of medical imaging data via blockchain consensus. *Health Informatics Journal*, 25(4), 1398–1411. DOI: 10.1177/1460458218769699 PMID: 29692204

Pearce, C., & Haikerwal, M. C. (2010). E-health in Australia: Time to plunge into the 21st century. *The Medical Journal of Australia*, 193(7), 397–398. DOI: 10.5694/j.1326-5377.2010.tb03967.x PMID: 20919969

Pilares, Iris Cathrina Abacan, et al. "Addressing the challenges of electronic health records using blockchain and ipfs." *Sensors* 22.11 (2022): 4032.

Pilares, Iris Cathrina Abacan, et al. "Addressing the challenges of electronic health records using blockchain and ipfs." *Sensors* 22.11 (2022): 4032.

Praveen, G., Singh, P. K., & Ranjan, P. (2024). A Blockchain Integrated IPFS-based System. *International Journal of Intelligent Systems and Applications in Engineering*, 12(13s), 288–301.

Reen, G. S., Mohandas, M., & Venkatesan, S. (2019, December). *Decentralized patient centric e-health record management system using blockchain and IPFS. In 2019 IEEE conference on information and communication technology*. IEEE.

Saberi, M. A., Adda, M., & Mcheick, H. (2022). Break-Glass Conceptual Model for Distributed EHR management system based on Blockchain, IPFS and ABAC. *Procedia Computer Science*, 198, 185–192. DOI: 10.1016/j.procs.2021.12.227

Sahama, T., Simpson, L., & Lane, B. (2013, October). Security and Privacy in eHealth: Is it possible? In *2013 IEEE 15th International Conference on e-Health Networking, Applications and Services (Healthcom 2013)* (pp. 249-253). IEEE.

Vimalachandran, P., Wang, H., Zhang, Y., & Zhuo, G. (2017). The Australian PCEHR system: ensuring privacy and security through an improved access control mechanism. *arXiv preprint arXiv:1710.07778.*

Xia, Q. I., Sifah, E. B., Asamoah, K. O., Gao, J., Du, X., & Guizani, M. (2017). MeDShare: Trust-less medical data sharing among cloud service providers via blockchain. *IEEE Access : Practical Innovations, Open Solutions*, 5, 14757–14767. DOI: 10.1109/ACCESS.2017.2730843

Xu, J., Gao, X., Sorwar, G., & Croll, P. (2013). Implementation of e-health record systems in Australia. *The International Technology Management Review*, 3(2), 92–104. DOI: 10.2991/itmr.2013.3.2.3

Zandieh, S. O., Yoon-Flannery, K., Kuperman, G. J., Langsam, D. J., Hyman, D., & Kaushal, R. (2008). Challenges to EHR implementation in electronic-versus paper-based office practices. *Journal of General Internal Medicine*, 23(6), 755–761. DOI: 10.1007/s11606-008-0573-5 PMID: 18369679

Chapter 8
Application of Cloud Computing Technology for Enhances E-Government Services in Edo State

Mary Ebele Idahosa
https://orcid.org/0009-0006-6745-640X
Idahosa University, Nigeria

Saadatu Eireyi-Edewede
Benson Idahosa University, Nigeria

Charles Ejesei Eruanga
Benson Idahosa University, Nigeria

ABSTRACT

Abstract This research looks closely on application of cloud computing technologies for enhanced e-Government services in Edo State. The government has a big responsibility to provide maximum service to citizens. The aim of many governments is to provide online services and make it reachable to beneficiaries as such many governments, therefore aim to develop government services by including cloud computing as a platform to provide services. However, technological developments, especially cloud computing, can be an alternative solution for effective information delivery. The hypothetical message of this research emphasizes the need to believe in digital infrastructure and cultural differences in the design and implementation of e-Government using cloud computing technology to achieve optimal equality of

DOI: 10.4018/979-8-3693-7678-2.ch008

access to government services. Several literature works were closely examined on the various e-government services in Edo State, the benefits of cloud computing in e-government services were discussed, challenges and possible solution were discussed.

INTRODUCTION

Digital age has transformed how governments operate, making its services easily accessible online through what's called E-Government Services. Governments around the world are now using cloud computing technology to make their services more efficient, easier for citizens to access, and more responsive. Cloud computing helps governments move away from old systems to more dynamic, online services focused on the needs of the people. This means everyone can access the services they need, reducing inequality and ensuring no one is left out.

E-Government Services are all about using technology to make it easier for people to access and use government services. It makes government interactions smoother and improves how citizens engage with government agencies and the quality of services received. The value of these digital services is huge. They make governments more accountable and open, give people more control over their dealings with public agencies, and help governments run more efficiently. By using technology wisely, governments can deliver better services, cut costs, and make citizens happier.

Edo State e-government service has ushered in a new era of governance characterized by transparency, efficiency, and citizen-centric service delivery. With streamlined processes and digital workflows, it has help to reduce the cumbersome movement of physical documents within MDAs. This makes information flows seamlessly across departments, leading to faster decision-making and improved service delivery to citizens. This transition in technology in Edo State had brought several awards to the state; one of it is the Edo State Information Communication Technology Agency (Edo ICTA). It has been honored with the prestigious "Best State ICT Agency" award by the Bureau of Public Service Reforms (BPSR) under the Presidency of Nigeria.

Technology, especially the internet and cloud computing, gives governments a flexible, secure way to store and manage a lot of information, and people access services anytime, anywhere. This not only helps different government departments work together better but also focuses on making life easier for citizens. The importance of cloud computing in e- government services is that it provides a robust foundation for hosting and managing digital tools and data. Cloud systems are flexible and secure, which means governments can scale services to meet demands without compromising sensitive information.

However, transitioning to e-government services isn't without its challenges. Issues like the digital divide mean security and privacy and keeping online services running smoothly is essential, as any downtime can disrupt important services. Overcoming these obstacles requires careful planning, investment in technology, and designing user-friendly platforms to ensure everyone can use these services. Inayatulloh & Maryani (2021) state that e-government is facing different types of challenges such as technical, organizational and economic challenges which puts governments under pressure to be innovative. Innovative means that the E-government should benefit from the latest ICTs (Information and Communication Technologies), which increase the efficiency and the effectiveness of the public sector. This article looks into how cloud computing is reshaping government services everywhere, making governance better for everyone.

LITERATURE REVIEW

E-Government Services

Government services are crucial functions of the government aimed at fulfilling the needs of the

Community and some challenges persist in the delivery of government services, particularly concerning disparities in access, this is the actual situation for citizens in remote areas and navigating through the bureaucratic difficulties of government services can be cumbersome for even urban settlers. This does not only destroy trust in governance but likewise hinders individual progress and social well-being. However, among these disparities, there is a bright solution for E-government. E-government provides a transformative route to bridge these gaps and aid the way for equal access for all (Durman, 2024) In Vietnam, the concept of e-government emerged in the middle of the 1990s and the government initiated implementing an e-government system in 2001 under the "Project 112" (Nguyen, 2007) .

E-Government services mark a significant change in how governments interact with citizens and offer public services. It has to do with the government providing e-services by depending on technology tools and building an integrated system to provide an easy way for the beneficiaries to complete their needs anywhere at any time. The first governor in Nigeria to introduce e-government services was Bola Ahmed Tinubu, who served as the Governor of Lagos State from 1999 to 2007. His administration implemented various digital initiatives aimed at improving governance, enhancing service delivery, and increasing transparency. These initiatives laid the groundwork for further e-governance developments in the country. E-government is officially defined in the Vietnam E-Government Architecture Framework Version

1.0 as “the government that applies information technology to improve the effectiveness and efficiency of state agencies, enhance publicity and transparency of information, and provide better public services to people and businesses Alkilani, .M and Kobziev. V. (2019) defined it as the use of technology tools as a platform for providing e-government services and increased the productivity of services for beneficiaries easily and accurately and efficiently. They identified four, main elements for e-government interaction as follow:

- Government-to-Government (G2G): G2G is referring to the communication and exchange of data among the government components, such as departments and agencies.
- Government-to- Employees (G2E): G2E refers to the relationship between the government and employees, G2E can be described as providing an e-services environment to the employees of government such as online training and paying utilities.
- Government-to-Citizen (G2C): G2C can be described as accessibility online to government services to retrieve needed information anywhere at any time.
- Government-to-Business (G2B): G2B can be described as the interaction between the government and business. Inayatulloh & Maryani (2021) state that there are four stages to developing e- government, there are: Attendance, Collaboration, Contract and Conversion.

1) Attendance, namely bringing up the regional web on the internet. In this phase, the elementary information desired by the public is shown on the government web.
2) Collaboration, specifically a regional website that delivers services for communication among the communal and resident government. In this phase, the information shown is extra diverse, such as transfer facilities and email communiqué on government websites;
3) Contracts, specifically resident government websites which in addition to having communication services are also equipped with community transaction services.
4) Conversion, specifically in this situation government facilities are increased in a combined means. Fakhour & Baker (2016), provide recommendations on how to enhance e-government implementation strategies and plans by incorporating facilitating conditions, trust in the government and trust in the internet as determinants of e-government adoption. The study by Vanya Verma (2021) explored the uptake of e-government services in India by integrating UTAUT with trust and citizen satisfaction, and the research findings indicated that UTAUT’s factors and two newly added factors are

antecedents of e-government service adoption. Nguyen et al. (2020) employed an extended version of UTAUT to explore the determinants affecting the adoption of e government services in Vietnam with small and medium enterprises as the study's context. The author identified that the introduction of new features and perceived benefits of time and money, facilitating conditions and especially website quality also induce citizens to use online government services. Edo state is currently operating e-government services and in this article we look at the various e-government services implemented in Edo State.

E-GOVERNMENT IMPLEMENTATION IN EDO STATE

Edo state leads Nigeria in E-government implementation towards paperless governance in modernizing governance and embracing technological advancement. This will help to curb the traditional bureaucratic structures from administration to citizens. According to Oriazowan, C. (2024). Edo state has successfully implemented its E-government initiative, known as **EdoGov**. This initiative marks a pivotal moment not only for the state but for Nigeria as a nation as it propels the nation towards a more efficient, transparent, and paperless government system. It has helped the government operations and has streamlined services, communication is facilitated, and services are delivered promptly to citizens. The deployment of **EdoGov** provided laptops for over 5000 across the various MDAs which serve as indispensable tools for employees to carry out their day-to-day tasks efficiently and effectively. He further illustrated that Edo State is empowering its workforce to embrace digital transformation and deliver services with enhanced productivity.

In addition provision of laptops, by Edo State government has brought about kiosk system within MDAs to further enhance the utilization of the **EdoGov** platform. These kiosks serve as accessible touch points for employees, by providing convenient access to essential government services and information to its citizens. Edo State is fostering a culture of digital inclusiveness and accessibility within its government agencies. Ministries, Departments & Agencies (2024). Edo state has undertaken the training of not less than 17,000 staff members on the **EdoGov** Enterprise Resource Planning (ERP) system. The training ensures that employees are equipped with the adequate skills needed to navigate and maximize the benefits of the e-government platform efficiently and effectively. Edo State has emerged as a trailblazer in Nigeria by becoming the first to launch a paperless government system.

The adoption of **EdoGov** has ushered in a new era of governance characterized by transparency, efficiency, and citizen-centric service delivery. With streamlined processes and digital workflows, it has help to reduce the cumbersome movement of physical documents within MDAs. This makes information flows seamlessly across departments, leading to faster decision-making and improved service delivery to citizens. The implementation of E-government success serves as a beacon of inspiration for the broader Nigerian context and the wider West African region. By embracing digital transformation and harnessing the power of technology, governments can unlock new opportunities for growth, innovation, and development.

Edo State's achievement in implementing **EdoGov** represents a significant milestone in Nigeria's journey towards a more efficient and transparent governance system. With its pioneering efforts in digitalization and paperless governance, Edo State stands as a shining example of the transformative potential of e-government initiatives. As other states and nations look to replicate this success, the future of governance in Africa is undoubted digital. Automation of government services in Edo has reduced the backlog and freed up government resources.

Consequently, application of cloud computing technologies for enhanced E-government services in Edo State is crucial for government services to stay relevant, improve service delivery, and effectively support its citizens. It involves usage of cloud computing technologies and making strategic decisions to implement cloud-based solutions that meet the specific needs and goals of the government. Some of the e-government services in Edo State are:

EDO TECH PARK

According to Oriazowan (2024) Edo State has marked a significant milestone in its journey towards becoming a hub of technological innovation and excellence with the commissioning of the state-of-the-art ICT infrastructure, the (Edo Tech Park) which is located at Enagwe campus (home of Edo Tech Park), Ohen Road, Main Road, off, Benin City, Nigeria. This groundbreaking initiative underscores the state government's unwavering commitment to fostering digital transformation, driving economic growth, and empowering its citizens through cloud computing technology.

The Edo Tech Park stands as a testament to the vision and foresight of the Governor, who recognized the pivotal role of cloud computing Technology in shaping the future of governance and socio-economic development. This elite facility is not just a physical space but a symbol of Edo State's determination to harness the power of innovation and entrepreneurship to propel itself onto the global stage.

At the heart of the Edo Tech Park lies an ambitious undertaking: the establishment of an elite software engineering and leadership-training institute. This institute aims to cultivate and nurture the next generation of technology talent, equipping them with the skills, knowledge, and mindset needed to thrive in the cloud technology economy. The institute represents a bold step towards addressing the growing demand for skilled ICT professionals both locally and internationally.

The curriculum at the software engineering institute was designed in collaboration with industry experts and leading academic institutions, ensuring that students receive cutting-edge training that is relevant, practical, and aligned with the evolving needs of cloud technology. From coding and programming languages to software development methodologies and leadership skills, students will undergo a rigorous and comprehensive training program that prepares them to excel in a rapidly changing and competitive global landscape.

Moreover, the Edo Tech Park is poised to serve as a catalyst for innovation, collaboration, and knowledge-sharing within the technology ecosystem. By providing state-of-the-art infrastructure, mentorship opportunities, and access to funding and resources, the park aims to foster a vibrant ecosystem where startups, entrepreneurs, and technology enthusiasts can thrive and succeed. Through incubation programs, hackathons, and networking events, the park will facilitate the exchange of ideas, the formation of partnerships, and the creation of innovative solutions that address pressing challenges and drive positive change.

In addition to its focus on talent development and innovation, the Edo Tech Park is also designed to catalyze economic growth and create job opportunities within the state. By attracting investments, fostering entrepreneurship, and nurturing a skilled workforce, the park has the potential to spur the growth of the local ICT industry, attract foreign investment, and position Edo State as a preferred destination for tech companies and investors.

As Edo State embarks on this transformative journey with the inauguration of the Edo Tech Park, it reaffirms its commitment to building a prosperous, inclusive, and technologically advanced society. By investing in ICT infrastructure, talent development, and innovation, the state is laying the foundation for a future where technology serves as a powerful enabler of progress and prosperity for all its citizens. With the launch of the software engineering institute, Edo State is not just building a brighter future for it but also contributing to the advancement of the global tech community, one software engineer at a time.

E-SECURITY SERVICE IN EDO STATE

In this technology era, the effective management of resources and the safeguarding of citizens' well-being are very curial. As such, it is important to use technological infrastructure in carrying out government services to ensure the smooth functioning of governmental operations, particularly in the area of security. In this light, according to Oriazowan, C. (2024) the Edo State Government has taken a significant move in the establishment of its Command-and-Control Center—an innovative hub designed to enhance security and foster seamless communication between citizens and authorities.

Situated at the heart of Edo State, the Command-and-Control Center serves as a beacon of technological advancement and proactive governance. It represents a **collaborative** effort between the government and its citizens, aiming to create a safer and more responsive environment for all residents. At its stand, the center operates as a citizen interface facility, **harnessing** the power of live streaming technology to monitor events round-the-clock, every day of the year (Igiekhume, Donatus 2022).

Before the introduction of e-security initiatives in Edo State, the security situation was characterized by several challenges. High crime rates, including armed robbery, kidnapping, and cult-related violence, were significant issues. These problems were exacerbated by limited resources and traditional policing methods, which struggled to effectively address the rising crime levels. Community unrest and a lack of trust in law enforcement also contributed to the overall insecurity. The state government recognized the need for a more modern approach to security, which eventually led to the introduction of e-security measures aimed at improving surveillance, data collection, and response times to incidents.

One of the key features of the Command-and-Control Center is its ability to facilitate real-time monitoring of incidents. Through a sophisticated network of cameras and sensors strategically positioned across the state, the center provides continuous surveillance of public spaces, critical infrastructure, and potential hotspots. This comprehensive coverage enables swift and informed decision-making by expert personnel stationed within the facility.

Additionally, the Command-and-Control Center acts as a conduit for the exchange of security intelligence between citizens and government agencies. By fostering community engagement, it empowers individuals to become essential contributors to the security framework. Through dedicated channels and platforms, citizens can report suspicious activities, share important information, and offer actionable insights to support law enforcement efforts.

The significance of citizen engagement cannot be over emphasized. In an era marked by evolving security challenges and dynamic threat landscapes, the collective vigilance of the populace emerges as a potent force multiplier. By empowering citizens to contribute to the safety and security of their neighborhoods, the Command and Control Center fosters a sense of ownership and accountability within the community.

Moreover, the Command and Control Center functions as a central hub for coordinating emergency responses and crisis management efforts. During times of crisis, it acts as the nerve center for organizing rescue operations, deploying resources, and communicating vital information to key stakeholders. This proactive strategy not only reduces response times but also strengthens the state's overall resilience against unexpected challenges.

In essence, the establishment of the Command and Control Center exemplifies Edo State's commitment to leveraging technology for the betterment of its citizens. By harnessing the power of real-time monitoring, citizen engagement, and expert intervention, the center heralds a new era of governance—one that is responsive, inclusive, and proactive in safeguarding the well-being of its populace.

As other regions face similar challenges, the groundbreaking initiatives in Edo State shine as a source of inspiration and innovation. By investing in advanced infrastructure development, governments can strengthen their connections with citizens, improve security measures, and create a brighter and safer future for everyone. In this context, the Command and Control Center exemplifies not just progress but also the transformative power of visionary leadership and **collaborative** partnerships.

EDOGIS

Edo State Geographical Information Service (EDOGIS) is saddled with the responsibility of data as regards lands and building across the geographical zone ensuring quality and standard in line with the land use Act. It is committed to service to all developers with utmost honesty delivered in a transparent, courteous and fair manner. As the bedrock of socio-economic growth, it regulates continuous, unbiased administration of land. With the introduction of the **E-Gov** registration and issuance of certificates of all land titles have become very easy with prompt response removing the usual government bureaucracy as a practice (Oriazowan, C. 2024). Upon commencement of the e-gov applicant can have access to information as regards the geographical information of Edo State with a physical visitation to the office just with the use of internet either through your Tablet, phone, or computer system. Processing and issuance of certificate of occupancy to landowners have become easy with the introduction of **e-Gov** as required by law. Every document of interest or title to Land in Edo State is registered in accordance with the provisions of the law including those previously registered with the Ministry of Lands and Surveys before the commencement of this administration. Persons who are entitled in law or equity to any land, are required by this law to apply to be registered as a landholder through the e-gov without stress under this administration bottlenecks have been removed to ease registration of land. With the online application for different categories applicants do not need to visit the physical office irrespective of your geographical location it allows multi-user access to the network, applicants can access the website at the comfort of your home with the use of the internet. Payments are not left out in this innovation with **e-Gov** payment can also be initiated and made through the quick teller platform with a designated link which is evidence of your payment and a receipt will be generated by the issuance of an e-receipt.

E-PROCUREMENT SERVICES IN EDO STATE.

Edo State has in the past six years, with the introduction of e-government using cloud computing technology has witnessed a paradigm shift in the way public procurement is conducted, elevating the state's procurement system and processes to unprecedented levels of efficiency, fairness and compliance.

Edo has become a model for other sub-nationals and countries since implementing landmark reforms by the governor to instill transparency and probity in its procurement processes as not less than 19 Nigerian States and two countries have visited the State to understudy the transformational changes.

The Managing Director noted: "The governor's support is the reason why we are able to achieve so much in public procurement in Edo State. Sometimes, they take a file to him and he asks if it has gone through procurement.

EDO STATE E-GOVERNMENT AWARD 2023

Edo State commitment to excellence and innovation in the field of Information Communication Technology (ICT), the Edo State Information Communication Technology Agency (Edo ICTA) has been honored with the prestigious "Best State ICT Agency" award by the Bureau of Public Service Reforms (BPSR) under the Presidency of Nigeria. This recognition, bestowed on 13th October 2023, is a testament to Do IT's remarkable strides in leveraging cloud computing technology to enhance public service delivery and drive socio-economic development within the state.

The Nigeria Govtech Public Service Award, administered by the BPSR, serves as a platform to celebrate and honour outstanding achievements in ICT-driven governance and public service delivery across Nigeria. Edo ICTA's receipt of the "Best State ICT Agency" award highlights its exemplary performance, innovative initiatives, and transformative impact on governance and citizen engagement.

Edo State has emerged as a frontrunner in leveraging cloud computing technology to address key challenges and propel progress under the visionary leadership of Governor Godwin Obaseki. Edo ICTA, has played a pivotal role in spearheading initiatives in digitizing government services, enhancing transparency, and fostering inclusive growth.

A key factor in Edo ICTA's success is its strategic emphasis on utilizing cloud technology to narrow the digital divide and empower residents. By implementing targeted programs and initiatives, the agency has diligently promoted digital literacy, enhanced internet access, and facilitated e-government services, ensuring that all citizens can access information and opportunities equally in the digital era.

Additionally, Edo ICTA has shown a strong dedication to promoting innovation and entrepreneurship within the ICT sector, establishing Edo State as a center for technological advancement and skilled talent. By cultivating a supportive environment for ICT startups and small to medium-sized enterprises, the agency has driven economic development, generated employment opportunities, and encouraged creativity and innovation throughout the state.

The acknowledgment given to Edo ICTA by the BPSR highlights the agency's commitment, vision, and unwavering pursuit of excellence in cloud technology-driven governance. This recognition inspires all stakeholders to remain focused on leveraging the transformative potential of cloud technology for the benefit of the community.

As Edo State advances in its digital transformation, guided by the values of innovation, inclusivity, and effective governance, Edo ICTA remains dedicated to fostering positive change and providing meaningful solutions for all citizens. This esteemed award acts as a catalyst for continued progress, positioning Edo State to reach new milestones in cloud technology development and serving as an exemplary model for others to emulate.

CONCEPT OF CLOUD COMPUTING TECHNOLOGY

Cloud computing is derived from the acronym CLOUD, which stands as C for "Computing resources", L for "Location independent", O for "Online accessibility", U for "Utility for users" and D for "Demand by users" (Swapna & Birader, 2017). Therefore, Cloud computing is a broad term that encompasses both technology and services. Various scholars have different viewpoints of the term "cloud" Hence, the concept of cloud computing can be defined as the sharing and use of applications and resources of a network environment to get work done without concern about ownership and management of the network's resources and applications" (Scale, 2009).

This implies that cloud computing is a technology model that has revolutionized the way businesses, individuals and government access, store; manage data, applications, and services over the internet. It involves the use of remote servers hosted in the internet to store, manage, and process data instead of relying on local servers or personal computers. Thus, cloud computing is the combination of servers, networks, connection, applications and resources. Similarly, Pettey & Forsling

(2009) affirmed that cloud computing is a style of computing with massive scalable and elastic IT-enabled capabilities that delivered service to external customers using Internet technologies. Furthermore, Rana (2010) defined cloud computing as a pool of abstracted highly scalable and managed computer infrastructure capable of hosting end-customer applications and billed by consumption.

The National Institute of Standards and Technology (NIST) also defined cloud computing as "a model that enables ubiquitous, convenient, on-demand network access to shared pool of configurable computing resources such as networks, servers, storage, applications, and services with minimal management effort or service provider interaction. Therefore, cloud computing requires remote server and internet to maintain and organize data and applications. In the same vein, Suciu Besiet al (2013) stated that cloud computing is the delivery of computing and storage capacity to serve community of end-user by combining user data, software and on demand computation resources over a network. Consequently, the components of cloud computing include servers, storage, networking, virtualization, and other technologies that form the foundation of cloud computing. Virtualization allows multiple virtual instances (virtual machines or containers) to run on a single physical server, optimizing resource utilization such as Hypervisors (VMware or Hyper-V), containerization technologies (Docker), and orchestration tools (Kubernetes).

Thus, cloud computing technology encompasses infrastructure, platforms, and software that enable cloud services. While cloud computing services are activities and functionalities provided to users through the internet. Hence, cloud computing is the combination of servers, network connections, applications and resources to work together for the delivery of scalable, on-demand computing resources and services over the internet. Besides, Cloud computing, is a parallel and distributed system consisting of interconnected and virtualized computers that provide unified computing resources based on service-level agreements established through negotiation between service providers and customers (Buyya, Yeo, & Venugopal, 2009). According to Sahu (2016) cloud computing relies on sharing computing resources rather than having local servers or personal devices to handle applications. Naone (2007) asserts that cloud computing is an act of using web browser on the internet to allocate or de- allocate access to remote computing resources based on users' demands. It also refers to paying for the real use of computing resources and facilities.

Qusayi (2011) affirms that cloud computing is an Internet-based computing that provides shared computer processing resources, data to computers and other devices on-demand. This implies that cloud computing refers to both applications delivered as services over the Internet and the hardware and systems software in the data centers that provide these services. Moreover, the National Institute of Standards and Technology (NIST) identified five essential characteristics of cloud computing such as on-demand service, broad network access, resource pooling, rapid elasticity and measured service. On-demand self-service does not require human interaction with service provider as customers can automatically engage in self-service using computing capabilities such as server time and network storage. Secondly, broad network access is provided over network and accessed through standard mechanisms to stimulate the use of various client platforms. Thirdly resource pooling is used to serve multiple consumers with the aid of diverse physical and virtual resources which are assigned to suit the needs of specific consumers. Fourthly, rapid elasticity is automatic scale that allows the purchase of any quantity at any given time. Lastly, measured service is the provision of services to monitor the benefit of users or costumers. Likewise,

Dutt (2017) enumerates the characteristics of clouds computing to include: - Resources shared among users are distributed very fast in computing environment. On-demand & quot provision of resources without assistance from engineers during peak periods. - It also ensures that work is efficiently shared by using common infrastructure with multiple users and multiple applications. - It reduces the cost of services as users can access resources globally through internet connection provided by a third-party. - The applications are easy to maintain as compared to individual applications because they are installed on a common platform and can be accessed from various locations. - There are minimum chances of infrastructure failure as servers are available and more reliable. - Besides, companies need not own infrastructure as there are cost reductions through pay-as-per usage of resources. Users can also access services by using Application Programming Interfaces (APIs) on the cloud and pay as per usage. Nevertheless, Sabiti, Sarika & amp; Bulu (2015) observed that modern technologies have led to tremendous transformation in almost all disciplines and spheres and government are not exempted from the race. Interestingly, governments are adopting new technologies to ensure that the goals of satisfying the public needs are achieved rapidly through cloud computing service (Wada, 2014).

However, cloud-based services are set to transform government activities from administrative burden to focus on innovative services for citizens. Cloud computing facilitates sharing information resources and services over the internet rather than local servers/ nodes or personal devices. Cloud computing is acting as a resource pooling technology for accessing infinite computing services and resources as per demand of users and can be compare with models of pay as you use and utility model can also be used for mobile services (Kumar (2015) stated that the idea of cloud computing is based on the fundamental principle of reusability of IT capabilities. Cloud computing broaden horizons across organizational boundaries compared to automatic, grid, utility, and distributed computing. Remarkably, cloud computing is the delivery of computing services over the internet to allow individuals and institutions to use software and hardware that are managed by third parties from remote locations. Cloud services include online file storage, social networking sites, webmail, online applications etc. In addition, cloud computing model allows access to information resources from anywhere that has available network connection.

There is no doubt that under the revolution of technology tools and the internet, many governments and private sectors using Creative Commons License Attribution 4.0 International (CC BY 4.0) aim to develop its e-services to be easy to reach and at any time. Implementing e-government without clouds is an old technique and is not too efficient. Cloud computing technology encompasses the infrastructure, platforms, and software that enable cloud services. While cloud computing services are the actual offerings and functionalities provided to users or organizations through the internet, using the underlying technology (Quddusim, 2014). Cloud computing offers several benefits for e- government services such as increased storage capacity, scalability, flexibility, collaboration opportunities, and cost savings services. (Microsoft 2021).. According to Seena & Sudhier, (2013). Cloud computing enhances the migration of desktop applications to web-based applications such as Gmail, Google Calendar, and Google Talk, Google Docs text files, spreadsheets. Inayatulloh, (2020) highlight five important features of cloud computing namely:

1. On-demand self-service. Consumers could control computing abilities unilaterally, equally server time and net storage, mechanically as desirable deprived of needful human communication with apiece service workers.
2. Wide-ranging network entrance. Abilities that are accessible over the network and retrieved via typical devices that introduce the usage of multiple stages.
3. Supply combining. A pool of computing properties owned by a provider to serve several different virtual customers, vigorously allocated and assigned allowing customer requests. Here is logic of site objectivity that the consumer commonly does not have a controller of the site of the resources providing, but it is possible to determine locations at a higher level.
4. Quick resistance. Abilities can be assigned in some cases performed mechanically to rapidly count out and enter on request. For customers, the available capabilities are frequently limitless and the quantity can be attuned.
5. Dignified Service. Cloud computing systems mechanically monitor and optimize resource usage by applying dimension capabilities at numerous stages according to the kind of service.

TYPES OF CLOUD COMPUTING DEPLOYMENT MODEL

According to Paul, karn, and Rajesh (2015, p. 31) Cloud computing deployment models means the delivery models in which cloud service are provided to the user or clients. This is a style of computing where several activities have been done. Cloud computing is classified as public, private, hybrid, community, infrastructure service, software as service. This is done based on the services which are mainly categorized on the basis of access and sizes.

Public Cloud: This is when the service provider opens up the cloud infrastructure to open use. It can also be referred to as cloud infrastructure that is located and accessed via the public network. The infrastructure will be on the premises of the service provider, but it will be operated by whoever is making use of it, be it government organization, business or academic institutions. The user of these services does not have any control over the location of the infrastructure. The main features of the public cloud are: reasonable level of security, easy to deploy, and very elastic, cost-effective, and low operational cost, this also requires online backup and restore type of solution (Paul, karn, and Rajesh 2015, p.31).

Private Cloud: As it implies it is owned by a particular institution or organization. Which is hosted internally or externally, Private cloud service offers better security, especially, for an organization that require excellent data management services and uptime requirements, it is also the best choice for organizations that need to manage their host applications and other applications used by their customer, clients, as the case maybe. Paul, Karn, and Rajesh (2015) has so many strengths out of which on demand capacity serviced based accessed are considered as important benefits in the deployment of cloud computing technologies. It is used by members of the organization which is owned and managed by the organization itself. It suitable for organizations that deal with sensitive data. The main features of private cloud include maximum level of reliability and scalability, and high level security, design for organizations and businesses, greater control over cloud infrastructure, and users get both network access and computational resources. There is no much difference in the design structure between the public cloud and the private for the level of security.

Hybrid Cloud: Paul, Karn, and Rajesh (2015) states that hybrid cloud computing, as the name implies is the mixture of private, public and community cloud service. It ensures safety, scalability and high performance but you really need a reputed hybrid cloud vendor to ensure reliability, especially because diverse environments are involved. It can definitely leverage the cost benefits to a great extent and even manage the vulnerabilities found in critical data applications. Many organizations/ businesses have adopted hybrid solution because it creates room for an establishment to bring their own device policy, while employees can access applications and information to improve collaboration. It promotes a more personalized approach. It provides better scale and the convenience of a public cloud and as well as reliability and infrastructure of private cloud computing. The elasticity of scale up and down is an important point in hybrid cloud computing.

Community Cloud: This is similar to the public cloud except that access is limited to specific consumers. According to Paul, Karn, and Rajesh (2015), this may also be owned by community members or third party cloud provider with limited access, the member cloud shares the responsibility for defining and evolving the community. Community cloud deployment model set up is mutually shared among many organizations that belong to a particular community, example of such are the universities. The aim of this is to achieve their goal, which can also be hosted externally or internally. Privacy is shared by community members; it also has saving cost. This type of deployment model is suitable for institutions or organizations that need a centralized cloud computing ability for managing and building. However, it is appropriate for organization or institution with shared interest and also with shared stored information.

Infrastructure as a Service (IaaS): This is a self-service code targeted at managing and monitoring remote datacenter infrastructure for the following functions: storage, networking and computing. Cloud service provider delivers the infrastructure while the clients get to decide on the operating system of their choice. They scale and spin virtual machines of their choice. The entire responsibility of scalability, initial provision of system and connectivity falls on the hands of the vendor. You need a team of system administrators to monitor and manage the system, its maintenance and firewall aspects. Companies using IaaS service have to manage their applications data loss, routine and middleware. Apart from the virtualization layer, cloud vendors in IaaS also provide messaging queues and databases as well. Amazon Web Service (AWS), Microsoft Azure are all perfect examples of IaaS.

Software as a Service (SaaS): According to Berry and Resiman (2012) it is perhaps the most commonly used cloud deployment model. This is because the web delivery model, eliminates the need to install and run applications on your computer. The model also makes it easier for businesses to streamline their maintenance and support. The vendor manages the service, including applications data, middleware, runtime, server, storage, virtualization, networking and even the operating systems. Google app, citrix Go To meeting and Cisco WebEx are all perfect examples of SaaS. Basically, the use of new technology in an organization or an institution must achieve the purpose for which it is being used. It is important to note the characteristics of cloud computing;

On-Demand Self-Service: As the name implies it enables the users or information seekers to manage their resources according to their information needs. Rapid Elasticity: It is an important feature in cloud computing because it enables users of the cloud to retrieve and use resources based on needs. Cloud ability automatically shrinks, and expands based on demand.

Broad Network Access: Cloud service can be accessed by any device connected to the internet that promotes use by inter-erogenous thick client platforms e.g. laptop, tablets, mobile phones, and desktops. Resources pooling: The providers of computing resources are pooled to serve multiple consumers at a time using multi-tenant model. Cloud users do not have knowledge of the exact location. Measured Service: Cloud systems automatically control and optimize resources used; it involves pay per use model. Usage of resources can be controlled, monitored for both the provider and consumer of the service.

ENHANCING E-GOVERNMENT SERVICES USING CLOUD COMPUTING

The rapid development of IT technology has a significant impact on how data is transferred, analyzed and processed. There are many cases where cloud computing technology helps the civic conversation necessary to Political democracy. For example, the Philippines Center for Investigative Journalism posted in 2003 on its website a study pointing out extravagant houses and luxury vehicles owned by Government officials who can't explain how they paid for them. There were also numerous applications by officials to change their birth records to delay their retirement, indicating how lucrative their modestly paid positions must be. Using cloud computing in e-government services will address the challenges of delivering services to citizens in rural areas. It will increase transparency and accountability .Citizens can access relevant information on government operations. Cloud computing in government services will foster trust in government and promote transparency in decision making.

Therefore, many governments aim to benefit from the development of cloud computing technology to improve e-services. The emergence of cloud computing technologies has led to major developments in e-government services which have made the information that beneficiaries need become more accessible. Alkilani, M and Kobziev. V. (2019) State that to ensure cloud computing is implemented in e-government services successfully, we have to understand the stages of e-government developing system, data type, and data flow process. The understanding of these points helps decision-maker to enhance e-government services by providing needed tools necessary for a successful e-government service. However, using cloud computing to enhancing e-government services us needs to clarify and understand the following points: Stages of developing e-government systems, data type and data flow process.

Stages of Developing E-Government Systems

1 Define the requirement of an e-government system: A System Requirement describes what is required to meet the users' needs. System requirements specify which actions the design must provide in order to benefit the system's users. The system requirements document should be precise. Should define exactly what is to be implemented. It also includes users of the system, the system's services, constraints and goals. These requirements are described and defined in detail, serving as the system specification.

2 Design functional requirements and roles: Designing the function of the system is a very important section to identify the permissions of each user on the system, designing the function of the system with its specific roles of each user contributes to exchanging the data easily and fast.

3 Develop Interface of e-government system: In the stage of developing the interface of the system, the design has to involve all the objects that a user sees and interacts with directly on their screen to complete a task or inquire. In the stage of designing the interface, all the details must be taken into consideration such as colors, links, buttons and ... etc. The interface of the system is the channel between citizens and services the government provides.

4 Testing the e-government system: This is the main focus of the life cycle of the system and is the longest stage of the system development life cycle, testing stage involves verifying that each unit meets its specification, and each function in the system meets the requirement designed for.

5 Deploy e-government system: This stage is the last stage in the system development process and can be defined as the implementation stage. Deploy stage come after the stage of testing, and confirm that the system meets the needed requirement, and all the functions of the e-government system work together probable

Benefits Of Cloud Computing Technology On E-Government Services

Cloud computing has numerous benefits in organizations. Mate (2016) states that cloud computing have a cost efficient method to use maintain and upgrade government functions because of its information, automatic software integration and quick deployment. Yuvarej (2013) and Yahaya (2009) affirm that cloud computing power, location and device independency, high scalability, less maintenance and indulgence, unlimited storage capacity, diverse support, faster deployment that enable government to provide effective services. These benefits have positive effects on government services and growth. Therefore, cloud computing is beneficial to government services (Agbontan, 2018).

Besides, cloud-based services eliminate the need for the government to invest in expensive hardware and software through budgetary allocation to enhance resources and services. Besides, there are two modes of payment in cloud computing namely, "Pay-as-you-go" & "Subscription". Cloud computing enables the government to save costs as they pay only for required services. Therefore, cloud computing technology is flexible and it enables the government to expand services anytime because numerous users can gain access to the same resources simultaneously. In the same vein, Oyeleye, Fagbola & Daramola (2014) affirmed that adopting cloud computing has key influence on cost-effectiveness, Similarly, Arpaci (2017) asserts that cloud computing adoption can be promoted if arms of government can increase the awareness of knowledge management.

In addition, installation and maintenance of cloud computing enable government organizations to procure hardware to run servers update software and solve other computing issues. Likewise, Wada (2018) affirms that implementing cloud computing in government services will reduce cost of maintaining systems, save energy and expose the government to multivariate information resources as well as optimize government services. Furthermore, cloud computing provides the government with flexible and scalable storage options to efficiently store and manage large amounts of data, digital resources and preservation of materials. The challenge of physical storage space inherent in traditional government is not a problem in cloud computing because space is conserved. Hence, there is increased storage in cloud computing than personal computers, servers' e.t.c. Moreover, cloud-based management systems are used to automate various government functions, streamline operations, enhance efficiency and allow staff and citizens to provide better user experiences. Besides, cloud computing enables the government to provide remote access to resources, increase access to digital collections and services for citizens anywhere and anytime. Remarkably, Internet connection is borderless without geographical boundaries and locations to one place or country are not limited but accessible throughout the world. Thus, cloud computing provides access 24/7 to governmental information resources anytime and anywhere.

Essentially, Cloud technologies facilitate collaboration between governments and enhance sharing of resources, expertise and digital collections, thereby increasing and providing robust government services to satisfy citizens' needs. This implies that cloud computing encourages participating governments to share their resources. As a result, the government can save costs and access more resources in one place through collaboration. Furthermore, retrieval of resources in cloud computing is quicker and faster than manual government services. The software also assists citizens to retrieve desired information quickly. The collection available in electronic format can be of any media format. In a cloud computing environment the interaction between citizens and government is frequent. In cloud computing there is no defined user group: Anybody can access electronic resources depending on data subscription.

Basically, the benefits of cloud computing technology in government services include efficiency of service, reduction of cost, unlimited storage capacity, ease of access to information, file sharing etc. Similarly, Agu (2014) and Remero (2012) found that economy of resources, ability to reuse, reduction of cost and maximization of utilities are positive effects of cloud computing for government services.

How Edo State Has Benefited From E-Governance

Acknowledging that no nation can reach its full potential without embracing digital tools, the Edo State Government has equipped its staff with essential technology. Furthermore, a range of training and educational programs focused on the practical use and maintenance of these tools has been introduced. The significant improvements seen in public service due to digital innovations have encouraged the State Government to incorporate digitalization into the everyday functions of its employees. Consequently, September 1st, 2023, marks the official shift to a fully paperless governance system in Edo, highlighting the State's strong commitment to advancing digital transformation. (Osayomore, Omoruyi P. 2023).

Digital training is also refer to as information and communication technology (ICT) training, has had through impact on the present-day public service in Edo state since the commencement of the administration of Governor Godwin Onaghehase Obaseki. Under Governor Godwin O. Obaseki leadership the immersion of digital skills among the workforce has ushered in numerous enhancements within the public service. The transformation compasses the creation of a more conducive working environment, along with the modernization of office spaces, policies implementation and the adoption of malleable approaches in execution of tasks through advanced internet connectivity that spans across all departments. Osayomore, P. Omoruyi (2023) pointed some ways whereby Edo State citizens have benefited from e-governance are:

Improved Service Delivery: Citizens can access government services more efficiently and conveniently online, reducing wait times and increasing responsiveness.

Transparency and Accountability: Digital platforms enhance transparency in government operations, allowing citizens to track services and access information easily, which foster greater accountability.

Increased Participation: E-Government initiatives facilitate greater citizen engagement in governance through online feedback mechanisms, surveys, and public consultations.

Cost Savings: Digital services often reduce the need for physical visits to government offices, saving citizens' time and travel expenses.

Enhanced Accessibility: E-Government makes services more accessible to individuals in remote areas, ensuring that all citizens can benefit regardless of their location.

Empowerment through Information: With access to online resources and information, citizens are better informed about their rights and services available to them, empowering them to make informed decisions.

Streamlined Processes: The digitization of processes minimizes bureaucracy, making it easier for citizens to navigate government services and reducing the chances of corruption.

Economic Opportunities: Improved digital infrastructure can foster economic growth by creating opportunities for local businesses and attracting investment in technology and services.

Quick Response to Issues: E-Government allows for faster reporting and resolution of public concerns, enabling the government to address issues in real time.

Digital Literacy Development: Initiatives aimed at improving digital literacy help equip citizens with the skills necessary to thrive in a digital economy, promoting overall community development.

Challenges of Cloud Computing Technology For E-Government Services

Despite the awareness, utilization and adoption of cloud computing for government services, there are catalog of challenges which include limited internet infrastructure, data security and privacy when migrating to the cloud, compliance with regulations and standards relating to data handling can be complex; vendor lock-in and managing cloud costs effectively and staff training to effectively manage cloud-based systems. Ristenpart et al. (2009) and Ashima & Popli (2016) identified inadequate number of computers, unstable Internet connectivity, and insufficient electricity; inadequate awareness and Internet skills; inadequate financial resources; and shortage of trained ICT staff. Lack of supportive policy or guidelines, lack of security and ownership of intellectual property of cloud computing services as challenges that affect cloud computing. Surprisingly, Alemayehu,(2010) found that the level of awareness of government personnel on the use of cloud computing is very low. According to him, the primary reason for lack of awareness could be due to limited exposure to training on cloud computing for government workers and administrators in Edo State. Furthermore, lack of awareness may also be attributed to lack of resources and initiatives aimed at promoting and disseminating information about cloud computing in Edo State. In addition, Mate (2016) affirms that security and privacy, application migration from one cloud to other; interoperability, computing performance, reliability and availability are challenges that affect cloud computing. Miller, Jeffrey & Neidecker-Lutz, (2010) enumerated the challenges of cloud computing to include constant internet connection, slow internet connections, limited features offering, security, danger of data loss or cloud vendor filing for bankruptcy. Likewise, Shen & Tong (2010) stated that the deployment of cloud computing technology security is a challenge due to availability of different systems that may be working in a multiple environment. Additionally, proliferation of mobile and personal devices such as smartphones and tablets have increased cloud-based storage services. Besides, Drive, Dropbox or Microsoft Dropbox has also raised the issue of data privacy and confidentiality putting the user at a legal risk. Thus, the government will need to assess cloud computing technologies by considering the security challenges associated with it. Similarly, Catteddu & Hoboken (2012) identified integrity, trust, privacy, expectations, control, regulations, intellectual property management, auditing, service-metering and performance as challenges affecting cloud computing. Mohammed, Tahiru & Abdullaziz (2019) found that security of data, inconsistency and cost of internet, lack of trust of cloud service providers were among the challenges that affect cloud computing.

However, there may be limited access to information and training materials, conferences, workshops or seminars that specifically focus on cloud computing for government services. Without access to these resources, government administrators may not be aware of latest technological advancements and be ignorant of potential opportunities that would facilitate cloud computing to improved government services. Ashima & Popli (2016) stressed that cloud computing services need stable power supply to function and be sustainable.

Besides, privacy and security of data affect ease of accessibility by citizens due to risks that threaten security of sensitive data. In addition, data stored in the cloud can be vulnerable to attacks from viruses, theft, etc. There is also the risk of data loss due to system failure and improper backup (Nazir, 2013). Notably, the physical location of servers can be difficult to locate. Hence, auditing of software and security can be problematic.

Nevertheless, network connectivity and bandwidth that are directly connected to internet connectivity can lead to failure when users cannot access services provided through the internet. This implies that more bandwidth will be required by most governments to address low-speed Internet connections. There could also be a lack of compatibility between different hardware and software.

Moreover, different state governments may face challenges relating to data sovereignty and compliance with local laws due to choice of cloud providers and location of data centers. However, there will be limited control over maintenance or customization of services provided by third parties. Therefore, it becomes very difficult to access the physical location of servers. Backup, updates, restore and disaster recovery as the government depends on service providers. It also has limited flexibility for users as cloud computing is provided by third parties.

More so, costs for technological infrastructure and cloud computing service could be higher. Sahu (2015) affirms that the initial cost of cloud computing is capital intensive and very high. As a result, many publishers are forced to calculate the expected profit before adopting cloud computing technologies (economic barriers) and this may also inhibit user's access to resources. Regrettably, cloud computing providers may increase cost of their services and organizations may end up paying higher charges due to high inflation rate. As a result, governments need to consider long-term sustainability and continuity of cloud services to ensure that service providers may not discontinue services or change pricing models.

Consequently, places in areas with limited or unreliable internet access may not be able to fully access cloud services, due to inadequate provision of uninterrupted services to users. Likewise, the process of migrating existing systems and workflows to the cloud can be complex and require planning, compatibility assessment, data migration, and staff training. In addition Cloud computing can encourage digital divide, as users without proper access to the internet or devices may face barriers in accessing cloud-based services. For instance, video clips can degenerate overtime (unless they are saved in specific formats that require Video clips which can be upgraded/updated overtime to avoid loss of resources. Digital resources can be more challenging to update than a reading list.

Knowledge and integration require the government to have their own IT staff that has knowledge of cloud computing to ease dependence on service providers. Likewise, it could be more difficult to integrate equipment used in data centers than peripheral equipment such as printers, USB drives used in organizations (Dutt, 2017). Likewise, applying cloud computing to government services in Nigeria could be very poor due to inadequacy of internet infrastructure. Significantly, multiple taxation from federal, state and local government as well as weak regulation, negatively affect cloud computing adoption in the Nigerian government. Although there are numerous negative effects of cloud computing; these challenges can be mitigated through careful planning, robust security measures, evaluating providers, ensuring data compliance, and addressing access issues for all citizens.

Nevertheless, Abdulsalam & Fatima (2011) found that unsteady power supply, cost of ownership, lack of access are challenges that affect cloud computing. Interestingly, Nag & Nikam (2016) found that poor Internet connection, unreliable power supply, and poor allocation of funds to state governments are major challenges that affect use of cloud computing services by the government. In the same vein, Raed, Fash, Chang (2015) found that data security, lock-in, privacy issues, regulatory compliance, data insecurity. Vendor lock-in: switching cloud providers or negotiating favorable terms, limiting flexibility and cost optimization options affect cloud computing.

This limited utilization of cloud computing hampers the potential benefits and advancements of cloud computing on government services. Besides, multiple taxation from federal, state and local government as well as weak regulation, are challenges that affect cloud computing adoption in Nigeria government.

Although cloud computing has revolutionized government services there are still challenges that affect privacy, security, connectivity, migration, sustainability and access that must be addressed. Therefore, by proactively addressing these challenges and adopting appropriate strategies, governments can maximize the benefits of cloud computing while ensuring the scalability, accessibility, and cost-efficiency.

Possible Solution To Challenges of E-Government Services

Infrastructure Development, Enhancing infrastructure is essential; this includes investing in strong technological systems to facilitate E-Government services and implementing digital literacy programs to empower both citizens and government staff.

Inclusive Design: Designing E-Government services with accessibility in mind to cater to diverse user needs.

Data Management: Implementing effective and efficient data management practices to safeguard information integrity.

Collaboration and Partnerships. Encourage partnerships among government, the private sector, civil society, and academic institutions to promote innovation in E-Government.

Continuous Improvement: continuous improving on E-Government processes to enhance efficiency and user satisfaction.

Green IT: Adopting environmentally sustainable practices in the deployment of E-Government solutions.

Citizen Engagement: Encouraging citizen participation in the co-creation of E-Government services.

Capacity Building: Providing training and development opportunities to enhance the skills of government personnel.

Monitoring and Evaluation: Establishing mechanisms for monitoring and evaluating the impact of E-Government initiatives.

Legal and Regulatory Framework: Establishing a robust legal and regulatory framework to govern E-Government operations.

Private Sector Involvement: Utilizing the expertise and resources of the private sector to enhance the implementation of E-Government initiatives.

Block-Chain Use of Cloud Computing In Transforming E-Government

Block chain are reforming e-government services with the use of cloud computing this offers a partnership for transforming e-government services. Block chain technology with the use of cloud computing transforms e-government services. This function is relevant to E-government system on data integrity and trust. (Ahmad, Lutfiani, Ahmad, Rahardja, & Aini, 2021). The fact that blocks chain technology is decentralized, it lowers the risks of data interfering and unauthorized access. It create an incorruptible records, modification of data is impossible which guarantee high level of privacy. It therefore, provides outstanding level of data security, thus promoting trust between government institutions and its citizens, such as citizens are assured of the validity and accuracy of public records. (Ølnes & Jansen, 2017). The middlemen interference is reduced with the use of block chain technologies the usually office bureaucracy and cost of governance is reduced and reduces (Elisa, Yangl, Chao, F., & Cao,, 2023). The automating governmental processes, such as payment of licenses, utility bills and tax payments is facilitated at convenient with the use of block chain. It has come to reduce delay in service delivering and ensures transparency and accountability through the availability of its transparent ledger, which allows real-time tracking of activities.

However this application of block chain technology is not without challenges, Merging with block chain technology requires meaningful changes in existing lawful and administrative structures. According to Elisa, Yang,, Li,, Chao,, & Naik, (2020) in this regard, state that new policies for data privacy, interoperability with the standing systems, and legal undertakings for the validity of block-chain based transactions have to be developed by the governments. Mustafa, Rafiq, Jhamat, & Arshad, (2024) state that in scalability of the relevant block-chain there is a direct association which has been found between a high volume of transactions and increased time and resource use in increasing the number of transactions, which could, in turn, place certain limitations on the use of block-chain in cases of high-volume public service.

The important of block chain in e-government services cannot be over emphases. According to --- the following are the benefit of block chain in e-government services:

Enhanced Security: Block-chain's decentralized nature and cryptographic security make it ideal for protecting sensitive citizen data and preventing unauthorized access.

Transparency and Trust: Transactions recorded on a block-chain are immutable and transparent, allowing citizens to track government activities, thus enhancing trust in public institutions.

Streamlined Identity Verification: Block-chain can facilitate secure digital identities, enabling citizens to authenticate their identities safely and easily across various government services.

Smart Contracts for Efficiency: Automated smart contracts can streamline processes like procurement and grant disbursement, reducing administrative overhead and speeding up service delivery.

Immutable Records: All transactions and interactions can be securely logged on a block-chain, providing a clear and auditable history that can be crucial for compliance and accountability.

Artificial Intelligence (AI) Use of Cloud Computing In Transforming E-Government

Artificial intelligence and cloud computing technology can drive significant improvements in government operations and policies. These two technologies have helped to reshape industries and government parastatals are not left out as well. AI is the application of computer programmed to performed human tasks based on it programmed. Government has come to accept AI block-chain that can improve governance, with improve government services. AI can be defined as the ability of a computer to imitate the intelligence of human behavior while improving its own performance. AI is not only robotics, rather an intelligent behavior of an autonomous machine that describes the brain of the machine and not its body; it can drive a car, play a game, and perform diverse sophisticated jobs. AI is a field that falls at the intersections of several other domains, including Machine Learning, Deep Learning, Natural Languages Processing, Context Awareness, Data Security and Privacy

The Benefits of AI in Cloud Computing for E-Government

As governments worldwide increasingly adopt digital solutions to improve public services, the integration of artificial intelligence (AI) with cloud computing has emerged as a transformative force in e-government. This synergy not only enhances service delivery but also increases efficiency, reduces costs, and fosters better engagement with citizens. According to Didier Ongena (2024) the key benefits of AI in cloud computing for e-government initiatives are:

Enhanced Data Management

One of the foremost advantages of AI in cloud computing is its ability to manage vast amounts of data effectively. Governments generate and collect enormous datasets from various sources, including social services, public health, and transportation. AI algorithms can analyze this data in real-time, helping governments to derive actionable insights, identify trends, and make informed decisions. Cloud computing facilitates the storage and processing of this data at scale, allowing for more efficient governance.

Improved Service Delivery

AI-powered Chabot's and virtual assistants are increasingly being deployed in e-government platforms to provide citizens with instant responses to their inquiries. By integrating these AI tools with cloud computing, governments can ensure that services are available 24/7, significantly improving accessibility. Moreover, AI can personalize services based on individual user data, leading to a more tailored citizen experience.

Cost Efficiency

Cloud computing allows governments to reduce their IT infrastructure costs by leveraging pay-as-you-go models. Coupled with AI, which can automate routine tasks and processes, this leads to significant savings. For example, AI can streamline administrative tasks, freeing up human resources to focus on more complex issues. This combination not only lowers operational costs but also enhances the overall efficiency of government operations.

Enhanced Security and Compliance

Data security is paramount in e-government, given the sensitive nature of the information involved. AI can bolster security measures by identifying potential threats and anomalies in real time. Cloud computing platforms often come equipped with advanced security protocols and compliance tools, ensuring that government data remains secure and adheres to regulatory standards. This dual approach significantly mitigates risks associated with data breaches and cyber threats.

Better Citizen Engagement

AI-driven analytics tools can help governments understand citizen needs and preferences by analyzing public feedback, social media interactions, and survey responses. This insight allows governments to tailor their services and communication strategies effectively. Additionally, cloud-based platforms enable real-time feedback mechanisms, fostering a more participatory approach to governance.

Streamlined Decision-Making

AI can assist government officials in making quicker, data-driven decisions. By analyzing historical data and predicting future trends, AI tools can provide insights that inform policy-making and resource allocation. Cloud computing enhances this capability by enabling access to data and analytical tools from anywhere, facilitating collaboration among different government departments and stakeholders.

CHALLENGES AND SOLUTIONS IN AI AND BLOCK-CHAIN FOR E-GOVERNMENT SERVICES

In exploring the benefits of AI implementation in government services, there is a need to acknowledge and address the challenges of this transformative technological shift. While AI holds the potential to act as a catalyst for development, especially in nations with low per capital incomes, certain challenges loom large (Khalifa Alhosani & Saadat M. Alhashmi 2024). Understanding and effectively managing these challenges becomes paramount for ensuring the successful integration of AI into public sector operations. One significant challenge lies in the need for capacity-building. While AI can revolutionize various facets of public service delivery, there is a shortage of field experts who can evaluate outcomes. This scarcity complicates the implementation process, making it imperative for public organizations to foster a more profound understanding of AI in terms of its technical aspects and broader implications (Carlsson B, Jacobsson S, Holmén M, Rickne 2022). Addressing the challenges of security, privacy, and the digital divide in AI and block-chain for e-government services is crucial for fostering trust and ensuring equitable access. By implementing robust security measures, enhancing privacy protections, and promoting digital inclusion, governments can create more effective and accessible digital services. As these technologies continue to evolve, proactive engagement with these challenges will be essential for building a fair and secure digital future for all citizens.

Security Challenges

Data Breaches: AI systems can be vulnerable to hacking, leading to unauthorized access to sensitive information.

Cyber-attacks on Block chain: While block chain is inherently secure, it is not immune to attacks such as 51% attacks, smart contract vulnerabilities, and phishing.

Insider Threats: Employees with access to sensitive systems may inadvertently or maliciously compromise security.

Solutions

Robust Cyber security Protocols: Implement comprehensive security frameworks that include encryption, intrusion detection systems, and regular security audits.

Smart Contract Audits: Regularly review and audit smart contracts for vulnerabilities before deployment to mitigate risks.

Access Controls: Implement strict role-based access controls (RBAC) to limit access to sensitive information and systems based on user roles.

Privacy Challenges

Data Usage Transparency: Citizens may be unaware of how their data is collected, used, and stored, leading to privacy concerns.

Regulatory Compliance: Ensuring compliance with various data protection regulations (e.g., GDPR, HIPAA) can be complex.

Data Anonymity: While block-chain provides transparency, it can inadvertently expose user identities if not properly anonymized.

Solutions

Clear Data Policies: Develop transparent data usage policies that inform citizens about data collection, processing, and storage practices.

Privacy-By-Design Principles: Incorporate privacy features into the design of AI and block-chain systems; ensuring data protection is a foundational element.

Anonymization Techniques: Use advanced cryptographic techniques (e.g., zero-knowledge proofs) to maintain user anonymity while ensuring data integrity.

Digital Divide Challenges

Access to Technology: Not all citizens have equal access to the internet or digital devices, which can hinder participation in e-government services.

Digital Literacy: Variations in digital literacy can create disparities in how effectively citizens engage with e-government platforms.

Socioeconomic Barriers: Individuals from lower socioeconomic backgrounds may face challenges in accessing and utilizing digital services.

Solutions

Infrastructure Investment: Governments should invest in expanding internet access and providing affordable technology to underserved communities.

Digital Literacy Programs: Implement training programs to improve digital literacy, ensuring citizens can effectively use e-government services.

User-Friendly Interfaces: Design e-government platforms with intuitive interfaces that accommodate users of varying technological skill levels, including support in multiple languages.

Interoperability Issues

E-government services often involve multiple systems and agencies. The lack of interoperability between existing systems and new AI and block-chain solutions can hinder effective implementation and data sharing.

Solution:

Develop standardized protocols and frameworks that facilitate interoperability among different platforms. Encourage collaboration between various government entities and technology providers to create unified systems that can seamlessly share data.

Resistance to Change

Implementing AI and block-chain may face resistance from government employees and citizens who are accustomed to traditional processes. Concerns about job displacement and a lack of understanding of new technologies can create barriers to acceptance.

Solution: Invest in training and education programs to equip employees with the necessary skills to work with AI and block-chain. Public awareness campaigns can also help inform citizens about the benefits of these technologies, fostering a culture of innovation and acceptance.

Regulatory and Legal Challenges

The rapid evolution of AI and block chain technologies often outpaces existing regulations. Governments may struggle to create appropriate legal frameworks to govern their use, leading to uncertainty.

Solution:

Governments should engage with stakeholders, including legal experts, technologists, and the public, to develop comprehensive regulatory frameworks that address the unique challenges posed by these technologies. Adaptive legislation that can evolve with technological advancements will be crucial.

Ethical Considerations

The use of AI in decision-making processes raises ethical concerns, particularly regarding bias and accountability. Block-chain, while transparent, may not address ethical issues related to data input and usage.

Solution: Establish ethical guidelines for AI development and usage within government services. Implement mechanisms for accountability, ensuring that decision-making processes are transparent and subject to oversight. Regularly review AI algorithms to identify and mitigate biases.

Case Studies

The extent to which various governments are applying AI in improving their service delivery can be seen in a number of case studies. Countries around the world are adopting AI solutions for their public services. Governments are investing heavily in AI to develop more innovative and better public services for the residents. Some of the applications of AI in the public sector to improve services include the following:

AI implementation in New South Wales (NSW) Revenue Department

Revenue NSW is utilizing artificial intelligence to identify and support disadvantaged customers who cannot pay their penalties. The programme has been in operation since 2018, diverts vulnerable clients from enforcement action, and gives other settlement choices. This means fewer needy individuals will be compelled to pay fines they cannot afford. It also improves the overall efficiency of the garnishee procedure. With many 46,000 consumers classified as 'vulnerable,' the community advantages of an efficient AI solution are significant (NSW), Previously, Revenue NSW could only learn that a customer was vulnerable after debt collection action was taken. This programme aids in predicting vulnerability and providing alternative resolution choices. Various indicators are assessed to determine susceptibility, such as how frequently they contact Revenue NSW, the number of major penalties they have, their age and expected socio-economic position, and the weekly payment amount if their debt is to be paid via an installment plan.

This forecast is intended to supplement, not replace, human decision-making. Revenue NSW employees can assess the program's forecasts and connect identified clients to more appropriate resolution channels that provide focused assistance. This may result in sanctions being lifted, enforcement being halted, repayment plans being established, or a labor and Development Order being implemented to allow customers to decrease their punishment by participating in unpaid labor, training, or therapy.

National Health Services (NHS) UK

Artificial intelligence has been used to improve healthcare significantly in various ways, including earlier disease detection and prevention and the support of clinical decision-making. With the help of AI, a patient's health may be tracked in real-time. We may warn professionals of possible threats by transmitting information about a patient's weight, height, blood sugar, stress levels, heart rate, etc., to artificial intelligence healthcare systems. Governments may use AI to deliver high-quality healthcare to their citizens. For instance, AI affected how the COVID-19 pandemic virus was identified and handled (Khalifa Alhosani & Saadat M. Alhashmi 2024). They further illustrate that the UK's National Health Service (NHS) has begun a data collection initiative for people with chronic obstructive pulmonary disease (COPD). The NHS created the National COVID-19 Chest Imaging Collection (NCCID) via various partnerships; it is an open-source collection of chest X-rays from COVID-19 patients throughout the UK. The NHS has also developed an AI tool that can diagnose heart disease in only 20 s, even while the patient is still inside an MRI scanner. A physician would need at least 13 min to examine the MRI scans of a patient personally.

Annotation of Buildings by the French Government

The French consulting firm Capgemini collaborated with Google, the search engine giant, to develop AI technology capable of analyzing pictures and locating previously unidentified buildings. The project uncovered twenty thousand previously unknown ponds throughout France. Because of this discovery, the French government received an additional €10 million in tax revenue. The government says it will use the scheme to uncover gazebos and patios that have not been registered. US federal departments and insurance companies utilize an analogous AI method to monitor physical assets for signs of tampering. According to Khalifa Alhosani & Saadat M. Alhashmi (2024). The artificial intelligence programme, Near Map, developed by an Australian company, can identify and partition geographic objects in aerial photos. More than 380,000 square kilometers of imagery from the United States and Australia were used to teach the Near Map AI. In conclusion, thanks to AI, governments can better monitor infrastructure for tax evasion and illicit property transfers.

Smarter Policy-Making by Belgium

Government agencies and politicians can leverage AI as a powerful tool for intelligent and public-interest policy-making. The utilization of AI technologies enables policymakers to conduct in-depth analyses of publicly accessible data, shedding light on novel issues relevant to both their constituents and geographic locations. According to Fabregue et al. (2021), the application of analytical information in policy-making yields two significant benefits: it expedites the process of polling and identifying the root causes of problems, leading to improved policy outcomes, and it enhances awareness of societal shifts, allowing for more timely policy adjustments. An illustrative example is the Belgian authorities' use of an AI crowdsourcing tool during the 2019 climate change rallies. Developed by the Belgian tech company Citizen Lab, this tool facilitated a better understanding of protesters' demands through public input. Consequently, Belgium prioritized 15 climate action initiatives based on the insights gained from the AI-driven analysis of public sentiment and concerns (Fabrègue B, Portal LJ, Cockshaw C.2023).

Estonia:

Digital Identity: Estonia is a pioneer in digital identity solutions, offering citizens a secure and verifiable e-ID that enables access to over 6,000 public services. The e-ID uses strong encryption and two-factor authentication, ensuring secure interactions.

Block-chain for Data Integrity: Estonia employs block-chain technology to secure its e-government systems. Each transaction is recorded on a block-chain, ensuring transparency and integrity in data management.

Singapore:

SingPass: Singapore's SingPass system is an integrated digital identity platform that allows citizens to access government services securely. It utilizes multi-factor authentication to enhance security.

Smart Nation Initiative: Singapore's initiative leverages technology, including block-chain, for secure transactions and data integrity across various services, fostering a transparent and efficient government.

Emerging Trends in Cloud Technologies for Government Services

Various emerging trends has emerged since the inception of technological advancement which has reshape how government interact and operate with its citizens. Relying on the power on artificial intelligence and cloud computing embracing mobile-first strategies and open data initiatives, these cutting-edge trends are sure to drive efficiency, and engagement of citizens. Below are the most promising digital trends to revolutionized government services.

Artificial Intelligence and Automation: AI and automation are revolutionizing digital government services by enhancing efficiency and decision-making. In public services, AI applications range from Chabot that provide instant customer support to predictive analytics for resources allocation and emergency response. For instance, AI-powered systems in social services can access eligibility for benefits and detect fraudulent claims, streamlining administrative tasks and ensuring accurate for benefits and detect fraudulent claims, streamlining administrative tasks and ensuring accurate resources distribution. In law enforcement, predictive policing algorithms analyze data to identify potential crime hotspots. Allowing for proactive measure to maintain public safety.

Block-chain Technology: this is a pivotal trend in digital government services, offering significant transparency and security benefits. By providing a decentralized and immutable ledger, block-chain ensures that government transactions are transparent and reducing the risk of fraud. This technology allows citizens to verify records independently.

Internet of Things (IOT): This is a transformative trend in Digital government services, playing a crucial role in developing smart cities and connected infrastructure. IoT enables the integration of various devices and sensors to collect and analyzed data in real time, enhancing and efficiency and responsiveness of public services. In smart cities, IoT applications include smart traffic management solutions that optimize collection routes and reduce costs. The impact of Internet of things enables proactive maintenance of infrastructure also reduces operational cost and improvement of citizens life.

Edge Computing

Edge computing involves processing data closer to the source (e.g., IoT devices) rather than relying solely on centralized cloud servers. This reduces latency and bandwidth usage. The implication for government services are:

Real-Time Data Processing: Edge computing enables real-time analytics for applications such as traffic management, public safety, and environmental monitoring, improving responsiveness and efficiency.

Enhanced Security: By processing sensitive data locally, edge computing can minimize exposure to potential breaches during data transmission, enhancing security for citizen data.

Support for IoT Initiatives: Governments can deploy IoT devices (like smart meters and surveillance cameras) that leverage edge computing for efficient data processing and immediate action.

5G Technology

5G is the fifth generation of wireless technology, offering significantly higher speeds, lower latency, and greater connectivity compared to previous generations. The implication for government services are:

Improved Connectivity: 5G allows for seamless connectivity for smart city initiatives, enhancing communication between devices and services, thus facilitating better urban management.

Enhanced Public Services: Faster data transmission can improve services like telemedicine, remote education, and emergency response systems, ensuring timely access to crucial resources.

Innovative Applications: The low latency and high capacity of 5G can support advanced technologies such as augmented reality (AR) for training public service workers and virtual consultations for citizens.

Server less Architectures

Server less computing allows developers to build and run applications without managing server infrastructure. Resources are automatically allocated based on demand. The implication for government services are:

Cost Efficiency: Governments can reduce costs by paying only for the resources they use, allowing for more efficient allocation of budgets to critical services.

Scalability: Server-less architectures automatically scale with demand, enabling government services to handle varying workloads, especially during peak times (e.g., tax season).

Faster Development Cycles: Developers can focus on coding rather than infrastructure management, leading to faster deployment of new applications and services that better meet citizen needs.

CONCLUSION

Cloud computing is actually working to help break down the barriers of many governments to enter a new phase of collaboration and partnering, sharing services, and pooling of resources. It offers an effective way to share information between citizens, reducing efforts in providing services, budget management and cost effectiveness. Developing e-government services and implementing it comes with a number of challenges that need to be addressed before they are implemented. To ensure cloud computing grants quick access to e-government services, there is a need for a deep understanding of all components of e-government in the development system process. Addressing the challenges of security, privacy, and the digital divide in AI and block-chain for e-government services is crucial for fostering, trust and ensuring equitable access. By implementing robust security measures, enhancing privacy protections, and promoting digital inclusion, governments can create more effective and accessible digital services. As these technologies continue to evolve, proactive engagement with these challenges will be essential for building a fair and secure digital future for all citizens. This paper gives insight on need to believe in digital infrastructure and cultural differences in the design and implementation of e-Government using cloud computing technology, Artificial Intelligence, and Blockchain to achieve optimal equality of access to government services.

APPENDIX I

Block-Chain Use of Cloud Computing In Transforming E-Government

Block chain are reforming e-government services with the use of cloud computing this offers a partnership for transforming e-government services. Block chain technology with the use of cloud computing transforms e-government services. This function is relevant to E-government system on data integrity and trust. (Ahmad, Lutfiani, Ahmad, Rahardja, & Aini, 2021). The fact that blocks chain technology is decentralized, it lowers the risks of data interfering and unauthorized access. It create an incorruptible records, modification of data is impossible which guarantee high level of privacy. It therefore, provides outstanding level of data security, thus promoting trust between government institutions and its citizens, such as citizens are assured of the validity and accuracy of public records. (Ølnes & Jansen, 2017). The middlemen interference is reduced with the use of block chain technologies the usually office bureaucracy and cost of governance is reduced and reduces (Elisa, Yangl, Chao, F., & Cao,, 2023). The automating governmental processes, such as payment of licenses, utility bills and tax payments is facilitated at convenient with the use of block chain. It has come to reduce delay in service delivering and ensures transparency and accountability through the availability of its transparent ledger, which allows real-time tracking of activities.

However this application of block chain technology is not without challenges, Merging with block chain technology requires meaningful changes in existing lawful and administrative structures. According to Elisa, Yang,, Li,, Chao,, & Naik, (2020) in this regard, state that new policies for data privacy, interoperability with the standing systems, and legal undertakings for the validity of block-chain based transactions have to be developed by the governments. Mustafa, Rafiq, Jhamat, & Arshad, (2024) state that in scalability of the relevant block-chain there is a direct association which has been found between a high volume of transactions and increased time and resource use in increasing the number of transactions, which could, in turn, place certain limitations on the use of block-chain in cases of high-volume public service.

The important of block chain in e-government services cannot be over emphases. According to --- the following are the benefit of block chain in e-government services:

Enhanced Security: Blockchain's decentralized nature and cryptographic security make it ideal for protecting sensitive citizen data and preventing unauthorized access.

Transparency and Trust: Transactions recorded on a blockchain are immutable and transparent, allowing citizens to track government activities, thus enhancing trust in public institutions.

Streamlined Identity Verification: Blockchain can facilitate secure digital identities, enabling citizens to authenticate their identities safely and easily across various government services.

Smart Contracts for Efficiency: Automated smart contracts can streamline processes like procurement and grant disbursement, reducing administrative overhead and speeding up service delivery.

Immutable Records: All transactions and interactions can be securely logged on a blockchain, providing a clear and auditable history that can be crucial for compliance and accountability.

Artificial Intelligence (AI) Use of Cloud Computing In Transforming E-Government

Artificial intelligence and cloud computing technology can drive significant improvements in government operations and policies. These two technologies have helped to reshape industries and government parastatals are not left out as well. AI is the application of computer programmed to performed human tasks based on it programmed. Government has come to accept AI block-chain that can improve governance, with improve government services. AI can be defined as the ability of a computer to imitate the intelligence of human behavior while improving its own performance. AI is not only robotics, rather an intelligent behavior of an autonomous machine that describes the brain of the machine and not its body; it can drive a car, play a game, and perform diverse sophisticated jobs. AI is a field that falls at the intersections of several other domains, including Machine Learning, Deep Learning, Natural Languages Processing, Context Awareness, Data Security and Privacy

The Benefits of AI in Cloud Computing for E-Government

As governments worldwide increasingly adopt digital solutions to improve public services, the integration of artificial intelligence (AI) with cloud computing has emerged as a transformative force in e-government. This synergy not only enhances service delivery but also increases efficiency, reduces costs, and fosters better engagement with citizens. According to Didier Ongena (2024) the key benefits of AI in cloud computing for e-government initiatives are:

Enhanced Data Management

One of the foremost advantages of AI in cloud computing is its ability to manage vast amounts of data effectively. Governments generate and collect enormous datasets from various sources, including social services, public health, and transportation. AI algorithms can analyze this data in real-time, helping governments to derive actionable insights, identify trends, and make informed decisions. Cloud computing facilitates the storage and processing of this data at scale, allowing for more efficient governance.

Improved Service Delivery

AI-powered Chabot's and virtual assistants are increasingly being deployed in e-government platforms to provide citizens with instant responses to their inquiries. By integrating these AI tools with cloud computing, governments can ensure that services are available 24/7, significantly improving accessibility. Moreover, AI can personalize services based on individual user data, leading to a more tailored citizen experience.

Cost Efficiency

Cloud computing allows governments to reduce their IT infrastructure costs by leveraging pay-as-you-go models. Coupled with AI, which can automate routine tasks and processes, this leads to significant savings. For example, AI can streamline administrative tasks, freeing up human resources to focus on more complex issues. This combination not only lowers operational costs but also enhances the overall efficiency of government operations.

Enhanced Security and Compliance

Data security is paramount in e-government, given the sensitive nature of the information involved. AI can bolster security measures by identifying potential threats and anomalies in real time. Cloud computing platforms often come equipped with advanced security protocols and compliance tools, ensuring that government data remains secure and adheres to regulatory standards. This dual approach significantly mitigates risks associated with data breaches and cyber threats.

Better Citizen Engagement

AI-driven analytics tools can help governments understand citizen needs and preferences by analyzing public feedback, social media interactions, and survey responses. This insight allows governments to tailor their services and communication strategies effectively. Additionally, cloud-based platforms enable real-time feedback mechanisms, fostering a more participatory approach to governance.

Streamlined Decision-Making

AI can assist government officials in making quicker, data-driven decisions. By analyzing historical data and predicting future trends, AI tools can provide insights that inform policy-making and resource allocation. Cloud computing enhances this capability by enabling access to data and analytical tools from anywhere, facilitating collaboration among different government departments and stakeholders.

Challenges and Solutions in AI and Blockchain for E-Government Services

In exploring the benefits of AI implementation in government services, there is a need to acknowledge and address the challenges of this transformative technological shift. While AI holds the potential to act as a catalyst for development, especially in nations with low per capital incomes, certain challenges loom large (Khalifa Alhosani & Saadat M. Alhashmi 2024). Understanding and effectively managing these challenges becomes paramount for ensuring the successful integration of AI into public sector operations. One significant challenge lies in the need for capacity-building. While AI can revolutionize various facets of public service delivery, there is a shortage of field experts who can evaluate outcomes. This scarcity complicates the implementation process, making it imperative for public organizations to foster a more profound understanding of AI in terms of its technical aspects and broader implications (Carlsson B, Jacobsson S, Holmén M, Rickne 2022). Addressing the challenges of security, privacy, and the digital divide in AI and blockchain for e-government services is crucial for fostering trust and ensuring equitable access. By implementing robust security measures, enhancing privacy protections, and promoting digital inclusion, governments can create more effective and accessible digital services. As these technologies continue to evolve, proactive engagement with these challenges will be essential for building a fair and secure digital future for all citizens.

Security Challenges

Data Breaches: AI systems can be vulnerable to hacking, leading to unauthorized access to sensitive information.

Cyber-attacks on Block chain: While block chain is inherently secure, it is not immune to attacks such as 51% attacks, smart contract vulnerabilities, and phishing.

Insider Threats: Employees with access to sensitive systems may inadvertently or maliciously compromise security.

Solutions

Robust Cyber security Protocols: Implement comprehensive security frameworks that include encryption, intrusion detection systems, and regular security audits.

Smart Contract Audits: Regularly review and audit smart contracts for vulnerabilities before deployment to mitigate risks.

Access Controls: Implement strict role-based access controls (RBAC) to limit access to sensitive information and systems based on user roles.

Privacy Challenges

Data Usage Transparency: Citizens may be unaware of how their data is collected, used, and stored, leading to privacy concerns.

Regulatory Compliance: Ensuring compliance with various data protection regulations (e.g., GDPR, HIPAA) can be complex.

Data Anonymity: While blockchain provides transparency, it can inadvertently expose user identities if not properly anonymized.

Solutions

Clear Data Policies: Develop transparent data usage policies that inform citizens about data collection, processing, and storage practices.

Privacy-By-Design Principles: Incorporate privacy features into the design of AI and blockchain systems; ensuring data protection is a foundational element.

Anonymization Techniques: Use advanced cryptographic techniques (e.g., zero-knowledge proofs) to maintain user anonymity while ensuring data integrity.

Digital Divide Challenges

Access to Technology: Not all citizens have equal access to the internet or digital devices, which can hinder participation in e-government services.

Digital Literacy: Variations in digital literacy can create disparities in how effectively citizens engage with e-government platforms.

Socioeconomic Barriers: Individuals from lower socioeconomic backgrounds may face challenges in accessing and utilizing digital services.

Solutions

Infrastructure Investment: Governments should invest in expanding internet access and providing affordable technology to underserved communities.

Digital Literacy Programs: Implement training programs to improve digital literacy, ensuring citizens can effectively use e-government services.

User-Friendly Interfaces: Design e-government platforms with intuitive interfaces that accommodate users of varying technological skill levels, including support in multiple languages.

Interoperability Issues

E-government services often involve multiple systems and agencies. The lack of interoperability between existing systems and new AI and blockchain solutions can hinder effective implementation and data sharing.

Solution:

Develop standardized protocols and frameworks that facilitate interoperability among different platforms. Encourage collaboration between various government entities and technology providers to create unified systems that can seamlessly share data.

Resistance to Change

Implementing AI and blockchain may face resistance from government employees and citizens who are accustomed to traditional processes. Concerns about job displacement and a lack of understanding of new technologies can create barriers to acceptance.

Solution: Invest in training and education programs to equip employees with the necessary skills to work with AI and blockchain. Public awareness campaigns can also help inform citizens about the benefits of these technologies, fostering a culture of innovation and acceptance.

Regulatory and Legal Challenges

The rapid evolution of AI and block chain technologies often outpaces existing regulations. Governments may struggle to create appropriate legal frameworks to govern their use, leading to uncertainty.

Solution:

Governments should engage with stakeholders, including legal experts, technologists, and the public, to develop comprehensive regulatory frameworks that address the unique challenges posed by these technologies. Adaptive legislation that can evolve with technological advancements will be crucial.

Ethical Considerations

The use of AI in decision-making processes raises ethical concerns, particularly regarding bias and accountability. Blockchain, while transparent, may not address ethical issues related to data input and usage.

Solution: Establish ethical guidelines for AI development and usage within government services. Implement mechanisms for accountability, ensuring that decision-making processes are transparent and subject to oversight. Regularly review AI algorithms to identify and mitigate biases.

Case studies

The extent to which various governments are applying AI in improving their service delivery can be seen in a number of case studies. Countries around the world are adopting AI solutions for their public services. Governments are investing heavily in AI to develop more innovative and better public services for the residents. Some of the applications of AI in the public sector to improve services include the following:

AI implementation in New South Wales (NSW) revenue department

Revenue NSW is utilizing artificial intelligence to identify and support disadvantaged customers who cannot pay their penalties. The programme has been in operation since 2018, diverts vulnerable clients from enforcement action, and gives other settlement choices. This means fewer needy individuals will be compelled to pay fines they cannot afford. It also improves the overall efficiency of the garnishee procedure. With many 46,000 consumers classified as 'vulnerable,' the community advantages of an efficient AI solution are significant (NSW), Previously, Revenue NSW could only learn that a customer was vulnerable after debt collection action was taken. This programme aids in predicting vulnerability and providing alternative resolution choices. Various indicators are assessed to determine susceptibility, such as how frequently they contact Revenue NSW, the number of major penalties they have, their age and expected socio-economic position, and the weekly payment amount if their debt is to be paid via an installment plan.

This forecast is intended to supplement, not replace, human decision-making. Revenue NSW employees can assess the program's forecasts and connect identified clients to more appropriate resolution channels that provide focused assistance. This may result in sanctions being lifted, enforcement being halted, repayment plans being established, or a labor and Development Order being implemented to allow customers to decrease their punishment by participating in unpaid labor, training, or therapy.

National health services (NHS) UK

Artificial intelligence has been used to improve healthcare significantly in various ways, including earlier disease detection and prevention and the support of clinical decision-making. With the help of AI, a patient's health may be tracked in real-time. We may warn professionals of possible threats by transmitting information about a patient's weight, height, blood sugar, stress levels, heart rate, etc., to artificial intelligence healthcare systems. Governments may use AI to deliver high-quality healthcare to their citizens. For instance, AI affected how the COVID-19 pandemic virus was identified and handled (Khalifa Alhosani & Saadat M. Alhashmi 2024). They further illustrate that the UK's National Health Service (NHS) has begun a data collection initiative for people with chronic obstructive pulmonary disease (COPD). The NHS created the National COVID-19 Chest Imaging Collection (NCCID) via various partnerships; it is an open-source collection of chest X-rays from COVID-19 patients throughout the UK. The NHS has also developed an AI tool that can diagnose heart disease in only 20 s, even while the patient is still inside an MRI scanner. A physician would need at least 13 min to examine the MRI scans of a patient personally.

Annotation of buildings by the French Government

The French consulting firm Capgemini collaborated with Google, the search engine giant, to develop AI technology capable of analyzing pictures and locating previously unidentified buildings. The project uncovered twenty thousand previously unknown ponds throughout France. Because of this discovery, the French government received an additional €10 million in tax revenue. The government says it will use the scheme to uncover gazebos and patios that have not been registered. US federal departments and insurance companies utilize an analogous AI method to monitor physical assets for signs of tampering. According to Khalifa Alhosani & Saadat M. Alhashmi (2024). The artificial intelligence programme, Near Map, developed by an Australian company, can identify and partition geographic objects in aerial photos. More than 380,000 square kilometers of imagery from the United States and Australia were used to teach the Near Map AI. In conclusion, thanks to AI, governments can better monitor infrastructure for tax evasion and illicit property transfers.

Smarter policy-making by Belgium

Government agencies and politicians can leverage AI as a powerful tool for intelligent and public-interest policy-making. The utilization of AI technologies enables policymakers to conduct in-depth analyses of publicly accessible data, shedding light on novel issues relevant to both their constituents and geographic locations. According to Fabregue et al. (2021), the application of analytical information in policy-making yields two significant benefits: it expedites the process of polling and identifying the root causes of problems, leading to improved policy outcomes, and it enhances awareness of societal shifts, allowing for more timely policy adjustments. An illustrative example is the Belgian authorities' use of an AI crowdsourcing tool during the 2019 climate change rallies. Developed by the Belgian tech company Citizen Lab, this tool facilitated a better understanding of protesters' demands through public input. Consequently, Belgium prioritized 15 climate action initiatives based on the insights gained from the AI-driven analysis of public sentiment and concerns (Fabrègue B, Portal LJ, Cockshaw C.2023).

Estonia:

Digital Identity: Estonia is a pioneer in digital identity solutions, offering citizens a secure and verifiable e-ID that enables access to over 6,000 public services. The e-ID uses strong encryption and two-factor authentication, ensuring secure interactions.

Blockchain for Data Integrity: Estonia employs blockchain technology to secure its e-government systems. Each transaction is recorded on a blockchain, ensuring transparency and integrity in data management.

Singapore:

SingPass: Singapore's SingPass system is an integrated digital identity platform that allows citizens to access government services securely. It utilizes multi-factor authentication to enhance security.

Smart Nation Initiative: Singapore's initiative leverages technology, including blockchain, for secure transactions and data integrity across various services, fostering a transparent and efficient government.

Emerging Trends in Cloud Technologies for Government Services

As technology advances, various emerging trends reshape how governments operate and interact with citizens. From leveraging the power of cloud computing and artificial intelligence to embracing mobile-first strategies and open data initiatives, these cutting-edge trends are poised to drive efficiency, transparency, and citizen engagement to new heights. Below are the most promising digital trends to revolutionize government services.

Artificial Intelligence and Automation

AI and automation are revolutionizing digital government services by enhancing efficiency and decision-making. In public services, AI applications range from chatbots that provide instant customer support to predictive analytics for resource allocation and emergency response. For instance, AI-powered systems in social services can assess eligibility for benefits and detect fraudulent claims, streamlining administrative tasks and ensuring accurate resource distribution. In law enforcement, predictive policing algorithms analyze data to identify potential crime hotspots, allowing for proactive measures to maintain public safety.

Furthermore, AI-driven automation in government services, such as processing tax returns and managing public records, significantly reduces processing times and human error, leading to more efficient service delivery. These advancements demonstrate the transformative potential of AI in enhancing government efficiency.

Blockchain Technology

Blockchain technology is a pivotal trend in digital government services, offering significant transparency and security benefits. By providing a decentralized and immutable ledger, blockchain ensures that government transactions are transparent and tamper-proof, reducing the risk of fraud and corruption. This technology enhances trust in public administration by allowing citizens to verify records' authenticity independently.

A notable case study is Estonia's e-Residency program, which utilizes blockchain to secure digital identities and facilitate cross-border business operations, ensuring data integrity and security.

Internet of Things (IoT)

The Internet of Things (IoT) is a transformative trend in digital government services, playing a crucial role in developing smart cities and connected infrastructure. IoT enables the integration of various devices and sensors to collect and analyze data in real time, enhancing the efficiency and responsiveness of public services. In smart cities, IoT applications include smart traffic management systems that reduce congestion, energy-efficient smart grids, and intelligent waste management solutions that optimize collection routes and reduce costs.

For example, Barcelona has implemented IoT-based solutions for street lighting, waste management, and parking, significantly improving urban efficiency and sustainability. The impact of IoT on public services is profound, as it enables proactive maintenance of infrastructure, reduces operational costs, and improves the quality of life for citizens by providing more responsive and data-driven services.

Edge Computing

Edge computing involves processing data closer to the source (e.g., IoT devices) rather than relying solely on centralized cloud servers. This reduces latency and bandwidth usage. The implication for government services are:

Real-Time Data Processing: Edge computing enables real-time analytics for applications such as traffic management, public safety, and environmental monitoring, improving responsiveness and efficiency.

Enhanced Security: By processing sensitive data locally, edge computing can minimize exposure to potential breaches during data transmission, enhancing security for citizen data.

Support for IoT Initiatives: Governments can deploy IoT devices (like smart meters and surveillance cameras) that leverage edge computing for efficient data processing and immediate action.

5G Technology

5G is the fifth generation of wireless technology, offering significantly higher speeds, lower latency, and greater connectivity compared to previous generations. The implication for government services are:

Improved Connectivity: 5G allows for seamless connectivity for smart city initiatives, enhancing communication between devices and services, thus facilitating better urban management.

Enhanced Public Services: Faster data transmission can improve services like telemedicine, remote education, and emergency response systems, ensuring timely access to crucial resources.

Innovative Applications: The low latency and high capacity of 5G can support advanced technologies such as augmented reality (AR) for training public service workers and virtual consultations for citizens.

Server less Architectures

Server less computing allows developers to build and run applications without managing server infrastructure. Resources are automatically allocated based on demand. The implication for government services are:

Cost Efficiency: Governments can reduce costs by paying only for the resources they use, allowing for more efficient allocation of budgets to critical services.

Scalability: Serverless architectures automatically scale with demand, enabling government services to handle varying workloads, especially during peak times (e.g., tax season).

Faster Development Cycles: Developers can focus on coding rather than infrastructure management, leading to faster deployment of new applications and services that better meet citizen needs.

The first governor in Nigeria to introduce e-government services was Bola Ahmed Tinubu, who served as the Governor of Lagos State from 1999 to 2007. His administration implemented various digital initiatives aimed at improving governance, enhancing service delivery, and increasing transparency. These initiatives laid the groundwork for further e-governance developments in the country.

Vanya Verma (2021) Role of e-governance and digital India in empowering Indian citizens

https://blog.ipleaders.in/role-e-governance-digital-india-empowering-indian-citizens

Enagwe campus (home of Edo Tech Park), **Ohen Road, Main Road, off, Benin City, NG.**

HOW EDO STATE HAS BENEFITED FROM E-GOVERNANCE.

Acknowledging that no nation can reach its full potential without embracing digital tools, the Edo State Government has equipped its staff with essential technology. Furthermore, a range of training and educational programs focused on the practical use and maintenance of these tools has been introduced. The significant improvements seen in public service due to digital innovations have encouraged the State Government to incorporate digitalization into the everyday functions of its employees. Consequently, September 1st, 2023, marks the official shift to a fully paperless governance system in Edo, highlighting the State's strong commitment to advancing digital transformation. (Osayomore, Omoruyi P. 2023)

Digital training, also known as Information and Communication Technology (ICT) training, has had a profound impact on the contemporary public service of Edo State since the inception of the administration of Governor Godwin Obaseki. Under his leadership, the infusion of digital skills among the workforce has ushered in numerous enhancements within the public service. The transformation encompasses the creation of a more conducive working environment, the modernization of office spaces, the streamlined implementation of policies, the adoption of flexible approaches to tasks execution, and a comprehensive organizational overhaul through advanced internet connectivity that spans across all departments. Osayomore, Omoruyi P. (2023)

Pointed out ways Edo State citizens has benefited from e-governance:

Improved Service Delivery: Citizens can access government services more efficiently and conveniently online, reducing wait times and increasing responsiveness.

Transparency and Accountability: Digital platforms enhance transparency in government operations, allowing citizens to track services and access information easily, which foster greater accountability.

Increased Participation: E-Government initiatives facilitate greater citizen engagement in governance through online feedback mechanisms, surveys, and public consultations.

REFERENCES

Adams, G. (2013). Calculating the cloud: Determing the true cost of hosting services in the cloud. Retrieved from Educause Quarterly: http://www.edecause.edu/educas

Ademodi, D. T. (2015). Empirical study of Awareness and Use of Reference Source by Undergraduate in Adekunle Ajasin University Library. Pp 10-17 Information and Knowledge Management Journal Agu, P.C. (2014). User and services of academic libraries. In F.C Ekere (ed). Administration of academic libraries: A book of reading (pp.120-128). Enugu: Praise House Publishers.

Ademodi, E. O & Adepoju (2009). Influence of information technology skills on library patronage Available at https://core.ac.uk/ download/pdf/ 21516248 3.pdf

Ahmad, D., Lutfiani, N., Ahmad, A. A., Rahardja, U., & Aini, Q. (2021). Blockchain Technology Immutability Framework Design in E-Government. Journal of Administration (Public Administration Journal), 32-41.

Ahmad, D., Lutfiani, N., Ahmad, A. A., Rahardja, U., & Aini, Q. (2021). Blockchain Technology Immutability Framework Design in E-Government. *Journal of Administration (Public Administration Journal)*, 32-41.

Ajibola, B. (2012). Cloud Cooputing Communication of the ACM. Retrieved from http://csrc.nistgov/organizations/fisseg/2009conference/prelentational/fissea09day3cloudcomputi ng.pdf.

Akuffo, M. N., & Budu, S. (2019). Use of electronic resources by students in a premier postgraduate theological university in Ghana. SAJIM, vol.21, n.1, pp.1-9. ISSN 1560-683X. http://dx.doi.org/ African Journal of Information Management Alemayehu, N. (2010). *Is Cloud Computing Really Read for Prime Time?* Retrieved from IEEE Computer Society: www.leavcom./pdf/cloudcomputing.DOI: 10.4102/ sajim.v21i1.1026.South

Al Kilani and Kobziev V. (2017) “An Overview Of E-government Concept, Econtechmod. An international quarterly journal, Vol. 06, No. 4, pp. 97-102.

Al-Omari, A., & Al-Omari, H. (2006). E-Government Readiness Assessment Model Ahmed Al-Omari and Hussein Al-Omari. *Journal of Computational Science*, 2(11), 841–845. DOI: 10.3844/jcssp.2006.841.845

AlAwadhi, S., & Morris, A. (2009). “Factors influencing the adoption of e-government services. Journal of Software Vol.4, 584-590.Retrieved fromhttps://www.researchgate.net/publication/373675400_Factors_Influencing_the_Adoption_of_E-Government_Services_A_Study_among_University_Students.

Ali, J. S., & Yong, J. (2014). *Impact of Cloud Computing Technology on E-Government.* DOI: 10.1007/978-3-319-11958-8_22

Alzahrani, N. (2013). Understanding reliability and validity in qualitative research. The

Ani, Okon E. and Ahiazu, B. (2018), 'Towards effective development of electronic information resources in Nigerian university libraries', Library Management, 29(6/7), 504 – 514

Annuj, D. (2017). Cloud Computing. Available at https://www.academia.ed /10200815/cloud_computing

Arpaci, I. (2017). Antecedents and consequences of cloud comuting adoption in education to achieve knowledge management. doi:.DOI: 10.1016/j.chb.2017.01.024

Ashima, W., & Popli, R. (2016). Comprehensive Study of Security and Privacy Challenges in the Era of Big Data. *Proceedings of ICICCT on Information Communication Technology*. Jagan Institute of Management Studies.

Bakare A. (2018). Awareness and Adoption of Cloud Computing in Nigeria Libraries: An Aid to Library Services.

Bamidele, I. A., Omeluzor, U. S., Amadi, U. H., & Abayomi, I. (2003). Training of Library Assistant in Academic Library: a Study of Babcock University Library, Nigeria Sage Open Publisher https://www.coursehero.com/file/236201902/bamidele-et-al-2013-training-of-library-assistants-in-academic-library-a-study-of-babcock-university/

Baum, C. a. (2000). Gartner's Four Phases of E-Government Model, Gartner, Research note.

Berry, R., & Reisman, M. (2012). Policy Challenges of Cross-border Cloud Computing. Journal of International Commerce and Economics. p. 1-38

Bullu, J. (2014). An exploratory study of Indian university students' use of social networking websites: Implication for the work place. *Business Communication Quarterly*, 72, 105–110. http://www.scimagojr.com/journalsearch.php?q=1990019254&

Carlsson B, Jacobsson S, Holmén M, Rickne (2022) A. Innovation systems: analytical and methodological issues. Res polic. 31(2):233–45.

Carter, L., & Bélanger, F. (2005). The utilization of e-government services: Citizen trust, innovation and acceptance factors. *Information Systems Journal*, 15(1), 5–25. DOI: 10.1111/j.1365-2575.2005.00183.x

Cattedu, D., & Hogben, G. (2009). Cloud Computing Benefits, Risk, and Recommendations for Information Security: the European network and information security agency (ENISA). Retrieved from www.resilience.enisa.europa.eu/cloud-security-and-resilience/publications/cloud-computing-benefits-risk-and-recommendations-for-information-security

Christian, R. O. (2008). Self-efficacy and use of electronic information as predictors of academic performance. Electronic Journal Of Academic and Special Librarianship, 8(2). Retrieved, from https://southernlibrarianship.icaap.org/content/v08n02/tella_a01.html

Dahunsi, F. M., & Owoseni, T. M. (2015). *Cloud Computing in Nigeria: The Cloud Ecosystem Perspective*. Nigeria Journal of Technology., DOI: 10.4314/njt.341.911

Dillon, T., & Wu, C., & Chang, E. (2010). Cloud Computing: Issues and Challenges. 24th IEEE International Conference on Advanced Information Networking and Applications, IEEE Computer Society. 27-33. DOI: 10.1109/AINA.2010.187

Dinev Tamara & Hu Qing, (2005). The Centrality of Awareness in the Formation of User Behavioral Intention toward Protective Information Technologies

Durman, O. (2024). Good governance–basis for building an effective public administration system.theoretical and empirical research in urban management, 37-43,. Retrieved from https://doi.org/DOI: 10.32836/2310-9653-

Elisa, N., Yang,, L., Li,, H., Chao,, F., & Naik, N. (2020). Consortium blockchain for security and privacy-preserving in E-government Systems. arXiv preprint, 451-479.

Elisa, N., Yang,, L., Li,, H., Chao,, F., & Naik, N. (2020). Consortium blockchain for security and privacy-preserving in E-government Systems. *arXiv preprint*, 451-479.

Elisa, N., Yangl, L., & Chao, F., & Cao, Y. A. (2023). A framework of blockchain-based secure and. wireless. *Network (Bristol, England)*, •••, 1005–1015.

Elisa, N., Yangl, L., Chao, F., & Cao, Y. A. (2023). A framework of blockchain-based secure and. *wireless. Network (Bristol, England)*, •••, 1005–1015.

Erhabor, E. D. (2012). Using Cloud Services for Library IT Infrastructure. Journal Code for Library. Retrieved from https://journal.code4lib.org/articles/2510

Eric, M. (2012). Winds of change: Libraries and cloud computing. *Multimedia Information and Technology*, 37, 24–28.

Ezeani, I., & amp; Igwesi, O. (2012). Using social media applications for educational outcome college teaching: Strucctural equation analysis. *British Journal of Educational Technology*, 44, 87–100.

Ezeani, I., & Igwesi, O. (2012). Using social media applications for educational outcome college teaching: Strucctural equation analysis. *British Journal of Educational Technology*, 44, 87–100.

Fabrègue B, Portal LJ, Cockshaw C.(2023) Using smart people to build smarter: How smart cities attract and retain highly skilled workers to drive innovation (Belgium, Denmark, the Netherlands, Poland). Smart Cities Reg Dev (SCRD) J. 7(1):9–30.

Fakhoury, R., & Baker, S. D. (2016). Governmental trust, active citizenship, and E-government acceptance in Lebanon. *Journal of Leadership, Accountability and Ethics*, •••, 36–52.

Fayemi, Y. (2013). IaaScloud Computing Service for Libraries: Cloud storage and virtual machines. In IaaScloud Computing Service for Libraries: Cloud storage and virtual machines (Vol. 29, 87-100). Bingley, West, Yorkshire, England: Emerald Group Publishing Limited.

Finlay, S. (2016). User profile for personalized information. Retrieved from Nova Education: http://www.nova.edu/ssss/QR/QR8-4/golafshani.pdf

Gbaje, S., & Aliyu, E. (2014). Application of Digital Libraries and Electronic Technologies in Uganda. *African Journal of Library Archives and Information Science*, 12, 145–154. Retrieved 2014, from

Gila Cohen Zilka (2017) Awareness of eSafety and Potential Online Dangers among Children and Teenagers Journal of Information Technology Education: Research pp. 319-338. https://doi.org/DOI: 10.28945/3864

Goldner, M. (2012). Wind of changes: Libraries and cloud computing. Retrieved from OCLC: htt://www.oclc.org/multimedia/2011files/-paper.pdf

Hung, Y. S., Chang, M. C., & amp; Kuo, R. S. (2013). User acceptance of mobile e-government services: an empirical Study. Turkey: Government Information Quarterly. doi:. giq2012.07.008DOI: 10.1016/j

Igiekhume, Donatus (2022) Why Edo State is Taking the Lead in E-government.

Inayatulloh & Maryani. (2021) Integrated E-Government Model with Cloud Computing Technology. Proceedings of the International Conference on Industrial Engineering and Operations Management Rome, Italy, August 2-5, 2021 © IEOM Society International 1661

Jeffrey S, & Omar A (2014). Challenges and Issues within Cloud Computing Technology:cloud computingThe 5th International Conference on Cloud Computing, GRIDs, and Virtualization pp. 55-63. Retrieved 2019, from http://researchgates .net/publication_

Jisc. (2014) Developing digital literacies. Available at https://jisc.ac.uk/guides / developing- Digital-literacy

Johnson, B. (2011). *Shaping The Internet Age: An essay on the evolution of internet and the technologies that are helping connect people to information.* Imternet Policy Institute.

Kaushik, A & Kumar, A (2013). Application of Cloud Computing in Libraries. International Journal of Information Dissemination and Technology,3(4), 270-273.

Kessler, A. (2012). Impact of internet use on agricultural research outputs in Nigeria universities of agriculature. Hi Tech NewsIncororating Online and CD notes, 44-52.

Khalifa Alhosani & Saadat M. Alhashmi. (2024) Opportunities, challenges, and benefits of AI innovation in government services: a review of Springer link vol 4 No 18.

Kinengyere, A. A. (2007). *The effect of information literacy on the Utilization of Electronic Information Resources in Selected Academic and Research Institutions in Uganda.* Emerald Insight Journal., DOI: 10.1108/02640470710754832

Kroski, E. (2009). Library cloud atlas: A guide to cloud computing and storage stacking. *Library Journal*, •••, 207. https://www.libraryjournal.com/article/ CA6695772.html

Krubuand, D., & Osawam, M. (2011). Avoiding the death zone: Choosing and running a library project in the cloud. *Emerald Group Publishing Limited*, 30, 418–427.

Kurfalı, M., Arifoglu, A., Tokdemir, G., & Paçin, Y. (2017). Adoption of e-government services in Turkey: Computers in Human Behavior. *Computers in Human Behavior*, 66, 168–178. DOI: 10.1016/j.chb.2016.09.041

Mahalakshmi, K. & Ally S, S.(2012). Awareness and application of cloud computing in Indian libraries: a study among librarians of engineering colleges of coimbatore district. International Conference on Cloud Computing Technologies, Applications and Management, ICCCTAM

Miller, M., & Jeffrey, K., & Neidecker-Lutz, B. (2009. (2010). The future of cloud opportunities. *European Cloud Cloud*, 2010, 66.

Ministries, Departments & Agencies. (2024). Home - Edo State Government.

Mosa, H. El-Bakry, and M. AbuElkheir, (2015) “Cloud Computing in EGovernment: A Survey Cloud Computing in E-Government: A Survey,” Int. J. Adv. Res. Comput. Sci. Technol., vol. 3,

Mustafa, G., Rafiq, W., Jhamat, N., & Arshad, Z. (2024). Blockchain-based governance models in e-government: a comprehensive framework for legal, technical, ethical and Security Consideration. International Journal of Law and Management, 521-541.

Mustafa, G., Rafiq, W., Jhamat, N., & Arshad, Z. (2024). Blockchain-based governance models in e-government: a comprehensive framework for legal, technical, ethical and Security Consideration. *International Journal of Law and Management*, 521-541.

Naone, E. (2007). Computer in the Cloud. Retrieved. *Technology Review*.

Ndou, V. D. (2004). Ndou, (2004) E – government for developing countries: Opportunities and challenges. *The Electronic Journal on Information Systems in Developing Countries*, 18(1), 1–24. DOI: 10.1002/j.1681-4835.2004.tb00117.x

Neethu & Vanaja (2017). Concepts & application of cloud computing in libraries. International Journal of Trend in Research and Development,1-4.

Nguyen, T. a. (2007). Grounding e-government in Vietnam: from antecedents to responsive government. Journal of Business Systems, Governance and Ethics, 35-52.

NSW R. (n.d.) Using machine technology. [Online] Revenue NSW. https://www .revenue.nsw.gov.au/news-media-releases/using-machine-technology. Accessed 20th October 2024.

Ølnes, S., & Jansen, A. (2017). Ølnes, S., & Jansen Blockchain technology as s support infrastructure in e-government. In Electronic Government. Ølnes, S., & Jansen, A. (2017). Blockchain technology as s support infrastructure in egovernment. In Electronic G International conference (pp. 215-227). Russia: Spring International Publishing.

Ølnes, S., & Jansen, A. (2017). Ølnes, S., & Jansen Blockchain technology as s support infrastructure in e-government. In Electronic Government. *Ølnes, S., & Jansen, A. (2017). Blockchain technology as s support infrastructure in egovernment. In Electronic G International conference* (pp. 215-227). Russia: Spring International Publishing.

Ongena, D. (2024). *4 foundational ways that AI is transforming government. Global Government Lead.* Microsoft.

Onuoha, F. R. (2012). Library in the Clouds: OCLC Systems and Services. *International Digital Library Perspectives*, 29, 762–776.

Oriazowan, C. (2024). Edo State Government Holds Workshop on E-Government Challenges and Sustainability. Benin City: ICTA Projects and Events, News. Retrieved fromhttps://icta.edostate.gov.ng/2024/05/10/edo-state-government-holds -workshop-on-e- government-challenges-and-sustainability/

Ossai-Ugbah, M. S. (2012). A social cognitive theory of internet use and gratifications: Towards a new model of media attendance. *Journal of Broadcasting & Electronic Media*, 48, 358–377.

Oyekan, A. (2007). The usage of intranet and its impact on organizational knowledge sharing: an explanatory investigation of a public hospital. Retrieved from Express Library: http://epress.lib.uts.edu.au/research/bitstream/handle/10453/20028/ 02Whole.df?sequence

Paul, P. B. Karn, R. Rajesh (2015) Cloud Computing and its Deployment Model: International Journal of Applied Science and Engineering DOI:DOI: 10.5958/2322-0465.2015.00005.2

Preeti, C., & Vinod, S. (2016, June). Cloud Computing a Survey Report. *International Journal of Recent Research Aspects*, 3, 139–142.

Qualitative Report-Nova Education, 8(4), 2013. Retrieved from http://www.nova .edu/ssss/QR/QR8-4/golafshani.pdf

Quddusi, S. U. H. (2014).. . *Document Management and Cloud Computing: the TQM Journal*, 26(2), 102–108.

Ramirez, M., Lans-Vargas, L., & Montes, H. M. (2022). Government influence on e-government adoption by citizens in Colombia. Latin America Journal, 25-45. doi:DOI: 10.1371/journal.pone.0264495

Rana, R. (2010). The future of cloud computing. *Analysis*, 1(1), 1–26.

Rastogi, (2010) A Model based approach to Implement Cloud Computing in E-Governance," Int. J. Comput. Appl., vol. 9, no. 7, pp. 15–18.

Reid, S. (2007). Communication channels and adoption of web-based courses by university

Ristenpart, T., Eran, T., Hovav, S., & Stefan, S. (2009). Hey You Get of My Cloud: exploring information leakage in third-party computer clouds retrieved 2019 www. cloud.riste.tech.cornell.edu/papers/clouds.pdf pp.1-14 preofessors. Journal of Interactive Online Learning, 6, 142-158.

Sabiti, M. Sarika Meher & Bulu, Maharana (2015). Awareness and usage of Cloud Computing Application among LIS Professionals: A case study of 17 Indian University Libraries. Library Philosophy and Practice. Retrieved from http://digitalcommons.unl. edu/cgi/viewcontent.cgi? article=3431& context=libphilprac.

Spacey, A. (2013). Library services in electronic environment:Changes, challenges issues and strtegies. Kaveri. doi:doi=10.1.1460.5639_pdf.

Suciu, G. (2013). Study on advantages and disadvantages of Cloud Computing: the advantages of telemetry applications in cloud. https://www.mobcomm.pub.ro/wp - content/uploads/2016/04/GeorgeSuciu_PhD-Thesis-Summary_v7.pdf

Swapna G & Biradar B. S (2017). Application of Cloud Computing Technology in Libraries: International Journal of library and information studies,7(1);52-61

Swapna, G., & Birader, B. S. (2017). *Information literacy model for higher education institutions in India*. International Journal of Digital Library Service.

Swapna, G. & Biradar (2007). Application of Cloud Computing Technology in Libraries, International Journal of Library & Information Science https://ijlis.org

Team, E. M. B. (2024). *Cloud Computing in E-Government Services*. Home Technology Cloud Computing in E-Government Services.

Theophilus, O. C. (2013). Information communication technology support for an e-learning environment at university of Lagos. Library Philosophy and Practice (e-journal). Retrieved from http://epress.lib.uts.edu.au/research/bitstream/handle/10453/20028/02Whole.pdf?sequenc e e=2.

Verma, V. (2021) Role of e-governance and digital India in empowering Indian citizens https://blog.ipleaders.in/role-e-governance-digital-india-empowering-indian -citizens

Wada, I. (2014). Cloud Computing Implementation in Libraries: A Synergy for Library Services Optimization. *International Journal of Library and Information Science*, 10(2), 17–27.

Wescott, C. G. (2023). *E-government and the applications of technology to. working paper of Pacific Basin Research Center, and chapter in Dennis A. Rondinelli.* Pacific Region., https://www.unapcict.org/sites/default/files/2019-01/e-Government%20and%20the%20Applications%20of%20Technology%20to%20Government%20Services.pdf

Yuvaraj, T. (2013). Modern Information Technologies: Their impact on Library Services. *Journal of Management Information Systems*, 11, 87–114.

KEY DEFINITION OF TERMS

Cloud Computing: this is the computing software that can be accessed over the network

rather than permanently installed on the desktop.:

Data-Flow: this is the transfer of information from one part of the system to another

Data-Type: this tells a computer system how to interpret its value

E-Governemnt: Is the use of technology in carrying and delivery services to its citizens.

Government Services: Is the activities and functions performed by government to its

citizens:

Implementation: this is the act of putting plan into execution.

Technology: this is the application of scientific knowledge in carrying out operations.

Chapter 9
Enhancing Cloud Security Strategies to Mitigate Critical Threats

Junaid Basaad
Sharda University, India

Vishal Jain
https://orcid.org/0000-0003-1126-7424
Sharda University, India

ABSTRACT

In cloud computing, there are several key security concerns, including data loss or leakage, misconfiguration, unauthorized access, insecure APIs, account hijacking, and cyberattacks, that it confronts. Data loss generally occurs when personal files on the cloud get exposed to leakage on breaching by a certain hacker. Misconfiguration is one of the leading causes of data breaches, in most cases exposing cloud-based resources to attackers due to the reliance of an organization on CSPs for configuration and security. Unauthorized access is a great risk, since cloud deployments differ from physical server infrastructures in that they are often directly accessible from the public networks, hence greater intrusion. Another threat may be insecure APIs provided by the CSPs-those that a customer fails to secure their cloud interfaces properly-an attacker may enable through vulnerabilities. Account hijacking-whereby stolen employee credentials are used to access sensitive data-is of most concern.

DOI: 10.4018/979-8-3693-7678-2.ch009

1. INTRODUCTION

In today's fast-paced world, new technologies are brought into existence every other day. The global community is seeking these demands to live an uncomplicated life. We as humans want to face the least number of challenges in order to achieve anything. The need for new technologies and algorithms is crucial, as these growing demands need to be served for the advancement of the community. A cloud infrastructure is nothing but a virtual storage that provides on- demand services to its users with add-on features. For ensuring a nation's overall development, it is mandatory for it to have e-governance related services provided to the people of that nation. This chapter aims to highlight the importance and impact of providing maximum security to a cloud system for a better result in its performance and to make it less vulnerable to threats and cyberattacks. An excellent example that comes into our minds is India's Aadhaar System. In the beginning, India faced real data breaches that affected the security of the service. The population began reporting problems and raising queries regarding the misuse of personal data and data leaks. In order to make sure that the issues faced by the public are being addressed, the Indian Government started implementing robust security measures that helped in the advancement of the e-Aadhaar Service, (Mudawi, Beloff, &White, 2019). This example is perfect as it fits the title of this paper quite well. Many more events have played key roles in the advancement of e-governance services like the implementations made by UK and US governments in their cloud platforms for e-governance services that will be discussed in the literature section of the chapter, (Kao *et al.*, 2012).

The paper provides an insight into the most common threats for cloud computing security, hence providing a proper understanding of risks associated with cloud deployments. Readers will learn about real-world incidents and the root causes of these security breaches, (Choudhary, Vyas, & Lilhore, 2023). Furthermore, it covers strategies and best practices to make the cloud more secure. Hence, it will be highly applicable for IT professionals, cloud administrators, and organizations using the services of the cloud.

Some effective ways to alleviate cloud computing security issues are by providing strong encryption of data during transmission or even static data, thus preventing unauthorized hacking and leakage, (Moghaddam, Karimi, & Alrashdan, 2013). Account hijacking could be prevented through comprehensive employee training in terms of cybersecurity, secure management of credentials, and the identification of phishing attempts, (Tirumala, Sathu, & Naidu, 2015). This way, threats can be identified with real-time continuous monitoring and incident response, with minimal damage. Finally, regular patching of systems means the constant updating of cloud services and software with security patches that have been addressed so far; this reduces their chances of being exploited based on any known vulnerabilities.

If these strategies are followed, an organization can almost double the security for their deployments on the cloud, protect from common threats, and ensure integrity and confidentiality of their data. Along with that, there are different legislations based on the data privacy of the users for any CSP. One of the most well-known techniques applied for securing data at rest or transit is the Advanced Encryption Standard. This technique was proposed by NIST in 2001, and it aimed at replacing the older techniques related to the encryption of data, like DES, (Thiyagarajan & Kamalakannan, 2014).

For a safe and private cloud environment, the need to ensure its safety arises. Cloud computing services provide vast features, but with that, our data's vulnerability also lies at stake. Various techniques are currently being implemented to prevent any kinds of data breaches. There also exist tools and machines that detect and block any data breaches by sensing any irregular movement of data and thus prevent data leakages. Techniques like cryptography have found to be useful to cloud users as it converts the user's data to an unreadable format and of no use for the intruder, (M. M. R. & A. T. P., 224). During storage and transmissions, the data being stored in the unreadable format known as Cipher text becomes of no use for an intruder. This has found to be quite an effective security measure. True enough, there are mechanisms under each service model that advance cloud security according to the needs of the users and applications. Let us consider how the three big service models, IaaS, PaaS, and SaaS, add up to enhanced security.

1. **Infrastructure as a Service (IaaS):** With virtualization technologies, IaaS providers can isolate workloads thus preventing any unauthorized access or data breaches between tenants. Fine-grained access controls might be the service from Identity and Access Management (IAM) in IaaS models, meaning that organizations can define who is supposed to have access to certain resources. It will be built-in for security purposes, such as firewalls, load balancers, and VPNs, to secure data that is being transmitted or traveled across computer networks. Monitoring mechanisms in IaaS environments usually enable organizations to monitor the activities of the users and ensure overall compliance with regulatory standards.
2. **Platform as a Service (PaaS):** In general, most of the PaaS providers handle many of the security-related tasks such as patch management and application security on the side, so that the developer can focus on building the application. PaaS environments include built-in security features like authentication, encryption, and API security and hence safer for applications from common vulnerabilities. PaaS allows developers to deploy applications in a safe environment so that they do not risk any type of danger before releasing the application.

The PaaS providers also provide data encryption at rest and in flight to ensure data integrity and confidence.

3. **Software as a Service (SaaS):** The provider of SaaS software updates regularly due to their desire to address security vulnerabilities; therefore, the chances of users running outdated software against an attack vector are reduced. In addition, most SaaS applications provide effective mechanisms for user authentication, which include MFA and SSO. These mechanisms enhance security since only the authorized individuals are able to access sensitive data. Most of the SaaS applications usually offer encryption of data in order to ensure that unauthorized parties and guarantee the integrity and confidentiality of their data cannot access sensitive information.

Most of the SaaS vendors adopt all the market rules and regulations, like GDPR and HIPAA, which ensure the organizations that their data will be protected and kept private. Many SaaS applications ensure fine access control features to define roles and entitlements for the users while keeping the access to sensitive information to the minimum number of people who actually have to view it, based on the principle of least privilege. SaaS platforms normally have an inbuilt monitoring and logging facility. Organizations can then monitor user activity as well as detect potential security incidents in real time with SaaS platforms. Most SaaS providers have robust backup and disaster recovery solutions that help restore data in the case of accidental deletion, data corruption or cyberattacks.

Organizations can leverage the unique security features of each service model to strengthen their general security posture. This demands a basic understanding on the shared responsibility model, wherein the provider and the consumer share the responsibilities in order to maintain security. Along with that, governance, data management, and user education best practices must be integrated to complement the security features offered by cloud service providers.

2. LITERATURE SURVEY

Cloud computing is extremely vulnerable to various types of security threats. Indeed, the most common and costly ones are data breaches. On the other hand, studies have pointed out that due to dynamic cloud environments—characterized by shared resources being assigned dynamically—the user is exposed to a greater risk. Misconfigured cloud storage, weak encryption protocols, and poor access controls remain the common reasons behind human-error breaches, as seen recently within organizations like Capital One and Verizon. Besides, cloud infrastructures also happen to be prime targets for APTs in order to utilize sophisticated, stealthy techniques in compromising sensitive information over extended periods, (Lai & Leu, 2015). DoS and DDoS attacks also exploit the elasticity in cloud resources, overwhelming resources with traffic, thus rendering them unusable, (Aishwarya & Malliga, 2024). Besides traditional attacks, new research puts a strong focus on the growing risk due to side-channel attacks and hypervisor vulnerabilities that leverage the sharing nature of multitenant environments to reach data across virtual machine, (Dhinakar *et al.*, 2023). Insider threats, both malicious and unintentional, also are harder to detect in a decentralized, complex cloud environment. These challenges highlight the need for robust, multi-faceted security to be designed, with a particular focus on the cloud.

In this regard, the literature puts forward a wide variety of technological improvements and best practices in the interest of hardening cloud environments. While encryption remains at the core of cloud security, end-to-end encryption, homomorphic encryption, and secure multi-party computation are some of the approaches that are considered under scrutiny to protect data at rest and in transit without undermining functionality, (Aparajit *et al.,* 2022). This is important in the implementation of ZTA, which through constant identity validation and stringent verification processes with every interaction on the network, tries to reduce insider threats and unauthorized access. AI and ML are also becoming very cardinal in cloud security because it allows real-time monitoring and automated threat detection that flags unusual behaviors and predicts the attack before it occurs, (Ahamad *et al.,* 2022). Another promising solution involves integrating the blockchain technology itself, which can provide a decentralized, tamper-proof way of managing data transactions and securing cloud infrastructure, (Pavithra, Ramya, Prathibha, 2019). Similarly, ABE-related research is gaining momentum; it allows for finer access control, hence helping the cloud service provider give permission over user-specific permissions without compromising a large-scale breach.

Confidential computing is one development area in cloud security where computations can be allowed in isolated environments even on shared infrastructures. Indeed, this would further reinforce cloud security to ensure data stays safe during its processing. Put together, all these pieces of innovation undergird the constantly shifting panorama of cloud security and direct ways to mitigate evolving threats while granting scalability, performance, and compliance to global data protection regulations. Securing data on a cloud server has become a revolution for any industry existing right now. From private all over to hybrid cloud servers, cloud has become a necessity for every individual, (Alkhonaini & El-Sayed, 2018). There is no need for a justification that can prove why the cloud environment is better than the traditional storage models. When it comes to security, cost factor and much more, people would not want to shift their important data from a secure cloud server to an unprotected or vulnerable physical server.

ALGORITHMS USING ENCRYPTION

2.1. DES (Data Encryption Standard)

In the early 1970s, Horst Feistel succeeded in developing the DES algorithm that was later on submitted to the National Bereau of Standards (NBS). This algorithm mainly targets the encryption of the user's data and therefore, enhances the overall security and reliance of the cloud server. In other terms, the main focuses of the DES algorithm is to use the same key for encrypting and decrypting data, blocking cipher by using encryption. DES uses 56-bit key for the whole encryption process. 64-bit is the original size of the key but the 8-bits are engaged in error detection and that leaves the rest 56-bits for encryption.

DES stands for Data Encryption Standard. It is a symmetric key operation that operates on blocks of 64 bits with 56-bit keys. It does the encryption of data in rounds - exactly 16 rounds using Feistel ciphers where key mixing, substitution by means of S-boxes, permutation, and division into left and right halves take place. It relies both on substitution and permutation steps in such a way as to satisfy confusion and diffusion properties for security, (Verma *et al.*, 2021). Rather historic, DES is no longer considered a very secure system because of the small key size, hence is vulnerable to brute-force attacks. AES, or Advanced Encryption Standard has for the most part, replaced it.

Figure 1. Working of DES (data encryption standard)

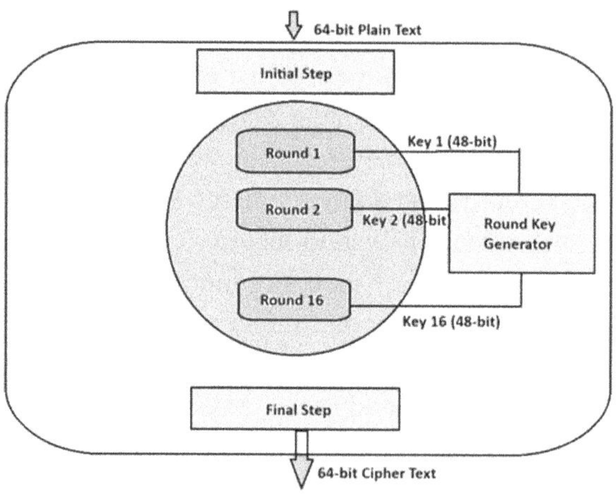

2.2. AES (Advanced Encryption Standard)

Back in 2001, NIST launched this encryption technique, which replaced the DES algorithm reason being, DES had its drawbacks and had become quite vulnerable at that time. It demanded a new technique like AES that is really well known for its efficiency and reliability. AES's working is the same as DES but with certain plus points. The multiple rounding of the encryption process highlighted these plus points for AES. Different key sizes corresponded to different number of rounds, (Sivakumar *et al.,* 2019).

Advanced Encryption Standard has found broad applications in various fields due to its strong and efficient security features, (Lee, Dewi, & Wajdi, 2018). The largest early adopter of AES applications was securing data for the U.S. government. In 2001, NIST officially picked AES as the official encryption standard of federal agencies and replaced DES.

Besides being used in government applications, AES has been broadly used in commercial sectors to protect financial transactions and online communications. For example, most of the online services running over the Internet, including most major financial institutions, rely on AES to encrypt data exchanged via SSL/TLS protocols for secure browsing and financial transactions, (Jaspin *et al.,* 2021). Down below is given a diagrammatic representation of the working and mechanism used in the AES encryption technique for maintaining a secure cloud environment.

Figure 2. Working of AES (advanced encryption standard)

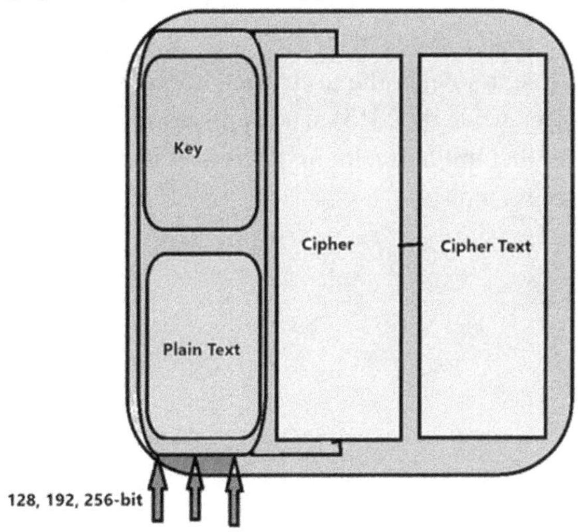

AES symmetric key encryption technique of data that encrypts the data into blocks. Each round is composed of four major steps: SubBytes for byte substitution using an S-box; ShiftRows, which performs a row shift to diffuse the data; MixColumns, column mixing for further diffusion and AddRoundKey, where the data is XORed with the encryption key. Initial and final rounds exclude MixColumns. AES itself is quite secure and efficient, hence finding wide applicability in securing sensitive data across different platforms, (Mohurle & Panchbhai, 2016).

It is robust in nature-as for efficiency and strong due to the presence of a series of well-defined substitution, permutation, and mixing operations. It is considered to be highly secure, and it is the encryption standard endorsed by the U.S. National Institute of Standards and Technology for applications in government and commerce.

IDENTITY AND ACCESS MANAGEMENT (IAM)

2.3. OAuth 2.0

A well-known protocol used for accessing a user's data or resources stored on a web or cloud server without having to enter the credentials for authentication. This framework is widely used for granting access to APIs in various web and mobile applications. Architecture used in this protocol is the client-server architecture. The server issues a token to the client that grants access to the client of the resource owner's data. OAuth 2.0 authorization framework enables a third-party application to access the user's resources without exposing the credentials of the user. It functions through a series of steps that involve an authorization server and a resource server. It starts when the user wants to grant access to the third-party application, (Pansotra & Singh, 2015). The application will redirect the user to the authorization server that initiates a login of the user and requests authorization for the application's access request.

Figure 3. OAuth 2.0 working

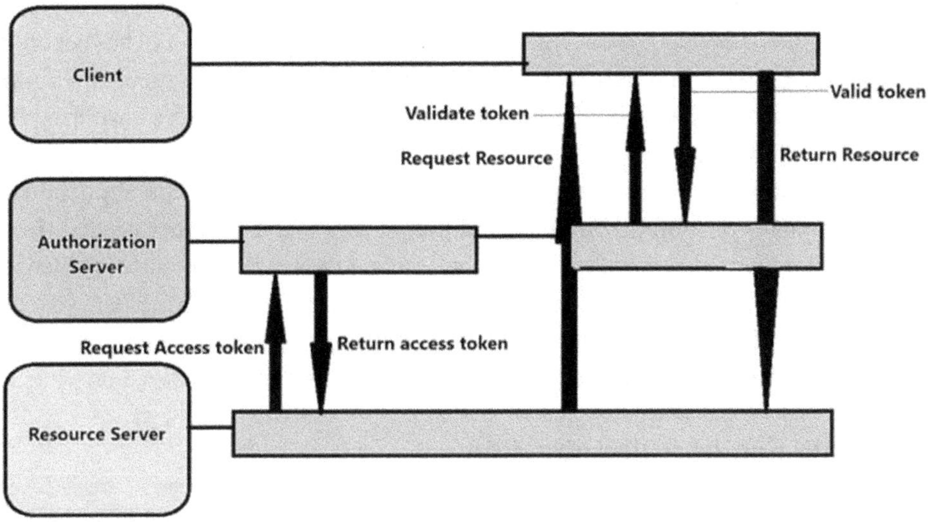

OAuth 2.0 evolves earlier security models to handle problems inherent in the direct authentication mechanism with username and password sharing. Previous systems, for instance, OAuth 1.0, are generally designed based on user input of credentials into third-party apps that use the credentials to communicate with protected resources. That model had several security issues: it was generally based on password sharing between many services, which increased the possibility of data leaking and complicated password revocation. If they wanted to revoke the access to any one service, they actually had to change their password-a propagated change that usually broke the access to other services relying on the same credentials, (Chung, Kim, & Kim, 2018). The original OAuth protocol, OAuth 1.0, emerged as a solution to this problem whereby third-party services could get access to resources on behalf of the user without ever having to handle or store passwords. In that aspect, OAuth 1.0 was a leap in security but had its own setbacks, which included the signature and token-generation process being cumbersome, (Upadhyaya & Bansal., 2015). This was difficult to implement, particularly in mobile applications, and did not really address the scaling needs for today's cloud applications and APIs. One of the reasons OAuth 2.0 was created was to simplify the process, making it more secure and fitting for a wider set of applications: web, mobile, and desktop clients.

OAuth 2.0 also moved away from the burden of cryptographic signatures for a lighter system based on tokens. It relied on HTTPS for security in their place, (Alsubaij, Hafez, & Alghathbar, 2013). It introduced access tokens, short-lived credentials that can be used by a third-party application to access certain resources, and refresh tokens that allow the application to request an access token anew without re-asking for the user's log-in credentials, thereby enhancing security and user experience. OAuth 2.0 massively improved on security and usability by decoupling user credentials from resource access. Fast-track to this day, the protocol has become the standard on which modern authentication and authorization systems are built, and major platforms like Google, Facebook, GitHub, and Microsoft have used it, (Sendor *et al.,* 2014).

Upon receiving consent, the authorization code is returned to the application, which exchanges the authorization code for an access token. Another typical flow is the implicit grant, destined for single-page applications, where the access token is given back directly to the application without going through an intermediate step of code exchange. In general, OAuth 2.0 allows flexibility in providing a secure way of including the user permissions among different applications and service providers.

2.4. Multi- Factor Authentication

MFA is a technique that authenticates users by requiring two or more authentication factors for access to a system, application, or account. This increases the level of security because it requires not only what a user remembers, but also a key user will have, like a smartphone, hardware token, or smart card, and something the user is. In this respect, MFA decreases possibility of unauthorized access to systems or accounts in cases when the compromising of one form of factor-a password-may occur, (Sharphathy & Sumalatha, 2024). Therefore, MFA is very common in systems dealing with sensitive information and has been an additional layer of protection against phishing, identity theft, and cyberattacks.

MFA is a security-enhancing measure that requires two or more different forms of verification by a user before access to an account or system can be obtained. This is quite different from single-factor authentication, where one generally uses only a password to gain access. MFA ties together several factor types: something the user knows-a password-something the user has, such as a smartphone or hardware token-and something the user is, biometric data including fingerprints or facial recognition. By demanding multiple forms of authentication, (Ashitha *et al.,* 2024), MFA adds layers of security that make it more difficult for attackers to gain access, even if they have compromised one factor. This helps in the multi-disciplinary approach towards various sectors for protection against information divulgence and protection of cybersecurity. Down below is given a representation of how any type of multi-factor authentication works and each process has been shown in detail.

Figure 4. Working of MFA

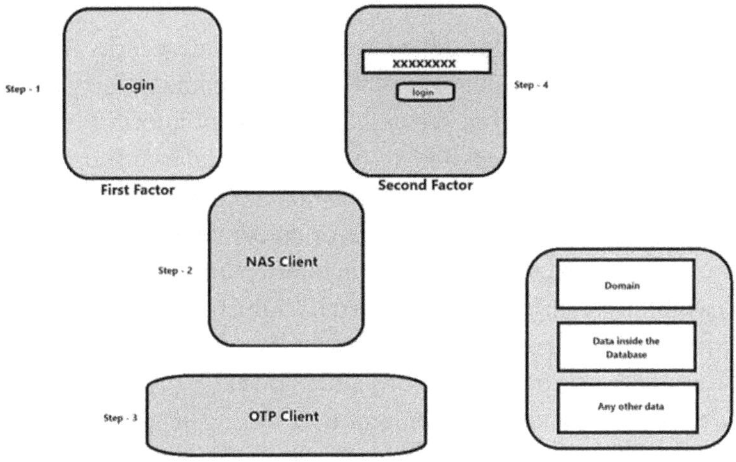

This authentication technique reinforces security by providing users with two or even more verification forms to validate identities when granting access to any system or service. Common approaches include something that users know, such as a password; something that the users have-anything from a smartphone to a security token-and something the users are, where fingerprinting and any other type of biometric data come into play. This multi-layered approach massively enhances security in that it makes access very hard for unauthorized persons, even if they have compromised a single factor, such as a password, (Nikam & Potey, 2016). MFA helps protect a host of threats from phishing attacks to credential theft by ensuring that any such form of access will require more than a single piece of information, thus providing an additional layer of defense.

2.5. Other Approaches for Cloud Security

Furthermore, approaches that combine or use the algorithms of Artificial Intelligence and Blockchain have also improved security of cloud servers significantly with a great impact. This approach may be applied for predictive AI concerning security threats and vulnerabilities at a time ahead, hence proactively keeping away from risks. Furthermore, AI can also automate the common and repetitive work of the security scene such as monitoring network traffic and scanning for vulnerabilities. This means freeing the human mind for more complex issues within security. For example, AI networks can create benchmark behaviors of normal behavior for users. This can allow them to identify anomalies as efficiently possible that might indicate suspected compromised accounts or insiders. AI-driven authentication procedures focusing on using biometrics and adaptive techniques for security adaptation can also be improved.

Blockchain technology offers other advantages toward security if applied to the cloud. Due to the decentralized nature underlying its technology, this provides advantages in that data received will be secured. The spread of information throughout a graph of nodes minimizes attacks and the breaching of data while improving redundancy and resiliency. However, once information has been written to a blockchain network, it becomes impossible to change or delete without getting a consensus from the network, which ensures integrity in information and makes it hard to mess with sensitive information by unknown users. Besides, blockchain offers transparent ledgers of transactions and data exchange, and therefore, organizations can track and review any access to sensitive information. This also provides transparency to regulatory compliance and the building of user trust. The smart contracts enable the execution of a defined action when particular conditions are met automatically, thus securing through pure rules established in advance that govern data access and transactions and cannot be accessed manually.

Furthermore, blockchain would improve identity management by developing decentralized digital identities controlled by the users, thereby reducing chances of identity theft or unauthorized access to cloud resources. It does combine AI and blockchain technologies to offer a formidable means for cloud security enhancement. To keep up with today's technology, the significant use of AI, Zero Trust or blockchain can be crucial for ensuring a secure, user-friendly and a much more reliable cloud server.

Securing cloud environments involves much more than the usage of traditional techniques involving encryption algorithms. Here are some of the latest technologies and strategies that organizations can utilize to strengthen cloud security. The core principle of a Zero Trust security model is the phrase "never trust, always verify." In the Zero Trust paradigm, strict verification must be conducted for every user and device attempting to access resources, not mattering where they come from. Core to any Zero Trust deployment involves continuous monitoring of user behavior, segmentation of networks to limit access to sensitive data, and highly developed multi-factor authentication (MFA) and identity management solutions.

Artificial Intelligence and Machine Learning algorithms can particularly add greatly to the security of cloud computing. AI/ML can identify anomaly-based user behavior patterns to point out potential threats or breaches. This technology may automatically react to a security incident, such as setting up affected systems in isolation or blocking the suspecting IP addresses. AI further analyzes vast amounts of data coming from different sources, identifying emerging threats and vulnerabilities to provide proactive security against them. As organizations increasingly adopt containerization for their application deployments, the security of these containerized environments is one of the critical parameters. The container runtime protection tools will do all the necessary checks on the running activities of a container and thereby keep track of suspicious activities at runtime. The other significant parameter is that the images of the containers should be scanned before deployment, which points out the vulnerabilities. Besides that, the stringent network policies set within the environment would limit the communication between these containers, and further restriction in lateral movement across the environment.

All the above characteristics of server-less computing lead to scalability and efficiency but introduce unique security challenges. Function-level security embraces the tools used while analyzing serverless functions for vulnerabilities and misconfigurations before they are deployed. Monitoring and logging solutions track function executions and watch out for anomalies or unauthorized access attempts. Since cloud applications heavily rely on APIs, it becomes very important to make those interfaces secure. In addition to traffic management, an API gateway may enforce various security policies like rate limiting or access controls. Applying API security solutions can detect attacks that are specific to the API, for instance, injection attacks or credential stuffing. IAM solutions arrive in a package to address user identities and manage rights to access. Role-Based Access Control is a security measure that controls access to sensitive resources based on user roles and the related responsibilities. Identity federation permits safe access across diverse systems and platforms without compromising a central approach to managing identity.

Automation can significantly scale cloud security operations. Real-time aggregation and analysis of security logs from SIEM solutions allow for real-time identification of live threats and incident response. SOAR platforms refers to the integration of multiple security tools in unison with automation of workflows to streamline processes in incident response. As organizations move toward multi-cloud strategy, securing those environments is important. Thus, the unified management tools for security across disparate cloud environments provide a centralized view of security. Consistent policies and configurations across all the cloud platforms reduce the risks. Decentralized identity solutions are also very critical in terms of security aspects because they control identities without any kind of central authority, therefore, bringing about security in such identities for use. It minimizes risks of stolen identities and provides genuine safe authentication without having to share critical information.

With the use of these latest technologies and strategies, organizations are able to significantly improve their posture for cloud security. An integrated approach of all these techniques together with traditional security methods, such as encryption, can provide a robust defense mechanism against burgeoning security threats in the cloud. Continuous assessment and updating of security protocol is necessary to move ahead against the possible vulnerability and attacks.

3. GOVERNMENT ASSISTANCE

The Government of India, in recent times, has taken some giant strides towards the much-needed security concerns with cloud computing, now that every activity relating to public administration, financial services, and healthcare has become increasingly dependent on digital services and cloud-based technologies. The Indian government that involves enforcement policies for data localization is laying down a key strategy. This policy insists that all critical and sensitive data, especially financial and personal information, must remain within the country's borders. For instance, the RBI has enforced strict regulations to ensure that the operators of the payment systems store data only in India to prevent unauthorized access and breach of data. The government is also taking the Personal Data Protection Bill forward that enumerates provisions with respect to the privacy and processing and storage of data amongst others in a manner that ensures Cloud service providers follow strict protocols with regard to data about Indian citizens, (Choudhari & Sasankar, 2021).

The Ministry of Electronics and Information Technology (MeitY) has also developed guidelines on cloud security through the initiative of GI Cloud (MeghRaj). The Guidelines will provide for the most efficient adoption of cloud in the government, ensuring security features in data management and deployment of various services on public and private clouds. The cloud service providers willing to avail cloud services with various Indian government agencies shall meet the strict security guidelines laid by MeitY, including occasional audits and threat assessments.

The UK has set out elaborate plans to curb the threats on cloud computing and protect data, especially government services, businesses, and infrastructural servicers. First is setting up the National Cyber Security Centre, which lays down in detail a set of guidelines and best practices that every organization using cloud computing must follow. Cloud service providers are accredited for use within government systems only after rigorous tests to meet the highest level of security. Setting this in concrete, the G-Cloud Framework is essentially a procurement system, whereby pre-vetted cloud-based services are availed to government organizations, (Choi, Seo, & Kwon, 2024). Only cloud providers meeting a high standard of security and compliance-like data encryption and vulnerability management-make their way into the G-Cloud catalog. This would enable government agencies to securely and efficiently transition into cloud services without exposure to risks due to cyber-attacks or data breaches. In addition, some of the crucial supporters of the cloud security enhancement strategy in the UK are Cyber Essentials and Cyber Essentials Plus; these standards enable any organization to implement the required security measures against cloud-based cyber threats. They range from a number of focuses; including firewalls, secure configuration, user access control, and malware protection. Cyber Essentials enable the organization to develop an understanding of the risks that come with cloud threats and set baseline security standards for them, while Cyber Essentials Plus provide more-detailed security assessments. Conformance to the GDPR regulation is another critical element in the UK's approach towards cloud security, (Michels & Walden, 2021). GDPR imposed strict privacy measures on organizations in respect of personal data and mechanisms for reporting breaches, thus providing a real framework for maintaining the integrity and security of personal data in cloud environments even beyond Brexit.

Cloud computing security issues have been paramount in the United States since the country relies highly on the cloud for nearly all government and private operations. One of the primary frameworks used in securing cloud services by U.S. federal agencies is called the Federal Risk and Authorization Management Program. FedRAMP has set very high standards that cloud service providers must meet before selling their services to federal agencies. The program continuous monitoring, management of vulnerabilities and periodic security testing of the cloud services serve to keep them safe from emerging threats. Strong protocols at FedRAMP serve to reduce risks by asking cloud providers to establish advanced encryption, multifactor authentication, and incident response mechanisms.

Major contributions towards the cloud security strategy in the U.S. are provided by NIST. They have in-depth recommendations on the right implementation of security in clouds. These range from data encryption, access control, and risk management to cloud architecture lockdown, (Hassan *et al.*, 2024). NIST is also involved in developing standards that have to do with the Zero Trust architecture, where it eliminates the implicit trust between users and systems by continuously verifying their access rights to cloud resources.

Various governments around the world have taken up cloud security and resorted to a set of initiatives in order to handle the unique challenges thrown up by cloud technologies. The Federal Risk and Authorization Management Program initiated by the United States government is one key initiative done for ensuring that CSPs are maintaining the most stringent security standards. FedRAMP allows the adoption of a standardized process related to security assessment and continuous monitoring regarding cloud services utilized within federal agencies. Such a policy helps ensure that sensitive government information remains secure. In an addition, NIST has come up with comprehensive guides; for instance, the NIST Special Publication 800-53 lays down recommendations on how to go about securing the cloud environments. In particular, these frameworks serve as critical references for both the public and private sectors in establishing the baseline for cloud security practices.

Meanwhile, cloud security has also been influenced by the European General Data Protection Regulation, entailing a stern set of standards for the storage, processing, and transfer of personal data. In addition, the European Union Agency for Cybersecurity has proposed a cloud computing security certification scheme to harmonize cloud security practices within member states. MeitY has issued a cloud adoption policy in India promoting safe deployment across governmental agencies, (Walden & Michels, 2024). Similarly, other countries such as Australia and Singapore have created cloud security frameworks, including ASD Certified Cloud Services List and Singapore MTCS Standard that classify CSPs based on their capability to satisfy certain requirements about security. These different initiatives taken by different nations symbolically reflect the commitment of the world towards ensuring cloud security, maintaining data privacy, and securing national interests in this digital era.

4. FUTURE SCOPE

In the future, enhancements in cloud security will be focused on several key points to tackle emerging challenges. Quantum-resistant encryption will become much more vital with the emergence of quantum computing, which might break up conventional encryption techniques. Artificial intelligence and machine learning can therefore, be used increasingly to refine threat detection and response, enabling the accurate identification of anomalies and threats in real time. A future Zero Trust extended architecture will be one with more granular access controls, continuous monitoring, and adaptive security policies working around the intricacies of a modern cloud environment. With the increased edge computing, a corresponding need to secure distributed data and applications at the edge of the network will be just as important. This will require new security measures designed to operate at the edge in these distributed environments. Blockchain technology can also help provide decentralized, tamper-proof systems for data integrity verification and enhance security. In addition, privacy-enhancing technologies and secure multi-party computation will emerge in an even broader way to protect sensitive information while maintaining data utility.

Patching prevailing gaps and preparing for upcoming vulnerabilities requires a holistic method in order to fortify cloud security. In this regard, the adoption of Zero Trust Architecture is imperative because it would introduce strict verification mechanisms for all users, devices, and applications from whatever origin, thereby reducing the chances of a breach to a minimum. AI and ML will continue to improve automated threat detection and response to identify and handle security incidents in real time. Strong encryption techniques include but are not limited to end-to-end and quantum-resistant encryption, which need to be implemented with the static data.

The future of cloud security will be progressively shaped through improvements in emerging technologies, coupled with the ever-increasing complexity of cloud environments. Included among the leading areas of concentration is the development of quantum-resistant encryption. Quantum computing, as it gets better and stronger, is predicted to undermine traditional methods of encryption and leave sensitive data vulnerable. The research on post-quantum cryptography will be critical in ensuring that cloud systems can keep the day-to-day advancement in quantum machines' computation power at bay through wide protection of stored and in-transit data. Another interesting piece is integrating AI with ML for real-time threat detection and response. AI and ML can analyze network traffic independently, recognize anomalies, and perform threat mitigation autonomously to reduce human interaction and increase the accuracy of implemented security. AI-driven autonomous SOCs could unleash a sea change in cloud security-where organizations could handle potential breaches more quickly and learn lessons from past incidents continuously.

Besides this, expanding deployments of IoT and multi-cloud architectures bring new challenges to be considered for future strategies in cloud security. With billions of devices connecting over cloud networks, the security of IoT devices would necessarily call for more secure authentication protocols and decentralized identity management systems. Blockchain can, therefore, provide a tamper-proof way of managing identities and performing access control across cloud environments. The increase in multi-cloud and hybrid cloud deployments further creates demand for standardized security protocols across cloud service providers. Research should aim at developing unified security frameworks wherein organizations enjoy consistent protection while leveraging flexibility due to multiple cloud platforms being in play. It would also confer so much importance to confidential computing in the near future, which is about protecting data while being used by trusted environments of execution. This will be very important for industries whose operations involve much sensitive data. Finally, the evolving landscape of data privacy regulations-like GDPR and CCPA-seeks automated solutions that ensure compliance in real time and hence mitigate legal risks while preserving security. It is in this view that cloud providers should embed a concept of security and privacy by design; hence, cloud infrastructures should be robust to meet the demands..

Updates of cloud security standards and certifications in respect of emerging threats enable maintaining high bars of security. The other important activities are enabling ongoing security training and awareness programs, securing APIs in the cloud with stringent measures, and investing in research and development in innovative technologies.

5. CONCLUSION

Enhanced cloud security is a process that will continue, whereby the cloud will see its adoption increased across industries and governments. The dynamic nature of cloud environments, together with ever-sophisticated cyber threats, establishes the need to develop continued sophisticated methods and frameworks in security. The effort will involve incorporating technologies like AI-driven threat detection, quantum-resistant encryption, and Blockchain, which will help to even elevate the posture of cloud security. However, governments worldwide are also doing their part-from FedRAMP to GDPR, and down to national cloud security frameworks-to ensure that cloud services meet the most restrictive standards of security and compliance.

Sustained innovation in technology and regulation will continue to reinforce cloud security in the future. These new challenges, ranging from the security of IoT devices to multi-cloud interoperability, need collaboration on different levels: governments, cloud providers, and the private sector. At the end, the adoption of robust security architectures and practices secures sensitive data and fosters trust in cloud computing, enabling the organizations to avail full benefits of the cloud with minimized risk. This can be summarized that cloud security topology has been changing fast to address complex demands, which have set newer challenges in the digital world. Innovative strategies toward addressing security challenges will become imperative when organizations and individuals continue with more dependence on cloud services. Some major improvements in quantum-resistant encryption, artificial intelligence, and ML in threat detection and the expansion of Zero Trust Architecture are some areas that would be crucial for data and application security. It will be secure with edge computing environments, blockchain for ensuring integrity extending to data, and integrating privacy-enhancing technologies. All these developments demand a head-on meet and call for collaboration across borders to create a robust and resilient cloud ecosystem in which the emerging threats are managed with ease to assure integrity and confidentiality for critical information.

Cloud security is undeniably one serious issue in this ever-evolving digital ecosystem. Scalability and efficiency, along with cost savings, have become the prime motivators for organizations in different sectors to make a shift toward cloud platforms. The agility provided by such migrations of clouds makes the requirement for a robust strategy related to security even more imperative. Admittedly, shifting to the cloud has its advantages, but on the other hand, it also opens the door for new vulnerabilities that could be utilized by cybercriminals. One breach may lead to the leakage of vital data, disruption of activities, and serious destruction of a company's reputation. With the cyber threats becoming advanced, the need is felt within organizations for continuously reshaping and updating their security protocols while keeping their defenses robust against new attack vectors. Security challenges have definitely become dynamic in nature, and hence, proactive rather than reactive approaches would be called for with regular assessment of risks, patching up vulnerabilities.

Ahead lies a future when even more cooperation and adaptability will be needed in cloud security. Security in the cloud is a question of shared responsibility, and it requires an extremely close collaboration between cloud providers and cloud users. Providers ensure the security of the infrastructure; an organization assumes the complete responsibility of its data and applications in the cloud. Moreover, the further clouds move into intricacy with the introduction of edge, serverless architectures, and quantum technologies, the more reason organizations would have to think again about their security strategy. These innovations come with both opportunities and risks. It will be those companies that are agile and forward-looking that will be in a better position to react to new challenges. A culture of continuous improvement and of cooperation, both internally within an organization and externally with experts in the field, can help ensure that business leader's future-proof their cloud security strategies in the most resilient ways. Ultimately, it will boil down to how much ability any business can adapt, innovate, and secure its cloud environments.

REFERENCES

Ahamad, S., Mohseni, M., Shekher, V., Smaisim, G. F., Tripathi, A., & Alanya-Beltran, J. (2022, April). A detailed analysis of the critical role of artificial intelligence in enabling high-performance cloud computing systems. In *2022 2nd International Conference on Advance Computing and Innovative Technologies in Engineering (ICACITE)* (pp. 156-159). IEEE.

Aishwarya, R., & Malliga, S. (2014, April). Intrusion detection system-An efficient way to thwart against Dos/DDos attack in the cloud environment. In *2014 International conference on recent trends in information technology* (pp. 1-6). Ieee.

Al Mudawi, N., Beloff, N., & White, M. (2019, August). Cloud computing in government organizations-towards a new comprehensive model. In *2019 IEEE SmartWorld, Ubiquitous Intelligence & Computing, Advanced & Trusted Computing, Scalable Computing & Communications, Cloud & Big Data Computing, Internet of People and Smart City Innovation (SmartWorld/SCALCOM/UIC/ATC/CBDCom/IOP/SCI)* (pp. 1473-1479). IEEE.

Alkhonaini, M., & El-Sayed, H. (2018, August). Migrating data between physical server and cloud: improving accuracy and data integrity. In *2018 17th IEEE International Conference On Trust, Security And Privacy In Computing And Communications/12th IEEE International Conference On Big Data Science And Engineering (TrustCom/BigDataSE)* (pp. 1570-1574). IEEE.

Alsubaih, A., Hafez, A., & Alghathbar, K. (2013, September). Authorization as a service in cloud environments. In *2013 International Conference on Cloud and Green Computing* (pp. 487-493). IEEE.

Aparajit, S., Shah, R., Chopdekar, R., & Patil, R. (2022, May). Data protection: The cloud security perspective. In *2022 3rd International Conference for Emerging Technology (INCET)* (pp. 1-5). IEEE.

Ashitha, U., Amulya, A. H. L. S., Sushma, G., Irfana, S., & Saibaba, C. M. (2024, May). Strengthening Cloud Security Through Multi-Factor Authentication: A Comprehensive Integration of Diverse Approaches. In *2024 International Conference on Electronics, Computing, Communication and Control Technology (ICECCC)* (pp. 1-8). IEEE.

Choudhari, N. V., & Sasankar, A. B. (2021, February). Architectural vision of cloud computing in the Indian government. In *2021 International Conference on Innovative Trends in Information Technology (ICITIIT)* (pp. 1-7). IEEE.

Choudhary, C., Vyas, N., & Lilhore, U. K. (2023, November). Cloud Security: Challenges and Strategies for Ensuring Data Protection. In *2023 3rd International Conference on Technological Advancements in Computational Sciences (ICTACS)* (pp. 669-673). IEEE.

Chung, S. H., Kim, J. H., & Kim, Y. (2018, October). Pragmatic approach using OAuth mechanism for IoT device authorization in cloud. In *2018 International Conference on Advances in Computing, Communication Control and Networking (ICACCCN)* (pp. 1-4). IEEE.

Dhinakar, N. M., Rao, K. K., Jayanath, N., Prasad, R. D. V., Jadala, V. C., & Chintala, R. R. (2023, March). Defending against Cache-based Side-Channel Attack using Virtual Machine Migration in Cloud. In *2023 International Conference on Sustainable Computing and Data Communication Systems (ICSCDS)* (pp. 239-242). IEEE.

Moghaddam, F. F., Karimi, O., & Alrashdan, M. T. (2013, November). A comparative study of applying real-time encryption in cloud computing environments. In *2013 IEEE 2nd International Conference on Cloud Networking (CloudNet)* (pp. 185-189). IEEE.

Ga-Yeong Choi. JeongEun Seo, and Hun-Yeong Kwon. (2024). "A Comparative Study of National Cloud Security Strategy and Governance." In Proceedings of the 25th Annual International Conference on Digital Government Research (dg.o '24). Association for Computing Machinery, New York, NY, USA, 241–250. https://doi.org/DOI: 10.1145/3657054.3657085

Hassan, O., Fatai, F., Aderibigbe, O., Akinde, A., Onasanya, T., Sanusi, M., & Odukoya, O. (2024). Enhancing Cybersecurity through Cloud Computing Solutions in the United States. *Intelligent Information Management*, 16(4), 176–193. DOI: 10.4236/iim.2024.164011

Jaspin, K., Selvan, S., Sahana, S., & Thanmai, G. (2021, March). Efficient and secure file transfer in cloud through double encryption using AES and RSA Algorithm. In *2021 international conference on emerging smart computing and informatics (ESCI)* (pp. 791-796). IEEE.

Kao, T. C., Mao, C. H., Chang, C. Y., & Chang, K. C. (2012, June). Cloud SSDLC: Cloud security governance deployment framework in secure system development life cycle. In *2012 IEEE 11th international conference on trust, security and privacy in computing and communications* (pp. 1143-1148). IEEE.

Lai, S. T., & Leu, F. Y. (2015, July). A security threats measurement model for reducing Cloud computing security risk. In *2015 9th International Conference on Innovative Mobile and Internet Services in Ubiquitous Computing* (pp. 414-419). IEEE.

Lee, B. H., Dewi, E. K., & Wajdi, M. F. (2018, April). Data security in cloud computing using AES under HEROKU cloud. In *2018 27th wireless and optical communication conference (WOCC)* (pp. 1-5). IEEE.

Michels, J. D., Walden, I., Cybersecurity, C., & Infrastructure, C. (May 1, 2021). C. Millard (ed.), Cloud Computing Law (2nd Edn, OUP 2021), Available at *SSRN*: https://ssrn.com/abstract=4204847 or http://dx.doi.org/DOI: 10.2139/ssrn.4204847

Mohurle, M., & Panchbhai, V. V. (2016, July). Review on realization of AES encryption and decryption with power and area optimization. In *2016 IEEE 1st International Conference on Power Electronics, Intelligent Control and Energy Systems (ICPEICES)* (pp. 1-3). IEEE.

Nikam, R., & Potey, M. (2016, December). Cloud storage security using multi-factor authentication. In *2016 international conference on recent advances and innovations in engineering (ICRAIE)* (pp. 1-7). IEEE.

Pansotra, E., & Singh, S. P. (2015). Cloud Security Algorithms. *International Journal of Security and Its Applications.*, 9(10), 353–360. DOI: 10.14257/ijsia.2015.9.10.32

Pavithra, S., Ramya, S., & Prathibha, S. (2019, February). A survey on cloud security issues and blockchain. In *2019 3rd International Conference on Computing and Communications Technologies (ICCCT)* (pp. 136-140). IEEE.

Sendor, J., Lehmann, Y., Serme, G., & de Oliveira, A. S. (2014, March). Platform-level support for authorization in cloud services with OAuth 2. In *2014 IEEE International Conference on Cloud Engineering* (pp. 458-465). IEEE.

Sharphathy, M. N., & Sumalatha, V. (2024, March). A Secure Multi Factor Authentication Framework in Cloud Computing. In *2024 5th International Conference on Intelligent Communication Technologies and Virtual Mobile Networks (ICICV)* (pp. 761-767). IEEE.

Sivakumar, P., NandhaKumar, M., Jayaraj, R., & Kumaran, A. S. (2019, March). Securing data and reducing the time traffic using AES encryption with dual cloud. In *2019 IEEE International Conference on System, Computation, Automation and Networking (ICSCAN)* (pp. 1-5). IEEE.

Thiyagarajan, B., & Kamalakannan, R. (2014, February). Data integrity and security in cloud environment using AES algorithm. In *International Conference on Information Communication and Embedded Systems (ICICES2014)* (pp. 1-5). IEEE.

Tirumala, S. S., Sathu, H., & Naidu, V. (2015, December). Analysis and prevention of account hijacking based incidents in cloud environment. In *2015 international Conference on Information Technology (ICIT)* (pp. 124-129). IEEE.

Upadhyaya, A., & Bansal, M. (2015, March). Deployment of secure sharing: Authenticity and authorization using cryptography in cloud environment. In *2015 International Conference on Advances in Computer Engineering and Applications* (pp. 852-855). IEEE.

Verma, V., Kumar, P., Verma, R. K., & Priya, S. (2021). *"A Novel Approach for Security in Cloud Data Storage Using AES-DES-RSA Hybrid Cryptography," 2021 Emerging Trends in Industry 4.0 (ETI 4.0)*. Raigarh., DOI: 10.1109/ETI4.051663.2021.9619274

Walden, I., & Michels, J. D. (2024). Getting Critical: Making Sense of the EU Cybersecurity Framework for Cloud Providers. In Carneiro Pacheco de Andrade, F. A., Fernandes Freitas, P. M., & de Sousa Covelo de Abreu, J. R. (Eds.), *Legal Developments on Cybersecurity and Related Fields. Law, Governance and Technology Series* (Vol. 60). Springer., DOI: 10.1007/978-3-031-41820-4_2

Chapter 10
TOGAF-Based Enterprise Architecture Framework for Nusantara Smart Governance Domain

Mustika Sari
https://orcid.org/0000-0003-3941-051X
Department of Civil Engineering, Faculty of Engineering, Universitas Indonesia, Indonesia

Mohammed Ali Berawi
Department of Civil Engineering, Faculty of Engineering, Universitas Indonesia, Indonesia

Ignasius Mario
Center for Sustainable Infrastructure Development, Faculty of Engineering, Universitas Indonesia, Indonesia

Gunawan Saroji
Department of Civil Engineering, Politeknik Negeri Bengkalis, Indonesia

ABSTRACT

Indonesia's new capital city, Nusantara, is being developed with the smart city concept, with Smart Governance (SG) as a domain outlined in the Nusantara Smart City Blueprint. SG refers to the government's utilization of information and communications technology (ICT) to improve decision-making by promoting better stakeholder collaboration. Establishing the SG domain in the greenfield Nusantara requires cooperation among the government, private sector, and citizens as the users. Hence, it is crucial to develop an Enterprise Architecture (EA) framework that

DOI: 10.4018/979-8-3693-7678-2.ch010

defines the business processes, technical infrastructure, and information systems to provide SG services successfully. Therefore, this research aims to develop the EA framework for Nusantara's SG domain, ensuring that the smart features within the domain are aligned to enhance the ease of doing business in Nusantara. To obtain its objective, this study utilized The Open Group Architecture Framework (TOGAF) as a comprehensive approach to the domain's planning, design, implementation, and management.

1. INTRODUCTION

Indonesia is currently developing its new capital city, Nusantara, on Kalimantan Island. This development was motivated by the need for economic transformation supported by human development and technological advancement to obtain the Indonesia 2045 vision, where the country becomes one of the top five global economies (Muhyiddin, 2019). Furthermore, the decision to relocate was encouraged by the fact that Jakarta, the current capital city, is no longer suitable as the nation's capital due to its high population density, severe traffic congestion, and environmental challenges, such as recurring floods and subsidence (Savin, 2020; Takagi et al., 2016). These challenges require the urgency to adopt innovative governance and development approaches.

Nusantara is envisioned as a global city, with the smart city concept as one of the core principles for its development. Beyond improving city operations and providing better public services, the integration of technological advancements in smart cities is essential for creating sustainable urban environments, as it focuses on the efficient use of resources, reducing environmental impacts, and improving the quality of life for the citizens (Bibri & Krogstie, 2017; Lin et al., 2019; Phung et al., 2022). Moreover, integrating sustainable practices, such as the optimized use of renewable energy, aligns with global targets such as the United Nations Sustainable Development Goals (SDGs) (Al-Nory, 2019). Furthermore, by considering social inclusion and economic sustainability, a smart city framework can help the city achieve long-term sustainable development (Danilina & Majorzadehzahiri, 2020).

Nusantara Smart City Blueprint, published by Nusantara Capital Authority (NCA) (2023), outlined the smart city framework that encompasses six (6) key smart domains, which include Smart Governance (SG), Smart Transportation and Mobility (STM), Smart Living (SL), Natural Resources and Energy (NRE), Industry and Human Resources (IHR); and Built Environment and Infrastructure (BEI). The SG domain is the philosophy of leveraging information and communication technology (ICT) to enhance governance and promote active public engagement in governmental affairs (Pereira et al., 2018). This domain helps governments improve service infrastructure and is the foundation for an accountable and participatory government (Demirel & Mülazımoğlu, 2022; Scholl & Scholl, 2014).

Within Nusantara's SG domain, four (4) subdomains were developed. The City Management and Planning Service subdomain features the Integrated Command Control Center (ICCC) for overseeing infrastructure and emergency management, a Centralized Citizen Reporting Center for issue reporting, and an Urban Planning System for data-driven urban planning and land use. The Digital Service for Citizen subdomain integrates a comprehensive platform for essential services, including resident administration, public feedback, environmental monitoring, and a centralized digital identity system. The Smart Permit System (SPS) feature simplifies business operations by facilitating permit applications, utility registrations, tax payments, job postings, and government assistance. The IKNOW App is a mobile application designed to enable engagement with the development of Nusantara with various functions related to the smart city initiative, such as providing information about the development, gathering feedback from users, and involving them in decision-making processes. This study focuses on the SPS, which aims to enhance the ease of business in Nusantara.

Implementing SG domain features is a complex task due to its dynamic nature that involves many sectors, various stakeholders, cross-sectoral collaboration, and interactive services (Javidroozi et al., 2014); hence, it is important to have a well-developed business plan and IT infrastructure design providing seamless integration of services (Pourzolfaghar et al., 2016). To manage the complex information system, processes, and infrastructure in a smart city organization, an enterprise architecture (EA) framework should be developed for Nusantara's SG domain (Bastidas et al., 2017). EA is a strategic framework that comprehensively aligns an enterprise's strategies, business processes, information systems, and technology infrastructure, ensuring that they work together to meet the enterprise's visions (Tamm et al., 2011). In the smart city context as an urban enterprise, the availability of the EA framework evidently can provide better strategic agility and stability in a constantly changing situation (Mamkaitis et al., 2016).

Previous studies have attempted to explore the development of EA for smart cities. Saluky (2017) demonstrated using The Open Group Framework Architecture (TOGAF) framework in developing an EA model for smart cities, emphasizing its role in facilitating communication among stakeholders and addressing population growth, challenges, and environmental concerns. The research shows that TOGAF can be used as a communication medium for all stakeholders in a smart city, helping manage challenges such as population growth, energy needs, and pollution levels. A study by Bastidas et al. (2023) highlighted the practical challenges of integrating EA into urban governance. It emphasized the need for further research to optimize its application in smart cities, which resulted in ten major research directions for applying EA in real-world smart cities. Kakarontzas et al. (2014) presented a conceptual EA framework centered on architectural patterns addressing the identified quality and functional requirements to support the development of software systems in smart cities. Lnenicka et al. (2017) proposed a government EA framework to analyze smart cities' big data analytics requirements, focusing on the public sector's interconnecting business and application architecture. Petersen et al. (2019) developed an EA framework for data management in smart cities through various virtual enterprises that enhance business collaboration, emphasizing data exchange to create value-added services for citizens.

Collectively, these studies highlight the role of EA in managing the complexity of smart cities, accommodating multiple stakeholder perspectives, and supporting various city governance requirements. It is also evidenced that mainly these EAs were developed using the TOGAF framework specifying a detailed method for EA development based on interrelated areas of specialization called architecture domains, which include Business Architecture (BA), Information System Architecture (ISA), and Technology Architecture (TA) (The Open Group, 2022). Nevertheless, limited studies were found to have ever presented the development of EA, particularly for the SG domain of smart cities. Therefore, this research aims to fill the gap in current research regarding the lack of discussion on well-defined EA for the SG domain in smart cities by developing a TOGAF-based EA Framework for the Nusantara SG Domain. The result of this study was expected to impact the ease of doing business and the overall effectiveness of SG, particularly in the context of Nusantara.

2. LITERATURE STUDY

2.1 Smart Governance

Defined as the capacity to use intelligent and adaptive actions to maintain and make decisions on various matters, SG is the foundation of a smart, open, and participatory government (Pereira et al., 2018). Since its increased adoption in 2005, SG has driven governments to adapt their supporting infrastructure and build better communication channels to meet public needs. The smart approach to governance emphasizes leveraging technological advancements to improve the quality of life, particularly in the context of smart cities (Demirel & Mülazımoğlu, 2022).

In a smart city, technology plays a crucial role as an interface between social and technological dimensions, empowering new production, distribution, and governance methods, facilitating organizational transformation and institutional restructuring, and shaping individual choices and behaviors (Anand & Navío-Marco, 2018; Berawi et al., 2022). Meijer and Bolivar (2016) identified three key concepts in implementing a smart city: a technology-driven approach supported by ICT, a human resources approach fostering local development and innovation, and a governance model facilitating collaboration and network relationships among local stakeholders from city residents to corporate entities. In this context, SG adopts a public administration perspective, addressing social issues through policies and administrative reforms (Demirel & Mülazımoğlu, 2022).

The application of technology in government services is already prevalent in many developed countries. Digitalization enhances public administration efficiency, reduces regulatory burdens, and facilitates interactions between government, businesses, and citizens (Campmas et al., 2022). The development of e-government and the use of ICT aim to enhance administrative efficiency, performance, citizen-centricity, and service delivery, laying a crucial foundation for the development of smart governance (Pereira et al., 2018). Digital governance has become particularly relevant in developing countries due to the need to enhance government effectiveness (Berawi et al., 2021). Eliminating bureaucratic processes to improve information access and evaluating the implementation of digitalized government services are common requirements in these regions (Shkarlet et al., 2020).

In Europe, various platforms facilitate public participation within the governance domain. For example, Stockholm collects direct public input to improve city services, while Vienna uses crowdsourcing to enhance government functions. Furthermore, nearly all European cities provide open data to the public, with the European Union actively promoting Open Data by integrating data platforms across European cities (Yang et al., 2021). In the Asia-Pacific region, Seoul offers participation services like those in Europe, including issue reporting, policy suggestion submissions, and public voting for policy decisions. Singapore focuses on urban data platforms and e-government, while Tokyo emphasizes smart city initiatives with less public participation. Melbourne's government services are more limited, similar to those in the United States (Yang et al., 2021). Estonia has been a notable example of digital government services since the early 2000s, exemplifying successful smart governance. The secure use of digital identities for transactions within the e-Estonia system has built strong public trust. Estonia's Digital Governance Model shows that SG thrives in small countries with a young population, high trust in institutions, and a need for technological modernization (Stephany, 2020).

2.2 Enterprise Architecture

EA is a field that focuses on the design and implementation of information system architectures, particularly within large organizations and major projects such as corporate planning and government construction (Zhou et al., 2020). EA is a guiding framework that systematically defines the current or future organizational environment while establishing structured, continuous development and maintenance processes. In strategic planning, EA is critical in guiding and optimizing an organization's IT investments, effectively translating business strategies into actionable technological solutions (Jonkers et al., 2006).

One of the key strengths of EA is its ability to provide a comprehensive perspective across the entire enterprise. Although different domains within an organization may have existing architectural practices with varying maturity levels, challenges often arise due to the diverse methods and techniques used to document these architectures. This diversity can obscure the interconnections among different domains, making it difficult to ensure alignment with the organization's overall goals. For example, while a highly optimized technical infrastructure may deliver impressive performance at a low cost, it might be too inflexible to support agile and rapidly evolving business processes (Jonkers et al., 2006).

EA concisely overviews an organization's business and IT systems, highlighting their interconnections. It consists of models and standards to analyze the current landscape, envision future conditions, and create strategic roadmaps. These models cover business processes, information, applications, and infrastructure, organized into layers according to stakeholder views. The adoption of EA is expected to generate organizational value by promoting interoperability, flexibility, agility, coherence, and alignment between business and IT (Gong & Janssen, 2019).

A well-crafted EA offers the insights necessary to balance these diverse requirements. It facilitates the translation of corporate strategy into daily operations, ensuring that the organization's technical infrastructure aligns with broader business objectives. Moreover, EA provides strategic solutions for managing the complexities of diverse systems and technologies, enabling organizations, including cities, to simplify and digitize public services. It is a cohesive framework for managing the overall IT system, aligning IT strategy with business goals and design needs, and providing a solid foundation for informed decision-making during development (Anthony Jnr et al., 2021).

One of the most used methods in EA is TOGAF, a detailed method equipped with tools for creating an EA. It follows a step-by-step process using proven techniques and reusable architectural assets. While TOGAF provides a set of principles, it also focuses on the rules for developing the right principles. Three levels of principles assist in decision-making across the organization. TOGAF offers guidance on the effective use of IT resources and supports the practical growth and application of architectural tenets (Dumitriu & Popescu, 2020). TOGAF encompasses several key views (see Figure 1). First, BA focuses on system user issues and describes the flow of information between people and business processes. Data Architecture (DA) details the data management capabilities organized to support both logical and physical assets necessary for applications. Applications Architecture illustrates the fundamental architecture, including architectural segments and their relationships with the organization's business processes. Lastly, Technology Architecture addresses the selection of components to support business processes, data processing, and application services, covering aspects such as IT infrastructure, middleware, communication networks, processing, and standards.

Figure 1. TOGAF enterprise architecture (Shoilekova et al., 2024)

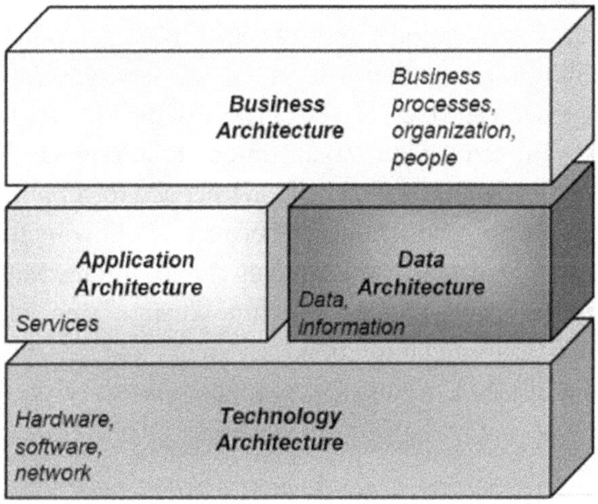

3. METHODOLOGY

This research undertook several stages to develop the EA for Nusantara's SG domain. The first stage was a comprehensive literature study conducted to collect data on the implementation of e-governance, particularly in business activities within Indonesia, by drawing on data provided by the Indonesia Investment Coordinating Board (BKPM). Furthermore, information regarding the planned developments in Nusantara was also collected to ensure that the EA design of the SG aligns with the existing plans for the new capital. A benchmarking study was also conducted by reviewing records and case studies of successful SG features implemented in other countries. This study was essential for understanding best practices that can be adapted for Nusantara.

After collecting the data, the next research stage was TOGAF modeling to develop the EA. Through its Architecture Development Method (ADM), TOGAF offers a framework for creating, managing, and implementing EA. The TOGAF ADM has several key characteristics. Firstly, it is one of the three widely used architectural design frameworks. Secondly, it is an open standard, meaning it can be freely used without interference or restrictions from other parties. Thirdly, it is open-source, allowing customization based on specific system design needs and conditions without reliance on a particular vendor (Rerung et al., 2020). Finally, all these characteristics make it easy to integrate into various systems (Lesnussa & Sitokdana, 2023).

The TOGAF modeling started with the Preliminary Phase, during which the architectural project's context, scope, and first framework are developed. Next, the Architecture Vision phase followed, whereby the architectural approach is harmonized with the organization's business objectives. Subsequently, the BA was established, providing a comprehensive outline of the organization's framework, procedures, management, and tactics. The purpose of the ISA was to ensure that data and applications are aligned with the organization's requirements. Then, the TA was designed to outline the technical infrastructure needed to support the information systems, including hardware, software, and networks. Following these phases, there are several more phases, such as Opportunities and Solutions, Migration Planning, Implementation Governance, and Architecture Change Management, which are used in the implementation and migration, as seen in Figure 2. This study will focus on the development of BA, ISA, and TA as the core layers of the TOGAF model.

Figure 2. TOGAF Architecture Development Method (ADM) (Adopted fromThe Open Group (2022))

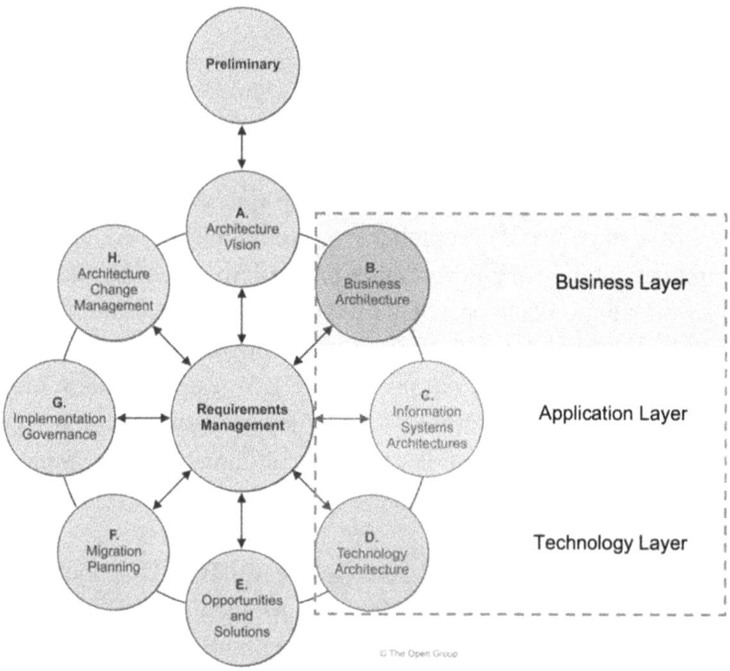

Building on the framework developed using the TOGAF method, the next research stage involves expert validation to ensure the robustness and applicability of the research results. This validation process was conducted through in-depth interviews with SG, EA, and public administration subject matter experts. The semi-structured interviews aim to gather insights and feedback on the proposed framework, focusing on its alignment with business processes, technological integration, and overall feasibility. Engaging with experts allowed for the refinement of the framework, addressing potential gaps, and enhancing its effectiveness in improving the ease of doing business in Nusantara. This process ensures that the SG domain is both practical and adaptable, tailored to meet the specific needs and challenges of the new capital. The research workflow is shown in Figure 3.

Figure 3. Research workflow

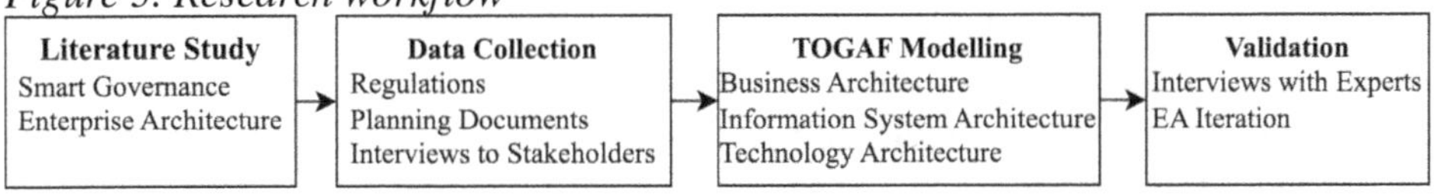

4. ENTERPRISE ARCHITECTURE FOR NUSANTARA'S SMART GOVERNANCE DOMAIN

4.1 Preliminary Phase and Architecture Vision

The SG domain services are designed to provide residents and businesses in Nusantara access to government services. Additionally, the centralized and integrated features of the SG will build transparency in the government's functionalities that require accessibility to information on policy, announcement, and administrative procedures. Digitalizing governmental processes eliminates bureaucratic entanglements, accelerates administrative workflows, saves citizens' time, and reduces government operational costs.

The SPS is one of the features in the SG domain, where businesses can apply for licenses to the NCA using a Single Sign-On (SSO) system. Companies can receive location recommendations based on their type and detailed spatial plans and check the 3D spatial intends to ensure compliance. Furthermore, businesses can report construction progress and receive government inspection schedules, while Artificial Intelligence (AI)-powered pre-screening of building permit applications accelerates the review and survey process. The system also allows businesses to monitor the progress of their licensing applications, providing a transparent and efficient process.

Beyond licensing, SG simplifies utility registration by allowing businesses to register utilities for their buildings via an integrated platform. It also streamlines tax and levy payments with customized submissions, payment reminders, and easy payment options. Additionally, businesses can post job vacancies on platforms integrated with the Smart Governance system, further supporting the economic ecosystem within Nusantara. The SG domain services also include government assistance programs tailored to business needs, where they can access publicly available government datasets to support decision-making and receive personalized information about relevant government programs, training, and incentives. It also includes access to incubator and accelerator programs designed to help startups and small and medium-sized enterprises (SMEs).

The EA for the SPS was developed in this study based on the business processes outlined in Presidential Regulation No. 12 of 2023 concerning the Granting of Business Licenses, Ease of Doing Business, and Investment Facilities for Business Actors in Nusantara. Furthermore, the Architecture Vision was also established based on the Presidential Regulation No. 63 of 2022, which emphasizes the goal for Nusantara to become a 'World Class City for All', as shown in Figure 4. The EA development has identified the end users as individuals or organizational representatives with specific roles related to initiating or performing activities based on their assigned tasks. These users include IKN residents, business owners, investors, government entities and employees, NCA employees, Public Service Agency (PSA), and ministerial officers.

Figure 4. Nusantara's vision, objectives, and enablers

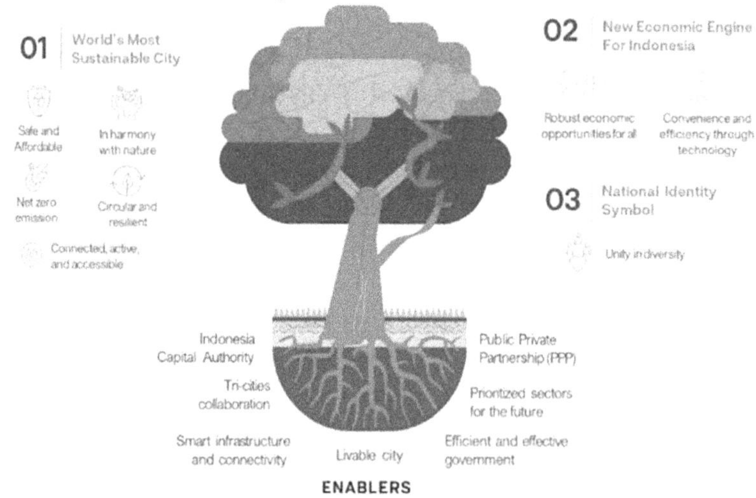

4.2 Business Architecture

BA establishes a consistent and effective security management framework within EA. It focuses on comprehensively understanding and modeling business strategies, governance structures, organizational frameworks, and key business processes. By aligning technological solutions with organizational goals and stakeholder needs, focusing on strategic objectives, leveraging value stream enablers, and ensuring robust interactions with government and other domains, Nusantara can provide residents with accountable and efficient government services. The BA encompasses several key components: strategic objectives, end users, channels, smart solutions, and value stream enablers. Figure 5 displays the developed BA diagram.

Figure 5. Business architecture

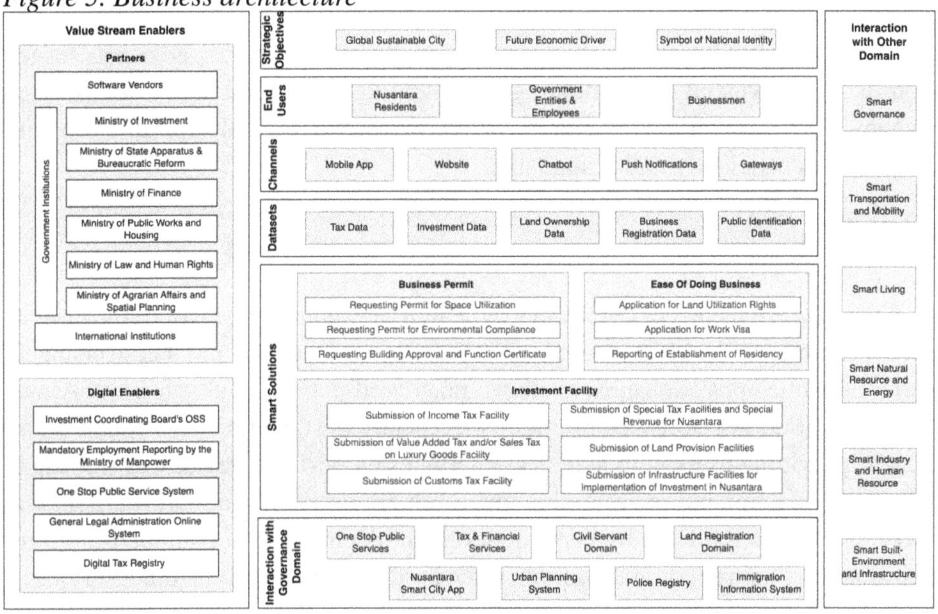

Strategic Objectives

Strategic Objectives define the long-term, overarching goals the NCA aims to achieve. These objectives act as guiding principles aligned with the organization's mission and vision, offering clear direction for decision-making and resource allocation. The vision of Nusantara has three strategic objectives: First, Nusantara is poised as an efficiently managed global city for sustainable living through good governance practices in various aspects of city life. Second, Nusantara aims to be

Indonesia's future economic locomotive, driven by social and economic change through innovation and technological development. Third, Nusantara will be a symbol of national identity that unites Indonesia's diverse socio-cultural characters.

End Users

End Users represent the primary beneficiaries of the SG domain services. Identifying end users is critical for designing services that are user-centric. These users include citizens, businesses, government employees, and visitors, ensuring that the services meet the diverse needs of all stakeholders. Nusantara residents are individuals from diverse backgrounds, such as children, homemakers, and the elderly, who expect safe, comfortable, and high-quality city facilities and services to support their daily lives. Businessmen include entrepreneurs and investors who seek a conducive business environment with access to markets, supportive infrastructure, and policies. Government entities and employees are comprised of employees from NCA, provincial and national government agencies, and the Public Service Agency (PSA), which require smart systems and technological support to operate city services efficiently and sustainably.

Channels

Channels are the access pathways by which SPS data, information, or services are communicated inside an organization or between other entities. These channels include mobile apps, websites, chatbots, push notifications, and gateways. A mobile application is a software program specifically designed for smartphones and tablets, providing users with features or services on portable devices. A website is a collection of web pages accessible via a web browser, offering information, services, or resources related to a specific domain. A chatbot is a computer program that simulates human communication, often used for automated customer service or information retrieval through text or voice interactions. Push notifications are alerts or messages sent directly to a user's device, delivering timely information, updates, or notifications even when the app is not in use. Gateways serve as central hubs for collecting and transmitting data, connecting various IoT devices and sensors to a network, enabling real-time data analysis, and the efficient management of urban services and infrastructure.

Smart Solutions

Smart Solutions encompass the processes within each business operation that constitute the system's core functionalities. These solutions are derived from Government Regulation No. 12 of 2023, which details the provision of business licenses, ease of doing business, and investment facilities for business actors in Nusantara Capital. These services are consolidated into smart solutions, which form the fundamental offerings of the system, streamlining business processes and enhancing service delivery efficiency.

Business Permit solution facilitates the business process by enhancing efficiency in obtaining various permits, including licenses for space usage, environmental compliance, construction approvals, and the issuance of functionality certifications. Integrating these processes into a unified system allows the NCA to effectively manage legal and regulatory requirements, reducing delays and boosting operational efficiency. The Ease of Doing Business solution simplifies essential administrative tasks for companies and individuals, including requesting land use rights, acquiring work permits, and officially registering residency. Investment Facility solution provides specialized support to investors, offering streamlined procedures for applying for income tax facilities, customs tax facilities, and Value Added Tax (VAT) or Sales Tax on luxury items. It also includes provisions for exclusive tax benefits, unique revenue sources for Nusantara, and the allocation of land and infrastructure facilities to support investment.

Value Stream Enablers

Value Stream Enablers provide the essential support and collaborative platforms necessary for effectively executing business processes within the system. These enablers are divided into two categories: Partners and Digital Enablers. Partners are entities selected based on their relevance to the required bodies, institutions, and organizations to construct the system, providing the critical data necessary for business process functions. They include the Ministry of Investment, Ministry of State Apparatus & Bureaucratic Reform, Ministry of Finance, Ministry of Public Works and Housing, Ministry of Law and Human Rights, and the Ministry of Agrarian Affairs and Spatial Planning, as well as international institutions and software vendors.

Meanwhile, Digital Enablers serve as supplementary systems that enhance the functionality of the business processes described in the smart solutions. These enablers integrate advanced technologies to improve operational efficiency and effectiveness. Key digital enablers include the Investment Coordinating Board's Online Single Submission (OSS), the Mandatory Employment Reporting system by the Ministry of Manpower, the One Stop Public Service System, the General

Legal Administration Online System, and the Digital Tax Registry. Together, these partners and digital enablers form a robust foundation that supports and optimizes the overall business process execution within the system.

Data Sets

Data Sets are the foundational elements crucial for supporting business process services. They are derived from the smart solutions' functionalities and outline the required data types. The primary data types include personal, business, transaction, geospatial, and performance data, all of which are vital for the efficient operation and management of various business processes. Key data sets for the developed BA include a wide range of categories, including tax data that tracks financial obligations and compliance, investment data that monitors investment activities and trends, land ownership data that records property rights and transactions, business registration data that ensures businesses are properly documented and regulated, and public identification data that verifies the identities of individuals interacting with the system.

Interaction with Government Domain

Interaction of SPS as a smart feature with other features within the SG domain involves relationships with various government entities, such as One Stop Public Services, Tax & Financial Services, Civil Service Administration, and Land Management Services, as well as the Nusantara Smart City App, Urban Planning System, Police Registry, and Immigration Information System. These interactions are crucial for the integrated functioning of the SG domain, ensuring seamless service delivery across different government entities.

Interaction with Other Domains

Interaction with Other Domains refers to the SPS's integration with the other five domains within the Nusantara smart city, with BEI and IHR as the domains it interacts with the most. For instance, in BEI, particularly the Smart Infrastructure feature, businessmen can report building progress and receive schedules on government inspections. Additionally, through SPS, they can apply for building permits, which AI will screen first to accelerate the review and survey process. In the IHR domain, particularly the Digital Service for SMEs feature, small and medium enterprises (SMEs) can access the SPS feature with SSO, apply for utility registration, Tax and Retribution payments, receive personalized information, and register for government programs training, incentives, including incubator and accelerator program for startups & SMEs.

4.3 Information Systems Architecture

The ISA can be defined as an information system blueprint that provides decision-making regarding the form of data, applications, and technology required by an organization to support the BA. Therefore, the primary objective of ISA is to develop the DA and AA that align with the Architecture Vision (Rerung et al., 2020).

4.3.1 Data Architecture

DA involves designing and managing organizational data assets, ensuring data quality, accessibility, and security. The development of DA is based on the components required for data processing. Broadly, data processing necessitates processes of acquisition, refinement, and consumption. Additionally, the data from applications needed by business processes are outlined according to each process (Carli et al., 2013). As displayed in Figure 6, the components in the DA include data acquisition, data refinery, data consumption, and application data.

The developed DA provides a structured approach to managing data assets and developing Nusantara's SG domain, particularly the SPS feature. By focusing on data acquisition, refinery, and consumption and understanding the application data requirements, the DA ensures that data quality, accessibility, and security are maintained. It supports efficient data management and enhances the overall effectiveness of SG initiatives, driving sustainable urban development and improving the quality of life for citizens.

Data Acquisition

Data Acquisition involves gathering data from various sources such as legacy systems, master data management, web, social media, open data, and software as a service (SaaS). This process represents general data acquisition, accommodating the interoperability service system. Effective data acquisition ensures that diverse and relevant data sources are integrated into the system, forming a comprehensive data foundation for SG.

Figure 6. Data architecture

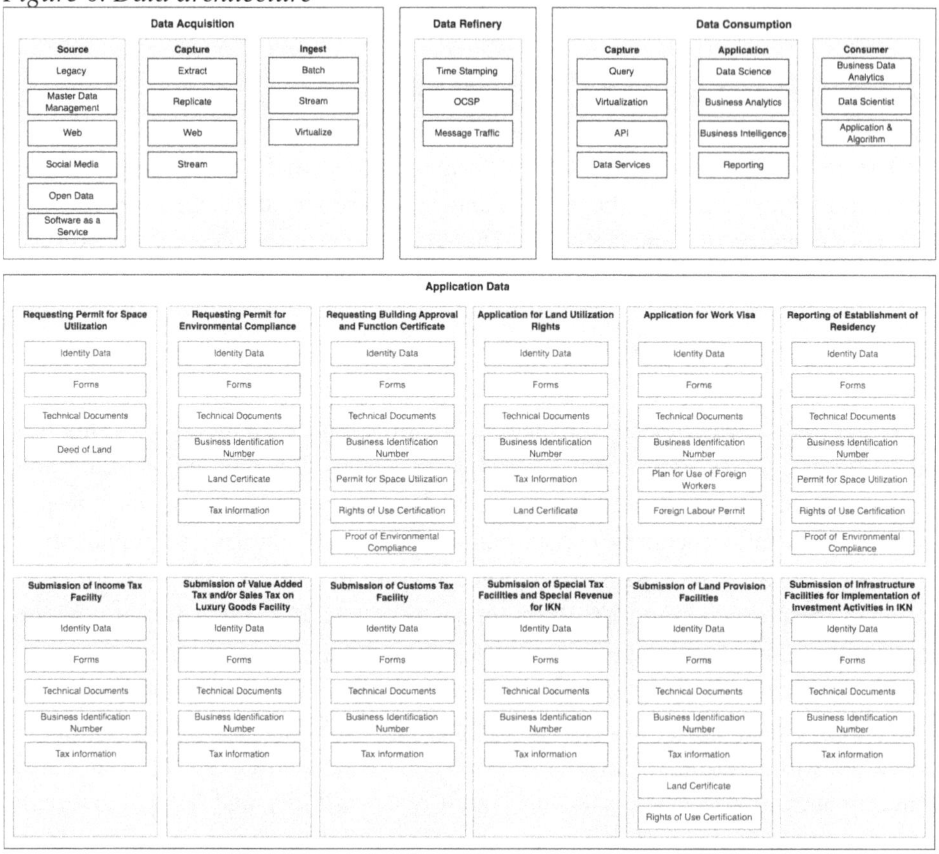

Data Refinery

Data Refinery purifies data through time stamping, Online Certificate Status Protocol (OCSP), and message traffic analysis to ensure data is accurate, secure, and usable. The refinement process is crucial for maintaining data integrity and security.

Data Consumption

Data Consumption relates to how data is captured, processed, and utilized. This phase includes batch processing, streaming, virtualization, and various ways to capture, query, and use data. It represents the general processes of data consumption from web-based service systems. Effective data consumption strategies enable the efficient use of data, providing valuable insights and supporting informed decision-making in smart governance.

Application Data

Different applications generate and consume specific data. For instance, in the context of a smart city, data related to permit applications, tax filings, and infrastructure development are critical. Application data is derived from Smart Solutions and elaborates on the specific data needed to execute business processes from Smart Solutions. Understanding application data requirements ensures that the data architecture supports the functional needs of smart governance, enabling seamless integration and interoperability across various applications.

4.3.2 Application Architecture

Application Architecture outlines the structure and behavior of software applications within an organization. Application architecture development is based on the services from business processes and benchmarking from existing smart governance systems. This Application Architecture framework provides a structured approach to developing and implementing Smart Governance in Nusantara. The framework ensures that applications are well-aligned with organizational needs and user expectations by focusing on security, business activities, services, user interaction channels, domain interactions, and infrastructure. This approach supports the creation of a sustainable and efficient smart city, enhancing the quality of life for its citizens and driving economic growth. The AA of the SPS in Nusantara, which involves security, business activities, services, channels, interaction with other domains, and infrastructure, is in Figure 7.

Security

The AA involves implementing security measures such as authentication, access control, encryption, and monitoring to protect sensitive information. These security components are derived from benchmarking the systems in the SG domain used by the National Institute for Information Security (NIIS). Ensuring robust security is crucial for maintaining data integrity and trust in digital services.

Activities

Business activities are translated into specific applications, such as those for business permits, ease of doing business, and investment facilities. Each activity has distinct processes and functions, which are supported by tailored applications to meet the specific needs of these processes. This ensures that business operations are efficiently managed and aligned with organizational goals.

Figure 7. Application architecture

Services

Applications provide various services, including digital document management, e-government services, data analysis and reporting, workflow automation, citizen engagement platforms, and transparency initiatives. These services are essential for enhancing operational efficiency, improving public service delivery, and fostering greater citizen participation in governance.

Channels

The AA determines how end-users interact with the system, selecting channels such as websites, mobile applications, chatbots, and push notifications to provide an optimal user experience. The architecture ensures that users can engage with services conveniently and effectively by offering multiple access points.

Interaction with Other Domains

Applications interact with the other five domains in Nusantara. This interaction ensures that applications are integrated and interoperable, supporting the holistic development of SG domain services.

Infrastructure

The technological backbone that supports the applications involves central services, security servers, timestamping authorities, information systems, and certification authorities. This infrastructure is designed based on benchmarking from the Smart Governance system of NIIS. A robust infrastructure is essential for ensuring the applications' reliability, scalability, and security, enabling them to function seamlessly and efficiently.

4.4 Technology Architecture

TA is designed based on the technological requirements needed to execute business processes outlined in the BA. This architecture is structured around the main components necessary for the technological support of the Smart Governance system. This Technology Architecture framework provides a structured approach to developing and implementing the technological elements of Smart Governance in Nusantara. By focusing on smart solutions, channels, end users, security, data management, operations, connectivity, integrations, and infrastructure, this framework ensures that the technological needs of the SG system are met comprehensively. This approach supports the creation of a robust, efficient, and secure smart city that enhances the quality of life for its citizens and promotes sustainable urban development. Figure 8 displays the TA for SPS in the SG domain of Nusantara, consisting of smart solutions, channels, users, security, data, operations, connectivity, integration, infrastructure, and end devices.

Figure 8. Technology architecture

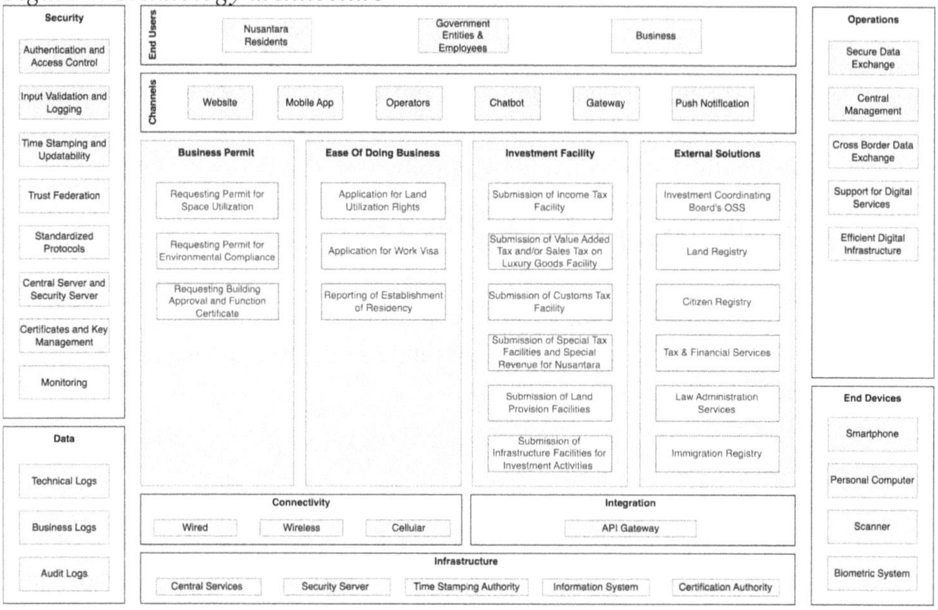

Smart Solutions

Smart solutions use advanced technologies to efficiently implement business processes, including technologies for managing business permits, facilitating ease of doing business, and managing investment facilities. These Smart Solutions are derived from Government Regulation No. 3 of 2022. The implementation of these technologies ensures streamlined operations and enhanced service delivery. For business permits, the smart solutions can request licenses for space utilization, request permits for environmental compliance, and request building approval and function certificates. As for ease of doing business, smart solutions can support and expedite the application for land utilization rights, work visas, and residency establishment reports. In the context of investment facility, the smart solutions help the submission of income tax facility, submission of value added tax and sales tax on luxury goods facility, submission of customs tax facility, submission of special tax facilities and special revenue for Nusantara, submission of land provision facilities, and submission of infrastructure facilities for investment activities. Several existing solutions exist from external government entities, including the Investment Coordinating Board's OSS, Land Registry, Citizen Registry, Tax & Financial Services, Law Administration Services, and Immigration Registry.

Channels

The technology layer supports various channels, including websites, mobile applications, operators, chatbots, gateways, and push notifications, ensuring seamless connectivity. This multi-channel approach guarantees users access to services through their preferred platforms, enhancing user engagement and satisfaction.

End Users

TA considers end users' devices, such as smartphones, personal computers, scanners, and biometric systems, ensuring compatibility and accessibility. By accommodating diverse devices, the architecture ensures that all users can efficiently interact with Nusantara's SPS.

Security

A crucial aspect of TA is ensuring system security through authentication, access control, timestamping, encryption, and monitoring. These security measures are benchmarked from the Smart Governance systems implemented by the National Institute for Information Security (NIIS). Robust security protocols are essential for protecting sensitive information and maintaining trust in the system. The security in the SG domain of Nusantara, particularly the SPS, encompasses Authentication and Access Control, Input Validation and Logging, Time Stamping and Updatability, Trust Federation, Standardized Protocols, Central Server and Security Server, Certificates and Key Management, and Monitoring.

Data

Managing various data types, including technical, business, and audit logs, is part of the technology layer. This layer also supports secure data exchange and efficient digital infrastructure. Effective data management ensures that all data is accurately recorded, securely stored, and easily accessible for analysis and reporting.

Operations

The technology layer supports secure data exchange, central management, cross-border data exchange, and digital service support. These operations are designed based on benchmarking from the Smart Governance systems implemented by NIIS. Efficient operational support ensures the smooth functioning of the system and high-quality service delivery.

Connectivity

Technology architecture involves selecting and implementing various connectivity options, including wired, wireless, and mobile, to ensure reliable communication and robust connectivity options that ensure the system remains accessible and operational under multiple conditions.

Integrations

Integrating with external systems is a critical part of Technology Architecture. This is achieved through API gateways, which facilitate seamless data exchange and interoperability with other systems. Effective integration ensures the Smart Governance system can collaborate with external services and platforms, enhancing its functionality and reach.

Infrastructure

Ensuring the resilience of the infrastructure, including central services, security servers, timestamp authorities, information systems, and certification authorities, is fundamental to the technology layer. This infrastructure is designed based on benchmarking from the Smart Governance systems implemented by NIIS. A resilient infrastructure ensures the system's reliability, scalability, and security, supporting its long-term sustainability.

End Devices

End devices include smartphones, personal computers, scanners, and biometric systems, which are critical for enabling user interaction with the system, facilitating data input, access, and authentication processes, and supporting the overall functionality of the SG domain's infrastructure.

4.5 Expert Validation

Expert evaluation is a key method used to assess the reliability of research results. In this study, expert validation was conducted through in-depth interviews and analysis with specialists in the technology field, with a particular focus on smart governance systems. Two experts with significant expertise in SG domain services of smart city development were interviewed for the validation process in this study. Expert 1 holds a Doctor of Philosophy in Information Systems and has two decades of experience in technology, digital media, and developing digital applications and services. Expert 1 provided insights into the enterprise architecture developed for the SG domain's features during validation. The expert confirmed that the BA adequately addresses the business processes related to business licensing and ease of doing business.

Furthermore, he observed that the DA effectively represents data services for business processes and meets the extract, transform load (ETL) requirements. Overall, Expert 1 acknowledged the progress towards a functional system but emphasized the need for more detailed explanations regarding the technology and application architectures. However, Expert 1 suggested the implementation of packaged business capabilities to ensure that the SG domain is not monolithic. Adopting a composable architecture would facilitate the development of the system in a more agile and decentralized manner, allowing for improvements without the necessity of a complete rebuild.

The second expert served as a high-level officer at the technology office of the Nordic Institute for Interoperability Solutions (NIIS). The expert has been involved in the X-Road project in Finland, which provides a centrally governed distributed platform that manages data exchange within an ecosystem. Expert 2 stated that using the EA model for the SG domain can emphasize its efficacy in facilitating stakeholder communications. Furthermore, Expert 2 highlighted the significance of digital identity systems as a critical component of the SG domain services. Additionally, Expert 2 emphasized the importance of integrating a data exchange layer into the SG domain. It was noted that the development of Nusantara's SG domain was similar to Estonia's experience in building its system from scratch. Expert 2 posited that the SG domain in Nusantara has significant potential to provide digital government services to all segments of society. This prospect bears a resemblance to the successes observed in Estonia.

The expert validation process has identified several key areas for consideration in developing the SG domain. Firstly, there is a need for more detailed explanations and clarity, particularly in the TA and AA, to ensure that all aspects of the system are thoroughly understood and effectively implemented. Secondly, composable architecture is crucial to avoid a monolithic system structure. This approach allows for greater agility and decentralization, facilitating easier updates and improvements. Moreover, the integration of robust digital identity systems is crucial for the success of the Smart Governance system, ensuring secure and reliable user identification and access. Finally, drawing parallels with Estonia's experience underscores the potential for implementing Nusantara successfully. Estonia's experience developing a comprehensive Smart Governance system provides valuable lessons and a benchmark for Nusantara's development.

5. CONCLUSION

The development of the SG domain in Nusantara smart city is important given its goals of improving the residents' quality of life, enhancing the efficiency of city operations, and increasing the performance of public services. Leveraging the principles of good governance and ICT is critical to strengthening decision-making, transparency, accountability, and citizen participation. Adopting an EA framework, particularly developed using the TOGAF method, is needed in developing the SG domain to align the technological solutions with business processes and ensure comprehensive integration across various government entities.

This research emphasizes the need for a holistic approach that includes BA, DA, AA, and TA, specifically designed for Nusantara SPS, to increase the ease of doing business in Nusantara. Each component is designed to address specific challenges and requirements of smart governance. BA focuses on aligning organizational goals with technological solutions, enhancing public service delivery, and fostering stakeholder collaboration. DA ensures data quality, accessibility, and security, supporting efficient data management and interoperability, while AA provides a structured approach to developing secure, efficient, and user-friendly software applications. Moreover, TA addresses the technological infrastructure required to support smart governance, including security, data management, and connectivity.

REFERENCES

Al-Nory, M. T. (2019). Optimal Decision Guidance for the Electricity Supply Chain Integration with Renewable Energy: Aligning Smart Cities Research with Sustainable Development Goals. *IEEE Access : Practical Innovations, Open Solutions*, 7, 74996–75006. Advance online publication. DOI: 10.1109/ACCESS.2019.2919408

Anand, P. B., & Navío-Marco, J. (2018). Governance and economics of smart cities: opportunities and challenges. In *Telecommunications Policy* (Vol. 42, Issue 10). DOI: 10.1016/j.telpol.2018.10.001

Anthony Jnr, B., Abbas Petersen, S., Helfert, M., & Guo, H. (2021). Digital transformation with enterprise architecture for smarter cities: A qualitative research approach. *Digital Policy. Regulation & Governance*, 23(4), 355–376. DOI: 10.1108/DPRG-04-2020-0044

Bastidas, V., Bezbradica, M., Bilauca, M., Healy, M., & Helfert, M. (2023). Enterprise Architecture in Smart Cities: Developing an Empirical Grounded Research Agenda. *Journal of Urban Technology*, 30(1), 47–70. DOI: 10.1080/10630732.2022.2122681

Bastidas, V., Bezbradica, M., & Helfert, M. (2017). Cities as enterprises: A comparison of smart city frameworks based on enterprise architecture requirements. *Lecture Notes in Computer Science (Including Subseries Lecture Notes in Artificial Intelligence and Lecture Notes in Bioinformatics), 10268 LNCS*. DOI: 10.1007/978-3-319-59513-9_3

Berawi, M. A., Sari, M., Addiani, F. A. F., & Madyaningrum, N. (2021). Developing a Blockchain-based Data Storage System Model to Improve Government Agencies' Organizational Performance. *International Journal of Technology*, 12(5), 1038. DOI: 10.14716/ijtech.v12i5.5237

Berawi, M. A., Susantono, B., & Sari, M. (2022). Fostering resilient and smart cities to enhance sustainable urban development. In *The Routledge Handbook of Sustainable Cities and Landscapes in the Pacific Rim* (pp. 704–719). Routledge., DOI: 10.4324/9781003033530-60

Bibri, S. E., & Krogstie, J. (2017). Smart sustainable cities of the future: An extensive interdisciplinary literature review. In *Sustainable Cities and Society* (Vol. 31). DOI: 10.1016/j.scs.2017.02.016

Campmas, A., Iacob, N., & Simonelli, F. (2022). How can interoperability stimulate the use of digital public services? An analysis of national interoperability frameworks and e-Government in the European Union. *Data & Policy*, 4, e19. Advance online publication. DOI: 10.1017/dap.2022.11

Carli, R., Dotoli, M., Pellegrino, R., & Ranieri, L. (2013). Measuring and managing the smartness of cities: A framework for classifying performance indicators. *Proceedings - 2013 IEEE International Conference on Systems, Man, and Cybernetics, SMC 2013*, 1288–1293. DOI: 10.1109/SMC.2013.223

Danilina, N., & Majorzadehzahiri, A. (2020). Social factors of sustainability for a smart city development. *IOP Conference Series. Materials Science and Engineering*, 869(2), 022027. Advance online publication. DOI: 10.1088/1757-899X/869/2/022027

Demirel, D., & Mülazımoğlu, M. E. (2022). How the smart governance model shapes cities? Cases from Europe. *Journal of Enterprising Communities*, 16(1), 8–25. DOI: 10.1108/JEC-08-2021-0115

Dumitriu, D., & Popescu, M. A. M. (2020). Enterprise architecture framework design in IT management. *Procedia Manufacturing*, 46, 932–940. DOI: 10.1016/j.promfg.2020.05.011

Gong, Y., & Janssen, M. (2019). The value of and myths about enterprise architecture. *International Journal of Information Management*, 46, 1–9. DOI: 10.1016/j.ijinfomgt.2018.11.006

Javidroozi, V., Shah, H., Amini, A., & Cole, A. (2014). Smart city as an integrated enterprise: a business process centric framework addressing challenges in systems integration. *3rd International Conference on Smart Systems, Devices and Technologies*. DOI: 10.13140/RG.2.1.2561.1921

Jonkers, H., Lankhorst, M. M., Ter Doest, H. W. L., Arbab, F., Bosma, H., & Wieringa, R. J. (2006). Enterprise architecture: Management tool and blueprint for the organisation. *Information Systems Frontiers*, 8(2), 63–66. DOI: 10.1007/s10796-006-7970-2

Kakarontzas, G., Anthopoulos, L., Chatzakou, D., & Vakali, A. (2014). A conceptual enterprise architecture framework for smart cities: A survey based approach. *ICE-B 2014 - Proceedings of the 11th International Conference on e-Business, Part of ICETE 2014 - 11th International Joint Conference on e-Business and Telecommunications*. DOI: 10.5220/0005021400470054

Lesnussa, J., & Sitokdana, M. N. N. (2023). Leveraging TOGAF ADM for Enterprise Architecture in West Seram Environment Agency. *Journal of Information Systems and Informatics*, 5(4), 1595–1608. Advance online publication. DOI: 10.51519/journalisi.v5i4.603

Lin, C., Zhao, G., Yu, C., & Wu, Y. (2019). Smart City Development and Residents' Well-Being. *Sustainability (Basel)*, 11(3), 676. DOI: 10.3390/su11030676

Lnenicka, M., Machova, R., Komarkova, J., & Pasler, M. (2017). Government enterprise architecture for big and open linked data analytics in a smart city ecosystem. *Smart Innovation. Systems and Technologies*, 75, 475–485. Advance online publication. DOI: 10.1007/978-3-319-59451-4_47

Mamkaitis, A., Bezbradica, M., & Helfert, M. (2016). Urban enterprise: A review of Smart City frameworks from an enterprise architecture perspective. *IEEE 2nd International Smart Cities Conference: Improving the Citizens Quality of Life, ISC2 2016 - Proceedings*. DOI: 10.1109/ISC2.2016.7580810

Meijer, A., & Bolívar, M. P. R. (2016). Governing the smart city: A review of the literature on smart urban governance. *International Review of Administrative Sciences*, 82(2), 392–408. DOI: 10.1177/0020852314564308

Muhyiddin, M. (2019). Future Challenges on Indonesia's Vision 2045. *Jurnal Perencanaan Pembangunan: The Indonesian Journal of Development Planning*, 3(1). Advance online publication. DOI: 10.36574/jpp.v3i1.63

Nusantara Capital Authority. (2023). *Cetak Biru Kota Cerdas Nusantara (Nusantara Smart City Blueprint)* (B. Susantono, M. A. Berawi, T. A. Setiono, A. Gunawan, Y. G. Sucahyo, M. Sari, G. Gunawan, & A. Mahendra, Eds.; 1st ed.). Otorita Ibu Kota Nusantara. https://www.ikn.go.id/storage/thd/blueprint/cetak_biru_kota_cerdas_nusantara.pdf

Pereira, G. V., Parycek, P., Falco, E., & Kleinhans, R. (2018). Smart governance in the context of smart cities: A literature review. In *Information Polity* (Vol. 23, Issue 2, pp. 143–162). IOS Press. DOI: 10.3233/IP-170067

Petersen, S. A., Pourzolfaghar, Z., Alloush, I., Ahlers, D., Krogstie, J., & Helfert, M. (2019). Value-Added Services, Virtual Enterprises and Data Spaces Inspired Enterprise Architecture for Smart Cities. *IFIP Advances in Information and Communication Technology*, 568, 393–402. Advance online publication. DOI: 10.1007/978-3-030-28464-0_34

Phung, S., Richards, A. C., & Mohammadzadeh, M. (2022). Smart Cities in the Pacific Rim: A mapping of urban evolution in the Pacific. In *The Routledge Handbook of Sustainable Cities and Landscapes in the Pacific Rim* (pp. 670–686). Taylor and Francis. DOI: 10.4324/9781003033530-58

Pourzolfaghar, Z., Bezbradica, M., & Helfert, M. (2016). Types of IT Architectures in Smart Cities – A review from a Business Model and Enterprise Architecture Perspective. *AIS Pre-ICIS Workshop on "IoT & Smart City Challenges and Applications" – ISCA 2016, 1*(1987).

Rerung, R. R., & Wahvuni, A., Rinasari, & Susrini, I. (2020). Blueprint of Smart Campus System Using TOGAF ADM. *6th International Conference on Computing, Engineering, and Design, ICCED 2020*. DOI: 10.1109/ICCED51276.2020.9415824

Saluky, S. (2017). Development of Enterprise Architecture Model for Smart City. [Information Technology Engineering Journals]. *ITE Journal*, 2(2), 12–18. Advance online publication. DOI: 10.24235/itej.v2i2.17

Savin, G. V. (2020). Quality indicator of the smart city transportation and logistics system. *Economic Analysis: Theory and Practice*, 19(11), 2116–2135. DOI: 10.24891/ea.19.11.2116

Scholl, H. J., & Scholl, M. C. (2014). *Smart Governance: A Roadmap for Research and Practice*. DOI: 10.9776/14060

Shkarlet, S., Oliychenko, I., Dubyna, M., Ditkovska, M., & Zhovtok, V. (2020). Comparative analysis of best practices in E-government implementation and use of this experience by developing countries. *Administratie Si Management Public*, 2020(34), 118–136. DOI: 10.24818/amp/2020.34-07

Shoilekova, K., Ivanova, B., & Andreeva, M. (2024). The Meaning of Business and Software Architecture in the Enterprise Architecture. *Lecture Notes in Networks and Systems, 935 LNNS*. DOI: 10.1007/978-3-031-54820-8_28

Stephany, F. (2020). It's Not Only Size That Matters: Determinants of Estonia's E-Governance Success. *Electronic Government, an International Journal, 16*(1), 1. DOI: 10.1504/EG.2020.10028669

Takagi, H., Esteban, M., Mikami, T., & Fujii, D. (2016). Projection of coastal floods in 2050 Jakarta. *Urban Climate*, 17, 135–145. DOI: 10.1016/j.uclim.2016.05.003

Tamm, T., Seddon, P. B., Shanks, G., & Reynolds, P. (2011). How does enterprise architecture add value to organisations? *Communications of the Association for Information Systems*, 28(1). Advance online publication. DOI: 10.17705/1CAIS.02810

The Open Group. (2022). The Open Group Standard The TOGAF® Standard, Version 10. In *The TOGAF® Standard, Version 10*.

Yang, J., Kwon, Y., & Kim, D. (2021). Regional Smart City Development Focus: The South Korean National Strategic Smart City Program. *IEEE Access : Practical Innovations, Open Solutions*, 9, 7193–7210. DOI: 10.1109/ACCESS.2020.3047139

Chapter 11
Integrating AI, Blockchain, and Cloud Computing for Enhanced E-Government Solutions

Batal Almutairi
Arab Open University, Kuwait

ABSTRACT

This chapter explores the integration of artificial intelligence (AI), blockchain, and cloud computing as a transformative force in modernizing e-government solutions. It highlights how these technologies synergize to enhance efficiency, transparency, and security in public administration. AI's ability to process large datasets and automate decision-making, Blockchain's secure and immutable ledger for trustworthy transactions, and cloud computing's scalable infrastructure collectively offer governments the tools needed to meet the growing demands of the digital age. This chapter examines practical applications like resource allocation, cybersecurity, and data analysis, emphasizing their role in enhancing trust and accountability in governance. Moreover, it showcases global case studies of successful e-government initiatives and provides a roadmap for implementing a holistic digital government strategy. This chapter serves as a comprehensive guide for policymakers and technologists involved in public sector digital transformation.

DOI: 10.4018/979-8-3693-7678-2.ch011

INTRODUCTION

The convergence of Artificial Intelligence (AI), Blockchain, and Cloud Computing represents not just a technological advancement but a fundamental shift in the way governments can deliver services, engage with citizens, and manage public resources. As governments across the globe navigate the complexities of the digital age, the integration of these three powerful technologies offers a transformative approach to modernizing e-Government solutions. This transformation is not simply about incorporating new tools; it is about fundamentally rethinking how governance is conducted in a world where citizens expect immediacy, transparency, and efficiency in all their interactions with the state.

AI, Blockchain, and Cloud Computing, when combined, form a synergistic trio that holds the potential to redefine public sector operations on multiple levels. AI's ability to process vast datasets and automate complex decision-making processes can revolutionize the efficiency of government operations, enabling faster, more informed responses to citizen needs. For instance, AI can be employed to optimize resource allocation during a crisis, predict trends in public health, or even streamline bureaucratic processes that historically have been cumbersome and slow.

Blockchain, on the other hand, provides the foundational security and integrity required to ensure that government transactions and records are trustworthy and transparent. Blockchain technology ensures that all governmental actions, whether they involve financial transactions, voting systems, or public record management, are recorded in a manner that is both tamper-proof and verifiable. This not only protects against fraud but also builds public trust by providing a clear, accessible record of government actions.

Cloud Computing complements these technologies by offering the scalable and flexible infrastructure necessary to support the vast and growing demands of digital governance. The move to cloud-based systems allows governments to handle large volumes of data with ease, scale their operations according to demand, and reduce the costs associated with maintaining physical IT infrastructure. Moreover, Cloud Computing enables the rapid deployment of AI and Blockchain technologies, ensuring that these innovations can be integrated seamlessly into existing government frameworks to be more adaptive and responsive to the changing needs of their citizens.

The adoption of these technologies also plays a critical role in addressing the complex societal challenges that modern governments face. From managing public health crises to ensuring equitable access to services, the integration of AI, Blockchain, and Cloud Computing can enhance a government's ability to respond effectively and efficiently. Furthermore, smart cities rely on real-time data analytics (powered by AI), secure and efficient transactions (enabled by Blockchain), and scalable IT infrastructure (provided by Cloud Computing).

Cybersecurity is another area where the integration of AI, Blockchain, and Cloud Computing can have a transformative impact. AI can detect and respond to threats in real-time, Blockchain can secure critical data and transactions, and Cloud Computing can provide the resilient infrastructure needed to protect against and recover from attacks. This multi-layered approach to security ensures that government systems remain protected and operational, even in the face of significant threats.

Finally, by leveraging AI to analyze public data, Blockchain to ensure the integrity of the decision-making process, and Cloud Computing to store and share information, governments can create policies that are not only more effective but also more transparent. This book aspires to be a pivotal reference for anyone involved in the digital transformation of the public sector, offering insights into how these technologies can be integrated to create more efficient, transparent, and responsive government systems. As governments worldwide continue to grapple with the challenges of digital transformation, the lessons and strategies outlined in this book will serve as a guide to building the resilient, agile, and citizen-centric governments of the future.

STRATEGIC IMPORTANCE OF INTEGRATING AI, BLOCKCHAIN, AND CLOUD COMPUTING IN E-GOVERNMENT

Focusing on the integration of AI, Blockchain, and Cloud Computing in e-Government solutions is important for several reasons:

1. Enhanced Security and Trust

In the era of increasing cyber threats, the security of government data and transactions is paramount. Blockchain technology, with its decentralized and immutable ledger, offers a robust solution to prevent fraud, unauthorized access, and data breaches. The immutability of Blockchain ensures that once data is recorded, it cannot be altered or deleted without the consensus of the network, providing a permanent and tamper-proof record of all transactions. This characteristic is particularly valuable in the public sector, where the integrity of records such as land titles, birth certificates, and financial transactions is crucial for legal and administrative purposes.

The role of Blockchain in enhancing security goes beyond just data integrity. By integrating Blockchain with Artificial Intelligence (AI), governments can create a multi-layered defense mechanism that not only protects data but also actively monitors and responds to potential threats in real-time. AI can be employed to analyze patterns and behaviors across the Blockchain network, identifying anomalies that may indicate fraudulent activity or unauthorized access attempts. For instance, if

AI detects a transaction that deviates from established norms, it can trigger an alert or even automatically initiate countermeasures to prevent a security breach (Shinde, K., et al., 2023).

This integration of AI and Blockchain is particularly effective in addressing the evolving nature of cyber threats. Traditional security systems often rely on predefined rules and patterns to detect and respond to threats. However, as cyber attackers become more innovative, these static defenses can be bypassed. AI can continuously analyze new data, learn from past incidents, and improve its detection capabilities over time. When combined with Blockchain's secure ledger, this creates a highly resilient security system that can anticipate and counteract threats before they cause damage.

Moreover, Blockchain's transparency and traceability play a significant role in building trust between governments and citizens. This is particularly important in areas such as voting, public procurement, and the management of social benefits, where trust in the system is essential for its legitimacy. The use of smart contracts, self-executing contracts with the terms of the agreement directly written into code, further enhances security and trust in government operations.

2. Improved Efficiency and Cost-Effectiveness

The integration of these technologies can significantly reduce operational costs and improve the efficiency of government processes. Cloud Computing provides the necessary infrastructure for scalable, on-demand access to computational resources, while AI can automate routine tasks, thus freeing up human resources for more strategic functions. This combination allows for more agile and responsive governance, which is critical in times of crisis or when rapid policy adjustments are required (Shinde, K., et al., 2023). By leveraging these technologies, governments can transition from traditional, often cumbersome, bureaucratic systems to more agile, responsive, and cost-effective models of governance.

Cloud Computing: A Foundation for Scalable and Cost-Effective Infrastructure

Cloud Computing plays a pivotal role in this transformation by providing the necessary infrastructure for scalable, on-demand access to computational resources. Unlike traditional government IT infrastructures, cloud platforms offer a virtualized environment where resources such as processing power, storage, and networking can be allocated dynamically based on current needs. This flexibility is particularly valuable during peak periods, such as during tax season or in the aftermath of a natural disaster, when the demand for government services may surge unexpectedly.

The ability to scale services up or down as required not only ensures that government systems remain operational under varying loads but also leads to significant cost savings. Moreover, cloud service providers often include maintenance, updates, and security as part of their offerings, further reducing the operational burden on government IT departments.

AI: Automating Routine Tasks to Enhance Efficiency

Artificial Intelligence complements the scalability of Cloud Computing by automating routine tasks, thereby freeing up human resources for more strategic functions. Governments handle a wide range of administrative tasks, from processing applications and managing records to responding to citizen inquiries. AI-powered automation can take over these routine tasks, processing them faster and with fewer errors than human workers. For example, AI can automate the processing of tax returns, speeding up the time it takes for citizens to receive refunds and reducing the workload on tax officials. In addition to automating routine tasks, AI can enhance decision-making processes by analyzing large datasets to identify trends, predict outcomes, and recommend actions. By making data-driven decisions, governments can respond more effectively to crises, allocate resources more efficiently, and improve the overall quality of public services (Shinde, K., et al., 2023).

Blockchain: Ensuring Security and Transparency

While Cloud Computing and AI focus on efficiency and cost reduction, Blockchain adds another layer of value by ensuring the security and transparency of government processes. By integrating Blockchain with Cloud Computing and AI, governments can ensure that their operations are not only efficient but also secure and transparent. This is particularly important in building public trust, as citizens need to be confident that their data is being handled securely and that government processes are fair and accountable (Karthikeyan, P., et al., 2023).

Agility and Responsiveness in Times of Crisis

The integration of these technologies is particularly critical in times of crisis or when rapid policy adjustments are required. For example, during the COVID-19 pandemic, governments around the world had to quickly adapt to unprecedented challenges, from managing public health responses to providing economic relief. The agility provided by Cloud Computing allowed governments to rapidly deploy new services, such as online health monitoring platforms and digital payment systems, to meet the urgent needs of their citizens. AI played a key role in analyzing data to inform policy decisions, such as predicting the spread of the virus and optimizing the distribution of medical supplies. Meanwhile, Blockchain ensured the transparency and security of these efforts, helping to maintain public trust during a time of uncertainty (Shinde, K., et al., 2023).

3. Transparency and Accountability

One of the most transformative aspects of Blockchain technology in e-Government is its ability to provide transparent and traceable records of all transactions. This capability significantly enhances accountability, reduces opportunities for corruption, and fosters greater citizen engagement. Blockchain introduces a decentralized ledger which ensures that all governmental actions, whether financial transactions, legislative processes, or public service delivery, are recorded securely and are open to scrutiny by stakeholders, including the public.

Blockchain's transparency is crucial in sectors like public procurement, where corruption and mismanagement are prevalent concerns. This not only ensures that the process is transparent but also that it is immutable, meaning once a record is created, it cannot be altered or deleted. Moreover, in e-voting systems, Blockchain can ensure that votes are cast, recorded, and counted transparently, reducing the risk of electoral fraud and increasing voter confidence. The technology's decentralized nature ensures that no single entity has control over the electoral process, which is essential for maintaining the integrity of democratic systems (Tyma, B., et al.(2022), Cointelegraph, 2023). Furthermore, in the public sector, smart contracts can be used to ensure that funds are released only when specific conditions are met, which can significantly reduce the risk of embezzlement or misappropriation of public resources (Tyma, B., et al., 2022).

4. Facilitating Digital Inclusion

Cloud-based services powered by AI can be made accessible to a broader population, including those in remote or underserved areas. This aligns with global efforts to bridge the digital divide and promote inclusive development (Li, W., et al., 2021). By leveraging these technologies, governments can create a more inclusive digital ecosystem that enables equitable participation in the digital economy, ensuring that no citizen is left behind. One of the most significant advantages of Cloud Computing is its ability to provide scalable and flexible infrastructure that can be accessed from virtually anywhere with an internet connection. This means that citizens in rural areas can access the same high-quality services as those in urban centers, breaking down geographical barriers and promoting greater equality in service delivery (Ali, K. E., et al., 2018).

Moreover, the integration of AI into these cloud-based services enhances their accessibility and usability. AI-powered tools, such as virtual assistants and automated systems, can provide personalized assistance to citizens, guiding them through complex processes and ensuring that they can access the services they need. This is particularly valuable for individuals with limited digital literacy, as it ensures that they can participate fully in the digital government services available to them (OECD, 2023). In addition to improving accessibility, cloud-based AI services can also provide critical support in local languages, making government services more inclusive for non-native speakers. This capability is essential in multilingual countries, where a lack of language support can often lead to the exclusion of minority groups from the benefits of digital services (Microsoft, 2023).

Cloud Computing and AI can also support broader efforts to build digital literacy and skills in underserved communities. Cloud-based platforms can host online training programs, educational resources, and virtual classrooms that are accessible to anyone with an internet connection. AI can tailor these resources to the needs of individual users, providing personalized learning experiences that help citizens develop the skills they need to thrive in the digital economy. This not only promotes digital inclusion but also contributes to economic empowerment and social mobility (Guo, B., et al., 2023). By ensuring that all citizens, regardless of their location or socioeconomic status, have access to digital government services, these technologies contribute to more equitable and inclusive societies. This is particularly relevant in the context of the United Nations Sustainable Development Goals (SDGs), which emphasize the need to reduce inequalities and ensure inclusive access to information and communication technologies (ICTs) (OECD, 2023).

5. Data-Driven Decision Making

The integration of Artificial Intelligence (AI), Blockchain, and Cloud Computing into government operations offers unprecedented opportunities to enhance decision-making processes, driving more informed and effective policy decisions. This convergence creates a robust framework for collecting, storing, and analyzing vast amounts of data, thereby enabling governments to respond more swiftly and accurately to the needs of their citizens.

AI's Role in Data Analysis and Predictive Modeling

AI's ability to analyze large datasets allows governments to uncover patterns and trends that might otherwise go unnoticed. This capability is particularly valuable in areas such as public health, economic policy, and urban planning, where data-driven insights can inform decisions that have far-reaching consequences. For instance, AI can analyze data from various sources, including social media, public records, and sensor networks, to predict outcomes such as the spread of infectious diseases, the impact of economic policies, or traffic congestion in cities. These predictive models enable policymakers to take proactive measures, thereby improving the efficiency and effectiveness of government interventions.

Blockchain's Secure Data Storage

Blockchain technology complements AI by providing a secure and transparent method for storing the data that AI systems analyze. The decentralized nature of Blockchain ensures that data is not stored in a single location but is distributed across a network of nodes, making it highly resistant to tampering and unauthorized access. In addition, Blockchain's immutability ensures that once data is recorded, it cannot be altered, providing a reliable audit trail that enhances transparency and accountability in government operations (Tsolakis, N. et al. 2023).

Scalability and Flexibility Through Cloud Computing

Cloud Computing provides the necessary infrastructure to support the storage and processing of large datasets generated by AI and secured by Blockchain. The scalability of cloud platforms allows governments to handle increasing amounts of data without the need for significant investments in physical infrastructure. Moreover, cloud-based systems offer the flexibility to scale resources up or down based on demand, ensuring that government services remain responsive even during periods of high usage, such as during natural disasters or public health emergencies (Bharanidharan & Jayalakshmi, 2021).

Enhanced Responsiveness and Agility

The combination of AI, Blockchain, and Cloud Computing creates an ecosystem that enables more agile and responsive governance. AI can provide real-time insights based on current data trends, Blockchain ensures that these insights are based on secure and verifiable data, and Cloud Computing allows these technologies to be deployed and scaled rapidly. This ecosystem is particularly valuable in crisis management, where timely and accurate decision-making is critical. For example, during the COVID-19 pandemic, governments that leveraged these technologies were able to quickly implement digital health solutions, track the spread of the virus, and allocate resources more effectively (Kaginalkar, Kumar, Gargava, & Niyogi, 2021).

Overall, the integration of AI, Blockchain, and Cloud Computing in e-Government not only enhances the ability of governments to make informed policy decisions but also ensures that these decisions are based on secure, reliable, and scalable data infrastructures. As these technologies continue to evolve, they will play an increasingly important role in shaping the future of digital governance, enabling more transparent, accountable, and effective public administration.

Advancing Predictive Maintenance With Fuzzy Estimators and AI

Predictive maintenance in e-Government systems is becoming increasingly sophisticated with the integration of fuzzy estimators and predictive modeling. These techniques, as highlighted by Abiad et al. (2024), offer governments tools to handle uncertain and imprecise data while optimizing resource utilization. By employing fuzzy estimators, governments can enhance the accuracy of failure predictions and ensure continuous service delivery, even in resource-constrained environments. Furthermore, integrating Blockchain ensures data security, while Cloud Computing enables scalable, real-time processing of predictive models. Together, these technologies represent a significant advancement in maintaining critical e-Government infrastructure.

The role of predictive maintenance in e-Government infrastructure is becoming increasingly sophisticated with the incorporation of advanced techniques such as fuzzy estimators and predictive modeling. As discussed by Abiad et al. (2024), fuzzy estimators provide a robust framework for handling uncertainty and imprecise data, which are common in large-scale government systems. These tools enable governments to anticipate equipment failures, optimize resource utilization, and ensure uninterrupted public services.

For example, in data centers managing sensitive e-Government transactions, predictive algorithms enhanced by fuzzy estimators can analyze sensor data to forecast failures and reduce downtime. By integrating these estimators with Blockchain's secure and immutable framework, governments can ensure the integrity of predictive data while enhancing transparency in maintenance operations. Furthermore, Cloud Computing's real-time data processing capabilities make it possible to deploy these models across distributed infrastructure, ensuring scalability and responsiveness even in underfunded environments.

Enriching Predictive Analytics in Public Administration With Fuzzy Estimators

Predictive analytics is an essential tool for modern e-Government systems, enabling governments to anticipate and address challenges proactively. Incorporating fuzzy estimators, as discussed by Abiad et al. (2024), can significantly enhance the accuracy and reliability of predictive models, particularly in the context of public administration where uncertainty and imprecise data are common.

Fuzzy estimators provide a mathematical framework to handle ambiguous or incomplete data, making them ideal for scenarios such as resource allocation, infrastructure maintenance, and disaster preparedness. For instance, in public transportation systems, fuzzy logic can be used to predict traffic congestion patterns, enabling authorities to optimize routes and schedules dynamically. Similarly, in healthcare, predictive models augmented by fuzzy estimators can forecast patient demand, improving resource management in hospitals and clinics.

In the context of Blockchain and AI integration, fuzzy estimators can enhance decision-making processes by refining the analysis of large datasets. For example, AI algorithms combined with fuzzy logic can assess citizen feedback to prioritize service improvements, while Blockchain ensures the security and integrity of the underlying data.

By leveraging these advanced predictive tools, governments can achieve greater resilience, efficiency, and responsiveness in their operations. This aligns closely with the successes observed in Estonia and Singapore, where data-driven decision-making has transformed public services.

Enhancing E-Government Resilience With Predictive Modeling

Recent advancements in predictive maintenance, such as the use of censored life data estimations discussed by Abiad et al. (2024), have introduced powerful tools for building resilient e-Government systems. Censored life data techniques allow for more accurate reliability analyses, particularly when dealing with incomplete or partially observed datasets-a common scenario in public administration. By applying these methods, governments can predict the lifespan of critical infrastructure components, ensuring timely maintenance and reducing unexpected failures.

For example, predictive models utilizing censored life data can be deployed in telecommunication networks and IoT systems integral to e-Government services. Combined with AI's machine learning capabilities, these models enable dynamic adjustments to maintenance schedules based on real-time data, enhancing system resilience. Blockchain's ability to provide immutable records ensures transparency and trust in maintenance processes, while Cloud Computing supports the storage and processing of large datasets required for such analyses.

Integrating predictive maintenance into e-Government strategies not only improves service continuity but also optimizes resource allocation, making it a cornerstone of digital resilience efforts in public administration.

ACTIONABLE FRAMEWORK FOR IMPLEMENTING PREDICTIVE MAINTENANCE IN E-GOVERNMENT

To facilitate the adoption of predictive maintenance in e-Government systems, governments can adapt the six-step framework proposed by Abiad et al. (2020). This framework provides a structured approach to integrating predictive maintenance technologies effectively:

1. **Define Maintenance Objectives**: Identify critical systems and establish clear objectives for predictive maintenance, such as reducing downtime or improving service reliability.
2. **Develop a Condition Monitoring Program**: Use IoT sensors and real-time monitoring tools to collect data on infrastructure performance and detect early signs of degradation.
3. **Leverage Predictive Algorithms**: Implement advanced predictive models, including time-to-failure (TTF) and censored life data estimations, to forecast potential issues and plan maintenance activities proactively.
4. **Invest in Technology Infrastructure**: Ensure robust computational resources and interoperability with legacy systems to handle large-scale data processing.
5. **Establish a Centralized Maintenance Management System**: Use a Computerized Maintenance Management System (CMMS) to integrate predictive insights into operational workflows and automate maintenance scheduling.
6. **Monitor Key Performance Indicators (KPIs)**: Track metrics such as Mean Time Between Failures (MTBF) and Mean Time to Repair (MTTR) to evaluate the effectiveness of predictive maintenance and identify areas for improvement.

Implementation Barriers to Digital Transformation in e-Government

While the integration of AI, Blockchain, and Cloud Computing offers significant benefits, several implementation barriers hinder the success of e-Government initiatives, particularly in developing nations and underfunded regions:

Digital Literacy

A lack of digital skills among public officials and citizens remains a major obstacle. Without adequate training programs, the full potential of these technologies cannot be realized. Governments must prioritize capacity-building initiatives to bridge the digital skills gap.

Infrastructure Gaps

Reliable internet connectivity, robust IT systems, and access to modern devices are essential for deploying e-Government solutions. However, in many regions, inadequate infrastructure limits scalability and accessibility. Strategic investment in infrastructure development is critical for overcoming this barrier.

Resistance to Change

Public administrations often face cultural and organizational resistance to adopting new technologies. Employees accustomed to traditional processes may view digital transformation as a threat to their roles or an unnecessary complication. Change management practices, including communication, stakeholder engagement, and incentives, are essential to overcome this resistance.

Financial Constraints

The high initial costs of implementing AI, Blockchain, and Cloud systems can be prohibitive for governments with limited budgets. Establishing international collaborations and leveraging public-private partnerships can help mitigate these financial challenges.

Regulatory and Policy Challenges

The absence of clear regulations for data privacy, cybersecurity, and technology governance creates uncertainty, delaying implementation. Governments must develop comprehensive policies to ensure ethical and secure use of digital tools.

Challenges and Risks Deploying AI, Blockchain, and Cloud Computing

While the benefits of integrating AI, Blockchain, and Cloud Computing in e-Government systems are compelling, the deployment of these technologies presents significant risks and challenges, particularly in developing nations and underfunded governments. One of the primary concerns is cybersecurity. Although Blockchain offers a high degree of data security, its adoption requires significant technical expertise and robust IT infrastructure, which may be lacking in resource-constrained settings. Without adequate safeguards, these systems remain vulnerable to cyberattacks and data breaches, undermining citizen trust.

Recent studies, such as Gura et al. (2023), emphasize the risks associated with Blockchain and AI in governance, which merit deeper exploration:

> **Blockchain Risks**: Although Blockchain offers transparency and data security, its decentralized nature can lead to governance challenges. The immutability of Blockchain records may conflict with privacy regulations, particularly in jurisdictions lacking comprehensive data protection laws. Additionally, the high energy consumption associated with some Blockchain technologies raises sustainability concerns.
>
> **AI Risks**: The adoption of AI in governance introduces risks of algorithmic bias, lack of transparency, and potential misuse of predictive capabilities. For instance, biased training datasets can perpetuate discrimination in public services, undermining equity and trust. Moreover, the reliance on AI for decision-making raises ethical questions about accountability when errors occur.

Addressing these risks requires governments to establish robust ethical guidelines, ensure compliance with international data protection standards, and invest in sustainable and transparent technologies.

Transparency, while a key advantage of Blockchain, also introduces risks. In some cases, the immutability of Blockchain records could expose sensitive citizen data if access controls are not carefully implemented. Additionally, AI systems, which often require vast datasets for training, may inadvertently amplify existing inequalities or biases in governance if not deployed responsibly.

In developing nations, financial constraints pose a critical barrier to adopting these technologies. The upfront costs of deploying and maintaining AI, Blockchain, and Cloud systems can be prohibitive, particularly in countries with competing priorities for limited public funds. Furthermore, the lack of local expertise may necessitate reliance on foreign vendors, raising concerns about data sovereignty and long-term sustainability.

To address these challenges, governments must adopt a phased approach to technology deployment, prioritize capacity building, and seek international partnerships for technical and financial support. These strategies can mitigate risks while enabling even underfunded governments to benefit from modern e-Government solutions.

Technological and Computational Challenges in Predictive Maintenance

Predictive maintenance relies on advanced algorithms to evaluate equipment conditions, forecast failures, and optimize maintenance schedules. As highlighted by Abiad et al. (2020), designing and implementing these algorithms involves several challenges, particularly for governments integrating them into e-Government infrastructure.

One key difficulty is the data dependency of predictive algorithms. Effective predictive maintenance requires extensive, high-quality datasets that reflect equipment conditions under normal, warning, and failure states. For governments with outdated or fragmented systems, data acquisition and cleaning can be significant hurdles. Furthermore, the computational intensity of predictive models, such as those based on time-to-failure (TTF) or mean-time-between-failure (MTBF), demands robust IT infrastructure, which may be unavailable in underfunded regions.

Another challenge is the model complexity required to account for dynamic and heterogeneous e-Government systems. Algorithms must process data from diverse sources, such as IoT devices and sensor networks, while remaining adaptive to evolving conditions. Interoperability with legacy systems further complicates implementation, requiring custom solutions that are both resource-intensive and costly.

CONCEPT AND IMPORTANCE OF INTEGRATING AI, BLOCKCHAIN, AND CLOUD SYSTEMS IN E-GOVERNMENT

The integration of Artificial Intelligence (AI), Blockchain, and Cloud Computing into e-Government systems is not merely a technological advancement; it is a transformative force that is reshaping the very foundations of public administration and governance. This integration signals a paradigm shift in how public sector services are conceptualized, delivered, and continuously improved. In the past, government services were largely characterized by manual processes, paper-based records, and face-to-face interactions, which often led to inefficiencies, delays, and a lack of transparency. However, as governments around the world navigate the complexities of digital transformation, the combined power of AI, Blockchain, and Cloud Computing provides a potent synergy that can significantly enhance the efficiency, transparency, and responsiveness of government operations.

This chapter probes into the core concepts of each of these technologies-AI, Blockchain, and Cloud Computing- and explores their collective impact on e-Government. It aims to provide a comprehensive guide for policymakers, technologists, and scholars who are involved in the digital transformation of the public sector. By understanding how these technologies can be integrated to create more efficient, transparent, and responsive government systems, stakeholders will be better equipped to drive innovation in public service delivery and meet the evolving expectations of citizens in the digital age.

AI, Blockchain, and Cloud Computing: The Pillars of Modern e-Government

Each of these technologies-AI, Blockchain, and Cloud Computing-brings distinct capabilities that are crucial for modernizing government operations. When integrated, they create a powerful synergy that enables governments to overcome the limitations of traditional administrative systems, paving the way for more efficient, transparent, and responsive governance.

Artificial Intelligence (AI)

Artificial Intelligence (AI) stands at the forefront of the digital transformation in the public sector, offering unprecedented opportunities to revolutionize the way government services are delivered. This transformative technology empowers governments to not only manage and analyze vast amounts of data but also to anticipate and respond to the needs of citizens with a level of precision and speed that was previously unimaginable (Rai et al., 2023). One of the most significant advantages of AI in the public sector is its ability to automate routine and complex processes, freeing up valuable human resources for more strategic tasks from processing applications and managing workflows to conducting initial screenings for social services eligibility. This automation not only reduces the time and cost associated with these tasks but also minimizes the potential for human error, ensuring that services are delivered more consistently and accurately.

Moreover, AI's ability to enhance decision-making processes is another critical factor in its integration into e-Government systems. AI algorithms can process and analyze complex datasets far more quickly and accurately than humans, providing government officials with insights that inform better policy decisions. Whether it's determining the allocation of funding, optimizing the delivery of public services, or crafting targeted interventions for at-risk populations, AI equips governments with the tools to make data-driven decisions that are more informed and effective. Additionally, AI can assist in monitoring the effectiveness of social programs, providing insights that can be used to refine and improve service delivery over time.

Public health management is another area where AI's impact is particularly profound. AI can analyze data from electronic health records, social determinants of health, and other sources to predict disease outbreaks, identify at-risk populations, and optimize the allocation of healthcare resources. This capability is especially important in responding to public health crises, such as pandemics, where timely and accurate information can save lives. AI's ability to process vast amounts of data in real-time allows public health officials to make informed decisions quickly, ensuring that interventions are both timely and effective.

Furthermore, AI's role in enhancing citizen engagement cannot be overlooked. For example, AI-powered chatbots and virtual assistants can provide citizens with instant access to information and services, answering queries, guiding them through application processes, and even helping them navigate complex bureaucratic procedures. As governments continue to embrace AI, the potential for innovation and improvement in public sector services is vast, paving the way for a new era of digital governance where speed, accuracy, and responsiveness are the norm.

Blockchain

As a decentralized and secure ledger system, Blockchain is particularly valuable in ensuring the integrity and transparency of government transactions. Blockchain can safeguard against fraud, enhance data security, and ensure that public records are immutable and accessible. This is critical in areas such as electoral processes, land registry management, and public procurement, where the accuracy and transparency of data are essential for maintaining public trust (Karthikeyan et al., 2023). Furthermore, Blockchain's ability to provide a tamper-proof record of transactions can significantly reduce the risk of corruption and enhance accountability across government operations (Pani et al., 2021).

One of the most significant applications of Blockchain in the public sector is in the management of electoral processes. Elections are the bedrock of democratic governance, and the integrity of the electoral process is critical to maintaining public trust. Blockchain technology can revolutionize how votes are cast, counted, and verified by providing a transparent and immutable record of every vote. This ensures that election results cannot be tampered with or altered, thus safeguarding the democratic process from fraud and manipulation. By using Blockchain, governments can also enhance voter confidence, knowing that their votes are securely recorded and accurately counted, which is vital for the legitimacy of the electoral outcomes (Karthikeyan et al., 2023).

Traditional land registry systems are often plagued by issues such as forged documents, disputes over land ownership, and bureaucratic delays. The immutability of Blockchain ensures that once a record is entered, it cannot be altered or deleted, thereby preventing fraud and ensuring that property rights are protected. Moreover, public procurement involves the allocation of significant government resources and is often susceptible to corruption, favoritism, and inefficiencies. Blockchain can streamline procurement processes by automating contract execution through smart contracts which ensure that contracts are only executed when predefined conditions are met, further reducing the risk of fraud and errors (Karthikeyan et al., 2023).

Beyond these specific applications, Blockchain's broader ability to provide a tamper-proof record of transactions can significantly reduce the risk of corruption across various government operations. By ensuring that all transactions are recorded on a secure, immutable ledger, Blockchain makes it much more difficult for corrupt activities to go undetected. In this way, Blockchain can play a crucial role in fostering a culture of integrity and accountability in the public sector, where the responsible management of public resources is essential for good governance (Pani et al., 2021).

Moreover, the decentralized nature of Blockchain means that no single entity controls the data, further enhancing the security and reliability of government operations. This decentralization reduces the risk of data breaches and cyber-attacks, which are increasingly common in centralized systems. In a Blockchain-based system, data is stored across a network of nodes, making it highly resilient to attacks and failures. This level of security is particularly important for sensitive government data, such as personal identification information, financial records, and national security data. By protecting this data from unauthorized access and tampering, Blockchain helps governments maintain the trust of their citizens and ensure the continuity of essential services (Karthikeyan et al., 2023).

Cloud Computing

Cloud Computing provides the scalable and flexible infrastructure necessary to support the vast amounts of data generated and processed by AI and Blockchain technologies. By migrating services to the cloud, governments can ensure that their digital infrastructure is resilient, cost-effective, and capable of scaling in response to changing needs. Cloud platforms enable the rapid deployment of services, reduce the costs associated with maintaining physical infrastructure, and offer robust security measures that protect sensitive government data (Haque, 2022).

Cloud Computing provides the scalable and flexible infrastructure necessary to support the vast amounts of data generated and processed by AI and Blockchain technologies. The flexibility of Cloud Computing ensures that these systems can adapt to varying workloads without compromising performance. By migrating services to the cloud, governments can ensure that their digital infrastructure is not only resilient but also cost-effective. Cloud platforms eliminate the need for large-scale, on-premises hardware by providing a virtualized environment where resources can be allocated on-demand. Moreover, cloud services come with built-in redundancy and disaster recovery capabilities, ensuring that government systems remain operational even in the face of hardware failures or natural disasters (Haque, 2022).

The security of sensitive government data is another paramount concern that Cloud Computing addresses effectively. With robust security measures, including encryption, multi-factor authentication, and continuous monitoring, cloud platforms offer a level of data protection that is often superior to traditional, on-premises systems. Cloud providers also regularly update their security features to address emerging threats, thereby providing governments with a continually evolving defense against cybersecurity risks.

Furthermore, Cloud Computing facilitates the seamless integration of AI and Blockchain into existing government systems, ensuring that these advanced technologies can be deployed quickly and effectively. The cloud's scalable nature allows governments to allocate the necessary computing power as needed, enabling AI to perform real-time data analysis and Blockchain to process and validate transactions without delay. This integration is crucial for enabling governments to implement innovative solutions, such as AI-driven predictive analytics for public health or Blockchain-based secure voting systems, without the need for extensive and costly infrastructure upgrades.

In taxation, cloud platforms can host AI-driven systems that analyze financial data to detect fraud, streamline tax collection processes, and enhance compliance. By moving these processes to the cloud, tax authorities can handle peak loads during filing seasons more effectively, reducing the likelihood of system crashes and ensuring that citizens have a smooth and reliable experience when filing taxes. This chapter underscores the importance of Cloud Computing as a critical component of e-Government, offering insights and practical guidance for those involved in the ongoing digital transformation of the public sector.

CASE STUDIES OF SUCCESSFUL INTEGRATION: LESSONS FROM LEADING E-GOVERNMENT INITIATIVES

The integration of Artificial Intelligence (AI), Blockchain, and Cloud Computing in e-Government solutions is fundamentally transforming public sector operations. A critical component in achieving sustained efficiency and reliability is predictive maintenance, a concept thoroughly explored in the telecommunications sector by Abiad et al. (2018). Predictive maintenance uses advanced analytics and condition-monitoring tools to anticipate equipment failures, minimizing downtime and optimizing resource allocation.

This section will present detailed case studies from leading e-Government initiatives worldwide, highlighting the practical application and benefits of integrating AI, Blockchain, and Cloud technologies. It will feature Estonia's e-Residency program, which utilizes Blockchain for secure identity management, AI for predictive services, and Cloud for scalable infrastructure, demonstrating enhanced security, efficiency, and citizen engagement (PWC, 2021). According to Thomson Reuters, the e-Residency program enables non-residents to access a secure digital identity and leverage Estonia's public and private digital services, ensuring data integrity and security through Blockchain technology (ThomsonrReuters.com, 2023).

Another notable example is Singapore's Smart Nation initiative, which integrates AI for data analytics, Blockchain for secure transactions, and Cloud for robust data storage and processing, illustrating the creation of a cohesive digital ecosystem. The Smart Nation initiative aims to harness technology to improve the quality of life for citizens, create more opportunities, and build stronger communities. The integration of these advanced technologies has enabled Singapore to develop a smart urban infrastructure, providing valuable lessons for other countries aiming to digitalize their public services.

(1) Estonia's e-Residency Program: Pioneering a Global Digital Identity Revolution

Estonia's e-Residency program is a pioneering example of how the integration of Blockchain, Artificial Intelligence (AI), and Cloud Computing can revolutionize public services, offering enhanced security, efficiency, and citizen engagement. Launched in 2014, Estonia's e-Residency program allows non-residents to obtain a secure digital identity that provides access to Estonia's extensive suite of public and private digital services. This initiative reflects Estonia's commitment to digital transformation and serves as a model for other nations seeking to modernize their public sector services.

Overview of Estonia's e-Residency Program

The e-Residency program was conceived as part of Estonia's broader e-Government strategy, which aims to create a seamless digital environment for both residents and global citizens. The program allows individuals from around the world to apply for e-Residency, granting them access to a digital identity issued by the Estonian government. The success of the e-Residency program is underpinned by the strategic integration of Blockchain, AI, and Cloud Computing technologies.

Blockchain for Secure Identity Management

Blockchain technology plays a critical role in the e-Residency program by ensuring the security and integrity of digital identities. Each e-resident's digital identity is stored on a Blockchain, providing a secure, tamper-proof record that is protected against unauthorized access and fraud. The use of Blockchain in identity management also enhances transparency and accountability. This transparency not only builds trust among e-residents but also ensures compliance with international data protection standards, such as the General Data Protection Regulation (GDPR).

AI for Predictive Services

Artificial Intelligence (AI) is integrated into the e-Residency program to provide predictive services that enhance the efficiency and responsiveness of Estonia's digital ecosystem. AI algorithms analyze data generated by e-residents' interactions with digital services, enabling the Estonian government to anticipate needs, streamline processes, and offer personalized services. This predictive capability not only improves the user experience but also reduces the administrative burden on government agencies, allowing them to allocate resources more effectively.

Cloud Computing for Scalable Infrastructure

Cloud Computing provides the scalable infrastructure that supports the e-Residency program, allowing it to handle a growing number of e-residents from around the world. The cloud's flexibility also allows Estonia to continuously update and improve its digital services without significant downtime or disruption. This scalability is particularly important as the e-Residency program expands, enabling Estonia to accommodate new e-residents and offer additional services as needed.

Visions and Implications for Digital Transformation

Estonia's e-Residency program provides valuable insights for governments looking to embark on digital transformation initiatives. By embracing digital identities and offering global citizens access to its digital ecosystem, Estonia has positioned itself as a leader in e-Government, attracting entrepreneurs, digital nomads, and investors from around the world. As digital transformation continues to reshape the public sector, the lessons learned from Estonia's e-Residency program will be invaluable for governments seeking to build more inclusive, efficient, and secure digital ecosystems.

Estonia's Approach to Overcoming Implementation Challenges in Digital Transformation

Estonia's successful implementation of its e-Residency Program and broader digital government initiatives was not without challenges. However, the country managed to overcome these obstacles through a combination of strategic foresight, strong leadership, collaboration, and an unwavering commitment to innovation and transparency. Below we present how Estonia addressed and overcame some of the key implementation challenges.

1. Building Trust in Digital Systems

One of the primary challenges was building trust in digital systems among both citizens and the global community. People needed assurance that their data would be secure and that the digital identity system would be reliable. The government implemented advanced encryption methods and utilized Blockchain technology to ensure that digital identities and transactions were secure and tamper-proof. Estonia also established strong legal frameworks to protect user data, ensuring compliance with international standards like the General Data Protection Regulation (GDPR).

2. Ensuring Interoperability Across Systems

Integrating various government services into a unified digital platform required ensuring that different systems could communicate and work together seamlessly. Interoperability was crucial for the success of Estonia's digital government strategy. Estonia developed the X-Road, a secure data exchange layer that facilitates interoperability between different government systems. X-Road allows various public and private sector organizations to exchange data securely, enabling the seamless integration of services across the digital ecosystem.

3. Addressing Legal and Regulatory Barriers

Implementing a digital identity program and other digital government services required changes to existing laws and regulations. Estonia undertook a comprehensive review of its legal and regulatory landscape to identify and address barriers to digital transformation. The government introduced new legislation to support digital identity, e-signatures, and electronic transactions, ensuring that these digital services were legally recognized and enforceable. Estonia also worked closely with international partners to align its regulations with global standards, which helped foster international trust and cooperation.

4. Promoting Digital Literacy and Adoption

Encouraging widespread adoption of digital services required raising digital literacy levels among citizens and ensuring that people were comfortable using new technologies. Estonia invested heavily in digital literacy programs and public awareness campaigns to educate citizens about the benefits of digital services and how to use them effectively. The government introduced digital skills training in schools and provided resources for adults to improve their digital competencies.

5. Managing Resistance to Change

As with any significant transformation, there was resistance to change from both within the government and among the general population. Estonia overcame resistance by involving key stakeholders in the development and implementation process. The government engaged with public servants, private sector partners, and citizens to gather feedback and address concerns. Estonia also implemented change management strategies, including training and support programs, to help public sector employees transition smoothly to new digital tools and processes.

6. Ensuring Scalability and Sustainability

Scaling digital services to accommodate a growing number of users, both domestically and internationally, posed significant challenges in terms of infrastructure and resource allocation. The cloud-based infrastructure allowed Estonia to expand its digital services without the need for costly physical infrastructure. Additionally, the government adopted a continuous improvement approach, regularly updating and optimizing its digital services to ensure they remained sustainable and responsive to changing needs.

7. Developing Innovation and Continuous Improvement

Maintaining momentum and continuously improving digital services was necessary to keep pace with technological advancements and changing user expectations. Estonia established a culture of innovation within its government, encouraging experimentation and the adoption of new technologies. The government set up innovation labs and pilot programs to test new ideas before scaling them up. This commitment to innovation ensured that Estonia's digital government services remained cutting-edge and met the evolving needs of its users.

8. International Collaboration and Partnerships

As a small country, Estonia faced the challenge of gaining international recognition and building a global reputation for its digital services. By engaging with global organizations, participating in international forums, and sharing its experiences, Estonia positioned itself as a leader in digital transformation. This not only helped Estonia gain international credibility but also allowed it to learn from and contribute to global best practices in digital governance.

9. Addressing Infrastructure Challenges

Building the necessary digital infrastructure to support widespread adoption of e-Government services required significant investment and coordination. Estonia prioritized the development of a robust digital infrastructure, including nationwide broadband access, secure data centers, and the X-Road data exchange layer. Estonia's investment in infrastructure laid the foundation for the successful implementation and scalability of its digital government programs.

Lessons Learned From Estonia's e-Residency Program for Successful Digital

Transformation Estonia's e-Residency Program offers several key lessons that can serve as valuable insights for other countries aiming to implement digital transformation initiatives. These lessons highlight the importance of strategic vision, technological integration, and user-centric design in building a successful digital government program.

1. Pioneering Digital Identity

Lesson: Estonia's e-Residency Program allows global citizens to access a range of Estonian public and private services, demonstrating the potential of digital identities to extend the reach of government services beyond geographical boundaries.
Application: Governments should consider developing secure digital identity solutions that enable broader access to public services, particularly for non-residents and expatriates.

2. Integration of Advanced Technologies

Lesson: The program's success is built on the strategic integration of Blockchain for secure data management, AI for personalized services, and Cloud Computing for scalable infrastructure.
Application: Integrating Blockchain, AI, and Cloud Computing can enhance security, improve service delivery, and ensure scalability, making digital services more resilient and responsive.

3. Focus on Security and Trust

Lesson: Blockchain technology is used in the e-Residency Program to ensure the integrity and security of digital identities and transactions.
Application: Governments must ensure that digital services are protected against fraud and unauthorized access, using technologies like Blockchain to build trust among users and safeguard sensitive data.

4. Global Accessibility and Economic Opportunity

Lesson: Estonia's e-Residency Program has attracted entrepreneurs and digital nomads, boosting Estonia's economy and positioning it as a hub for global digital business.
Application: By providing digital tools that enable global citizens to engage with a country's economy, governments can stimulate economic growth and increase their global influence.

5. User-Centric Design and Ease of Use

Lesson: The e-Residency Program is designed to be user-friendly, with a focus on making it easy for users to access services online, manage their business, and interact with the Estonian government.
Application: Digital government services should be designed with the user in mind, prioritizing ease of use and accessibility. Simplifying the user experience can lead to higher adoption rates and better overall satisfaction with government services.

6. Scalability and Flexibility

Lesson: The use of Cloud Computing in Estonia's e-Residency Program allows the system to scale as needed, accommodating the growing number of e-residents.
Application: Cloud-based solutions offer the necessary scalability to handle surges in demand and support continuous growth.

7. Legal and Regulatory Framework

Lesson: Estonia's success with e-Residency is supported by a strong legal and regulatory framework that facilitates digital transactions and protects user data.
Application: Governments should develop policies that support digital transactions, protect user data, and encourage innovation while ensuring compliance with international standards.

8. Continuous Improvement and Adaptation

Lesson: Estonia continues to evolve its e-Residency Program by incorporating new technologies and responding to user feedback allowing the program to stay relevant and effective in meeting the needs of its users.
Application: By actively seeking feedback and staying abreast of technological advancements, governments can ensure their digital services remain effective and user-focused.

9. Promoting Digital Literacy and Awareness

Lesson: Estonia has successfully promoted digital literacy among its e-residents, ensuring that users can fully utilize the digital services available to them.
Application: Governments should invest in educational initiatives that help users understand and effectively use digital tools and platforms.

10. International Collaboration and Innovation

Lesson: Estonia's e-Residency Program has positioned the country as a leader in digital innovation and has led to collaborations with other nations and international organizations
Application: Governments should seek international collaborations to share best practices, co-develop digital solutions, and promote their digital initiatives on the global stage.

(2) Building a Digital Future: Singapore's Smart Nation Initiative

Singapore's Smart Nation initiative stands as a shining example of how a country can successfully integrate advanced technologies like Artificial Intelligence (AI), Blockchain, and Cloud Computing to create a cohesive and innovative digital ecosystem. Launched in 2014, the Smart Nation initiative aims to harness the power of technology to improve the quality of life for its citizens, create new economic opportunities, and build stronger, more connected communities. This ambitious project has positioned Singapore as a global leader in digital transformation, providing valuable insights for other countries seeking to modernize their public services.

AI for Data Analytics and Urban Management

A cornerstone of the Smart Nation initiative is the use of AI for data analytics, which plays a critical role in managing Singapore's urban infrastructure. AI-driven analytics are employed to monitor and optimize various aspects of city life, including traffic management, public health, and environmental sustainability. For instance, AI algorithms analyze data from sensors deployed across the city to predict traffic congestion and adjust traffic signals in real-time, thereby improving the flow of vehicles and reducing commute times. Similarly, by analyzing data from healthcare facilities, social services, and even social media, AI can identify emerging health trends and potential outbreaks, enabling the government to respond proactively.

Blockchain for Secure Transactions and Digital Identity

Blockchain technology is another key component of Singapore's Smart Nation initiative, particularly in the realm of secure transactions and digital identity. Blockchain provides a secure, decentralized ledger that is used to record and verify transactions across various sectors, including finance, healthcare, and public services. This technology ensures that all transactions are transparent, immutable, and resistant to tampering, which is essential for maintaining trust in digital government services. One of the most significant applications of Blockchain in Singapore's Smart Nation initiative is in the area of digital identity. This system not only simplifies interactions with the government but also enhances security by reducing the risk of identity theft and fraud.

Cloud Computing for Scalable Infrastructure

To support the vast amounts of data generated by AI and Blockchain technologies, Singapore's Smart Nation initiative relies heavily on Cloud Computing for scalable data storage and processing. Cloud platforms provide the necessary infrastructure to handle the city-state's growing digital needs, allowing for the efficient management of data across various government agencies and public services. Moreover, Cloud Computing facilitates the integration of AI and Blockchain across different sectors to enable more coordinated and efficient governance.

Insights and Lessons for Digital Transformation

Singapore's Smart Nation initiative provides several key insights for other countries looking to embark on digital transformation journeys. By combining AI, Blockchain, and Cloud Computing, Singapore has created a robust digital infrastructure that supports a wide range of public services, enhances security, and fosters innovation. This focus on user experience is evident in the development of the National Digital Identity system, AI-driven public health management, and smart urban infrastructure, all of which are designed to make life easier, safer, and more convenient for Singaporeans. Finally, the success of the Smart Nation initiative is largely due to the Singaporean government's commitment to embracing innovation and its willingness to invest in the necessary infrastructure and skills development. For other countries, this underscores the importance of strategic planning and investment in building the foundations for a successful digital future.

Valuable Lessons From Singapore's Smart Nation Initiative for Governments Embarking on Digital Transformation

There are so many Valuable Lessons learned from Singapore's Smart Nation initiative, which can be applied to other governments seeking to embark on digital transformation journeys.

1. Comprehensive Integration of Advanced Technologies

Lesson: The successful integration of AI, Blockchain, and Cloud Computing is crucial for creating a cohesive and efficient digital ecosystem to enhance public services, increase operational efficiency, and ensure secure transactions. **Application**: Governments should prioritize the adoption of a range of advanced technologies, ensuring that they are not just implemented in isolation but integrated into a broader digital strategy that maximizes their collective impact.

2. Strong Leadership and Vision

Lesson: The success of the Smart Nation initiative is driven by strong government leadership and a clear, strategic vision for digital transformation.
Application: Governments should ensure that their leaders articulate a clear vision for digital initiatives and actively support the implementation of digital strategies.

3. Focus on Citizen-Centric Design

Lesson: By designing services that are user-friendly and accessible, the Smart Nation initiative has effectively engaged the public and increased the adoption of digital services which improved the quality of life for its citizens.
Application: Digital government strategies should prioritize the needs and experiences of citizens, ensuring that digital services are accessible, easy to use, and responsive to public needs.

4. Commitment to Data Security and Privacy

Lesson: Singapore's use of Blockchain technology in securing digital transactions and identities highlights the importance of data security and privacy in digital transformation.
Application: Governments must implement robust security measures, including the use of Blockchain for secure data storage and identity management, to protect sensitive information and build public trust in digital services.

5. Scalable and Flexible Infrastructure

Lesson: Singapore's ability to scale its digital infrastructure as needed has been critical in maintaining the resilience of its digital services.
Application: Governments should invest in scalable and flexible digital infrastructure, such as Cloud Computing, to ensure that their digital services can grow and adapt to changing demands without compromising service quality or security.

6. Encouraging Innovation and Continuous Improvement

Lesson: Singapore has fostered a culture of innovation, continuously experimenting with new technologies and refining its digital services.

Application: Governments should create an environment that encourages innovation, such as through the establishment of innovation labs or pilot projects, and be committed to continuous improvement by regularly updating and optimizing digital services.

7. Effective Public-Private Partnerships

Lesson: By partnering with technology companies, academic institutions, and other stakeholders, Singapore has been able to leverage external expertise and resources.
Application: Governments should actively seek partnerships with private sector organizations and other stakeholders to gain access to the latest technologies, knowledge, and innovations, thereby enhancing their digital transformation efforts.

8. Global Outlook and Competitiveness

Lesson: By positioning itself as a global leader in digital transformation, Singapore has attracted international businesses, talent, and investment.
Application: Governments should adopt a global perspective in their digital strategies, considering how digital transformation can enhance their country's competitiveness on the world stage and attract global investment and talent.

Blueprint for Digital Excellence: Replicating Singapore's Smart Nation Success

To replicate Singapore's success in digital transformation through initiatives like the Smart Nation program, other countries can adopt several key strategies. These strategies encompass leadership, technological integration, policy development, and citizen engagement. Here's how other countries can follow Singapore's success:

1. Strong Vision and Leadership
   (i) **Establish a Clear Vision:** Countries should begin by articulating a clear vision for digital transformation, setting ambitious but achievable goals that align with national priorities.
   (ii) **Government Commitment:** Ensure that top-level government leaders are committed to driving digital transformation. This includes securing the necessary political will and resources to implement long-term digital strategies.
2. Comprehensive Digital Strategy

(i) **Develop a National Digital Strategy:** Countries should create a comprehensive digital strategy that outlines the integration of AI, Blockchain, and Cloud Computing into public services. This strategy should include specific objectives, timelines, and key performance indicators (KPIs) to track progress.

(ii) **Prioritize Interoperability:** Developing standards for interoperability ensures that different systems can work together seamlessly, enabling a cohesive digital ecosystem.

3. Citizen-Centric Approach

(i) **Focus on User Experience:** Countries should prioritize the needs of their citizens by designing digital services that are intuitive, accessible, and responsive to user feedback.

(ii) **Promote Digital Literacy:** Singapore invests in educating its population about digital tools, and other countries should similarly provide training and resources to help citizens and businesses engage with digital services.

4. Investment in Infrastructure

(i) **Build Robust Digital Infrastructure:** Countries aiming to replicate this success must invest in reliable and scalable infrastructure, such as high-speed broadband, secure data centers, and cloud computing capabilities.

(ii) **Adopt Cloud Computing:** Leveraging Cloud Computing allows for scalable and flexible data storage and processing, which is essential for managing large amounts of data generated by AI and other technologies.

5. Secure and Transparent Data Management

(i) **Implement Strong Data Governance:** Like Singapore, countries should prioritize data security and privacy by implementing robust data governance frameworks. This includes protecting citizens' data through encryption, secure storage, and strict access controls.

(ii) **Utilize Blockchain for Security**: Blockchain technology can be employed to secure transactions and ensure the integrity of government data.

6. Developing Innovation and Collaboration

(i) **Encourage Public-Private Partnerships:** Like Singapore, other countries should foster collaboration with tech companies, startups, and universities to drive innovation in digital government services.

(ii) **Create Innovation Hubs:** Establish innovation labs or hubs where new technologies can be tested and developed in a controlled environment.

7. Agility and Adaptability

(i) **Embrace Agile Methodologies:** To keep pace with rapidly evolving technologies, countries should adopt agile methodologies in their digital projects.

(ii) **Continuous Improvement:** Regularly assess the performance of digital initiatives and make necessary improvements to ensure that digital services remain relevant and effective.

8. Policy and Regulatory Support
   (i) **Update Legal Frameworks**: Countries should update their legal and regulatory frameworks to support digital transformation. This includes creating laws that recognize digital identities, e-signatures, and electronic transactions.
   (ii) **Promote Open Data:** By making government data publicly accessible, countries can increase transparency and encourage innovation.
9. Public Trust and Engagement
   (i) **Build Public Trust:** Countries should focus on transparency, data protection, and ethical use of AI and other technologies to build and maintain public trust.
   (ii) **Engage with Citizens**: Regular engagement with citizens through consultations, surveys, and feedback mechanisms ensures that digital services are aligned with public needs and expectations.
10. Long-Term Sustainability
    (i) **Plan for Sustainability:** Countries should ensure that their digital strategies are sustainable by securing long-term funding, investing in workforce development, and planning for future technological advancements.
    (ii) **Monitor and Evaluate:** Establish clear metrics and regularly evaluate the impact of digital initiatives. This helps in identifying areas for improvement and ensuring that the country remains on track to achieve its digital goals.

DEVELOPING A HOLISTIC DIGITAL GOVERNMENT STRATEGY: BEST PRACTICES AND FRAMEWORKS

The final section will focus on formulating a comprehensive digital government strategy. It will outline best practices and frameworks for effectively integrating AI, Blockchain, and Cloud technologies within the public sector. This part will provide practical guidelines for policymakers and public administrators, detailing essential steps for developing a digital transformation roadmap. It will highlight key considerations for policy development, such as regulatory compliance, data privacy, and cross-departmental coordination. Additionally, strategies for fostering innovation and building public trust will be discussed, including stakeholder engagement, transparency initiatives, and continuous improvement processes. By offering actionable insights and a structured approach, this section aims to equip government leaders with the tools necessary to drive successful digital transformation and enhance public service delivery.

Developing a Holistic Digital Government Strategy: Best Practices and Frameworks

As governments worldwide embrace digital transformation, the development of a holistic digital government strategy is crucial for effectively integrating advanced technologies like Artificial Intelligence (AI), Blockchain, and Cloud Computing within the public sector. This final section of the chapter focuses on formulating a comprehensive digital government strategy by outlining best practices and frameworks that can guide policymakers and public administrators through the digital transformation process.

Formulating a Comprehensive Digital Government Strategy

The development of a digital government strategy begins with a clear understanding of the goals and objectives that the government aims to achieve through digital transformation. These goals may include improving the efficiency and effectiveness of public services, enhancing data security and privacy, promoting transparency, and increasing citizen engagement. Once these goals are established, the next step is to identify the key technologies -such as AI, Blockchain, and Cloud Computing- that will enable the government to achieve these objectives.

1. Vision and Leadership

A successful digital government strategy requires strong leadership and a clear vision. Government leaders must articulate a compelling vision for digital transformation that resonates with both policymakers and citizens. This vision should outline the long-term benefits of digital transformation, including how it will improve public services and enhance the quality of life for citizens.

2. Regulatory Compliance and Data Privacy

Governments must ensure that their digital initiatives comply with national and international regulations, such as data protection laws and cybersecurity standards. This requires a thorough assessment of the legal and regulatory landscape, as well as the development of policies and procedures that protect citizens' data while enabling innovation. Data privacy should be a core component of the strategy, with clear guidelines on how data is collected, stored, and used by government agencies.

3. Cross-Departmental Coordination

Effective digital transformation requires seamless coordination across government departments and agencies. Cross-departmental coordination can be achieved through the establishment of a centralized digital transformation office or task force, which is responsible for overseeing the implementation of the digital government strategy. This office should work closely with all relevant stakeholders, including IT departments, policy advisors, and external partners, to ensure alignment and consistency across the government.

4. Innovation and Public Trust

Raising innovation is essential for driving digital transformation in the public sector. Governments should create an environment that encourages experimentation and the adoption of new technologies. This can be achieved by establishing innovation labs, providing funding for pilot projects, and collaborating with the private sector and academic institutions. Building public trust is equally important, as citizens must feel confident that digital government services are secure, reliable, and beneficial.

5. Continuous Improvement

Digital transformation is an ongoing process that requires continuous monitoring and improvement. Governments should establish mechanisms for regularly assessing the performance of digital initiatives and making necessary adjustments. This may involve collecting feedback from citizens, conducting performance audits, and staying informed about emerging technologies and best practices.

BEST PRACTICES AND FRAMEWORKS FOR DIGITAL GOVERNMENT STRATEGY

As governments around the world increasingly recognize the potential of digital technologies to enhance efficiency, transparency, and citizen engagement, it is essential to establish robust frameworks and best practices that guide these efforts. This document explores key best practices and frameworks that governments can adopt to effectively navigate the complexities of digital transformation, from establishing clear governance structures and prioritizing data privacy to fostering innovation and building public trust. By implementing these strategies, governments can create a resilient and forward-looking digital infrastructure that serves the evolving demands of the 21st century.

Figure 1. Framework for Digital Government Strategy

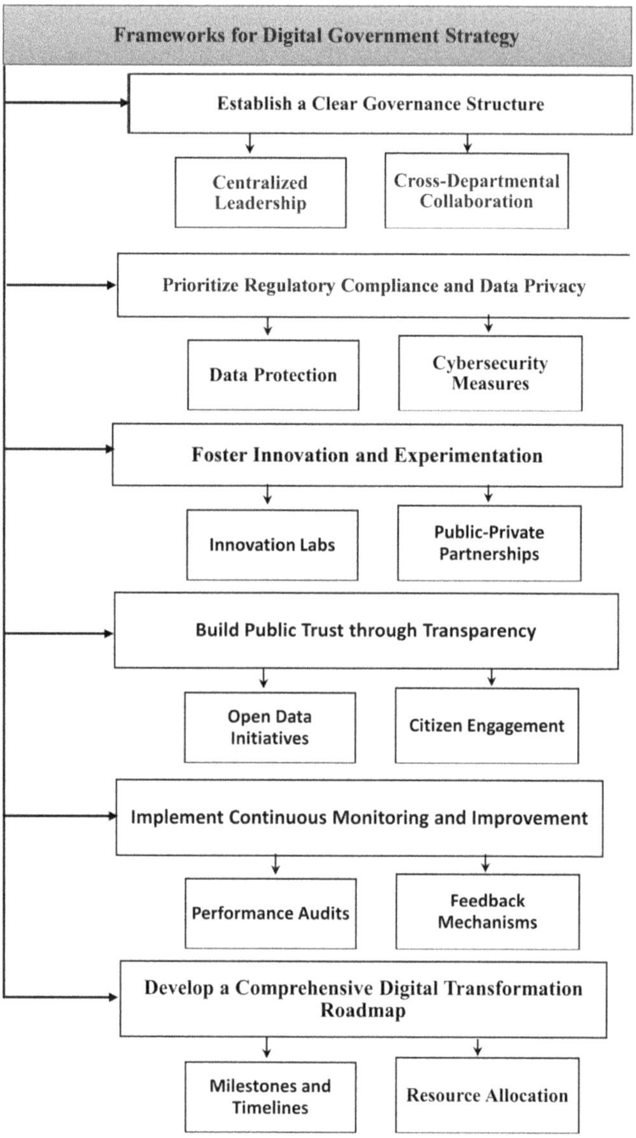

Legal Frameworks and Policy Requirements

Successfully adopting AI, Blockchain, and Cloud Computing in e-Government necessitates comprehensive legal frameworks and policies to address ethical, operational, and technical concerns. Governments must focus on the following areas:

Data Protection and Privacy

Clear regulations are needed to govern the collection, processing, and sharing of citizen data. Laws akin to the GDPR can serve as a benchmark, ensuring that personal data is safeguarded while enabling necessary data exchanges for digital services.

Cybersecurity Standards

Robust cybersecurity policies are crucial to protect critical e-Government systems from cyberattacks and unauthorized access. These policies should include threat detection, response protocols, and mandatory audits.

Technology Standardization

Interoperability across government departments is essential for seamless integration. Standardizing data formats, communication protocols, and system architectures can reduce implementation costs and complexity.

Ethical AI Guidelines

To address biases and ensure fairness in AI decision-making, governments must establish ethical guidelines for AI deployment. These should cover transparency, accountability, and the avoidance of discriminatory practices.

Public-Private Collaboration Policies

Many governments rely on private sector expertise for technology adoption. Clear policies should define terms for data ownership, intellectual property, and service level agreements to ensure sustainable partnerships.

Establishing a clear governance structure begins with the creation of a centralized leadership body to ensure that digital initiatives are guided by a unified vision and executed with consistency across all levels of government. Moreover, fostering cross-departmental collaboration is crucial for the cohesive and efficient implementation of these initiatives. By breaking down silos and encouraging cooperation among different government departments, digital transformation efforts can be more seamlessly integrated into existing structures and processes, maximizing their impact and sustainability.

Regulatory compliance and data privacy are paramount in the digital age, particularly for government entities that handle sensitive information. It is imperative to develop comprehensive data protection policies that not only adhere to national regulations but also align with international standards. In doing so, governments can build a secure digital environment that fosters trust among citizens and stakeholders.

Governments should establish innovation labs where new technologies can be explored and pilot projects can be developed. These labs serve as incubators for cutting-edge ideas that can be tested and refined before being implemented on a larger scale. By collaborating with the private sector, academic institutions, and other stakeholders, governments can leverage external expertise and resources to accelerate their digital transformation efforts.

Building public trust through transparency is a foundational element of any digital government strategy. Open data initiatives are an effective way to increase transparency, allowing citizens to access and engage with government data. This openness not only empowers citizens but also holds government accountable for its actions. This engagement fosters a sense of ownership among citizens and strengthens the legitimacy of digital initiatives.

Continuous monitoring and improvement are essential to ensuring the long-term success of digital government strategies. Regular performance audits provide an objective assessment of the effectiveness of digital initiatives, highlighting areas of success as well as opportunities for improvement. Feedback mechanisms, both from citizens and stakeholders, are invaluable in identifying challenges and refining strategies.

Finally, developing a comprehensive digital transformation roadmap is crucial for guiding the implementation of digital initiatives. Resource allocation is another critical aspect, as ensuring that adequate resources-whether financial, human, or technological-are available is necessary to support digital transformation efforts. A well-planned and resourced roadmap not only provides direction but also ensures that digital initiatives are implemented effectively, leading to sustainable and impactful digital government transformation.

By offering a structured approach to developing a holistic digital government strategy, this section equips policymakers and public administrators with the tools and insights necessary to drive successful digital transformation. The best practices and frameworks outlined here provide a roadmap for integrating AI, Blockchain, and Cloud Computing technologies within the public sector, ensuring that digital initiatives are aligned with broader government objectives, comply with regulatory requirements, and foster innovation and public trust. As governments around the world continue to embrace digital transformation, these guidelines will serve as a valuable reference for enhancing public service delivery and building resilient, future-ready governments.

REFERENCES

Abiad, M., & Ionescu, S. (2020). *Building an algorithm for predictive maintenance*. UPB Scientific Bulletin, Series D. *Mechanical Engineering (New York, N.Y.)*, 337–348.

Abiad, M., Kadry, N., & Ionescu, S. (2018). *Preventive & predictive maintenance of telecommunication equipment: A review*. 2018 4th International Conference on Applied and Theoretical Computing and Communication Technology (iCATccT), 154–159. https://api.semanticscholar.org/CorpusID:211244649

Abiad, M., Shafiq, M., Habib, S., & Atif, M. (2024). *On the Development of Fuzzy Estimators for Life Time Distributions based on Censored Fuzzy Life Times*. International Journal of Neutrosophic Science, 198-209. DOI: 10.54216/IJNS.240217

Ali, K. E., & Alonso-Monsalve, S. (2018). *A Study of Cloud Computing Adoption in Universities as a Guideline to Cloud Migration*. Sage Journals.

Bharanidharan, G., & Jayalakshmi, S. (2021). Predictive scaling for elastic compute resources on public cloud utilizing deep learning-based long short-term memory. *International Journal of Advanced Computer Science and Applications*, 12(10), 73–81.

Guo, B., Feng, Y., & Lin, J. (2023). Digital inclusive finance and digital transformation of enterprises. *Finance Research Letters*, 57, 104270. DOI: 10.1016/j.frl.2023.104270

Gura, K., AlAkoum, A., Melenciuc, M., & Henley, S. (2023). Mobile Biometric and Sentiment Data, Generative Artificial Intelligence and Behavior Tracking Tools, and Wearable Sensor-based and Connected Monitoring Devices in Immersive Interconnected 3D Worlds. *Analysis and Metaphysics*, 22(0), 255–273. DOI: 10.22381/am22202314

Haque, E. (2022). *Enterprise Service Management (ESM): The art of ESM in the era of AI, Blockchain and metaverse*. Lulu.com.

Kaginalkar, A., Kumar, S., Gargava, P., & Niyogi, D. (2021). Review of urban computing in air quality management as smart city service: An integrated IoT, AI, and cloud technology perspective. *Urban Climate*, 39, 100972. DOI: 10.1016/j.uclim.2021.100972

Karthikeyan, P., Pande, H. M., & Sarveshwaran, V. (2023). *Artificial Intelligence and Blockchain in Digital Forensics*. DOI: 10.1201/9781003374671

Kumar, S., Lim, W. M., Sivarajah, U., & Kaur, J. (2023). Artificial Intelligence and Blockchain Integration in Business: Trends from a Bibliometric-Content Analysis. *Information Systems Frontiers*, 25, 871–896. DOI: 10.1007/s10796-022-10279-0 PMID: 35431617

Li, W., Wu, J., Cao, J., Chen, N., Zhang, Q., & Buyya, R. (2021). Blockchain-based trust management in cloud computing systems: A taxonomy, review and future directions. *Journal of Cloud Computing (Heidelberg, Germany)*, 10(1), 35. DOI: 10.1186/s13677-021-00247-5

Microsoft. (2023). *Changing the government landscape with cloud and AI*. Microsoft.

OECD. (2023). OECD Digital Government Index. OECD iLibrary.

Pani, S. K., Lau, S. L., & Liu, X. (2021). *Blockchain and AI Technology in the Industrial Internet of Things*. Springer. DOI: 10.4018/978-1-7998-6694-7

PWC. (2021). *Estonia – the Digital Republic Secured by Blockchain*. Retrieved from https://www.pwc.com/gx/en/services/legal/tech/assets/estonia-the-digital-republic-secured-by-blockchain.pdf

Rai, B. K., Kumar, G., & Balyan, V. (2023). *AI and Blockchain in Healthcare*. SpringerLink., DOI: 10.1007/978-981-99-0377-1

Shinde, N. K., Seth, A., & Kadam, P. (2023). Exploring the Synergies: A Comprehensive Survey of Blockchain Integration with Artificial Intelligence, Machine Learning, and IoT for Diverse Applications. In Shastri, A. S., Shaw, K., & Singh, M. (Eds.), *Machine Learning and Optimization for Engineering Design* (pp. 1–27). Springer. DOI: 10.1007/978-981-99-7456-6_7

ThomsonReuters.com. (2023). *e-Estonia: The Power and Potential of Digital Identity*. Retrieved from https://www.thomsonreuters.com/en-us/posts/news-and-media/e-estonia-power-potential-digital-identity/

Tsolakis, N., Schumacher, R., Dora, M., & Kumar, M. (2023). Artificial intelligence and blockchain implementation in supply chains: A pathway to sustainability and data monetisation? *Annals of Operations Research*, 327(1), 157–210. DOI: 10.1007/s10479-022-04785-2 PMID: 35755830

Tyma, B., Dhillon, R., Sivabalan, P., & Wieder, B. (2022). Understanding accountability in blockchain systems. *Accounting, Auditing & Accountability Journal*, 35(7), 1625–1655. DOI: 10.1108/AAAJ-07-2020-4713

Chapter 12

Knowledge Management in Public Sector Innovation Optimized by Artificial Intelligence

Rosane Malvestiti
https://orcid.org/0000-0002-4927-5721
Universidade Federal de Santa Catarina, Brazil

Laura Pertile
https://orcid.org/0009-0006-8077-8542
Universidade Federal de Santa Catarina, Brazil

Murilo Pedro Demarchi
https://orcid.org/0000-0003-1941-6340
Universidade Federal de Santa Catarina, Brazil

Gertrudes Aparecida Dandolini
Universidade Federal de Santa Catarina, Brazil

Andreia De Bem Machado
https://orcid.org/0000-0002-4404-0341
Universidade Federal de Santa Catarina, Brazil

ABSTRACT

Given the rapid transformations brought about by artificial intelligence across all sectors and in lifestyle, knowledge is ever-present, and its management is essential. Therefore, public services need to innovate to meet social and organizational demands, focusing on solving complex problems that require new knowledge and

DOI: 10.4018/979-8-3693-7678-2.ch012

effective governmental strategies. This chapter details, through a scoping review, how knowledge management (KM) is used in public sector innovation (PSI) and how artificial intelligence (AI) facilitates this interaction. As a result, it was evident that KM, facilitated by AI, offers a promising path for public organizations, enabling the creation of more adaptive, efficient, and citizen-centered solutions. However, the successful integration of AI and KM still requires ongoing efforts to adapt to new technologies, develop digital skills and competencies of public servants, and implement inclusive public policies that consider the ethical and social implications of these technologies. Future studies should focus on research about Ethics and Transparency in AI.

1. INTRODUCTION

In recent years, the world has faced significant challenges that have altered the course of human history. Still recovering from the devastating impacts of the COVID-19 pandemic, global economies have been affected by large-scale conflicts such as Russia's invasion of Ukraine. Amidst this chaotic and uncertain scenario, millions of lives have been drastically affected, resulting in disruptions in energy and food markets, alongside rising inflation. Faced with these adversities, governments are compelled to adopt effective strategies to manage changes across all sectors. Additionally, they confront issues such as climate change, poverty, social inequality, and the promotion of digital inclusion (OECD, 2023).

These issues, known as "wicked problems," present challenges for governments in developing and implementing strategies. Attempts to solve these problems often lead to unexpected consequences, reflecting the complexity and uncertainty inherent in these challenges. Moreover, such problems are heavily influenced by the specific context in which they occur, requiring adaptive and innovative approaches from governments (Zivkovic, 2018).

Within the field of knowledge management (KM), there is a direct relationship with solving organizational problems. However, it is increasingly clear that organizations need to reconceptualize KM not only as an internal tool for organizational improvement but as a strategy that can contribute to societal improvement as a whole. This approach requires an analysis focused on social problems and possibilities for innovation that transcend traditional organizational boundaries (Dumay, 2019). To expedite and enhance this process, innovation is identified as a promising path, especially when facilitated using artificial intelligence. In this context, public agencies face an imperative need to innovate and digitally transform how services are delivered, aiming to add value and agility to increasingly complex social demands (Malischeski et al., 2021).

The chapter presents practical examples that illustrate the application of these strategies in different contexts. For instance, co-innovation networks in China have facilitated the flow of knowledge among universities, companies, and the government, promoting an environment conducive to continuous innovation (Zhang, Sun, Fan, & Weng, 2023). Moreover, it highlights the need for ongoing efforts to adapt and improve these practices through new technologies and collaboration, aiming for outcomes that are centered on society's needs. Therefore, it is proposed to explore these dynamics by investigating how knowledge management and artificial intelligence can be integrated to drive significant transformation in the public sector.

In summary, this chapter presents a scoping review of the literature and aims to provide a comprehensive, critical, and detailed overview of the research conducted on the use of knowledge management in public sector innovation, as well as exploring the role of artificial intelligence in facilitating and enhancing the processes that occur in this context. The conduct of this review has allowed for the identification and analysis of the methods used and their applications in various innovative public sectors, highlighting the importance of knowledge management and artificial intelligence as catalysts for innovation in the public sector. Based on this analysis, it was possible to identify gaps in the existing knowledge and point to directions for future studies, suggesting areas where improvements are necessary to face contemporary challenges. It also reveals how the integration of knowledge management and artificial intelligence can significantly transform public administration, and promote greater efficiency, transparency, and citizen focus.

2. THEORETICAL REFERENCE

2.2. Knowledge Management in The Public Sector

Recent research on strategic management highlights significant changes in ideas that ensure competitive advantage. Strategies developed by top management and approaches focused on internal resources are being replaced by a new perspective. This new approach centers on knowledge creation, developing new competencies, integrating external and internal knowledge within the organization (cooperation), and developing strategic actions that allow the organization to innovate. It also promotes the use of new management modalities, such as knowledge management (Carayannis, Alexander & Ioannidis, 1999).

Knowledge Management (KM), a recent and interdisciplinary area, presents different definitions and perspectives on its essence and purpose. In this study, KM is defined as a process involving the creation, sharing, storage, and application of knowledge. The main goal is to enhance productivity, performance, and promote organizational advancement (ISO, 2018).

The study of KM was intensely discussed during the 1990s. Gonzalez and Martins (2017), studying processes related to KM, observed two main perspectives: the first, called the flow based on organizational development, focuses on promoting an increase in knowledge storage as well as the reuse of knowledge repositories; the second, in the flow based on processes, highlights the contribution of information technology as a tool to stimulate individuals' creativity in creating value. Analyzing organizational development. Kariyado (2016) emphasizes that the essence of KM is to enable knowledge to be available to those who wish to use it.

In this knowledge economy or society, organizations, public or private, must be prepared to learn, remember, unlearn, and act according to the best information, knowledge, and know-how available (Dalkir, 2011). However, as it is still a relatively new field of study, it has been observed that about 80% of KM implementation programs in organizations (public or private) tend to not succeed. Among the main reasons are the failure to implement KM with an operational focus and as a program of change in structures and work methods; the absence of the right people who can deliver such changes; the lack of involvement of other stakeholders; the implementation of part of the solution and not the solution as a whole; the failure to incorporate KM into organizational processes and activities; and low effectiveness of sponsors (Barnes & Milton, 2015).

Specifically regarding KM in the public sector, in a systematic literature review developed by researchers Massaro, Dumay & Garlatti (2015), who sought to understand the state of the art of KM research in the public sector and the development of a future research agenda, it was observed that among the most studied research themes, those related to processes (36%) and KM strategies (15%) stand out, with a small number of authors who have developed studies in KM in the public sector, and the focus of the research being linked to the areas of education and research centers (Massaro, Dumay & Garlatti, 2015).

As a discipline, the main contribution of KM in the public sector is to increase the capacity of civil servants and the organization in creating, sharing, and applying knowledge so that quality public services are provided to society, especially in this digital era (Batista, 2012).

2.2. Public Sector Innovation

Governments around the world have faced challenges in delivering public services. The COVID-19 pandemic and tensions between Russia and Ukraine have profoundly impacted the lives of millions of people and societies, intensifying the need for innovation in the public sector. The main reasons for this include changes in the social environment, reflecting new societal needs and expectations; emerging technological challenges, such as the advancement of artificial intelligence; and resource scarcity, which are limited (Malischeski, 2023; OECD, 2023).

Although technological leverage introduces new complexities to be assimilated by organizations, it also brings to light opportunities that can be exploited. In a context marked by climate change, urban mobility issues, refugee integration, protection of natural resources, and reduction of social inequalities, governments need to develop innovative solutions that go beyond conventional approaches. This requires a level of responsiveness that enables governments to understand, test, and incorporate new ways of addressing these challenges (Torfing & Ansell, 2017).

In studies on economic development, the economist and political scientist Joseph Schumpeter (1961) was one of the first to highlight the importance of innovation. He associated it with the creation of something new or the improvement of processes and products, especially in the private sector, and identified it as a driving force for economic growth and country development. Peter Drucker, on the other hand, was one of the first to discuss the need for innovation in organizations, including public ones, as early as the 1950s and 1960s. He argued that innovation is crucial not only for companies but also for governmental organizations in the pursuit of efficiency and effectiveness. However, it was not until the beginning of this century that research on public sector innovation began to stand out.

Although there is no convergence on the definition of public sector innovation and its typologies, it can be understood as the introduction of new elements into the public sector, whether through new knowledge, reorganization, or the development of new management or service provision skills, representing a significant discontinuity with past practices (Osborne and Brown, 2011). This change not only renews the existing structure but also instigates a critical evolution in management methodologies and service provision within the public sector. Regarding the typologies of public sector innovation, Morales and Dandolini (2022), through an integrative review, identified five groups: 1) products (goods and services); 2) processes; 3) management; 4) by mission, conceptual; paradigm; and 5) policy, governance, partnerships, and citizen.

2.3. Artificial Intelligence

Digital innovation, especially those involving Artificial Intelligence (AI), enables an organization to gain a competitive advantage by improving operational capability through the analysis of large-scale data and information. In this research, the term "Artificial Intelligence" is defined as the ability of computer systems to perform tasks like human intelligence, which involves a complex activity of processing and analyzing data (Yuwono, Tjondronegoro, Riverola & Loy; 2024).

In the field of digital government, AI is still a relatively new area. However, there has been a steady increase in the adoption and use of this type of technology in various contexts, such as predictive policing; cybersecurity and regulatory enforcement; adjudication of government benefits and privileges; chatbots to answer citizen queries; and filling, searching, and drafting documents (Mellouli, Janssen & Ojo; 2024).

In this universe, although different applications and benefits can be observed in the governmental context, social, ethical, and legal challenges are also created, which require a combination of technical and institutional solutions (Mellouli et al. 2024).

Among the benefits observed in the scientific literature, Mellouli et al. (2024) list the increase in productivity and the automation of repetitive tasks; digital assistance; creativity through the creation of new content; real-time monitoring; development of evidence-based policies more quickly and effectively; and solving complex problems by automating tasks and enabling more rational decision-making. Regarding challenges or risks, they highlight the obsolescence of some types of work; the creation of misinformation and fake news; loss of human experience and knowledge (tacit knowledge); lack of capacity to think "outside the box"; increased energy consumption due to computational capabilities; replication of human errors; bias in data handling; and less fair and inclusive political decisions (Melloulíet al. 2024).

3. METHODOLOGY

The methodology adopted in this chapter was the scoping review, an approach aimed at understanding the fundamental concepts that underpin a specific research area. This methodology is particularly useful for examining the extent, range, and nature of existing investigations; determining whether a full systematic review is feasible or not; summarizing and disseminating the results of scientific studies, and finally, identifying gaps in the literature on a topic (Arksey; O'Malley, 2005).

In the context of this chapter, the scoping review was chosen to examine knowledge management in public sector innovation, with a special focus on optimizing these processes through artificial intelligence. To ensure the rigor and integrity of the review process, the research followed the guidelines proposed by PRISMA, adapted for the scoping review branch (Tricco et al., 2018). A specific protocol was developed and divided into three main stages. Thus, the recommended checklist was followed, ensuring the consistency and validity of the findings (Tricco et al., 2018).

This protocol guided the entire conduct of the review, ensuring that the information collected was comprehensive and accurately reflected the current state of the literature on the contributions of artificial intelligence and knowledge management in public sector innovation that drive and expedite problem-solving and increase the availability of government service offerings. Figure 1 presents the stages of the scoping review, an overview of the methodology of this study.

Figure 1. Stages of the scoping review (Developed by the authors (2024), according to Tricco et al. (2018))

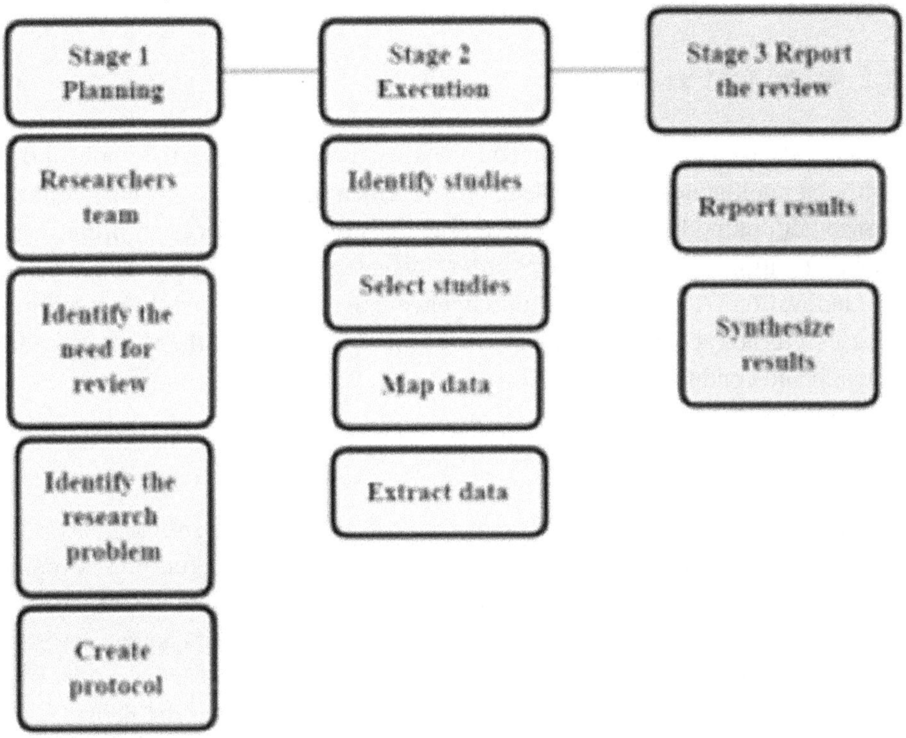

3.1. Stage 1 - Planning

As shown in Figure 1, this stage involves four phases: (a) forming the research team with their roles previously determined, (b) identifying and justifying the need for the study; (c) defining the research question that will guide the entire research, and (d) creating the scoping review protocol, which will be supported by the research question and directs the steps to be followed. More details on each phase of this stage are provided below.

3.1.1. Researchers team

To initiate the review, a research team was defined, consisting of five members with pre-established roles. Thus, one researcher was assigned the role of judge to decide in case of doubts, a translator, a coordinator, and two researchers designated for screening and data extraction in a blind manner. This type of approach ensures that during the eligibility screening of articles and data extraction, the researchers do not communicate and are unaware of each other's results, allowing them to remain focused solely on the content and free from influences to ensure impartiality in document selection and data extraction.

3.1.2. Need for the review

This study is justified by the need to find answers aiming at the applicability of artificial intelligence and knowledge management in public sector innovation to optimize both individual and collective potentials of such services. A preliminary search for relations between the keywords ("management knowledge" AND "public sector innovation" AND "artificial intelligence") in the Scopus and Web of Science databases returned no reviews or isolated studies, which indicated the need to broaden the search and conduct the review.

3.1.3. Research question

To define the strategy for this research, the Problem, Concept, and Context (PCC) mnemonic was considered, which is used to help identify and delineate key topics. Thus, this strategy was adopted to formulate the research question for this scoping review and to identify studies, analyze and systematize the data, show the paths taken, indicate new research activities, highlight gaps, and publish the results (The Joanna Briggs Institute, 2015). For each letter, the following was defined:

P = analyze the scientific production of national and international articles on knowledge management, public sector innovation, and artificial intelligence.

C = research in totality how knowledge management in public sector innovation (in its various scenarios of action) can be optimized by AI.

C = number of publications, degree of recommendation, and evidence of the studies, which public service utilizes knowledge management and AI, whether the publications are uni or multi-professional, and the most researched themes/public sector.

Leading to the following question: How is KM being applied in public sector innovation and optimized by AI?

3.1.4. Protocol

Following the development of the research question, the protocol was defined in detail.

- Choice of databases

The selected databases were Scielo, IEEE, Scopus, and Web of Science (WoS). Scielo was chosen as it is the largest database in the native language of the researchers. IEEE (Institute of Electrical and Electronics Engineers - https://www.ieee.org/) was selected because it is a database with full texts related to engineering and computer technology in English, with a portfolio of more than five million documents, including over three hundred journals, with approximately twenty thousand new documents added monthly, and most importantly, it is a peer-reviewed database. Scopus and WoS both provide access to comprehensive multidisciplinary academic citation data. They are the two largest peer-reviewed databases.

- Formatting the Boolean equation

For a better understanding of the keywords, an initial study was conducted by the three researchers designated for the screening and data extraction. After this initial study, a librarian and thesaurus expert from the Federal University of Santa Catarina (UFSC) was consulted. The three researchers participated in the meeting, which lasted one hour, analyzing and discussing the formulation of the equation, with the goal of achieving significant coverage, resulting in this Boolean equation:

("artificial intelligence" OR "generative AI" OR "generative language model" OR "large language model" OR "learning systems" OR chatgpt OR "Intelligent Systems") AND ("public sector" OR "public administration" OR government OR "public service" OR "public policy" OR "municipal administration" OR "state administration" OR "federal administration" OR "public institutions" OR "government agencies" OR "public management" OR "government operations" OR "public organizations" OR "public finance" OR "local government" OR "national government" OR "regional government") AND ("knowledge management" OR "knowledge creation" OR "knowledge storage" OR "knowledge sharing" OR "knowledge identification" OR "knowledge application" OR "knowledge transfer" OR "knowledge retention" OR "intellectual capital" OR "knowledge dissemination" OR "knowledge development" OR "knowledge acquisition" OR "knowledge exchange" OR "knowledge integration" OR "knowledge systems" OR "knowledge processes") AND (innovation OR innovative OR creativity OR invention OR novelty OR advancement OR transformation OR breakthrough OR improvement OR disruption OR disruptive)

- Eligibility criteria

The eligibility criteria were:

First screening - (a) inclusion - all documents associating KM, PSI, and AI; all dates;

(b) exclusion - all documents not associating KM, PSI, and AI;

Second screening - (a) inclusion - articles published in journals associating KM, PSI, and AI;

(b) exclusion - documents that were not journal articles, such as conference papers or proceedings, extended abstracts, book chapters; articles that did not associate KM, PSI, and AI.

3.2. Stage 2 - Execution

This stage marks the commencement of the actual research. However, even after the protocol is finalized, it is updated as necessary. As illustrated in Figure 1, the first phase of this stage is to identify all studies from the previously chosen databases, followed by the phase of selecting studies according to the eligibility criteria directed by the research question, as defined in the protocol. This phase was conducted by the team in a blind review. The third phase, data analysis, involves extracting data from each study through a full read of each document considered, also performed in a blind review format. Below are these phases in detail.

3.2.1. Identifying the studies

The searches in the databases were conducted in May 2024. All returned documents were considered for the first screening according to eligibility criteria. Thus, the Boolean equation was used in the databases with the field "all fields", specifically in Scopus under "Article title, Abstract, Keywords". Table 1 shows the return quantity from each database.

Table 1. Boolean equation

Boolean Equation	Databases Number of Documents			
	Scielo	IEEE	Wos	Scopus
("artificial intelligence" OR "generative AI" OR "generative language model" OR "large language model" OR "learning systems" OR chatgpt OR "Intelligent Systems") AND ("public sector" OR "public administration" OR government OR "public service" OR "public policy" OR "municipal administration" OR "state administration" OR "federal administration" OR "public institutions" OR "government agencies" OR "public management" OR "government operations" OR "public organizations" OR "public finance" OR "local government" OR "national government" OR "regional government") AND ("knowledge management" OR "knowledge creation" OR "knowledge storage" OR "knowledge sharing" OR "knowledge identification" OR "knowledge application" OR "knowledge transfer" OR "knowledge retention" OR "intellectual capital" OR "knowledge dissemination" OR "knowledge development" OR "knowledge acquisition" OR "knowledge exchange" OR "knowledge integration" OR "knowledge systems" OR "knowledge processes") AND (innovation OR innovative OR creativity OR invention OR novelty OR advancement OR transformation OR breakthrough OR improvement OR disruption OR disruptive)	0	60	186	116
	Total = 362 documents			

Source: Developed by the authors, 2024.

3.2.2. Selecting the Studies

The 362 documents retrieved from the databases were placed into the bibliographic reference manager EndNote Web (https://web.endnote.com/), a software that assists in removing duplicates, organizing citations, and automatically generating references. After removing duplicates, the remaining documents were transferred to Rayyan (https://www.rayyan.ai/). Rayyan is an online application from the Qatar Foundation used for systematic review research, which speeds up the first screening among other functions, allowing researchers to review the articles in blind review. EndNote found one duplicate, and Rayyan found another 40, totaling 41 duplicates, leaving 321 documents.

At this point, the first screening phase began, with two researchers reading the titles and abstracts of each article, adhering to the eligibility criteria for this phase. All documents were kept assessing the possibilities for inclusion. The judge's role was invoked due to 84 conflicts. It is important to justify that the inclusion of all types of documents at this stage was based on understanding the constructs studied and the attempt to obtain as many documents as possible for analysis. However, this approach did not yield positive results, leading to a change in the eligibility criteria and, consequently, a second screening. After resolving the conflicts from the first screening, 35 documents remained for the second screening. In this phase, only articles published in journals were considered, and those that did not provide any significant contribution to the study were excluded. No conflicts arose during this stage, leaving 16 journal articles for data extraction via a synthesis matrix (Klopper,

Lubbe, & Rugbeer, 2007). Based on the reviewers' suggestions, two articles were added, numbers 13 and 18 in Table 2, requiring new analysis. The flowchart, Figure 2, presents the stages of document eligibility.

Figure 2. Flowchart of the document selection stages (Developed by the authors, 2024)

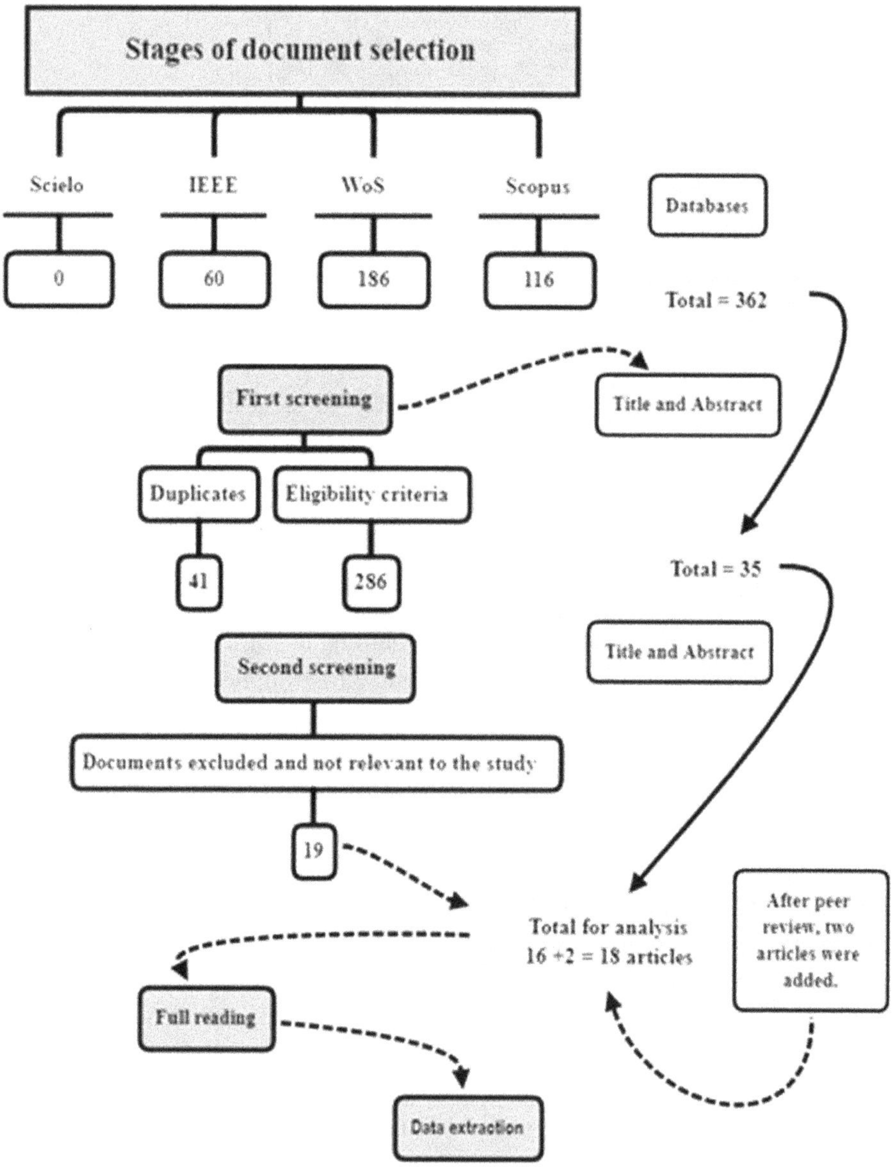

3.2.3. Data mapping

Data mapping was conducted using the 18 selected articles. This phase was designed to provide a structured dataset aimed at summarizing all the data found in the selected articles. For example, publication year, type of research, public sector studied, and the type of AI used. This synthesis of data was performed using a synthesis matrix (Klopper, Lubbe, & Rugbeer, 2007) generated in Excel. From this mapping, it was possible to write an interpretation of the main findings and directions of the research.

3.2.4. Data extraction

Researchers created a standard list for the process of data extraction and mapping. After creating this checklist, it was tested with one article to see if there would be conflicts between reviewers, and upon finding none, they proceeded to extract data from all selected articles. Each researcher-reviewer checked the list individually, however, there was interaction allowing changes, agreement, and updates to the checklist as necessary, to ensure that no relevant information was missed, with direct quotations extracted from the articles. Various data were extracted such as publication year, type of publication, type of contribution to KM, PSI, and AI, public sector research, methodology, etc. Finally, the data were combined through thematic analysis (Braun & Clarke, 2006).

3.3. Stage 3 - Reporting the Scoping Review

This stage is characterized by the synthesis of results as shown in Figure 1, detailed in the following subsection. Continuing with the text of this scoping review, the results, discussion, and final considerations are described.

3.3.1. Reporting the results

For the interim results, the synthesis matrix proposed by Klopper, Lubbe, & Rugbeer (2007) was used. Thus, a standard synthesis matrix was generated in Excel (spreadsheet software developed by Microsoft) that allowed organizing the articles so that researchers could extract the data while maintaining a blind review, for comparing articles and the information extracted, identifying research gaps, areas of consensus, and subsequent synthesis.

3.3.2. Synthesis of results

Both the mapping and the data extraction were performed to provide a structured dataset, such as publication year, methodologies used, contributions, and the relationships among the constructs (KM, SPI, and AI), to enable the writing of this scoping review. The synthesis was carried out from data extraction through filling out the spreadsheet, which generated a body of knowledge. From this, a coherent narrative with the results found, the researchers' interpretation, and the identification of research gaps were written by the team, enabling the sharing of the findings. Figure 3 shows a partial analysis of the selected articles.

Figure 3. Partial analysis of data (Developed by the authors, 2024)

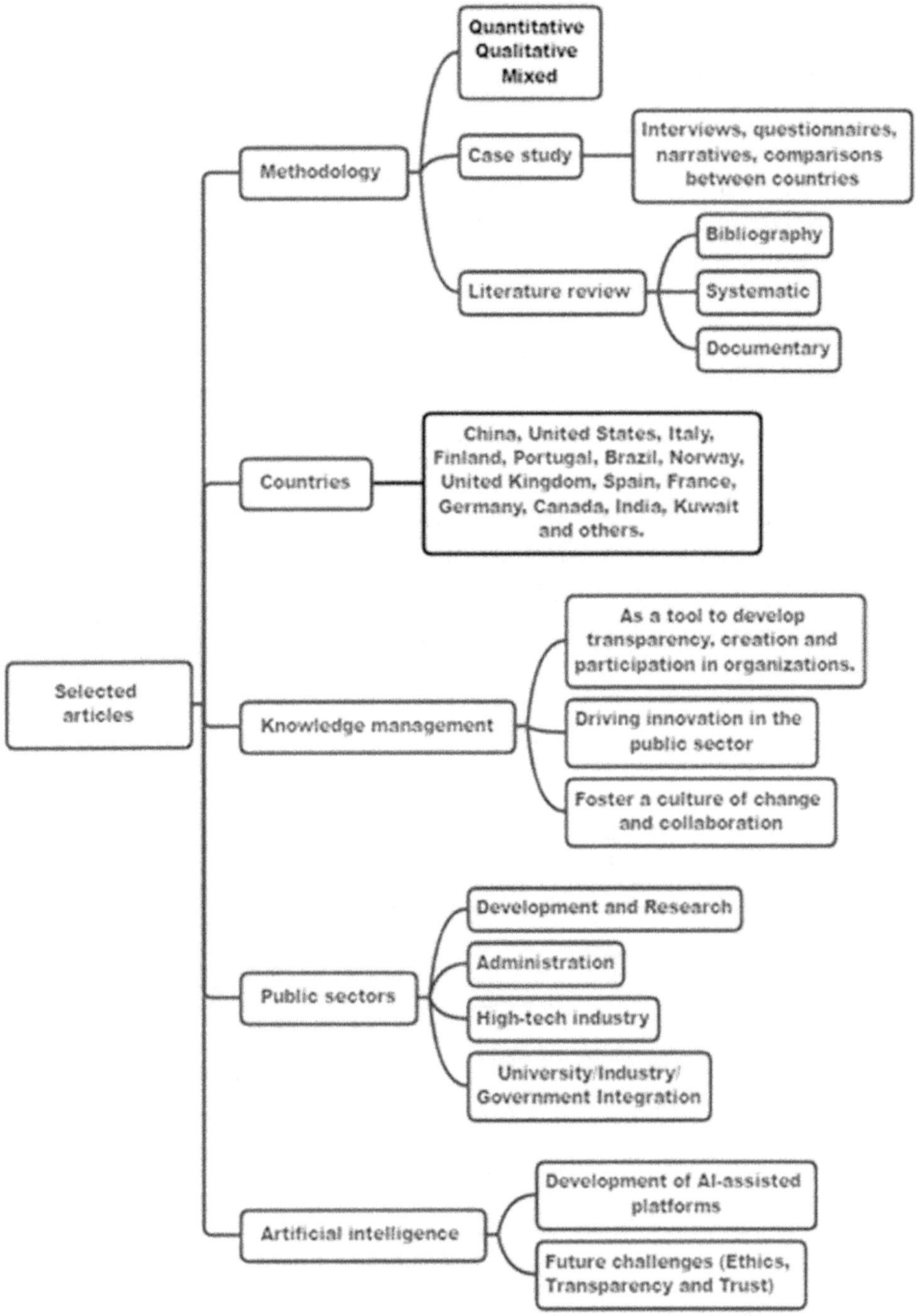

4. RESULTS

Figure 2 provided an overview of the article selection process for this scoping review. Initially, there were 362 articles from scientific databases which were analyzed by researcher-reviewers with the help of the Rayyan software. The software automatically generates a list of duplicates which is reviewed and manually excluded one by one. After the removal of duplicates, the review began in a double-blind manner, culminating with 16 articles, two more articles added after peer-review, total 18 articles, as shown in Table 2 with the titles, authors, and year of publication.

Table 2. Articles selected for data extraction

Nº	Titles	Authors	Year
1	Leveraging knowledge, learning, and innovation in forming strategic government-university-industry (GUI) R&D partnerships in the US, Germany, and France	Carayannis, E. G., Alexander, J., Ioannidis, A.	2000
2	Digital library research in the US: an overview with a knowledge management perspective	Chen, HC.	2004
3	Increasing synergies between institutions and technology developers: Lessons from marine energy	Corsatea, T. D.	2014
4	Performance improvement in public administrations by organizational learning	Stoll, M., Laner, D.	2014
5	Inter-partner control, trust, and radical innovation of IJVs in China: A contingent governance perspective	Wang, LW, Jin, JL, Yang, DF, Zhou, KZ.	2020
6	Theoretical foundations in support of small and medium towns	De Noronha, T., Vaz, E.	2020
7	Analysis of Drivers of Digital Learning in COVID-19 and Post-COVID-19 Scenario Using an ISM Approach	Agrawal, R., Wankhede, V. A., Nair, R. S.	2021
8	The How data shape actor relations in artificial intelligence innovation systems: an empirical observation from Chinaof ICTs-related innovation on public values in public sector: A meta-analysis	Yu, Z, Liang, Z, Wu, PY.	2021
9	Intellectual Structure of Knowledge Management: A Bibliometric Analysis of the Journal of Information and Knowledge Management	García-González, MS, Paniagua-Arís, E, Martínez-Béjar, R, López-Caballero, JA, Gasparetto, A.	2022
10	An Artificial Intelligence-Based Model for Knowledge Evaluation and Integration in Public Organizations	García-González, MS, Paniagua-Arís, E, Martínez-Béjar, R, López-Caballero, JA, Gasparetto, A.	2023
11	Transforming Talent Development: a Reflective Analysis of the Innovative Government-School Cooperation Model Under the Paradigm of Knowledge Innovation	Zhang, S, Sun, ZW, Fan, ZY, Weng, SY.	2023
12	Understanding the evolution of open government data research: towards open data sustainability and smartness	Gao, YY, Janssen, M, Zhang, CC.	2023
13	The use of blockchain technology to build smart cities- creating public value in Kuwait	Alkhaldi, Afnan; Alrashidi, Huda; Alhasan, Khawla; Alsadeeqi, Ahmad; Alshami, Abdullah	2023

continued on following page

Table 2. Continued

Nº	Titles	Authors	Year
14	Description of Crowdsourcing and AI-Based Tool for Knowledge Management and Systems Change in Public Servicesretations for reflexive policy practices	Ulmanen, S, Hirvonen, M, Tattersall, P, Ristikari, T, Kuo, VC, Virta, P, Jurvonen, T, Niemelä, M.	2024
15	Digital Transformation in the Public Administrations: A Guided Tour for Computer Scientists	Ciancarini, P., Giancarlo, R., Grimaudo, G.	2024
16	Meio Ambiente, Políticas de Inovação e Tecnologia: Relações e Correlações nos Últimos Dez Anos no Brasil	de Menezes, E. E., Oliveira, M. R., Silva, C. H. C., e Silva, S. D.	2024
17	Synergizing Technology and Tradition: A Pathway to Intelligent Village Governance and Sustainable Rural Development	Xiao, M, Luo, ST, Yang, SS.	2024
18	Digital transformation on the design and implementation of virtual political campaigns in Kuwait- perceptions and attitudes of politicians and campaign managers for bold innovation and social impact in Kuwait	Alhaimer, Rashed	2024

Source: Developed by the authors, 2024.

From the 18 articles, data were extracted using the synthesis matrix proposed by Klopper et al. (2007). The main topics covered include: authors, year of publication, countries, research context, public sector in focus, the relationship of knowledge management with the public sector, innovative aspects, methodologies employed, as well as the results and conclusions. Regarding the year of publication (Table 2), although no start date was defined in the eligibility criteria for inclusion or exclusion, the articles proved to be recent, as shown in Figure 4.

Figure 4. Years of article publications (Developed by the authors, 2024)

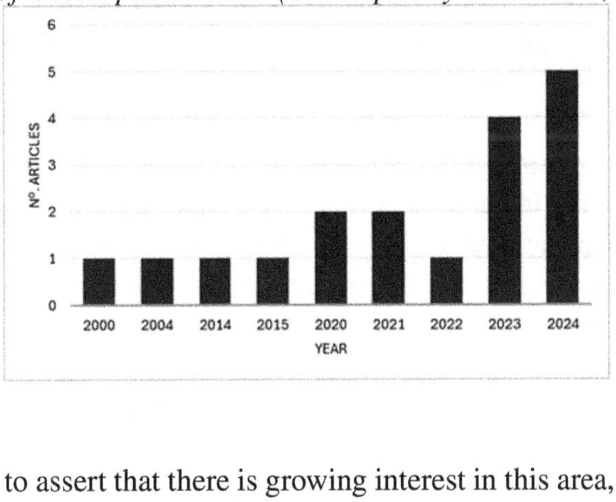

It is possible to assert that there is growing interest in this area, considering the challenges faced by the public sector in complex contexts, which generate a need for knowledge creation and innovation that can benefit from the integration of KM (Knowledge Management) and artificial intelligence.

Regarding the countries, as can be seen in Figure 5 below, China had five publications; followed by the United States of America with three; France, Germany, Italy, Portugal, Spain, India, and Global Analysis (Paris, Lebanon, Dubai, Palestine, Bahrain) with two each; and the rest with one each, including Brazil, Denmark, Ireland, Norway, Sweden, UK, Austria, Finland, Canada, Developing Countries (Israel/Georgia/Uzbekistan/Japan/Netherlands/Saudi Arabia/USA/EU/China/India) and Kuwait.

Figure 5. Countries most represented in this scoping review (Developed by the authors, 2024)

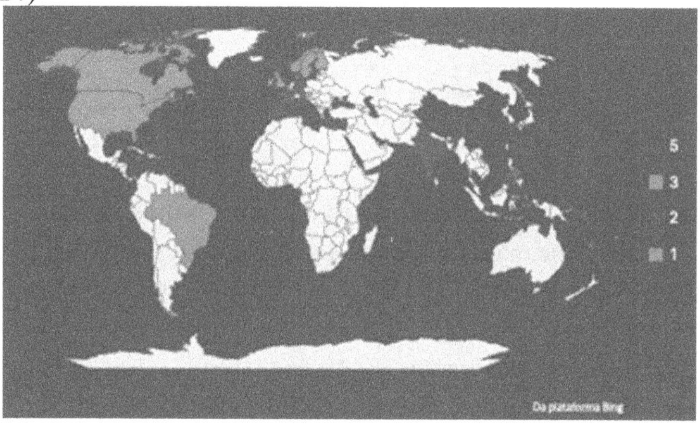

During the data extraction, the methodological diversity of the analyzed studies was observed, as they simultaneously adopted both theoretical (Gao, Janssen, & Zhang, 2023) and empirical approaches (Yu, Liang, & Wu, 2021; Alkhaldi et al., 2023; Alhaimer, 2924). They also involved questionnaires and interviews (García-González et al., 2023; Yu, Liang, & Wu, 2021; Alkhaldi et al., 2023). Some studies suggest new ways to solve problems through the creation of AI-based interactive platforms to promote integration between academia, government, and society, or to improve communication among the involved parties (Zhang, Sun, Fan, & Weng, 2023; Xiao, Luo, & Yang, 2024). These platforms integrated knowledge management with innovations in the public sector. Additionally, field research was conducted to validate conceptual and structural models, whether qualitative (Carayannis, Alexander, & Ioannidis, 2000; Alkhaldi et al., 2023), quantitative (Wang, Lu, Jin, Yang, & Zhou, 2020; Alhaimer, 2924), or mixed-methods (Corsatea, 2014).

Figure 6 below illustrates the findings of this review.

Figure 6. Methodologies used (Developed by the authors, 2024)

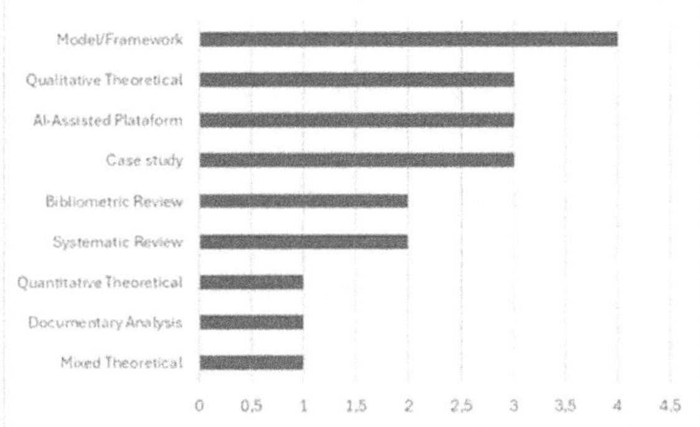

To complement the analysis and data extraction, another characteristic observed was the public sectors in which the research was developed. The following Figure 7 illustrates the most frequent public sectors in the research of this review: Education (5), Social Sciences (4), Innovation (4), AI (4), Administration (3), Sustainable Agribusiness (3), Computer Science (2), Technology (2), Organizations/Industries (2), Sustainable Development (2), Digital Learning (1), Microelectronics (1), Health (1), Environmental Public Policies (2), Biological Sciences (1), Law (1), Livestock (1), Open Government Data (1), Marine Energy (1), Smart cities (1) and Library Science (1).

Figure 7. Prominent public sector (Developed by the authors, 2024)

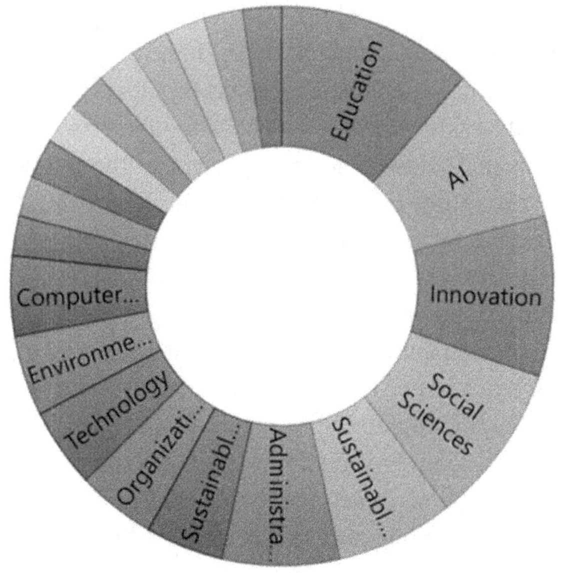

The discussion of the results is presented below.

5. DISCUSSION

The discussion was structured based on a thematic analysis of the data according to the method of Braun and Clarke (2006), resulting in three central themes: the relationship between AI and knowledge management; the application of AI in public sector innovation; and the role of AI in knowledge management as a facilitator of innovation in the public sector. The analysis of selected studies highlights the growing importance of integrating knowledge management (KM) and artificial intelligence (AI) as catalysts for innovation in the public sector. The results indicate that multiple approaches to knowledge management have been used to foster various types of innovation in the public sector, ranging from digital transformation to increasing citizen engagement. However, the implementation of these technologies faces a series of challenges and barriers that need to be overcome to maximize their benefits.

Digital transformation, which involves integrating technologies and promoting digital solutions across all activities of a public organization, impacts not only citizens but also all governmental and administrative processes, altering the very nature of the social contract. In this regard, it requires the integration of new knowledge and skills, especially in relation to co-creation and the development of digital competencies. AI has been seen as a key technology in this new era, particularly in the creation of smart cities and data governance (Ciancarini, Giancarlo & Grimaudo, 2024).

The analysis of the articles reveals a diversity of perspectives on how different nations have implemented and adopted Artificial Intelligence (AI) in areas like innovation and knowledge management. These findings show how public policies, technological infrastructures, and distinct cultural contexts impact the effectiveness and reach of AI initiatives. Identifying the challenges and barriers in implementing AI-based innovations and knowledge management in the public sector is crucial for developing effective strategies that can mitigate these obstacles. The inherent complexity of the public sector, combined with the specifics of each regional and national context, requires a careful and detailed analysis of these challenges.

Finland and China stand out for their strong integration of AI into their public sector knowledge management and innovation strategies. Finland, for example, is a notable case of high adherence to the application of AI for public administration. The Itla View platform, highlighted by Ulmanen et al. (2024), exemplifies how AI can be effectively used to convert tacit knowledge into strategic decisions in public services. This level of adoption reflects the country's technological advancement and the Finnish government's readiness to adopt cutting-edge AI solutions to optimize public management.

In China, as demonstrated by Gao, Janssen, and Zhang (2021), AI is widely used to enhance the administration of open government data. Besides promoting transparency, the continuous development of open data policies, combined with the extensive use of AI, drives innovation, especially in the development of smart cities. These examples are linked to nations with robust digital infrastructures and well-established public policies that support technological innovation.

However, one of the central points highlighted in the study by Xiao et al. (2021), is the difficulty of integrating emerging technologies with established governmental practices. Resistance to change, especially in organizations with rigid structures, hinders the advancement of digital transformation initiatives. To overcome this barrier, it is crucial to promote an organizational culture that values innovation and encourages experimentation. Additionally, policies that facilitate interoperability between legacy systems and new technological platforms are essential for ensuring a smooth and efficient transition.

Countries like the United States and China face specific challenges that limit the effectiveness of AI in certain contexts. The study by Wang et al. (2020) on radical innovation in multinational joint ventures in China emphasizes the institutional and cultural obstacles that prevent the full incorporation of AI in knowledge management processes. They highlight issues such as trust and control among partners as critical to the success of these ventures and often limit radical innovation in these contexts.

India and the United States are progressively incorporating AI into knowledge management and innovation practices but face distinct challenges. In the United States, as per Ciancarini et al. (2024), the use of AI in public administrations demonstrates a strong commitment to technological innovation, especially in smart city projects. However, the same authors note that the full potential of these initiatives is still restricted by challenges related to data governance and system interoperability, which requires effective knowledge management.

In India, according to Agrawal et al. (2021), AI played a crucial role in enabling digital learning during the COVID-19 pandemic, however, the implementation of these innovations is limited by the country's socioeconomic complexities and inequalities. These authors also emphasize the urgency of improving digital infrastructure, particularly in disadvantaged regions. Inequality in technology access exacerbates educational disparities, underscoring the need for significant investments in infrastructure. Additionally, empowering educators and students to adapt to new forms of learning is essential to maximize the benefits of digitization in the educational sector (Agrawal et al. 2021).

The work conducted in Brazil by Menezes Júnior et al. (2024) highlights the fragmentation of public policies as a significant barrier to sustainable innovation. Coordination between different levels of government is essential to create a cohesive and favorable environment for innovation. Without this coordination, isolated initiatives run the risk of failing or being limited in their impact. Political stability and policy continuity are equally important to attract investments and ensure long-term success. (Menezes Júnior et al., 2024).

5.1. AI and Knowledge Management

Artificial Intelligence (AI) is emerging as a critical tool for Knowledge Management (KM), fostering significant evolution in the field, as detailed by Nasrallah et al. (2022). According to these authors, bibliometric analysis reveals that KM is undergoing rapid transformation, largely influenced by the increasing role of AI. This technology facilitates the analysis and interpretation of large volumes of data, promoting innovation and enhancing decision-making in various organizational contexts.

Automation of Knowledge Creation and Storage: AI aids in the creation and storage of knowledge by automating information capture processes. AI tools, such as natural language processing (NLP) systems, are capable of analyzing large volumes of textual data, extracting insights, and organizing this information into accessible databases. Studies like that of Wang et al. (2020) show that this automation allows organizations to store and access knowledge in a more structured manner, reducing the dependence on human experts for information organization.

Dissemination and Sharing of Knowledge: AI also plays a crucial role in the dissemination and sharing of knowledge. AI platforms can recommend relevant content to users based on their profiles and previous activities, facilitating access to useful and up-to-date information. The study by Ulmanen et al. (2024) highlights the use of AI to create knowledge networks within public organizations, connecting employees to relevant information sources and promoting a culture of knowledge sharing.

Challenges in Implementing AI in KM: Despite advancements, the articles also point out significant challenges in implementing AI for knowledge management. Yu et al. (2021), for example, discuss the risks associated with algorithmic bias, where AI systems can perpetuate existing prejudices if not properly supervised. Additionally, reliance on AI for KM may lead to the loss of nuances and contexts that can only be understood by human experts. Furthermore, the research by Ulmanen et al. (2024) complements this view by exploring the use of AI-based crowdsourcing tools in digital governance. They reveal the complexity of engaging citizens in democratic governance processes, underlining that citizen participation is crucial for the success of these initiatives. However, for this participation to be fully realized, it is critical to build trust regarding privacy and data security. Ensuring that data is protected and used transparently is vital for increasing public acceptance and involvement in digital platforms. Furthermore, the paper addresses the digital divide by emphasizing that despite the advantages of digital learning, the lack of accessible infrastructure and resources negatively impacts the education of many students. During the COVID-19 pandemic, this digital divide became evident as many students did not have adequate access to digital platforms. The research identifies drivers for digital learning, such as low-cost internet and government support, which are seen as crucial to reducing the digital divide and enabling a more inclusive learning environment. The framework proposed in the paper suggests that implementing these drivers could promote more equal access to digital education, especially benefiting students in regions or contexts with fewer technological resources (Ulmanen et al. 2024).

AI as a Facilitator of Innovation: Another highlighted point is how AI not only enhances knowledge management but also acts as a facilitator of innovation. AI's ability to process and analyze large volumes of data in real time allows organizations to identify innovation opportunities that might be overlooked by traditional methods. The research by Menezes Júnior et al. (2024) exemplifies how the combination of AI and KM can lead to significant advancements in public policies and government services.

5.2. AI and Public Sector Innovation

One of the main challenges is the resistance to change within public organizations, a recurring theme in various studies, as highlighted by Xiao et al. (2021). This resistance is often associated with rigid organizational structures and a lack of a culture of innovation. To mitigate this issue, it is essential to promote an organizational culture that values experimentation and is open to adopting new technologies. Creating policies that facilitate interoperability between legacy systems and new technological platforms is also necessary to ensure a smooth and efficient transition.

The reviewed articles emphasize that the application of artificial intelligence (AI) in the public sector has been one of the main drivers of innovation in public services. AI is being used to enhance administrative efficiency, improve decision-making, and provide more personalized services to citizens.

Digital Transformation, Automation, and Decision Making: Xiao et al. (2021) highlight how AI is being implemented to automate bureaucratic processes, which not only reduces operational costs but also speeds up the response time of public institutions. This automation has the potential to transform how governments interact with citizens, making services more accessible and efficient.

García-González et al. (2023) report that the use of AI in public administrations in Spain, through the application of ontologies, has allowed for more effective knowledge integration, promoting consistency and eliminating redundancies in management practices. This AI-based approach was particularly successful in the context of sustainable agricultural practices, where the integration of different knowledge perspectives was crucial for the development of more efficient public policies.

In the article "Synergizing Technology and Tradition: A Pathway to Intelligent Village Governance and Sustainable Rural Development" by Xiao, Luo, and Yang (2024), the authors highlight the critical role that artificial intelligence (AI) plays in enhancing the governance of rural communities. Used to promote cooperation among stakeholders and increase information transparency, AI enables more informed and efficient decision-making processes. The platform mentioned in the study discusses how AI can provide access to timely and accurate information, increasing accountability and transparency in decision-making (Matheus et al., 2020; Watts, 2015).

Alhaimer's (2024) study analyzes how digital transformation has impacted political campaigns in Kuwait, especially during the COVID-19 pandemic. The research found that factors such as perceived ease of use (PEOU), perceived usefulness (PU), and perceived convenience (PC) positively influenced the adoption of virtual campaigns. In their analysis, a positive impact on perceived usefulness was observed, which suggests that the more convenient and accessible a technology is, the greater its perceived usefulness, and therefore, its adoption. Furthermore, the use of a user-friendly interface increases the perception of convenience and usefulness, highlighting the impotence of the user experience in virtual campaigns, making it a useful strategy to replace in-person events, as was the case during the COVID-19 pandemic.

Furthermore, when it comes to the challenges and disadvantages of virtual political campaigns, as well as considering the ethical issues related to the use of AI in the public sector, the author highlights the need for politicians to be aware of issues of privacy and data confidentiality, in addition to the potential for security breaches, in sections that address the use of social networks for political campaigns and the associated risks; the risk of manipulation of data and public opinion, which can lead to undue influence and psychological manipulation; and the accessibility and moderation of content, with concerns about the accessibility of campaigns to individuals who may hold extreme views, as well as the difficulty of moderating inappropriate content, which can have a negative impact, especially on minors (Alhaimer, 2024).

Citizen Engagement and Transparency: Another important application of AI in the public sector is in increasing transparency and facilitating citizen engagement. AI-based crowdsourcing tools, discussed in the study by Ulmanen et al. (2024), are allowing citizens to actively participate in governance, contributing ideas, voting on proposals, and collaborating directly with public administrations. This not only strengthens participatory democracy but also improves public trust in governmental institutions.

When it comes to disruptive technologies, such as the use of blockchain in the public sector, Alkhaldi et al. (2023) analyzed the study of this technology in the development of smart cities and the way they can add public value and improve the efficiency of government services. In their study, it was observed that the use of this technology can overcome operational and bureaucratic challenges in Kuwait, bringing more reliability and security, speed, resource savings, transparency and connection with the citizen.

Public-Private Partnerships: In terms of public-private partnerships, Wang et al. (2020) point to the need to balance control and trust between partners. Radical innovation depends on an environment where partners can collaborate openly, but this is only possible when there are clear and reliable mechanisms to ensure that the interests of all parties are protected. In this context, governance policies must be strengthened to promote effective collaboration.

Remarkably, to foster deeper stakeholder engagement and more inclusive and participatory governance practices, the use of advanced communication technologies such as augmented reality and virtual reality (Caputo et al., 2023) is crucial. These technologies, combined with AI, allow rural communities to merge traditional knowledge with technological innovations, creating an environment conducive to sustainable development and intelligent governance.

Regulatory Frameworks and Data: Yu et al. (2021) discuss the concentration of power in digital platforms, raising questions about equity and the distribution of benefits resulting from innovation. According to the authors, data centralization can stifle competition and limit the development of new solutions. Therefore, it is imperative to develop regulatory frameworks that encourage healthy competition and ensure that data are used in a way that benefits society as a whole.

Challenges and Risks: Despite the advantages, the articles also highlight the challenges and risks associated with the use of AI in the public sector. Issues such as data privacy, algorithmic bias, and the centralization of power in the hands of a few technology providers are central concerns. The work of Yu et al. (2021) highlights that without proper regulation, AI can reinforce inequalities and create new ethical and social challenges.

Future of AI in the Public Sector: The reviewed literature suggests that the future of AI in the public sector depends on how governments will balance innovation with the protection of citizens' rights. Creating policies that encourage responsible innovation while ensuring privacy and equity will be key to the success of AI in the public sector.

5.3. AI in Knowledge Management and Innovation in the Public Sector

Studies also show that the incorporation of AI in knowledge management is a successful tactic for promoting innovation in the public sector. According to Zhang et al. (2024), China's tripartite cooperation model—supported by AI—among the government, educational institutions, and businesses has proven essential for coordinating talent development with market demands. Learning can be more individualized and efficient when using cognitive maps and artificial intelligence (AI) to help visualize and integrate knowledge.

Agrawal et al. (2021) provide another example of how artificial intelligence was used to combine data from multiple sources during the COVID-19 pandemic, allowing Indian government administrations to respond to the outbreak more quickly and efficiently. These results demonstrate how AI can play a significant role in the development of flexible, data-driven public policies.

While the benefits of AI in knowledge management and innovation are evident, the findings also point to a number of challenges and limitations. For instance, Menezes Júnior et al. (2024) highlight the complexity of implementing AI systems in existing governmental infrastructures, as well as concerns about data privacy and security. These challenges need to be carefully managed to maximize the benefits of AI in the public sector.

Facilitating Innovation through Knowledge Management: Research by Nohade Nasrallah et al. (2022) reveals that AI is emerging as a central element in the evolution of KM, especially in contexts where innovation is a strategic priority. By automating the analysis of large volumes of data, AI enables public organizations to extract valuable insights from their daily operations, which can be used to inform and shape new innovative policies and practices. AI's ability to identify patterns and predict trends becomes a crucial resource for knowledge managers, aiding in more informed decision-making and anticipating future needs.

Studies suggest that KM can be optimized by artificial intelligence through the use of digital platforms that facilitate the sharing of knowledge (tacit and explicit) across different organizational levels, as was the case with the Itla View platform in Finland. This platform was specifically used in the areas of education, social services, and health and allowed for organizational renewal and an increased capacity to respond to changes. It uses AI to analyze and process large volumes of data, facilitating the identification of relevant phenomena and supporting informed decision-making. Moreover, it improved communication and collaboration within public service organizations, enabling decisions to be made based on local knowledge and up-to-date data, as well as promoting continuous learning (Ulmanen et al., 2024).

AI as a Factor in Organizational Agility: AI also contributes to increasing the agility of public organizations, allowing for quicker adaptation to changes in the external environment. This is particularly relevant in contexts where innovation must be continuous and responsive to new social and technological demands. Research by Yu et al. (2021) highlights how AI, when used in KM, can accelerate the introduction of new technologies and practices in the public sector, ensuring that organizations remain competitive and effective.

To assess and integrate knowledge in public organizations, García-González et al. (2023) described an AI and ontology-based method for representing knowledge and enabling the comparison and integration of different views. The study was developed in Spain, set in the context of sustainable practices in agriculture and livestock in the Mediterranean biogeographic region, specifically in Murcia. By integrating different expert ontologies, the authors observed that creating a more integrated view maximizes both relational and conceptual support and enables the execution of automatic knowledge assessments, integrating it consistently and without redundancies.

Innovation in Governance and Citizen Participation: The study by Ulmanen et al. (2024) complements this view by exploring how AI is being used to promote innovation in public governance, particularly through citizen engagement. AI tools are employed to facilitate the crowdsourcing of ideas and the collection of feedback from the population, allowing public institutions to develop solutions more aligned with the expectations and needs of citizens. This approach not only improves the effectiveness of public policies but also reinforces public trust in government institutions, promoting a culture of participatory innovation.

Overcoming Structural Challenges: The implementation of AI in KM also helps overcome structural barriers that traditionally limit innovation in the public sector. Wang et al. (2020), for example, discuss how the integration of AI and KM can mitigate challenges related to bureaucracy and information fragmentation. By centralizing and systematizing knowledge, AI allows public employees to have quicker and more accurate access to the necessary information, facilitating interdepartmental collaboration and the implementation of innovative practices.

It was observed that, in Chinese communities, one of the alternatives to improve the integration of cutting-edge technologies with the traditional governance system of these communities was the use of technologies like the Internet of Things and cloud computing to demonstrate how AI can support intelligent governance. In this scenario, integration promoted an improvement in information transparency, negotiation between parties, and ensured quicker responses. It is important to highlight the participation of different stakeholders in the process, as well as social supervision, which allowed for the cultural preservation of that region alongside economic growth. (Xiao et al., 2024).

6. CONCLUSION

This chapter explored the integration of Knowledge Management (KM) and Artificial Intelligence (AI) as tools to enhance innovation in the public sector. In a global scenario characterized by complex challenges such as climate change, economic crises, and increasing social demands, public organizations are increasingly pressured to adopt innovative actions that can accelerate the delivery of public services and improve organizational efficiency. This scoping review has shown that KM, facilitated by AI, offers a promising path to meet these challenges, enabling the creation of more adaptive, efficient, and citizen-centered solutions.

The importance of innovation in the public sector cannot be underestimated, especially in a world where social demands and economic challenges are constantly evolving. AI and KM emerge as powerful tools to meet these challenges, offering potential to transform the way governments operate and how public services are delivered to the population. However, despite existing practices, there is still a significant gap in the literature on how these technologies can be optimized and effectively implemented in different public contexts.

The application of AI in the public sector, as demonstrated by various international examples, has the potential not only to enhance KM but also to transform how public services are developed and delivered to society. However, successful integration of AI and KM requires an ongoing effort to adapt to new technologies, develop digital skills and competencies of public servants, and implement inclusive public policies that consider the ethical and social implications of these technologies.

The current literature lacks studies that address the long-term impacts of AI and KM on public innovation integratively. While there are promising practices, the lack of a systemic approach and the need for greater coordination between public policies and emerging technologies indicate that there is still much to be explored and understood. Thus, for public sector innovation to truly reach its potential, a continuous research effort is required, focused not only on implementing new technologies but also on critically evaluating their ethical, social, and operational implications.

The research also revealed significant gaps in the examined literature, indicating the need for future research that explores different ways of applying AI in KM and its potential to drive innovation in the public sector. Future studies should focus on developing integrated models that combine AI and KM, examine the impact of these technologies in varied governmental contexts, and investigate the empowerment strategies needed to prepare public servants for this new digital era.

Ethics and transparency in the use of artificial intelligence in the public sector are essential to ensure fairness, privacy, and accountability in serving citizens. However, clear guidelines and regulations for this use are still being defined, leaving open challenges to achieving responsible and trustworthy implementation of these technologies in government.

In summary, the integration of KM and AI in the public sector represents a new way of thinking about the provision of public services capable of transforming public administration, promoting a more innovative, transparent, and effective environment. However, to take advantage of these opportunities, a continued commitment to research, training, and innovation that respond to the emerging needs of society and ensure the delivery of quality public services is highlighted.

6.1. FUTURE RESEARCH SUGGESTIONS

Despite the advances, there are several gaps in the research and practice of knowledge management and innovation with AI in the public sector. Some areas that require attention include:

1. **Ethics and Transparency in AI**: Future studies should address ethical issues related to the use of AI in the public sector, ensuring transparency, fairness, and accountability in automated decisions.
2. **Training and Adaptation**: Investigating how to train civil servants to use AI tools and adapt to technological changes is crucial for the successful implementation of digital innovation.
3. **Data Security**: The protection of personal and sensitive data should be a priority. Research should explore best practices and technologies to ensure data security and privacy in the use of AI.
4. **Social Impact of AI**: Assessing the social impact of introducing AI into public services, including possible inequalities and digital exclusions, it is key to creating inclusive and equitable solutions for public service offerings and innovations, both for servers and users.

Although the integration of artificial intelligence (AI) in knowledge management and innovation in the public sector has significantly advanced, there are still substantial gaps that need to be addressed in future research. Firstly, it is essential to delve deeper into the ethical and transparency issues in the use of AI. The adoption of this technology in governmental processes requires a careful analysis of how the principles of transparency, fairness, and accountability are being applied, ensuring that automated decisions are fair and understandable to all citizens.

Training public servants for the effective use of AI is a critical area that requires more attention. Technological adaptation is one of the biggest challenges faced by public organizations, and therefore, investigating the best training practices and barriers that prevent a smooth transition is crucial for the success of these initiatives. Another crucial aspect to be explored is data security, especially in a context where the protection of sensitive information is paramount. Future research should focus on developing and evaluating technologies and policies that ensure the privacy and integrity of data used by AI, without compromising the functionality and efficiency of public services.

The social impact of AI is another area that demands investigation. With the increasing introduction of digital technologies in public services, it is vital to assess how these innovations are affecting the population, especially in terms of inequality and digital exclusion. Understanding these impacts will allow the creation of more inclusive and equitable solutions, benefiting both public servants and citizens.

It is imperative to explore more deeply the governance of AI in the public sector and the intersection between AI and knowledge management. The creation of effective and adaptable governance policies can determine the success of AI initiatives, while optimizing the integration of AI with knowledge management can further boost innovation in public services. Future research addressing these themes will help develop initiatives that can balance innovation with security, transparency, and accountability, ensuring that AI becomes a truly transformative tool in public administration.

ACKNOWLEDGMENT

This research was supported by two Organization:

- Coordination for the Improvement of Higher Education Personnel - CAPES - Brazil - Financing Code 001.
- Santa Catarina State Research and Innovation Support Foundation - FAPESC (20/2024).

REFERENCES

Agrawal, R., Wankhede, V. A., & Nair, R. S. (2021). Analysis of drivers of digital learning in COVID-19 and post-COVID-19 scenario using an ISM approach. *Journal of the Institution of Engineers (India)*: Series B, 102, 1143–1155. https://doi.org/ DOI: 10.1007/s40031-020-00528-8

Alhaimer, R. (2024). Digital transformation on the design and implementation of virtual political campaigns in Kuwait: perceptions and attitudes of politicians and campaign managers for bold innovation and social impact in Kuwait. *Journal of Science and Technology Policy Management*. https://doi.org/DOI: 10.1108/JSTPM-11-2023-0212

Alkhaldi, A., Alrashidi, H., Alhasan, K., Alsadeeqi, A., & Alshami, A. (2023). The use of blockchain technology to build smart cities- creating public value in Kuwait. *Journal Global Knowledge, Memory and Communication*, V. ahead-of-print (ahead-of-print), 1-15. https://doi-org.ez46.periodicos.capes.gov.br/10.1108/GKMC-11-2022-0263

Arksey, H., & O'Malley, L. (2005). Scoping studies: Towards a methodological framework. *International Journal of Social Research Methodology*, 8(1), 19–32. DOI: 10.1080/1364557032000119616

Barnes, S., & Milton, N. (2015). *Designing a successful KM strategy: a guide for the knowledge management professional*. Information Today, Inc.

Batista, F. F. (2012). *Modelo de gestão do conhecimento para a administração pública brasileira: como implementar a gestão do conhecimento para produzir resultados em benefício do cidadão*. Ipea.

Braun, V., & Clarke, V. (2006). Using thematic analysis in psychology. *Qualitative Research in Psychology*, 3(2), 77–101. DOI: 10.1191/1478088706qp063oa

Carayannis, E. G., Alexander, J., & Ioannidis, A. (2000). Leveraging knowledge, learning, and innovation in forming strategic government–university–industry (GUI) R&D partnerships in the US, Germany, and France. *Technovation*, 20(9), 477–488. DOI: 10.1016/S0166-4972(99)00162-5

Chen, H. (2004). Digital library research in the US: An overview with a knowledge management perspective. Program. *Electronic Library and Information Systems*, 38(3), 157–167. DOI: 10.1108/00330330410547205

Ciancarini, P., Giancarlo, R., & Grimaudo, G. (2024). Digital transformation in the public administrations: A guided tour for computer scientists. *IEEE Access : Practical Innovations, Open Solutions*, 12(99), 1–1. DOI: 10.1109/ACCESS.2024.3363075

Corsatea, T. D. (2014). Increasing synergies between institutions and technology developers: Lessons from marine energy. *Energy Policy*, 74, 682–696. DOI: 10.1016/j.enpol.2014.07.006

Creswell, J. W. (2010). *Projeto de pesquisa: métodos qualitativo, quantitativo e misto*. (3rd ed.; Artmed, ed.). Porto Alegre: Artmed.

Dalkir, K. (2011). Knowledge Management in Theory and Practice Second Edition. *In Knowledge Management in Theory and Practice*.

de Menezes Junior, E. E., Dutra e Silva, S., Oliveira, M. R., & Silva, C. H. C. (2024). Meio Ambiente, Políticas de Inovação e Tecnologia: Relações e Correlações nos Últimos Dez Anos no Brasil. Fronteira: *Journal of Social, Technological and Environmental Science*, 13(1), 213–226. Recuperado de https://periodicos.unievangelica.edu.br/index.php/fronteiras/article/view/7175

Gao, Y., Janssen, M., & Zhang, C. (2021). Understanding the evolution of open government data research: Towards open data sustainability and smartness. *International Review of Administrative Sciences*, 89(1), 59–75. Advance online publication. DOI: 10.1177/00208523211009955

García-González, M. S., Paniagua-Arís, E., Martínez-Béjar, R., López-Caballero, J. A., & Gasparetto, A. (2023). An artificial intelligence-based model for knowledge evaluation and integration in public organizations. *Applied Sciences (Basel, Switzerland)*, 13(21), 11796. DOI: 10.3390/app132111796

Gonzalez, R. V. D., & Martins, M. F. (2017). Knowledge management process: A theoretical-conceptual research. *Gestão & Produção*, 24(2), 248–265. DOI: 10.1590/0104-530x0893-15

ISO. (2018). *ISO 30401:2018*, Knowledge Management Systems, Requirements. Em 61010-1 © Iec:2001.

Kariyado, M. Y. (2016). Proposta e aplicação de uma sistemática baseada na gestão do conhecimento para a melhoria do processo de compras públicas. Universidade Federal de São Carlos. São Carlos: UFSCar, 2016. 140 p. Dissertação (Mestrado) - Universidade Federal de São Carlos, 2016.

Klopper, R., Lubbe, S., & Rugbeer, H. (2007). The Matrix Method of Literature Review. *Alternation (Durban)*, 14(1), 262–276. DOI: 10.1002/asia.200900414

Koenig, M. E. D. (2011). Knowledge Management in Theory and Practice (2nd ed.). *Journal of the American Society for Information Science and Technology*, 62(10). https://doi.org/DOI: 10.1002/asi.21613

Malischeski, K. (2023). Colaboração e inovação no setor público: diretrizes aos i-Labs [Universidade Federal de Santa Catarina]. https://repositorio.ufsc.br/handle/123456789/253749

Martin, F., Zhuang, M., & Schaefer, D. (2024). Systematic review of research on artificial intelligence in K-12 education (2017–2022). *Computers and Education: Artificial Intelligence*, 6(May 2023), 100195. https://doi.org/DOI: 10.1016/j.caeai.2023.100195

Massaro, M., Dumay, J., & Garlatti, A. (2015). Public sector knowledge management: A structured literature review. *Journal of Knowledge Management*, 19(3), 530–558. DOI: 10.1108/JKM-11-2014-0466

Mellouli, S., Janssen, M., & Ojo, A. (2024). Introduction to the Issue on Artificial Intelligence in the Public Sector: Risks and Benefits of AI for Governments. *Digital Government: Research and Practice*, 5(1), 1–6. DOI: 10.1145/3636550

Morales, P. D. A. e Dandolini, G. A.Tipologias da inovação no setor público: uma revisão integrativa da literatura In: de Bem Machado, et al. (2022). Inovação no setor público: desafios e possibilidades. *Pimenta Cultural*. DOI: DOI: 10.31560/pimentacultural/2022.95835

Nasrallah, N., Atayah, O. F., El Khoury, R., Hamdan, A., & Obaid, S. (2022). Intellectual structure of knowledge management: A bibliometric analysis of the Journal of Information and Knowledge Management. *Journal of Information & Knowledge Management*, 21(01), 2250001. DOI: 10.1142/S0219649222500010

Noronha, T., & Vaz, E. (2020). Theoretical foundations in support of small and medium towns. *Sustainability (Basel)*, 12(13), 5312. DOI: 10.3390/su12135312

OCDE. (2023). Global Trends in Government Innovation 2023. *OCDE*. https://www.oecd-ilibrary.org/sites/0655b570-en/index.html?itemId=/content/publication/0655b570-en&_csp_=81514dda47e6d6cb4cb62f97e5c3e4e4&itemIGO=oecd&itemContentType=book

Osborne, S. P., & Brown, L. (2011). Innovation, public policy and public services delivery in the UK. The word that would be king? *Public Administration*, 89(4), 1335–1350. DOI: 10.1111/j.1467-9299.2011.01932.x

Stoll, M., & Laner, D. (2014). *Performance improvement in public administrations by organizational learning*. Springer., DOI: 10.1007/978-3-319-06773-5_1

The Joanna Briggs Institute. (2015). The Joanna Briggs Institute Reviewers' Manual 2015 Methodology for JBI Scoping Reviews. Retrieved May 6, 2024, from The Joanna Briggs Institute website: https://reben.com.br/revista/wp-content/uploads/2020/10/Scoping.pdf

Torfing, J., & Ansell, C. (2017). Strengthening political leadership and policy innovation through the expansion of collaborative forms of governance. *Public Management Review*, 19(1), 37–54. DOI: 10.1080/14719037.2016.1200662

Tricco, A. C., Lillie, E., Zarin, W., O'Brien, K. K., Colquhoun, H., Levac, D., Moher, D., Peters, M. D. J., Horsley, T., Weeks, L., Hempel, S., Akl, E. A., Chang, C., McGowan, J., Stewart, L., Hartling, L., Aldcroft, A., Wilson, M. G., Garritty, C., & Straus, S. E. (2018). PRISMA Extension for Scoping Reviews (PRISMA-ScR): Checklist and Explanation. *Annals of Internal Medicine*, 169(7), 467–473. DOI: 10.7326/M18-0850 PMID: 30178033

Ulmanen, S., Hirvonen, M., Tattersall, P., Ristikari, T., Kuo, V., Virta, P., Jurvonen, T., & Niemelä, M. (2024). Description of crowdsourcing and AI-based tool for knowledge management and systems change in public services. *International Journal on Management of Innovation & Technology*, 21(04), 2450027. DOI: 10.1142/S0219877024500275

Wang, L., Jin, J. L., Yang, D., & Zhou, K. Z. (2020). Inter-partner control, trust, and radical innovation of IJVs in China: A contingent governance perspective. *Industrial Marketing Management*, 88, 70–83. DOI: 10.1016/j.indmarman.2020.04.018

Xiao, M., Luo, S., & Yang, S. (2024). Synergizing technology and tradition: A pathway to intelligent village governance and sustainable rural development. *Journal of the Knowledge Economy*. Advance online publication. DOI: 10.1007/s13132-024-01937-6

Yu, Z., Liang, Z., & Wu, P. (2021). How data shape actor relations in artificial intelligence innovation systems: An empirical observation from China. *Industrial and Corporate Change*, 30(1), 251–267. DOI: 10.1093/icc/dtaa063

Yuwono, E. I., Tjondronegoro, D., Riverola, C., & Loy, J. (2024). Co-creation in action: Bridging the knowledge gap in artificial intelligence among innovation champions. *Computers and Education: Artificial Intelligence*, 7(May), 100272. DOI: 10.1016/j.caeai.2024.100272

Zhang, S., Sun, Z., Fan, Z., & Weng, S. (2023). Transforming talent development: A reflective analysis of the innovative government-school cooperation model under the paradigm of knowledge innovation. *Journal of the Knowledge Economy*, 15(3), 15176–15201. Advance online publication. DOI: 10.1007/s13132-023-01677-z

KEY TERMS AND DEFINITIONS

Algorithmic Transparency: The principle that advocates for clarity and openness in automated decision-making processes, allowing stakeholders to understand how decisions are made by AI.

Artificial Intelligence (AI): Technology that enables computer systems to perform tasks that typically require human intelligence, such as voice recognition, decision-making, and language translation.

Data Security: Practices and technologies used to protect personal and sensitive data against unauthorized access, ensuring the privacy and integrity of information.

Ethics in AI: A set of principles that guide the responsible use of artificial intelligence, ensuring transparency, fairness, and accountability in automated decisions.

Knowledge Management (KM): The process of creating, sharing, storing, and applying knowledge within an organization to improve efficiency and innovation.

Public Sector Innovation: The introduction of new methods, ideas, or products in the public sector aimed at enhancing the efficiency, effectiveness, and quality of public services.

Social Impact of AI: The consequences of using artificial intelligence in public services, including potential inequalities and digital exclusions, and its implications on society.

Technological Adaptation: The process of training and empowering public servants to adapt to technological changes, especially in the use of AI tools.

Chapter 13
Delivering Public Service in the Age of Digital Era Governance:
The Potentials of AI for Smart Government Applications Qatar

Ahmed Badran
https://orcid.org/0000-0002-9346-1927
Qatar University, Qatar

ABSTRACT

This chapter examines how to restructure service provision processes in government organizations using modern ICT. Precisely, the chapter discusses the role of smart governance in improving service delivery by focusing on smart applications. The chapter emphasizes that the practice has gone beyond the traditional e-government. At present, smart governance initiatives focus, in addition to services availability, on the idea of integrating various types of public services. The chapter also emphasizes that the application of the AI-augmented smart government would enhance the process of designing and providing government services. AI-augmented smart government applications also enhance the level of transparency in government agencies and advance the values of accountability and integrity in the various activities of the state's administrative apparatus.

DOI: 10.4018/979-8-3693-7678-2.ch013

1- INTRODUCTION

Many researchers link the development in the field of ICT, with the idea of Smart Government (SG) as a tool to improve service delivery. This chapter attempts to build on previous research in the field of e-governance and government services by analysing SG as one of e-governance models. This should help to understanding the reality of SG and clarify its relationship to e-governance. This also should help underlining the role that e-governance and SGs play in improving service delivery processes. In this context, it can be noted that improving service delivery mechanisms has been a major challenge for public policy-makers particularly in developing countries. Many governments have tried to benefit from e-governance to bring about a qualitative shift in service delivery. Nonetheless, despite this great interest in the idea of e-governance the rates of success and failure have varied. The SG initiative in Qatar represents a transition from e-government to a more advanced form of interaction models between the government and the citizen. The project places service recipients at the heart of designing and delivering government services. Nonetheless, the recent advances in AI cast some shadows on the future of SG initiatives. This prompts us to ask about the potential role of AI applications in supporting the existing SG projects. More precisely, the chapter answers the following research question: Can the revolution in AI applications help supporting SG initiatives? What are the opportunities and challenges that may result from adopting AI to enhance such initiatives? In answering this question, the chapter addresses the role of AI technology and its potential implications for the Qatari SG initiatives. The discussion also addresses the role of e-governance in establishing the values and pillars of justice, transparency and combating corruption within government administrative bodies (Bertot et al., 2010). From this perspective, the chapter emphasizes the need to adopt e-governance by employing smart ICT as one of the strategic approaches for improving service delivery. In this regard, we should note that the progress in smart technologies has helped many countries to go beyond the concept and applications of e-government in its traditional form. Many governments have tried to re-engineer and redesign public services in a more integrated manner.

The quest for new creative service delivery mechanisms has become a major concern for policy-makers. This was fuelled by the continuous governmental efforts to employ e-governance as a strategic approach to improve service delivery. It has also been motivated by the continuous pressure on administrative agencies to improve the level of quality of services provided. In this context, the notion of SG is used interchangeably with the concept of e-government. Therefore, conceptual clarity is needed in order to understand the similarities and differences between the two notions. This conceptualisation of SG helps to remove ambiguity and confusion between this concept and the idea of e-government. The importance of a theoretical basis of SG increases in light of its modernity and the lack of an agreed upon definition that outline its dimensions, mechanisms and approaches. In addition, the concept of SG contributes to linking such a notion with the broader framework of digital governance as presented by Patrick Dunleavy and Helen Margetts as a post-new public management paradigm (Białożyt, 2017).

The chapter will be divided into five sections plus the introduction and the conclusion. Following on from section one, the introduction, in section two, a theoretical framework of AI and E-governance will be provided. The aim is to analyse the key concepts and explain the main components and related theoretical and conceptual issues. Section three, focuses on the evolution of e-government initiatives in an attempt to distinguish between the different phases via which such initiatives and projects were developed. The aim is to find out how we ended up talking about smart-governments as a key mechanism for modernising public service delivery in the age of digital era governance. In section four, the notion of AI and its potential impact and application on the process of service deign and delivery will be discussed. The crux of the discussion in this section revolves around the ways in which AI applications can be used to augment and enhance public servicers. The discussion in this section also covers the opportunities and challenges of AI applications in the realm of public services modernisation. Global examples and future directions for AI-augmented transitions in Qatar are proposed in section five. The discussion in this section addresses the main requirements for a successful transition towards AI-augmented public services systems.

2- AI AND E-GOVERNANCE: A CONCEPTUAL FRAMEWORK

The discussion in this section aims at unpacking the key theoretical and conceptual issues related to AI and E-governance developments. Such a conceptual and theoretical clarity is key in understanding the underlying foundations of such new constricts and pave the way for a more in-depth analysis of

2.1- AI and Public Service Delivery: Ethical, Social, Economic, and Regulatory Considerations

Artificial intelligence is the latest technological revolution, and includes the ability of a system to accurately interpret external data, and employ knowledge in order to achieve a set of specific goals and tasks in a way that ensures flexible adaptation in the end (Margets & Dorobantu, 2019). From a smart governance perspective, AI can be understood as the process by which technology is employed in the process of collecting and analysing data, and then presenting it in an attractive way that meets the tastes and interests of the receiving audience, while saving time, effort and costs (Badran, 2021b). In this regard, a number of factors that influence the application of AI in the field of e-governance can be identified. Technological factors, the most important of which is the availability of technologies, devices, equipment and programs necessary for the success of work within the SG environment. It can be said that this challenge is one of the most important challenges related to this field, considering that other factors are related to this factor. Economic factors, especially the availability of the necessary budget and expenses allocated to purchase devices and equipment, and thus the ability to achieve the goals required for the transformation to SGs enhanced by AI applications. Government support and the degree of response by government agencies. The greater the government support, the better the results will be in terms of the transformation towards SGs enhanced by AI applications. Because this government support facilitates the transformation process by solving many of the problems facing government agencies. Motivating employees in the government sector, as the digital work environment includes employees with a high degree of accuracy and skill, so their wages should be paid and incentives provided to them in order to encourage them to provide their best in this field. Professional factors, most notably working hours, working conditions, work environment, and other issues that can be considered a basic condition for the success of the application of AI in the field of e-governance. Factors related to the government institution itself, such as the degree of flexibility, response to modern changes, available infrastructure, working conditions, and others (Badran, 2023).

From an ethical perspective, AI technology presents several key ethical dilemmas that should be considered as it plays a role in modernizing service delivery mechanisms. The key challenges in this area include privacy and surveillance (Devineni, 2024). AI systems often rely on massive amounts of data to function effectively, which can lead to violations of individuals' privacy (Bartneck et al., 2021). For example, facial recognition and data tracking can lead to widespread surveillance, raising concerns about consent, autonomy, and how personal data is used. Furthermore, bias and fairness provides another ethical dilemma that service delivery organization need to tackle (González-Sendino et al., 2023). AI algorithms are susceptible to biases present in training data, which can lead to unfair outcomes. Bias in AI can result in discrimination in areas such as employment, law enforcement, lending, and healthcare (Varona & Suárez, 2022). Ensuring fairness and avoiding harmful biases is a key ethical challenge. AI ethical challenges also include accountability and responsibility for actions (Novelli et al., 2024). Determining liability when an AI system goes wrong or causes harm is complex, especially in areas such as medical AI, where errors can have serious consequences. The question of determining liability remains whether it is on the developer or the user or the system itself is an unclear issue (Loi & Spielkamp, 2021). Transparency and interpretability in AI operations presents another major ethical consideration in AI-driven service delivery mechanisms (Cheong, 2024). Many AI models, especially those based on deep learning, are considered black boxes (Papadouli, 2022). That means their decision-making process is difficult to understand or interpret. The lack of transparency in AI can lead to a lack of trust and poses a particular challenge in areas that require understanding the reasons behind decisions, such as health care or criminal justice. Additionally, AI systems, especially those that make independent decisions, can interfere with the freedom of individuals by making decisions on their behalf or influencing behaviour, such as advertising targeting or social media algorithms. This raises ethical concerns about preserving the autonomy of individuals and avoiding sole dependence on machines (Prunkl, 2024). At the economic level, AI is likely to automate some tasks, which may cause the loss of certain jobs and lead to economic changes (Rawashdeh, 2023). Despite the potential for new AI to create, there are concerns about the ability of the workforce to adapt quickly enough and about the extent to which these new opportunities are available to all (Tiwari, 2023). From a decision-making point of view, making ethical and moral decisions in scenarios such as healthcare, AI systems may need to make decisions that involve ethical judgments including triaging patients or acting in emergencies (Zhang et al., 2022). Designing AI to handle such complex ethical decisions faces significant challenges, as it requires encoding human values and balancing conflicting ethical principles (Kim et al., 2022). The potential use of AI in specific areas such as autonomous weapons or surveillance tools is a major ethical and security concern (Dresp-Langley, 2023). The idea of killer robots or AI-powered warfare raises many questions about the ethics of delegating life decisions to machines (Nobles, 2024). Developments in AI also raise existential questions about the long-term impact of AI and the existential risks it may pose to humans (Growiec, 2024). AI may exceed human control, creating potential risks to the future of humanity. Although this concern is still more hypothetical, it remains a topic of debate in ethical circles and AI research.

Public trust in AI is essential for its widespread acceptance and successful integration into public service organizations. However, achieving this remains a complex challenge (Robles & Mallinson, 2023). AI systems are becoming an integral part of many areas, from health care and food supply to criminal justice, where their decisions significantly influence people's lives. For the public to trust these systems there must be a level of transparency and accountability (Shan et al., 2022). People need to understand how AI makes decisions, especially in sensitive areas. However, because many AI models operate as black boxes, the decision-making process is often difficult to interpret, even for developers. This lack of transparency can lead to doubts and concerns about the fairness and reliability of AI, especially when biases appear in the training data that lead to flawed or discriminatory decisions (Hao Qin & Zhi Li, 2024). As AI evolves, transparency will become a matter of perception in building and maintaining public trust. Building public trust also requires addressing concerns about data privacy and the ethical standards of AI, given that AI often relies on large datasets, including sensitive personal information (Oh & Jung, 2023). Issues such as unauthorized access or misuse of data can undermine public trust. Ethical AI practices, such as ensuring unbiased decision-making and prioritizing privacy protections, are essential to mitigate these concerns. Regulatory action can help set standards for responsible AI use, demonstrating to the public that there are procedures in place to protect their rights and interests. When AI is aligned with transparent practices, ethical guidelines, and strong governance, public trust can grow, allowing AI to be a positive force for society (Robertson & Ridge-Newman, 2022).

It is worth noting in this regard that the characteristics of AI make it difficult for government to intervene in the traditional reactive regulatory fashion in order to regulate its activities. The traditional regulatory methods including product licensing, research and development oversight, and tort liability will not be as effective and as productive in regulating AI developments, as is the case with other sectors. The first challenge for AI regulators is to determine what is meant by such a slippery concept. In other words, the first step to create a common regulatory ground is to get some clarity on the notion of AI (Badran, 2021b). Despite the problematic features of AI, there is a good reason to believe that government regulation could be used to protect the public interest and to reduce public risks. Nonetheless, in such a complex and fragmented AI environment, the government intervention through regulation should be cautious and calculated in a way that avoids the possible negative consequences for the AI sectors, the regulators, and for end-users. Petit has identified some of major pitfalls of government regulation for AI systems including disabling and knee-Jerk regulation, rent-seeking and regulatory capture; besides regulatory timing. Government regulation for AI can either be enabling or disabling for AI activities. Given the aforementioned benefits of AI applications, it would not be wise for a government to put in place too much regulation that stifles the development of the entire sector. A balanced approach is needed that weighs-up the pros and cons of government intervention in each case. Added to this, responding to potential regulatory risks by developing a heavy-handed regulatory system which prohibit specific AI activities or research in an automatic or unthinking fashion 'knee-Jerk regulation' would definitely impact negatively on the AI sector (Badran, 2023).

Existing regulatory frameworks including the General Data Protection Regulation (GDPR) and the OECD AI principles could be helpful in providing some guidance into the ways in which AI might be regulated. In this respect, the OECD AI principles provides an important example of intergovernmental collaboration aiming at providing AI regulatory standards. The OECD AI principles have been issued in 2019 and updated in 2024. Five main values have been identified in order to develop fair, innovative, and trustworthy AI regulatory frameworks. The aim is to shaping a human-centric approach to AI based on the core values of human rights and democracy (OECD, 2024). The initiative has been widely adopted by the OECD countries and many other partners worldwide. At the heart of the initiative come key values including safety and security, accountability, transparency, fairness, and privacy. As such, the OECD AI principles provide a practical guidance to AI policy-makers on how to navigate thorny ethical, social, and economic issues. Focusing in data protection in the age of AI, the GDPR framework shed light on how privacy and security could be compromised by AI applications and provide insights on the ways of protecting such an important element. In this regard, a seminal study by the European Parliament indicated how AI is regulated in the GDPR. The paper examined the extent to which AI fits into the GDPR conceptual framework. The discussion demonstrated the tensions and proximities between AI and data protection principles considering the legal bases for AI applications and their impact on personal data. Profiling and automated decision-making have been underlined as key concerns that might interfere with data protection, security, and privacy. Additionally, data subjects' rights, including the rights to access, erasure, portability and object have been mentioned as cornerstones for data protection under AI (European Parliament. Directorate General for Parliamentary Research Services, 2020). The study concluded that AI could be deployed in a way that is consistent with the GDPR. Nonetheless, the GDPR does not provide sufficient guidance for regulators and policy-makers. Consequently, the GDPR need to be expanded and concretised.

The above discussion indicates that AI notions and applications interferes with many thorny issues. Those issues do not confine themselves to technical problems but they extend to cover diverse ethical, social, and economic difficulties. With issues such as privacy, security, and AI ethics at stake, the regulation of such an important growing field has become necessary.

2.2- Conceptualising E-governance: a Quest for Public Services Modernisation

Regarding the notion of e-governance, there are many definitions of this concept. Those definitions revolve in its entirety around the way governments practice the governance process, which in turn explains the way countries and governments manage their affairs, resources and relations with citizens. To govern in that sense is to exercise power and influence by the government and its institutions as well as the rest of the societal parties. In this context, e-governance can be described as the practice of governance through electronic means to achieve efficiency, speed and transparency in the process of communicating information to the public and to other government agencies. From this angle, e-governance can be considered as "a tool to empower citizens and increase transparency rates in government work by employing ICT in a way that leads to raising the level of efficiency in the provision of government services" (Kumar et al., 2014). In the same vein, e-government can be broadly perceived as a form of government, which reflects the nature of the relationship between state authority and its institutions on the one hand, and non-governmental societal parties on the other. The definition focused on ways to enhance the ways of participation by citizens through e-democracy, as well as ways to develop government services through e-government applications.

The contributions of ICT in the field of e-governance are evident through the emphasis on concepts and practices such as e-democracy at the political level and e-government at the level of services and e-commerce with regard to businesses and companies. Together, these areas constitute the main parts of e-governance at the societal level. By focusing on the government administrative apparatus and the process of services provision, we can identify the elements of e-governance as follows (Savoldelli et al., 2013):

- **E-administration**: refers to government efforts to enhance transparency and accountability in the government administrative apparatus through the application of ICT.
- **E-services:** that includes all government efforts to automate public services and provide them to citizens through electronic media using the Internet, in order to provide the service with a higher degree of efficiency and effectiveness (Luna-Reyes & Gil-Garcia, 2014).
- **E-participation**: refers to government efforts to build bridges of communication with citizens and recipients of public services. The aim is to evaluate service delivery processes and hold administrative bodies accountable for their actions. Today, the citizen is no longer satisfied with being a mere recipient of government services. Citizens also try to become a partner in the process of designing and delivering services.

In order to achieve the previous three components, governments should develop an appropriate and supportive legislative environment, as well as providing the necessary infrastructure. Access to the Internet is an essential part of implementing e-governance. Thus, ICT plays a pivotal role in e-governance as it helps to change patterns and processes of governance. It also creates new structures and modern patterns of interaction between the state and the citizen. In addition, ICT expands the scope of the process of governance and interaction with citizens and recipients of social services to include sectors of society that were previously excluded. E-governance is also a tool to accomplish the information society and to solidify the principals of good governance with its core are the values of transparency, accountability, integrity and impartiality (Bertot et al., 2016). Thus, the application of ICT through e-governance helps to overcome the spatial and temporal, boundaries of services provision.

Given the basic principles on which e-governance is founded, service delivery can be enhanced via openness and transparency, accountability and control, integrity and impartiality. A good e-governance system is open and transparent in its transactions with all societal parties. This openness would enhance trust between the citizen and government agencies, as well as confidence in the government administrative apparatus. This trust is built by providing accurate information about government agencies for citizens so that they can evaluate the government's performance with a degree of accuracy. This in turn helps citizens to participate effectively in improving the performance of public organizations. The spread of administrative corruption and the absence of accountability mechanisms in government agencies can be indicators of the weakness of the e-governance system. Accountability for actions and decisions are integral parts of e-governance and require the establishment of mechanisms for oversight and follow-up (Cornforth, 2002).

It may be useful, before concluding this section, to distinguish between e-government and e-governance, as many researchers and practitioners use both terms interchangeably. Despite the fact that the use of ICT is a common denominator between the two terms, the term e-government, as it will become clear later, is narrower than the concept of e-governance. The latter is concerned with a larger number of issues that focus on the interaction between the government and its institutions on the one hand, and between citizens and recipients of government services on the other. In other words, while e-government applications focus on the aspect related to services delivery in health, education and other fields, the concept of e-governance focuses on the way to manage the participatory relationship between the governments on the one hand and the citizen on the other. The aim is to clarify the impact of e-government applications on the state's relationship with the citizen (Misuraca & Viscusi, 2014).

Following on from the above theoretical and conceptual discussions of the main concepts, the next section will explain the evolution of smart-government projects. The notion of digital era governance will be critically evaluated in an attempt to underline the main phases of smart-governments initiatives.

3- MODERNISING PUBLIC SERVICES DELIVERY: THE ROLE OF E-GOVERNANCE INITIATIVES

It is difficult to treat all aspects related to services design and delivery in one chapter. Therefore, the discussion in the following parts will focus on the processes of delivering government services through the application of modern technologies in the field of ICT (Linders, 2012). The concept of the Digital Era Governance (DEG) refocuses on the role ICT in improving government performance in general and services provision in particular. The DEG notion was suggested by post-new public management researchers as a new paradigm (Margetts & Dunleavy, 2013). According to their views, The New Public Management (NPM) reforms have retreated in favour of DEG applications. In this regard, three main features distinguish the DEG have been identified: re-integration of government services; an organizational rearrangement depends on holistic government structures; besides the application of modern technology (Białożyt, 2017). Considering features of DEG it can be noted that this notion does not represent a paradigm shift in the field of government performance and service delivery (Margetts & Dunleavy, 2013). The NPM movement with its focus on the idea of e-government originated the main idea of their claim about making ICT at the heart of administrative reform processes and the redesign of administrative services. Consequently, we can raise some question marks about characterizing DEG as the new paradigm of the post-NPM movement. Nevertheless, we should clarify that DEG converges with the idea of SG in many points. Perhaps the most important of these points is the pivotal role of ICT in improving services delivery. In this regard, DEG proponents called for the centralization of the service delivery process through a unified platform, which is what Dunleavy defined as re-centralization (Margetts & Dunleavy, 2013). This idea of recentralization of service delivery contrasts with the idea of decentralization, which the NPM approach emphasized.

3.1- E-Government Evolution: From One-Way Communication to Smart Government

Many researchers and international institutions have provided different definitions of e-Government (Alhosh, 2006). These definitions revolve around using ICT and internet to reduce the gap between government agencies, citizens, and private sector companies. As such, e-government as “a process of changing and transforming relationships between institutions and citizens through ICT” (Vlahovic & Vracic, 2015). From this perspective, e-government aims to provide high-quality services by enabling access to information. The application of e-government also helps fighting corruption and increasing productivity of the administrative apparatus. Focusing on the concept of efficiency and effectiveness, e-government can be defined as “the use of digital technologies to achieve a transformation in government operations in a manner that improves efficiency, effectiveness and the level of quality of services provided” (Nam, 2019). Additionally, many international organizations have also defined e-government. For instance, the United Nations Economic and Social Commission for Western Asia (ESCWA) regarded e-government from a holistic perspective as "the use of ICT to improve job performance and government services" (ESCWA, 2014). From the World Bank's perspective, e-government refers to "the government's use of ICT (such as wide networks, the Internet, and mobile computing), which has the potential to bring about a change in the relationship with citizens, the business sector, and the rest of government agencies" (the World Bank, 2016). While the definition of the World Bank focused on the services that ICT can provide to the citizen, the definition of the Organization for Economic Cooperation and Development (OECD) focuses on the ability of modern technological developments to link the different parts of the government apparatus. In that sense, e-government provides opportunities to develop the service delivery process and increase the efficiency and effectiveness of administrative processes (OECD, 2001).

By reviewing the previous definitions, it becomes clear that the main goal behind the application of e-government is to provide better access to government services. Hence, the application of e-government has results in a number of improvements in governments including the following (Hartley, 2010):

- Faster services for citizens around the clock.
- More efficient and economically effective services.
- More flexible and responsive services to customers' needs.
- Services characterized by transparency and equality among service recipients.
- Lower levels of administrative corruption.

From this stance, e-government applications help in fostering the foundations of good governance including accountability, transparency and fighting corruption. Furthermore, e-governments enable citizens not only to become recipients of service but participants in decision-making processes as well. At the level of implementation, e-government has gone through three main stages. The first stage was the one-way communication from governments to citizens. During that early stage, many governments provided information about public services and ways to obtain them via official websites. Electronic websites of government organizations also provided some forms related to service provision. Hence, many government agencies' websites were filled with useful information. Nonetheless, citizens did not have the opportunity to communicate with these authorities to inquire or to submit requests electronically. That means the communication was one-way from the government to the citizen. Despite the inability to communicate electronically with government agencies, this early stage of e-government represented a major shift in the way citizens deal with governments. For example, it became possible to identify the services provided by each agency and the paperwork required to obtain those services. That means citizens are no longer required to go to those agencies in order to inquire about the required documents.

In a more advanced step, thanks to the progress in ICT, the e-government entered its second phase. This phase enabled citizens to communicate with government agencies electronically. In other words, in addition to providing information, during this stage it became possible for the citizen and the service applicant to submit the request directly to the concerned authority through its website and obtain the desired service without physically moving to the sites of these authorities. It has also become possible for citizens requesting the service to evaluate the process of provision and provide feedback to service providers. Service providers may benefit from such feedback and citizens' complaints about deficiencies in knowing the level of services quality and then working on improving them. Many countries have passed the first stage of the e-government implementation to the second stage. However, the majority of those countries have not yet passed to the third stage, which is the SG stage. The SG is the highest stage of e-government maturity, where smart applications are relied upon that provide integrated services to customers around the clock. It allows users the opportunity to participate in the design of government services through feedback processes. Such an integration in the process of providing government services helps in vanishing the borders between government departments. In other words, SG initiatives encourage government agencies to cooperate with each other so that the user can obtain the service directly without the need to contact and follow up with each agency separately.

3.2- What is a Smart Government? How is it Different from E-Government?

According to Gartner, SGs apply and integrate modern technologies in order to enhance planning, management and operation processes across various levels and administrative processes. The ultimate aim is to reach a sustainable public value derived from the process of technological transformation within the government organization. This definition does not differ much in its content from the aforementioned e-government definitions (Badran, 2021a). Nevertheless, what distinguishes the SG from e-government is the focus on what smart technologies such as mobile phones and can provide as facilitating factors working between governments on the one hand, and other parties dealing with them, such as the citizen and the private sector, on the other. In this context, smart technologies can help integrate government services platforms and enable service access 24/7 (Badran, 2019). In essence, the SG goes beyond just developing a set of modern applications to deal with societal parties through smart mobile devices. It provides a comprehensive strategy for restructuring and integrating government services provided through the websites of public institutions. SGs also rely on a unified platform for the government as a whole through which the customer can access various types of services and communicate with various government agencies. Such an integrative perspective of the concept of SG will make the government closer to the citizen. The smart applications connected to the government information network will also enable administrative government agencies to benefit from the vast amount of data available on all aspects of economic and social activities. This in turn should activate the ability of the state's administrative apparatus to design and implement policies, programs and services that meet the needs of the citizen and fulfil the demands of the community (Anthopoulos & Reddick, 2016).

The SG is a social government. That means SGs are in constant and continuous interaction with the various governmental and non-government parties in the society. SGs also benefit from the data generate via social interactions in designing and delivering public services. In addition, the SG is an agile government that is flexible and mobile and responds to the demands of societal parties of different backgrounds. The SG is also a government that relies in its decisions, actions, policies and services on careful analysis of the evidence and information available in the society. The SG works within a framework of radical openness and transparency with all parties of society, as if it performs its work and services in a glasshouse. Such transparency and openness to all actors in society would help making the most of the available data and information in developing better services and improving the standard of living of society as a whole. Finally yet importantly, one of the most important features of SG is that it is based on mutual trust between all parties. This trust needs a period of time to build through various transactions between formal and informal parties, but it is the cement that binds the various parts and components of the SG (Alzahrani et al., 2017).

The SG is based, in essence, on re-designing work procedures within government agencies and institutions in an integrated manner. That integration is facilitated by the use of ICT and smart devices in a way that allows the flow of information and data between the various government units. SGs enables the use of information in designing and providing services that satisfy customers in addition to facilitating the process of interaction between societal actors and government agencies (Badran, 2019). Accordingly, the successful application of SG projects requires a full attention and consideration of the patterns of interaction between users and government agencies. Based on such patterns, governments should determine the preferences of the users regarding the type of services they receive and the way these services are provided. From this perspective, and contrary to what many researchers believe, it can be said that the SG and its applications are nothing but an extension of the e-government model that many Arab countries have known during the last decade of the 20th century. To put it another way, SG is not a new type of government and does not represent a break from the idea of e-government (Badran, 2021a).

As is the case with e-government, the implementation of the idea of SG passes through specific stages in which the maturity of the SG increases over time. In general, it can be noticed that SGs represent the highest stages of maturity of e-government applications. The idea of e-government has developed to provide better services to the citizen than the traditional government, which was characterized by limited services provided and limited use of ICT. In this context, mobile government is a stage that separates e-government and SG, which is. This stage is characterized by a high degree of ambiguity and lack of clarity. In other words, the notion of mobile government carries the initial premonitions of the idea of SG in terms of using mobile technology to provide government services. Nonetheless, it has not reached the maturity level of SG that depends on the integration of the services provided.

The maturity level of SG can be measured by looking at three main indicators (Anthopoulos et al., 2021). Firstly, the degree of citizen participation. In general, the more citizens are involved in the process of designing and providing government services, the more mature the SG model is. Secondly, the extent of transparency in providing information to the user. According to this indicator, the initial stages of the implementation of the SG may witness the availability of a large amount of information. However, a mature model of SGs provide this information regardless of time and place limits. It also provides each user with information that benefits him/her personally according to their interests and the nature of services they seeks to obtain it. From this perspective, the SG is a transparent government and provides information to customers according to their personal preferences. The third and final indicator is related to the level of cooperation between various government agencies in order to provide integrated services to the user. In this regard, the greater the degree of cooperation and coordination between government departments, the more mature a SG model becomes. The highest stage of maturity according to this indicator is what is known as 360 Degrees citizen service. At this level, government services become highly responsive to change in customers' tastes and demands. Based on the information and real-time data governments receive about such changes services are redesigned immediately to meet customers' needs (Badran, 2019).

3.3- The Requirements for a Successful Application of Smart Government

By reviewing the concept presented to the SG, it becomes clear that SG represents a more advanced stage of e-government. Accordingly, the transformation from e-government to the SG needs to take place through an action plan. This plan should accurately explains the requirements and stages of the transformation process in a way that ensures a successful transition from relying on web technology and electronic portals to implement smart tools and sensors that enable governments to deal in real time with data and information received from the community. The following requirements for the successful transformation to the SG model can be identified (Netten et al., 2016):

- Using the data and information available on the portals and websites of government agencies in developing smart applications for government services.
- Developing the general framework that governs the process of collecting and classifying government data and information to become more flexible and more able to deal in real time data and information received in a way that maximizes the benefits of using this information.
- Forming partnerships with various actors in society in order to develop smart applications for government services. For example, taking advantage of the databases available with government agencies in the economic, social and health fields and in the field of transportation by making them available to smart application developers. This should enable developers to design useful applications tailored for those dealing with government agencies.
- Providing guiding frameworks for SG users that explain how to deal with the services provided and how to obtain those services through smart applications.
- Develop guiding frameworks for government agencies on how to convert the provided services into smart services, while leaving the freedom for each of these agencies to develop what they see fit as applications and technologies for the transformation of the SG model.
- Investing in developing smart applications and providing financial encouragement to software and application developers to update already existing applications, such as electronic payment applications, or develop new applications for services that did not exist before.

By reviewing these requirements, it becomes clear that the process of moving from e-government to the SG model is not easy. On the contrary, it is a challenging process, which requires rethinking the existing electronic structure in an attempt to benefiting from them in developing new smart tools and applications. Such smart tools and applications enable better communications among government agencies and the rest of the societal actors. In other words, the shift to the SG model does not mean the recycling and reproduction of existing ministries and government websites through smart mobile devices. A successful SG model is based on restructuring and integrating government services. It requires the removal of any existing overlapping between governments unites. It also makes easier for service applicants to deal with all government agencies at once through a single platform to get access to all services around the clock. This transformation necessitates a good management of the various stages of the transition. It also calls for a clear and specific planning for what is to be accomplished and the period for which this transformation is expected to be completed. Finally, the resources required to complete the transition come at the heart of a successful SG model (Badran, 2021a).

Having said that, it is also important to denote the need to a shift from simply focusing on SGs to move to the notion of smart cities. It is inconceivable to have a SG in an environment characterized by backwardness, stagnation and reactionary. In other words, the SG model flourishes in smart cities that seek to achieve sustainability in economic growth by providing a modern ICT infrastructure. Through such an infrastructure, governments can provide services to citizens with a high degree of quality, efficiency and effectiveness (Badran, 2019).

3.4- Smart Governance Models

SG models are very similar to e-government ones. Although the two models differ in the application mechanism and in the technological media used to communicate with government agencies, SG models can be summarized by looking at the parties involved in the interaction and communication processes into three models. The first model, from government to citizen. This model refers to the government's interaction with citizens through electronic media in order to provide information and services. Accordingly, there are many services and information that the government can provide to citizens. That includes but not limited to services related to submitting applications, and obtaining various approvals in addition to issuing licenses and providing information about administrative rules, decisions, and laws. As such, this first model of e-governance allows citizens participation in public affairs through consultation, deliberation and electronic voting.

The second model from government to the business community. Through this model, the government interacts with the business community and companies as one of the important groups within society that have a number of demands and services of their own. In addition to providing information, companies and non-governmental organizations need electronic systems that enable them to complete their registration procedures, as well as organize daily transactions such as payments, practices, and bids. Through this model, the government provides a number of electronic systems that enable companies to complete sales and purchases electronically. These systems include the e-procurement system, e-customs services system, and e-commerce system. The third model represents the communications between government agencies: from government to government. The first and second models express the electronic/SG as seen by those dealing with the government entity, whether they are individuals or companies. This is known as Front Offices, which represent the interface of electronic interaction with users. However, success in providing high-quality electronic services depends at the same time on what happens within the government and between its various departments. These interactions take place in what is known as the back offices. Hence, the SG needs to rearrange the workload between government departments and ministries in a way that ensures effective co-ordination among them and increases the productivity of back offices. The process of arranging government back offices is based on the idea of integration and coordination between all activities and services. It requires an integrated system to link all government units at central and local levels, in addition to sharing information, ideas and decision-making mechanisms. South Korea provides a successful model in how to coordinate and link different government systems at central and local levels in a way that enables the provision of a set of integrated services to citizens.

This discussion of SG models makes it evident that, among other things, how government back offices (from one government to another) interact with the electronic interface that consumers view determines how well integrated services are delivered to them using smart electronic media.

. In other words, success at the smart electronic level is preceded by a very important requirement, which is to rearrange work systems within government agencies and ministries in a way that remove overlapping and repetition in the services provided. It is inconceivable that there is a successful SG in the cybernetic space supported by a rigid and paper-based bureaucratic government.

The aforementioned discussion of E-governance and smart-government notion indicated that the application of ICT in the domain of public services is not new. There have been several initiatives and divers projects to make a good use of technology in modernising public services. Such initiatives have gone through different phases including what we call today smart-governments. The following section will focus on a new development in the journey of E-governance developments that is AI applications. The emergence of AI and the widespread utilisation in different sectors including public services delivery ushers a new phase of E-governance developments as it carries many opportunities and poses diverse threats.

4- AI-AUGMENTED SMART GOVERNMENT: OPPORTUNITIES AND CHALLENGES

Talking about AI-Augmented SG applications requires that we first identify the most important advantages that AI applications can provide to the work of governments in general and with regard to the process of designing and delivering services in particular. The AI revolution helps in dealing with the databases available to government institutions in a more effective and efficient manner (Barbero, 2016). The progress made in the field of AI applications and the algorithms associated with them that have the ability to deal with large databases can greatly analyse the available data and use the results reached through this analysis in redesigning the processes of delivering public services. Furthermore, the speed at which AI applications work helps in a more efficient manner in reducing the time required to deliver government services and reducing the complexity associated with those services. This aspect has been facilitated by the various progresses in the field of e-governance, which are linked to the discussed models, whether related to e-government or SG. However, what AI provides in this regard lies in the ability to quickly process a huge volume of data and identify the most important elements that can be used in developing government services (Margets & Dorobantu, 2019). In other words, the cognitive technologies and deep learning capabilities available to AI applications enable them to take advantage of the databases available to government organizations in a better way than applications used within the framework of SG initiatives. From this perspective, AI can be considered an enhancing factor for SG applications rather than being considered a development unrelated to such initiatives (Lips, 2024).

In addition to the above advantages, AI applications provide multiple opportunities for SG initiatives. Among these opportunities is increasing the ability of SG projects to predict the future. AI applications have a great ability to identify recurring patterns in large databases and predict some of the complex phenomena that government organizations deal with. At this point, databases of users and recipients of government services can be used to identify the general patterns of behaviour of these individuals and design service delivery processes based on those patterns. It is also possible to predict the possibility of any future changes to those patterns and to hedge against the problems that may result from this change that government organizations may face and negatively affect the process of providing services to citizens. In addition, AI applications based on cognitive technology can identify the most important patterns of government service recipients. Some of these applications can explain the reasons behind their choice of these patterns and suggest to the decision-maker the next steps that he should take to deal with the problems of delivering services to citizens. In this context, these applications become an important factor that affects the decision-making processes in government (Al-Besher & Kumar, 2022).

In terms of simplifying procedures, AI applications can help SG initiatives get rid of the paper-based culture and the associated burdens on government service providers and citizens dealing with these organizations. The process of obtaining some services requires preparing and submitting many forms needed to receive the service. This constitutes a burden on the government employee and the recipient of the service. In this context, AI applications can interact with recipients of government services instantly and can answer any inquiries raised by these individuals. AI applications can also save time and effort for government service providers and for recipients of these services by simplifying procedures and reducing the amount of documents required to obtain the service. AI applications can also maximize the use of available resources for government organizations. In light of the scarcity of resources that many of these organizations suffer from, dealing efficiently and effectively with available resources becomes essential. In this context, AI applications can perform many of the tasks that government service providers perform faster and on a larger scale, which can redistribute the resources available to public service organizations so that the human element can be used in jobs that AI applications cannot perform.

AI applications can deal with data collected through various smart applications such as cameras and sensors in an automated manner. Dealing with data generated in real time can solve many problems. For example, AI applications can solve many traffic problems based on their ability to collect and analyse data generated in real time, thus alleviating the severity of traffic congestion on roads. These applications can also predict the possibility of traffic accidents or increased traffic density on some roads based on the data they collect and analyse in real time. In addition, AI applications that track some behavioural patterns or some diseases can predict the possibility of these diseases developing in the future in a way that represents a threat to the lives of individuals, and thus this can help improve the health of individuals in society.

From a citizen engagement perceptive, AI can transform citizen engagement in the design and delivery of public services by facilitating more inclusive, responsive, and data-driven approaches (Alhaimer, 2024a). Through AI-powered data profiling, governments can gain real-time insights into citizens' needs, preferences, and challenges, enabling them to tailor public services accordingly. This can be achieved through Chabot, predictive profiling, and digital feedback systems that efficiently collect and analyse large amounts of citizen input. For example, Singapore is using AI to aggregate and profile feedback on municipal services, allowing agencies to respond more effectively to community needs by making government services more adaptable and targeted. AI can help shift from a one-size-fits-all approach to a more personalized, citizen-centric model (Alhaimer, 2023). AI also enhances engagement by creating accessible platforms for civic engagement, such as interactive apps and online forums where residents can contribute ideas and provide feedback on policy initiatives. It can also break down the Natural language driven by AI breaks down language barriers, allowing diverse communities to easily participate in discussions about public service delivery. This in turn enables citizens to be active in shaping services from healthcare and education to transportation and urban planning. In this context, studies indicate that the application of smart technologies had a significant impact on the development of higher education systems during the COVID-19 period. During this period, the application of smart education technology helped build more durable and more resistant education systems (Alkhaldi et al., 2024). Additionally, machine-learning algorithms can identify trends in citizen feedback, providing governments with insights into long-term needs and emerging issues. As a result, AI not only enhances the efficiency of public services, but also strengthens the democratic process by making citizen input an integral part of the design and implementation of public policies (Alhaimer, 2024b).

The above advantages of applying AI technology should not lead us to say that the process of transformation towards SGs supported by these applications is completely free of problems. Among the main challenges, facing the process of transformation towards SGs supported by AI applications is the lack of the skills required for this transformation among government employees. For long periods, governments have become accustomed to working with a specific mechanism and their employees have been trained in the skills required to perform the work according to this mechanism. With the transformation towards e-government and smart applications, there has become an urgent need to retrain employees in the government sector in the new skills required to deal with smart technologies, especially technologies related to AI. This lack of skills required to deal with SGs enhanced by AI applications may push many government departments to outsource the services they provide to the private sector. This outsourcing is not evil in itself if it is done within a framework of partnership between government departments and private institutions and aims primarily to transfer skills and expertise to government employees. However, if this framework of partnership is not available, the situation may end up in a situation where government departments have outsourced many services to private sector institutions at a time when these departments do not have mechanisms to control the service provision process and monitor the performance levels of the private sector. This, in turn, may harm the service provision process and may harm applicants for public services (Agarwal, 2018).

AI-Augmented SG faces another challenge related to the potential negative effects of AI applications on the future of government employees. It is expected that the expansion of the application of AI in government organizations will lead to many government employees losing their jobs. This poses a fundamental challenge for government organizations that should find alternative jobs for these individuals or train them for new jobs that are compatible with smart applications (Jarrahi, 2018). On the technical level, some studies indicate that despite the start of e-government initiatives in many countries decades ago, many government departments are still lagging behind in terms of SG technology. This delay in developing smart applications that can be used via mobile phones makes it difficult to advance in this field to integrate AI within these initiatives. In addition to this technical problem, there is another dimension related to the lack of integration and interconnection between the different AI systems within the government system. Smart technologies are multiple, including, for example, tracking and monitoring systems, sensing systems, and other smart technologies that work to collect and analyse information from different sources. What hinders the application of AI within SG initiatives is the lack of integration and integration between these systems, which work as isolated islands from each other.

In addition to the above, information security and privacy provides another challenge facing the adoption of AI-Augmented SG. Many smart applications, such as surveillance cameras, collect information about individuals all the time. This may constitute a breach of the privacy of these individuals, especially since these individuals are not always aware of the nature of the information collected about them, nor the way in which this information is dealt with, nor the parties who benefit from it (European Parliament. Directorate General for Parliamentary Research Services., 2020). It is worth noting that the concept of privacy requires that information about individuals be obtained after their explicit consent to do so. However, with the spread of smart technologies, the process of collecting information is done automatically all the time without necessarily obtaining this prior permission from those about whom the information is collected. In addition to this dimension related to privacy, there is the problem of data confidentiality. The information and data that are collected are stored in databases that may in turn become a target for cyber hacking operations, which exposes individuals' data to risk.

From an environmental sustainability perspective, the advent of AI applications poses a challenge in terms of energy consumption. While AI applications can enhance energy conservation, the work of these smart applications and the associated electronic system based on collecting, analysing and storing data in large databases in turn consumes a large amount of energy, which may have a negative environmental impact from a sustainability perspective. The expansion of the use of AI also raises many ethical concerns related to how to deal with the data collected, especially in the case of smart applications that operate independently of human intervention. Self-driving cars, for example, can assess the situation and make decisions without human intervention. Likewise, autonomous weapons represent a major ethical problem, especially if we consider the ability of these weapons to operate independently and make individual decisions.

From the previous discussion, it is clear that adopting AI applications within the framework of SG initiatives should be done through a balanced approach that can identify the advantages and disadvantages resulting from this matter. The application of AI provides many opportunities for government agencies and institutions to develop service delivery processes for citizens, but in order to benefit from these opportunities, the challenges and risks that may result from adopting these smart applications should be dealt with. In the end, any development in the field of SGs, including the use of AI, has the emotional goal of improving the lives of individuals in society. Therefore, if the focus is on the advantages and opportunities and the risks and challenges are neglected, the final result may be a decline or deterioration in the services provided and harm to the service seeker instead of developing these processes in a way that serves citizens.

The discussion of AI opportunities and threats paves the way for exploring some global examples and providing some policy recommendations for a smooth and successful transition towards AI-augmented smart-government.

5- TRANSITION TO AI-AUGMENTED SMART GOVERNMENT: GLOBAL EXAMPLES AND RECOMMENDATIONS FOR QATAR

To give context to Qatar's efforts to employ AI to enhance government effectiveness, case studies from other countries can provide valuable insights. We start with Singapore, which has sought to improve public services through AI solutions (Ta et al., 2022). In this context, Singapore has adopted AI across various government functions to streamline services, particularly through the Smart Nation initiative (Foong et al., 2024). AI is used in areas such as healthcare, transportation, and city planning. For example, the Singaporean government uses AI to predict traffic and manage accidents. In the field of public health, the smart Chabot was launched to answer citizens' inquiries about government services, which enhanced ease of access and speed of response (Goode et al., 2023). As a result, government services have become more efficient and citizen satisfaction with these services has increased, as surveys have shown high satisfaction rates, indicating that integrating AI into public systems can enhance citizen satisfaction and increase government effectiveness (Koh et al., 2023).

The United Kingdom offers another example of AI application in the public health and social services sector. In this context, the National Health Service (NHS) in the United Kingdom has integrated AI to address challenges related to the efficiency and accessibility of healthcare (Fazakarley et al., 2023). AI algorithms help predict patient needs and improve staff allocation. They also contribute to improving the accuracy of diagnoses through medical imaging. The NHS has introduced AI-powered Chabot to deal with patient inquiries and determine priorities, which reduces waiting times and enhances patient satisfaction by reducing administrative defects and improving response times. These AI-powered improvements have contributed to increasing public satisfaction with healthcare services and providing resources for critical medical cases (Kalidindi & Gandhi, 2023).

In the field of using artificial intelligence in law enforcement and interaction with citizens, the United States of America has witnessed major developments supported by artificial intelligence applications in the field of public safety and law enforcement (Joh, 2022). In this regard, crime prediction tools are used to analyse data, which helps police departments allocate resources and prevent crimes. In addition, some local governments use Chabot powered by artificial intelligence to facilitate communication with citizens, allowing them to report non-emergency problems or request information quickly. For example, the city of Los Angeles uses Chabot to answer residents' inquiries about municipal services. These initiatives have improved public interaction with local authorities and made services more responsive, which has enhanced customer satisfaction with these government agencies (Rani, 2024). Through these studies, it becomes clear how artificial intelligence can enhance government responsiveness, ease of access to services, and their efficiency, leading to increased public satisfaction. As for Qatar, these applications can be used to improve artificial intelligence strategies to improve service delivery, simplify administrative processes, and enhance public trust.

The abovementioned examples indicate that the ability of governments to govern in the future depends, to a large extent, on their success in achieving a greater degree of communication with stakeholders in society via SG applications (Badran, 2019). This applies to the SG initiatives in all countries including Qatar. SG in Qatar, which was built on the vision of the political leadership that a successful government is one that reaches users wherever they are. Therefore, it has become necessary to deal with the challenges imposed by the AI developments in the current DEG. It is equally important to benefit from the opportunities provided by AI technologies and ICT fields. The aim should be to constructing a government that is more communicative with societal stakeholders and more responsive to the demands of citizens, private sector companies, and non-governmental organizations. To this end, decision-makers at the local level should develop an integrated strategy for the transformation process towards AI-Augmented SG. Such a strategy should be based on developing AI technologies and tools that suit the nature of the local Qatari community. This is needed to ensure that AI applications are appropriate for the needs of customers in Qatar. In this context, a number of recommendations can be made to decision-makers regarding the aspects that should be taken into account to ensure a successful transformation from the e-government stage to the AI-Augmented SG model. That includes the following:

- **Continuous Support and Follow-Up by the Political Leadership:** perhaps one of the most important factors for the success of the AI-Augmented SG experience in Qatar, if not the most important of all, is the support that the SG initiative received from the highest levels of political leadership within the country. The launch of the initiative by, the Qatari officials had a significant impact on many government institutions. In this context, government departments have strived to implement the SG directives in light of the QNV 2030.

The follow-up to the transformation process to the SG model and setting a time frame for completing that process also had an impact in emphasizing the determination of the political leadership to successfully complete the transformation process.

- **Changing the Prevailing Mental Image in Government:** Many government institutions hold a certain image about the nature of public services and the methods of providing them. AI-Augmented SG is primarily linked to providing smart solutions to problems related to service provision, not just developing smart applications. Therefore, to transform into smart departments, government departments need to think smart and change the mental image associated with the service provision process and its relationships with customers. AI-Augmented SG also requires higher levels of integration, coordination and cooperation between different government agencies in a way that enables the provision of integrated and easier services and greater returns to the user. In other words, enabling the user to obtain more than one service at the same time and with the same levels of quality and efficiency.
- **Increasing Connectivity and Developing an Information Security Framework:** AI-Augmented SG requires increasing connectivity to the Internet in public places. This can be done by creating hotspots to connect to the World Wide Web. Smart services will not be accessible to the user unless he is connected to the information network. Additionally, because of the cyber risks associated with the development of AI-Augmented SG, there is a need to develop information security framework. That includes standards and systems for the security and safety of information related to electronic services provided in a way that protects the user from the risks of hacking and theft of personal and banking data. This step is of great importance to build trust between the citizen and the AI-Augmented SG. This recommendation becomes even more important when we consider that many of the technologies used to protect the security and safety of users have become outdated and do not keep pace with the rapid development of information hackers in developing modern software that can hack users' personal accounts.
- **Developing the Regulatory Environment:** From a public interest's perspective, there is too much at stake that requires government intervention in the form of AI regulations. AI applications may result in breaches in the areas of individual privacy and may expose personal data to unwanted third party. Cyber-Security threats provide another reason for governments to intervene in order to minimize the risks of using AI applications. The users of AI applications might be more open to the idea of having a legitimate fair and impartial regulatory body that protect their interests rather than leaving the task of AI regulation to the industry itself because of the potential conflict

of interests between AI developers and manufacturers on the one hand and the users on the other. To this end, AI regulators should enjoy certain powers chief among them is their ability to approve new AI applications and devices before entering the market. This will ensure the public that any devices or applications have been properly tested before being deployed to end-users. AI regulators should also have the power to sanction non-complaints and impose penalties and fines on AI stakeholders that do not conform to regulations. Such a balanced and centralized approach for AI regulation would secure the development of the sector in a harmonized and coordinated fashion while protecting the public interests by reducing the potential harm resulting from using AI applications and machines. In this context, the legislative and regulatory framework is required to ensure that no legislations hinder the transition from e-government to AI-Augmented SG (Badran, 2022). This includes ensuring the availability of all legislations and legal frameworks that guarantee the integrity of transactions conducted through AI-Augmented SG applications. It is also needed to protect the rights of individuals and establishments from any violations that may be exposed to as a result of electronic transactions. That might include but not limited to violations of intellectual property rights. This legislative framework is necessary to legitimize AI-Augmented SG and the transactions that take place through its platform. It is also necessary to develop the institutional framework by establishing regulatory bodies concerned with monitoring and implementing electronic legislation. Such a regulator should be equipped by the necessary expertise and powers in order to perform their role to the fullest extent.

- **Achieving a Citizen Centric Government:** A customer-oriented government can be realised by increasing users' awareness of new applications, their benefits, and how to use them. In addition, AI-Augmented SG can benefit from users' feedback in developing methods of service delivery. At the heart of this process is building trust with customers by emphasizing the confidentiality of information and data, ensuring system security, and achieving higher levels of coordination and cooperation with internal customers (other government departments) and external customers (the private sector and users) in order to develop integrated electronic services.
- **Building capacity in Qatar:** capacity building is required in order to address the challenges of AI to ensure the country can leverage the benefits of these applications while mitigating the associated risks As AI technology evolves and spreads across sectors, Qatar faces opportunities for transformational growth but also requires skilled expertise, strong infrastructure, and ethical governance. Capacity building in this area involves training local talent, enhancing technical skills, and developing a strong base of professionals

who can innovate and effectively manage AI-based systems. By investing in education and specialized training programs, Qatar can develop a qualified workforce in the areas of machine learning, data science, and AI ethics, strengthening its position as a leading AI leader. Therefore, with the rapid adoption of AI across sectors such as healthcare, finance, and public services, Qatar needs to ensure that it has the infrastructure and knowledge to responsibly apply these technologies. Capacity building includes establishing research institutions, funding AI projects, and collaborating with global technology leaders to share best practices. By creating policies and risk management to address the ethical implications of AI, Qatar can commit to principles of fairness, privacy, and transparency, which will enhance public trust in AI systems. In addition, developing local expertise will help to mitigate reliance on external expertise and ensure that AI solutions are adapted to fit Qatar's cultural and economic context. Local professionals with a deep understanding of global trends and the country's needs can lead AI solutions that are aligned with Qatar's goals in sustainability, economic diversification, and social development as outlined in Vision 2030. By prioritizing capacity building, Qatar enhances its readiness to meet AI challenges and opens up prospects for economic growth, technological leadership, and resilient governance in an increasingly AI-dependent world.

CONCLUSION

This chapter discussed the developments that e-government initiatives have gone through in the context of e-governance and advances in the field of AI. In this context, the chapter attempted to shed light on the idea of e-governance as a theoretical and conceptual framework that can be used to analyse the concepts and tools for using ICT to improve government services. The chapter reviewed the stages through which e-government models developed to SG initiatives. The chapter also discussed the potential role of AI in improving the efficiency and effectiveness of SG initiatives. The chapter offered the idea of a SG enhanced by AI and discussed the opportunities and challenges posed by this model. The study concluded that AI offers many opportunities to improve the efficiency and effectiveness of SGs in the field of service provision. However, the study stressed the need to consider the challenges posed by the model of SG enhanced by AI and develop solutions to the problems that may arise from the application of AI in the field of government service provision.

REFERENCES

Agarwal, P. K. (2018). Public Administration Challenges in the World of AI and Bots. *Public Administration Review*, 78(6), 917–921. DOI: 10.1111/puar.12979

Al-Besher, A., & Kumar, K. (2022). Use of artificial intelligence to enhance e-government services. *Measurement. Sensors*, 24, 100484. DOI: 10.1016/j.measen.2022.100484

Alhaimer, R. (2023). *Impact of governmental social media campaigns on citizens' attitudes towards Kuwait's vision 2035*. Global Knowledge, Memory and Communication., DOI: 10.1108/GKMC-06-2023-0209

Alhaimer, R. (2024a). Digital transformation on the design and implementation of virtual political campaigns in Kuwait: Perceptions and attitudes of politicians and campaign managers for bold innovation and social impact in Kuwait. *Journal of Science and Technology Policy Management*. DOI: 10.1108/JSTPM-11-2023-0212

Alhaimer, R. (2024b). Exploring the Attitudes of Kuwait's Residents Toward the Role of Corruption and Anti-Corruption Entities (Nazaha) in Kuwait. *Public Integrity*, 26(3), 305–321. DOI: 10.1080/10999922.2023.2176054

Alhosh, A. (2006). *E-government reality and prospects*. Arab Nile Publishing Group.

Alkhaldi, A., Malik, S., Alhaimer, R., Alshaheen, A., & Lytras, M. D. (2024). Translating a value-based framework for resilient e-learning impact in post COVID-19 times: Research-based Evidence from Higher Education in Kuwait. *Heliyon*, 10(2), e24271. DOI: 10.1016/j.heliyon.2024.e24271 PMID: 38298680

Alzahrani, L., Al-Karaghouli, W., & Weerakkody, V. (2017). Analysing the critical factors influencing trust in e-government adoption from citizens' perspective: A systematic review and a conceptual framework. *International Business Review*, 26(1), 164–175. DOI: 10.1016/j.ibusrev.2016.06.004

Anthopoulos, L., Sirakoulis, K., & Reddick, C. G. (2021). Conceptualizing Smart Government: Interrelations and Reciprocities with Smart City. *Digital Government: Research and Practice*, 2(4), 1–28. DOI: 10.1145/3465061

Badran, A. (2019). Smart-Governments for Smart Cities: The Case of Dubai Smart-Government. In Samad, W. A., & Azar, E. (Eds.), *Smart Cities in the Gulf* (pp. 59–82). Springer Nature Singapore., DOI: 10.1007/978-981-13-2011-8_5

Badran, A. (2021a). Developing Smart Cities: Regulatory and Policy Implications for the State of Qatar. *International Journal of Public Administration*, ●●●, 1–14. DOI: 10.1080/01900692.2021.2003811

Badran, A. (2021b). Thoughts and Reflections on the Case of Qatar: Should Artificial Intelligence Be Regulated? In Azar, E., & Haddad, A. N. (Eds.), *Artificial Intelligence in the Gulf* (pp. 69–92). Springer Singapore., DOI: 10.1007/978-981-16-0771-4_5

Badran, A. (2022). Independent regulators in the Middle East. In *Handbook on Regulatory Authorities*. Edward Elgar Publishing.

Badran, A. (2023). Artificial Intelligence between Government and Self-Regulation Policies: A Theoretical Approach. . DOI: 10.31430/IJZH4708

Barbero, M. C. (2016). *Big data analytics for policy making. European Commission*. Big data analytics for policy making. European Commission.

Bartneck, C., Lütge, C., Wagner, A., & Welsh, S. (2021). Privacy Issues of AI. In C. Bartneck, C. Lütge, A. Wagner, & S. Welsh, *An Introduction to Ethics in Robotics and AI* (pp. 61–70). Springer International Publishing. DOI: 10.1007/978-3-030-51110-4_8

Bertot, J. C., Estevez, E., & Janowski, T. (2016). Digital public service innovation: Framework proposal. *Proceedings of the 9th International Conference on Theory and Practice of Electronic Governance*, 113–122. DOI: 10.1145/2910019.2910108

Bertot, J. C., Jaeger, P. T., & Grimes, J. M. (2010). Using ICTs to create a culture of transparency: E-government and social media as openness and anti-corruption tools for societies. *Government Information Quarterly*, 27(3), 264–271. DOI: 10.1016/j.giq.2010.03.001

Białożyt, W. (2017). Digital Era Governance – a new chapter of public management theory and practice Wojciech Białożyt. *MAZOWSZE Studia Regionalne*, 22(22), 117–129. DOI: 10.21858/msr.22.08

Cheong, B. C. (2024). Transparency and accountability in AI systems: Safeguarding wellbeing in the age of algorithmic decision-making. *Frontiers in Human Dynamics*, 6, 1421273. DOI: 10.3389/fhumd.2024.1421273

Cornforth, C. (Ed.). (2002). *The Governance of Public and Non-Profit Organizations* (0 ed.). Routledge., DOI: 10.4324/9780203167571

Dresp-Langley, B. (2023). The weaponization of artificial intelligence: What the public needs to be aware of. *Frontiers in Artificial Intelligence*, 6, 1154184. DOI: 10.3389/frai.2023.1154184 PMID: 36967833

ESCWA. (2014). *E-Government: Policies, Strategies and Applications*. Academy of Information and Communication Technologies for Development for Government Sector Leaders in the Arab Countries.

European Parliament. Directorate General for Parliamentary Research Services. (2020). *The impact of the general data protection regulation on artificial intelligence*. Publications Office. https://data.europa.eu/doi/10.2861/293

Fazakarley, C. A., Breen, M., Leeson, P., Thompson, B., & Williamson, V. (2023). Experiences of using artificial intelligence in healthcare: A qualitative study of UK clinician and key stakeholder perspectives. *BMJ Open*, 13(12), e076950. DOI: 10.1136/bmjopen-2023-076950 PMID: 38081671

Foong, Y. P., Pidani, R., Sithira Vadivel, V., & Dongyue, Y. (2024). Singapore Smart Nation: Journey into a New Digital Landscape for Higher Education. In Kwok, A. O. J., & Teh, P.-L. (Eds.), *Emerging Technologies in Business* (pp. 281–304). Springer Nature Singapore., DOI: 10.1007/978-981-97-2211-2_13

González-Sendino, R., Serrano, E., Bajo, J., & Novais, P. (2023). A Review of Bias and Fairness in Artificial Intelligence. *International Journal of Interactive Multimedia and Artificial Intelligence, In press*(In press), 1. DOI: 10.9781/ijimai.2023.11.001

Goode, K., Kim, H. M., & Deng, M. (2023). *Examining Singapore's AI Progress*. Center for Security and Emerging Technology., DOI: 10.51593/2021CA014

Growiec, J. (2024). EXISTENTIAL RISK FROM TRANSFORMATIVE AI: AN ECONOMIC PERSPECTIVE. *Technological and Economic Development of Economy*, 0(0), 1–27. DOI: 10.3846/tede.2024.21525

Hartley, J. (2010). Innovation in governance and public services: Past and present. *Public Money & Management*, 25(1), 27–34.

Jarrahi, M. H. (2018). Artificial intelligence and the future of work: Human-AI symbiosis in organizational decision making. *Business Horizons*, 61(4), 577–586. DOI: 10.1016/j.bushor.2018.03.007

Kalidindi, S., & Gandhi, S. (2023). Workforce Crisis in Radiology in the UK and the Strategies to Deal With It: Is Artificial Intelligence the Saviour? *Cureus*. Advance online publication. DOI: 10.7759/cureus.43866 PMID: 37608900

Kim, M. J., Theriault, J., Hirschfeld-Kroen, J., & Young, L. (2022). Reframing of moral dilemmas reveals an unexpected "positivity bias" in updating and attributions. *Journal of Experimental Social Psychology*, 101, 104310. DOI: 10.1016/j.jesp.2022.104310

Koh, F. H., Ladlad, J., Foo, F.-J., Tan, W. J., Sivarajah, S. S., Ho, L. M. L., Ng, J.-L., Koh, F. H., Chong, C., Aw, D., Kam, J.-H., Tan, A. Y. H., Tan, C.-C., Yeung, B. P. M., Wong, W.-K., Toh, B.-C., Ladlad, J., Barco, J., Chue, K.-M., & Foo, F.-J. (2023). Real-time artificial intelligence (AI)-aided endoscopy improves adenoma detection rates even in experienced endoscopists: A cohort study in Singapore. *Surgical Endoscopy*, 37(1), 165–171. DOI: 10.1007/s00464-022-09470-w PMID: 35882667

Kumar, P., Kumar, D., & Kumar, N. (2014). E-Governance in India: Definitions, Challenges and Solutions. *International Journal of Computer Applications*, 101(16), 6–8. DOI: 10.5120/17769-7408

Linders, D. (2012). From e-government to we-government: Defining a typology for citizen coproduction in the age of social media. *Government Information Quarterly*, 29(4), 446–454. DOI: 10.1016/j.giq.2012.06.003

Lips, M. (2024). Digital transformation in the public sector. In Verhoest, K., Hammerschmid, G., Rykkja, L. H., & Klijn, E. H. (Eds.), *Collaborating for Digital Transformation* (pp. 13–30). Edward Elgar Publishing., DOI: 10.4337/9781803923895.00010

Loi, M., & Spielkamp, M. (2021). Towards Accountability in the Use of Artificial Intelligence for Public Administrations. *Proceedings of the 2021 AAAI/ACM Conference on AI, Ethics, and Society*, 757–766. DOI: 10.1145/3461702.3462631

Luna-Reyes, L. F., & Gil-Garcia, J. R. (2014). Digital government transformation and internet portals: The co-evolution of technology, organizations, and institutions. *Government Information Quarterly*, 31(4), 545–555. DOI: 10.1016/j.giq.2014.08.001

Margets, H., & Dorobantu, C. (2019). Rethink government with AI. *Nature*, 568(7751), 163–165. DOI: 10.1038/d41586-019-01099-5 PMID: 30967667

Margetts, H., & Dunleavy, P. (2013). The second wave of digital-era governance: A quasi-paradigm for government on the Web. *Philosophical Transactions of the Royal Society A: Mathematical, Physical and Engineering Sciences, 371*(1987), 20120382. DOI: 10.1098/rsta.2012.0382

Misuraca, G., & Viscusi, G. (2014). *Digital governance in the public sector: Challenging the policy-maker's innovation dilemma* (I. Proceedings, Ed.; pp. 146–154). of the 8th International Conference on Theory and Practice of Electronic Governance. ACM.

Nam, T. (2019). Does E-Government Raise Effectiveness and Efficiency?: Examining the Cross-National Effect. *Journal of Global Information Management*, 27(3), 120–138. DOI: 10.4018/JGIM.2019070107

Netten, N., Bargh, M. S., Van Den Braak, S., Choenni, S., & Leeuw, F. (2016). On Enabling Smart Government: A Legal Logistics Framework for Future Criminal Justice Systems. *Proceedings of the 17th International Digital Government Research Conference on Digital Government Research*, 293–302. DOI: 10.1145/2912160.2912180

Nobles, C. (2024). The Weaponization of Artificial Intelligence in Cybersecurity: A Systematic Review. *Procedia Computer Science*, 239, 547–555. DOI: 10.1016/j.procs.2024.06.206

Novelli, C., Taddeo, M., & Floridi, L. (2024). Accountability in artificial intelligence: What it is and how it works. *AI & Society*, 39(4), 1871–1882. DOI: 10.1007/s00146-023-01635-y

OECD. (2024). *AI principles*. OECD. https://www.oecd.org/en/topics/ai-principles.html

Oh, P., & Jung, Y. (2023). A machine-learning approach to assessing public trust in AI-powered technologies. In Nah, S. (Ed.), *Research Handbook on Artificial Intelligence and Communication* (pp. 193–213). Edward Elgar Publishing., DOI: 10.4337/9781803920306.00021

Papadouli, D. J. V. (2022). *Transparency in Artificial Intelligence: A Legal Perspective. 4.*

Prunkl, C. (2024). Human Autonomy at Risk? An Analysis of the Challenges from AI. *Minds and Machines*, 34(3), 26. DOI: 10.1007/s11023-024-09665-1

Qin, H., & Li, Z. (2024). *A Study on Enhancing Government Efficiency and Public Trust: The Transformative Role of Artificial Intelligence and Large Language Models*. DOI: 10.5281/ZENODO.12619360

Rani, M. (2024). Impacts and ethics of using Artificial Intelligence (AI) by the Indian Police. *Public Administration and Policy*, 27(2), 182–192. DOI: 10.1108/PAP-06-2023-0081

Rawashdeh, A. (2023). The consequences of artificial intelligence: An investigation into the impact of AI on job displacement in accounting. *Journal of Science and Technology Policy Management*. DOI: 10.1108/JSTPM-02-2023-0030

Robertson, C., & Ridge-Newman, A. (2022). The Potential of Artificial Intelligence to Rejuvenate Public Trust in Journalism. In Manninen, V. J. E., Niemi, M. K., & Ridge-Newman, A. (Eds.), *Futures of Journalism* (pp. 127–142). Springer International Publishing., DOI: 10.1007/978-3-030-95073-6_9

Robles, P., & Mallinson, D. J. (2023). Artificial intelligence technology, public trust, and effective governance. *Review of Policy Research*, ropr.12555. DOI: 10.1111/ropr.12555

Savoldelli, A., Misuraca, G., & Codagnone, C. (2013). Measuring the Public value of e-Government: The eGEP2. 0 model. *Electronic Journal of E-Government*, 11(1), 373–388.

Shan, Y., Ji, M., Xie, W., Lam, K.-Y., & Chow, C.-Y. (2022). Public Trust in Artificial Intelligence Applications in Mental Health Care: Topic Modeling Analysis. *JMIR Human Factors*, 9(4), e38799. DOI: 10.2196/38799 PMID: 36459412

Ta, A. W. A., Goh, H. L., Ang, C., Koh, L. Y., Poon, K., & Miller, S. M. (2022). Two Singapore public healthcare AI applications for national screening programs and other examples. *Health Care Science*, 1(2), 41–57. DOI: 10.1002/hcs2.10 PMID: 38938890

Tiwari, R. (2023). The Impact of AI and Machine Learning on Job Displacement and Employment Opportunities. *INTERANTIONAL JOURNAL OF SCIENTIFIC RESEARCH IN ENGINEERING AND MANAGEMENT*, 07(01). Advance online publication. DOI: 10.55041/IJSREM17506

Varona, D., & Suárez, J. L. (2022). Discrimination, Bias, Fairness, and Trustworthy AI. *Applied Sciences (Basel, Switzerland)*, 12(12), 5826. DOI: 10.3390/app12125826

Vlahovic, N., & Vracic, T. (2015). An Overview of E-Government 3.0 Implementation. *In Encyclopedia of Information Science and Technology, Third Edition (p*, 2700–2708. Zhang, Z., Chen, Z., & Xu, L. (2022). Artificial intelligence and moral dilemmas: Perception of ethical decision-making in AI. *Journal of Experimental Social Psychology, 101*, 104327. DOI: 10.1016/j.jesp.2022.104327

ADDITIONAL READINGS

Acemoglu, D., & Restrepo, P. (2018). The Race between Man and Machine: Implications of Technology for Growth, Factor Shares, and Employment. *The American Economic Review*, 108(6), 1488–1542. DOI: 10.1257/aer.20160696

Al Thani, D., Hassan, A., Chalghoumi, H., Othman, A., & Hammad, S. (2021). Addressing the Digital Gap for the Older Persons and their caregivers in the State of Qatar: A Stakeholders' Perspective. *2021 8th International Conference on ICT & Accessibility (ICTA)*, 01–06. DOI: 10.1109/ICTA54582.2021.9809430

De Vries, H., Bekkers, V., & Tummers, L. (2016). Innovation in The Public Sector: A Systematic Review and Future Research Agenda. *Public Administration*, 94(1), 146–166. DOI: 10.1111/padm.12209

Gobble, M. M. (2016). Defining disruptive innovation. *Research Technology Management*, 59(4), 34–46. DOI: 10.1080/08956308.2016.1185347

Grozea, I.-L., & Troancă, D. (2023). Digital Transformation and the Financial Sector: A Comprehensive Perspective. *Sciendo*, 56(2), 56–63. DOI: 10.2478/saec-2023-0018

Hatsu, S., & Ngassam, E. K. (2016). A framework for the monitoring and evaluation of e-governance projects in developing countries. *2016 IST-Africa Week Conference*, 1–7. DOI: 10.1109/ISTAFRICA.2016.7530619

Hinings, B., Gegenhuber, T., & Greenwood, R. (2018). Digital innovation and transformation: An institutional perspective. *Information and Organization*, 28(1), 52–61. DOI: 10.1016/j.infoandorg.2018.02.004

Janowski, T. (2015). Digital government evolution: From transformation to contextualization. *Government Information Quarterly*, 32(3), 221–236. DOI: 10.1016/j.giq.2015.07.001

Rykkja, H. L., Hammerschmid, G., Hans Klijn, E., & Verhoest, K. (2024). Introduction: Collaborating for digital transformation in the public sector. In K. Verhoest, G. Hammerschmid, L. H. Rykkja, & E. H. Klijn (Eds.), *Collaborating for Digital Transformation* (pp. 2–12). Edward Elgar Publishing. DOI: 10.4337/9781803923895.00009

Yassin, F. E., & El Nahlawy, H. (2023). *Driving digital transformation in the Arab region.* UNDP. https://www.undp.org/arab-states/stories/driving-digital-transformation-arab-region

Chapter 14
Impact of Digital Technologies on Tourist Arrival in Selected Economies

Meenakshi Gupta
https://orcid.org/0000-0002-7866-4961
Department of Economics, Faculty of Management, Shri Mata Vaishno Devi University, Katra, India

Bhoomika Sharma
Department of Economics, Faculty of Management, Shri Mata Vaishno Devi University, Katra, India

Ajay Kumar Singh
https://orcid.org/0000-0003-0429-0925
Department of Humanities and Social Sciences, Graphic Era University, Dehradun, India

ABSTRACT

This chapter assesses the significance of digital technologies on tourist arrivals in Australia, France, India, Italy, Japan and Saudi Arabia during 2009 – 2020. It developed a linear regression equation to observe role of digital technologies in tourism sector. The results based on Panel FGLS model infer that broadband subscription, use of internet, IT investment and mobile phone subscription showed a significant impact on tourist arrivals. Digital technologies like broadband subscription, internet access, internet expenditure and mobile subscription are essential to promote tourism sector. It suggests policy implications to increase digital technologies for further development of the tourism industries. Digital technologies are also positive

DOI: 10.4018/979-8-3693-7678-2.ch014

to increase smart tourism, and sustainable development in these countries. Smart tourism is favourable for achieving SDGs in the mentioned countries. Scope of further research directions in the area of digital technologies and tourism industries are also identified in this chapter.

1. INTRODUCTION

Digital technologies are crucial tools for increasing social and economic development through creating new business, new products, new markets, and increasing customer and producers' relationship (Bak et al., 2022; Singh et al., 2023). Hence, digital technologies are supportive to create growth opportunities in multiple sectors including, social communication, education tourism and transport, and green growth (Jiang & Phoong, 2023; Jyoti & Singh, 2023). Digital technologies are also crucial drivers to increase sustainability in the resources (Singh, 2025). Singh et al. (2024e) found a crucial impact of digitalization on environmental sustainability across countries. Digital technologies are also bringing innovation and new growth opportunities in the tourism sector (Li et al., 2023). These are also worthy for tourists to make their travel plan with minimum costs. Use of digital technologies help to increase the movement of a country towards a digital economy. Digital economy is supportive to increase tourism development effectively (Tang, 2023). Digital economy is also playing a prime role to enhance the tourism industry and its sustainability (Barashok et al., 2021). Digital technologies are also helping to create a digital platform for campaigning of political parties in elections (Alhaimer, 2023).

Digital technologies develop an online ecosystem to meet the diverse requirements of travellers to make travel plans and can book travel tickets, and hotels. Digital technologies also enhance green growth (Singh et al., 2024b). Behra et al. (2023) investigated the understanding of domestic and foreign tourists towards green hotels in india. Further, the tourism sector is playing a positive and significant role for improving livelihood security and social welfare of the people. Tourism is a situation which provides the motivation of individuals to be moved from one geographical location to another for entertainment purpose or cultural or religious purpose (Hamid et al., 2021). Tourism industry also generates foreign revenue for the government and creates infrastructural development. It is a significant driver to increase inclusion in the cultures of different communities. Digitalization also attracts FDI that will also boost the tourism sector (Singh & Kumar, 2022). Digitalization nurtures a favourable benefit for the tourism sector and its growth (Barashok et al., 2021). The growth and development of the tourism industry depend on multiple indicators including ICT, social security and legal protection, infrastructural development, government policies, and globalization. Further, the growth of tourism industries is highly imperative to make a holistic change in social, economic and cultural sectors (Barashok et al., 2021).

The development of the tourism industry has significantly increased after globalization worldwide. Tourism is a key service industry and it is a vital strategy for promoting global economic growth and development (Selimi et al., 2017). Tourism created through digitalization may be more effective to increase social development, and participation of tourists in digital technologies (Jiang & Phoong, 2023). Tourism industry has a positive impact on domestic consumption and foreign exchange earnings. It also helps to reduce unemployment, poverty and income inequality (Steiner, 2006). Tourism is a significant activity to generate foreign exchange and employment in many developing countries (Lopez-Cordova, 2020). Digitalization also creates new markets for better growth of the tourism sector. Human and physical capital also improve as growth and volume of the tourism industry increases (Hye & Khan, 2012). It is also evidence of a snowball effect of economic growth on the tourism sector (Honey, 2009; Selimi et al., 2017). This occurs when new tourist sites are developed that also create new enterprises and non- governmental organizations. As a result, providing tourism services is a key activity for stimulating the economic growth of a nation (Selimi et al., 2017).

Recently, research on tourism has focused on the newly created usage of high technology such as smartphones, apps, and virtual reality for marketing objectives. The use of virtual reality constitutes one of most innovative media among the numerous other uses. Nowadays, the tourism sector is highly dependent on the application of ICT and other digital technologies (Iorio et al., 2020). Internet and mobile technologies are playing an effective role to increase the success of this sector (Bak et al., 2022). The dependency of foreign travellers on digital platforms are also significantly increased worldwide (Lopez-Cordova, 2020). Digital platforms could be helpful to reduce the cost of travel tickets and it also minimize the time of traveller to decide a place for visits (Lopez-Cordova, 2020). These technologies also promote smart tourism. Hence, rapid technological development is essential to increase smart tourism (Tee, 2024). Smart tourism works as a crucial tool to sustain a dynamic tourism ecosystem (Tee, 2024). It is also associated with better experience of tourists, and maintains digital connectivity and sustainability (Tee, 2024). However, inequalities in digital technologies may be caused to reduce growth of the tourism sector across countries. Tourism is a significant industry that is also adopting e-tourism (Li et al., 2023). The term smart tourism reflects the present state of tourism development and it also provides appropriate facilities to the travellers (Xiang & Fesenmaier, 2017). Smart tourism is also highly information intensive due to its huge dependency on ICT and other digital devices. The use of ICT facilitates easy access to information which is an essential feature of smart tourism (Zhou & Li, 2012). ICT, thus, changed the development of the tourism sector worldwide (Bak et al., 2022). It comprises smart tourist destinations, smart businesses and smart experiences (Singh & Jyoti, 2023b).

Smart tourism is helpful to increase the reliance of tourists on ICT (Gretzel et al., 2015). Integration of ICT with digital and physical tourism infrastructure is essential for sustainable growth of the tourism industry. Sustainable growth of this industry also leads to an increased green tourism industry. While the green tourism industry would be useful to increase sustainable development in future. This increases the attractiveness of tourist destinations due to more convenience, personalization, interaction and efficiency thereby attracting more visitors. ICT in the tourism sector promotes most SDGs directly or indirectly. It creates more job opportunities; thus, it is contributing to poverty reduction (SDG1). Lopez-Cordova (2020) also claimed that digital tools help to increase employment and contribute to increase GDP. It also promotes SDG3 and SDG4 through investment in health and education. Business organizations created through ICT ensure decent work for people through development of online job platforms (Singh & Jyoti, 2023d). These organizations also use ICT for marketing and promotion that attracts tourists and thus increase their revenues.

Digital technologies also stimulate economic growth and contribute to the achievement of SDG8. Similarly, to support ICT-based tourism services, both public and private investment is done in improving the digital infrastructure viz., internet, mobile networks, and broadband connectivity. Thus, tourism industries also contribute towards SDG9 and SDG17. Besides, it also contributes to SDG12 by promoting responsible consumption by encouraging the use of online booking systems prioritizing eco-friendly tourism practices. Moreover, with the use of ICT in this sector, data on tourist behaviour, resource usage and environmental effects can be collected and analysed. This can also provide feedback to different stakeholders of the sector that may empower them to make well- informed decisions that favour SDG11 (sustainable cities and communities) and SDG13 (adapt to climate change) (Singh & Jyoti, 2023a; Singh, 2020). Furthermore, it enables collaboration and communication among different stakeholders and communities. Thus, the tourism sector also promotes SDG5 (social inclusion) and SDG10 (reduced inequality) (Bak et al., 2022).

Objectives and Scope of this Chapter

While going through the literature, ICT in the tourism sector has brought challenges along with opportunities (Buhalis & Law, 2008; Egge et al., 2020; Gretzel et al., 2020; Gursoy et al., 2022; Pencarelli, 2020). However, past literature could not highlight the drawback of tourism industries. Also, earlier scholars did not explore the implications of different digital technologies on the tourism sector. Hence, this chapter is an attempt to find out how ICT contributes to the tourism sector in the selected economies? Accordingly, it examines the impact of different digital technologies on the tourism sector in selected countries using the EGLS model. Thereupon, it also suggests policy proposals to increase the development of the tourism sector. Finally, it also describes further research direction in the tourism sector and its affecting activities. The scope of this chapter is not concise in digital technologies and its association with the tourism sector. The chapter makes an interconnection of digital technologies with the tourism sector. Thereupon, it makes a conceptual framework to observe the association of the tourism sector with SDGs.

2. REVIEW OF LITERATURE

Tourism sector is essential for increasing the economic growth and development through creating employment opportunities and increasing foreign reserves (Bak et al., 2022). In the context of African countries, Fayissa et al. (2007) reported a positive implication of the tourism sector on economic growth. Tourism industry contributes a significant share in GDP, job creation and provides foreign exchange in the world (Lopez-Cordova, 2020). Similar association between tourism sector and economic growth is also detected by Samimi et al. (2011) in developing countries. Mishra et al. (2011) also found a causal association between tourism sector and economic growth in India. Existing studies also claimed that tourism industries bring multiple opportunities to reduce poverty income inequalities and social diversity (Steiner, 2006). Tourism may be significant to increase financial development and velocity of money. For instance, it is a fast-growing industry and helps to increase the economic growth and social welfare of communities in India (Venkatesh et al., 2016). Tourism sector is beneficial to increase infrastructural development, money flow and promote new management practices in the environmental sector (Shiji, 2016). Butler (2015) also highlighted that increasing equipment, infrastructure, and basic amenities in the tourism sector due to digitalization. Hence, the tourism sector has provided huge benefits in the past three decades across countries. Higham et al. (2013) examined the psychological and social factors leading to tourist mobility.

Tourism sector also enhances development of hotels, resorts, and restaurants, healthcare facilities, and transport infrastructure i.e., road, shipping, aviation and railways. The tourism industry depends on multiple activities like geographical location, weather conditions, social safety, government norms, easy transport, destination loyalty, and hotel availability (Chen & Gursoy, 2001). Per capita income is a significant driver that provides the motivation to increase travel plans. Tourism motivation also promotes tourism industries and it also provides the sustainable growth of the tourism sector (Vila et al., 2024). Foreign exchange earnings also lead to increased tourism industries. Exports also lead to increased employment and competition across firms. It also enhances investment and technological advancement. Culture, heritage and landscape also attract tourists to travel in other countries (Vila et al., 2024). Destination choice has now become a crucial aspect in tourism marketing which in turn leads to tourist satisfaction. Choice of the destination and spots has now been an important decision being discussed by various researchers (Ajzen & Driver, 1992; Chen, 2001; Fesenmaier, 1988; Um & Crompton, 1990).

Indian tourism marketers are based on traditional techniques (Ahmed & Krohan, 1992). In the modern day, technology is transforming the traditional tourist experience. The quick growth of digital technologies like artificial intelligence, ICT, mobile apps are promoting the digital economy (Brennen & Kreiss, 2016). The "ubiquity" of the internet has been facilitated by its growing use (Robert et al., 2021). The internet-based economy has a power to alter the rate of expansion of the world economy and increase all factors' productivity (Hu et al., 2021).

Internet and information technologies work as crucial drivers to increase appropriate marketing, and increase communication among the suppliers, consumers and suppliers (Li et al., 2023). Information technology (IT) is useful to increase tourism marketing, distribution and promotion of the tourism sector (Bayram, 2020). IT is significant for selecting the management way in the tourism sector (Bayram, 2020). The internet and social media are crucial to increase communication among the people (Hoffman, 2000; Gozgor et al., 2024). Social media could be an effective and risk minimise medium for communication during COVID-19 (Alhaimer, 2023). Social media is a medicator to increase the interaction among the producers and consumers in the tourism and other industries (Bak et al., 2022; Singh et al., 2024c), and it also boosts business opportunities (Singh et al., 2024c). These technologies also promote e-tourism and maintain the commercial link across tourism traders (Li et al., 2023). Bak et al. (2022) examined the implications of ICT on operation of the tourism sector in European countries.

ICT also seemed useful to increase transportation, leisure and hospitality. The efficiency of the tourism sector also improved with the use of ICT tools. Hence, ICT has changed human life (Egger et al., 2020). Barashok et al. (2021) also noted the significant contribution of digitalization in the tourism sector. Digitalization appears useful to increase sustainability of tourism business. Most countries are focusing on and developing the digital economy as a component that promotes growth (Nakatani, 2021). Digital economy is playing a positive role in increasing the economic power of development (Hu et al., 2021). Based on estimates from the World Bank, the digital economy today accounts for 15% of all global GDP and it has expanded at a rate of 2.5 times greater than the GDP of the real world over the past 10 years.

Within a few years, the mysterious computers that once took up entire rooms evolved into vital instruments for several businesses. Compared to earlier traditional techniques, computer-enforced labour procedures took greatly less time, and data retrieval, organization, and storage became easier. A worldwide information flow mechanism could be achieved using computer networking. Since the development of written media, the internet has been the most significant invention (Hoffman, 2000). The travel industry has effectively entered a new phase with the advent of digital technology: the digital technology tourism age. According to researchers, according to the UN Secretary-General of the International Digital Cooperative Organization (DCO), the digital economy would have grown to 30% of the world GDP and employ 30 million people by 2030.

In both wealthy and developing countries, the digital economy has expanded to various degrees, helping in the economic recovery and bridging the gap between them (Kononova et al., 2021; Kononova et al., 2020). The digital marketplace is expected to expand at the fastest rate in the years to come and have the greatest upside due to its reliance on constantly evolving technology for the Internet, equitable development, and creative business models (Jinghua & Xianmei, 2021). Technological adoption is also helpful to address the issues of climate change in agricultural and other sectors (Singh et al., 2020). It's also essential for achieving rapid economic development.

Massive amounts of data, short films, and the use of virtual reality are creating new tourism industries that accelerate the creation of individualized consumption modes and creative tourism consumption scenarios, coinciding with a shift in how humans interact and consume. The tourism industry is greatly benefited by these improvements (Maslova et al., 2020).

Lopez-Cordova (2020) also recognized a remarkable impact of digital tools on tourism. Adoption of digital platforms by consumers and services providers are supportive to increase international travel (Lopez-Cordova, 2020). Digital platforms could be effective to reduce the costs of traveling. Jiang and Phoong (2023) assessed the impact of digitalization on the tourism sector and it reported that digitalization appeared to increase product development, tourism consumption and industrial development. Tang (2023) examined the impact of digital technology on tourism development in the United Kingdom. It observed that the regional growth of the tourism sector improved due to transformation of the digital economy. Archi et al. (2023) highlighted the role of digital technologies in sustainable growth of the tourism sector using bibliometric analysis.

Ethical and Regulatory Challenges posed by digital technologies: The use of digital technologies has given rise to digital inequality. Tang (2023) emphasizes the significance of accessibility. It has been argued that digital platforms have the potential to further worsen inequality by denying opportunities to those who are already at risk (Lopez-Cordova 2020). Furthermore, it also raises the issues of privacy. Customers frequently have little influence over how these digital platforms use their personal data, so they feel insecure. By analysing the role of public trust in digital governance, Alhaimer (2024) argued that as more services are moved online, trust becomes a critical issue. Solove (2006) deliberated over the risk of data breaches along with privacy concerns. The rise of cyber threats is another issue in digitalization. It is essential to practice ethical considerations in cyber security to mitigate financial risks (Anderson & Moore, 2006). AI and other advanced tools have also posed a threat to the traditional job market (Brynjolfsson & McAfee, 2014).

Environmental and Socio-Political Costs of tourism: Sustainability is another issue in digitalization. In their study on tourist sustainability, Archi et al. (2023) showed how digital platforms can either facilitate or hinder sustainable behaviours? This study also argued that although technology can improve visitor experiences and maximize resource utilization but poor management of it can also result in environmental degradation due to over tourism The literature highlights that the increased visitors disturb the local ecosystem and results in loss of biodiversity (Higham et al., 2014). Thus, extensive tourism may increase ecological footprint and carbon footprint. Moreover, a great inflow of tourists generates increased waste and it contributes to pollution (Gössling *et al.,* 2012). It also strains local resources. Behra and Jatav (2022) examined the waste management practices in small hotels in India. Water shortages in some places are caused by tourists' excessive use, which affects local and natural ecosystems (Peeters et al., 2018). Tourism sector also has a significant implication of fresh water consumption (Gössling et al., 2012). The literature also highlights that it can worsen the climate change effects as the tourism sector is a significant contributor of GHGs (IPCC, 2018). Thus, it has adverse impact on livelihood security of people in all sectors (Singh et al. 2019). Though the impacts of over tourism are primarily environmental, however, the impacts can be extended to cultural and social dimensions also. Digital platforms increase cultural understanding and in turn foster community engagement and intercultural dialogue (Cohen & Cohen, 2012). Moreover, it enables local stakeholders to participate in tourism decision making, thus highlighting social equity (Wanjiru & Liu, 2018). The use of digital can also shape political landscapes (Alhaimer, 2023). Destinations that use digital tools can better address the needs of the tourists and thus it leads to improved political accountability and governance.

Table 1 presents the summary of relevant literature in the area of digital technologies and their implications of tourism sectors in different countries.

Table 1. Summary of relevant review of literature

Author(s)	Study Area	Main Objectives	*DVs/IVs*/Methods	Main Findings
Fayissa et al. (2007)	42 African countries	Impact of tourism sector on GDP	OLS and GLS model	Tourism sector is positive to increase GDP
Mishra et al. (2011)	India	Association of tourism and economic growth	Granger causality test	Tourism sector is favourable to increase economic growth
Hye and Khan (2012)	Pakistan	Relationship between tourism and economic growth	ARDL model	Tourism sector have positive impact on economic growth
Kuang and Tsai (2016)	Taiwan	Role of tourism sector in economic growth	Quantile regression model	Positive impact of tourism sector on economic growth
Selimi et al. (2017)	Developing countries	Impact of tourism development on economic growth	P-VAR approach	Positive association between tourism development and economic growth
Zhuo et al. (2017)	China	Association of tourism specialization and economic growth	Linear regression model	It is non-linear association between tourism sector and economic growth
Sharma (2018)	India	Causal association between tourism receipts and economic growth	Augmented Dickey-Fuller (ADF) test	It is a unidirectional relationship between tourism sector and economic growth
Midoun and Nardjess (2019)	Maghreb countries	Association of tourism inflows and GDP	Regression analysis	Tourism inflows is positive to increase economic growth
Bayram (2020)	Across countries	Implication of information technology (IT) on tourism	Review of literature	IT created new application areas for tourism industry
Kumar Shekhar (2020)	India	Examine tourism industry affecting factors as giving more focus on digitalization	Social media, digitalization	Social media is crucial contributor to increase use of digitalization in tourism sector
Barashok et al. (2021)	Across countries	Examine the role of digitalization in the tourism sector	Review of literature	Digitalization is seemed favourable to increase tourism business more flexible
Bak et al. (2022)	European countries	Examine the contribution of ICT in the operation of tourism sector	Review of literature	ICT could be helpful to make the significant changes in the tourism sector
Tang (2023)	United Kingdom	Examine the impact of digital economy on tourism development	Linear regression model	Regional growth of tourism development increased due to digital economy

continued on following page

Table 1. Continued

Author(s)	Study Area	Main Objectives	*DVs/IVs*/Methods	Main Findings
Archi et al. (2023)	Across countries	Explore the role of adoption of digital technologies in sustainable tourism	Bibliometric analysis	Digital technologies are conducive to increase tourism industries
Alhaimer (2023)	Kuwait	Examine the role of virtual platform in political election	Descriptive analysis	Virtual platform could be useful for political parties in election campaigns.
Jiang and Phoong (2023)	Across countries	Digitalization and sustainability in tourism sector	Systematic review of existing literature	Digitalization is useful to increase industrial development in tourism sector
Gozgor et al. (2024)	151 countries	Assess the contribution of digital governance in tourism sector	Fixed-effect model	Social media monitoring hinders inbound tourism.

Source: Author's compilation as per the findings of previous literature.

3. RESEARCH METHODOLOGY

3.1. Study Area and Data Sources

This chapter includes Australia, France, India, Italy, Japan and Saudi Arabia. These countries are selected as per the number of international tourists, percentage share of revenue generated through tourism, and share of tourism revenue in gross national income. These are the most popular travel countries in the world. Australia has a good reputation for tourists and it provides safety to them. Australia provides the working visa to the tourists without any complication. Sydney, Melbourne, Brisbane, Perth and Adelaide are major cities of Austria in which most tourists visit throughout the year. France has 1st rank in the tourism sector in the world. Paris is a famous city for international tourists in France. The country generates the largest revenue through tourism sectors as compared to other countries. India is also a good place for international tourists and it has 15th position to attract the perception of international tourists to visit in this country.

Figure 1. Number of tourists arrivals (in Million) (https://www.worlddata.info/tourism.php)

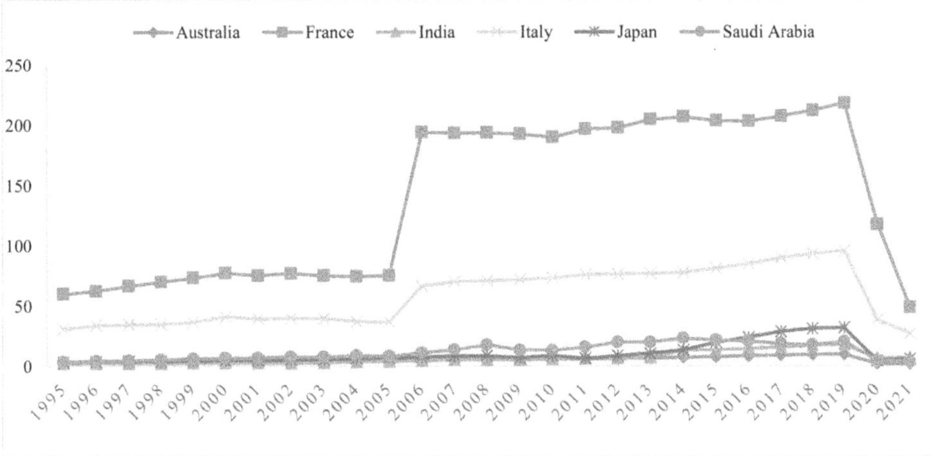

India has a good position in the development of the tourism sector among the G20 region. Japan has 5th ranking for providing a destination to international tourists. Japan has 29th ranking in the absolute term of international tourists. Tokyo and Osaka are the prime cities for international travellers in Japan. Saudi Arabia has 25th ranking in the number of international tourists. Saudi Arabia also generates significant revenue through international travellers. The progress of these countries in various indicators of the tourism sector is provided in Figure 1, Figure 2 and Figure 3. Figure 1 explores the trend in the number of tourist arrivals in the above-mentioned countries. Figure 2 explains the trend in the revenue generated through the tourism sector in the undertaken countries. The percentage share of the tourism sector in gross national product (GNP) of these countries is presented in Figure 3. These figures demonstrated the development of the tourism sector in these countries consistently increased during 2000 – 2019. However, the number of tourist arrivals and percentage share of the tourism sector in GNP of these countries declined after 2019 due to COVID-19 pandemics.

Figure 2. Revenue received through international tourists' arrivals (in Billion US$) (https://www.worlddata.info/tourism.php)

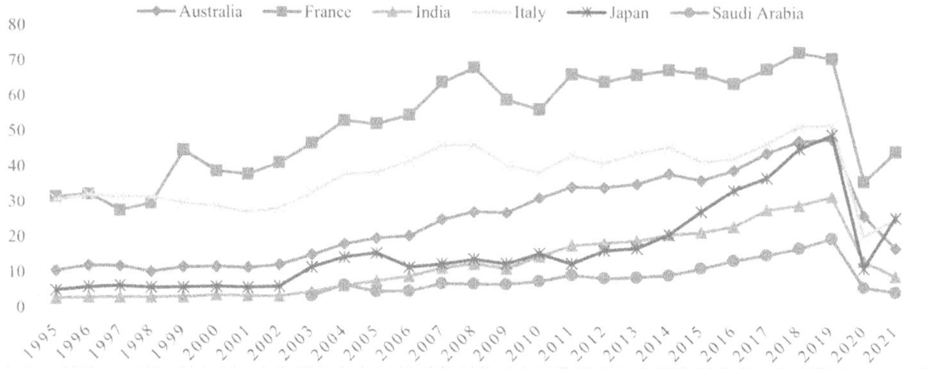

Figure 3. Percentage share of tourism sector in GNP (https://www.worlddata.info/tourism.php)

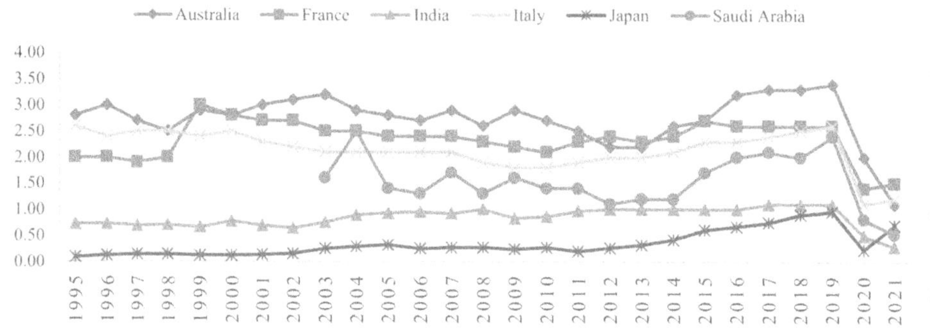

The useful statistical data for selected variables is taken from secondary sources. The secondary data for this chapter is taken from the following databases: The World Bank Group (World Bank Group - International Development, Poverty, & Sustainability), Our World in Data (Our World in Data) & Data.gov.in (Home | Open Government Data (OGD) Platform India), and https://www.worlddata.info/tourism.php.

3.2. Explanation of Variables

The chapter used the number of tourist arrivals (*ARRIVAL*) as dependent variable in the statistical analysis. The variable is considered as a proxy indicator to explain the progress of tourism industries in selected countries. While some certain indicators in the area of digital technologies are composed as independent variables. Broadband subscription, internet access, internet expenditure, mobile subscription and automated teller machine have significant influence on the tourism sector (Singh & Jyoti, 2023a; Gozgor et al., 2024). These are the crucial indicators to create a favourable digital platform in a country. Hence, these variables are applied as independent variables in this research. The description of variables is highlighted in Table 2. The rationality of the above-mentioned variables is explained as:

Table 2. Description of variables

Variable	Description	Source
ln(BBSUB)	Broadband Subscriptions	Our World in Data
ln(INTERNET)	Internet Access	The World Bank Group
ln(INTEXP)	Internet Expenditure	Our World in Data
ln(MOBSUB)	Mobile Subscription	Our World in Data
ln(ATM)	Automated Teller Machine	Our World in Data
ln(ARRIVAL)	The Tourist's Arrival	The World Bank Group

Source: Author's compilation.

***Tourist Arrival* (*ARRIVAL*):** The earlier studies considered different variables to define the development of the tourism sector (Sharma, 2018). Sharma (2018) considered tourism receipts; Midoun and Nardjess (2019) applied tourist inflows as proxy variables for tourism industries. Lopez-Cordova (2020) also detects the association of tourist arrival and size of travel. Statistical data on this variable for selected countries are available during 2009 to 2020. It offers detailed information of travel patterns and tourism developments in these economies. It also shows how the development of infrastructure and transportation has attracted the tourists in these countries. It also indicates the evolution of developing nations through tourism development and the influence of various favourable policies, technology use and other innovations on travel and sustainable tourism (Archi et al., 2023). Thus, tourism arrival is an important variable to realize the functioning of the tourism sector in a country (Zhuo et al., 2017). Zhuo et al. (2017) also used the percentage share of tourists in total population for tourism specialization. Accordingly, Zhuo et al. (2017) studied the association of tourism specialization with economic growth in China.

***Broadband Subscription* (*BBSUB*):** This is an important variable in the era of digitalization. It is also a useful digital technology (Singh et al., 2023). The data on this variable indicates the role of internet connectivity on tourist behaviour and destination choices. It also reflects the dependency of people on the internet for making their travelling plans. Increased digital involvement by travellers is linked to higher rates of broadband adoption, which can have an effect on marketing tactics, visitor experiences, and the competitiveness of travel destinations. Using this data, policymakers and stakeholders in the tourism industry may improve digital infrastructure, advertise online for tourism- related products and services, and guarantee that travellers from all backgrounds have greater access to travel information.

***Internet Access* (*INTERNET*):** Internet accessibility is also vital to promote digitalization (Lopez-Cordova, 2020). Accessibility of the internet could be useful to increase the participation of economic agents in marketing (Bak et al., 2022; Tang, 2023). Internet usage has a big impact on tourism. It also has an influence on the tourism industry and destination experiences of tourists. Reliability in internet connectivity draws in tech-savvy tourists and raises visitor satisfaction. Additionally, internet connectivity promotes digital marketing initiatives, facilitates contact between travellers and service providers, and increases traveller spending. Ensuring fair tourist opportunities for all requires addressing inequities in access.

***Internet Expenditure* (*INTEXP*):** Tourism internet expenditure pertains to the total amount of money that travellers spend on internet-related amenities and services while on vacation. This includes payments for digital entertainment, mobile apps, Wi-Fi access, and internet-connected destinations. As travellers depend more on technology for planning and interaction, internet expenditure has grown to be a substantial portion of total travel expenses. Tech-savvy tourists can be drawn to businesses or destinations that offer dependable internet access and digital service access, which can enhance their overall experience. Revenue from tourism can also be increased by using digital marketing strategies and online booking platforms. Hence, internet expenditure is also helpful to promote tourism industries.

***Mobile Subscription* (*MOBSUB*):** Using this variable as an independent variable will indicate the available connectivity level to tourists (Tang, 2023). If there are more mobile subscriptions, then there is better access to communication (Singh & Jyoti, 2023a). Thus, it has a significant influence on travel decisions. This can also help to track the tourist movement and behaviour. It offers insights into tourist choices and possible opportunities for investment in the tourism sector.

Automated Teller Machine (*ATM*): ATMs in the travel industry are a dual-edged hazard in terms of digitization. On the one hand, they restrict digital payment methods by maintaining the reliance on cash and transaction fees. However, they are accessible in places without digital infrastructure and give tourists a recognizable way to make payments. ATMs continue to be essential for guaranteeing banking accessibility and security despite their errors, especially in areas with a lack of digital infrastructure. Hence, it is also working as a crucial tool to promote tourism industries effectively.

3.3. Model Specification

Previous studies used diverse forms of empirical models to assess the impact of tourism on economic growth (Samimi et al., 2011). Fayissa et al. (2007) applied OLS and GLS model to explore the impact of tourism on GDP in African countries. Samimi et al. (2011) pursued a P-VAR approach to examine the association of tourism development with economic growth. Hye and Khan (2012) applied ARDL model to explore the relationship between tourism and economic growth in Pakistan. Kuang and Tsai (2016) also examined the association of tourism sector with economic growth using quantile regression model. Zhuo et al. (2017) preferred linear regression model to explore the association between tourism specialization and economic growth in China. Thereupon, Tang (2023); Gozgor et al. (2024) also applied various forms of empirical model to analysis the impact of digital technologies and digital governance on tourism sector.

For developing an empirical model, the chapter assumes that digital connection metrics including the density of ATMs, internet expenses, broadband subscriptions, internet access, and mobile subscriptions have a greater influence on travel plan of tourists. These variables also affect travel plans, destination preferences and spending patterns of the number of tourists who arrive in a specific country. Therefore, investments like digital infrastructure can be given top priority by policymakers and the reason is to improve visitor experiences. Following regression equation is adopted to examine the impact of aforesaid variables on number of tourist arrivals:

$$ln(ARRIVAL)_{it}$$

$$= \alpha + \beta_1 ln(BBSUB)_{it} + \beta_2 ln(INTERNET)_{it} + \beta_3 ln(\text{INTEXP})_{it} + \beta_4 ln(MOBSUB)_{it} + \beta_5 ln(ATM)_{it} + \mu_i + \nu_t + \varepsilon_{it} \quad (1)$$

The above specified model is used to examine the impact of digital technologies on tourism's "$ln(ARRIVAL)_{it}$" in a certain nation (i) over a specified duration (t). It looks at the impact of specified variables on tourist arrivals. The impact on these factors on tourist arrivals is represented by the coefficients (α, $\beta_1 - \beta_5$), while the fixed effects for characteristics particular to a nation and time period are represented by μ_i and v_t, respectively. Unobserved factors affecting tourist arrivals are taken into account by the error term (ε_{it}) in equation (1).

3.4. Applied Process for Selecting Appropriate Model

***Unit Root Test*:** In analysis of time series data, the notion of unit roots is essential, especially when attempting to comprehend the characteristics of non-stationary processes. A time series variable with a stochastic trend is said to have a unit root if the variations from its mean are long-lasting and do not eventually return to a constant level (Singh et al., 2024a). A fundamental tenet of many time series models is stationarity, which is the foundation of the idea of unit roots. A time series that exhibits stable statistical attributes over a given period of time is said to be steady. If unit root is presented in the time series data, then the variable is non-stationary. If the variable is not moving closer to a balanced position, because of that the behavior will remain unpredictable. The test is used to find the unit roots for time series and if we are talking about a technique that is statistical to check the unit root then it will be Bai and Nag in 2004 PANIC unit root test (Sharma, 2018). If there is no stationarity in panels' datasets then the PANIC test takes place.

The steps included in the PANIC unit roots test, firstly estimating a regression model with the given variables in the panel and then, changing it into common or unique components. To evaluate the stationary qualities of panel data, researchers enable the PANIC test that helps to fully understand the common and unique source of non-stationary data. This test is very helpful. Null hypothesis can be written as:

> **H_0:** The unit root is presented in the panel data and it has common and unique components.
> **H_1:** The unit root is presented in the panel data and the components are not common and unique.

By demonstrating that the variables were stationary regardless of common or unique components, or both, rejecting the null assumption offers evidence against the existence of root units in the set of data. This affects how econometric models that are fitted to panel data are specified and interpreted.

***Co-integration*:** Co-integration describes the long-term relationship between variables and that is observed over time as well as across different entities in panel data analysis. The factors of interest have a consistent, long-term relationship in the case of panel data as per co-integration tool. It also means that there is a strong relationship between entities and changes in one variable and that can also be replaced or substituted with another variable.

Panel co-integration analysis is used to find the long-term relationships between the variables. It also explains that what types of social or economic factors influence outcome. The hypothesis of cointegration tells, if the variables have the interesting long-term connection or not. If there is absence of the long-term relationships in the variables then it is considered as the null hypothesis. Following hypothesis are formulated:

H_0: There is no cointegration relationship between the variables.
H_1: There is a co-integrating relationship between the variables.

The researchers test their hypotheses on co-integration to learn more about the constantly changing relationships and fundamental economic or social processes of the variables.

***Hausman Test*:** Hausman test is used to evaluate the estimators' consistency in the panel data models. It facilitates researchers in selecting between fixed effects (FE) and random effect (RE) models according to the degree at which the presumptions of each one are met (Lopez-Cordova, 2020). The random effect (RE) estimator's consistency and efficiency, or its ability to produce objective estimates of the coefficients, is the null hypotheses of the Hausman test. The fixed effect (FE) estimator is deemed preferred based on the alternative premise because the random effect (RE) estimator is inaccurate and wasteful. The null theory can be stated formally as follows:

H_0: The random effect (RE) estimator shows efficiency and consistency.

The estimates derived from the fixed-effect (FE) model and the random effect (RE) model are compared using the Hausman test. The random effect (RE) model is thought to be adequate if the estimations are comparable. On the other hand, researchers ought to employ the fixed effect (FE) model in place of the random effect (RE) estimator if there are notable disparities between the estimates, suggesting that the latter model is inconsistent. Following hypothesis is formulated:

H_1: The fixed effect (FE) estimator is more efficient and consistent than the random effect (RE) estimate.

***Random Effect Model*:** The model is used for checking the heterogeneity of different entities within panel data analysis (Selimi et al., 2017). Time-dependent and time-varying both factors incorporate and it allows for more accuracy in forecasting outcomes and efficient parameter estimation. No relationships between individual-specific impacts and the variables that explain them which is unpredictable and not always true but they still rely on the presumption. Despite these drawbacks, this model is still a useful tool for solving the different variables like endogenous and omitted variables. Numerical expression for the basic random effects model is as follows:

$$Y_{\text{it}} = \alpha + \beta X_{\text{it}} + \mu_i + \varepsilon_{\text{it}} \tag{2}$$

Here, the variable that is dependent for entity *i* in the period of time *t* is represented by *Y*(*it*); The symbol "*X*" indicates the independent variable(s) of unit "*i*" during time period "*t*"; the intercept term is α; the coefficient(s) for the independent variable(s) are denoted by β; the random effect for entity *i*, which captures unobserved individual-specific effects is μ_i; and the error term stands for random noise and unobserved components is ε_{it} in equation (2). This model captures entity-specific effects that are unique to each individual and assumes; μ_i=0 is a random variable. By estimating the variance of μ_i, the random effects method provides information about the degree of personal level variation in the data.

Random effect model is especially useful for representing the differences that occur inside and between individual entities over time, enabling a more complex sense of its underlying dynamics. For the expansion of the random effects model on the conventional linear regression framework, adding random effects for both distinct entities and time periods can help and that allows for the accounting of the hidden variation at both levels. Mathematically expressed model as follows:

$$Y_{\text{it}} = \alpha + \beta X_{\text{it}} + \gamma t_{\text{it}_i} \tag{3}$$

Here, for entity *i* in time period *t*; Y_{it} stands for the dependent variable; X_{it} for the independent variable(s); α (the intercept term) and β (the coefficients) represent the independent variables; effects that change over time and among entities, the model additionally includes random effects, denoted as γ_i for each entity and δ_t over time periods; ε_{it} denotes as the error term in equation (3). Moreover, the two-way random effect model, the null hypothesis can be stated as follows:

H_0: There are no continuous random effects for items and time periods.

Put differently, the null hypothesis suggests that the explanatory variables of the model are not able to account for any individual-specific variation between entities or temporal-specific variation across time periods. Then, the alternative hypothesis (H_1) is finalized as:

H_1: Random effects are present continuously for entities and/or temporal periods.

The hypothesis in two-way random effects model usually concerns the existence of random effects for both time periods (time-series units) and entities (cross-sectional units). When observations are performed on the same objects over a number of time periods, panel data is analysed using the model.

The alternative would show whether random effects on entities thus/or time periods are important sources of variations in the variable that is dependent, proving their significance in the model and rejecting the null theory in favour of it.

4. RESULTS AND DISCUSSION

The present study uses Unit Root Bai and Ng in 2004 PANIC test for testing the stationarity of the data. These tests, however, might not fully reflect the fluctuation of panel data, which is a collection of observations made over time on a number of things. An example of the second-generation unit root examination created especially for panel data includes the Bai and Ng in 2004 PANIC test. By accommodating both typical and unique non-stationary in panel datasets, it expands on the capabilities of conventional unit root tests. There are some steps that need to be done if anyone wants to perform a PANIC test, firstly a regression model with panels (estimated), then the residuals must be divided into components like common and unique.

4.1. Hypothesis

H_0: The unit root is presented in the panel data and it has common and unique components.

H_1: The unit root is presented in the panel data and the components are not common and unique.

Table 3 presents the results of unit root. The results demonstrate that most variables (excluding, *ln(INTERNET)*, *ln(MOBSUB)*) are found non-stationary.

Table 3. Results for Unit Root Bai and Ng in 2004 PANIC test

Variables	Level	
	value	***p*-value**
ln(BBSUB)	0.08798	0.92989
ln(INTERNET)	1.75089	0.07996
ln(INTEXP)	0.28031	0.77924
ln(MOBSUB)	3.46787	0.00052

Variables	Level	
	value	*p*-value
ln(*ATM*)	-0.40092	0.68848
ln(*ARRIVAL*)	-0.83874	0.40162

Source: Author's Estimation.

4.2. Results for Kao Residual Co-integration Test

It is a statistical technique for determining if co-integration exists in panel data models. For the determination of residuals, the panel regression model must be estimated. The hypothesis of Kao residual cointegration, if the variables have the interesting long-term connection or not and if there is absence of the long-term relationships in the variables then it is considered as the null hypothesis. On the other hand, if there is an interesting long-term connection then we will reject the null hypothesis and accept the alternative hypothesis, which suggests that each of the variables are restricted by long-term relationship. Here, we tested following hypothesis:

H_0: Co-integration doesn't exist.
H1: Co-integration exists

Table 4. Results for Kao residual cointegration test

Model	T-stat	Prob.
	-2.848055	0.0022

Source: Author's Estimation.

It is reported in Table 4 that the probability value is 0.0022. Therefore, we reject null hypothesis and accept alternative hypothesis. Also, the t- statistic value of model 1 is -2.848055 which means the variables have a negative long- term relationship with each other's.

4.3. Hausman Test

The Hausman test examines the efficiency and consistency of estimators for panel data models. It specifically assists researchers in selecting between fixed effects (FE) and random effects (RE) frameworks based on the estimator features and model assumptions. The test contrasts the estimates obtained using the random effect (RE) model, that presupposes the individual-specific effects have no correlation with the responses', with the fixed effects (FE) framework, which takes individual-specific effects into account. The random effect (RE) estimator's consistency and efficiency, or its ability to produce objective estimates of the coefficients, are the null hypotheses of the Hausman test. Researchers ought to switch to the fixed effects (FE) model, nevertheless, if the estimates derived from both the random effect (RE) and fixed effect (FE) models show a substantial difference, suggesting that the random effect (RE) estimator is inconsistent. Considering the assumptions and characteristics of the estimators, the Hausman test aids researchers in selecting the best models for use with panel data analysis. Following hypothesis are validated under the random and fixed-effect models:

$H_{0:}$ Random effect models are better in comparison with fixed effect models.

H_1: Fixed effect models are better in comparison with random effect models.

Table 5. Results for correlated random effects – Hausman test

Test Summary		
Cross-Section Random	Chi-Sq. Statistic	0.000000
	Chi-Sq. d. f.	5
	Prob.	1.0000
Period Random	Chi-Sq. Statistic	0.000000
	Chi-Sq. d. f.	5
	Prob.	1.0000
Cross-Section and Period Random	Chi-Sq. Statistic	0.000000
	Chi-Sq. d. f.	5
	Prob.	1.0000

Source: Author's Estimation.

According to the results of the Hausman test, the total number of regressors in Model are 5 as shown by chi-sq. Degree of freedom in Table 5. In model, the probability value of chi-sq. statistic is 1.0000 which is not statistically significant at 5% level. This indicates that the null hypothesis of a fixed effect model is better than the random effect model, thus it can be rejected. Therefore, the random effect model is best suited for estimating the model. Also, chi-sq. statistics is 0.0000 signifying that the random effect model holds perfectly in this scenario.

4.4. Two-way Random Effect Model

Random effect model enables the capture of heterogeneity that is not observed and that differs between entities and time. Hence, the results estimated through this model is given in Table 6.

Table 6. Results for random effect estimation method

Dependent variable is *ln*(*ARRIVAL*)
Method is Panel *FGLS* (Two-way Random Effect)
Period: 2009-2020
Cross sections included: 6
Total panel (balanced) observation: 72
Swamy as well as Arora estimator of component variances

Variable	Coefficient	Std. Error	t-Statistic	Prob.
ln(*BBSUB*)	1.633400	0.169341	9.645613	0.0000
ln(*INTERNET*)	0.388544	0.098427	3.947542	0.0002
ln(*INTEXP*)	1.822716	0.175528	10.38419	0.0000
ln(*MOBSUB*)	2.7415710	0.345307	6.995824	0.0000
ln(*ATM*)	-2.795194	0.272190	-10.26928	0.0000
Constant coefficients	-37.31936	5.392160	-6.921041	0.0000

Source: Author's estimation.

The model allows the estimation of average impacts on variables across entities and time periods while adjusting for individual-specific or time-specific characteristics by taking these random effects into consideration. Table 6 shows the results that is estimated through for random effect estimation method. Increasing number of Internet broadband subscription rates can lead to increase good connectivity for the travellers. If travellers have more access to the internet, then they may find it simpler to plan and organize their vacations, access travel-related resources, reserve accommodation, and take part in digital promotional activities for locations. Internet facilities lead to an increase in visitors' visits because now they know about the destination they're going for traveling. Overall, the positive correlation with *ln*(*ARRIVAL*) and *ln*(*BBSUB*) highlights the importance of broadband infrastructure in determining the dynamics of the tourist industry and indicates efforts to promote and grow destinations.

Another, positive relationship exists among *ln*(*ARRIVAL*) and *ln*(*INTERNET*). This result implies that traveller arrivals typically rise with the rising internet usage. This research suggests that the desire for or activities related to tourism may be stimulated by internet usage. It may be seen as a sign that travellers are becoming more dependent on the internet for assessing desire information, reservations, and make communication around travel, which helps them make travel-related decisions and makes them more likely to visit destinations. The significance of digitization as well as internet presence in boosting tourism and drawing tourists is highlighted by this beneficial link. In order to improve the overall tourist experience and take advantage of the growing trend for internet-dependent travel behaviour, policymakers, managers of destinations, and tourism businesses can make use of this insight by making investments in digital marketing strategies, upgrading internet infrastructure, and offering online services.

ln(*ARRIVAL*) and *ln*(*INTEXP*) are found to be positively correlated. It means that there is a direct correlation between rising internet spending and rising visitor numbers. It is also possible that greater internet spending will boost demand for tourism or activities related to tourism. Improved internet availability and usage may facilitate travellers' access to details about trip locations, lodging options, activities, or travel services. Through the strategic utilization of digital technologies and online resources, destinations can improve their competitiveness, expand their market reach, and leverage the changing preferences of consumers in the digital age which is the new era of digitalization.

A strong relationship has been discovered among *ln*(*ARRIVAL*) and *ln*(*MOBSUB*). This result suggests that cell phone subscriptions could act as a stand-in for technology connectedness and information availability, which could have a favourable impact on traveller demand. Travelers may depend on their cell phones for communication, planning, navigation, and information access about destinations as smart phone technology becomes more commonplace. Because travellers perceive mobile services to be more convenient and connected, places with greater mobile subscriptions rates may draw more visitors. It is possible to better inform destination partners about the value of investing in digital services, mobile- friendly tourism experiences, and mobile infrastructure by recognizing the positive correlation between *ln*(*ARRIVAL*) and *ln*(*MOBSUB*).

The correlation that is negative among *ln*(*ARRIVAL*) with LNATM can be linked to the impact of digitalization on the dynamics of tourism. With the progress of digitization, travellers are becoming less dependent on hard currency from ATMs and more reliant on digital forms of payment like credit cards, smart phones, and internet transactions. As a result, the number of tourists may decline as ATMs become more widely available.

Additionally, digitalization makes transactions smooth and transparent, enabling travellers to access their money and make purchases online without having to withdraw cash in person. Because of this convenience, the significance of ATM availability in determining traveller demand declines. Therefore, the inverse connection between *ln*(*ARRIVAL*) and *ln*(*ATM*) is an indication of how travellers' tastes and habits are evolving in reaction to the digital revolution. Overall, the negative correlation between *ln*(*ARRIVAL*) as *ln*(*ATM*) emphasizes how digital technologies are transforming the nature of tourism and how destinations must modify their offerings to accommodate the demands of increasingly knowledgeable about technology visitors.

5. CONCLUSION

This research focuses on the factors influencing tourism in a few chosen countries. By trying to utilize accurate econometric techniques including unit root analysis, Hausman tests, as well as two-way random effect models, it has shown an important relationship between a number of important variables with tourism outcomes. ICT enables travel demand and improves destination accessibility, as evidenced by variables like broadband subscription and internet access. The study also clearly indicated that ICT allows more tourist arrivals. This may be attributed to the fact that ICT in the tourism sector allows the tourists to plan their trips in an efficient manner. Internet accessibility and broadband subscription make them well-versed with their travel choices and travel destinations. Moreover, due to ICT there is improved communication between the travelers and the service providers which result in smoother travel experiences among tourists and thus lead to increased travel demand.

6. SIGNIFICANCE AND POLICY IMPLICATIONS OF THE CHAPTER

The chapter has significance in the existing theoretical and empirical literature in various perspectives. Firstly, the review of literature explains the importance of digital technologies in development and progress of tourism industries across countries. Secondly, it develops linear regression equations to explore the selected independent variables in the tourism sector. Thirdly, it estimates the regression coefficients of variables using random and effect models. Fourthly, it provides the statistical interpretation of results as per the estimated coefficients of explanatory variables. Fifthly, it suggests that digital technologies are effective to increase the growth of the tourism sector. Sixthly, it also develops a connection of the tourism sector with SDGs. Seventh, it proposes scope of further research directions in the area of digital technologies and tourism.

As seeing the positive impact of ICT on tourism, the present study suggests the following policy implications: It is recommended that more investment should be made in digital infrastructure such as broadband networks and internet access to strengthen the tourism sector. The government should provide safe and secure transactions, and successful facilities to the international travelers. Policy makers should establish an environment that is favorable to the digital innovations in the tourism sector. Government can set up standards for digital platforms and this can lead to enhanced travel experience. A comprehensive policy has to be framed by involving policy support, research and collaboration among all the stakeholders to fully realize the potential of ICT for sustainable development (Singh & Jyoti, 2023c). Policymakers may also use mobile technology to boost visitor experiences, advertise travel, and boost economic growth in areas where tourism is important. The government should provide more technological opportunities to the people for using digital technologies for travel purposes (Bak et al., 2022). Smart tourism may be promoted through creating digital infrastructure, data utilization and increasing collaboration across stakeholders (Tee, 2024). The developing countries should pay significant attention to increase sustainable tourism development to get benefits from this sector in the long-term (Butler, 2015).

7. LIMITATION AND SCOPE OF FURTHER RESEARCH DIRECTIONS

The chapter examined the digital technologies of the tourism sector in selected countries. However, the growth of the tourism sector depends on other variables like tourism policies, per capita income, foreign exchange, inflation, infrastructural development, geographical location, social safety, and privacy. While this chapter could not include these variables in the regression analysis. Existing researchers can observe the contribution of these variables to increase the growth of the tourism sector. Thereupon, the development of the tourism sector brings negative externalities for the environmental sector. For example, extensive tourism may be harmful for water resources. Extensive development of the tourism industry may be accountable for more environmental degradation and climate change. Although, this chapter could not examine the impact of the tourism sector on different indicators of environmental sector and climate change. Hence, it is a significant research area in which existing researchers can observe the implications of digital technologies to minimize the negative impact of the tourism sector on environmental sustainability (Archi et al., 2023). The association of digital technologies and the tourism market may be examined in further research.

REFERENCES

Ahmed, Z. U., & Krohan, F. B. (1992). Marketing India as a tourist destination in North America—Challenges and opportunities. *International Journal of Hospitality Management*, 11(2), 89–98. DOI: 10.1016/0278-4319(92)90003-E

Ajzen, I., & Driver, B. E. (1992). Applied of the theory of planned behavior to leisure choice. *Journal of Leisure Research*, 24(3), 207–224. DOI: 10.1080/00222216.1992.11969889

Alhaimer, R. (2023). *Comparing virtual political campaigns with traditional political campaigns: evidence from Kuwait during the COVID-19 pandemic. Global Knowledge, Memory and Communication*. Global Knowledge, Memory and Communication., DOI: 10.1108/GKMC-07-2022-0182

Alhaimer, R. (2024). Unveiling the digital persona image: the influence of social media on political candidates' brand personality and voter behaviour in Kuwait. https://www.researchgate.net/publication/376617959_Unveiling_the_digital_persona_image_the_influence_of_social_media_on_political_candidates'_brand_personality_and_voter_behaviour_in_Kuwait Anderson, R., & Moore, T. (2006). The economics of information security. *Science*, New Series, 314(5799), 610-613. https://www.jstor.org/stable/20031627

Archi, Y. E., Benbba, B., Kabil, M., & Dávid, L. D. (2023). Digital technologies for sustainable tourism destinations: State of the art and research agenda. *Administrative Sciences*, 13(8), 1–21. DOI: 10.3390/admsci13080184

Bak, I., Barej-Kaczmarek, E., & Sulikowski, P. (2022). Impact of information and communication technologies on the tourism sector. *European Research Studies*, 25(3), 595–606. DOI: 10.35808/ersj/3052

Barashok, I. V., Rudenko, L. L., Shumakova, E. V., & Orlovskaia, I. V. (2021). Digitalization: New possibilities for the tourism industry. *IOP Conference Series. Earth and Environmental Science*, 666(06259), 1–6. DOI: 10.1088/1755-1315/666/6/062059

Bayram, G. E. (2020). Impact of information technology on tourism. In Hassan, A., & Sharma, A. (Eds.), *The Emerald Handbook of ICT in Tourism and Hospitality* (pp. 243–257). Emerald Publishing Limited., DOI: 10.1108/978-1-83982-688-720201015

Behra, A., & Jatav, S. S. (2022). Waste management practices of small hotels in Dehradun. *Journal of Tourism Insights*, 12(1), 1–16. https://scholarworks.gvsu.edu/jti/vol12/iss1/3/

Behra, A., Jatav, S. S., Amit, K. Y., & Kiran, B. B. (2023). How do domestic and foreign tourists understand the concept of 'green hotels' and its practices in India? *Journal of Survey in Fisheries Sciences*, 10(4S), 2551–2559. https://sifisheriessciences.com/journal/index.php/journal/article/view/1614

Brennen, J. S., & Kreiss, D. (2016). Digitalization. *The International Encyclopedia of Communication Theory and Philosophy*, 1(1), 1–11. DOI: 10.1002/9781118766804.wbiect111

Brynjolfsson, E., & McAfee, A. (2014). *The second machine age: work, progress, and prosperity in a time of brilliant technologies*. WW Norton & Company.

Buhalis, D., & Law, R. (2008). Progress in information technology and tourism management: 20 years on and 10 years after the internet—the state of e-Tourism research. *Tourism Management*, 29(4), 609–623. DOI: 10.1016/j.tourman.2008.01.005

Butler, R. (2015). The evolution of tourism and tourism research. *Tourism Recreation Research*, 40(1), 16–27. DOI: 10.1080/02508281.2015.1007632

Chen, J. S. (2001). A case study of Korean outbound travellers' destination images by using correspondence analysis. *Tourism Management*, 22(4), 345–350. DOI: 10.1016/S0261-5177(00)00066-2

Chen, J. S., & Gursoy, D. (2001). An investigation of tourists' destination loyalty and preferences. *International Journal of Contemporary Hospitality Management*, 13(2), 79–85. DOI: 10.1108/09596110110381870

Cohen, E., & Cohen, S. A. (2012). Authentication: Hot and cool. *Annals of Tourism Research*, 39(3), 1295–1314. DOI: 10.1016/j.annals.2012.03.004

Egger, I., Lei, S. I., & Wassler, P. (2020). Digital free tourism – an exploratory study of tourist motivations. *Tourism Management*, 79(1), 1–10. DOI: 10.1016/j.tourman.2020.104098

Fayissa, B., Nsiah, C., & Tadasse, B. (2008). Impact of tourism on economic growth and development in Africa. *Tourism Economics*, 14(4), 807–818. DOI: 10.5367/000000008786440229

Fesenmaier, D. R. (1988). Integrating activity pattern into destination choice models. *Journal of Leisure Research*, 20(3), 175–191. DOI: 10.1080/00222216.1988.11969771

Gössling, S., Peeters, P., Hall, C. M., Ceron, J. P., Dubois, G., Lehmann, L. V., & Scott, D. (2012). Tourism and water use: Supply, demand, and security. An international review. *Tourism Management*, 33(1), 1–15. DOI: 10.1016/j.tourman.2011.03.015

Gozgor, G., Lau, C. K., Lin, Z., & Zeng, Y. (2024). The impact of digital governance on tourism development. *Journal of Digital Economy*, 3(1), 1–13. DOI: 10.1016/j.jdec.2024.05.003

Gretzel, U., Fuchs, M., Baggio, R., Hoepken, W., Law, R., Neidhardt, J., & Xiang, Z. (2020). E-Tourism beyond COVID-19: A call for transformative research. *Information Technology & Tourism*, 22(2), 187–203. DOI: 10.1007/s40558-020-00181-3

Gretzel, U., Sigala, M., Xiang, Z., & Koo, C. (2015). Smart tourism: Foundations and developments. *Electronic Markets*, 25(3), 179–188. DOI: 10.1007/s12525-015-0196-8

Gursoy, D., Malodia, S., & Dhir, A. (2022). The metaverse in the hospitality and tourism industry: An overview of current trends and future research directions. *Journal of Hospitality Marketing & Management*, 31(5), 527–534. DOI: 10.1080/19368623.2022.2072504

Hamid, R. A., Albahri, A. S., Alwan, J. K., Al-quaysi, Z. T., Albahri, O. S., Zaidan, A. A., Alnoor, A., Almoodi, A. H., & Zaidan, B. B. (2021). How smart is e-tourism? A systematic review of smart tourism recommendation system applying data management. *Computer Science Review*, 39(1), 1–13. DOI: 10.1016/j.cosrev.2020.100337

Higham, J., Cohen, S. A., Peeters, P., & Gössling, S. (2013). Psychological and behavioural approaches to understanding and governing sustainable mobility. *Journal of Sustainable Tourism*, 21(7), 949–967. DOI: 10.1080/09669582.2013.828733

Hoffman, D. L. (2000). The revolution will not be televised: Introduction to the special issue on marketing science and the Internet. *Marketing Science*, 19(1), 1–3. https://www.jstor.org/stable/193255. DOI: 10.1287/mksc.19.1.1.15181

Honey, M., & Gilpin, R. (2009). *Tourism in the developing world: Promoting peace and reducing poverty*. United States Institute of Peace., https://www.usip.org/sites/default/files/tourism_developing_world_sr233_0.pdf

Hu, L., Yao, S., Zhou, Z., & Miao, N. (2021). The Importance of the construction of digital economy major under the background of new liberal arts. *World Scientific Research Journal*, 7(8), 104–111. DOI: 10.6911/WSRJ.202108_7(8).0020

Hye, Q. M. A., & Khan, R. E. A. (2013). Tourism-led growth hypothesis: A case study of Pakistan. *Asia Pacific Journal of Tourism Research*, 18(4), 303–313. DOI: 10.1080/10941665.2012.658412

Iorio, C., Pandolfo, G., D'Ambrosio, A., & Siciliano, R. (2020). Mining big data in tourism. *Quality & Quantity*, 54(1), 1655–1669. https://link.springer.com/article/10.1007/s11135-019-00927-0. DOI: 10.1007/s11135-019-00927-0

IPCC (2018). Global Warming of 1.5°C.An IPCC Special Report on the impacts of global warming of 1.5°C above pre-industrial levels and related global greenhouse gas emission pathways, in the context of strengthening the global response to the threat of climate change, sustainable development, and efforts to eradicate poverty [Masson-Delmotte, V., P. Zhai, H.-O. Pörtner, D. Roberts, J. Skea, P.R. Shukla, A. Pirani, W. Moufouma-Okia, C. Péan, R. Pidcock, S. Connors, J.B.R. Matthews, Y. Chen, X. Zhou, M.I. Gomis, E. Lonnoy, T. Maycock, M. Tignor, and T. Waterfield (eds.)].

Jiang, C., & Phoong, S. W. (2023). A ten-year review analysis of the impact of digitization on tourism development (2012-2022). *Humanities & Social Sciences Communications*, 10(1), 665. Advance online publication. DOI: 10.1057/s41599-023-02150-7 PMID: 37192942

Jinghua, Y., & Xianmei, S. (2021). Political economics analysis of competition and monopoly in the digital economy era. *Economic Review Journal*, 3(1), 18–26.

Jyoti, B., & Singh, A. K. (2023). Does digitalization have a causal relationship with economic development? an experience from a country-wise panel data statistical analysis. In R. Sine Nazlı & G. Sari (Eds.), *Handbook of Research on Perspectives on Society and Technology Addiction* (pp. 34-61). IGI Global. DOI: 10.4018/978-1-6684-8397-8.ch003

Kononova, O., Prokudin, D., & Ryabysko, J. (2021). The vision and the perspective of digital tourism. 22nd Conference on Scientific Services & Internet (SSI-2020), Novorossiysk-Abrau (online), Russia. DOI: 10.48550/arXiv.2109.09795

Kononova, O., Prokudin, D., & Tupikina, E. (2020). From e-Tourism to digital tourism. https://ceur-ws.org/Vol-2784/rpaper13.pdf

Kuang, T., & Tsai, Y. F. (2016). The effect of tourism growth on economic growth: A quantile regression analysis. https://hdl.handle.net/20.500.14394/48202

Kumar, S., & Shekhar, . (2020). Digitalization: A strategic approach for development of tourism industry in India. *Paradigm*, 24(1), 93–108. DOI: 10.1177/0971890720914111

Li, P., Zho, Y., & Huang, S. (2023). Role of information technology in the development of e-tourism marketing: A contextual suggestion. *Economic Analysis and Policy*, 78(1), 307–318. DOI: 10.1016/j.eap.2023.03.010

Lopez-Cordova, E. (2020). Digital platforms and the demand for international tourism services. Policy Research Working Paper, 9147, Finance, Competitiveness and Innovation Global Practice, World Bank Group. https://www.worldbank.org/prwp

Maslova, T., Pletneva, N., Althonayan, A., Tarasova, E., & Krasnov, A. (2020). Transformation of consumer behavior in the tourism industry in the conditions of digital economy. *IOP Conference Series. Materials Science and Engineering*, 940(1), 1–8. DOI: 10.1088/1757-899X/940/1/012070

Midoun, S., & Nardjess, F. (2019). Tourism-led growth hypothesis: A case study of some North African countries. *African Journal of Hospitality, Tourism and Leisure*, 8(5), 1–13. www.ajhtl.com/uploads/7/1/6/3/7163688/article_86_8_5__2019_algeria.pdf

Mishra, P. K., Rout, H. B., & Mohapatra, S. S. (2011). Causality between tourism and economic growth: Empirical evidence from India. *European Journal of Soil Science*, 18(4), 518–527.

Nakatani, R. (2021). Total factor productivity enablers in the ICT industry: A cross-country firm-level analysis. *Telecommunications Policy*, 45(9), 10–21. DOI: 10.1016/j.telpol.2021.102188

Peeters, P. M., Gössling, S., Klijs, J., Milano, C., Novelli, M., Dijkmans, C. H. S., & Mitas, O. (2018). Research for TRAN Committee-Overtourism: Impact and possible policy responses. European Parliament, Directorate General for Internal Policies, Policy Department B: Structural and Cohesion Policies, Transport and Tourism. *European Union*.

Pencarelli, T. (2020). The digital revolution in the travel and tourism industry. *Information Technology & Tourism*, 22(3), 455–476. DOI: 10.1007/s40558-019-00160-3

Robert, A., Valerie, J., Vincent, L., Filippos, P., Ieva, R., & Lara, V. (2021). The digital economy and the Euro area. *Economic Bulletin Articles, European Central Bank*, 8. https://www.ecb.europa.eu/press/economic bulletin/articles/2021/html/ecb.ebart202008_03~da0f5f792a.en.html#:~:text=Most%20euro%20area%20countries%20have,States%20(see%20Chart%201)

Samimi, A. J., Sadeghi, S., & Sadeghi, S. (2011). Tourism and economic growth in developing countries: P-VAR approach. *Middle East Journal of Scientific Research*, 10(1), 28–32. https://www.idosi.org/mejsr/mejsr10(1)11/5.pdf

Selimi, N., Sadiku, M., & Sadiku, L. (2017). The impact of tourism on economic growth in the Western Balkan countries: An empirical analysis. *International Journal of Business and Economic Sciences Applied Research*, 10(2), 19–25. DOI: 10.25103/ijbesar.102.02

Sharma, N. (2018). Tourism led growth hypothesis: Empirical evidence from India. *African Journal of Hospitality, Tourism and Leisure*, 7(2), 1–11. https://www.ajhtl.com/uploads/7/1/6/3/7163688/article_7_vol_7__2__2018.pdf

Shiji, O. (2016). Economic impact of tourism in India. *The International Journal of Social Sciences (Islamabad)*, 5(1), 35–46. https://ndpublisher.in/admin/issues/IJSSV5N1f.pdf. DOI: 10.5958/2321-5771.2016.00013.2

Singh, A. K. (2025). Causality of digitalization with social sustainability in selected countries. In Siyal, S. (Ed.), *Impact of Digitalization on Education and Social Sustainability* (pp. 39–78). IGI Global., DOI: 10.4018/979-8-3693-1854-6.ch002

Singh, A. K., & Jyoti, B. (2023a). Empirical evidence from different income group countries on the interdependency between digitalization and economic development. In Patricia Ordóñez de Pablos and Xi Zhang (Eds.), 5G, Artificial Intelligence, and Next Generation Internet of Things: Digital Innovation for Green and Sustainable Economies, (pp. 44-85). IGI Global. DOI: DOI: 10.4018/978-1-6684-8634-4.ch003

Singh, A. K., & Jyoti, B. (2023b). Does digitalization have a bi-directional causal relationship with the entrepreneurship ecosystem? Evidence from a country-wise panel data analysis. In Yanamandra, R., & Indiran, L. (Eds.), *Handbook of Research on Designing Sustainable Strategies to Develop Entrepreneurial Intention* (pp. 178–172). IGI Global., DOI: 10.4018/978-1-6684-8781-5.ch007

Singh, A. K., & Jyoti, B. (2023c). Impact of digitalization on global sustainable development across countries. *Green and Low-carbon Economy*, 4(2), 1–20. DOI: 10.47852/bonviewGLCE32021482

Singh, A. K., & Jyoti, B. (2023d). Empirical investigation for assessing the causality of entrepreneurship ecosystem with entrepreneurial behavior and attitudes across countries. In Abe, E., & Abe, I. (Eds.), *Cases on the Interplay Between Family, Society, and Entrepreneurship* (pp. 315–353). IGI Global., DOI: 10.4018/978-1-6684-8748-8.ch012

Singh, A. K., & Kumar, S. (2022). Factors influencing entrepreneurship ecosystem and economic development: Evidence from cross-sectional country-wise imbalanced panel data analysis. *The IUP Journal of Entrepreneurship Development*, 19(3), 24–47.

Singh, A. K., Kumar, S., & Gupta, M. (2024e). Relationship between digitalization and environmental sustainability in selected countries. In Yıldırım, S., Yıldırım, D., Demirtaş, I., & Kandpal, V. (Eds.), *Green Transition Impacts on the Economy, Society, and Environment* (pp. 83–107). IGI Global., DOI: 10.4018/979-8-3693-3985-5.ch006

Singh, A. K., Kumar, S., & Jyoti, B. (2023). Does entrepreneurship ecosystem have a causal relationship with economic development? A country-wise imbalanced panel data investigation. In Magd, H., Khan, S. A., Nte, N. D., & Sarim, M. (Eds.), *Entrepreneurship and Economic Sustainability* (pp. 1–15)., https://www.researchgate.net/publication/366353165_Does_Entrepreneurship_Ecosystem_have_a_Causal_Relationship_with_Economic_Development_A_Country-wise_Imbalanced_Panel_Data_Investigation

Singh, A. K., Singh, R., & Singh, R. (2024a). Impact of digitalization on sustainable development in G20 countries. In Ahmed, E. (Ed.), *Developing Digital Inclusion Through Globalization and Digitalization* (pp. 287–335). IGI Global., DOI: 10.4018/979-8-3693-4111-7.ch013

Singh, A. K., Singh, S., & Gupta, M. (2024c). A literature review for the association of social media with micro and small enterprises in India. In Hossain, S. (Ed.), *Cases on Social Media and Entrepreneurship* (pp. 38–62). IGI Global., DOI: 10.4018/979-8-3693-1781-5.ch003

Singh, A. K., Singh, S., & Sankaranarayanan, K. G. S. (2024b). A comparative performance of green technology, green growth, social, and economic development in India and China. In Ordóñez de Pablos, P. (Ed.), *Digital Technologies for a Resource Efficient Economy* (pp. 107–141). IGI Global., DOI: 10.4018/979-8-3693-2750-0.ch006

Singh, N. P., Bhawna, A., Surendra, S., & Arshad, Kh. (2019). Mainstreaming climate adaptation in Indian rural developmental agenda: A micro-macro convergence. *Climate Risk Management*, 29(1), 30–41. https://www.sciencedirect.com/science/article/pii/S221209631830130X. DOI: 10.1016/j.crm.2019.04.003

Singh, N. P., Srivastava, S. K., Sharma, S., Anand, Bh., Singh, S., & Ranjith, C. P. (2020). Dynamics of socio-economic factors affecting climate vulnerability and technology adoption: Evidence from Jodhpur district of Rajasthan. *Indian Journal of Traditional Knowledge*, 19(1), 192-196. http://op.niscpr.res.in/index.php/IJTK/article/view/30867/465477393

Singh, S. (2020). Farmers' perception of climate change and adaptation decisions: A micro-level evidence from Bundelkhand Region, India. *Ecological Indicators*, 116(1), 1–10. https://www.sciencedirect.com/science/article/abs/pii/S1470160X2030412X. DOI: 10.1016/j.ecolind.2020.106475

Solove, D. J. (2006). The digital person and the future of privacy. In Strandburg, K. J., & Raicu, D. S. (Eds.), *Privacy and Technologies of Identity*. Springer., DOI: 10.1007/0-387-28222-X_1

Steiner, C. (2006). Tourism, poverty reduction and the political economy: Egyptian perspectives on tourism's economic benefits in a semi-rentier state. *Tourism and Hospitality Planning & Development*, 3(3), 161–177. DOI: 10.1080/14790530601132286

Tang, R. (2023). Digital economy drives tourism development—Empirical evidence based on the UK. *Ekonomska Istrazivanja*, 36(1), 2003–2020. DOI: 10.1080/1331677X.2022.2094443

Tee, M. K. (2024). Malaysia's smart tourism framework. In Kumar, S., Talukder, M. B., & Pego, A. (Eds.), *Utilizing Smart Technology and AI in Hybrid Tourism and Hospitality* (pp. 51–78). IGI Global., DOI: 10.4018/979-8-3693-1978-9.ch003

Um, S., & Crompton, J. L. (1990). Attitude determinations in tourism destination choice. *Annals of Tourism Research*, 17(1), 432–448. DOI: 10.1016/0160-7383(90)90008-F

Venkatesh, M., & Raj, D. J. (2016). Impact of tourism in India. *International Journal of Scientific Engineering and Applied Science*, 2(1), 167–184. https://ijseas.com/volume2/v2i1/ijseas20160119.pdf

Vila, N. A., Cardoso, L., Archi, Y. E., & Brea, J. A. F. (2024). The role of digital technology and sustainable practices in tourists' decision making. In El Archi, Y., Benbba, B., Dávid, L. D., & Cardoso, L. (Eds.), *Promoting Responsible Tourism with Digital Platforms* (pp. 1–19). IGI Global., DOI: 10.4018/979-8-3693-3286-3.ch003

Wanjiru, I. R., & Xiaoguang, L. (2021). Evaluating University–Community Engagement Through a Community-Based Lens: What Indicators Are Suitable? *Journal of Higher Education Outreach & Engagement*, 25(4), 133–146.

Xiang, Z., & Fesenmaier, D. R. (2017). Big data analytics, tourism design and smart tourism. In D. R. Xiang, Zheng, Fesenmaier (Eds.), *Analytics in Smart Tourism Design, Concepts and Methods*, pp. 299–307. Springer International Publishing Switzerland. DOI: 10.1007/978-3-319-44263-1_17

Zhou, K. Z., & Li, C. B. (2012). How knowledge affects radical innovation: Knowledge base, market knowledge acquisition, and internal knowledge sharing. *Strategic Management Journal*, 33(9), 1090–1102. DOI: 10.1002/smj.1959

Zuo, B., & Huang, S. (2018). Revisiting the tourism-led economic growth hypothesis: The case of China. *Journal of Travel Research*, 57(2), 151–163. DOI: 10.1177/0047287516686725

Chapter 15
E-Health Transforming Healthcare Delivery With AI, Blockchain, and Cloud

Rajat Singhal
https://orcid.org/0009-0002-8017-2306
Sharda University, India

Vishal Jain
https://orcid.org/0000-0003-1126-7424
Sharda University, India

Dharm Raj
https://orcid.org/0000-0001-8363-0515
Sharda School of Engineering and Technology, India

ABSTRACT

An Electronic Health Records System is a digitized version of a patient's medical records that are stored electronically. The current system that Hospitals use to store digital patient information and medical records faces numerous obstacles.These systems fail to balance data security and open threats to hackers and unauthorized access which can lead to cyberattacks. The chapter explores how AI, Blockchain and Cloud Computing are combined to overcome these challenges. Blockchain creates a decentralized, transparent, and immutable system providing a robust framework for secure and efficient management of patient records by using Hyperledger Fabric, Amazon Web Service with a React.js front-end to deliver a great experience to users. This proposed architecture provides data security, improves integration issues, operational costs and provides a safe, scalable, and patient-centric approach, and represents a substantial development in healthcare data management with the in-

DOI: 10.4018/979-8-3693-7678-2.ch015

tegration of serverless computing with blockchain technology.

1. INTRODUCTION

Electronic Health Records (EHRs) have changed the healthcare industry by digitizing patient records, making it easier to access, share, and manage medical information. Traditionally, information about a patient is recorded on paper and then entered into one central digital database, which raises a myriad of issues related to accessibility, integrity, and security of data. In the future, EHRs will continue to advance with the evolution of cloud and serverless computing, and thus be more secure with better data integrity, aided by blockchain technology(Seymour et al., 2012).

1.1 Role of Electronic Health Records (EHRs) in Healthcare

EHRs have transformed healthcare from a traditional, paper-based model into a very sophisticated digital system. Integrating patient information in EHRs into a single record allows for quality and safety of care, facilitating appropriate and timely provision of relevant information to health practitioners. Reducing errors and increasing diagnosis accuracy is also great teamwork among health providers. In addition to driving down costs and increasing efficiency, EHRs allow for faster administrative processes associated with, for example, scheduling and billing. They enable insights from data through analysis tools and further population health management via aggregation for trend analysis and preventive health initiatives(Jabali et al., 2022a).

1.1.1 Improved Patient Care: EHRs allow healthcare providers to immediately access information on patients that is accurate and current, which are elements important to making informed clinical decisions. An EHR provides an overall perspective into a patient's history that may reduce the risk of medical errors, such as improper medication or misdiagnosis. Additionally, EHRs further support evidence-based decision-making by incorporating accessible clinical guidelines and support tools that help lead the healthcare provider to give the best possible care(Aguirre et al., 2019).

1.1.2 Enhanced Care Coordination: Moreover, in a traditional healthcare setting, the information about the patient is fragmented in different locations and is maintained in different formats. The coordination of care is thus very difficult to handle. The EHR allows sharing of patient information among different service providers and institutions seamlessly. Due to this interoperability, every member of a patient's care team will have the same information, thus making the care for the patient better coordinated, especially for those patients with chronic conditions requiring multiple specialists(Jabali et al., 2022b).

1.1.3 Increased Efficiency and Cost-saving: EHRs manage administrative procedures well; they minimize the time and effort taken while charting, performing billing, and handling prescriptions. Automating such processes, EHRs lighten the administrative load of healthcare providers and hence give them more time to attend to patients. Finally, EHRs facilitate cost savings in large measures through a reduction in paper-based records, elimination of duplicate testing, and better resource management.

1.1.4 Public Health and Research: EHRs also play a very important role in public health and medical research. Aggregated EHR data from large numbers of patients enable researchers to learn about the trends, track the spread of diseases, and develop new treatments. In the context of public health, EHRs support population health management with real-time data on outbreaks of diseases, vaccination rates, and other health indicators(Jones et al., 2014).

1.2 Problems with Current EHR Systems

The EHR systems face many more difficulties concerning data privacy, security, integration, and scalability. These challenges continue to increase with the rising volume of medical information, which, in this case, is a consequence of the rapidly expanding population of patients and healthcare providers using digital systems for their electronic medical records. In these connected healthcare times, the need for a secure, scalable, and efficient EHR has never been more critical(Ozair et al., 2015).

1.2.1 Data Security Issues: One of the major concerns for the currently running EHR systems is related to the security of the patient data, which is very sensitive and valuable, hence becoming the prime target for any cyberattack. Hacking in healthcare may lead to serious consequences of identity theft, financial loss, and damage to the organizational image. Security of patient data is not just a legally, but also an ethically, indispensable requirement for healthcare providers.

1.2.2 Interoperability Concerns: Integration of EHR systems is difficult due to the inconsistency of existing systems due to different healthcare providers using different data and formats. This complicates the flow of information between them in terms of its exchange and integration. In doing so, this causes inefficiency, duplicated tests, and probably gaps in patient care.

1.2.3 Scalability and Performance Issues: Scalability and performance in EHR systems are serious issues with the increment of quantity of data related to patients, resulting in slow response time and system downtime that hamper effective healthcare delivery. Large amounts of data require correspondingly high-performance levels for management. Most conventional EHR systems, besides requiring huge infrastructure investments in things like hardware and maintenance may be difficult to scale and rather expensive.

1.2.4 Usability and User Experience: Two major challenges with EHRs concern usability and user experience, which could be difficult to master by health professionals due to complicated, incomprehensible user interfaces. As such, this results in increased time for training, user frustration, and even mistakes regarding data entry.

1.3 Overview of AI, Cloud, and Blockchain in Healthcare

These are three dynamic technologies of healthcare transformation in AI, Cloud Computing, and Blockchain, which help in addressing major concerns of EHR systems. Certainly, this has to do with security challenges, interoperability, scalability, and data quality.

The application of technology and artificial intelligence (AI) in healthcare has the potential to address some challenges. Artificial Intelligence in technologies ensures data security with real-time threat detection and predictive analytics, with early warnings of potential cyber threats. On interoperability, the AI ensures the integration of different EHR systems smoothly and is translated through Natural Language Processing and machine learning. AI also supports the quality and integrity of data by automating its input, information validation, and checking inconsistencies—everything to ensure that patient records are absolutely accurate and reliable(Davenport & Kalakota, 2019; Devadass et al., 2017a).

In particular, cloud computing provides enormous assistance to electronic health record systems in the areas of scalability, security, interoperability, and financial-based limitations. It offers a scalable infrastructure that automatically scales up in real time to match the increasing demand for patient data while remaining operationally effective and accessible whenever requirements increase. Better data security includes encryption, access control strategies, and real-time updating regularly to ensure the safety of sensitive health information and compliance with regulating legislation. Cloud platforms enable improved interoperability through the seamless exchange and sharing of data between EHR systems that have common standards for APIs and protocols (Devadass et al., 2017a).

Blockchain offers several advantages to Electronic Health Records (EHR) systems through improved security in the data, ease in interoperability, and scalability. The decentralized, tamper-evident ledger assures stability and safety for a patient's information because all transactions are recorded, unchangeable, and highly diminished against risks of unauthorized changes and data breaches. It also supports scalable data management to handle large volumes of data without performance compromise or reliability issues (Sharma et al., 2023).

Here, we summarize recent breakthroughs in the application of AI, cloud, and Blockchain in healthcare, describe a roadmap to building an effective EHR system, and discuss the possible future direction of these technologies in healthcare systems.

2. ARTIFICIAL INTELLIGENCE IN HEALTHCARE

The introduction of AI into the healthcare sector is one of the exciting new developments toward movement in the medical practice and delivery of healthcare services. AI in health, powered by machine learning, natural language processing, and advanced analytics, opens a new page in this industry by driving diagnostic accuracy further, making care more personalized, and advancing operational excellence. That is likely to dull long-established worries on the part of healthcare providers and make medical treatment accurate, efficient, and focused on the patient(Bajwa et al., 2021).

2.1 Machine Learning – Neural Network and Deep Learning

Machine Learning is a statistical technique for fitting models to data and to 'learn' by training models with data. Machine learning trains algorithms to make inferences or predictions about new cases based on prior examples or background cases. In health, it works best in processing many other electronic health records, medical images, and genomic data to come up with the most accurate diagnosis and treatment effects. Unsupervised learning detects concealed patterns in patient information, thereby facilitating the early detection of diseases and personalization of care(Angra & Ahuja, 2017).

A neural network is a more complex form of machine learning that has been available since the 1960s and has been well-established in healthcare by enhancing the ability to analyze complex data and improve decision-making processes. Neural networks, by design, are structures of the form of the human brain. They then become computational models that involve a series of interconnected nodes or "neurons." In health care, they are utilized to recognize patterns and make predictions from complex data sets. For example, in medical imaging, neural networks detect abnormalities such as tumors or fractures by images taken from X-rays, MRI, and CT scans. Hence, such networks can detect small features and aberrations that might be easily missed by human observers after sifting through huge databases of tagged images in medicine. Its increased ability to collaborate and analyze large data sets made it such an instrumental tool in improving diagnostic accuracy and in the treatment of patients(Uhrig, n.d.).

The most complex form of machine learning is the deep learning associated with neural networks that have more than one hidden layer; this allows complex data representation and feature extraction. Deep learning techniques have truly revolutionized areas like medical imaging and genomics within healthcare. For instance, deep learning models have marked the state-of-the-art results in the classification of high-dimensional data, with features represented as pixel values from medical images or nucleotide sequence reads. For example, convolutional neural networks are applied to handle the medical image toward enhancing its image quality to optimally detect abnormalities(Angra & Ahuja, 2017).

Using deep learning algorithms in genomics involves the analysis of genetic data to identify biomarkers associated with diseases for use in predicting patient response to treatments. Deep learning architectures are deep enough and elaborate to do things that ordinary machine learning methodologies cannot. It empowers progress in diagnostic fronts, formulation of treatment strategies, and therefore, personalized healthcare(Nand et al., 2023).

2.2 Types of Machine Learning

There are three different types of Machine Learning(Oladipupo, 2010)

2.2.1 Supervised Learning: Trained models, using labelled data, predict outcomes or classify data. It is used in healthcare to predict disease progression, classify diagnoses informed by medical images, and analyze records of patients for determining treatment responses.

2.2.2 Unsupervised Learning: Unlabelled data analysis provides patterns in the data and groups it according to similarities. These processes have proven invaluable for clustering patient data, finding hidden patterns within medical records, and segmenting populations to offer personalized care.

2.2.3 Reinforcement Learning: Trains models to decide by rewarding desirable and penalizing undesirable actions. It has also been applied in optimizing treatment plans and making adaptive algorithms for personalized medicine.

Figure 1. Types of machine learning

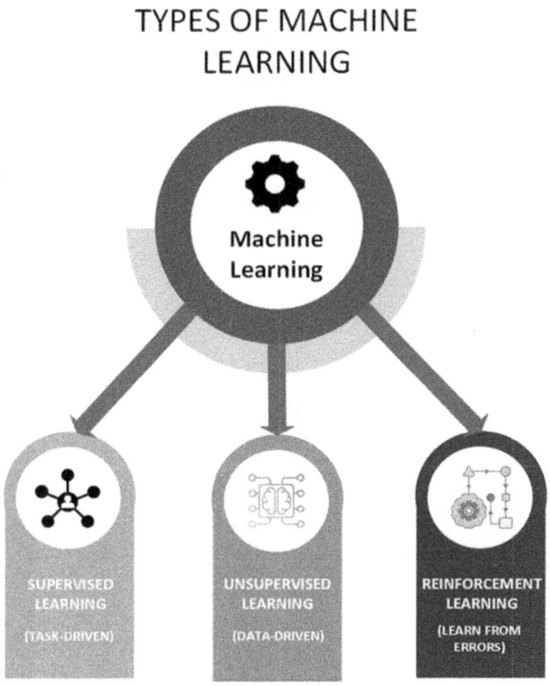

2.3 Essential Equations in Machine Learning

2.3.1 Linear Regression

Linear regression predicts the target variable y based on the input variables x:

$$Y = \omega_0 + \omega_1 x_1 + \omega_2 x_2 + \ldots + \omega_n x_n + \varepsilon$$

Where:

- ω_0 is the intercept,
- $\omega_1, \omega_2, \ldots \omega_n$ are the coefficients (weights) for each features,
- ε is the error term.

2.3.2 Cost Function for Linear Regression

The Mean Squared Error(MSE) is used as a cost function for linear regression, measuring the average squared difference between actual and predicted values:

$$J(\omega) = \frac{1}{m}\sum_{i=1}^{m}(y_1 - y_2)^2$$

- Where:
- y_1 is the actual value,
- y_2 is the predicted value,
- m is the number of samples.

2.3.3 F1 Score for Model Evaluation

The F1 score is the harmonic mean of precision and recall:

$$F1 = 2 \times \frac{Precision \times Recall}{Precision + Recall}$$

Where:

- Precision $= \frac{TP}{TP + FP}$
- Recall $= \frac{TP}{TP + FN}$

• TP, FP, and FN are true positives, false positives, and false negatives, respectively.

2.4 Natural Language Processing

Natural language processing (NLP) is that part of artificial intelligence dedicated to developing the interaction approaches between the computational system and human linguistic expressions. NLP in health is applied to interpret and analyze large volumes of unstructured data that normally include clinical documentation, patient records, and published literature. For instance, an NLP system may crawl patient records for closely related medical history, symptoms, and treatments that enable good decision-making and efficient management of the patients.

In healthcare, NLP matters range from text generation to understanding and classification, mostly in clinical documentation and scientific papers. NLP systems, thus, find use cases in reading unstructured clinical notes on a patient, generating summaries like radiological findings, transcribing conversations with patients, and even powering conversational AI. This capability is at the core of uniting human language with machine-understandable articulation, making both stronger: delivery of healthcare services and research efforts through NLP(Luo et al., 2017).

Figure 2. Different types of AI used in Healthcare sector

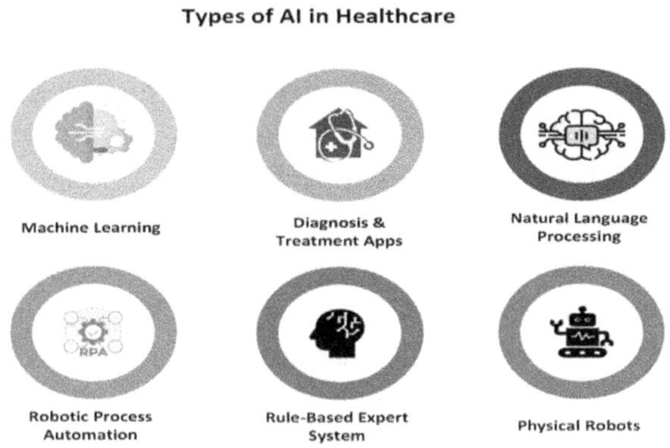

3. CLOUD COMPUTING IN HEALTHCARE

Cloud computing has risen as a very powerful agent of change in the provision of healthcare services in adaptable and expandable solutions that better the rendering of medical services, improve patient outcomes, and reduce operational costs. Using cloud-based platforms, healthcare providers can securely store and administer huge lots of patient information so that it becomes available to any authorized person from anywhere at any time. This access is, therefore paramount value to telemedicine, remote patient monitoring, and collaborative care, which makes quick decisions based on real-time data and treatment efforts. The National Institute of Standards and Technology stated five important elements, three service models, and four deployment models. The five important elements are stated(De La Torre-Díez et al., 2012):

3.1 Characteristics of Cloud Computing

3.1.1 On-demand Self-Service: Server time and network storage can automatically self-provision items by users. This does away with the human element at the service provider. Such non-personnel service capabilities really help to elastically and quickly use resources to the needed amount.

3.1.2 Broad network access: Cloud-based services are services made available over a network through standard protocols usable by a plethora of devices, such as smartphones, tablets, laptops, and desktops. It ensures that the service is of wide access and functional on many platforms.

3.1.3 Resource Pooling: A provider pools computing resources, responding to demand across several consumers in a multi-tenant model, where resources are physically and virtually assigned and reassigned on demand, such as storage, processing, memory, and network bandwidth.

3.1.4 Rapid elasticity: Cloud resources, are provisioned and released elastically–often automatically–to scale out rapidly and scale in correspondingly, on-demand. In many cases, the capabilities available to the consumer appear limitless and hence can be bought in any size amount at any time.

3.1.5 Measured service: Cloud systems control and optimize resource use in an automatic way, therefore providing ways to measure, monitor, and report consumption of resources, thus ensuring transparent provision to the level suitable for both the provider and the consumer.

Figure 3. Types of cloud computing

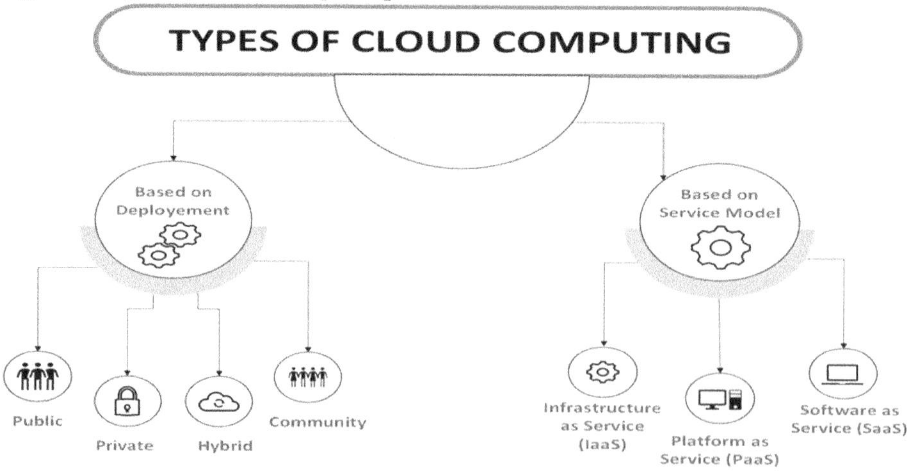

3.2 Service Models of Cloud Computing

Three types of services are being used under cloud computing:

3.2.1 Infrastructure as a Service (IaaS): Cloud computing model that offers virtualized computing resources over the internet. Through IaaS, an organization is able to rent its IT infrastructure—servers, storage, networking capacities—on an as-soonest basis. This does away with expensive hardware in-company premises and offers flexibility, scalability, and independence to change dynamically computing resources at the companies' requirements. IaaS performs very well with workloads that need high availability, disaster recovery, and dynamic scaling; as such, it will be the cynosure for those organizations looking up to improved IT operations. In other words, it has increasingly been the answer for the majority of outfits when it comes to enhancing IT operations with more superior and cost-effective tools(Guo et al., 2012).

3.2.2 Platform as a Service (PaaS): Cloud Computing that gives an application developer a full-fledged environment in terms of creating, deploying, and managing his applications without the headaches of taking care of the underlaying infrastructure. A PaaS service allows full-fledged facilities in terms of development and deployment environments in the cloud, enabling programming, testing, and integration of applications with the relevant features for managing database and analytics In such a model, ease in shortening the development cycle brings a corresponding ease in collaboration and scaling, two qualities yearned for in software development teams. Some examples of the PaaS offerings are: Google App Engine, Microsoft Azure, AWS Elastic Beanstalk(Guo et al., 2012).

3.2.3 Software as a Service (SaaS): This service refers to a cloud computing model whereby applications are provided via the internet. Most likely, this will be without the need for installation, maintenance-free, and outside personal control of the supporting infrastructure. The customary hosting in a SaaS application is by a third-party provider, with access through a web browser then availed by subscription. Through this model, organizations would avoid capital investments in hardware, software, and IT resources that come with the same and would instead focus on its core business operations. Typical examples of such popular SaaS applications are Google Workspace, Salesforce, Microsoft Office 365, and Dropbox(Guo et al., 2012).

3.3 Deployment Models of Cloud Computing

There are four types of models that are deployed under cloud computing:

3.3.1 Public Cloud: The public cloud refers to cloud infrastructure, where services are offered over the internet by a third party. Common types of these third-party providers include AWS, Microsoft Azure, Google Cloud, and others. If taken in this way, it is going to be shared between multiple businesses for exceptional scaling and affordability. These features have made this model extremely ideal for decreasing information technology costs and increasing capacity at will, with absolutely no management overhead of the physical infrastructure.

3.3.2 Private Cloud: The private cloud model is the only one that should be used when dealing with an organisation's use of computing resources. In contrast with a public cloud, resources allocated to a private cloud offer more control, customization, and security. Private cloud infrastructure lies on-premise setup of an organisation that is deployed over a hosted model, or isn't shared with other organisations. Organisational control over their environments in private clouds might lend some ability to customize those environments for their specific needs, ensuring adherence to industry standards while keeping sensitive information secured within a controlled environment.

3.3.3 Community Cloud: It is a cloud computing model in which the infrastructure is shared between organizations with common requirements in areas such as security, compliance, performance requirements, etc. In these kinds of clouds, various organizations would come and share infrastructure and related operational resources to achieve configurations specific to them that result in different goals. Most businesses in this model offer distinct mandates of regulatory or operational value, for example, health, government, or financial sectors.

3.3.4 Hybrid Cloud: A hybrid cloud is an integrated computing environment with the mix of public and private clouds as one unit, allowing organizations to get desirable benefits from either according to requirements. In this environment, sensitive data or applications remain in a private cloud, offering additional security, governance, and regulatory compliance, while less sensitive or less important workloads run in a public cloud. With its flexibility and extensibility, the approach allows better resource efficiency and higher economic viability for organizations.

4. EMERGENCE OF BLOCKCHAIN TECHNOLOGY IN HEALTHCARE

Blockchain, initially conceived to enable digital, mysterious currencies such as Bitcoin, is rapidly becoming a powerful force for change in many sectors, including—if not especially—the field of healthcare. Quite basically, blockchain works by providing a decentralized, distributed ledger that has recorded numerous transactions at different nodes in a secure, transparent, and unalterable way. Each transaction is put together inside a "block" and then added to a "chain" of previous transactions, forming a permanent, verifiable record(Haleem et al., 2021).

Developed on decentralized structures, blockchain is a technology whereby many participants head common ledgers, normally updating in real-time, through a typical system of authentication via consensus protocols, meaning those participating have the same information. In blockchain technology, there isn't any central body to govern its operations because of decentralization; hence, this reduces the risk associated with a single failure point of any kind and also increases data security(Agbo et al., 2019).

4.1 What is Blockchain?

Blockchain is a type of decentralized, distributed digital ledger technology that allows transactions to be recorded across a network of computers in such a way that data security, transparency, and immutability are guaranteed. Transactions are structured one after another, in a chain-a reason it's called "blockchain." This is how users will engage in operations with each other securely without any necessity for a third party since all parties in the system have a copy of one universal ledger. Blockchain finds its application in the worlds of finance, cryptocurrencies, healthcare-secure patient records, tracking goods along the supply chain, and wherever secure, transparently acquired, and decentralized transaction records are required(Zhang et al., 2018).

The key features of blockchain include:

4.1.1 Decentralization: While traditional databases have a single central authority, blockchains are a network of nodes computing devices where the network works in a decentralized manner. Because each node gets a complete copy of the entire blockchain, there's no single point that will lead to a failure(Sun et al., 2018).

4.1.2 Transparency: Blockchain presents all the transactions visible to the participants of the network, accountability and therefore transparency are guaranteed.

4.1.3 Security: Cryptographic protection is applied to the transactions passing through a blockchain. Following this addition process, a block cannot be altered without further alterations to all following blocks down the chain; this requires the consensus of most participants in the network.

4.1.4 Immutability: Once something is recorded onto the blockchain, it's very difficult to change or delete. This is what gives the blockchain its record permanence and tamper-proof characteristics, some of the key requisites that make blockchain especially useful in applications such as financial transactions, supply chain management, and medical records.

4.1.5 Consensus Mechanism: Blockchain networks depend on consensus mechanisms such as PoW (Proof-of-Work) or PoS (Proof-of-Stake) to attain an agreement on the validity of transactions. This is what guarantees that only transactions meeting extremely rigid criteria of validity find their way into the blockchain.

4.2 How Blockchain Works:

Blockchain is a form of digital record-keeping system, decentralized and distributed over a network of computers. The functional mechanism of blockchain works in the following manner in sequence(Attaran, 2022; Huang et al., 2021):

Figure 4. Visual Infographic workflow of Blockchain

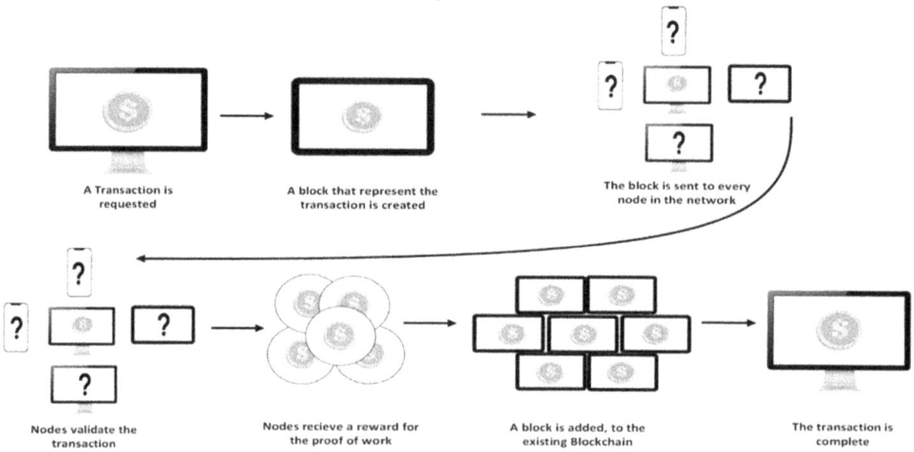

4.2.1 Transition Initiation: A user initiates a transaction—a transaction that could involve sending some cryptocurrencies, recording information to the blockchain, or executing a smart contract.

4.2.2 Transition Broadcast: The transaction propagates through the decentralized network of computers where all nodes in this network hold the full copy of the blockchain and are able to verify the validity of the transaction

4.2.3 Validation: Nodes confirm the transaction by using one of the following common consensus mechanisms.

- **Proof of Work:** Basically, several nodes were competing to be the one to crack a difficult math problem. Whichever node cracks it first gets that block of transactions added to the blockchain and gets a reward.

Proof of Stake: Validators compete to create blocks on a chain based on the number of coins they have, combined with the act of "staking" these coins as equity collateral. It is combined with other transactions into a block upon successful verification.

4.2.4 Block Creation: Validated transactions are then collected to build a block. A block consists of a set of transactions, a timestamp, a link to the previous block, and a hash—the solution for the consensus mechanism, like the solved puzzle in Proof of Work.

4.2.5 Chain Addition: In this way, the newly mined block is added to the existing blockchain, thereby creating an immutable record. This block is connected to the previous block by means of a cryptographic hash, hence the chain of the reason why it was called a blockchain.

4.2.6 Distribution and Synchronization: The modified blockchain is broadcast on the whole network. All the nodes implement updating of the copy of the blockchain with a new block added. Therefore, all copies of the blockchain will be the same and up to date.

4.2.7 Immutability and Security: If one of the added blocks in a blockchain is tampered with, it would require the redoing of the consensus mechanism of that block and all that followed. In PoW, this would be done with a majority of computing power or the majority stakes in PoS; hence, it makes Blockchain highly tamper-proof and secure.

4.2.8 Completion: The transaction is done, and now the data gets recorded into the blockchain for a lifetime. Then the data would be available to everybody with the right permission for that blockchain, provided it is public or private.

4.3 Potential to Address EHR Challenges

Blockchain technology can really help solve some very serious problems in healthcare data security, interoperability, and trust. It would thus be valuable for developing a decentralized, secure, and unchangeable record of patients' data within the domain of health. This, therefore, makes information tamper-proof, yet accessible to persons of authority. This heightened level of security ensures that sensitive information about health is well guarded against cyber threats and unauthorized access—surely a major concern within the modern digital space(Attaran, 2022).

4.3.1 Data Security and Integrity:

Immutable records are an intrinsic feature of blockchain, data once stored become incurable for the rest of the time without network agreement. This maintains very high levels of data integrity, which counters the issues associated with breaches in data or unauthorized modifications in EHR systems. Data stored in a decentralized way across different nodes minimizes the risk of centralization, to say the least. Even if one node is compromised, data integrity across a network will be ensured under the power of consensus and replication.

4.3.2 Interoperability and Data Exchange:

Interoperability can only be worked out through the provision of a standardized framework for data exchange. Besides smart contracts, dApps shall design automated mechanisms of sharing agreements of data toward smooth integration between different EHR systems. Using blockchain technology, patients and health services may access their medical records both transparently and with controlled sharing. The technology enables secure sharing of patient data between different health service providers while maintaining privacy and consent(Zhang et al., 2017).

4.3.3 Scalability and Efficiency:

In the management of patient records, a single source of truth is made possible through blockchain. Less fragmented data ensures this approach along with a reduction in redundant entry, which thereby ensures better efficiency. Blockchain technology provides an indelible record of all activities regarding data through its immutability. This ensures greater transparency and accountability, which is important in tracking and changing data through compliance with imposed regulations in order to build trust between stakeholders(Saeed et al., 2022).

4.4 Hyperledger Fabric – A Blockchain Framework

By design, Hyperledger Fabric is an open-source blockchain framework for enterprise use. Conversely, most public blockchain platforms, such as Bitcoin or Ethereum, by design, are created to be open to participation in a decentralized fashion. Permissioned and thus optimized to create private blockchain networks is Hyperledger Fabric itself. It is a part of the Hyperledger project hosted by the Linux Foundation aimed at providing enterprise-grade blockchain solutions(Wang & Qin, 2021).

4.4.1 How Hyperledger Fabric Works

4.4.1.1 Transaction Flow:

- A client sends the proposed transaction to endorsing peers.

- The endorsing peers simulate the transaction and send the endorsements back with the proposal without committing to the ledger.
- A client collects the endorsements and sends the transaction to the ordering service.
- The ordering service puts the transactions into blocks and delivers it to all peers for validation.
- Peers validate transactions and apply valid transactions to the ledger(ledgers & 2016, n.d.).

4.4.1.2 Endorsement and Validation: Transactions in Hyperledger Fabric had to be endorsed by a set of designated peers before they could be valid. Upon endorsement, the transaction is then sent to the ordering service for ordering into a block and subsequently validated by all network peers before it gets committed into ledger.

4.4.1.3 Consensus Mechanism: The public blockchains make use of either Proof of Work or Proof of Stake consensus mechanism. In the case of Hyperledger Fabric, a pluggable consensus model is applied. This opens up the possibility of taking into consideration several consensus algorithms, which can have the capability for the network to be more effective, especially in environments where not all participants are supposed to validate every transaction.

Figure 5. Working process of Hyperledger fabric - a blockchain framework

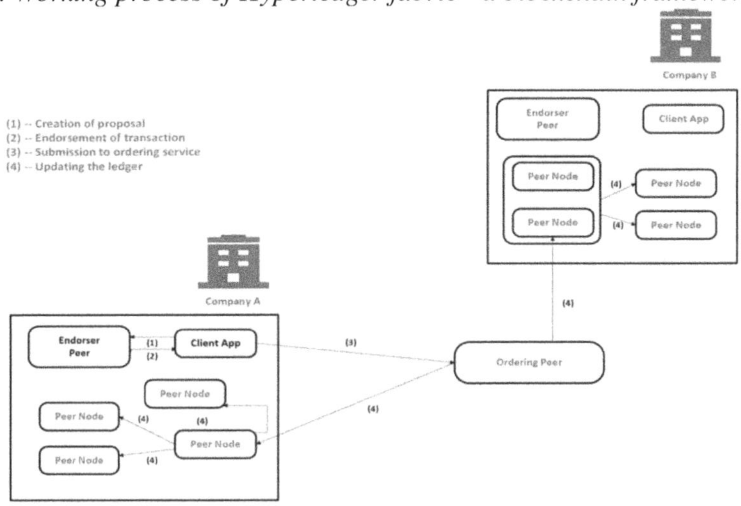

4.5 Smart Contacts on Blockchain

Smart contracts can be considered as self-executing agreements in which the rules of a contract are reduced to computer code. As a result, smart contracts automatically enforce and execute obligations of the parties after some preconditions have been met. Smart contracts run on decentralized blockchain platforms, such as Ethereum, ensuring, by implication, security, transparency, and their nonfungibility(Griggs et al., 2018).

4.5.1 How Smart Contract Works?

Smart contracts work by coding the terms into a series of "if-then" statements. Consider an example of a very simple smart contract: "In case party A sends X sum of cryptocurrency to party B, then transfer asset Y ownership to party A." The moment such a payment is made, the smart contract will self-execute and arrange the very transfer of ownership of the asset to the buyer. It comes as a result of the workability behind the blockchain, where the entire network of nodes verifies whether the stipulations, which the smart contract has put forth, have indeed set the specifications as being met(Mohanta et al., 2018).

Figure 6. How smart contracts are secure than traditional transaction

4.5.2 Advantages of Smart Contracts

Table 1. Advantages of smart contracts

Speed	**Automates processes, therefore reducing the time taken to execute agreements, such as financial transactions or legal agreements.**
Cost-Efficiency	No intermediaries, such as lawyers and brokers, involves less spending on transactions and administrative related matters.
Security	This holds in regard to the security features of blockchain, making the smart contracts tamper-proof and hard to hack because verification is decentralized.
Transparency	The terms are transparent and verifiable by all parties, hence increasing transparency and reducing the chances of disputes or misunderstandings.

(Saini et al., 2021)

4.5.3 Essential Equations in Blockchain Technology

4.5.3.1 Probability of an Event

The probability of a specific event occurring, such as a malicious attack, can be represented by:

$$P(A) = \frac{Number\ of\ favourable\ outcomes}{Total\ number\ of\ possible\ outcomes}$$

Where $P(A)$ is the Probability of the event occurring

4.5.3.2 Throughput in Blockchain Network

Throughput in a blockchain system measured as the number of transactions per second (TPS), can be expressed as:

$$T = \frac{N_{Transactions}}{t_{block}}$$

Where $N_{transactions}$ is the number of transactions in a block, and t_{block} is the time taken to add a block to the blockchain.

4.5.3.3 Data Storage in Blockchain

The total data storage S required by a blockchain network after n blocks is given by:

$$S = n \times S_{block}$$

Where S_{block} is the average size of each block.

5. RELATED WORK

Table 2 represents the comprehensive literature review, focus areas, techniques and methods used, and proposed future work by researchers –

Table 2. Literature review

Paper Title	Reference	Authors	Publication Year	Focus Area	Techniques/ Methods Used	Proposed Future Work
Blockchain in Healthcare: Portal for Electronic Health Records	(L. Kumar et al., 2024)	Lakshya Kumar, Aayush Sharma, Harshal Sharma and Swati Sharma	2024	Analysis of Blockchain Applications in Healthcare and focus on secure data transmission.		Need of blockchain in the healthcare industry to enhance privacy concern
Immersive Virtual and Augmented Reality in Healthcare: An IoT and Blockchain Perspective	(R. Kumar et al., 2023)	Rajendra Kumar, Vishal Jain, Garry Tan Wei Han and Abderezak Touzene	2023	Implementation of cost-effective and real-time solution for healthcare problem by using IOT, Blockchain, augmented reality and virtual reality	Frameworks for designing or upgrading healthcare system by increase security and data privacy	
Hyperledger fabric platform for healthcare trust relations—Proof-of-Concept	(Nedaković et al., 2023)	Aleksandar Nedaković, Anton Hasselgren, Katina Kralevska and Danilo Gligoroski	2023	Proposed Hyperledger fabric-based platform and the usage of blockchain technology	WebApp in the NextJS framework, Hyperledger fabric and smart contacts	
Applications of blockchain technology in medicine and healthcare: Challenges and future perspectives	(Siyal et al., 2019)	Ali Asad Siyal, Aisha Zahid Junejo, Muhammad Zawish, Aiman Khali and Georgia Soursou	2019	Generalized workflow of blockchain and its applications in the healthcare industry.		Distributed ledger of Blockchain technology to provide numerous advantages to medical industry.
The potential for artificial intelligence in healthcare	(Davenport & Kalakota, 2019)	Thomas Davenport and Ravi Kalakota	2019	Relevance of Artificial Intelligence and other related technologies in healthcare		Role of AI to address the greatest challenge in healthcare domain

continued on following page

Table 2. Continued

Paper Title	Reference	Authors	Publication Year	Focus Area	Techniques/ Methods Used	Proposed Future Work
A systematic review of the use of blockchain in healthcare	(Hölbl et al., 2018)	Marko Hölbl, Marko Kompara, Aida Kamisalic and Lili Nemec Zlatolas	2018	Highlighted the Challenges in Blockchain Adoption and proposed models to facilitate blockchain adoption	Data from multiple research paper and analysis of quality assessment	Integration and Scalability solutions to implement in real-world
A natural language processing system that links medical terms in electronic health record notes to lay definitions: System development using physician reviews	(Chen et al., 2018)	Jinying Chen, Emily Druhl, Balaji Polepalli Ramesh, Thomas K. Houston, Cynthia A. Brandt, Donna M. Zulman, Varsha G. Vimalananda and Samir Malkani	2018	Web Based natural language processing system that links medical system terms in EHR notes		
Implementation of a nationwide electronic health record (EHR): The international experience in 13 countries	(Fragidis & Chatzoglou, 2018)	Leonidas L Fragidis and Prodromos D Chatzoglou	2018	Identification of Best Practices applied in Electronic health record (EHR) system.		
Leveraging Blockchain Technology to Enhance Supply Chain Management in Healthcare:	(Clauson et al., 2018)	Kevin A. Clauson, Elizabeth A. Breeden, Cameron Davidson and Timothy K. Mackey	2018	Analysis of blockchain for the pharmaceutical supply chain	Focused on IoHT a subset of Internet of Things (IoT) on health and wellness.	
Cloud Computing in Healthcare	(Devadass et al., 2017b)	Lingkiswaran Devadass, Sugalia Santhira Sekaran and Rajermani Thinakaran	2017	Highlighted the review of some proposed cloud-based e-healthcare architecture.		

6. SYSTEM DESIGN AND ARCHITECTURE FOR INTEGRATING AI, CLOUD COMPUTING, AND BLOCKCHAIN IN HEALTHCARE

Implementing a healthcare system integrated with AI, cloud computing, and blockchain shall ensure its scalability, security, and interoperability. The architecture of the system has to meet the diversified needs of the stakeholders in terms of healthcare provisions, patients, and other involved parties. Summarized below is a discussion of the design and architecture of the system:

6.1 Architecture Overview

Figure 7 shows the visualized architecture as a multi-layered system with the following key layers -

Figure 7. Visualised architecture of multi-layered system

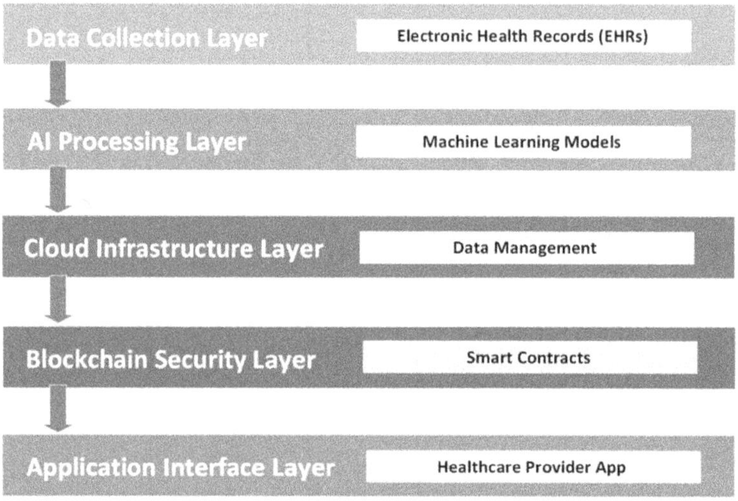

6.1.1 Data Collection Layer

The Data Collection Layer is an essential component of the system and would involve the sources having electronic health records, Internet of Things-enabled medical devices, wearable health monitoring devices, imaging technologies, and patient engagement portals. This layer essentially can be said to collect raw data for medical histories, data on the real-time patient monitoring, genetic data, among other health-related information.

6.1.2 AI Processing Layer

AI Processing Layer consists of tons of building blocks that include machine learning models, neural networks, NLP tools, and algorithms, tailor-made for diagnoses, predictive analytics, and individual treatment plans. Its main purpose is to analyze incoming data in the prediction of diseases, course, and outcome of treatment, the recognition of anomalies in medical images, and deep analysis of patient data.

6.1.3 Cloud Infrastructure Layer

The Infrastructure Layer of the Cloud refers to the public, private, or hybrid cloud services providing very basic storage, computing power, and networking resources. This is what enables AI processing—through the delivery of scalable computing resources necessary to store, process, and back up data so that AI algorithms may run effectively. It also houses information management services that consider unstructured data, databases management, and processing data in real-time to ensure that huge volumes of data are well managed and put to practice within the system.

6.1.4 Blockchain Security Layer

The Blockchain Security Layer encompasses blockchain nodes, smart contracts, consensus algorithms, and encryption protocols as an assurance measure toward the security, integrity, and transparency of data. This layer helps create the immutability of records in all transactions of data so that the log produced becomes tamper-resistant, improving auditability. It ensures that only authorized personnel access sensitive health information through smart contracts acting as regulatory mechanisms for access control.

6.1.5 Application Interface Layer

The Application Interface Layer implements user interfaces, dashboards, mobile applications, telemedicine platforms, and APIs, and, in short, provides the point of entry for interaction with the system by healthcare providers, patients, researchers, and other interested end-users who would like to enable telemedicine consultation for the real-time monitoring of patients, data representation, and access to EHR.

6.2 System Workflow

Figure 8. Workflow diagram of proposed system

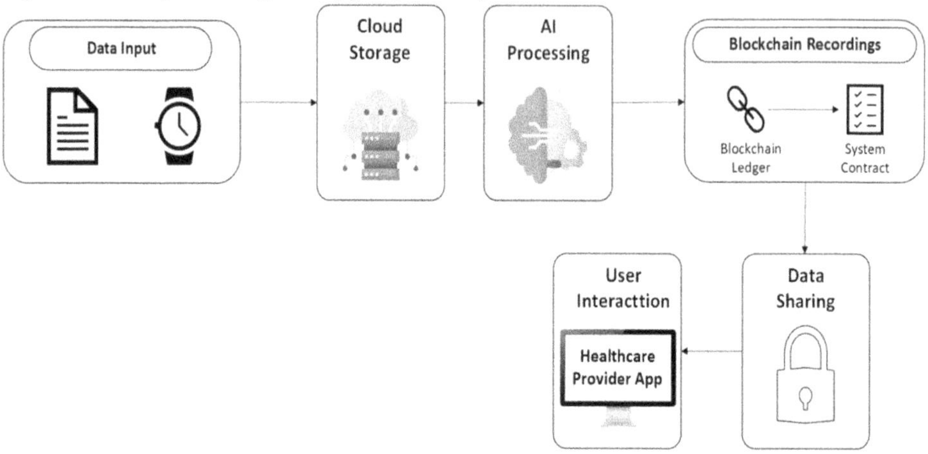

6.2.1 Data Input: Patient data from multiple sources is pulled and transmitted to the cloud for storage and preliminary processing: EHRs and wearable devices.

6.2.2 AI Processing: The AI layer processes the data, performing tasks such as diagnostics, disease prediction, and treatment personalization. AI models analyze the data in real-time, with results being stored and managed in the cloud.

6.2.3 Blockchain Recording: All important transactions and changes are recorded in the blockchain as processes of data. Smart contracts enforce the rules of access to data, allowing the manipulation of the data with access only to authorized users.

6.2.4 Data Storage and Management: Processed information and its corresponding blockchain entries are stored securely in the cloud. Moreover, the cloud infrastructure ensures that there are facilities for the system's scalability to handle large volumes of data.

6.3.5 User Interaction: Processed information and its corresponding blockchain entries are stored securely in the cloud. Moreover, the cloud infrastructure ensures that there are facilities for the system's scalability to handle large volumes of data.

6.3.6 Data Sharing and Interaction: Blockchain-powered secured data sharing allows smooth and easy patient information exchange across healthcare systems, thereby greatly facilitating collaboration by various organizations and systems.

7. IMPLEMENTATION METHODOLOGY

The development of this proposed system is developed as a series of structured steps that must be able to guarantee the interaction of every component in concert with others within an integrated system. The following section defines the major steps in setting up the development environment, initiating the blockchain network, managing serverless computing using AWS Lambda, setting up API Gateway, developing the user interface utilizing React.js, and combining all the components into one system.

7.1 Setting Up the Development Environment

To Setup the Development Environment follow the steps mentioned below:

7.1.1 Installing Hyperledger Fabric: Install Hyperledger Fabric in either the local environment or the cloud. Installation encompasses downloads of the binaries, Docker images, and sample networks. Core development tools in Fabric encompass utilities such as cryptogen, configtxgen used in the construction or management of the blockchain network, and peer commands.

7.1.2 Configuring AWS CLI and SDKs: The AWS Command Line Interface should be installed along with the necessary SDKs in a proper way so that one can deal properly with AWS services. These will be required for deploying and managing AWS Lambda functions and API Gateway configurations.

7.1.3 Installing React.js and Supporting Libraries: Set up a development environment with Node.js and npm for React.js. Install the required libraries and frameworks: for routing, React Router; HTTP request management, Axios; and so on.

7.1.4 Setting Up Version Control: Employ Git as a version control system to keep all code orderly via branches for development, testing, and production.

7.2 Deploying the Blockchain Network on AWS

Deploying the blockchain network on AWS involves the following steps:

7.2.1 Creating and Amazon EC2 Instance: Develop and deploy chaincode (smart contracts) on the Fabric network. Chaincode should be designed to handle the specific requirements of Electronic Health Records (EHR) management, including data validation, access control, and transaction processing.

7.2.2 Configuring the Blockchain Network: On the EC2 instance, initialize and configure the Hyperledger Fabric network by defining the network's peers, orders, and channels. Use docker-compose to bring up the network components, ensuring that each component can communicate effectively.

7.2.3 Deploying Chaincode: Design and implementation of smart contracts-chaincode are done on the Fabric network. The chaincode design shall aim to address some special needs brought forth by EHR management, such as data validation, access control, and transaction processes.

7.3 Creating and Managing Lambda Functions

AWS Lambda provides serverless computing for various backend tasks, without managing the servers. The Implementation is listed below:

7.3.1 Writing Lambda function: Develop Lambda functions using Node.js or Python that interact with the Hyperledger Fabric network. These functions will handle tasks such as querying the blockchain, submitting transactions, and managing user authentication.

7.3.2 Configuring Execution Roles and Permissions: Assign IAM roles to all AWS Lambda functions accordingly, so that they receive permissions to call any other AWS Service currently in use; this may include DynamoDB, S3, and API Gateway where necessary.

7.3.3 Setting Up the Triggers: Accomplish automatic event-triggering of Lambda functions, be it an HTTP request via the API Gateway, or change within a DynamoDB table, or even S3 file upload.

7.4 Building and Testing the API Gateway

7.4.1 Creating RESTful APIs: Design correct APIs on the API Gateway to expose the functionality supported by the Lambdas. Such APIs must serve the requests regarding patient records, User Authentication, and communication with blockchain technology.

7.4.2 Configuring CORS and Security Policies: Enable CORS to allow your frontend application to interact with it. Configure the APIs with security mechanisms, including one of the following: API keys, IAM roles, or JSON Web Token authentication.

7.4.3 Testing the API Gateway: Test the functionality of APIs using tools like Postman to ensure they return the expected results. Do load testing in order to look at how APIs will behave under different usage scenarios.

7.5 Developing the User Interface with React.js

The frontend interface is developed using React.js, providing a responsive and user-friendly experience. The implementation includes:

7.5.1 Designing UI Components: Create reusable React components for the various sections of the application, such as patient dashboards, record management interfaces, and user authentication.

7.5.2 Integrating APIs: Use Axios or Fetch API to connect the frontend application with the API Gateway, ensuring that user actions trigger the appropriate backend processes.

7.5.3 Implementing state management: Use React-specific state management tools in managing application-wide states; this is to say, user sessions, form data, and statuses of transactions.

7.5.4 Testing and Debugging: The unit tests the functionality of individual components, but the application should be tested for its end-to-end usability on a wide range of devices and browsers.

7.6 Integrating All Components into a Cohesive System

The final step is to integrate all the components, ensuring they work together as a cohesive system:

7.6.1 Orchestrating Frontend and Backend Communication:

Ensure that the React.js frontend optimally interfaces backend APIs and blockchain networks directly with API Gateway and Lambda functions.

7.6.2 Deploying the Application: Host static files on frontend services like AWS S3. Run the whole system in a production environment. Deploy with an AWS CloudFormation application to make sure there is cohesion and repeatability in the deployment.

7.6.3 Monitoring and Maintenance: Monitoring tools Provide AWS CloudWatch will measure the performance of an application in addition to its health. Set up logging and alerting to rapidly identify issues should they occur in production, to resolve those issues in the shortest time possible.

8. FUTURE TRENDS IN HEALTHCARE

This rapid, radical transformation of health care is being driven by technological innovation, evolving patient expectations, and the urgent demand for more effective and efficient ways of delivering care. Trends affecting how healthcare services will be delivered, accessed, and managed are going to probably shape the future. These include the continued uptake of adoption in digital health solutions, the integration of AI and machine learning, the rise of personalized medicine, the adoption of blockchain, and a strong focus on patient-centered care.

8.1 Digital Health and Telemedicine

Digital health technology, including telemedicine, will be pivotal in the future landscape of healthcare delivery. Indeed, the COVID-19 pandemic has ramped up this curve, which is likely to keep on rising in the desire of both patients and providers across the continuum of healthcare provision as they realize the convenience, effectiveness, and patient-oriented features provided by remote care. Future developments in telemedicine will further release advanced forms of virtual consultations, monitor chronic conditions remotely, and make use of AI in diagnoses for greater accuracy, along with personalized treatment.

8.2 Artificial Intelligence and Machine Learning

Creates a revolution in health care by providing better and more precise diagnostics, the forecast of patient outcomes, and optimization of treatment protocols, among others. Through deep analyses of the huge volumes of information from EHRs, medical imaging, and genomics by AI-based tools, patterns, and insights that could at least be hard for humans to grasp are showcased. In this context, in the future, AI will be directed towards perfecting decision support systems, administrative activities, and precision medicine in order to manage treatment for a certain patient considering his or her genetic profile and history.

8.3 Virtual and Augmented Reality

Virtual and augmented reality technologies will soon revolutionize medical education, the training of surgeons, and ultimately patient care. (Whig et al., 2023) VR is able to realistically simulate even such complicated surgical procedures that earlier were unrealizable as simulations. AR adds to the experience of a surgeon's real-time overlay of the most important information in the surgical field. Both these innovations find their place in patient therapy, such as in the VR-based rehabilitation programs for stroke patients and in the AR-assisted exercises of physical therapy(Ong et al., 2023).

8.4 Global Health Initiatives and Collaborative Care

Consequently, most of the health-related challenges are global and thus would need increased international cooperation through experience and expertise sharing. Global health programs will put much focus on disparities in accessibility and quality of care in low- and middle-income countries. A better future in healthcare delivery would entail increased coordination in the fight against such global health threats as pandemics and better strategies for the delivery of healthcare services in disadvantaged areas.

9. CONCLUSION

This chapter reviewed the transformational force accelerated by EHRs in the health industry, which considered the role pre-assumed for emerging technologies like AI, cloud computing, and blockchain. Innovations accelerate a chain of activities at unprecedented speed in—leveraging healthcare data management, security, and usage for the improvement of patient health outcomes and the enhancement and democratization of health services. AI intervention in health service delivery holds great promise for redefining diagnosis, personalized medicine, and patient care. The phenomenal capacity of AI in the analysis of vast amounts of data, in synergy with new vistas in the field of precision medicine, opens up the possibilities for proactive management of healthcare. The ever-increasing volume of health data has been made scalable and flexible for easy collaboration and real-time patient information access across multiple geographies and health providers through cloud computing.

Blockchain technology, intrinsically connected with security and transparency, now chose to apply its potential in solving some of the hot-button problems of the medical healthcare industry: data privacy, interoperability, and trust. It assures that on decentralization, immutable records shall ensure integrity and confidentiality of sensitive patient information, hence opening up new opportunities toward a safe and more effective health care system. However, it is not without a hitch in their implementation, as many issues are linked with these technologies about data privacy and regulatory compliance for widespread adoption. However, it is expected that these challenges will be answered by continued research and innovation with the full cooperation of stakeholders as healthcare moves forward.

The future of health care will be an ecosystem in which AI, cloud computing, and blockchain technologies continue to integrate and mature. Further maturity in this regard will transform the landscape even more into a patient-centered, evidence-based, and efficient one. For the way ahead on all of these, there must be technological innovations accompanied by careful consideration of their ethical, legal, and social implications so that the benefits from such advances may be realized equitably across populations. This confluence of artificial intelligence, cloud computing, and blockchain represents a critical shift toward a new overall well-connected, secure, and efficient system. As we move forward with these cutting-edge technologies, new avenues are opened to further enhance patient care, reduce costs, and tackle some of the key global health problems currently arising simultaneously. Moving forward, the drive, innovation, and collaboration need to continue with the fervor of exploiting fully all that the humungous transformative potential these technologies hold under the aegis of healthcare.

REFERENCES

Agbo, C. C., Mahmoud, Q. H., & Eklund, J. M. (2019). Blockchain technology in healthcare: A systematic review. *Healthcare (Basel)*, 7(2), 56. Advance online publication. DOI: 10.3390/healthcare7020056 PMID: 30987333

Aguirre, R. R., Suarez, O., Fuentes, M., & Sanchez-Gonzalez, M. A. (2019). Electronic Health Record Implementation: A Review of Resources and Tools. *Cureus*, 11(9). Advance online publication. DOI: 10.7759/cureus.5649 PMID: 31700751

Angra, S., & Ahuja, S. (2017). Machine learning and its applications: A review. *Proceedings of the 2017 International Conference On Big Data Analytics and Computational Intelligence, ICBDACI 2017*, 57–60. DOI: 10.1109/ICBDACI.2017.8070809

Attaran, M. (2022). Blockchain technology in healthcare: Challenges and opportunities. *International Journal of Healthcare Management*, 15(1), 70–83. DOI: 10.1080/20479700.2020.1843887

Bajwa, J., Munir, U., Nori, A., & Williams, B. (2021). Artificial intelligence in healthcare: Transforming the practice of medicine. *Future Healthcare Journal*, 8(2), e188–e194. DOI: 10.7861/fhj.2021-0095 PMID: 34286183

Chen, J., Druhl, E., Ramesh, B. P., Houston, T. K., Brandt, C. A., Zulman, D. M., Vimalananda, V. G., Malkani, S., & Yu, H. (2018). A natural language processing system that links medical terms in electronic health record notes to lay definitions: System development using physician reviews. *Journal of Medical Internet Research*, 20(1), e26. Advance online publication. DOI: 10.2196/jmir.8669 PMID: 29358159

Clauson, K. A., Breeden, E. A., Davidson, C., & Mackey, T. K. (2018). Leveraging Blockchain Technology to Enhance Supply Chain Management in Healthcare. *Blockchain in Healthcare Today*. Advance online publication. DOI: 10.30953/bhty.v1.20

Davenport, T., & Kalakota, R. (2019). The potential for artificial intelligence in healthcare. *Future Healthcare Journal*, 6(2), 94–98. DOI: 10.7861/futurehosp.6-2-94 PMID: 31363513

De La Torre-Díez, I., Díaz-Pernas, F. J., Fernández, G., Antón-Rodríguez, M., Martínez-Zarzuela, M., González-Ortega, D., & Boto-Giralda, D. (2012). Analysis of the benefits and constraints for the implementation of Cloud Computing over an EHRs system. *Proceedings of the 6th Euro American Conference on Telematics and Information Systems, EATIS 2012*. DOI: 10.1145/2261605.2261628

Devadass, L., Sekaran, S. S., & Thinakaran, R. (2017a). CLOUD COMPUTING IN HEALTHCARE. *International Journal of Students'. Research Technology Management*, 5(1), 25–31. DOI: 10.18510/ijsrtm.2017.516

Devadass, L., Sekaran, S. S., & Thinakaran, R. (2017b). CLOUD COMPUTING IN HEALTHCARE. *International Journal of Students'. Research Technology Management*, 5(1), 25–31. DOI: 10.18510/ijsrtm.2017.516

Fragidis, L. L., & Chatzoglou, P. D. (2018). Implementation of a nationwide electronic health record (EHR): The international experience in 13 countries. *International Journal of Health Care Quality Assurance*, 31(2), 116–130. DOI: 10.1108/IJHCQA-09-2016-0136 PMID: 29504871

Griggs, K. N., Ossipova, O., Kohlios, C. P., Baccarini, A. N., Howson, E. A., & Hayajneh, T. (2018). Healthcare Blockchain System Using Smart Contracts for Secure Automated Remote Patient Monitoring. *Journal of Medical Systems*, 42(7), 130. Advance online publication. DOI: 10.1007/s10916-018-0982-x PMID: 29876661

Guo, Y., Kuo, M. H., & Sahama, T. (2012). Cloud computing for healthcare research information sharing. *CloudCom 2012 - Proceedings: 2012 4th IEEE International Conference on Cloud Computing Technology and Science*, 889–894. DOI: 10.1109/CloudCom.2012.6427561

Haleem, A., Javaid, M., Singh, R. P., Suman, R., & Rab, S. (2021). Blockchain technology applications in healthcare: An overview. *International Journal of Intelligent Networks*, 2, 130–139. DOI: 10.1016/j.ijin.2021.09.005

Hölbl, M., Kompara, M., Kamišalić, A., & Zlatolas, L. N. (2018). A systematic review of the use of blockchain in healthcare. *Symmetry*, 10(10), 470. Advance online publication. DOI: 10.3390/sym10100470

Huang, G., Al Foysal, A., Huang, G., & Al Foysal, A. (2021). Blockchain in Healthcare. *Technology and Investment*, 12(3), 168–181. DOI: 10.4236/ti.2021.123010

Jabali, A. K., Waris, A., Khan, D. I., Ahmed, S., & Hourani, R. J. (2022a). Electronic health records: Three decades of bibliometric research productivity analysis and some insights. *Informatics in Medicine Unlocked*, 29, 100872. DOI: 10.1016/j.imu.2022.100872

Jabali, A. K., Waris, A., Khan, D. I., Ahmed, S., & Hourani, R. J. (2022b). Electronic health records: Three decades of bibliometric research productivity analysis and some insights. *Informatics in Medicine Unlocked*, 29, 100872. DOI: 10.1016/j.imu.2022.100872

Jones, S. S., Rudin, R. S., Perry, T., & Shekelle, P. G. (2014). Health information technology: An updated systematic review with a focus on meaningful use. *Annals of Internal Medicine*, 160(1), 48–54. DOI: 10.7326/M13-1531 PMID: 24573664

Kumar, L., Sharma, A., Sharma, H., & Sharma, S. (2024). Blockchain in Healthcare:Portal for Electronic Health Records. SSRN *Electronic Journal*. https://doi.org/DOI: 10.2139/SSRN.4492411

Kumar, R., Jain, V., Han, G. T. W., & Touzene, A. (2023). Immersive virtual and augmented reality in healthcare: An IoT and blockchain perspective. *Immersive Virtual and Augmented Reality in Healthcare: An IoT and Blockchain Perspective*, 1–223. DOI: 10.1201/9781003340133

Cachin, C. (2016, July). Architecture of the hyperledger blockchain fabric. In *Workshop on distributed cryptocurrencies and consensus ledgers* (Vol. 310, No. 4, pp. 1-4).

Luo, Y., Thompson, W. K., Herr, T. M., Zeng, Z., Berendsen, M. A., Jonnalagadda, S. R., Carson, M. B., & Starren, J. (2017). Natural Language Processing for EHR-Based Pharmacovigilance: A Structured Review. *Drug Safety*, 40(11), 1075–1089. DOI: 10.1007/s40264-017-0558-6 PMID: 28643174

Mohanta, B. K., Panda, S. S., & Jena, D. (2018). An Overview of Smart Contract and Use Cases in Blockchain Technology. *2018 9th International Conference on Computing, Communication and Networking Technologies, ICCCNT 2018*. DOI: 10.1109/ICCCNT.2018.8494045

Nand, P., Jain, V., Le, D.-N., Chatterjee, J. M., Kannan, R., & Verma, A. S. (Eds.). (2023). *Deep Learning for Healthcare Services* (Vol. 11). BENTHAM SCIENCE PUBLISHERS., DOI: 10.2174/97898150802301230201

Nedaković, A., Hasselgren, A., Kralevska, K., & Gligoroski, D. (2023). Hyperledger fabric platform for healthcare trust relations—Proof-of-Concept. *Blockchain: Research and Applications*, 4(4), 100156. DOI: 10.1016/j.bcra.2023.100156

Oladipupo, T. (2010). *Types of Machine Learning Algorithms*. New Advances in Machine Learning., DOI: 10.5772/9385

Ong, E. T., Pang, Y. J., Talib, C. A., Setiawan, R., Ng, J. H., & Por, F. P. (2023). Industrial Revolution (IR) and exemplary AR/ VR-based technological tools in preventive health education: The past, present, and future. *Immersive Virtual and Augmented Reality in Healthcare: An IoT and Blockchain Perspective*, 1–27. DOI: 10.1201/9781003340133-1

Ozair, F. F., Jamshed, N., Sharma, A., & Aggarwal, P. (2015). Ethical issues in electronic health records: A general overview. *Perspectives in Clinical Research*, 6(2), 73. DOI: 10.4103/2229-3485.153997 PMID: 25878950

Saeed, H., Malik, H., Bashir, U., Ahmad, A., Riaz, S., Ilyas, M., Bukhari, W. A., & Khan, M. I. A. (2022). Blockchain technology in healthcare: A systematic review. *PLoS One*, 17(4), e0266462. Advance online publication. DOI: 10.1371/journal.pone.0266462 PMID: 35404955

Saini, K., Roy, A., Chelliah, P. R., & Patel, T. (2021). Blockchain 2.O: A Smart Contract. *2021 International Conference on Computational Performance Evaluation,* ComPE 2021, 524–528. DOI: 10.1109/ComPE53109.2021.9752021

Seymour, T., Frantsvog, D., & Graeber, T. (2012). Electronic Health Records (EHR). [AJHS]. *American Journal of Health Sciences*, 3(3), 201–210. DOI: 10.19030/ajhs.v3i3.7139

Sharma, G. K., Bhardwaj, A., Arya, S., & Singhal, M. (2023). Blockchain in healthcare: Some use cases. *Immersive Virtual and Augmented Reality in Healthcare: An IoT and Blockchain Perspective*, 206–220. DOI: 10.1201/9781003340133-11

Siyal, A. A., Junejo, A. Z., Zawish, M., Ahmed, K., Khalil, A., & Soursou, G. (2019). Applications of blockchain technology in medicine and healthcare: Challenges and future perspectives. *Cryptography*, 3(1), 1–16. DOI: 10.3390/cryptography3010003

Sun, Y., Zhang, R., Wang, X., Gao, K., & Liu, L. (2018). A decentralizing attribute-based signature for healthcare blockchain. *Proceedings - International Conference on Computer Communications and Networks, ICCCN, 2018-July*. DOI: 10.1109/ICCCN.2018.8487349

Uhrig, R. E. (n.d.). Introduction to artificial neural networks. *Proceedings of IECON '95 - 21st Annual Conference on IEEE Industrial Electronics, 1*, 33–37. DOI: 10.1109/IECON.1995.483329

Wang, Q., & Qin, S. (2021). A hyperledger fabric-based system framework for healthcare data management. *Applied Sciences (Basel, Switzerland)*, 11(24), 11693. Advance online publication. DOI: 10.3390/app112411693

Whig, P., Kouser, S., Sharma, A., Bhatia, A. B., & Nadikattu, R. R. (2023). AR/VR revolutions in future healthcare. *Immersive Virtual and Augmented Reality in Healthcare: An IoT and Blockchain Perspective*, 96–118. DOI: 10.1201/9781003340133-6

Zhang, P., Schmidt, D. C., White, J., & Lenz, G. (2018). Blockchain Technology Use Cases in Healthcare. *Advances in Computers*, 111, 1–41. DOI: 10.1016/bs.adcom.2018.03.006

Zhang, P., Walker, M. A., White, J., Schmidt, D. C., & Lenz, G. (2017). Metrics for assessing blockchain-based healthcare decentralized apps. *2017 IEEE 19th International Conference on E-Health Networking, Applications and Services, Healthcom 2017, 2017-December*, 1–4. DOI: 10.1109/HealthCom.2017.8210842

Chapter 16

Impact of COVID-19 on Electronic-Governance Adoption:

Building Resilient and Inclusive Digital Societies

Kehinde Adewole Oyeniran
https://orcid.org/0000-0003-1754-6184
International Centre for Genetic Engineering and Biotechnology, South Africa

Mobolaji O. Tenibiaje
https://orcid.org/0009-0009-7248-970X
Bamidele Olumilua University of Education Science and Technology, Nigeria

Morenikeji A. Oke
https://orcid.org/0000-0001-7075-5239
Bamidele Olumilua University of Education Science and Technology, Nigeria

Busayo M. Olowe
https://orcid.org/0000-0003-0953-4140
Bamidele Olumilua University of Education Science and Technology, Nigeria

Olubukola H. Oyeniran
https://orcid.org/0000-0001-5262-7487
Federal University, Oye, Nigeria

Muftau K. Oladunmoye
Federal University of Technology, Akure, Nigeria

ABSTRACT

The global spread of the COVID-19 pandemic clearly altered the trajectory of the electronic governance adoption, also known as e-governance. In response to this challenge, governments, organisations, and individuals swiftly adopted various strategic digital coping and adaptation mechanisms. This chapter examines the global

DOI: 10.4018/979-8-3693-7678-2.ch016

efforts of some countries to adopt e-governance, their level of preparedness, and the challenges they face. The areas of health, education, and finances are important because of their significant direct and indirect impact on individual well-being. However, there are challenges related to data management, security, and privacy. Regardless of the existence of a pandemic, governments worldwide must consistently evaluate their readiness for pandemics by formulating favourable policies that can achieve reliable and inclusive implementation of future digital solutions.

1.0 INTRODUCTION

It is a well-established fact that history has a tendency to repeat itself. The coronavirus disease, also known as COVID-19, emerged a century later, following the 1918–1919 flu pandemic that claimed about 21 million lives globally within 12 months (Kumar et al., 2021; Morens et al., 2020; Ohadike, 1991). The virus was first detected in the city of Wuhan, China, with a likely origin traced to a wet seafood market in the city (Kumar et al., 2021). Unlike the flu pandemic of 1919, the COVID-19 pandemic presented unusual challenges to governments worldwide, primarily due to the technological advancement of the present age that makes a rapid spread of pathogens to places other than their origin in a short period of time possible. This makes handling pandemic events more difficult, requiring swift and effective responses to mitigate their impacts on the society.

1.1 E-governance, the COVID-19 Pandemic, and Associated Challenges

More important than ever, e-governance has emerged as a crucial tool for tackling the pandemic and fostering sustainable development (Amosun et al., 2022; Ullah et al., 2021; Ullah et al., 2022). E-governance involves the utilisation and application of information and communication technologies by governments to provide public services, engage with citizens, and improve governance processes that foster better livelihoods for their citizens (Figure 1).

Figure 1. A model of e-governance digital transformation in handling various areas of governance, including pandemic situations, such as COVID-19. Double arrows show useful adaptive conditions in which the process can learn to perform better with improved efficiency

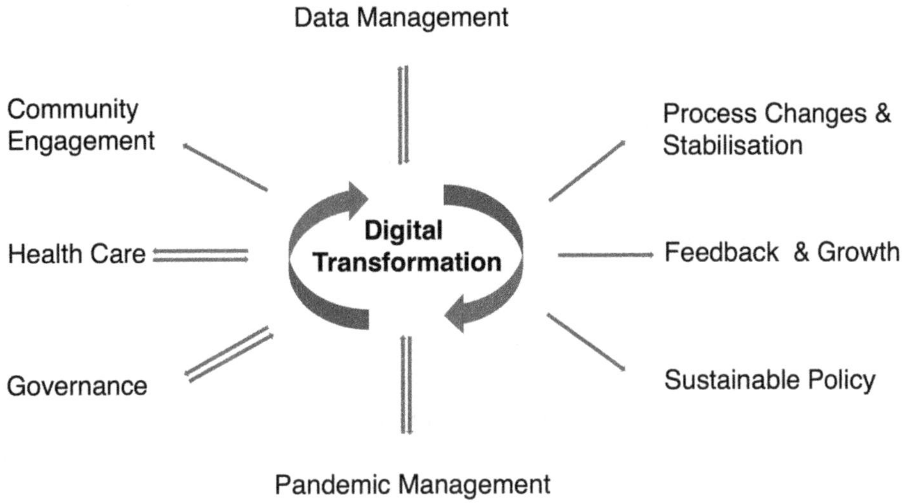

The COVID-19 pandemic has shown the weaknesses and disparities that exist in communities worldwide with swift transitions from conventional work settings to remote work, online education, and digital service provision (Flood et al., 2021). Following the pandemic, the governments and institutions quickly adapted to the new demands of adopting online platforms, leaving behind individuals without the essential digital skills or access to devices and internet connectivity, worsening pre-existing disparities and the need for proper planning (Onyema et al. 2020; Murray, 2022; Yun et al. 2022). The COVID-19 epidemic has exposed the significant disparities in digital inclusion, particularly affecting marginalised groups such as older adults, low-income individuals, and those with impairments. These groups face disproportionate difficulties in accessing and utilising digital technologies.

The importance of e-governance during the COVID-19 era, and its ability to impact citizen engagement, foster trust, and sharpen decision-making processes cannot be overemphasised (Ceesay et al., 2020; Mansoor, 2021; Avotra et al., 2021; Vardavas et al., 2021; Mensah et al., 2021). One crucial aspect of adjusting to a pandemic like COVID-19 is the potential for implementing novel strategies to address its numerous obstacles, including the utilisation of scientific advancements and technological innovations.

1.2 Technology Based Interventions and Challenges

The COVID-19 pandemic has led to the emergence of technology-driven inventive methods that expand the boundaries of logical thinking by exploring previously unexplored areas for creative progress. Hence, it is crucial to reevaluate our comprehension of digital solutions that have significant ramifications for the public throughout a pandemic to ensure efficient sustenance, regardless of a pandemic scenario or not. Pandemics can exert diverse impacts on the preexisting infrastructure of a nation. The magnitude of these consequences will primarily depend on the pre-pandemic economic and technological states of such a nation.

Further, challenges like data privacy, resistance to change, and the need for infrastructure upgrades to ensure service quality can hinder the adoption of e-governance during crises like the COVID-19 pandemic. This is often due to the natural resistance or initial reluctance to embrace change in the society (Mensah et al., 2021; Nguyen, 2023). Government must adopt e-governance tools, such as social networking websites, and strive to establish trust by actively working towards implementing impactful governance practices, such as transparent decision-making processes, accountability mechanisms, and citizen engagement initiatives. This would help foster public support for programmes aimed at driving positive change (Achmad, 2022).

Here, we examine the influence of COVID-19 on e-governance and how some countries gradually embraced the unavoidable aspects of e-governance opportunities, challenges, and the ultimate aim of establishing and maintaining resilient and inclusive digital societies. The chapter is organised into the following sections: e-governance acceleration during the pandemic crisis, inclusive digital services, cybersecurity and data privacy, long-term implications, and policy recommendations for sustainability. Figure 2 presents the conceptual summary of this chapter.

Figure 2. A conceptual summary of digital transformation for e-governance, in pandemic situations, such as COVID-19

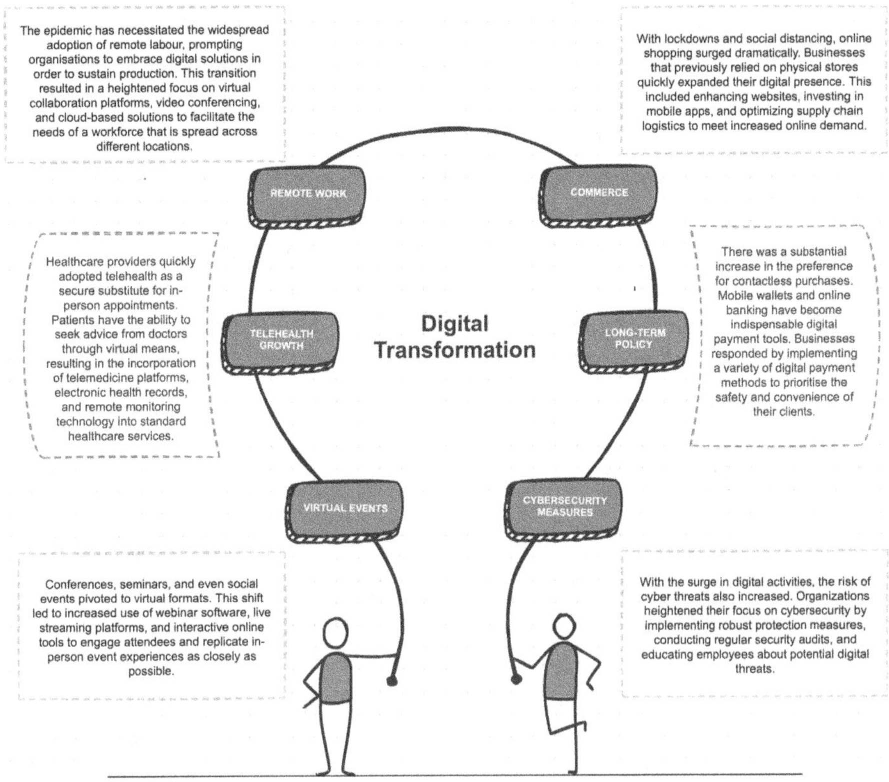

2.0 ACCELERATION OF E-GOVERNANCE ADOPTION IN COVID-19 PANDEMIC

E-governance measures are those digital innovations or initiatives that seek to adapt existing frameworks electronically for improved administrative purposes, with the goal of reducing interpersonal contacts in pandemic conditions. This is a significant departure from the pre-pandemic norms, where, for instance, people attended onsite offices for job activities and required little or no dependence on electronic based administration. A major advantage of electronic-based administration or governance systems is flexibility, scalability, and the potential for greater performance efficiency. Leveraging the potentials of e-governance can result in a win-win situation for the government and the populace, make governance seamless despite the pandemic, and produce a society that benefits immensely from the pandemic implemented training and skills acquisition programmes.

Following the COIVD-19 pandemic, countries in Africa and other parts of the world witnessed a significant increase in the development and deployment of various digital solutions in the form of e-governance for pandemic management (Demirag et al., 2020; Dubois, 2021; Jejeniwa, 2024; Nnenna, 2024b; Obasa et al., 2020). The adoption of e-governance services during the COVID-19 pandemic in Indonesia focused on the regulating roles of trust in the Health Belief Model (HBM), a digital-based initiative for health care administration in the country (Sihotang et al., 2023). Trust is found to enhance the effects of public acceptance and efficiency. Human behaviour and mindset, including concerns about data security and the convenience of online transactions, have a significant impact on individuals' willingness to use government electronic services during the pandemic. Trust is identified as a key component in enhancing this influence.

2.1 Rwanda and India

In Rwanda, the government demonstrated early preparedness through the deployment of mobile-based contact tracing applications for tracking positive cases of secondary transmission patterns of COVID-19. These proactive efforts underline the significance of innovative technology and comprehensive surveillance approaches through data-driven strategies and real-time monitoring for policy decision-making in the health sector, including pharmaceuticals (Feroz et al., 2021; Uwizeyimana et al., 2021, 2023). Another mobile application-based tool deployed to manage the pandemic situation is mobile health (mHealth), a community-based COVID-19 screening by community health workers (CHWs) in Rwanda. Findings from Omorou (2023) have revealed high levels of awareness, use, and satisfaction among the CHWs, with mHealth being perceived as a valuable tool for generating information on COVID-19 and curbing the spread of the pandemic in Rwanda. The research further provides valuable insights into the role of e-governance strategies, such as mHealth interventions and WelTel (a short message(SMS)-based digital platform that improves access and adherence to infection prevention and control measures, understands transmission dynamics, and informs public health decision-making regarding home-based care), in improving COVID-19 management and response efforts in Rwanda (Babili et al., 2023).

Like in Rwanda, the use of mobile phone applications also played a key role in the accelerated adoption of e-governance measures in India. In their study, Goyal et al. (2021) investigate the impact of privacy concerns and convenience values on the adoption of an e-governance initiative during a pandemic like crisis in India. The research posited that significance of convenience, perceived severity of the pandemic, and practical advantages had key roles in enhancing the acceptance of contact-tracing apps.

Interestingly, various service delivery frameworks and business services offered valuable perspectives on leveraging e-governance technologies using handheld mobile devices during public health crises like the COVID-19 pandemic, as observed in these countries. Effective e-governance strategies for pandemic situations have far-reaching coverage for diverse sectors and socio-economic demographics, signifying the possibility of broader acceptance and influence in distinct domains.

2.2 China and Indonesia

The promotion of Sustainable Development Goals (SDGs) during the COVID-19 pandemic in China can provide insights into the effective practices and experiences of the country in implementing SDGs amidst the crisis (Al-Dabbagh, 2020; Liu, 2022; Wang & Huang, 2021). Guan (2023) expounds on the valuable lessons from China for global governance and suggests strategies that governments worldwide can adopt to enhance post-pandemic SDG promotion. This submission can be very useful for comprehending the effective implementation of e-governance projects that align with the SDGs during crises like the COVID-19 pandemic. Further, the perceived usefulness of predicting citizens' intentions to adopt and recommend COVID-19 informational e-governance services accentuates the importance of tailored e-government services in tackling pandemics (Mensah et al., 2021).

In Indonesia, the significant influence of the urgent nature of the COVID-19 pandemic on governance processes and measures of accountability and the need to develop and adopt transformative e-governance measures to counter these pandemic-associated challenges at the various tiers of government received a timely focus (Haitami & Rengganis, 2021; Hartanto et al., 2021; Rafi et al., 2022). Warsono et al. (2023) offer significant insights into implementing e-governance in response to the COVID-19 pandemic, specifically on how local governments in Indonesia can address financial accountability through improved administrative capability and transparency measures despite the pandemic difficulties.

2.3 Sub-Saharan Africa

South Africa, despite having one of the largest economies in sub-Saharan Africa (Asubiaro & Onaolapo, 2023; Sadiq et al., 2023), also had its fair share of the various COVID-19-associated challenges, most especially in the smooth implementation of digital-based solutions to mitigate the pandemic effects. Galushi & Malatji (2022) and Mohale (2024) explore the transition from manual to technology-based service delivery methods, emphasising the implications for society, particularly for rural communities in South Africa. The results discuss the benefits of digital transformation in public administration, such as improved service delivery efficiency, cost-effectiveness, and accessibility. In Nigeria, e-governance measures for COVID-19 began with establishing a committee to draft an action plan, creating an e-governance technology development hub, implementing a unified national data management system, and fostering political will to effectively combat the virus (Barredo et al., 2022; David et al., 2022).

Further, the role of e-government in enhancing ethical practices, reducing corruption risks, and promoting user-friendly services is key to ensuring a smooth transition to e-governance. However, challenges such as disparities in digital access, leadership readiness, information technology (IT) infrastructure costs, low technological literacy, human capacity, poverty, cultural diversity, legal frameworks, and internet connectivity are still common barricades to e-government adoption in sub-Saharan Africa (Mensah et al., 2020; Nnenna, 2024a; Nokele, 2024; Okereke et al., 2020). Additional insights from some countries in Asia, the Middle East, and sub-Saharan Africa revealed these countries leveraged digital technology to develop a blockchain-powered blood system through which patients and health professionals could access safer blood (Ajadi and Drury, 2021).

3.0 INCLUSIVE DIGITAL SERVICES

Inclusive digital services refer to the provision of digital services that range from health, education, and financial products to society, especially the middle class and the less privileged, enabling them to access and utilise survival dependent services through digital devices or tools (Feroz et al., 2021; Golinelli et al., 2020; Reifels & Murray, 2022). Making digital services inclusive will ensure complete coverage for everyone in society by bridging the existing digital and economic divides between the financially excluded and the mainstream financial system. This can be attained by leveraging digital technologies to increase access, affordability, and convenience, making financial services more accessible and affordable during challenging times like the COVID-19 pandemic.

To achieve the right results, these digital interventions must be customised to address specific needs like the management of employee systems and public needs during the COVID-19 pandemic (Willem et al., 2021). Following the customisation of tools, training is another important aspect that must be addressed. For any digital tools to be truly inclusive, society must be familiar with their usage. Therefore, adequate training and orientations must be organised continuously to educate end users, mostly via incorporation into the school syllabus for learners to build the necessary skills for long-term sustenance.

3.1 Inclusive Digital Services in Action

3.1.1 Business and Education

National internet portals can serve as inclusive online platforms that play a vital role in disseminating crucial information regarding any pandemic condition to the public, offering easy access to essential updates and guidance. Other information, like travel restrictions, practical guidance on protection, and governmental response regarding the outbreak and control measures, can be monitored through these online portals (Sujan et al., 2022).

In developing countries like Nigeria, digital platforms and IT systems have provided emergency income to about eight million people, while universal lesson (uLesson) has created a virtual learning environment for primary and secondary school students (Tochukwu et al., 2021). The pandemic has also seen a significant increase in the utilisation of digital telecommunication platforms and educational technology, like Zoom for virtual meetings, Google Meet for conferences, and Google Classroom for online learning. Social media platforms have been used to promote services, information, and education, with corporate organisations like museums promoting artworks and conducting virtual tours (Agostino et al., 2021).

3.1.2 Agriculture

The agricultural industry has experienced enhanced accessibility to digital services through the adoption of technologies such as artificial intelligence (AI) for crop monitoring, internet of things (IoT) for data collection, blockchain for supply chain transparency, drones for precision farming, cloud data solutions for storage, and more (Panganiban, 2019). Crop death, mapping of farmland, and collecting essential agro-data have been made easier and more accessible through drone technology like Beat Drone (Barredo et al., 2022). Digital solutions have improved agricultural performance by connecting farmers to financial institutions, supporting financial inclusion, and building resilience between farmers and tractor owners. YouTube and Zoom have become digital platforms for farmers to learn new farming techniques, while Facebook and Twitter have been used to boost agribusiness and promote inclusion and sustainable development. Finally, the government must strive to achieve equal access to these digital tools for everyone by providing quality and affordable internet services for its citizens.

4.0 CYBERSECURITY AND DATA PRIVACY

The adoption of digital tools for COVID-19 management across the globe, with applications ranging from health care to finance, is not without its attendant challenges. Health systems rapidly shifted to telehealth and remote care models to maintain continuity of care while implementing social distancing measures. Similarly, governments and public institutions leveraged digital platforms to deliver essential services and information to citizens, often for the first time. For many organisations, the pandemic caused a "business unusual" approach, spurring the rapid integration of emerging technologies like artificial intelligence, big data analytics, and blockchain to facilitate remote work, virtual collaboration, and automated processes (Yallop & Aliasghar, 2020). However, the deployment of these digital technologies presented various challenges to organisations in areas relating to the ethical implications of increased data collection and use, heightened cybersecurity threats, and concerns around privacy and data governance.

With the rapid expansion of digital services, there are growing concerns about data privacy, security, and fair access (Renn et al., 2021). Navigating the trade-off between the advantages of digital transformation and the risks of data exploitation and exclusion poses a significant challenge for policymakers in the post-pandemic era. Gasser et al. (2020) opines the ensuing debate so far seems to be framed generically as a binary choice between using digital technologies to save lives versus respecting individual privacy and civil liberties.

4.1 Navigating the Data Privacy and Ethical Landscape

Establishing a nuanced, context-driven approach to data ethics and governance will be crucial to ensuring that the pandemic driven digital transformation benefits all members of the society rather than entrenching existing inequalities. The pandemic has also intensified public concerns about government and corporate use of data, which can undermine trust in digital institutions and services. The proliferation of misinformation and online manipulation tactics, such as fake news and targeted disinformation campaigns, have fostered division and undermined public trust in democratic processes (Azer and Samir, 2024; Rajasegar, 2024).

4.1.1 Challenges of Personal Data Protection

Protecting personal data and ensuring privacy are critical components of building inclusive and resilient digital societies (Renn et al., 2021). As more personal health information, financial records, and other sensitive data are collected and stored digitally, robust data governance frameworks are essential. This is crucial in low- and middle-income countries, where unregulated private technology sectors increase the risks of data commodification and unauthorised use (Mitgang et al., 2021). The COVID-19 pandemic has highlighted the delicate balance that policymakers and public health authorities must strike between leveraging data to inform rapid, evidence-based decision-making and safeguarding individual privacy and data rights.

Immediate provision of data on the epidemic's dynamics can support timely intervention but must be balanced against the risks of over-collection, improper use, or unauthorised disclosure of sensitive information (Nafi'ah, 2021). Calls have been made for digital contact tracing tools to prioritise privacy and user consent over maximising public health utility. The risk of inappropriate uses must be reduced by ensuring stringent requirements for data security, access, as well as clear legal protections and recourse for any violations (Kahn, 2020).

The increased reliance on remote communication and online services during the pandemic has emphasised the critical role of secure digital identity solutions. The rapid shift to virtual interactions has heightened the need for robust identity verification mechanisms to protect against fraud, enable trusted transactions, and facilitate access to essential services. Many countries have accelerated the deployment of digital ID systems, often drawing on biometric data, to support COVID-19 response efforts (Parng et al. 2023: Miller et al. 2020).

4.2 Practical Measures for Attaining Data Privacy

Implementing digital transformation must be done with careful consideration of privacy, security, and equity concerns to avoid further marginalisation of vulnerable groups. To harness the benefits of digital technologies while mitigating the risks, policymakers must develop a comprehensive data privacy and human rights-compliant framework. These could include the following elements:

i. Clearly defined policies and procedures to ensure that the collection, storage, and use of personal data is lawful, necessary, and proportionate to legitimate public health aims, with robust safeguards against unauthorised access or misuse.
ii. Meaningful consent mechanisms that empower individuals to make informed choices about the use of their data, with the ability to access, correct, and delete their information as needed.
iii. Robust data security measures, including encryption, access controls, and audit trails, are implemented to protect against data breaches and cyber threats.
iv. Equitable access to digital services and technologies, with targeted support for marginalised communities, to prevent the exacerbation of existing inequalities.

v. Transparent and accountable governance structures that involve civil society, privacy advocates, and affected communities in the design and implementation of data-driven initiatives.

Using technologies like contact tracing applications, digital surveillance, and biometrics for monitoring and responding to the pandemic has raised serious concerns about privacy and data protection (Raskar et al., 2020). While these tools can provide valuable public health benefits, they are often beset with the risk of infringing on individual rights, disproportionately impacting marginalised communities, and entrenching discriminatory practices (Min-Allah et al., 2021; Riemer et al., 2020; Rowe, 2020; Pratt et al., 2022). E-governance frameworks must carefully weigh the potential public health benefits of certain data-driven interventions against the risks to privacy and civil liberty. Achieving the right balance requires input from diverse stakeholders, robust legal frameworks, and strong enforcement mechanisms to prevent misuse or overreach. (Jeremy et al., 2022).

4.3 Safeguarding Digital Interaction

Recommended best practices for safeguarding digital interactions include the immediate cessation or reversal of exceptional data use after a crisis, which includes strict limits on data collection, retention, robust anonymization and de-identification protocols. Governments and corporations should provide comprehensive transparency regarding data practices, along with meaningful public consultation and democratic oversight. For empowered and independent data protection, authorities should have the resources and mandates to monitor and enforce compliance. Incorporating privacy-by-design principles in the development of all digital services and infrastructure is important. Beyond data protection, the pandemic has also revealed the critical need to ensure universal and fair access to digital public services and platforms. Vulnerable populations, including older adults, low-income individuals, and those with disabilities, have faced significant barriers to accessing essential services that have moved online.

5.0 LONG-TERM IMPLICATIONS

Considering the numerous initiatives aimed at swiftly implementing e-governance for managing the COVID-19 pandemic, it is imperative to work towards a society that progresses in ways that benefit its people. Therefore, governments should explore the positive progress made in e-governance to promote post-pandemic economic growth and development. To do this, we must embrace a proactive, policy-driven, and enduring transformative approach with the goal of establishing a robust and all-encompassing digital society. The attainment of these long-term implications and their benefits can be accomplished through the following guidelines:

i. Enhanced Digital Infrastructure and Services

The urgent need for remote access to government services during the pandemic prompted rapid investments in digital infrastructure. Governments have expanded broadband access, improved online platforms, and integrated advanced technologies such as AI and blockchain to deliver services efficiently (Agarwal et al., 2024). This infrastructure enhancement is expected to continue, ensuring that digital services are robust, secure, and capable of handling increased demand.

ii. Increased Citizen Engagement and Participation

Electronic governance has facilitated universal access to information and government services, hence enhancing citizen engagement in governance. The pandemic highlighted the importance of transparency and responsiveness, leading to the development of platforms that facilitate citizen feedback and involvement in decision-making processes. This trend may likely persist, fostering a more engaged and informed citizenry (Wilson & Tewdwr-Jones, 2021).

iii. Increased Efficiency and Transparency

Digital platforms enable more efficient service delivery and improved transparency in government operations. Automated processes reduce the time required for administrative tasks, while digital records enhance accountability and reduce opportunities for corruption. This increased transparency can foster greater trust between citizens and their governments (Schoper et al. 2023; Kramer et al. 2024).

iv. Data-driven Decision Making

E-governance facilitates the collection and analysis of large volumes of data, which can inform policy decisions and improve service delivery. The ability to leverage real-time data enhances the responsiveness and effectiveness of government actions. However, this also necessitates strong data governance frameworks to protect privacy and ensure the ethical use of data (Nel et al. 2023).

v. Promotion of Digital Inclusion

COVID-19 exposed the digital divide, emphasising the need for inclusive digital policies. Governments are now more aware of the importance of ensuring that all citizens, regardless of socio-economic status, have access to digital services (Vasylieva et al., 2021). Efforts to offer cost-effective internet connection, educational programs on digital skills, and help for marginalised communities are essential for achieving inclusive digital societies. These efforts will help bridge the digital gap and ensure that everyone benefits from e-governance (Farooqi et al., 2022).

vi. Resilience Against Future Crises

The pandemic has further emphasised the need for resilient systems capable of withstanding crises. E-governance provides a framework for the continuity of government operations during emergencies. By digitising processes and services, governments can maintain functionality and support citizens even in times of disruption. This resilience is crucial for handling future crises, whether they are health-related, natural disasters, or other unforeseen events (Tabuga et al., 2020).

vii. Economic Growth and Innovation

The shift towards digital governance can drive economic growth and innovation. E-governance platforms facilitate business operations, reduce administrative burdens, and create a conducive environment for startups and entrepreneurs (Wibowo, 2023). Additionally, the data generated through digital interactions can be leveraged to develop new services and products, fostering a culture of innovation.

viii. Privacy and Security Considerations

As digital interactions increase, so do concerns about privacy and security. Governments must prioritise the protection of personal data and implement robust cybersecurity measures to safeguard against threats (Shah et al., 2022). Building trust in e-governance systems is essential for their long-term success, and this requires transparent policies, accountability, and continuous improvements in security protocols (Smidt and Jokonya, 2021; Akinsanmi & Salami, 2021).

ix. Social and Cultural Shifts

The adoption of e-governance also brings about social and cultural changes. It requires citizens to become more digitally literate and adaptable to new technologies. Governments must invest in digital education and awareness programmes to ensure that all citizens can effectively engage with e-governance platforms (Mustafa et al., 2021).

x. Global Collaboration and Standards

The pandemic has shown that global challenges require collaborative solutions. E-governance can benefit from international cooperation, with countries sharing best practices, technologies, and standards. Harmonising e-governance frameworks globally can facilitate cross-border digital interactions, enhance interoperability, and support international trade and cooperation (Naqvi et al., 2021).

6.0 POLICY RECOMMENDATIONS

Challenges posed by the COVID-19 crises, particularly in public administration and leadership, necessitate the need for robust e-governance strategies. Achieving a robust and long-lasting e-governance strategies is a function of strong and useful policy that can stand the test of times. Therefore, formulating policy recommendations for a long-lasting e-governance adoption during, and after a pandemic is essential (Avotra et al., 2021). The task of recommending policies for effective digital governance implementation when adopting, for instance, health related interventions during the COVID-19 pandemic may shed light on the synergy of information exchange between government policymakers and public service providers (Peng, 2023). Effective health risk communication strategies, which advocate for the delivery of accurate information by government communication, will mitigate public confusion and errors (Kim & Kreps, 2020; Ullah et al., 2022). For instance, long-lasting policy recommendation may seek to further encourage or empower the use of social media, such as Instagram and Facebook, in a manner that makes real time, pandemic related information readily available (Sukmono & Kencana, 2023).

6.1 Legal Framework and Public Acceptance

To achieve a strong and inclusive implementation of e-governance, the government must first seek appropriate legal validation by consulting the relevant legislative arm of the government. In doing so, e-governance policies such as those with direct impacts on health sector and the well-being of individuals will have long-term, post pandemic benefits (Bostancı & Yıldırım, 2022). Policy recommenders should do a thorough, and unbiased job with real-world scenarios that include applicable data from social media to give policymakers useful information for making good e-governance plans that prioritises strong crisis related communication via strong leadership, control, and social media awareness (Zhong et al., 2022).

Convenience, conditional value, and functional value all play roles in the acceptance and success of e-governance initiatives, particularly the adoption of contact-tracing mobile applications during the COVID-19 pandemic (Goyal et al., 2021). It is therefore of utmost importance to factor these end user values into any pandemic related policy. Therefore, the functional value of such digital interventions should be enhanced through convenience and context-specific features to promote their acceptance. By examining the challenges, successes, and public discourse surrounding these digital interventions, policymakers can derive recommendations for effective technology adoption and legal support to ensure the longevity of these initiatives. This will offer valuable guidance for government frameworks in understanding public perceptions and the emphasis on the need for proactive measures to ensure effective utilisation of digital solutions in pandemic response and health protection regulations (Akinnuwesi et al., 2022; Amann et al., 2021).

6.2 Formulating Effective and Favourable Policies

Government policymakers must consider technology benefits, solution accuracy, privacy considerations, and mobile-related costs when formulating policies (Redmiles, 2020). This supports the importance of inciting variables to drive acceptance and use of such technologies, sensitising the populace, and planning for the digitalization of pandemic protective measures. For instance, the significant impact of social influence, performance expectancy, effort expectancy, perceived fear, facilitating conditions and usage behaviour can influence the intention to use food delivery applications (Puriwat & Tripopsakul, 2021b).

In a study that integrates the technology acceptance model (TAM) and perceived risk theory (PRT), a model was proposed for understanding citizens' intentions to key into e-governance during the COVID-19 pandemic in Vietnam. The findings perceived the pandemic influenced the citizen intentions to adopt and recommend such services (Mensah et al., 2021; Nguyen, 2023). Hence, it is important to ensure that e-governance services for pandemics are perceived as valuable and beneficial to users. Likewise, the impact of trustworthiness and technology acceptance on the utilisation of e-government services cannot be over emphasised.

The pressing need to implement work system changes for adaptive public service delivery during the COVID-19 pandemic is central to addressing technical challenges in public service setting (Ibad & Lolita, 2020). The adoption of work-from-home practices enabled by digital technologies offers valuable perspectives on how government-mandated lockdowns influenced the adoption of technology in the workplace, which can strongly inform the development of government policy frameworks for technology adoption during crises like COVID-19 (Peter, 2024).

6.3 Establishing Balanced Policies

6.3.1 Business

For business continuity, leveraging information technology and government support to ensure continuity and efficiency in governance practices cannot be overemphasised (Ahdadou et al., 2022). Technology organisation environment (TOE) model has shown that technological, organisational, and environmental factors influence the adoption of digital marketing by micro, small, and medium enterprises (MSMEs) (Ayundyayasti et al., 2023; Kraft et al., 2022). It is therefore important to consider these factors in implementing COVID-19-compliant operating procedures, utilising digital technology for virtual communication, adapting health guidelines for construction activities, embracing digital transformation in work processes, and developing human resources. Government can also provide stimuli like tax relaxation, and financial aids to address challenges such as increased material and operational costs, rising unemployment rates, order cancellations, delayed payments, and heightened transportation costs (Al-Sarafi & Najeh, 2022; Chowdhury et al., 2023). The usefulness, susceptibility, and satisfaction perceived by these technologies may positively influence consumer behaviour during and after the pandemic (Puriwat & Tripopsakul, 2021).

6.3.2 Health

Governments could adopt a comprehensive framework for integrating informatics and digital technologies to support public healthcare to identify requirements and gaps in public health informatics, offering valuable insights for policymakers in developing pandemic based sustainable technology adoption (Snowdon et al., 2021; Wang et al., 2021). Given the health implications of increased e-learning and reduced outdoor activities during the COVID-19 pandemic could lead to myopia development among school-age children, balancing screen time with outdoor exercise to mitigate the risks associated with myopia progression is important. Hence, implementing e-learning strategies, coupled with the need for measures to promote outdoor activities and regulate screen time to safeguard the visual health of the youth, is highly recommended (Liu et al., 2021).

Further, a conceptual framework for standardising policy and technology responses in the immediate aftermath of a pandemic, focusing on government interventions and technological strategies, could also be developed. This will categorise government policy directives implemented during the pandemic and offer insights into the impact of these interventions on epidemiological and economic outcomes (Moy et al., 2023). To navigate the challenges posed by the pandemic, effective implementation of various legal regulations, criminal sanctions for violators, electronic trial systems, corruption prevention policies, and workplace regulations is crucial for robust e-governance (Widodo et al., 2021). This emphasises the crucial role of government policymakers and legislative bodies in maintaining these policies over a long-term period, guaranteeing a successful post pandemic implementation and continuity.

7.0 CONCLUSION

The urgent nature of response to COVID-19 pandemic has greatly impacted governance processes and accountability measures, shifting from manual to technology-based service delivery techniques. E-governance methods offer significant benefits like flexibility, scalability, and the possibility for improved performance efficiency, and can enhance administrative operations and minimise interpersonal interactions, particularly during the pandemic. Some African countries demonstrated early preparedness for COVID-19 transmission by implementing mobile-based contact tracking applications, establishing committees to write action plans, building e-governance technology development hubs, and fostering political will. Inclusive digital services enable the middle-class and underprivileged individuals to easily access essential resources such as healthcare, education, and financial products. By implementing inclusive digital services, we can effectively close the gaps in both digital access and economic opportunities. Privacy considerations, as well as the functional, convenience, and conditional values, had a role in determining the intention to employ an e-governance effort in times of crisis. Governments should prioritise the attainment of equitable access to digital resources through the provision of training, high-quality, and cost-effective internet services, while utilising policies within the ambit of the law.

ACKNOWLEDGMENT

Kehinde Oyeniran is grateful to the International Centre for Genetic Engineering and Biotechnology (ICGEB) for sponsorship.

REFERENCES

Achmad, M. (2022). Hasan Aydin The Governments' Use of Social Networking Sites (SNS) to Promote Citizens' Trust During the COVID-19. *Journal of Ethnic and Cultural Studies*, 9(4), 156–186. DOI: 10.29333/ejecs/1383

Agarwal, P., Swami, S., & Malhotra, S. K. (2024). Artificial Intelligence Adoption in the Post COVID-19 New-Normal and Role of Smart Technologies in Transforming Business: A Review. *Journal of Science and Technology Policy Management*, 15(3), 506–529. DOI: 10.1108/JSTPM-08-2021-0122

Agostino, D., Arnaboldi, M., & Lema, M. D. (2021). New development: COVID-19 as an accelerator of digital transformation in public service delivery. *Public Money & Management*, 1–4(1), 69–72. Advance online publication. DOI: 10.1080/09540962.2020.1764206

Ahdadou, M., Aajly, A., & Tahrouch, M. (2022). *Information Technology Governance: Lessons Learned From the Covid-19 Crisis*. International Journal of Business and Technology Management., DOI: 10.55057/ijbtm.2022.4.1.1

Ajadi, S., & Drury, P. (2021). *Health Systems, Digital Health and COVID-19: Insights from Bangladesh*. GSMA Mobile for Development.

Akinnuwesi, B. A., Uzoka, F.-M. E., Fashoto, S. G., Mbunge, E., Odumabo, A., Amusa, O. O., Okpeku, M., & Owolabi, O. (2022). *A Modified UTAUT Model for the Acceptance and Use of Digital Technology for Tackling COVID-19*. Sustainable Operations and Computers., DOI: 10.1016/j.susoc.2021.12.001

Akinsanmi, T., & Salami, A. (2021). Evaluating the trade-off between privacy, public health safety, and digital security in a pandemic. *Data & Policy*, 3(17), e27. DOI: 10.1017/dap.2021.24

Al-Dabbagh, Z. S. (2020). Sustainable development and its role in containing crises: Corona virus pandemic crisis (COVID-19) in China as a model. *Journal of Public Affairs*, 20(4), e2339. DOI: 10.1002/pa.2339 PMID: 32904918

Al-Sarafi, A. H., & Najeh, T. (2022). Post COVID-19 Pandemic Possible Business Continuity Strategies for Construction Industry Revival a Preliminary Study in the Malaysian Construction Industry. *International Journal of Disaster Resilience in the Built Environment*. Advance online publication. DOI: 10.1108/IJDRBE-11-2021-0147

Amann, J., Sleigh, J., & Vayena, E. (2021). Digital Contact-Tracing During the Covid-19 Pandemic: An Analysis of Newspaper Coverage in Germany, Austria, and Switzerland. *PLoS One*, 16(2), e0246524. Advance online publication. DOI: 10.1371/journal.pone.0246524 PMID: 33534839

Amosun, T. S., Chu, J., Rufai, O. H., Muhideen, S., Shahani, R., & Gonlepa, M. K. (2022). Does e-government help shape citizens' engagement during the COVID-19 crisis? A study of mediational effects of how citizens perceive the government. *Online Information Review*, 46(5), 846–866. DOI: 10.1108/OIR-10-2020-0478

Asubiaro, T. V., & Onaolapo, S. (2023). A comparative study of the coverage of African journals in Web of Science, Scopus, and CrossRef. *Journal of the Association for Information Science and Technology*, 74(7), 745–758. DOI: 10.1002/asi.24758

Ayundyayasti, P., Sarana, S., Sadida, A., Sugiarti, S., & Suwondo, A. (2023). Analysis of the Adoption of Digital Marketing in MSMEs in the Era of the Covid-19 Pandemic. Journal of Applied Business Administration. https://doi.org/DOI: 10.30871/jaba.v7i1.4867

Azer, M. A., & Samir, R. (2024). Overview of the Complex Landscape and Future Directions of Ethics in Light of Emerging Technologies. *IJACSA). International Journal of Advanced Computer Science and Applications*, 15(7). Advance online publication. DOI: 10.14569/IJACSA.2024.01507142

Babili, A., Nsanzimana, S., Rwagasore, E., & Lester, R. (2023). SMS-based Digital Health Intervention in Rwanda's Home-Based Care Program for Remote Management of COVID-19 Cases and Contacts: A Qualitative Study of Sustainability and Scalability. *Frontiers in Digital Health*, 4, 1071790. Advance online publication. DOI: 10.3389/fdgth.2022.1071790 PMID: 36714610

Barredo, L., Olawale Benjamin, O., & Oluwatoyin Foye, V. (2022). Inclusion, Organizational Resilience, and Sustainable Development in Nigeria: The Role of Digital Innovations. Environmental Sciences Proceedings 2022, Vol. 15, Page 27, 15(1), 27. https://doi.org/DOI: 10.3390/environsciproc2022015027

Bostancı, S. H., Yıldırım, S., & Erdoğan, F. (2022). Covid-19 Pandemi Sürecinde Hastane Bilgi Sistemi Açısından E-Devlet Portalı'nın Hizmetleri Üzerine Bir Derleme. *Konuralp Tip Dergisi*, 14(S1), 271–279. Advance online publication. DOI: 10.18521/ktd.1036010

Budd, J., Miller, B. S., Manning, E. M., Lampos, V., Zhuang, M., Edelstein, M., Rees, G., Emery, V. C., Stevens, M. M., Keegan, N., Short, M. J., Pillay, D., Manley, E., Cox, I. J., Heymann, D., Johnson, A. M., & McKendry, R. A. (2020). Digital technologies in the public-health response to COVID-19. *Nature Medicine 2020 26:8, 26*(8), 1183–1192. https://doi.org/DOI: 10.1038/s41591-020-1011-4

Ceesay, L. B., Bojang, M. B. S., Malang, &, & Bojang, B. S. (2020). Global Journal of Management and Business Research: A Administration and Management Embracing E-Government during the Covid-19 Pandemic and Beyond: Insights from the Gambia Embracing E-Government during the Covid-19 Pandemic and Beyond: Insights from the Gambia.

Chowdhury, N. R., Janan, F., Mahmud, P., Liza, S. A., & Paul, S. K. (2023). Assessing Strategies to Mitigate the Impacts of a Pandemic in Apparel Supply Chains. Operations Management Research. https://doi.org/DOI: 10.1007/s12063-022-00345-w

David, O. A., Cyril Onyepuemu, N. O., & Qazeem, I. B. (2022). *E-Governance Response in Tackling Covid-19 in Nigeria*. Perspektif., DOI: 10.31289/perspektif.v11i3.7249

Demirag, I., Fırtın, C. E., & Bilbil, E. T. (2020). Managing Expectations With Emotional Accountability: Making City Hospitals Accountable During the COVID-19 Pandemic in Turkey. Journal of Public Budgeting Accounting \&. *Journal of Public Budgeting, Accounting & Financial Management*, 32(5), 889–901. Advance online publication. DOI: 10.1108/JPBAFM-07-2020-0097

Dubois, E. (2021). African Women, ICT and Neoliberal Politics, by Assata Zerai: A Review by Elisabeth Dubois. *Information Polity*, 26(2), 211–213. Advance online publication. DOI: 10.3233/IP-219003

Farooqi, A., Khalid, U., & Khan, A. M. (2022). Understanding the Digital Divide in the. Contemporary Digital World. *Global Political Review*, VII(IV), 7–14. DOI: 10.31703/gpr.2022(VII-IV).02

Feroz, A. S., Khoja, A., & Saleem, S. (2021). Equipping Community Health Workers With Digital Tools for Pandemic Response in LMICs. *Archives of Public Health*, 79(1), 1. Advance online publication. DOI: 10.1186/s13690-020-00513-z PMID: 33390163

Flood, J., Shingleton, J., Bennett, E., Walker, B., Amin-Chowdhury, Z., Oligbu, G., Avis, J., Lynn, R. M., Davis, P., Bharucha, T., Pain, C. E., Jyothish, D., Whittaker, E., Dwarakanathan, B., Wood, R., Williams, C., Swann, O., Semple, M. G., Ramsay, M. E., & Ladhani, S. N. (2021). Paediatric multisystem inflammatory syndrome temporally associated with SARS-CoV-2 (PIMS-TS): Prospective, national surveillance, United Kingdom and Ireland, 2020. *The Lancet Regional Health. Europe*, 3, 100075. Advance online publication. DOI: 10.1016/j.lanepe.2021.100075 PMID: 34027512

Galushi, L. T., & Malatji, T. L. (2022). Digital Public Administration and Inclusive Governance at the South African Local Government. In *Depth Analysis of E-Government and Service Delivery in Musina Local Municipality*. Academic Journal of Interdisciplinary Studies., DOI: 10.36941/ajis-2022-0154

Gasser, U., Ienca, M., Scheibner, J., Sleigh, J., & Vayena, E. (2020). Digital tools against COVID-19: Taxonomy, ethical challenges, and navigation aid. *The Lancet. Digital Health*, 2(8), e425–e434. DOI: 10.1016/S2589-7500(20)30137-0 PMID: 32835200

Golinelli, D., Boetto, E., Carullo, G., Nuzzolese, A. G., Landini, M. P., & Fantini, M. P. (2020). Adoption of Digital Technologies in Health Care During the COVID-19 Pandemic: Systematic Review of Early Scientific Literature. J Med Internet Res 2020;22(11):E22280 Https://Www.Jmir.Org/2020/11/E22280, 22(11), e22280. https://doi.org/DOI: 10.2196/22280

Goyal, S., Pillai, A., & Chauhan, S. (2021). E-Governance Using Mobile Applications: A Case Study of India During the COVID-19 Pandemic. *AJIS. Australasian Journal of Information Systems*, 25. Advance online publication. DOI: 10.3127/ajis.v25i0.3129

Guan, H. (2023). *Why Can China Still Promote the SDGs During the COVID-19 Pandemic*. Lecture Notes in Education Psychology and Public Media., DOI: 10.54254/2753-7048/15/20231069

Haitami, M., & Rengganis, A. (2021). The Dilemma of Good Governance Implementation in Indonesia during the Pandemic of Corona Virus Disease (COVID-19). *JASSP*, 1(1), 55–67. DOI: 10.23960/jassp.v1i1.25

Hartanto, D., Agussani, A., & Dalle, J. (2021). Hasan Aydin Antecedents of Public Trust in Government During the COVID-19 Pandemic in Indonesia. *Journal of Ethnic and Cultural Studies*, 8(4), 321–341. DOI: 10.29333/ejecs/975

Ibad, S., & Lolita, Y. W. (2020). Development and Urgency of Public Services Through E-Government in the Middle of Pandemi Covid-19. Journal of Public Administration and Governance. https://doi.org/DOI: 10.5296/jpag.v10i4.17867

Jejeniwa, T. O. (2024). *Conceptualizing E-Government Initiatives: Lessons Learned From Africa-Us Collaborations in Digital Governance*. International Journal of Applied Research in Social Sciences., DOI: 10.51594/ijarss.v6i4.1066

Kahn, J. P. (2020). *Digital Contact Tracing for Pandemic Response: Ethics and Governance Guidance*. Digital Contact Tracing for Pandemic Response., DOI: 10.1353/book.75831

Kim, D. K., & Kreps, G. L. (2020). An Analysis of Government Communication in the United States During the COVID-19 Pandemic: Recommendations for Effective Government Health Risk Communication. World Medical \&. *Health Policy (Amsterdam)*, 12(4), 398–412. Advance online publication. DOI: 10.1002/wmh3.363 PMID: 32904935

Kraft, C., Lindeque, J. P., & Peter, M. K. (2022). The Digital Transformation of Swiss Small and Medium-Sized Enterprises: Insights From Digital Tool Adoption. *Journal of Strategy and Management*, 15(3), 468–494. Advance online publication. DOI: 10.1108/JSMA-02-2021-0063

Krämer, D., Brachem, E., Schneider-Reuter, L., D'Angelo, I., Vollmann, J., & Haltaufderheide, J. (2024). The Role of Transparency in Digital Contact Tracing During COVID-19: Insights from an Expert Survey. *Health Care Analysis*. Advance online publication. DOI: 10.1007/s10728-024-00485-z PMID: 38909332

Kumar, A., Singh, R., Kaur, J., Pandey, S., Sharma, V., Thakur, L., Sati, S., Mani, S., Asthana, S., Sharma, T. K., Chaudhuri, S., Bhattacharyya, S., & Kumar, N. (2021). Wuhan to World: The COVID-19 Pandemic. *Frontiers in Cellular and Infection Microbiology*, 11, 596201. DOI: 10.3389/fcimb.2021.596201 PMID: 33859951

Liu, J., Li, B., Chen, Q. Y., & Dang, J. (2021). Student Health Implications of School Closures During the COVID-19 Pandemic: New Evidence on the Association of E-Learning, Outdoor Exercise, and Myopia. *Health Care*, 9(5), 500. Advance online publication. DOI: 10.3390/healthcare9050500 PMID: 33922486

Liu, S. (2022). Higher Education and Sustainable Development Goals during Covid-19: Coping Strategies of a University in Wuhan, China. Https://Doi.Org/10.4081/Jphr.2020.1933, 9(s1), 16–17. DOI: 10.4081/jphr.2020.1933

Mansoor, M. (2021). Citizens' trust in government as a function of good governance and government agency's provision of quality information on social media during COVID-19. *Government Information Quarterly*, 38(4), 101597. DOI: 10.1016/j.giq.2021.101597 PMID: 34642542

Mennis, J., Matthews, K. A., & Huston, S. L. (2022). Geospatial Perspectives on the Intersection of Chronic Disease and COVID-19. *Preventing Chronic Disease*, 19, 220145. DOI: 10.5888/pcd19.220145 PMID: 35772034

Mensah, I. K., Adams, S., Adjei, J. K., & Mwakapesa, D. S. (2021). Drivers of Egovernment Adoption Amidst COVID-19 Pandemic: The Information Adoption Model (IAM) Approach. *Information Development*. Advance online publication. DOI: 10.1177/02666669211010872

Mensah, R., Cater-Steel, A., & Toleman, M. (2020). Factors Affecting E-government Adoption in Liberia: A Practitioner Perspective. *The Electronic Journal on Information Systems in Developing Countries*. Advance online publication. DOI: 10.1002/isd2.12161

Michael Onyema, E., Chika Eucheria, N., Ayobamidele Obafemi, F., Sen, S., Grace Atonye, F., Sharma, A., & Omar Alsayed, A. (2020). Journal of Education and Practice www.iiste.org ISSN. 11(13). https://doi.org/DOI: 10.7176/JEP/11-13-12

Min-Allah, N., Alahmed, B. A., Albreek, E. M., Alghamdi, L. S., Alawad, D. A., Alharbi, A. S., Al-Akkas, N., Musleh, D., & Alrashed, S. (2021). A survey of COVID-19 contact-tracing apps. *Computers in Biology and Medicine*, 137, 104787. DOI: 10.1016/j.compbiomed.2021.104787 PMID: 34482197

Mitgang, E. A., Blaya, J. A., & Chopra, M. (2021). Digital Health in Response to COVID-19 in Low- and Middle-income Countries: Opportunities and Challenges. *Global Policy*, 12(S6), 107–109. DOI: 10.1111/1758-5899.12880 PMID: 34230840

Mohale, C. (2024). *The Role of E-Government in the Promotion of Municipal Service Delivery in South Africa*. International Journal of Social Science Research and Review., DOI: 10.47814/ijssrr.v7i3.1992

Morens, D. M., Breman, J. G., Calisher, C. H., Doherty, P. C., Hahn, B. H., Keusch, G. T., Kramer, L. D., LeDuc, J. W., Monath, T. P., & Taubenberger, J. K. (2020). The Origin of COVID-19 and Why It Matters. *The American Journal of Tropical Medicine and Hygiene*, 103(3), 955–959. DOI: 10.4269/ajtmh.20-0849 PMID: 32700664

Moy, N., Antonini, M., Kyhlstedt, M., Fiorentini, G., & Paolucci, F. (2023). Standardising Policy and Technology Responses in the Immediate Aftermath of a Pandemic: A Comparative and Conceptual Framework. *Health Research Policy and Systems*, 21(1), 10. Advance online publication. DOI: 10.1186/s12961-022-00951-x PMID: 36698139

Murray, C. J. L. (2022). COVID-19 will continue but the end of the pandemic is near. *Lancet*, 399(10323), 417–419. DOI: 10.1016/S0140-6736(22)00100-3 PMID: 35065006

Mustafa, K., Mustafa, R., & Ahmedi, B. (2021) *The Impact of the COVID 19 Pandemic on the Digitalization of Municipal Administration, the Development of E-Governance.* Asian Journal of Research in Computer Science, 10 (2). pp. 1-21. ISSN 2581-8260

Nafi'ah, B. A. (2021). Data Governance Mechanisms in Indonesia's Covid-19 Data Integration System. *Sosiohumaniora*, 23(3), 339. DOI: 10.24198/sosiohumaniora.v23i3.28437

Nel, E., MacLachlan, A., Ballinger, O., Cole, H., & Cole, M. (2023). Data-Driven Decision Making in Response to the COVID-19 Pandemic: A City of Cape Town Case Study. *Sustainability (Basel)*, 15(3), 1853. DOI: 10.3390/su15031853

Nnenna, U. J. (2024a). *Challenges and Opportunities in Implementing Open Government Data Initiatives in East Africa.* Iaa JSS., DOI: 10.59298/IAA-JSS/2024/102.111.00000

Nnenna, U. J. (2024b). *Evaluating the Effectiveness of E-Government Platforms in East Africa.* Iaa Jah., DOI: 10.59298/IAAJAH/2024/11.11017.11

Nokele, S. K. (2024). An Empirical Study of the Uptake of Electronic Government Services by the Limpopo Department of Home Affairs. Advances in Politics and Economics. https://doi.org/DOI: 10.22158/ape.v7n1p32

Obasa, A. E., Singh, S., Chivunze, E., Burgess, T., Masiye, F., Mtande, T., Ochieng, J., Chalwe, V., Mokgatla, B., Rennie, S., & Moodley, K. (2020). Comparative Strategic Approaches to COVID-19 in Africa: Balancing Public Interest With Civil Liberties. *South African Medical Journal*, 110(9), 858. Advance online publication. DOI: 10.7196/SAMJ.2020.v110i9.14934 PMID: 32880268

Ohadike, D. C. (1991). Diffusion and physiological responses to the influenza pandemic of 1918-19 in Nigeria. *Social Science & Medicine*, 32(12), 1393–1399. DOI: 10.1016/0277-9536(91)90200-V PMID: 1871611

Okereke, M., Williams, A. E., Nzeribe, E., Ashinedu, N. U., & Mairaj, M. W. (2020). COVID-19: Challenges Affecting the Uptake of E-Learning in Pharmacy Education in Africa. *The Pan African Medical Journal*, 35(Supp 2). Advance online publication. DOI: 10.11604/pamj.supp.2020.35.2.23910 PMID: 33623594

Omorou, A. Y. (2023). Feasibility, Acceptability, Satisfaction and Challenges of mHealth for Community-Based COVID-19 Screening by Community Health Workers in Rwanda: Insight From the E-ASCov Project (Preprint). *JMIR mHealth and uHealth*. Advance online publication. DOI: 10.2196/50745 PMID: 39401131

Panganiban, G. G. F. (2019). E-governance in agriculture: Digital tools enabling Filipino farmers. *Journal of Asian Public Policy*, 12(1), 51–70. DOI: 10.1080/17516234.2018.1499479

Peng, Z., Namyalo, P. K., Chen, X., Lv, M., & Coyte, P. C. (2023). What Motivates Individuals to Share Information With Governments When Adopting Health Technologies During the COVID-19 Pandemic? *BMC Public Health*, 23(1), 2527. Advance online publication. DOI: 10.1186/s12889-023-17437-2 PMID: 38110945

Peter, M. K., Wuersch, L., Neher, A., Lindeque, J. P., & Mändli Lerch, K. (2024). The Workplace of the Future: The COVID-19 Pandemic And working From Home In Swiss small Businesses. *Journal of Strategy and Management*, 17(4), 707–729. Advance online publication. DOI: 10.1108/JSMA-09-2023-0248

Pratt, B., Parker, M., & Bull, S. (2022). Equitable Design and Use of Digital Surveillance Technologies During COVID-19: Norms and Concerns. *Journal of Empirical Research on Human Research Ethics; JERHRE*, 17(5), 573–586. DOI: 10.1177/15562646221118127 PMID: 36069118

Puriwat, W., & Tripopsakul, S. (2021a). Explaining an Adoption and Continuance Intention to Use Contactless Payment Technologies: During the COVID-19 Pandemic. *Emerging Science Journal*, 5(1), 85–95. Advance online publication. DOI: 10.28991/esj-2021-01260

Puriwat, W., & Tripopsakul, S. (2021b). Understanding Food Delivery Mobile Application Technology Adoption: A UTAUT Model Integrating Perceived Fear of COVID-19. *Emerging Science Journal*, 5, 94–104. Advance online publication. DOI: 10.28991/esj-2021-SPER-08

Rafi, M., Suswanta, S., Handoko, T., & Effendi, G. N. (2022). Transformation of Public Services through Digital Services in the Covid-19 Era: Efforts Towards Good Governance in Indonesia. International Conference on Public Organization (ICONPO 2021), 209(Iconpo 2021), 168–176. https://doi.org/DOI: 10.2991/AEBMR.K.220209.022

Rajasegar, R. S., Gouthaman, P., Ponnusamy, V., Arivazhagan, N., & Nallarasan, V. (2024). Data Privacy and Ethics in Data Analytics. *Studies in Big Data*, 145, 195–213. DOI: 10.1007/978-981-97-0448-4_10

Ralison Avotra, A. A., Ye, C., Sandra Marcelline, T. R., Ali, A., & Yingfei, Y. (2021). Examining the Impact of E-Government on Corporate Social Responsibility Performance: The Mediating Effect of Mandatory Corporate Social Responsibility Policy, Corruption, and Information and Communication Technologies Development During the COVID Era. *Frontiers in Psychology*, 12, 737100. Advance online publication. DOI: 10.3389/fpsyg.2021.737100 PMID: 34712183

Raskar, R., Nadeau, G., Werner, J., Barbar, R., Mehra, A., Harp, G., Leopoldseder, M., Wilson, B., Flakoll, D., Vepakomma, P., Pahwa, D., Beaudry, R., Flores, E., Popielarz, M., Bhatia, A., Nuzzo, A., Gee, M., Summet, J., Surati, R., & Louisy, K. (2020). COVID-19 Contact-Tracing Mobile Apps: Evaluation and Assessment for Decision Makers. https://arxiv.org/abs/2006.05812v1

Redmiles, E. M. (2020). *User Concerns \&Amp; Tradeoffs in Technology-Facilitated COVID-19 Response*. Digital Government Research and Practice., DOI: 10.1145/3428093

Reifels, L., & Murray, V. (2022). Digital Health Emergency Management—Pandemics and Beyond. *JAMA Network Open*, 5(2), e220218–e220218. DOI: 10.1001/jamanetworkopen.2022.0218 PMID: 35195700

Renn, O., Beier, G., & Schweizer, P. J. (2021). The opportunities and risks of digitalisation for sustainable development: a systemic perspective. GAIA - Ecological Perspectives for Science and Society, 30(1), 23–28. https://doi.org/DOI: 10.14512/gaia.30.1.6

Riemer, K., Ciriello, R., Peter, S., Schlagwein, D., Ågerfalk, P., Conboy, K., & Myers, M. (2020). Digital contact-tracing adoption in the COVID-19 pandemic: IT governance for collective action at the societal level. *European Journal of Information Systems*, 29(6), 731–745. DOI: 10.1080/0960085X.2020.1819898

Rowe, F. (2020). Contact tracing apps and values dilemmas: A privacy paradox in a neo-liberal world. *International Journal of Information Management*, 55, 102178. DOI: 10.1016/j.ijinfomgt.2020.102178 PMID: 32836636

Sadiq, M. S., & Singh, I. P., M., A. M., & A., I. M. (. (2023). Identification of the Leading Economic Sectors of Nigeria: A Typology Juxtapose of Nigerian Economy Vis-À-Vis African Economies. *Jordan Journal of Economic Sciences*, 10(2), 101–115. DOI: 10.35516/jjes.v10i2.1396

Schöpper, H., Schnelle, J., Kersten, W. (2023) COVID-19: A Catalyst for Digitalization and Transparency?. Industry 4.0 Science, 39. Jg.,Nr. 1, S.72-79. https://doi.org/DOI: 10.30844/I4SE.23.1.72

Shah, I. A., Wassan, S., & Usmani, M. H. (2022). E-Government Security and Privacy Issues: Challenges and Preventive Approaches. Https://Services.Igi-Global.Com/Resolvedoi/Resolve.Aspx?Doi=10.4018/978-1-7998-9624-1.Ch004, 61–76. https://doi.org/DOI: 10.4018/978-1-7998-9624-1.ch004

Sihotang, D. M., Andriqa, M. R., Alfahmi, F. N., Wahyudi, A. S., Herdin Besila, M. A., Yulianang, M. A., Diana, E., & Hidayanto, A. N. (2023). The Moderating Role of Trust in Government Adoption E-Service During Covid-19 Pandemic: Health Belief Model Perspective. *International Journal of Information Technology : an Official Journal of Bharati Vidyapeeth's Institute of Computer Applications and Management*, 15(3), 1545–1553. Advance online publication. DOI: 10.1007/s41870-023-01203-z PMID: 37056795

Smidt, H. J., & Jokonya, O. (2021). The challenge of privacy and security when using technology to track people in times of COVID-19 pandemic. *Procedia Computer Science*, 181, 1018–1026. DOI: 10.1016/j.procs.2021.01.281 PMID: 33643498

Snowdon, J. L., Kassler, W., Karunakaram, H., Dixon, B. E., & Rhee, K. (2021). Leveraging Informatics and Technology to Support Public Health Response: Framework and Illustrations Using COVID-19. *Online Journal of Public Health Informatics*, 13(1). Advance online publication. DOI: 10.5210/ojphi.v13i1.11072 PMID: 33936521

Stephen Tochukwu, N., Methodius Ugwu, C., & Oluchukwu Wogu, J. (2021). Digital Learning in Post COVID-19 Era: Policy Options and Prospects for Quality Education in Nigeria. Library Philosophy and Practice, 1–18, 1–18. https://digitalcommons.unl.edu/libphilprac

Sujan, M. S. H., Tasnim, R., Islam, M. S., Ferdous, M. Z., Haghighathoseini, A., Koly, K. N., & Pardhan, S. (2022). Financial hardship and mental health conditions in people with underlying health conditions during the COVID-19 pandemic in Bangladesh. *Heliyon*, 8(9), e10499. Advance online publication. DOI: 10.1016/j.heliyon.2022.e10499 PMID: 36060462

Sukmono, F. G., & Surya Kencana, A. P. (2023). *Pola Baru Pengelolaan Media Digital Dalam Instagram @Humasjogja. Mediator*. Jurnal Komunikasi., DOI: 10.29313/mediator.v15i2.10705

Syed Aun, M. (2021). *Naqvi, Tahir Alyas, Nadia Tabassum, Abdallah Namoun, H. H. N.* Post Pandemic World and Challenges for E-Governance Framework. International Journal of Advanced Trends in Computer Science and Engineering., DOI: 10.30534/ijatcse/2021/1571032021

Tabuga, A. D., Domingo, S. N., Diokno-Sicat, C. J., Ulep, V., & Gilbert, T. (2020). Innovating governance: Building resilience against COVID-19 pandemic and other risks. Philippine Institute for Development Studies (PIDS), Quezon City. https://www.econstor.eu/handle/10419/241012

Truc Nguyen, T. T. (2023). Citizens' Intentions to Use E-Government During the COVID-19 Pandemic: Integrating the Technology Acceptance Model and Perceived Risk Theory. *Kybernetes*, 52(7), 2329–2346. Advance online publication. DOI: 10.1108/K-07-2022-1023

Ullah, A., Pinglu, C., Ullah, S., Abbas, H. S. M., & Khan, S. (2021). The Role of E-Governance in Combating COVID-19 and Promoting Sustainable Development: A Comparative Study of China and Pakistan. *Chinese Political Science Review*, 6(1), 86–118. DOI: 10.1007/s41111-020-00167-w

Ullah, S., Khan, F. U., Trifan, V. A., Spînu, A. E., & Sanda, G. (2022). Modeling Key Strategies for Reducing Socio-Economic and Health Crisis: Perspective From COVID-19 Pandemic. *International Journal of Environmental Research and Public Health*, 19(21), 14127. Advance online publication. DOI: 10.3390/ijerph192114127 PMID: 36361010

Uwizeyimana, T., Hashim, H. T., Kabakambira, J. D., Mujyarugamba, J. C., Dushime, J., Ntacyabukura, B., Ndayizeye, R., Adebisi, Y. A., & Lucero-Prisno, D. E.III. (2021). Drug Supply Situation in Rwanda During COVID-19: Issues, Efforts and Challenges. *Journal of Pharmaceutical Policy and Practice*, 14(1), 12. Advance online publication. DOI: 10.1186/s40545-021-00301-2 PMID: 33472702

Uwizeyimana, T., Manirambona, E., Musa, S. S., Uwiringiyimana, E., Bazimya, D., & Mathewos, K. (2023). Achieving COVID-19 Herd Immunity in Rwanda, Africa. *Public Health Challenges*, 2(1), e75. Advance online publication. DOI: 10.1002/puh2.75

Vardavas, C., Odani, S., Nikitara, K., El Banhawi, H., Kyriakos, C., Taylor, L., & Becuwe, N. (2021). Public perspective on the governmental response, communication and trust in the governmental decisions in mitigating COVID-19 early in the pandemic across the G7 countries. *Preventive Medicine Reports*, 21, 101252. DOI: 10.1016/j.pmedr.2020.101252 PMID: 33364149

Vasylieva, T. A., Kryklii, O. A., & Petrushenko, Y. M. (2021). Digital inclusion of population: economic, social, educational determinants in the COVID-19 era. Centre of Sociological Research. https://essuir.sumdu.edu.ua/handle/123456789/86161

Wang, Q., & Huang, R. (2021). The impact of COVID-19 pandemic on sustainable development goals – A survey. *Environmental Research*, 202, 111637. DOI: 10.1016/j.envres.2021.111637 PMID: 34233155

Wang, Q., Su, M., Zhang, M., & Li, R. (2021). Integrating Digital Technologies and Public Health to Fight Covid-19 Pandemic: Key Technologies, Applications, Challenges and Outlook of Digital Healthcare. *International Journal of Environmental Research and Public Health*, 18(11), 6053. Advance online publication. DOI: 10.3390/ijerph18116053 PMID: 34199831

Warsono, H., Hanani, R., & Rahman, A. Z. (2023). *Local Governments' Financial Accountability Responses in Critical Time: Reflection From Intergovernmental Management in Indonesia During the Early Covid-19 Pandemic*. Academic Journal of Interdisciplinary Studies., DOI: 10.36941/ajis-2023-0025

Wibowo, A. (2023). Enhancing Digital Transformation through Digital Innovation in the Context of Economic Advancement in the Era of Economic Society 5.0. Proceeding of Applied Science. *Educational Technology*, 1(1), 1–13. https://conferences.unusa.ac.id/index.php/paset/article/view/1313

Widodo, J. S., Kristiawanto, K., & Chandra, T. Y. (2021). *The Study of Implementation Effectiveness in the Various Criminal Law Policies During the Covid-19 Pandemic*. Kanun Jurnal Ilmu Hukum., DOI: 10.24815/kanun.v23i3.21912

Willem, L., Abrams, S., Libin, P. J. K., Coletti, P., Kuylen, E., Petrof, O., Møgelmose, S., Wambua, J., Herzog, S. A., Faes, C., Beutels, P., & Hens, N. (2021). The impact of contact tracing and household bubbles on deconfinement strategies for COVID-19. Nature Communications 2021 12:1, 12(1), 1–9. https://doi.org/DOI: 10.1038/s41467-021-21747-7

Wilson, A., & Tewdwr-Jones, M. (2021). Digital participatory planning: Citizen engagement, democracy, and design. Digital Participatory Planning: Citizen Engagement, Democracy, and Design, 1–292. https://doi.org/DOI: 10.4324/9781003190639/DIGITAL-PARTICIPATORY-PLANNING-ALEXANDER-WILSON-MARK-TEWDWR-JONES

Yallop, C. A., & Aliasghar, O. (2020). No business as usual: A case for data ethics and data governance in the age of coronavirus. *Online Information Review*, 44(6), 1217–1221. DOI: 10.1108/OIR-06-2020-0257

Yu, T.-C., Parng, I.-M., Yeh, J.-S., Cao, G.-W., & Wang, F.-C. (2023). A Digital Certificate System That Complies with International Standards: Taiwan Digital COVID-19 Certificate. *Standards 2023, Vol. 3, Pages 341-355, 3*(4), 341–355. DOI: 10.3390/standards3040024

Yun, J. Y., Sim, J. A., Lee, S., & Yun, Y. H. (2022). Stronger association of perceived health with socio-economic inequality during COVID-19 pandemic than pre-pandemic era. *BMC Public Health*, 22(1), 1–13. DOI: 10.1186/s12889-022-14176-8 PMID: 36114525

Zhao, W., Yin, C., Hua, T., Meadows, M. E., Li, Y., Liu, Y., Cherubini, F., Pereira, P., & Fu, B. (2022). Achieving the Sustainable Development Goals in the Post-Pandemic Era. *Humanities & Social Sciences Communications*, 9(1), 258. Advance online publication. DOI: 10.1057/s41599-022-01283-5 PMID: 35967482

Zhong, W., Hu, Q., & Kapucu, N. (2022). Robust Crisis Communication in Turbulent Times: Conceptualization and Empirical Evidence From the United States. *Public Administration*. Advance online publication. DOI: 10.1111/padm.12855

ADDITIONAL READING

Bhuvana, M., & Vasantha, S. (2021). The Impact of COVID-19 on Rural Citizens for Accessing E-Governance Services: A Conceptual Model Using the Dimensions of Trust and Technology Acceptance Model. In Al-Emran, M., & Shaalan, K. (Eds.), *Recent Advances in Technology Acceptance Models and Theories. Studies in Systems, Decision and Control* (Vol. 335). Springer., DOI: 10.1007/978-3-030-64987-6_27

Blom, P. P., & Uwizeyimana, D. E. (2020). Assessing the Effectiveness of e-Government and e-Governance in South Africa: During National Lockdown 2020. *Review of World Economics*, 11(5), 208. DOI: 10.5430/rwe.v11n5p208

Gavrilu ă, N., Stoica, V., & Fârte, G.-I. (2022). The Official Website as an Essential E-Governance Tool: A Comparative Analysis of the Romanian Cities' Websites in 2019 and 2022. *Sustainability (Basel)*, 14(11), 6863. DOI: 10.3390/su14116863

Patel, M., & Patel, M. (2022). An Integrated GIS/GPS Based e-Governance Approach for Different Agencies to Fight Against COVID-19. In Nayak, J., Naik, B., & Abraham, A. (Eds.), *Understanding COVID-19: The Role of Computational Intelligence. Studies in Computational Intelligence* (Vol. 963). Springer., DOI: 10.1007/978-3-030-74761-9_20

KEY TERMS AND DEFINITIONS

CHWs: Community Health Workers
HBM: Health Belief Model
IoT: Internet of Things
MSMEs: Micro, Small, and Medium Enterprises
PRT: Perceived Risk Theory
SDG: Sustainable Development Goals
TAM: Technology Acceptance Model
ULesson: Universal Lesson

Compilation of References

Abhishek, G. (2019). *Property registration and land record management via blockchains*. Indian Institute of Technology Kanpur.

Abiad, M., Kadry, N., & Ionescu, S. (2018). *Preventive & predictive maintenance of telecommunication equipment: A review*. 2018 4th International Conference on Applied and Theoretical Computing and Communication Technology (iCATccT), 154–159. https://api.semanticscholar.org/CorpusID:211244649

Abiad, M., Shafiq, M., Habib, S., & Atif, M. (2024). *On the Development of Fuzzy Estimators for Life Time Distributions based on Censored Fuzzy Life Times*. International Journal of Neutrosophic Science, 198-209. DOI: 10.54216/IJNS.240217

Abiad, M., & Ionescu, S. (2020). *Building an algorithm for predictive maintenance*. UPB Scientific Bulletin, Series D. *Mechanical Engineering (New York, N.Y.)*, 337–348.

Achmad, M. (2022). Hasan Aydin The Governments' Use of Social Networking Sites (SNS) to Promote Citizens' Trust During the COVID-19. *Journal of Ethnic and Cultural Studies*, 9(4), 156–186. DOI: 10.29333/ejecs/1383

Adams, G. (2013). Calculating the cloud: Determing the true cost of hosting services in the cloud. Retrieved from Educause Quarterly: http://www.edecause.edu/educas

Ademodi, D. T. (2015). Empirical study of Awareness and Use of Reference Source by Undergraduate in Adekunle Ajasin University Library. Pp 10-17 Information and Knowledge Management Journal Agu, P.C. (2014). User and services of academic libraries. In F.C Ekere (ed). Administration of academic libraries: A book of reading (pp.120-128). Enugu: Praise House Publishers.

Ademodi, E. O & Adepoju (2009). Influence of information technology skills on library patronage Available at https://core.ac.uk/ download/pdf/ 21516248 3.pdf

Afzal, M., & Panagiotopoulos, P. (2024). Data in Policing: An Integrative Review. *International Journal of Public Administration*, •••, 1–20. DOI: 10.1080/01900692.2024.2360586

Agarwal, P. K. (2018). Public Administration Challenges in the World of AI and Bots. *Public Administration Review*, 78(6), 917–921. DOI: 10.1111/puar.12979

Agarwal, P., Swami, S., & Malhotra, S. K. (2024). Artificial Intelligence Adoption in the Post COVID-19 New-Normal and Role of Smart Technologies in Transforming Business: A Review. *Journal of Science and Technology Policy Management*, 15(3), 506–529. DOI: 10.1108/JSTPM-08-2021-0122

Agbo, C. C., Mahmoud, Q. H., & Eklund, J. M. (2019). Blockchain technology in healthcare: A systematic review. *Healthcare (Basel)*, 7(2), 56. Advance online publication. DOI: 10.3390/healthcare7020056 PMID: 30987333

Agostino, D., Arnaboldi, M., & Lema, M. D. (2021). New development: COVID-19 as an accelerator of digital transformation in public service delivery. *Public Money & Management*, 1–4(1), 69–72. Advance online publication. DOI: 10.1080/09540962.2020.1764206

Agrawal, R., Wankhede, V. A., & Nair, R. S. (2021). Analysis of drivers of digital learning in COVID-19 and post-COVID-19 scenario using an ISM approach. *Journal of the Institution of Engineers (India)*: Series B, 102, 1143–1155. https://doi.org/ DOI: 10.1007/s40031-020-00528-8

Aguirre, R. R., Suarez, O., Fuentes, M., & Sanchez-Gonzalez, M. A. (2019). Electronic Health Record Implementation: A Review of Resources and Tools. *Cureus*, 11(9). Advance online publication. DOI: 10.7759/cureus.5649 PMID: 31700751

Ahamad, S., Mohseni, M., Shekher, V., Smaisim, G. F., Tripathi, A., & Alanya-Beltran, J. (2022, April). A detailed analysis of the critical role of artificial intelligence in enabling high-performance cloud computing systems. In *2022 2nd International Conference on Advance Computing and Innovative Technologies in Engineering (ICACITE)* (pp. 156-159). IEEE.

Ahdadou, M., Aajly, A., & Tahrouch, M. (2022). *Information Technology Governance: Lessons Learned From the Covid-19 Crisis*. International Journal of Business and Technology Management., DOI: 10.55057/ijbtm.2022.4.1.1

Ahmad, D., Lutfiani, N., Ahmad, A. A., Rahardja, U., & Aini, Q. (2021). Blockchain Technology Immutability Framework Design in E-Government. *Journal of Administration (Public Administration Journal)*, 32-41.

Ahmad, D., Lutfiani, N., Ahmad, A. A., Rahardja, U., & Aini, Q. (2021). Blockchain Technology Immutability Framework Design in E-Government. Journal of Administration (Public Administration Journal), 32-41.

Ahmad, S. F., Alam, M. M., Rahmat, M. K., Mubarik, M. S., & Hyder, S. I. (2022). Academic and Administrative Role of Artificial Intelligence in Education. In *Sustainability* (Vol. 14, Issue 3). DOI: 10.3390/su14031101

Ahmed, Z. U., & Krohan, F. B. (1992). Marketing India as a tourist destination in North America—Challenges and opportunities. *International Journal of Hospitality Management*, 11(2), 89–98. DOI: 10.1016/0278-4319(92)90003-E

Ahn, M. J., & Chen, Y.-C. (2022). Digital transformation toward AI-augmented public administration: The perception of government employees and the willingness to use AI in government. *Government Information Quarterly*, 39(2), 101664. https://doi.org/https://doi.org/10.1016/j.giq.2021.101664. DOI: 10.1016/j.giq.2021.101664

Aishwarya, R., & Malliga, S. (2014, April). Intrusion detection system-An efficient way to thwart against Dos/DDos attack in the cloud environment. In *2014 International conference on recent trends in information technology* (pp. 1-6). Ieee.

Ajadi, S., & Drury, P. (2021). *Health Systems, Digital Health and COVID-19: Insights from Bangladesh*. GSMA Mobile for Development.

Ajibola, B. (2012). Cloud Cooputing Communication of the ACM. Retrieved from http://csrc.nistgov/organizations/fisseg/2009conference/prelentational/fissea09day3cloudcomputi ng.pdf.

Ajwani-Ramchandani, R., Figueira, S., Torres de Oliveira, R., & Jha, S. (2021). Enhancing the circular and modified linear economy: The importance of blockchain for developing economies. *Resources, Conservation and Recycling*, 168, 105468. DOI: 10.1016/j.resconrec.2021.105468

Ajzen, I., & Driver, B. E. (1992). Applied of the theory of planned behavior to leisure choice. *Journal of Leisure Research*, 24(3), 207–224. DOI: 10.1080/00222216.1992.11969889

Akinnuwesi, B. A., Uzoka, F.-M. E., Fashoto, S. G., Mbunge, E., Odumabo, A., Amusa, O. O., Okpeku, M., & Owolabi, O. (2022). *A Modified UTAUT Model for the Acceptance and Use of Digital Technology for Tackling COVID-19*. Sustainable Operations and Computers., DOI: 10.1016/j.susoc.2021.12.001

Akinsanmi, T., & Salami, A. (2021). Evaluating the trade-off between privacy, public health safety, and digital security in a pandemic. *Data & Policy*, 3(17), e27. DOI: 10.1017/dap.2021.24

Akter, S., Michael, K., Uddin, M. R., McCarthy, G., & Rahman, M. (2022). Transforming business using digital innovations: The application of AI, blockchain, cloud and data analytics. *Annals of Operations Research*, 308(1), 7–39. DOI: 10.1007/s10479-020-03620-w

Akuffo, M. N., & Budu, S. (2019). Use of electronic resources by students in a premier postgraduate theological university in Ghana. SAJIM, vol.21, n.1, pp.1-9. ISSN 1560-683X. http://dx.doi.org/ African Journal of Information Management Alemayehu, N. (2010). *Is Cloud Computing Really Read for Prime Time?* Retrieved from IEEE Computer Society: www.leavcom./pdf/cloudcomputing.DOI: 10.4102/sajim.v21i1.1026.South

Al Kilani and Kobziev V. (2017) "An Overview Of E-government Concept, Econtechmod. An international quarterly journal, Vol. 06, No. 4, pp. 97-102.

Al Mudawi, N., Beloff, N., & White, M. (2019, August). Cloud computing in government organizations-towards a new comprehensive model. In *2019 IEEE SmartWorld, Ubiquitous Intelligence & Computing, Advanced & Trusted Computing, Scalable Computing & Communications, Cloud & Big Data Computing, Internet of People and Smart City Innovation (SmartWorld/SCALCOM/UIC/ATC/CBDCom/IOP/SCI)* (pp. 1473-1479). IEEE.

Alam, K. M., Rahman, J. A., Tasnim, A., & Akther, A. (2022). A blockchain-based land title management system for Bangladesh. *Journal of King Saud University. Computer and Information Sciences*, 34(6), 3096–3110. DOI: 10.1016/j.jksuci.2020.10.011

Alarie, B., Niblett, A., & Yoon, A. H. (2018). How artificial intelligence will affect the practice of law. *University of Toronto Law Journal*, 68(1, supplement 1), 106–124. https://doi.org/https://doi.org/10.3138/utlj.2017-0052. DOI: 10.3138/utlj.2017-0052

Alassaf, N., Alkazemi, B., & Gutub, A. (2003). Applicable light-weight cryptography to secure medical data in IoT systems. *Arabia (London, England)*, 2(2), 50–58.

Alassaf, N., & Gutub, A. (2019). Simulating light-weight-cryptography implementation for IoT healthcare data security applications. [IJEHMC]. *International Journal of E-Health and Medical Communications*, 10(4), 1–15. DOI: 10.4018/IJEHMC.2019100101

AlAwadhi, S., & Morris, A. (2009). "Factors influencing the adoption of e-government services. Journal of Software Vol.4, 584-590.Retrieved fromhttps://www.researchgate.net/publication/373675400_Factors_Influencing_the_Adoption_of_E-Government_Services_A_Study_among_University_Students.

Al-Besher, A., & Kumar, K. (2022). Use of artificial intelligence to enhance e-government services. *Measurement. Sensors*, 24, 100484. DOI: 10.1016/j.measen.2022.100484

Al-Dabbagh, Z. S. (2020). Sustainable development and its role in containing crises: Corona virus pandemic crisis (COVID-19) in China as a model. *Journal of Public Affairs*, 20(4), e2339. DOI: 10.1002/pa.2339 PMID: 32904918

Alhaimer, R. (2024). Digital transformation on the design and implementation of virtual political campaigns in Kuwait: perceptions and attitudes of politicians and campaign managers for bold innovation and social impact in Kuwait. Journal of Science and Technology Policy Management. DOI: 10.1108/JSTPM-11-2023-0212

Alhaimer, R. (2024). Unveiling the digital persona image: the influence of social media on political candidates' brand personality and voter behaviour in Kuwait. https://www.researchgate.net/publication/376617959_Unveiling_the_digital_persona_image_the_influence_of_social_media_on_political_candidates'_brand_personality_and_voter_behaviour_in_Kuwait Anderson, R., & Moore, T. (2006). The economics of information security. *Science*, New Series, 314(5799), 610-613. https://www.jstor.org/stable/20031627

Alhaimer, R. (2023). *Comparing virtual political campaigns with traditional political campaigns: evidence from Kuwait during the COVID-19 pandemic. Global Knowledge, Memory and Communication.* Global Knowledge, Memory and Communication., DOI: 10.1108/GKMC-07-2022-0182

Alhaimer, R. (2023a). Exploring the Attitudes of Kuwait's Residents Toward the Role of Corruption and Anti-Corruption Entities (Nazaha) in Kuwait. *Public Integrity*, 26(3), 305–321. DOI: 10.1080/10999922.2023.2176054

Alhaimer, R. (2023b). *Impact of governmental social media campaigns on citizens' attitudes towards Kuwait's vision 2035.* Global Knowledge, Memory and Communication., DOI: 10.1108/GKMC-06-2023-0209

Alhitmi, H. K., Mardiah, A., Al-Sulaiti, K. I., & Abbas, J. (2024). Data security and privacy concerns of AI-driven marketing in the context of economics and business field: An exploration into possible solutions. *Cogent Business & Management*, 11(1), 2393743. DOI: 10.1080/23311975.2024.2393743

Alhosh, A. (2006). *E-government reality and prospects*. Arab Nile Publishing Group.

Ali, D. A., Deininger, K., & Goldstein, M. (2014). Environmental and gender impacts of land tenure regularization in Africa: Pilot evidence from Rwanda. *Journal of Development Economics*, 110, 262–275. DOI: 10.1016/j.jdeveco.2013.12.009

Ali, J. S., & Yong, J. (2014). *Impact of Cloud Computing Technology on E-Government*. DOI: 10.1007/978-3-319-11958-8_22

Ali, K. E., & Alonso-Monsalve, S. (2018). *A Study of Cloud Computing Adoption in Universities as a Guideline to Cloud Migration*. Sage Journals.

Alipio, R. H., & Balahadia, F. F. (2020). DSS Framework: A Proposal for Disaster Logistic Support System for the Province of Laguna. *Recoletos Multidisciplinary Research Journal, 8*(2 SE-Articles), 51–62. DOI: 10.32871/rmrj2008.02.04

Ali, T., Nadeem, A., Alzahrani, A., & Jan, S. (2020, February). A transparent and trusted property registration system on permissioned blockchain. In *2019 International conference on advances in the emerging computing Technologies (AECT)* (pp. 1-6). IEEE. DOI: 10.1109/AECT47998.2020.9194222

Alkhaldi, A., Alrashidi, H., Alhasan, K., Alsadeeqi, A., & Alshami, A. (2023). The use of blockchain technology to build smart cities- creating public value in Kuwait. *Journal Global Knowledge, Memory and Communication*, V. ahead-of-print (ahead-of-print), 1-15. https://doi-org.ez46.periodicos.capes.gov.br/10.1108/GKMC-11-2022-0263

Alkhaldi, A., Malik, S., & Lytras, M. D. (2024). Transformative Leadership in Kuwait Direct Investment Promotion Authority: Investing in Talent, Innovation and the Next Generation. In S. Baroudi & M. D. Lytras, M. D. (Eds.), Transformative Leadership and Sustainable Innovation in Education: Interdisciplinary Perspectives (27-38). Emerald Publishing Limited. DOI: 10.1108/978-1-83753-536-120241003

Alkhaldi, A., Alrashidi, H., Alhasan, K., Alsadeeqi, A., & Alshami, A. (2023). *The use of blockchain technology to build smart cities: creating public value in Kuwait*. Global Knowledge, Memory and Communication., DOI: 10.1108/GKMC-11-2022-0263

Alkhaldi, A., Malik, S., Alhaimer, R., Alshaheen, A., & Lytras, M. D. (2024). Translating a value-based framework for resilient e-learning impact in post COVID-19 times: Research-based Evidence from Higher Education in Kuwait. *Heliyon*, 10(2), e24271. DOI: 10.1016/j.heliyon.2024.e24271 PMID: 38298680

Alkhonaini, M., & El-Sayed, H. (2018, August). Migrating data between physical server and cloud: improving accuracy and data integrity. In *2018 17th IEEE International Conference On Trust, Security And Privacy In Computing And Communications/12th IEEE International Conference On Big Data Science And Engineering (TrustCom/BigDataSE)* (pp. 1570-1574). IEEE.

Al-Nory, M. T. (2019). Optimal Decision Guidance for the Electricity Supply Chain Integration with Renewable Energy: Aligning Smart Cities Research with Sustainable Development Goals. *IEEE Access : Practical Innovations, Open Solutions*, 7, 74996–75006. Advance online publication. DOI: 10.1109/ACCESS.2019.2919408

Al-Omari, A., & Al-Omari, H. (2006). E-Government Readiness Assessment Model Ahmed Al-Omari and Hussein Al-Omari. *Journal of Computational Science*, 2(11), 841–845. DOI: 10.3844/jcssp.2006.841.845

Alruqi, A. S., & Aksoy, M. S. (2023). The Use of Artificial Intelligence for Disasters. *Ozean Journal of Applied Sciences*, 13(5), 731–738. DOI: 10.4236/ojapps.2023.135058

Al-Sarafi, A. H., & Najeh, T. (2022). Post COVID-19 Pandemic Possible Business Continuity Strategies for Construction Industry Revival a Preliminary Study in the Malaysian Construction Industry. *International Journal of Disaster Resilience in the Built Environment*. Advance online publication. DOI: 10.1108/IJDRBE-11-2021-0147

AlShaikh, F., & Hewahi, N. (2021). AI and Machine Learning Techniques in the Development of Intelligent Tutoring System: A Review. *2021 International Conference on Innovation and Intelligence for Informatics, Computing, and Technologies (3ICT)*, 403–410. DOI: 10.1109/3ICT53449.2021.9582029

Alsubaih, A., Hafez, A., & Alghathbar, K. (2013, September). Authorization as a service in cloud environments. In *2013 International Conference on Cloud and Green Computing* (pp. 487-493). IEEE.

Alzahrani, N. (2013). Understanding reliability and validity in qualitative research. The

Alzahrani, L., Al-Karaghouli, W., & Weerakkody, V. (2017). Analysing the critical factors influencing trust in e-government adoption from citizens' perspective: A systematic review and a conceptual framework. *International Business Review*, 26(1), 164–175. DOI: 10.1016/j.ibusrev.2016.06.004

Al-Zubaidie, M., Zhang, Z., & Zhang, J. (2019). PAX: Using pseudonymization and anonymization to protect patients' identities and data in the healthcare system. *International Journal of Environmental Research and Public Health*, 16(9), 1490.

Amado, J. A., Dayson, C. J. P., Gipaya, P. N., Hipos, A. M. G., Ortile, F. F., & Digo, G. S. (2024). Assessing the Impact of AI Generative Tools on Administrative and Supervisory Practices in Education. *Asia Pacific Journal of Management and Sustainable Development, 12*(1), 32–40. https://research.lpubatangas.edu.ph/wp-content/uploads/2024/07/3.-APJMSD-2024-06.pdf

Amann, J., Sleigh, J., & Vayena, E. (2021). Digital Contact-Tracing During the Covid-19 Pandemic: An Analysis of Newspaper Coverage in Germany, Austria, and Switzerland. *PLoS One*, 16(2), e0246524. Advance online publication. DOI: 10.1371/journal.pone.0246524 PMID: 33534839

Amosun, T. S., Chu, J., Rufai, O. H., Muhideen, S., Shahani, R., & Gonlepa, M. K. (2022). Does e-government help shape citizens' engagement during the COVID-19 crisis? A study of mediational effects of how citizens perceive the government. *Online Information Review*, 46(5), 846–866. DOI: 10.1108/OIR-10-2020-0478

Anand, A., McKibbin, M., & Pichel, F. (2016, March). Colored coins: Bitcoin, blockchain, and land administration. In *Annual world bank conference on land and poverty* (pp. 20-24).

Anand, P. B., & Navío-Marco, J. (2018). Governance and economics of smart cities: opportunities and challenges. In *Telecommunications Policy* (Vol. 42, Issue 10). DOI: 10.1016/j.telpol.2018.10.001

Anderson, J., & Rainie, L. (2023, June 21). As AI Spreads, Experts Predict the Best and Worst Changes in Digital Life by 2035 [Report]. Pew Research Center. https://www.pewresearch.org/internet/wp-content/uploads/sites/9/2023/06/PI_2023.06.21_Best-Worst-Digital-Life_2035_FINAL.pdf

Angra, S., & Ahuja, S. (2017). Machine learning and its applications: A review. *Proceedings of the 2017 International Conference On Big Data Analytics and Computational Intelligence, ICBDACI 2017*, 57–60. DOI: 10.1109/ICBDACI.2017.8070809

Ani, Okon E. and Ahiazu, B. (2018), 'Towards effective development of electronic information resources in Nigerian university libraries', Library Management, 29(6/7), 504 – 514

Ankolekar, A., Eppings, L., Bottari, F., Pinho, I. F., Howard, K., Baker, R., Nan, Y., Xing, X., Walsh, S. L. F., Vos, W., Yang, G., & Lambin, P. (2024). Using artificial intelligence and predictive modelling to enable learning healthcare systems (LHS) for pandemic preparedness. *Computational and Structural Biotechnology Journal*, 24, 412–419. https://doi.org/https://doi.org/10.1016/j.csbj.2024.05.014. DOI: 10.1016/j.csbj.2024.05.014 PMID: 38831762

Annuj, D. (2017). Cloud Computing. Available at https://www.academia.ed/10200815/cloud_computing

Anthony Jnr, B., Abbas Petersen, S., Helfert, M., & Guo, H. (2021). Digital transformation with enterprise architecture for smarter cities: A qualitative research approach. *Digital Policy. Regulation & Governance*, 23(4), 355–376. DOI: 10.1108/DPRG-04-2020-0044

Anthopoulos, L., Sirakoulis, K., & Reddick, C. G. (2021). Conceptualizing Smart Government: Interrelations and Reciprocities with Smart City. *Digital Government: Research and Practice*, 2(4), 1–28. DOI: 10.1145/3465061

Aparajit, S., Shah, R., Chopdekar, R., & Patil, R. (2022, May). Data protection: The cloud security perspective. In *2022 3rd International Conference for Emerging Technology (INCET)* (pp. 1-5). IEEE.

Archi, Y. E., Benbba, B., Kabil, M., & Dávid, L. D. (2023). Digital technologies for sustainable tourism destinations: State of the art and research agenda. *Administrative Sciences*, 13(8), 1–21. DOI: 10.3390/admsci13080184

Arksey, H., & O'Malley, L. (2005). Scoping studies: Towards a methodological framework. *International Journal of Social Research Methodology*, 8(1), 19–32. DOI: 10.1080/1364557032000119616

Arnaboldi, M., & Azzone, G. (2020). Data science in the design of public policies: Dispelling the obscurity in matching policy demand and data offer. *Heliyon*, 6(6), e04300. DOI: 10.1016/j.heliyon.2020.e04300 PMID: 32637693

Arpaci, I. (2017). Antecedents and consequences of cloud comuting adoption in education to achieve knowledge management. doi:.DOI: 10.1016/j.chb.2017.01.024

Arrieta, A. B., Díaz-Rodríguez, N., Del Ser, J., Bennetot, A., Tabik, S., Barbado, A., & Herrera, F. (2020). Explainable Artificial Intelligence (XAI): Concepts, taxonomies, opportunities and challenges toward responsible AI. *Information Fusion*, 58, 82–115. DOI: 10.1016/j.inffus.2019.12.012

Arruñada, B. (2012). *Institutional foundations of impersonal exchange: Theory and policy of contractual registries*. University of Chicago Press. DOI: 10.7208/chicago/9780226028354.001.0001

Arun Kumar, B. R., & Rohith, B. (2020). Designing Safe and Secure Land Registration-Ownership Using Blockchain Technology with a Focus on Mutual Authentication. In *Sustainable Communication Networks and Application: ICSCN 2019* (pp. 509-516). Springer International Publishing. DOI: 10.1007/978-3-030-34515-0_53

Ashima, W., & Popli, R. (2016). Comprehensive Study of Security and Privacy Challenges in the Era of Big Data. *Proceedings of ICICCT on Information Communication Technology*. Jagan Institute of Management Studies.

Ashitha, U., Amulya, A. H. L. S., Sushma, G., Irfana, S., & Saibaba, C. M. (2024, May). Strengthening Cloud Security Through Multi-Factor Authentication: A Comprehensive Integration of Diverse Approaches. In *2024 International Conference on Electronics, Computing, Communication and Control Technology (ICECCC)* (pp. 1-8). IEEE.

Asor, J., & Sapin, S. (2020). Implementation of predictive crime analytics in municipal crime management system in Calauan, Laguna, Philippines. *International Journal of Advanced Trends in Computer Science and Engineering, 9*(1.3), 150–157. https://doi.org/https://doi.org/10.30534/ijatcse/2020/2291.32020

Asubiaro, T. V., & Onaolapo, S. (2023). A comparative study of the coverage of African journals in Web of Science, Scopus, and CrossRef. *Journal of the Association for Information Science and Technology*, 74(7), 745–758. DOI: 10.1002/asi.24758

Atabekov, A. R. (2023). Issues in the implementation of predictive law in law enforcement activities: a comparative legal study. *Vestnik of the St. Petersburg University of the Ministry of Internal Affairs of Russia, 2023*(3), 67–75.

Attaran, M. (2022). Blockchain technology in healthcare: Challenges and opportunities. *International Journal of Healthcare Management*, 15(1), 70–83. DOI: 10.1080/20479700.2020.1843887

Augustinus, C., & Tempra, O. (2021). Fit-for-purpose land administration in violent conflict settings. *Land (Basel)*, 10(2), 139. DOI: 10.3390/land10020139

Avantaggiato, M., & Gallo, P. (2019, June). Challenges and opportunities using multichain for real estate. In *2019 IEEE International Black Sea Conference on Communications and Networking (BlackSeaCom)* (pp. 1-5). IEEE. DOI: 10.1109/BlackSeaCom.2019.8812780

Ayundyayasti, P., Sarana, S., Sadida, A., Sugiarti, S., & Suwondo, A. (2023). Analysis of the Adoption of Digital Marketing in MSMEs in the Era of the Covid-19 Pandemic. Journal of Applied Business Administration. https://doi.org/DOI: 10.30871/jaba.v7i1.4867

Azaria, A., ... "Medrec: Using blockchain for medical data access and permission management." *2016 2nd international conference on open and big data (OBD)*. IEEE, 2016. DOI: 10.1109/OBD.2016.11

Azbeg, K., Ouchetto, O., & Andaloussi, S. J. (2022). BlockMedCare: A healthcare system based on IoT, Blockchain and IPFS for data management security. *Egyptian Informatics Journal*, 23(2), 329–343. DOI: 10.1016/j.eij.2022.02.004

Azer, M. A., & Samir, R. (2024). Overview of the Complex Landscape and Future Directions of Ethics in Light of Emerging Technologies. *IJACSA). International Journal of Advanced Computer Science and Applications*, 15(7). Advance online publication. DOI: 10.14569/IJACSA.2024.01507142

Babili, A., Nsanzimana, S., Rwagasore, E., & Lester, R. (2023). SMS-based Digital Health Intervention in Rwanda's Home-Based Care Program for Remote Management of COVID-19 Cases and Contacts: A Qualitative Study of Sustainability and Scalability. *Frontiers in Digital Health*, 4, 1071790. Advance online publication. DOI: 10.3389/fdgth.2022.1071790 PMID: 36714610

Badran, A. (2023). Artificial Intelligence between Government and Self-Regulation Policies: A Theoretical Approach. . DOI: 10.31430/IJZH4708

Badran, A. (2019). Smart-Governments for Smart Cities: The Case of Dubai Smart-Government. In Samad, W. A., & Azar, E. (Eds.), *Smart Cities in the Gulf* (pp. 59–82). Springer Nature Singapore., DOI: 10.1007/978-981-13-2011-8_5

Badran, A. (2021a). Developing Smart Cities: Regulatory and Policy Implications for the State of Qatar. *International Journal of Public Administration*, •••, 1–14. DOI: 10.1080/01900692.2021.2003811

Badran, A. (2021b). Thoughts and Reflections on the Case of Qatar: Should Artificial Intelligence Be Regulated? In Azar, E., & Haddad, A. N. (Eds.), *Artificial Intelligence in the Gulf* (pp. 69–92). Springer Singapore., DOI: 10.1007/978-981-16-0771-4_5

Badran, A. (2022). Independent regulators in the Middle East. In *Handbook on Regulatory Authorities*. Edward Elgar Publishing.

Bag, A., Roy, S., & Pandey, A. (2024). Harnessing the Power of Artificial Intelligence in Law Enforcement: A Comprehensive Review of Opportunities and Ethical Challenges. In Ara, A., & Ara, A. (Eds.), *Exploring the Ethical Implications of Generative AI* (pp. 121–145). IGI Global., DOI: 10.4018/979-8-3693-1565-1.ch008

Bajwa, J., Munir, U., Nori, A., & Williams, B. (2021). Artificial intelligence in healthcare: Transforming the practice of medicine. *Future Healthcare Journal*, 8(2), e188–e194. https://doi.org/https://doi.org/10.7861/fhj.2021-0095. DOI: 10.7861/fhj.2021-0095 PMID: 34286183

Bakare A. (2018). Awareness and Adoption of Cloud Computing in Nigeria Libraries: An Aid to Library Services.

Bak, I., Barej-Kaczmarek, E., & Sulikowski, P. (2022). Impact of information and communication technologies on the tourism sector. *European Research Studies*, 25(3), 595–606. DOI: 10.35808/ersj/3052

Balahadia, F. (2020). Intelligent Investigation on Crime Incident Reports in the Province of Laguna through Predictive Model Development. *International Journal of Advanced Trends in Computer Science and Engineering, 9*(1.3), 139–144. https://doi.org/https://doi.org/10.30534/ijatcse/2020/2091.32020

Balahadia, F. F., Dadiz, B. G., Ramirez, R. R., Luvett, M., Lalata, J. P., & Lagman, A. C. (2019). Application of Data Mining Approach for Profiling Fire Incidents Reports of Bureau of Fire and Protection. *2019 International Conference on Computational Intelligence and Knowledge Economy (ICCIKE)*, 713–717. DOI: 10.1109/ICCIKE47802.2019.9004420

Bamidele, I. A., Omeluzor, U. S., Amadi, U. H., & Abayomi, I. (2003). Training of Library Assistant in Academic Library: a Study of Babcock University Library, Nigeria Sage Open Publisher https://www.coursehero.com/file/236201902/bamidele-et-al-2013-training-of-library-assistants-in-academic-library-a-study-of-babcock-university/

BARAI, V. (2024). BLOCKCHAIN IN LAND REGISTRY FOR TRANSFORMING LAND ADMINISTRATION. *Journal of Theoretical and Applied Information Technology*, 102(3).

Barashok, I. V., Rudenko, L. L., Shumakova, E. V., & Orlovskaia, I. V. (2021). Digitalization: New possibilities for the tourism industry. *IOP Conference Series. Earth and Environmental Science*, 666(06259), 1–6. DOI: 10.1088/1755-1315/666/6/062059

Barbero, M. C. (2016). *Big data analytics for policy making. European Commission.* Big data analytics for policy making. European Commission.

Bari, L. F., Ahmed, I., Ahamed, R., Zihan, T. A., Sharmin, S., Pranto, A. H., & Islam, M. R. (2023). Potential Use of Artificial Intelligence (AI) in Disaster Risk and Emergency Health Management: A Critical Appraisal on Environmental Health. *Environmental Health Insights*, 17, 11786302231217808. DOI: 10.1177/11786302231217808 PMID: 38089525

Barnes, S., & Milton, N. (2015). *Designing a successful KM strategy: a guide for the knowledge management professional.* Information Today, Inc.

Barredo, L., Olawale Benjamin, O., & Oluwatoyin Foye, V. (2022). Inclusion, Organizational Resilience, and Sustainable Development in Nigeria: The Role of Digital Innovations. Environmental Sciences Proceedings 2022, Vol. 15, Page 27, 15(1), 27. https://doi.org/DOI: 10.3390/environsciproc2022015027

Bartneck, C., Lütge, C., Wagner, A., & Welsh, S. (2021). Privacy Issues of AI. In C. Bartneck, C. Lütge, A. Wagner, & S. Welsh, *An Introduction to Ethics in Robotics and AI* (pp. 61–70). Springer International Publishing. DOI: 10.1007/978-3-030-51110-4_8

Bastidas, V., Bezbradica, M., & Helfert, M. (2017). Cities as enterprises: A comparison of smart city frameworks based on enterprise architecture requirements. *Lecture Notes in Computer Science (Including Subseries Lecture Notes in Artificial Intelligence and Lecture Notes in Bioinformatics), 10268 LNCS*. DOI: 10.1007/978-3-319-59513-9_3

Bastidas, V., Bezbradica, M., Bilauca, M., Healy, M., & Helfert, M. (2023). Enterprise Architecture in Smart Cities: Developing an Empirical Grounded Research Agenda. *Journal of Urban Technology*, 30(1), 47–70. DOI: 10.1080/10630732.2022.2122681

Batista, F. F. (2012). *Modelo de gestão do conhecimento para a administração pública brasileira: como implementar a gestão do conhecimento para produzir resultados em benefício do cidadão*. Ipea.

Batubara, F. R., Ubacht, J., & Janssen, M. (2018). Challenges of blockchain technology adoption for e-government: a systematic literature review. In *Proceedings of the 19th Annual International Conference on Digital Government Research: Governance in the Data Age*, 1-9. DOI: 10.1145/3209281.3209317

Baum, C. a. (2000). Gartner's Four Phases of E-Government Model, Gartner, Research note.

Bayram, G. E. (2020). Impact of information technology on tourism. In Hassan, A., & Sharma, A. (Eds.), *The Emerald Handbook of ICT in Tourism and Hospitality* (pp. 243–257). Emerald Publishing Limited., DOI: 10.1108/978-1-83982-688-720201015

Beer, D. (2018). Envisioning the power of data analytics. *Information Communication and Society*, 21(3), 465–479. DOI: 10.1080/1369118X.2017.1289232

Behra, A., & Jatav, S. S. (2022). Waste management practices of small hotels in Dehradun. *Journal of Tourism Insights*, 12(1), 1–16. https://scholarworks.gvsu.edu/jti/vol12/iss1/3/

Behra, A., Jatav, S. S., Amit, K. Y., & Kiran, B. B. (2023). How do domestic and foreign tourists understand the concept of 'green hotels' and its practices in India? *Journal of Survey in Fisheries Sciences*, 10(4S), 2551–2559. https://sifisheriessciences.com/journal/index.php/journal/article/view/1614

Belk, R. (2021). Ethical issues in service robotics and artificial intelligence. *Service Industries Journal*, 41(13–14), 860–876. DOI: 10.1080/02642069.2020.1727892

Benet, J. (2014). Ipfs-content addressed, versioned, p2p file system. *arXiv preprint arXiv:1407.3561.*

Berawi, M. A., Sari, M., Addiani, F. A. F., & Madyaningrum, N. (2021). Developing a Blockchain-based Data Storage System Model to Improve Government Agencies' Organizational Performance. *International Journal of Technology*, 12(5), 1038. DOI: 10.14716/ijtech.v12i5.5237

Berawi, M. A., Susantono, B., & Sari, M. (2022). Fostering resilient and smart cities to enhance sustainable urban development. In *The Routledge Handbook of Sustainable Cities and Landscapes in the Pacific Rim* (pp. 704–719). Routledge., DOI: 10.4324/9781003033530-60

Berk, R. A. (2021). Artificial Intelligence, Predictive Policing, and Risk Assessment for Law Enforcement. *Annual Review of Criminology, 4*(Volume 4, 2021), 209–237. DOI: 10.1146/annurev-criminol-051520-012342

Berry, R., & Reisman, M. (2012). Policy Challenges of Cross-border Cloud Computing. Journal of International Commerce and Economics. p. 1-38

Bertot, J. C., Estevez, E., & Janowski, T. (2016). Digital public service innovation: Framework proposal. *Proceedings of the 9th International Conference on Theory and Practice of Electronic Governance*, 113–122. DOI: 10.1145/2910019.2910108

Bertot, J. C., Jaeger, P. T., & Grimes, J. M. (2010). Using ICTs to create a culture of transparency: E-government and social media as openness and anti-corruption tools for societies. *Government Information Quarterly*, 27(3), 264–271. DOI: 10.1016/j.giq.2010.03.001

Bhagat, S. V., & Kanyal, D. (2024). Navigating the Future: The Transformative Impact of Artificial Intelligence on Hospital Management- A Comprehensive Review. *Cureus*, 16(2), e54518. DOI: 10.7759/cureus.54518 PMID: 38516434

Bharanidharan, G., & Jayalakshmi, S. (2021). Predictive scaling for elastic compute resources on public cloud utilizing deep learning-based long short-term memory. *International Journal of Advanced Computer Science and Applications*, 12(10), 73–81.

Bhattacharya, P., Tanwar, S., Shah, R., & Ladha, A. (2020). Mobile edge computing-enabled blockchain framework—a survey. In *Proceedings of ICRIC 2019: Recent Innovations in Computing* (pp. 797-809). Springer International Publishing.

Białożyt, W. (2017). Digital Era Governance – a new chapter of public management theory and practice Wojciech Białożyt. *MAZOWSZE Studia Regionalne*, 22(22), 117–129. DOI: 10.21858/msr.22.08

Bibri, S. E., & Krogstie, J. (2017). Smart sustainable cities of the future: An extensive interdisciplinary literature review. In *Sustainable Cities and Society* (Vol. 31). DOI: 10.1016/j.scs.2017.02.016

Biju, P. r., & Gayathri, O. (2024). Analytical state: A framework for thinking about artificial intelligence and algorithms for state power. *Electronic Government, an International Journal, 20*(4), 459–478. DOI: 10.1504/EG.2024.139503

Binhammad, M., Alqaydi, S., Othman, A., & Abuljadayel, L. H. (2024). The Role of AI in Cyber Security: Safeguarding Digital Identity. *Journal of Information Security*, 15(2), 245–278. https://doi.org/https://doi.org/10.4236/jis.2024.152015. DOI: 10.4236/jis.2024.152015

Borgeaud, A. (2024) Global Al Cybersecurity Market Size 2030, Statista. Available at: https://www.statista.com/statistics/1450963/global-ai-cybersecurity-market-size/

Bostancı, S. H., Yıldırım, S., & Erdoğan, F. (2022). Covid-19 Pandemi Sürecinde Hastane Bilgi Sistemi Açısından E-Devlet Portalı'nın Hizmetleri Üzerine Bir Derleme. *Konuralp Tip Dergisi*, 14(S1), 271–279. Advance online publication. DOI: 10.18521/ktd.1036010

Braun, V., & Clarke, V. (2006). Using thematic analysis in psychology. *Qualitative Research in Psychology*, 3(2), 77–101. DOI: 10.1191/1478088706qp063oa

Brayne, S., & Christin, A. (2021). Technologies of Crime Prediction: The Reception of Algorithms in Policing and Criminal Courts. *Social Problems*, 68(3), 608–624. DOI: 10.1093/socpro/spaa004 PMID: 38250480

Brennen, J. S., & Kreiss, D. (2016). Digitalization. *The International Encyclopedia of Communication Theory and Philosophy*, 1(1), 1–11. DOI: 10.1002/9781118766804.wbiect111

Bright, D., Brewer, R., & Morselli, C. (2021). Using social network analysis to study crime: Navigating the challenges of criminal justice records. *Social Networks*, 66, 50–64. DOI: 10.1016/j.socnet.2021.01.006

Brillantes, K. D. B., Jr. A. C. O., Francisco-Abrigo, K. A., Capones, E. M., & Jovellanos, J. B. B. (2019). *Status of Senior High School Implementation: A Process Evaluation*. https://www.econstor.eu/bitstream/10419/240964/1/pidsdps1913.pdf

Bringula, R. P. (2020). Intelligent Tutoring Systems for Filipino Learners: Current Research, Gaps, and Opportunities. In Habib, M. (Ed.), *Revolutionizing Education in the Age of AI and Machine Learning* (pp. 152–172). IGI Global., https://doi.org/http://doi:10.4018/978-1-5225-7793-5.ch008 DOI: 10.4018/978-1-5225-7793-5.ch008

Bringula, R., & Balahadia, F. (2019). A spatiotemporal analysis of fire incidents in Manila from 2011-2016: Implications for fire prevention. *Disaster Prevention and Management*, 28(2), 201–215. DOI: 10.1108/DPM-05-2018-0147

Broekhuizen, T., Dekker, H., de Faria, P., Firk, S., Nguyen, D. K., & Sofka, W. (2023). AI for managing open innovation: Opportunities, challenges, and a research agenda. *Journal of Business Research*, 167, 114196. https://doi.org/https://doi.org/10.1016/j.jbusres.2023.114196. DOI: 10.1016/j.jbusres.2023.114196

Brożek, B., Furman, M., Jakubiec, M., & Kucharzyk, B. (2024). The black box problem revisited. Real and imaginary challenges for automated legal decision making. *Artificial Intelligence and Law*, 32(2), 427–440. DOI: 10.1007/s10506-023-09356-9

Brynjolfsson, E., & McAfee, A. (2014). *The second machine age: work, progress, and prosperity in a time of brilliant technologies.* WW Norton & Company.

Budd, J., Miller, B. S., Manning, E. M., Lampos, V., Zhuang, M., Edelstein, M., Rees, G., Emery, V. C., Stevens, M. M., Keegan, N., Short, M. J., Pillay, D., Manley, E., Cox, I. J., Heymann, D., Johnson, A. M., & McKendry, R. A. (2020). Digital technologies in the public-health response to COVID-19. *Nature Medicine 2020 26:8, 26*(8), 1183–1192. https://doi.org/DOI: 10.1038/s41591-020-1011-4

Buhalis, D., & Law, R. (2008). Progress in information technology and tourism management: 20 years on and 10 years after the internet—the state of e-Tourism research. *Tourism Management*, 29(4), 609–623. DOI: 10.1016/j.tourman.2008.01.005

Bullu, J. (2014). An exploratory study of Indian university students' use of social networking websites: Implication for the work place. *Business Communication Quarterly*, 72, 105–110. http://www.scimagojr.com/journalsearch.php?q=1990019254&

Buterin, V. (2014). A next-generation smart contract and decentralized application platform. *white paper, 3*(37), 2-1.

Butler, R. (2015). The evolution of tourism and tourism research. *Tourism Recreation Research*, 40(1), 16–27. DOI: 10.1080/02508281.2015.1007632

Butt, U. M., Letchmunan, S., Hassan, F. H., Ali, M., Baqir, A., Koh, T. W., & Sherazi, H. H. R. (2021). Spatio-Temporal Crime Predictions by Leveraging Artificial Intelligence for Citizens Security in Smart Cities. *IEEE Access : Practical Innovations, Open Solutions*, 9, 47516–47529. DOI: 10.1109/ACCESS.2021.3068306

Cabaluna, C. (2024). *AI and the Law Forum Explores Future of Legal Practice in the Philippines.* Lexagle. https://www.lexagle.com/news-en-sg/ai-and-law-event-philippines-lexagle

Cachin, C. (2016, July). Architecture of the hyperledger blockchain fabric. In *Workshop on distributed cryptocurrencies and consensus ledgers* (Vol. 310, No. 4, pp. 1-4).

Cadiz, N., Mariano, K. L. S., Dumalag, J. B. L. C., Retamar, A. E., & Aceron, J. C. (2023). Information, Education, and Communication Campaign in the Philippines: Capacitating Academic Institutions and Government Agencies using Geographic Information System, Radar Remote Sensing, and Artificial Intelligence. *2023 Asian Conference on Remote Sensing (ACRS2023)*. https://www.researchgate.net/publication/380177949_Information_Education_and_Communication_Campaign_in_the_Philippines_Capacitating_Academic_Institutions_and_Government_Agencies_using_Geographic_Information_System_Radar_Remote_Sensing_and_Artificial_I

Caldwell, M., Andrews, J. T. A., Tanay, T., & Griffin, L. D. (2020). AI-enabled future crime. *Crime Science*, 9(1), 14. DOI: 10.1186/s40163-020-00123-8

Calo, R., & Citron, D. K. (2021). The Automated Administrative State: A Crisis of Legitimacy. *Emory Law Journal*, 70(4), 797–844. https://scholarlycommons.law.emory.edu/elj/vol70/iss4/1?utm_source=scholarlycommons.law.emory.edu%2Felj%2Fvol70%2Fiss4%2F1&utm_medium=PDF&utm_campaign=PDFCoverPages

Campana, P., & Meneghini, C. (2024). Organised crime movement across local communities: A network approach. *Trends in Organized Crime*, 27(3), 286–313. Advance online publication. DOI: 10.1007/s12117-024-09531-7

Campmas, A., Iacob, N., & Simonelli, F. (2022). How can interoperability stimulate the use of digital public services? An analysis of national interoperability frameworks and e-Government in the European Union. *Data & Policy*, 4, e19. Advance online publication. DOI: 10.1017/dap.2022.11

Capraro, V., Lentsch, A., Acemoglu, D., Akgun, S., Akhmedova, A., Bilancini, E., Bonnefon, J.-F., Brañas-Garza, P., Butera, L., Douglas, K. M., Everett, J. A. C., Gigerenzer, G., Greenhow, C., Hashimoto, D. A., Holt-Lunstad, J., Jetten, J., Johnson, S., Kunz, W. H., Longoni, C., & Viale, R. (2024). The impact of generative artificial intelligence on socioeconomic inequalities and policy making. *PNAS Nexus*, 3(6), pgae191. DOI: 10.1093/pnasnexus/pgae191 PMID: 38864006

Carayannis, E. G., Alexander, J., & Ioannidis, A. (2000). Leveraging knowledge, learning, and innovation in forming strategic government–university–industry (GUI) R&D partnerships in the US, Germany, and France. *Technovation*, 20(9), 477–488. DOI: 10.1016/S0166-4972(99)00162-5

Carli, R., Dotoli, M., Pellegrino, R., & Ranieri, L. (2013). Measuring and managing the smartness of cities: A framework for classifying performance indicators. *Proceedings - 2013 IEEE International Conference on Systems, Man, and Cybernetics, SMC 2013*, 1288–1293. DOI: 10.1109/SMC.2013.223

Carlsson B, Jacobsson S, Holmén M, Rickne (2022) A. Innovation systems: analytical and methodological issues. Res polic. 31(2):233–45.

Carter, L., & Bélanger, F. (2005). The utilization of e-government services: Citizen trust, innovation and acceptance factors. *Information Systems Journal*, 15(1), 5–25. DOI: 10.1111/j.1365-2575.2005.00183.x

Casino, F., Dasaklis, T. K., & Patsakis, C. (2019). A systematic literature review of blockchain-based applications: Current status, classification and open issues. *Telematics and Informatics*, 36, 55–81. DOI: 10.1016/j.tele.2018.11.006

Cattedu, D., & Hogben, G. (2009). Cloud Computing Benefits, Risk, and Recommendations for Information Security: the European network and information security agency (ENISA). Retrieved from www.resilience.enisa.europa.eu/cloud-security-and-resilience/publications/cloud-computing-benefits-risk-and-recommendations-for-information-security

Ceesay, L. B., Bojang, M. B. S., Malang, &, & Bojang, B. S. (2020). Global Journal of Management and Business Research: A Administration and Management Embracing E-Government during the Covid-19 Pandemic and Beyond: Insights from the Gambia Embracing E-Government during the Covid-19 Pandemic and Beyond: Insights from the Gambia.

Chamola, V., Goyal, A., Sharma, P., Hassija, V., Binh, H. T. T., & Saxena, V. (2023). Artificial intelligence-assisted blockchain-based framework for smart and secure EMR management. *Neural Computing & Applications*, 35(31), 22959–22969. DOI: 10.1007/s00521-022-07087-7 PMID: 35310553

Chang, V., Baudier, P., Zhang, H., Xu, Q., Zhang, J., & Arami, M. (2020). How Blockchain can impact financial services–The overview, challenges and recommendations from expert interviewees. *Technological Forecasting and Social Change*, 158, 120166. DOI: 10.1016/j.techfore.2020.120166 PMID: 32834134

Charles, V., Rana, N. P., & Carter, L. (2022). Artificial Intelligence for data-driven decision-making and governance in public affairs. *Government Information Quarterly*, 39(4), 101742. https://doi.org/https://doi.org/10.1016/j.giq.2022.101742. DOI: 10.1016/j.giq.2022.101742

Chavez-Dreyfuss, G. (2016). Sweden tests blockchain technology for land registry. *Reuters*, (June), 16.

Chen, H. (2004). Digital library research in the US: An overview with a knowledge management perspective. Program. *Electronic Library and Information Systems*, 38(3), 157–167. DOI: 10.1108/00330330410547205

Chen, J. S. (2001). A case study of Korean outbound travellers' destination images by using correspondence analysis. *Tourism Management*, 22(4), 345–350. DOI: 10.1016/S0261-5177(00)00066-2

Chen, J. S., & Gursoy, D. (2001). An investigation of tourists' destination loyalty and preferences. *International Journal of Contemporary Hospitality Management*, 13(2), 79–85. DOI: 10.1108/09596110110381870

Chen, J., Druhl, E., Ramesh, B. P., Houston, T. K., Brandt, C. A., Zulman, D. M., Vimalananda, V. G., Malkani, S., & Yu, H. (2018). A natural language processing system that links medical terms in electronic health record notes to lay definitions: System development using physician reviews. *Journal of Medical Internet Research*, 20(1), e26. Advance online publication. DOI: 10.2196/jmir.8669 PMID: 29358159

Chen, L., Chen, P., & Lin, Z. (2020). Artificial Intelligence in Education: A Review. *IEEE Access : Practical Innovations, Open Solutions*, 8, 75264–75278. DOI: 10.1109/ACCESS.2020.2988510

Chen, S., & Zhang, Y. (2021). Ethical considerations of artificial intelligence in public administration. *Journal of Public Administration: Research and Theory*, 31(4), 627–645. DOI: 10.1093/jopart/muab028

Chen, Y., & Bellavitis, C. (2020). Blockchain disruption and decentralized finance: The rise of decentralized business models. *Journal of Business Venturing Insights*, 13, e00151. DOI: 10.1016/j.jbvi.2019.e00151

Cheong, B. C. (2024). Transparency and accountability in AI systems: safeguarding wellbeing in the age of algorithmic decision-making. *Frontiers in Human Dynamics, 6*. https://www.frontiersin.org/journals/human-dynamics/articles/10.3389/fhumd.2024.1421273

Cheong, B. C. (2024). Transparency and accountability in AI systems: Safeguarding wellbeing in the age of algorithmic decision-making. *Frontiers in Human Dynamics*, 6, 1421273. DOI: 10.3389/fhumd.2024.1421273

Choudhari, N. V., & Sasankar, A. B. (2021, February). Architectural vision of cloud computing in the Indian government. In *2021 International Conference on Innovative Trends in Information Technology (ICITIIT)* (pp. 1-7). IEEE.

Choudhary, C., Vyas, N., & Lilhore, U. K. (2023, November). Cloud Security: Challenges and Strategies for Ensuring Data Protection. In *2023 3rd International Conference on Technological Advancements in Computational Sciences (ICTACS)* (pp. 669-673). IEEE.

Chowdhury, N. R., Janan, F., Mahmud, P., Liza, S. A., & Paul, S. K. (2023). Assessing Strategies to Mitigate the Impacts of a Pandemic in Apparel Supply Chains. Operations Management Research. https://doi.org/DOI: 10.1007/s12063-022-00345-w

Christian, R. O. (2008). Self-efficacy and use of electronic information as predictors of academic performance. Electronic Journal Of Academic and Special Librarianship, 8(2). Retrieved, from https://southernlibrarianship.icaap.org/content/v08n02/tella_a01.html

Chui, M., Hazan, E., Roberts, R., Singla, A., Smaje, K., Sukharevsky, A., Yee, L., & Zemmel, R. (2023, June 14). Economic potential of generative AI: The next productivity frontier [McKinsey & Company]. Retrieved from https://www.mckinsey.com/capabilities/mckinsey-digital/our-insights/the-economic-potential-of-generative-ai-the-next-productivity-frontier?cid=eml-web

Chung, S. H., Kim, J. H., & Kim, Y. (2018, October). Pragmatic approach using OAuth mechanism for IoT device authorization in cloud. In *2018 International Conference on Advances in Computing, Communication Control and Networking (ICACCCN)* (pp. 1-4). IEEE.

Ciancarini, P., Giancarlo, R., & Grimaudo, G. (2024). Digital transformation in the public administrations: A guided tour for computer scientists. *IEEE Access : Practical Innovations, Open Solutions*, 12(99), 1–1. DOI: 10.1109/ACCESS.2024.3363075

Clauson, K. A., Breeden, E. A., Davidson, C., & Mackey, T. K. (2018). Leveraging Blockchain Technology to Enhance Supply Chain Management in Healthcare. *Blockchain in Healthcare Today*. Advance online publication. DOI: 10.30953/bhty.v1.20

Cohen, E., & Cohen, S. A. (2012). Authentication: Hot and cool. *Annals of Tourism Research*, 39(3), 1295–1314. DOI: 10.1016/j.annals.2012.03.004

Cornforth, C. (Ed.). (2002). *The Governance of Public and Non-Profit Organizations* (0 ed.). Routledge., DOI: 10.4324/9780203167571

Corsatea, T. D. (2014). Increasing synergies between institutions and technology developers: Lessons from marine energy. *Energy Policy*, 74, 682–696. DOI: 10.1016/j.enpol.2014.07.006

Creswell, J. W. (2010). *Projeto de pesquisa: métodos qualitativo, quantitativo e misto*. (3rd ed.; Artmed, ed.). Porto Alegre: Artmed.

Crosby, M., Pattanayak, P., Verma, S., & Kalyanaraman, V. (2016). Blockchain technology: Beyond bitcoin. *Applied innovation, 2*(6-10), 71.

Dadios, E. P., Culaba, A. B., Albert, J. R. G., Paqueo, V. B., Orbeta, A. C., Serafica, R. B., Bandala, A. A., & Bairan, J. C. A. C. (2018). Preparing the Philippines for the fourth industrial revolution: A scoping study. In *PIDS Discussion Paper Series, No. 2018-11.*

Dahunsi, F. M., & Owoseni, T. M. (2015). *Cloud Computing in Nigeria: The Cloud Ecosystem Perspective*. Nigeria Journal of Technology., DOI: 10.4314/njt.341.911

Dakalbab, F., Abu Talib, M., Abu Waraga, O., Bou Nassif, A., Abbas, S., & Nasir, Q. (2022). Artificial intelligence & crime prediction: A systematic literature review. *Social Sciences & Humanities Open*, 6(1), 100342. https://doi.org/https://doi.org/10.1016/j.ssaho.2022.100342. DOI: 10.1016/j.ssaho.2022.100342

Dalkir, K. (2011). Knowledge Management in Theory and Practice Second Edition. *In Knowledge Management in Theory and Practice.*

Danilina, N., & Majorzadehzahiri, A. (2020). Social factors of sustainability for a smart city development. *IOP Conference Series. Materials Science and Engineering*, 869(2), 022027. Advance online publication. DOI: 10.1088/1757-899X/869/2/022027

Davenport, T. H., & Ronanki, R. (2019). Artificial intelligence for the real world: Don't start with AI. *Harvard Business Review*, 97(1), 108–116. DOI: 10.1111/j.1468-0327.2011.00239.x

Davenport, T., & Kalakota, R. (2019). The potential for artificial intelligence in healthcare. *Future Healthcare Journal*, 6(2), 94–98. DOI: 10.7861/futurehosp.6-2-94 PMID: 31363513

David, O. A., Cyril Onyepuemu, N. O., & Qazeem, I. B. (2022). *E-Governance Response in Tackling Covid-19 in Nigeria*. Perspektif., DOI: 10.31289/perspektif.v11i3.7249

Davis, F. D. (1989). Perceived usefulness, perceived ease of use, and user acceptance of information technology. *Management Information Systems Quarterly*, 13(3), 319–340. DOI: 10.2307/249008

Davis, F. D., Bagozzi, R. P., & Warshaw, P. R. (1992). Extrinsic and intrinsic motivation to use computers in the workplace 1. *Journal of Applied Social Psychology*, 22(14), 1111–1132. DOI: 10.1111/j.1559-1816.1992.tb00945.x

De Filippi, P. (2018). *Blockchain and the Law: The Rule of Code*. Harvard University Press.

De La Torre-Díez, I., Díaz-Pernas, F. J., Fernández, G., Antón-Rodríguez, M., Martínez-Zarzuela, M., González-Ortega, D., & Boto-Giralda, D. (2012). Analysis of the benefits and constraints for the implementation of Cloud Computing over an EHRs system. *Proceedings of the 6th Euro American Conference on Telematics and Information Systems, EATIS 2012*. DOI: 10.1145/2261605.2261628

de Leon, A. P., & Miranda, J. P. P. (2022). A Spatiotemporal Analysis of Fire Incidents in Pampanga Province of Philippines: Inputs for Fire Prevention Programs. *International Transaction Journal of Engineering, Management, and Applied Sciences and Technologies, 13*(10), 1–17. https://doi.org/http://doi.org/10.14456/ITJEMAST.2022.193

de Marcellis-Warin, N., & Warin, T. (2020). Government 4.0 and evidencebased policies: AI and data analytics to the rescue. In *Handb. Of Artificial Intelligence and Robotic Process Automation: Policy and Gov. Applic.* (pp. 31–39). Anthem Press; Scopus. https://www.scopus.com/inward/record.uri?eid=2-s2.0-85110815942&partnerID=40&md5=fccfa75b2db834014490044524b97dcb

de Menezes Junior, E. E., Dutra e Silva, S., Oliveira, M. R., & Silva, C. H. C. (2024). Meio Ambiente, Políticas de Inovação e Tecnologia: Relações e Correlações nos Últimos Dez Anos no Brasil. Fronteira: *Journal of Social, Technological and Environmental Science*, 13(1), 213–226. Recuperado de https://periodicos.unievangelica.edu.br/index.php/fronteiras/article/view/7175

Deininger, K., & Feder, G. (2009). Land registration, governance, and development: Evidence and implications for policy. *The World Bank Research Observer*, 24(2), 233–266. DOI: 10.1093/wbro/lkp007

Deininger, K., Selod, H., & Burns, A. (2012). *The Land Governance Assessment Framework: Identifying and monitoring good practice in the land sector*. World Bank Publications.

Deloitte. (2022). *State of AI in the Enterprise, 5th Edition*. Retrieved from https://www2.deloitte.com/us/en/insights/focus/cognitive-technologies/state-of-ai-and-intelligent-automation-in-business-survey.html

Demaidi, M. N. (2023). Artificial intelligence national strategy in a developing country. *AI & Society*. Advance online publication. DOI: 10.1007/s00146-023-01779-x

Demirag, I., Fırtın, C. E., & Bilbil, E. T. (2020). Managing Expectations With Emotional Accountability: Making City Hospitals Accountable During the COVID-19 Pandemic in Turkey. Journal of Public Budgeting Accounting \&. *Journal of Public Budgeting, Accounting & Financial Management*, 32(5), 889–901. Advance online publication. DOI: 10.1108/JPBAFM-07-2020-0097

Demirel, D., & Mülazımoğlu, M. E. (2022). How the smart governance model shapes cities? Cases from Europe. *Journal of Enterprising Communities*, 16(1), 8–25. DOI: 10.1108/JEC-08-2021-0115

Department of Education. (2019). *PISA 2018: National report of the Philippines*. https://www.deped.gov.ph/wp-content/uploads/2019/12/PISA-2018-Philippine-National-Report.pdf

Desouza, K. C., Dawson, G. S., & Chenok, D. (2020). Designing, developing, and deploying artificial intelligence systems: Lessons from and for the public sector. *Business Horizons*, 63(2), 205–213. DOI: 10.1016/j.bushor.2019.11.004

Desouza, K. C., & Jacob, B. (2017). Big data in the public sector: Lessons for practitioners and scholars. *Administration & Society*, 49(7), 1043–1064. DOI: 10.1177/0095399714555751

Devadass, L., Sekaran, S. S., & Thinakaran, R. (2017a). CLOUD COMPUTING IN HEALTHCARE. *International Journal of Students'. Research Technology Management*, 5(1), 25–31. DOI: 10.18510/ijsrtm.2017.516

Devlieghere, J., Gillingham, P., & Roose, R. (2022). Dataism versus relationshipism: A social work perspective. *Nordic Social Work Research*, 12(3), 328–338. DOI: 10.1080/2156857X.2022.2052942

Dhinakar, N. M., Rao, K. K., Jayanath, N., Prasad, R. D. V., Jadala, V. C., & Chintala, R. R. (2023, March). Defending against Cache-based Side-Channel Attack using Virtual Machine Migration in Cloud. In *2023 International Conference on Sustainable Computing and Data Communication Systems (ICSCDS)* (pp. 239-242). IEEE.

Dhirani, L. L., Mukhtiar, N., Chowdhry, B. S., & Newe, T. (2023). Ethical Dilemmas and Privacy Issues in Emerging Technologies: A Review. In *Sensors* (Vol. 23, Issue 3). DOI: 10.3390/s23031151

Dillon, T., & Wu, C., & Chang, E. (2010). Cloud Computing: Issues and Challenges. 24th IEEE International Conference on Advanced Information Networking and Applications, IEEE Computer Society. 27-33. DOI: 10.1109/AINA.2010.187

Dinev Tamara & Hu Qing, (2005). The Centrality of Awareness in the Formation of User Behavioral Intention toward Protective Information Technologies

Dresp-Langley, B. (2023). The weaponization of artificial intelligence: What the public needs to be aware of. *Frontiers in Artificial Intelligence*, 6, 1154184. DOI: 10.3389/frai.2023.1154184 PMID: 36967833

Duberry, J. (2022). *AI and information dissemination: Challenging citizens access to relevant and reliable information*. Edward Elgar Publishing., DOI: 10.4337/9781788977319.00008

Dubois, E. (2021). African Women, ICT and Neoliberal Politics, by Assata Zerai: A Review by Elisabeth Dubois. *Information Polity*, 26(2), 211–213. Advance online publication. DOI: 10.3233/IP-219003

Dumitriu, D., & Popescu, M. A. M. (2020). Enterprise architecture framework design in IT management. *Procedia Manufacturing*, 46, 932–940. DOI: 10.1016/j.promfg.2020.05.011

Durman, O. (2024). Good governance–basis for building an effective public administration system.theoretical and empirical research in urban management, 37-43,. Retrieved from https://doi.org/DOI: 10.32836/2310-9653-

Dwivedi, Y. K., Hughes, L., Ismagilova, E., Aarts, G., Coombs, C., Crick, T., Duan, Y., Dwivedi, R., Edwards, J., Eirug, A., Galanos, V., Ilavarasan, P. V., Janssen, M., Jones, P., Kar, A. K., Kizgin, H., Kronemann, B., Lal, B., Lucini, B., & Williams, M. D. (2021). Artificial Intelligence (AI): Multidisciplinary perspectives on emerging challenges, opportunities, and agenda for research, practice and policy. *International Journal of Information Management*, 57, 101994. DOI: 10.1016/j.ijinfomgt.2019.08.002

Edmunds, M., Peddicord, D., & Frisse, M. E. (2016). Ten reasons why interoperability is difficult. *Healthcare information management systems: Cases, strategies, and solutions*, 127-137.

Egger, I., Lei, S. I., & Wassler, P. (2020). Digital free tourism – an exploratory study of tourist motivations. *Tourism Management*, 79(1), 1–10. DOI: 10.1016/j.tourman.2020.104098

Ejjami, R. (2024). Public Administration 5.0: Enhancing Governance and Public Services with Smart Technologies. *International Journal For Multidisciplinary Research, 6*(4), 1–35. https://doi.org/https://doi.org/10.36948/ijfmr.2024.v06i04.26086

Elisa, N., Yang,, L., Li,, H., Chao,, F., & Naik, N. (2020). Consortium blockchain for security and privacy-preserving in E-government Systems. *arXiv preprint*, 451-479.

Elisa, N., Yang,, L., Li,, H., Chao,, F., & Naik, N. (2020). Consortium blockchain for security and privacy-preserving in E-government Systems. arXiv preprint, 451-479.

Elisa, N., Yangl, L., & Chao, F., & Cao, Y. A. (2023). A framework of blockchain-based secure and. wireless. *Network (Bristol, England)*, •••, 1005–1015.

Engstrom, D. F., Ho, D. E., Sharkey, C. M., & Cuéllar, M.-F. (2020). *Government by Algorithm: Artificial Intelligence in Federal Administrative Agencies*. https://law.stanford.edu/wp-content/uploads/2020/02/ACUS-AI-Report.pdf

Erhabor, E. D. (2012). Using Cloud Services for Library IT Infrastructure. Journal Code for Library. Retrieved from https://journal.code4lib.org/articles/2510

Eric, M. (2012). Winds of change: Libraries and cloud computing. *Multimedia Information and Technology*, 37, 24–28.

ESCWA. (2014). *E-Government: Policies, Strategies and Applications*. Academy of Information and Communication Technologies for Development for Government Sector Leaders in the Arab Countries.

European Commission. (2020). *Blockchain Strategy*. Retrieved from https://ec.europa.eu/digital-strategy/our-policies/blockchain-strategy_en

European Parliament and the Council of the European Union. (2016). Regulation (EU) 2016/679 of the European Parliament and of the Council of 27 April 2016 on the protection of natural persons with regard to the processing of personal data and on the free movement of such data, and repealing Directive 95/46/EC (General Data Protection Regulation). *Official Journal of the European Union, L*, 119, 1–88. https://eur-lex.europa.eu/legal-content/EN/TXT/PDF/?uri=CELEX:32016R0679&from=EN

European Parliament. (2024, June 18). EU's AI Act: First regulation on artificial intelligence. https://www.europarl.europa.eu/topics/en/article/20230601STO93804/eu-ai-act-first-regulation-on-artificial-intelligence

European Parliament. Directorate General for Parliamentary Research Services. (2020). *The impact of the general data protection regulation on artificial intelligence*. Publications Office. https://data.europa.eu/doi/10.2861/293

Ezeani, I., & amp; Igwesi, O. (2012). Using social media applications for educational outcome college teaching: Strucctural equation analysis. *British Journal of Educational Technology*, 44, 87–100.

Fabito, B. S., Balahadia, F. F., & Cabatlao, J. D. N. (2016). AppLERT: A mobile application for incident and disaster notification for Metro Manila. *2016 IEEE Region 10 Symposium (TENSYMP)*, 288–292. DOI: 10.1109/TENCONSpring.2016.7519420

Fabrègue B, Portal LJ, Cockshaw C.(2023) Using smart people to build smarter: How smart cities attract and retain highly skilled workers to drive innovation (Belgium, Denmark, the Netherlands, Poland). Smart Cities Reg Dev (SCRD) J. 7(1):9–30.

Fakhoury, R., & Baker, S. D. (2016). Governmental trust, active citizenship, and E-government acceptance in Lebanon. *Journal of Leadership, Accountability and Ethics*, •••, 36–52.

Farhad, A., & Pyun, J. Y. (2023). AI-ERA: Artificial intelligence-empowered resource allocation for LoRa-enabled IoT applications. *IEEE Transactions on Industrial Informatics*, 19(12), 11640–11652. DOI: 10.1109/TII.2023.3248074

Faris, M. (2023). Use of AI in Communication and Dissemination Statistics. *UNECE Expert Meeting on Dissemination and Communication of Statistics 2023*. https://unece.org/sites/default/files/2023-10/DissComm2023_S3_Indonesia_Faris_Paper.pdf

Farooqi, A., Khalid, U., & Khan, A. M. (2022). Understanding the Digital Divide in the. Contemporary Digital World. *Global Political Review*, VII(IV), 7–14. DOI: 10.31703/gpr.2022(VII-IV).02

Fayemi, Y. (2013). IaaScloud Computing Service for Libraries: Cloud storage and virtual machines. In IaaScloud Computing Service for Libraries: Cloud storage and virtual machines (Vol. 29, 87-100). Bingley, West, Yorkshire, England: Emerald Group Publishing Limited.

Fayissa, B., Nsiah, C., & Tadasse, B. (2008). Impact of tourism on economic growth and development in Africa. *Tourism Economics*, 14(4), 807–818. DOI: 10.5367/000000008786440229

Fazakarley, C. A., Breen, M., Leeson, P., Thompson, B., & Williamson, V. (2023). Experiences of using artificial intelligence in healthcare: A qualitative study of UK clinician and key stakeholder perspectives. *BMJ Open*, 13(12), e076950. DOI: 10.1136/bmjopen-2023-076950 PMID: 38081671

Feroz, A. S., Khoja, A., & Saleem, S. (2021). Equipping Community Health Workers With Digital Tools for Pandemic Response in LMICs. *Archives of Public Health*, 79(1), 1. Advance online publication. DOI: 10.1186/s13690-020-00513-z PMID: 33390163

Fesenmaier, D. R. (1988). Integrating activity pattern into destination choice models. *Journal of Leisure Research*, 20(3), 175–191. DOI: 10.1080/00222216.1988.11969771

Ficara, A., Curreri, F., Fiumara, G., & De Meo, P. (2023). Human and Social Capital Strategies for Mafia Network Disruption. *IEEE Transactions on Information Forensics and Security, 18*, 1926–1936. *IEEE Transactions on Information Forensics and Security*. Advance online publication. DOI: 10.1109/TIFS.2023.3256706

Finlay, S. (2016). User profile for personalized information. Retrieved from Nova Education: http://www.nova.edu/ssss/QR/QR8-4/golafshani.pdf

Fırat, M. (2023). Integrating AI Applications into Learning Management Systems to Enhance e-Learning. *Instructional Technology and Lifelong Learning*, 4(1), 1–14. DOI: 10.52911/itall.1244453

Flood, J., Shingleton, J., Bennett, E., Walker, B., Amin-Chowdhury, Z., Oligbu, G., Avis, J., Lynn, R. M., Davis, P., Bharucha, T., Pain, C. E., Jyothish, D., Whittaker, E., Dwarakanathan, B., Wood, R., Williams, C., Swann, O., Semple, M. G., Ramsay, M. E., & Ladhani, S. N. (2021). Paediatric multisystem inflammatory syndrome temporally associated with SARS-CoV-2 (PIMS-TS): Prospective, national surveillance, United Kingdom and Ireland, 2020. *The Lancet Regional Health. Europe*, 3, 100075. Advance online publication. DOI: 10.1016/j.lanepe.2021.100075 PMID: 34027512

Floridi, L., Cowls, J., Beltrametti, M., Chatila, R., Chazerand, P., Dignum, V., Luetge, C., Madelin, R., Pagallo, U., Rossi, F., Schafer, B., Valcke, P., & Vayena, E. (2018). AI4People—An Ethical Framework for a Good AI Society: Opportunities, Risks, Principles, and Recommendations. *Minds and Machines*, 28(4), 689–707. DOI: 10.1007/s11023-018-9482-5 PMID: 30930541

Foong, Y. P., Pidani, R., Sithira Vadivel, V., & Dongyue, Y. (2024). Singapore Smart Nation: Journey into a New Digital Landscape for Higher Education. In Kwok, A. O. J., & Teh, P.-L. (Eds.), *Emerging Technologies in Business* (pp. 281–304). Springer Nature Singapore., DOI: 10.1007/978-981-97-2211-2_13

Fragidis, L. L., & Chatzoglou, P. D. (2018). Implementation of a nationwide electronic health record (EHR): The international experience in 13 countries. *International Journal of Health Care Quality Assurance*, 31(2), 116–130. DOI: 10.1108/IJHCQA-09-2016-0136 PMID: 29504871

Fran. (2021). *The Top Skills in the Philippines for Employability*. Future Learn. https://www.futurelearn.com/info/futurelearn-international/top-skills-in-the-philippines

Fredriksson, C., Mubarak, F., Tuohimaa, M., & Zhan, M. (2017). Big Data in the Public Sector: A Systematic Literature Review. *Scandinavian Journal of Public Administration*, 21(3), 3. DOI: 10.58235/sjpa.v21i3.11563

Fu, X., & Fu, X. (Maggie), Ghauri, P., & Hou, J. (2022). International collaboration and innovation: Evidence from a leading Chinese multinational enterprise. *Journal of World Business, 57*(4), 101329. https://doi.org/https://doi.org/10.1016/j.jwb.2022.101329

Gabriel, A. G., Alcantara, G. M., & Alvarez, J. D. G. (2020). How Do Millennial Managers Lead Older Employees? The Philippine Workplace Experience. *SAGE Open*, 10(1), 2158244020914651. DOI: 10.1177/2158244020914651

Galushi, L. T., & Malatji, T. L. (2022). Digital Public Administration and Inclusive Governance at the South African Local Government. In *Depth Analysis of E-Government and Service Delivery in Musina Local Municipality*. Academic Journal of Interdisciplinary Studies., DOI: 10.36941/ajis-2022-0154

Gamage, H. T. M., Weerasinghe, H. D., & Dias, N. G. J. (2020). A survey on blockchain technology concepts, applications, and issues. *SN Computer Science*, 1(2), 1–15. DOI: 10.1007/s42979-020-00123-0

Gao, Y., Janssen, M., & Zhang, C. (2021). Understanding the evolution of open government data research: Towards open data sustainability and smartness. *International Review of Administrative Sciences*, 89(1), 59–75. Advance online publication. DOI: 10.1177/00208523211009955

García-González, M. S., Paniagua-Arís, E., Martínez-Béjar, R., López-Caballero, J. A., & Gasparetto, A. (2023). An artificial intelligence-based model for knowledge evaluation and integration in public organizations. *Applied Sciences (Basel, Switzerland)*, 13(21), 11796. DOI: 10.3390/app132111796

Garg, S., & Sharma, S. (2020). Impact of Artificial Intelligence in Special Need Education to Promote Inclusive Pedagogy. *International Journal of Information and Education Technology (IJIET)*, 10(7), 523–527. Advance online publication. DOI: 10.18178/ijiet.2020.10.7.1418

Garg, V., Jain, N., & Kumar, V. (2023). Cloud computing in the public sector: Case studies and future prospects. *Public Administration Review*, 83(1), 15–28. DOI: 10.1111/puar.13547

Gartner. (2024, April 16). Gartner Announces the Top Government Technology Trends for 2024. [Press release]. https://www.gartner.com/en/newsroom/press-releases/2024-04-16-gartner-announces-the-top-government-technology-trends-for-2024

Gaskins, N. (2023). Interrogating Algorithmic Bias: From Speculative Fiction to Liberatory Design. *TechTrends*, 67(3), 417–425. DOI: 10.1007/s11528-022-00783-0 PMID: 36160677

Gasser, U., Ienca, M., Scheibner, J., Sleigh, J., & Vayena, E. (2020). Digital tools against COVID-19: Taxonomy, ethical challenges, and navigation aid. *The Lancet. Digital Health*, 2(8), e425–e434. DOI: 10.1016/S2589-7500(20)30137-0 PMID: 32835200

Ga-Yeong Choi. JeongEun Seo, and Hun-Yeong Kwon. (2024). "A Comparative Study of National Cloud Security Strategy and Governance." In Proceedings of the 25th Annual International Conference on Digital Government Research (dg.o '24). Association for Computing Machinery, New York, NY, USA, 241–250. https://doi.org/DOI: 10.1145/3657054.3657085

Gbaje, S., & Aliyu, E. (2014). Application of Digital Libraries and Electronic Technologies in Uganda. *African Journal of Library Archives and Information Science*, 12, 145–154. Retrieved 2014, from

Gelera, A. M., & Dajao, E. S. (2022). Crime Mapping Approach for Crime Pattern Identification: A Prototype for the Province of Cavite. *Proceedings of Sixth International Congress on Information and Communication Technology. Lecture Notes in Networks and Systems*. https://doi.org/https://doi.org/10.1007/978-981-16-2380-6_79

Gila Cohen Zilka (2017) Awareness of eSafety and Potential Online Dangers among Children and Teenagers Journal of Information Technology Education: Research pp. 319-338. https://doi.org/DOI: 10.28945/3864

Goldner, M. (2012). Wind of changes: Libraries and cloud computing. Retrieved from OCLC: htt://www.oclc.org/multimedia/2011files/-paper.pdf

Golinelli, D., Boetto, E., Carullo, G., Nuzzolese, A. G., Landini, M. P., & Fantini, M. P. (2020). Adoption of Digital Technologies in Health Care During the COVID-19 Pandemic: Systematic Review of Early Scientific Literature. J Med Internet Res 2020;22(11):E22280 Https://Www.Jmir.Org/2020/11/E22280, 22(11), e22280. https://doi.org/DOI: 10.2196/22280

Gong, Y., & Janssen, M. (2019). The value of and myths about enterprise architecture. *International Journal of Information Management*, 46, 1–9. DOI: 10.1016/j.ijinfomgt.2018.11.006

Gonzalez, R. V. D., & Martins, M. F. (2017). Knowledge management process: A theoretical-conceptual research. *Gestão & Produção*, 24(2), 248–265. DOI: 10.1590/0104-530x0893-15

González-Sendino, R., Serrano, E., Bajo, J., & Novais, P. (2023). A Review of Bias and Fairness in Artificial Intelligence. *International Journal of Interactive Multimedia and Artificial Intelligence, In press*(In press), 1. DOI: 10.9781/ijimai.2023.11.001

Goode, K., Kim, H. M., & Deng, M. (2023). *Examining Singapore's AI Progress*. Center for Security and Emerging Technology., DOI: 10.51593/2021CA014

Gössling, S., Peeters, P., Hall, C. M., Ceron, J. P., Dubois, G., Lehmann, L. V., & Scott, D. (2012). Tourism and water use: Supply, demand, and security. An international review. *Tourism Management*, 33(1), 1–15. DOI: 10.1016/j.tourman.2011.03.015

Goyal, S., Pillai, A., & Chauhan, S. (2021). E-Governance Using Mobile Applications: A Case Study of India During the COVID-19 Pandemic. *AJIS. Australasian Journal of Information Systems*, 25. Advance online publication. DOI: 10.3127/ajis.v25i0.3129

Gozgor, G., Lau, C. K., Lin, Z., & Zeng, Y. (2024). The impact of digital governance on tourism development. *Journal of Digital Economy*, 3(1), 1–13. DOI: 10.1016/j.jdec.2024.05.003

Greely, H. T. (2022). Governing emerging technologies—Looking forward with horizon scanning and looking back with technology audits. *Global Public Policy and Governance*, 2(3), 266–282. DOI: 10.1007/s43508-022-00045-y

Gretzel, U., Fuchs, M., Baggio, R., Hoepken, W., Law, R., Neidhardt, J., & Xiang, Z. (2020). E-Tourism beyond COVID-19: A call for transformative research. *Information Technology & Tourism*, 22(2), 187–203. DOI: 10.1007/s40558-020-00181-3

Gretzel, U., Sigala, M., Xiang, Z., & Koo, C. (2015). Smart tourism: Foundations and developments. *Electronic Markets*, 25(3), 179–188. DOI: 10.1007/s12525-015-0196-8

Griggs, K. N., Ossipova, O., Kohlios, C. P., Baccarini, A. N., Howson, E. A., & Hayajneh, T. (2018). Healthcare Blockchain System Using Smart Contracts for Secure Automated Remote Patient Monitoring. *Journal of Medical Systems*, 42(7), 130. Advance online publication. DOI: 10.1007/s10916-018-0982-x PMID: 29876661

Growiec, J. (2024). EXISTENTIAL RISK FROM TRANSFORMATIVE AI: AN ECONOMIC PERSPECTIVE. *Technological and Economic Development of Economy*, 0(0), 1–27. DOI: 10.3846/tede.2024.21525

Guan, H. (2023). *Why Can China Still Promote the SDGs During the COVID-19 Pandemic*. Lecture Notes in Education Psychology and Public Media., DOI: 10.54254/2753-7048/15/20231069

Guo, Y., Kuo, M. H., & Sahama, T. (2012). Cloud computing for healthcare research information sharing. *CloudCom 2012 - Proceedings: 2012 4th IEEE International Conference on Cloud Computing Technology and Science*, 889–894. DOI: 10.1109/CloudCom.2012.6427561

Guo, B., Feng, Y., & Lin, J. (2023). Digital inclusive finance and digital transformation of enterprises. *Finance Research Letters*, 57, 104270. DOI: 10.1016/j.frl.2023.104270

Gupta, N., Das, M. L., & Nandi, S. (2019, December). Landledger: Blockchain-powered land property administration system. In *2019 IEEE International conference on advanced networks and telecommunications systems (ANTS)* (pp. 1-6). IEEE.

Gura, K., AlAkoum, A., Melenciuc, M., & Henley, S. (2023). Mobile Biometric and Sentiment Data, Generative Artificial Intelligence and Behavior Tracking Tools, and Wearable Sensor-based and Connected Monitoring Devices in Immersive Interconnected 3D Worlds. *Analysis and Metaphysics*, 22(0), 255–273. DOI: 10.22381/am22202314

Gursoy, D., Malodia, S., & Dhir, A. (2022). The metaverse in the hospitality and tourism industry: An overview of current trends and future research directions. *Journal of Hospitality Marketing & Management*, 31(5), 527–534. DOI: 10.1080/19368623.2022.2072504

Habib, G., Sharma, S., Ibrahim, S., Ahmad, I., Qureshi, S., & Ishfaq, M. (2022). Blockchain technology: Benefits, challenges, applications, and integration of blockchain technology with cloud computing. *Future Internet*, 14(11), 341. DOI: 10.3390/fi14110341

Haddad, A., Habaebi, M. H., Suliman, F. E. M., Elsheikh, E. A., Islam, M. R., & Zabidi, S. A. (2023). Generic patient-centered blockchain-based EHR management system. *Applied Sciences (Basel, Switzerland)*, 13(3), 1761.

Haitami, M., & Rengganis, A. (2021). The Dilemma of Good Governance Implementation in Indonesia during the Pandemic of Corona Virus Disease (COVID-19). *JASSP*, 1(1), 55–67. DOI: 10.23960/jassp.v1i1.25

Hakimi, M., Hamidi, M. S., Miskinyar, M. S., & Sazish, B. (2023). Integrating Artificial Intelligence into E-Government: Navigating Challenges, Opportunities, and Policy Implications. *International Journal of Academic and Practical Research*, 2(2), 1–1.

Haleem, A., Javaid, M., Singh, R. P., Suman, R., & Rab, S. (2021). Blockchain technology applications in healthcare: An overview. *International Journal of Intelligent Networks*, 2, 130–139. DOI: 10.1016/j.ijin.2021.09.005

Hamid, R. A., Albahri, A. S., Alwan, J. K., Al-quaysi, Z. T., Albahri, O. S., Zaidan, A. A., Alnoor, A., Almoodi, A. H., & Zaidan, B. B. (2021). How smart is e-tourism? A systematic review of smart tourism recommendation system applying data management. *Computer Science Review*, 39(1), 1–13. DOI: 10.1016/j.cosrev.2020.100337

Haque, E. (2022). *Enterprise Service Management (ESM): The art of ESM in the era of AI, Blockchain and metaverse*. Lulu.com.

Harry, A., & Sayudin, S. (2023). Role of AI in Education. *Injuruty:Interdiciplinary-JournalandHumanity*, 2(3), 260–268. DOI: 10.58631/injurity.v2i3.52

Hartanto, D., Agussani, A., & Dalle, J. (2021). Hasan Aydin Antecedents of Public Trust in Government During the COVID-19 Pandemic in Indonesia. *Journal of Ethnic and Cultural Studies*, 8(4), 321–341. DOI: 10.29333/ejecs/975

Hartley, J. (2010). Innovation in governance and public services: Past and present. *Public Money & Management*, 25(1), 27–34.

Hassan, O., Fatai, F., Aderibigbe, O., Akinde, A., Onasanya, T., Sanusi, M., & Odukoya, O. (2024). Enhancing Cybersecurity through Cloud Computing Solutions in the United States. *Intelligent Information Management*, 16(4), 176–193. DOI: 10.4236/iim.2024.164011

Henman, P. (2020). Improving public services using artificial intelligence: Possibilities, pitfalls, governance. *Asia Pacific Journal of Public Administration*, 42(4), 209–221. DOI: 10.1080/23276665.2020.1816188

Higgins, B. W. (2022). Legal Elements of an AI Regulatory Permit Program. In *The Oxford Handbook of AI Governance*.

Higham, J., Cohen, S. A., Peeters, P., & Gössling, S. (2013). Psychological and behavioural approaches to understanding and governing sustainable mobility. *Journal of Sustainable Tourism*, 21(7), 949–967. DOI: 10.1080/09669582.2013.828733

Hoffman, D. L. (2000). The revolution will not be televised: Introduction to the special issue on marketing science and the Internet. *Marketing Science*, 19(1), 1–3. https://www.jstor.org/stable/193255. DOI: 10.1287/mksc.19.1.1.15181

Hölbl, M., Kompara, M., Kamišalić, A., & Zlatolas, L. N. (2018). A systematic review of the use of blockchain in healthcare. *Symmetry*, 10(10), 470. Advance online publication. DOI: 10.3390/sym10100470

Honey, M., & Gilpin, R. (2009). *Tourism in the developing world: Promoting peace and reducing poverty*. United States Institute of Peace., https://www.usip.org/sites/default/files/tourism_developing_world_sr233_0.pdf

Ho, S. H., Lim, J. T., Ong, J., Hapuarachchi, H. C., Sim, S., & Ng, L. C. (2023). Singapore's 5 decades of dengue prevention and control—Implications for global dengue control. *PLoS Neglected Tropical Diseases*, 17(6), e0011400. DOI: 10.1371/journal.pntd.0011400 PMID: 37347767

Howell, S. T., Kuchler, T., Snitkof, D., Stroebel, J., & Wong, J. (2024). Lender automation and racial disparities in credit access. *The Journal of Finance*, 79(2), 1457–1512. DOI: 10.1111/jofi.13303

Hoxha, V., & Sadiku, S. (2019). Study of factors influencing the decision to adopt the blockchain technology in real estate transactions in Kosovo. *Property Management*, 37(5), 684–700. DOI: 10.1108/PM-01-2019-0002

Huang, G., Al Foysal, A., Huang, G., & Al Foysal, A. (2021). Blockchain in Healthcare. *Technology and Investment*, 12(3), 168–181. DOI: 10.4236/ti.2021.123010

Huang, L., & Zhou, T. (2024). How does blockchain technology enhance firm operation and cooperation? *International Review of Economics & Finance*, 92, 34–49. DOI: 10.1016/j.iref.2024.01.049

Huang, X., Wu, J., & Zhao, Y. (2021). Blockchain technology for securing public records: Applications and challenges. *Government Information Quarterly*, 38(2), 101–112. DOI: 10.1016/j.giq.2020.101513

Hu, L., Yao, S., Zhou, Z., & Miao, N. (2021). The Importance of the construction of digital economy major under the background of new liberal arts. *World Scientific Research Journal*, 7(8), 104–111. DOI: 10.6911/WSRJ.202108_7(8).0020

Hung, Y. S., Chang, M. C., & amp; Kuo, R. S. (2013). User acceptance of mobile e-government services: an empirical Study. Turkey: Government Information Quarterly. doi:. giq2012.07.008DOI: 10.1016/j

Hung, T. W., & Yen, C. P. (2023). Predictive policing and algorithmic fairness. *Synthese*, 201(6), 206. DOI: 10.1007/s11229-023-04189-0

Hwang, S., Nam, T., & Ha, H. (2021). From evidence-based policy making to data-driven administration: Proposing the data vs. value framework. *International Review of Public Administration*, 26(3), 291–307. DOI: 10.1080/12294659.2021.1974176

Hye, Q. M. A., & Khan, R. E. A. (2013). Tourism-led growth hypothesis: A case study of Pakistan. *Asia Pacific Journal of Tourism Research*, 18(4), 303–313. DOI: 10.1080/10941665.2012.658412

Ibad, S., & Lolita, Y. W. (2020). Development and Urgency of Public Services Through E-Government in the Middle of Pandemi Covid-19. Journal of Public Administration and Governance. https://doi.org/DOI: 10.5296/jpag.v10i4.17867

Igiekhume, Donatus (2022) Why Edo State is Taking the Lead in E-government.

Inayatulloh & Maryani. (2021) Integrated E-Government Model with Cloud Computing Technology. Proceedings of the International Conference on Industrial Engineering and Operations Management Rome, Italy, August 2-5, 2021 © IEOM Society International 1661

Iorio, C., Pandolfo, G., D'Ambrosio, A., & Siciliano, R. (2020). Mining big data in tourism. *Quality & Quantity*, 54(1), 1655–1669. https://link.springer.com/article/10.1007/s11135-019-00927-0. DOI: 10.1007/s11135-019-00927-0

IPCC (2018). Global Warming of 1.5°C.An IPCC Special Report on the impacts of global warming of 1.5°C above pre-industrial levels and related global greenhouse gas emission pathways, in the context of strengthening the global response to the threat of climate change, sustainable development, and efforts to eradicate poverty [Masson-Delmotte, V., P. Zhai, H.-O. Pörtner, D. Roberts, J. Skea, P.R. Shukla, A. Pirani, W. Moufouma-Okia, C. Péan, R. Pidcock, S. Connors, J.B.R. Matthews, Y. Chen, X. Zhou, M.I. Gomis, E. Lonnoy, T. Maycock, M. Tignor, and T. Waterfield (eds.)].

ISO. (2018). *ISO 30401:2018*, Knowledge Management Systems, Requirements. Em 61010-1 © Iec:2001.

Jabali, A. K., Waris, A., Khan, D. I., Ahmed, S., & Hourani, R. J. (2022a). Electronic health records: Three decades of bibliometric research productivity analysis and some insights. *Informatics in Medicine Unlocked*, 29, 100872. DOI: 10.1016/j.imu.2022.100872

Janssen, M., Brous, P., Estevez, E., Barbosa, L. S., & Janowski, T. (2020). Data governance: Organizing data for trustworthy Artificial Intelligence. *Government Information Quarterly*, 37(3), 101493. DOI: 10.1016/j.giq.2020.101493

Jarrahi, M. H. (2018). Artificial intelligence and the future of work: Human-AI symbiosis in organizational decision making. *Business Horizons*, 61(4), 577–586. DOI: 10.1016/j.bushor.2018.03.007

Jaspin, K., Selvan, S., Sahana, S., & Thanmai, G. (2021, March). Efficient and secure file transfer in cloud through double encryption using AES and RSA Algorithm. In *2021 international conference on emerging smart computing and informatics (ESCI)* (pp. 791-796). IEEE.

Javidroozi, V., Shah, H., Amini, A., & Cole, A. (2014). Smart city as an integrated enterprise: a business process centric framework addressing challenges in systems integration. *3rd International Conference on Smart Systems, Devices and Technologies*. DOI: 10.13140/RG.2.1.2561.1921

Jawaid, S. A. (2023). Artificial Intelligence with Respect to Cyber Security.

Jayabalan, J., & Jeyanthi, N. (2022). Scalable blockchain model using off-chain IPFS storage for healthcare data security and privacy. *Journal of Parallel and Distributed Computing*, 164, 152–167. DOI: 10.1016/j.jpdc.2022.03.009

Jeffrey S, & Omar A (2014). Challenges and Issues within Cloud Computing Technology:cloud computingThe 5th International Conference on Cloud Computing, GRIDs, and Virtualization pp. 55-63. Retrieved 2019, from http://researchgates .net/publication_

Jejeniwa, T. O. (2024). *Conceptualizing E-Government Initiatives: Lessons Learned From Africa-Us Collaborations in Digital Governance*. International Journal of Applied Research in Social Sciences., DOI: 10.51594/ijarss.v6i4.1066

Jiang, C., & Phoong, S. W. (2023). A ten-year review analysis of the impact of digitization on tourism development (2012-2022). *Humanities & Social Sciences Communications*, 10(1), 665. Advance online publication. DOI: 10.1057/s41599-023-02150-7 PMID: 37192942

Jinghua, Y., & Xianmei, S. (2021). Political economics analysis of competition and monopoly in the digital economy era. *Economic Review Journal*, 3(1), 18–26.

Jisc. (2014) Developing digital literacies. Available at https://jisc.ac.uk/guides / developing- Digital-literacy

Johansson-Pajala, R.-M., & Gustafsson, C. (2022). Significant challenges when introducing care robots in Swedish elder care. *Disability and Rehabilitation. Assistive Technology*, 17(2), 166–176. DOI: 10.1080/17483107.2020.1773549 PMID: 32538206

Johnson, B. (2011). *Shaping The Internet Age: An essay on the evolution of internet and the technologies that are helping connect people to information*. Imternet Policy Institute.

Johnson, L., & Miller, R. (2024). Cloud computing and public sector innovation: An overview. *International Journal of Cloud Computing and Services Science*, 12(2), 103–118. DOI: 10.1155/2024/1086224

Jolly, R. (2011). *The E health revolution: easier said than done*. Parliamentary Library.

Jones, S. S., Rudin, R. S., Perry, T., & Shekelle, P. G. (2014). Health information technology: An updated systematic review with a focus on meaningful use. *Annals of Internal Medicine*, 160(1), 48–54. DOI: 10.7326/M13-1531 PMID: 24573664

Jonkers, H., Lankhorst, M. M., Ter Doest, H. W. L., Arbab, F., Bosma, H., & Wieringa, R. J. (2006). Enterprise architecture: Management tool and blueprint for the organisation. *Information Systems Frontiers*, 8(2), 63–66. DOI: 10.1007/s10796-006-7970-2

Joshi, S., Rambola, R. K., & Churi, P. (2021). Evaluating Artificial Intelligence in Education for Next Generation. *Journal of Physics: Conference Series*, 1714(1), 12039. DOI: 10.1088/1742-6596/1714/1/012039

Jyoti, B., & Singh, A. K. (2023). Does digitalization have a causal relationship with economic development? an experience from a country-wise panel data statistical analysis. In R. Sine Nazlı & G. Sari (Eds.), *Handbook of Research on Perspectives on Society and Technology Addiction* (pp. 34-61). IGI Global. DOI: 10.4018/978-1-6684-8397-8.ch003

Kaginalkar, A., Kumar, S., Gargava, P., & Niyogi, D. (2021). Review of urban computing in air quality management as smart city service: An integrated IoT, AI, and cloud technology perspective. *Urban Climate*, 39, 100972. DOI: 10.1016/j.uclim.2021.100972

Kahin, B. (2016). Digitization and the Digital Economy. *Available at SSRN* 2782906.

Kahn, J. P. (2020). *Digital Contact Tracing for Pandemic Response: Ethics and Governance Guidance*. Digital Contact Tracing for Pandemic Response., DOI: 10.1353/book.75831

Kakarontzas, G., Anthopoulos, L., Chatzakou, D., & Vakali, A. (2014). A conceptual enterprise architecture framework for smart cities: A survey based approach. *ICE-B 2014 - Proceedings of the 11th International Conference on e-Business, Part of ICETE 2014 - 11th International Joint Conference on e-Business and Telecommunications*. DOI: 10.5220/0005021400470054

Kalenzi, C. (2022). Artificial Intelligence and Blockchain: How Should Emerging Technologies Be Governed? *Frontiers in Research Metrics and Analytics*, 7, 801549. DOI: 10.3389/frma.2022.801549 PMID: 35224423

Kalidindi, S., & Gandhi, S. (2023). Workforce Crisis in Radiology in the UK and the Strategies to Deal With It: Is Artificial Intelligence the Saviour? *Cureus*. Advance online publication. DOI: 10.7759/cureus.43866 PMID: 37608900

Kao, T. C., Mao, C. H., Chang, C. Y., & Chang, K. C. (2012, June). Cloud SSDLC: Cloud security governance deployment framework in secure system development life cycle. In *2012 IEEE 11th international conference on trust, security and privacy in computing and communications* (pp. 1143-1148). IEEE.

Kariyado, M. Y. (2016). Proposta e aplicação de uma sistemática baseada na gestão do conhecimento para a melhoria do processo de compras públicas. Universidade Federal de São Carlos. São Carlos: UFSCar, 2016. 140 p. Dissertação (Mestrado) - Universidade Federal de São Carlos, 2016.

Karthigha, M., Padmavathy, C., & Akshaya, V. S. (2022, December). Blockchain based Healthcare Data Management. In *2022 International Conference on Automation, Computing and Renewable Systems (ICACRS)* (pp. 392-396). IEEE.

Karthikeyan, P., Pande, H. M., & Sarveshwaran, V. (2023). *Artificial Intelligence and Blockchain in Digital Forensics*. DOI: 10.1201/9781003374671

Kaur, J., Rani, R., & Kalra, N. (2023). Attribute-based access control scheme for secure storage and sharing of EHRs using blockchain and IPFS. *Cluster Computing*, •••, 1–15.

Kaur, R., Gabrijelčič, D., & Klobučar, T. (2023). Artificial intelligence for cybersecurity: Literature review and future research directions. *Information Fusion*, 97, 101804. DOI: 10.1016/j.inffus.2023.101804

Kaushik, A & Kumar, A (2013). Application of Cloud Computing in Libraries. International Journal of Information Dissemination and Technology,3(4), 270-273.

Kazimzade, G., Patzer, Y., & Pinkwart, N. (2019). In Knox, J., Wang, Y., & Gallagher, M. (Eds.), *Artificial Intelligence in Education Meets Inclusive Educational Technology—The Technical State-of-the-Art and Possible Directions BT - Artificial Intelligence and Inclusive Education: Speculative Futures and Emerging Practices* (pp. 61–73). Springer Singapore., DOI: 10.1007/978-981-13-8161-4_4

Kempe, M. (2016). The land registry in the blockchain: A development project with lantmäteriet, telia company, chromaway and kairos future. *White Paper. Estocolmo.*

Keshta, I., & Odeh, A. (2020). Security and privacy of electronic health records: Concerns and challenges. *Egypt. Inform. J.*, 22(2), 177–183. DOI: 10.1016/j.eij.2020.07.003

Kessler, A. (2012). Impact of internet use on agricultural research outputs in Nigeria universities of agriculature. Hi Tech NewsIncororating Online and CD notes, 44-52.

Khalifa Alhosani & Saadat M. Alhashmi. (2024) Opportunities, challenges, and benefits of AI innovation in government services: a review of Springer link vol 4 No 18.

Khan, Z., & Vorley, T. (2017). Big data text analytics: An enabler of knowledge management. *Journal of Knowledge Management*, 21(1), 18–34. DOI: 10.1108/JKM-06-2015-0238

Kheshaifaty, N., & Gutub, A. (2021). Engineering Graphical Captcha and AES Crypto Hash Functions for Secure Online Authentication. *Journal of Engineering Research*. Advance online publication. DOI: 10.36909/jer.13761

Kim, D. K., & Kreps, G. L. (2020). An Analysis of Government Communication in the United States During the COVID-19 Pandemic: Recommendations for Effective Government Health Risk Communication. World Medical \&. *Health Policy (Amsterdam)*, 12(4), 398–412. Advance online publication. DOI: 10.1002/wmh3.363 PMID: 32904935

Kim, G.-H., Trimi, S., & Chung, J.-H. (2014). Big-data applications in the government sector. *Communications of the ACM*, 57(3), 78–85. DOI: 10.1145/2500873

Kim, M. J., Theriault, J., Hirschfeld-Kroen, J., & Young, L. (2022). Reframing of moral dilemmas reveals an unexpected "positivity bias" in updating and attributions. *Journal of Experimental Social Psychology*, 101, 104310. DOI: 10.1016/j.jesp.2022.104310

Kinengyere, A. A. (2007). *The effect of information literacy on the Utilization of Electronic Information Resources in Selected Academic and Research Institutions in Uganda*. Emerald Insight Journal., DOI: 10.1108/02640470710754832

King, T. C., Aggarwal, N., Taddeo, M., & Floridi, L. (2020). Artificial Intelligence Crime: An Interdisciplinary Analysis of Foreseeable Threats and Solutions. *Science and Engineering Ethics*, 26(1), 89–120. DOI: 10.1007/s11948-018-00081-0 PMID: 30767109

Klopper, R., Lubbe, S., & Rugbeer, H. (2007). The Matrix Method of Literature Review. *Alternation (Durban)*, 14(1), 262–276. DOI: 10.1002/asia.200900414

Koenig, M. E. D. (2011). Knowledge Management in Theory and Practice (2nd ed.). *Journal of the American Society for Information Science and Technology*, 62(10). https://doi.org/DOI: 10.1002/asi.21613

Koh, F. H., Ladlad, J., Foo, F.-J., Tan, W. J., Sivarajah, S. S., Ho, L. M. L., Ng, J.-L., Koh, F. H., Chong, C., Aw, D., Kam, J.-H., Tan, A. Y. H., Tan, C.-C., Yeung, B. P. M., Wong, W.-K., Toh, B.-C., Ladlad, J., Barco, J., Chue, K.-M., & Foo, F.-J. (2023). Real-time artificial intelligence (AI)-aided endoscopy improves adenoma detection rates even in experienced endoscopists: A cohort study in Singapore. *Surgical Endoscopy*, 37(1), 165–171. DOI: 10.1007/s00464-022-09470-w PMID: 35882667

Komalavalli, C., Saxena, D., & Laroiya, C. (2020). Overview of blockchain technology concepts. In *Handbook of research on blockchain technology* (pp. 349–371). Academic Press. DOI: 10.1016/B978-0-12-819816-2.00014-9

Kononova, O., Prokudin, D., & Ryabysko, J. (2021). The vision and the perspective of digital tourism. 22nd Conference on Scientific Services & Internet (SSI-2020), Novorossiysk-Abrau (online), Russia. DOI: 10.48550/arXiv.2109.09795

Kononova, O., Prokudin, D., & Tupikina, E. (2020). From e-Tourism to digital tourism. https://ceur-ws.org/Vol-2784/rpaper13.pdf

Kowalska-Pyzalska, A. (2024). Diffusion of Innovative Energy Services: Consumers' Acceptance and Willingness to Pay. Elsevier Science & Technology.

Kraft, C., Lindeque, J. P., & Peter, M. K. (2022). The Digital Transformation of Swiss Small and Medium-Sized Enterprises: Insights From Digital Tool Adoption. *Journal of Strategy and Management*, 15(3), 468–494. Advance online publication. DOI: 10.1108/JSMA-02-2021-0063

Krämer, D., Brachem, E., Schneider-Reuter, L., D'Angelo, I., Vollmann, J., & Haltaufderheide, J. (2024). The Role of Transparency in Digital Contact Tracing During COVID-19: Insights from an Expert Survey. *Health Care Analysis*. Advance online publication. DOI: 10.1007/s10728-024-00485-z PMID: 38909332

Kroski, E. (2009). Library cloud atlas: A guide to cloud computing and storage stacking. *Library Journal*, •••, 207. https://www.libraryjournal.com/article/CA6695772.html

Krubuand, D., & Osawam, M. (2011). Avoiding the death zone: Choosing and running a library project in the cloud. *Emerald Group Publishing Limited*, 30, 418–427.

Krupa, K. S., & Akhil, M. S. (2019). Reshaping the real estate industry using blockchain. In *Emerging Research in Electronics, Computer Science and Technology:Proceedings of International Conference, ICERECT 2018* (pp. 255-263). Springer Singapore. DOI: 10.1007/978-981-13-5802-9_24

Kshetri, N. (2017). Blockchain's roles in strengthening cybersecurity and protecting privacy. *Telecommunications Policy*, 41(10), 1027–1038. DOI: 10.1016/j.telpol.2017.09.003

Kshetri, N. (2017). Can blockchain strengthen the internet of things? *IT Professional*, 19(4), 68–72. DOI: 10.1109/MITP.2017.3051335

Kshetri, N. (2021). Blockchain and sustainable supply chain management in developing countries. *International Journal of Information Management*, 60, 102376. DOI: 10.1016/j.ijinfomgt.2021.102376

Kshetri, N., & Voas, J. (2022). Blockchain adoption in public administration: Regulatory and technical challenges. *Journal of Information Technology*, 37(3), 233–247. DOI: 10.1177/02683962221095425

Kuang, T., & Tsai, Y. F. (2016). The effect of tourism growth on economic growth: A quantile regression analysis. https://hdl.handle.net/20.500.14394/48202

Kumar, L., Sharma, A., Sharma, H., & Sharma, S. (2024). Blockchain in Healthcare:Portal for Electronic Health Records. SSRN *Electronic Journal*. https://doi.org/DOI: 10.2139/SSRN.4492411

Kumar, R., Jain, V., Han, G. T. W., & Touzene, A. (2023). Immersive virtual and augmented reality in healthcare: An IoT and blockchain perspective. *Immersive Virtual and Augmented Reality in Healthcare: An IoT and Blockchain Perspective*, 1–223. DOI: 10.1201/9781003340133

Kumar, A., Singh, R., Kaur, J., Pandey, S., Sharma, V., Thakur, L., Sati, S., Mani, S., Asthana, S., Sharma, T. K., Chaudhuri, S., Bhattacharyya, S., & Kumar, N. (2021). Wuhan to World: The COVID-19 Pandemic. *Frontiers in Cellular and Infection Microbiology*, 11, 596201. DOI: 10.3389/fcimb.2021.596201 PMID: 33859951

Kumar, P., Kumar, D., & Kumar, N. (2014). E-Governance in India: Definitions, Challenges and Solutions. *International Journal of Computer Applications*, 101(16), 6–8. DOI: 10.5120/17769-7408

Kumar, S., Lim, W. M., Sivarajah, U., & Kaur, J. (2023). Artificial Intelligence and Blockchain Integration in Business: Trends from a Bibliometric-Content Analysis. *Information Systems Frontiers*, 25, 871–896. DOI: 10.1007/s10796-022-10279-0 PMID: 35431617

Kumar, S., & Shekhar, . (2020). Digitalization: A strategic approach for development of tourism industry in India. *Paradigm*, 24(1), 93–108. DOI: 10.1177/0971890720914111

Kurfalı, M., Arifoglu, A., Tokdemir, G., & Paçin, Y. (2017). Adoption of e-government services in Turkey: Computers in Human Behavior. *Computers in Human Behavior*, 66, 168–178. DOI: 10.1016/j.chb.2016.09.041

Kuziemski, M., & Misuraca, G. (2020). AI governance in the public sector: Three tales from the frontiers of automated decision-making in democratic settings. *Telecommunications Policy*, 44(6), 101976. https://doi.org/https://doi.org/10.1016/j.telpol.2020.101976. DOI: 10.1016/j.telpol.2020.101976 PMID: 32313360

Lacity, M. C. (2020). *Blockchain foundations: for the internet of value*. Epic Books.

Lada, A., Wang, M., & Yan, T. (2021). *How machine learning powers Facebook's News Feed ranking algorithm*. Engineering at Meta. https://engineering.fb.com/2021/01/26/ml-applications/news-feed-ranking/

Lai, S. T., & Leu, F. Y. (2015, July). A security threats measurement model for reducing Cloud computing security risk. In *2015 9th International Conference on Innovative Mobile and Internet Services in Ubiquitous Computing* (pp. 414-419). IEEE.

Lee, B. H., Dewi, E. K., & Wajdi, M. F. (2018, April). Data security in cloud computing using AES under HEROKU cloud. In *2018 27th wireless and optical communication conference (WOCC)* (pp. 1-5). IEEE.

Lemieux, V. L. (2016). Trusting records: Is Blockchain technology the answer? *Records Management Journal*, 26(2), 110–139. DOI: 10.1108/RMJ-12-2015-0042

Lepri, B., Oliver, N., & Pentland, A. (2021). Ethical machines: The human-centric use of artificial intelligence. *iScience*, 24(3), 102249. https://doi.org/https://doi.org/10.1016/j.isci.2021.102249. DOI: 10.1016/j.isci.2021.102249 PMID: 33763636

Lesnussa, J., & Sitokdana, M. N. N. (2023). Leveraging TOGAF ADM for Enterprise Architecture in West Seram Environment Agency. *Journal of Information Systems and Informatics*, 5(4), 1595–1608. Advance online publication. DOI: 10.51519/journalisi.v5i4.603

Li, J., Wang, Q., & Sun, Y. (2024). Future prospects of AI and blockchain in public administration: Emerging trends and innovations. *Journal of Emerging Technologies in Public Administration*, 15(1), 55–72. DOI: 10.1080/2050124X.2024.2162908

Lin, C., Zhao, G., Yu, C., & Wu, Y. (2019). Smart City Development and Residents' Well-Being. *Sustainability (Basel)*, 11(3), 676. DOI: 10.3390/su11030676

Linders, D. (2012). From e-government to we-government: Defining a typology for citizen coproduction in the age of social media. *Government Information Quarterly*, 29(4), 446–454. DOI: 10.1016/j.giq.2012.06.003

Li, P., Zho, Y., & Huang, S. (2023). Role of information technology in the development of e-tourism marketing: A contextual suggestion. *Economic Analysis and Policy*, 78(1), 307–318. DOI: 10.1016/j.eap.2023.03.010

Lips, M. (2024). Digital transformation in the public sector. In Verhoest, K., Hammerschmid, G., Rykkja, L. H., & Klijn, E. H. (Eds.), *Collaborating for Digital Transformation* (pp. 13–30). Edward Elgar Publishing., DOI: 10.4337/9781803923895.00010

Liu, S. (2022). Higher Education and Sustainable Development Goals during Covid-19: Coping Strategies of a University in Wuhan, China. Https://Doi.Org/10.4081/Jphr.2020.1933, 9(s1), 16–17. DOI: 10.4081/jphr.2020.1933

Liu, J., Li, B., Chen, Q. Y., & Dang, J. (2021). Student Health Implications of School Closures During the COVID-19 Pandemic: New Evidence on the Association of E-Learning, Outdoor Exercise, and Myopia. *Health Care*, 9(5), 500. Advance online publication. DOI: 10.3390/healthcare9050500 PMID: 33922486

Li, W., Wu, J., Cao, J., Chen, N., Zhang, Q., & Buyya, R. (2021). Blockchain-based trust management in cloud computing systems: A taxonomy, review and future directions. *Journal of Cloud Computing (Heidelberg, Germany)*, 10(1), 35. DOI: 10.1186/s13677-021-00247-5

Lnenicka, M., Machova, R., Komarkova, J., & Pasler, M. (2017). Government enterprise architecture for big and open linked data analytics in a smart city ecosystem. *Smart Innovation. Systems and Technologies*, 75, 475–485. Advance online publication. DOI: 10.1007/978-3-319-59451-4_47

Loi, M., & Spielkamp, M. (2021). Towards Accountability in the Use of Artificial Intelligence for Public Administrations. *Proceedings of the 2021 AAAI/ACM Conference on AI, Ethics, and Society*, 757–766. DOI: 10.1145/3461702.3462631

López Jiménez, D., Dittmar, E. C., & Vargas Portillo, J. P. (2021). Self-regulation of sustainability as a manifestation of corporate social responsibility. *Revista de Ciencias Sociales*, 27(3), 16–29. DOI: 10.31876/rcs.v27i3.36750

López Jiménez, D., Dittmar, E. C., & Vargas Portillo, J. P. (2022). The trusted third party or digital notary in Spain: Effect on virtual transactions. *International Review of Law Computers & Technology*, 36(3), 453–469. DOI: 10.1080/13600869.2021.2004760

Lopez-Cordova, E. (2020). Digital platforms and the demand for international tourism services. Policy Research Working Paper, 9147, Finance, Competitiveness and Innovation Global Practice, World Bank Group. https://www.worldbank.org/prwp

Loukis, E. N., Maragoudakis, M., & Kyriakou, N. (2020). Artificial intelligence-based public sector data analytics for economic crisis policymaking. *Transforming Government: People. Transforming Government*, 14(4), 639–662. DOI: 10.1108/TG-11-2019-0113

Luna-Reyes, L. F., & Gil-Garcia, J. R. (2014). Digital government transformation and internet portals: The co-evolution of technology, organizations, and institutions. *Government Information Quarterly*, 31(4), 545–555. DOI: 10.1016/j.giq.2014.08.001

Luo, Y., Thompson, W. K., Herr, T. M., Zeng, Z., Berendsen, M. A., Jonnalagadda, S. R., Carson, M. B., & Starren, J. (2017). Natural Language Processing for EHR-Based Pharmacovigilance: A Structured Review. *Drug Safety*, 40(11), 1075–1089. DOI: 10.1007/s40264-017-0558-6 PMID: 28643174

Lv, Y., Hu, S., Liu, F., & Qi, J. (2022, August). Research on users' trust in customer service chatbots based on human-computer interaction. In China National Conference on Big Data and Social Computing (pp. 291-306). Singapore: Springer Nature Singapore. DOI: 10.1007/978-981-19-7532-5_19

Mackey, T. K., Kuo, T.-T., Gummadi, B., Clauson, K. A., Church, G., Grishin, D., Obbad, K., Barkovich, R., & Palombini, M. (2019). 'Fit-for-purpose?'—Challenges and opportunities for applications of blockchain technology in the future of healthcare. *BMC Medicine*, 17(1), 1–17. DOI: 10.1186/s12916-019-1296-7 PMID: 30914045

Madan, R., & Ashok, M. (2023). AI adoption and diffusion in public administration: A systematic literature review and future research agenda. *Government Information Quarterly*, 40(1), 101774. https://doi.org/https://doi.org/10.1016/j.giq.2022.101774. DOI: 10.1016/j.giq.2022.101774

Madhurya, J. A., Pillai, B. G., Dayananda Lal, N., & Jeena Jacob, I. (2020). Property registration framework using Ethereum blockchain. *International Journal of Emerging Trends in Engineering Research*, 8(9), 5209–5213. DOI: 10.30534/ijeter/2020/51892020

Madsen, L. B. (2014). *Data-driven healthcare: how analytics and BI are transforming the industry*. John Wiley & Sons.

Mahalakshmi, K. & Ally S, S.(2012). Awareness and application of cloud computing in Indian libraries: a study among librarians of engineering colleges of coimbatore district. International Conference on Cloud Computing Technologies, Applications and Management, ICCCTAM

Makridakis, S. (2017). The forthcoming Artificial Intelligence (AI) revolution: Its impact on society and firms. *Futures*, 90, 46–60. DOI: 10.1016/j.futures.2017.03.006

Makridis, C. A., & Mishra, S. (2022). Artificial Intelligence as a Service, Economic Growth, and Well-Being. *Journal of Service Research*, 25(4), 505–520. DOI: 10.1177/10946705221120218

Malik, G., Tayal, D. K., & Vij, S. (2019). An Analysis of the Role of Artificial Intelligence in Education and Teaching BT - Recent Findings in Intelligent Computing Techniques. In Sa, P. K., Bakshi, S., Hatzilygeroudis, I. K., & Sahoo, M. N. (Eds.), *Recent Findings in Intelligent Computing Techniques* (pp. 407–417). Springer Singapore. DOI: 10.1007/978-981-10-8639-7_42

Malischeski, K. (2023). Colaboração e inovação no setor público: diretrizes aos i-Labs [Universidade Federal de Santa Catarina]. https://repositorio.ufsc.br/handle/123456789/253749

Mamkaitis, A., Bezbradica, M., & Helfert, M. (2016). Urban enterprise: A review of Smart City frameworks from an enterprise architecture perspective. *IEEE 2nd International Smart Cities Conference: Improving the Citizens Quality of Life, ISC2 2016 - Proceedings*. DOI: 10.1109/ISC2.2016.7580810

Mani, V., Manickam, P., Alotaibi, Y., Alghamdi, S., & Khalaf, O. I. (2021). Hyperledger healthchain: Patient-centric IPFS-based storage of health records. *Electronics (Basel)*, 10(23), 3003.

Mansoor, M. (2021). Citizens' trust in government as a function of good governance and government agency's provision of quality information on social media during COVID-19. *Government Information Quarterly*, 38(4), 101597. DOI: 10.1016/j.giq.2021.101597 PMID: 34642542

Margetts, H., & Dunleavy, P. (2013). The second wave of digital-era governance: A quasi-paradigm for government on the Web. *Philosophical Transactions of the Royal Society A: Mathematical, Physical and Engineering Sciences, 371*(1987), 20120382. DOI: 10.1098/rsta.2012.0382

Margetts, H., & Dorobantu, C. (2019). Rethink government with AI. *Nature*, 568(7751), 163–165. DOI: 10.1038/d41586-019-01099-5 PMID: 30967667

Martin, F., Zhuang, M., & Schaefer, D. (2024). Systematic review of research on artificial intelligence in K-12 education (2017–2022). *Computers and Education: Artificial Intelligence*, 6(May 2023), 100195. https://doi.org/DOI: 10.1016/j.caeai.2023.100195

Mary Sowjanya, A., & Srividya, K. (2024). NLP-Driven Chatbots: Applications and Implications in Conversational AI. *Conversational Artificial Intelligence*, 713-725.

Maslej, N., Fattorini, L., Perrault, R., Parli, V., Reuel, A., Brynjolfsson, E., Etchemendy, J., Ligett, K., Lyons, T., Manyika, J., Niebles, J. C., Shoham, Y., Wald, R., & Clark, J. (April 2024). "The AI Index 2024 Annual Report," AI Index Steering Committee, Institute for Human-Centered AI, Stanford University, Stanford, CA, Retrieved from https://aiindex.stanford.edu/wp-content/uploads/2024/04/HAI_2024_AI-Index-Report.pdf

Maslova, T., Pletneva, N., Althonayan, A., Tarasova, E., & Krasnov, A. (2020). Transformation of consumer behavior in the tourism industry in the conditions of digital economy. *IOP Conference Series. Materials Science and Engineering*, 940(1), 1–8. DOI: 10.1088/1757-899X/940/1/012070

Massaro, M., Dumay, J., & Garlatti, A. (2015). Public sector knowledge management: A structured literature review. *Journal of Knowledge Management*, 19(3), 530–558. DOI: 10.1108/JKM-11-2014-0466

Mayer-Schönberger, V., & Cukier, K. (2013). *Big data: A revolution that will transform how we live, work, and think.* Houghton Mifflin Harcourt.

McLoughlin, I. P., Garrety, K., & Wilson, R. (2017). *The digitalization of healthcare: Electronic records and the disruption of moral orders.* Oxford University Press. DOI: 10.1093/acprof:oso/9780198744139.001.0001

Megas, K. (2024). *Managing Cybersecurity and Privacy Risks in the Age of Artificial Intelligence: Launching a New Program at NIST.* National Institute of Standards and Technology. https://www.nist.gov/blogs/cybersecurity-insights/managing-cybersecurity-and-privacy-risks-age-artificial-intelligence

Meijer, A., & Bolívar, M. P. R. (2016). Governing the smart city: A review of the literature on smart urban governance. *International Review of Administrative Sciences*, 82(2), 392–408. DOI: 10.1177/0020852314564308

Mellouli, S., Janssen, M., & Ojo, A. (2024). Introduction to the Issue on Artificial Intelligence in the Public Sector: Risks and Benefits of AI for Governments. *Digital Government: Research and Practice*, 5(1), 1–6. DOI: 10.1145/3636550

Memarian, B., & Doleck, T. (2023). Fairness, Accountability, Transparency, and Ethics (FATE) in Artificial Intelligence (AI) and higher education: A systematic review. *Computers and Education: Artificial Intelligence, 5*, 100152. https://doi.org/https://doi.org/10.1016/j.caeai.2023.100152

Memarian, B., & Doleck, T. (2023). Fairness, Accountability, Transparency, and Ethics (FATE) in Artificial Intelligence (AI), and higher education: A systematic review. *Computers and Education: Artificial Intelligence*, 100152.

Mennis, J., Matthews, K. A., & Huston, S. L. (2022). Geospatial Perspectives on the Intersection of Chronic Disease and COVID-19. *Preventing Chronic Disease*, 19, 220145. DOI: 10.5888/pcd19.220145 PMID: 35772034

Mensah, I. K., Adams, S., Adjei, J. K., & Mwakapesa, D. S. (2021). Drivers of Egovernment Adoption Amidst COVID-19 Pandemic: The Information Adoption Model (IAM) Approach. *Information Development.* Advance online publication. DOI: 10.1177/02666669211010872

Mensah, R., Cater-Steel, A., & Toleman, M. (2020). Factors Affecting E-government Adoption in Liberia: A Practitioner Perspective. *The Electronic Journal on Information Systems in Developing Countries.* Advance online publication. DOI: 10.1002/isd2.12161

Michael Onyema, E., Chika Eucheria, N., Ayobamidele Obafemi, F., Sen, S., Grace Atonye, F., Sharma, A., & Omar Alsayed, A. (2020). Journal of Education and Practice www.iiste.org ISSN. 11(13). https://doi.org/DOI: 10.7176/JEP/11-13-12

Michels, J. D., Walden, I., Cybersecurity, C., & Infrastructure, C. (May 1, 2021). C. Millard (ed.), Cloud Computing Law (2nd Edn, OUP 2021), Available at *SSRN*: https://ssrn.com/abstract=4204847 or http://dx.doi.org/DOI: 10.2139/ssrn.4204847

Microsoft. (2023). *Changing the government landscape with cloud and AI.* Microsoft.

Midoun, S., & Nardjess, F. (2019). Tourism-led growth hypothesis: A case study of some North African countries. *African Journal of Hospitality, Tourism and Leisure*, 8(5), 1–13. www.ajhtl.com/uploads/7/1/6/3/7163688/article_86_8_5__2019_algeria.pdf

Mikhaylov, S. J., Esteve, M., & Campion, A. (2018). Artificial intelligence for the public sector: Opportunities and challenges of cross-sector collaboration. *Philosophical Transactions. Series A, Mathematical, Physical, and Engineering Sciences*, 376(2128), 20170357. DOI: 10.1098/rsta.2017.0357 PMID: 30082303

Miller, M., & Jeffrey, K., & Neidecker-Lutz, B. (2009. (2010). The future of cloud opportunities. *European Cloud Cloud*, 2010, 66.

Min-Allah, N., Alahmed, B. A., Albreek, E. M., Alghamdi, L. S., Alawad, D. A., Alharbi, A. S., Al-Akkas, N., Musleh, D., & Alrashed, S. (2021). A survey of COVID-19 contact-tracing apps. *Computers in Biology and Medicine*, 137, 104787. DOI: 10.1016/j.compbiomed.2021.104787 PMID: 34482197

Ministries, Departments & Agencies. (2024). Home - Edo State Government.

Miranda, J. P. P., & Bringula, R. P. (2023). Towards the Development of a Model to Detect Learned Helplessness Among Grade 6 Mathematics Students. *2023 IEEE International Conference on Advanced Learning Technologies (ICALT)*, 373–375. DOI: 10.1109/ICALT58122.2023.00115

Miranda, J. P. P., & De Leon, A. P. (2017). Datasets of Fire and Crime Incidents in Pampanga, Philippines. *International Journal of Computing Sciences Research*, 7, 1637–1646. DOI: 10.25147/ijcsr.2017.001.1.121

Miranda, J. P. P., Dianelo, R. F. B., Gamboa, A. B., Bansil, J. A., Regala, A. R., & Simpao, L. S. (2024). Identification, validity, and reliability of the 21st-century workplace skills for on-the-job training practicum. *International Journal of Evaluation and Research in Education*, 10(5), 3485–3492. DOI: 10.11591/ijere.v13i5.28919

Mishra, P. K., Rout, H. B., & Mohapatra, S. S. (2011). Causality between tourism and economic growth: Empirical evidence from India. *European Journal of Soil Science*, 18(4), 518–527.

Misuraca, G., & Viscusi, G. (2014). *Digital governance in the public sector: Challenging the policy-maker's innovation dilemma* (I. Proceedings, Ed.; pp. 146–154). of the 8th International Conference on Theory and Practice of Electronic Governance. ACM.

Mitgang, E. A., Blaya, J. A., & Chopra, M. (2021). Digital Health in Response to COVID-19 in Low- and Middle-income Countries: Opportunities and Challenges. *Global Policy*, 12(S6), 107–109. DOI: 10.1111/1758-5899.12880 PMID: 34230840

Mittelstadt, B. D., Allo, P., Taddeo, M., Wachter, S., & Floridi, L. (2016). The ethics of algorithms: Mapping the debate. *Big Data & Society*, 3(2), 2053951716679679. DOI: 10.1177/2053951716679679

Moghaddam, F. F., Karimi, O., & Alrashdan, M. T. (2013, November). A comparative study of applying real-time encryption in cloud computing environments. In *2013 IEEE 2nd International Conference on Cloud Networking (CloudNet)* (pp. 185-189). IEEE.

Mohale, C. (2024). *The Role of E-Government in the Promotion of Municipal Service Delivery in South Africa.* International Journal of Social Science Research and Review., DOI: 10.47814/ijssrr.v7i3.1992

Mohamed, N. (2023). Current trends in AI and ML for cybersecurity: A state-of-the-art survey. *Cogent Engineering*, 10(2), 2272358. DOI: 10.1080/23311916.2023.2272358

Mohanta, B. K., Panda, S. S., & Jena, D. (2018). An Overview of Smart Contract and Use Cases in Blockchain Technology. *2018 9th International Conference on Computing, Communication and Networking Technologies, ICCCNT 2018*. DOI: 10.1109/ICCCNT.2018.8494045

Mohurle, M., & Panchbhai, V. V. (2016, July). Review on realization of AES encryption and decryption with power and area optimization. In *2016 IEEE 1st International Conference on Power Electronics, Intelligent Control and Energy Systems (ICPEICES)* (pp. 1-3). IEEE.

Montasari, R. (2023). The application of big data predictive analytics and surveillance technologies in the field of policing. In *countering cyberterrorism: the confluence of artificial intelligence, cyber forensics and digital policing in US and UK National Cybersecurity* (pp. 81-114). Cham: Springer International Publishing. DOI: 10.1007/978-3-031-21920-7_5

Morales, P. D. A. e Dandolini, G. A.Tipologias da inovação no setor público: uma revisão integrativa da literatura In: de Bem Machado, et al. (2022). Inovação no setor público: desafios e possibilidades. *Pimenta Cultural*. DOI: DOI: 10.31560/pimentacultural/2022.95835

Morens, D. M., Breman, J. G., Calisher, C. H., Doherty, P. C., Hahn, B. H., Keusch, G. T., Kramer, L. D., LeDuc, J. W., Monath, T. P., & Taubenberger, J. K. (2020). The Origin of COVID-19 and Why It Matters. *The American Journal of Tropical Medicine and Hygiene*, 103(3), 955–959. DOI: 10.4269/ajtmh.20-0849 PMID: 32700664

Morselli, C. (2009). The Criminal Network Perspective. In Morselli, C. (Ed.), *Inside Criminal Networks* (pp. 1–21). Springer., DOI: 10.1007/978-0-387-09526-4_1

Mosa, H. El-Bakry, and M. AbuElkheir, (2015) "Cloud Computing in EGovernment: A Survey Cloud Computing in E-Government: A Survey," Int. J. Adv. Res. Comput. Sci. Technol., vol. 3,

Moses, L. B., & Chan, J. (2014). Using big data for legal and law enforcement decisions: Testing the new tools. *The University of New South Wales Law Journal*, 37(2), 643–678. https://search.informit.org/doi/10.3316/informit.613165001799453

Moy, N., Antonini, M., Kyhlstedt, M., Fiorentini, G., & Paolucci, F. (2023). Standardising Policy and Technology Responses in the Immediate Aftermath of a Pandemic: A Comparative and Conceptual Framework. *Health Research Policy and Systems*, 21(1), 10. Advance online publication. DOI: 10.1186/s12961-022-00951-x PMID: 36698139

Muhyiddin, M. (2019). Future Challenges on Indonesia's Vision 2045. *Jurnal Perencanaan Pembangunan: The Indonesian Journal of Development Planning*, 3(1). Advance online publication. DOI: 10.36574/jpp.v3i1.63

Mukherjee, P., & Pradhan, C. (2021). Blockchain 1.0 to blockchain 4.0—The evolutionary transformation of blockchain technology. In *Blockchain technology: applications and challenges* (pp. 29–49). Springer International Publishing. DOI: 10.1007/978-3-030-69395-4_3

Mullis, I. V. S., Martin, M. O., Foy, P., Kelly, D. L., & Fishbein, B. (2020). *TIMSS 2019 International Results in Mathematics and Science*. https://timss2019.org/reports/wp-content/themes/timssandpirls/download-center/TIMSS-2019-International-Results-in-Mathematics-and-Science.pdf

Murikah, W., Nthenge, J. K., & Musyoka, F. M. (2024). Bias and ethics of AI systems applied in auditing - A systematic review. *Scientific African*, 25, e02281. https://doi.org/https://doi.org/10.1016/j.sciaf.2024.e02281. DOI: 10.1016/j.sciaf.2024.e02281

Murray, C. J. L. (2022). COVID-19 will continue but the end of the pandemic is near. *Lancet*, 399(10323), 417–419. DOI: 10.1016/S0140-6736(22)00100-3 PMID: 35065006

Mustafa, G., Rafiq, W., Jhamat, N., & Arshad, Z. (2024). Blockchain-based governance models in e-government: a comprehensive framework for legal, technical, ethical and Security Consideration. *International Journal of Law and Management*, 521-541.

Mustafa, G., Rafiq, W., Jhamat, N., & Arshad, Z. (2024). Blockchain-based governance models in e-government: a comprehensive framework for legal, technical, ethical and Security Consideration. International Journal of Law and Management, 521-541.

Mustafa, K., Mustafa, R., & Ahmedi, B. (2021) *The Impact of the COVID 19 Pandemic on the Digitalization of Municipal Administration, the Development of E-Governance*. Asian Journal of Research in Computer Science, 10 (2). pp. 1-21. ISSN 2581-8260

Nafi'ah, B. A. (2021). Data Governance Mechanisms in Indonesia's Covid-19 Data Integration System. *Sosiohumaniora*, 23(3), 339. DOI: 10.24198/sosiohumaniora.v23i3.28437

Nakatani, R. (2021). Total factor productivity enablers in the ICT industry: A cross-country firm-level analysis. *Telecommunications Policy*, 45(9), 10–21. DOI: 10.1016/j.telpol.2021.102188

Nam, T. (2019). Does E-Government Raise Effectiveness and Efficiency?: Examining the Cross-National Effect. *Journal of Global Information Management*, 27(3), 120–138. DOI: 10.4018/JGIM.2019070107

Nand, P., Jain, V., Le, D.-N., Chatterjee, J. M., Kannan, R., & Verma, A. S. (Eds.). (2023). *Deep Learning for Healthcare Services* (Vol. 11). BENTHAM SCIENCE PUBLISHERS., DOI: 10.2174/97898150802301230201

Naone, E. (2007). Computer in the Cloud. Retrieved. *Technology Review*.

Narayanan, A., Shah, N. H., & Williams, S. (2021). Blockchain for transparency and anti-corruption: A public administration perspective. *Journal of Digital Government*, 10(3), 213–228. DOI: 10.1080/2050277X.2021.1985823

Nasrallah, N., Atayah, O. F., El Khoury, R., Hamdan, A., & Obaid, S. (2022). Intellectual structure of knowledge management: A bibliometric analysis of the Journal of Information and Knowledge Management. *Journal of Information & Knowledge Management*, 21(01), 2250001. DOI: 10.1142/S0219649222500010

Nassar, A., & Kamal, M. (2021). Ethical Dilemmas in AI-Powered Decision-Making: A Deep Dive into Big Data-Driven Ethical Considerations. *International Journal of Responsible Artificial Intelligence, 11*(8 SE-Articles), 1–11. https://neuralslate.com/index.php/Journal-of-Responsible-AI/article/view/43

National Institute of Standards and Technology. (2023). Artificial Intelligence Risk Management Framework (AI RMF 1.0). https://nvlpubs.nist.gov/nistpubs/ai/nist.ai.100-1.pdf

National Science and Technology Council. (2023, May). National Artificial Intelligence Research and Development Strategic Plan: 2023 Update. Retrieved from https://www.whitehouse.gov/ostp/nsc/ai/national-artificial-intelligence-research-and-development-strategic-plan-2023-update/

Ndou, V. D. (2004). Ndou, (2004) E – government for developing countries: Opportunities and challenges. *The Electronic Journal on Information Systems in Developing Countries*, 18(1), 1–24. DOI: 10.1002/j.1681-4835.2004.tb00117.x

Nedaković, A., Hasselgren, A., Kralevska, K., & Gligoroski, D. (2023). Hyperledger fabric platform for healthcare trust relations—Proof-of-Concept. *Blockchain: Research and Applications*, 4(4), 100156. DOI: 10.1016/j.bcra.2023.100156

Neethu & Vanaja (2017). Concepts & application of cloud computing in libraries. International Journal of Trend in Research and Development,1-4.

Nel, E., MacLachlan, A., Ballinger, O., Cole, H., & Cole, M. (2023). Data-Driven Decision Making in Response to the COVID-19 Pandemic: A City of Cape Town Case Study. *Sustainability (Basel)*, 15(3), 1853. DOI: 10.3390/su15031853

Netten, N., Bargh, M. S., Van Den Braak, S., Choenni, S., & Leeuw, F. (2016). On Enabling Smart Government: A Legal Logistics Framework for Future Criminal Justice Systems. *Proceedings of the 17th International Digital Government Research Conference on Digital Government Research*, 293–302. DOI: 10.1145/2912160.2912180

Ngandee, S., & Taparugssanagorn, A. (2023). Improved information dissemination services for the agricultural sector in Thailand: Development and evaluation of a machine learning based rice crop yield prediction system. *Information Development*, 02666669231208017, 02666669231208017. Advance online publication. DOI: 10.1177/02666669231208017

Nguyen, T. a. (2007). Grounding e-government in Vietnam: from antecedents to responsive government. Journal of Business Systems, Governance and Ethics, 35-52.

Nikam, R., & Potey, M. (2016, December). Cloud storage security using multi-factor authentication. In *2016 international conference on recent advances and innovations in engineering (ICRAIE)* (pp. 1-7). IEEE.

Nnenna, U. J. (2024a). *Challenges and Opportunities in Implementing Open Government Data Initiatives in East Africa*. Iaa JSS., DOI: 10.59298/IAA-JSS/2024/102.111.00000

Nnenna, U. J. (2024b). *Evaluating the Effectiveness of E-Government Platforms in East Africa*. Iaa Jah., DOI: 10.59298/IAAJAH/2024/11.11017.11

Nobles, C. (2024). The Weaponization of Artificial Intelligence in Cybersecurity: A Systematic Review. *Procedia Computer Science*, 239, 547–555. DOI: 10.1016/j.procs.2024.06.206

Nokele, S. K. (2024). An Empirical Study of the Uptake of Electronic Government Services by the Limpopo Department of Home Affairs. Advances in Politics and Economics. https://doi.org/DOI: 10.22158/ape.v7n1p32

Noronha, T., & Vaz, E. (2020). Theoretical foundations in support of small and medium towns. *Sustainability (Basel)*, 12(13), 5312. DOI: 10.3390/su12135312

Norta, A., Fernandez, C., & Hickmott, S. (2018, July). Commercial property tokenizing with smart contracts. In *2018 International Joint Conference on Neural Networks (IJCNN)* (pp. 1-8). IEEE.

Novelli, C., Taddeo, M., & Floridi, L. (2024). Accountability in artificial intelligence: What it is and how it works. *AI & Society*, 39(4), 1871–1882. DOI: 10.1007/s00146-023-01635-y

NSW R. (n.d.) Using machine technology. [Online] Revenue NSW. https://www.revenue.nsw.gov.au/news-media-releases/using-machine-technology. Accessed 20th October 2024.

Nusantara Capital Authority. (2023). *Cetak Biru Kota Cerdas Nusantara (Nusantara Smart City Blueprint)* (B. Susantono, M. A. Berawi, T. A. Setiono, A. Gunawan, Y. G. Sucahyo, M. Sari, G. Gunawan, & A. Mahendra, Eds.; 1st ed.). Otorita Ibu Kota Nusantara. https://www.ikn.go.id/storage/thd/blueprint/cetak_biru_kota_cerdas_nusantara.pdf

O'Neil, C. (2016). *Weapons of math destruction: How big data increases inequality and threatens democracy*. Crown Publishing Group.

Oatley, G. C. (2022). Themes in data mining, big data, and crime analytics. *Wiley Interdisciplinary Reviews. Data Mining and Knowledge Discovery*, 12(2), e1432. https://doi.org/https://doi.org/10.1002/widm.1432. DOI: 10.1002/widm.1432

Obasa, A. E., Singh, S., Chivunze, E., Burgess, T., Masiye, F., Mtande, T., Ochieng, J., Chalwe, V., Mokgatla, B., Rennie, S., & Moodley, K. (2020). Comparative Strategic Approaches to COVID-19 in Africa: Balancing Public Interest With Civil Liberties. *South African Medical Journal*, 110(9), 858. Advance online publication. DOI: 10.7196/SAMJ.2020.v110i9.14934 PMID: 32880268

OCDE. (2023). Global Trends in Government Innovation 2023. *OCDE*. https://www.oecd-ilibrary.org/sites/0655b570-en/index.html?itemId=/content/publication/0655b570-en&_csp_=81514dda47e6d6cb4cb62f97e5c3e4e4&itemIGO=oecd&itemContentType=book

Odeyemi, O., Mhlongo, N. Z., Nwankwo, E. E., & Soyombo, O. T. (2024). Reviewing the role of AI in fraud detection and prevention in financial services. *International Journal of Science and Research Archive*, 11(1), 2101–2110. https://doi.org/https://doi.org/10.30574/ijsra.2024.11.1.0279. DOI: 10.30574/ijsra.2024.11.1.0279

OECD. (2019). *PISA 2018 Results (Volume 1): What students know and can do.* OECD Publishing. https://doi.org/https://doi.org/10.1787/5f07c754-en

OECD. (2023). OECD Digital Government Index. OECD iLibrary.

OECD. (2024). *AI principles.* OECD. https://www.oecd.org/en/topics/ai-principles.html

OECD. (2024, May 14). Using artificial intelligence in public financial management [Report No. GOV/SBO(2024)14]. Retrieved from https://one.oecd.org/document/GOV/SBO(2024)14/en/pdf

Offner, K. L., Sitnikova, E., Joiner, K., & MacIntyre, C. R. (2020). Towards understanding cybersecurity capability in Australian healthcare organisations: A systematic review of recent trends, threats and mitigation. *Intelligence and National Security*, 35(4), 556–585. DOI: 10.1080/02684527.2020.1752459

Ohadike, D. C. (1991). Diffusion and physiological responses to the influenza pandemic of 1918-19 in Nigeria. *Social Science & Medicine*, 32(12), 1393–1399. DOI: 10.1016/0277-9536(91)90200-V PMID: 1871611

Oh, P., & Jung, Y. (2023). A machine-learning approach to assessing public trust in AI-powered technologies. In Nah, S. (Ed.), *Research Handbook on Artificial Intelligence and Communication* (pp. 193–213). Edward Elgar Publishing., DOI: 10.4337/9781803920306.00021

Okereke, M., Williams, A. E., Nzeribe, E., Ashinedu, N. U., & Mairaj, M. W. (2020). COVID-19: Challenges Affecting the Uptake of E-Learning in Pharmacy Education in Africa. *The Pan African Medical Journal*, 35(Supp 2). Advance online publication. DOI: 10.11604/pamj.supp.2020.35.2.23910 PMID: 33623594

Oladipupo, T. (2010). *Types of Machine Learning Algorithms.* New Advances in Machine Learning., DOI: 10.5772/9385

Olatunde-Aiyedun, T. G. (2024). Artificial Intelligence (AI) in Education: Integration of AI Into Science Education Curriculum in Nigerian Universities. *International Journal of Artificial Intelligence for Digital*, 1(1), 1–14. https://papers.ssrn.com/sol3/papers.cfm?abstract_id=4733349

Olawade, D. B., Wada, O. J., David-Olawade, A. C., Kunonga, E., Abaire, O., & Ling, J. (2023). Using artificial intelligence to improve public health: A narrative review. *Frontiers in Public Health*, 11, 1196397. https://www.frontiersin.org/journals/public-health/articles/10.3389/fpubh.2023.1196397. DOI: 10.3389/fpubh.2023.1196397 PMID: 37954052

Olha, L., & Pavlo, T. (2024). Artificial Intelligence in Law Enforcement : Current State and Development Prospects. *Proceedings of 10th Socratic Lectures 2024*, 120–124. https://www.zf.uni-lj.si/images/zalozba/Sokratska_10_II/12_Lunhol_Olha.pdf

Ølnes, S., & Jansen, A. (2017). Ølnes, S., & Jansen Blockchain technology as s support infrastructure in e-government. In Electronic Government. *Ølnes, S., & Jansen, A. (2017). Blockchain technology as s support infrastructure in egovernment. In Electronic G International conference* (pp. 215-227). Russia: Spring International Publishing.

Ølnes, S., & Jansen, A. (2017). Ølnes, S., & Jansen Blockchain technology as s support infrastructure in e-government. In Electronic Government. Ølnes, S., & Jansen, A. (2017). Blockchain technology as s support infrastructure in egovernment. In Electronic G International conference (pp. 215-227). Russia: Spring International Publishing.

Ølnes, S., Ubacht, J., & Janssen, M. (2017). Blockchain in government: Benefits and implications of distributed ledger technology for information sharing. *Government Information Quarterly*, 34(3), 355–364. DOI: 10.1016/j.giq.2017.09.007

Omorou, A. Y. (2023). Feasibility, Acceptability, Satisfaction and Challenges of mHealth for Community-Based COVID-19 Screening by Community Health Workers in Rwanda: Insight From the E-ASCov Project (Preprint). *JMIR mHealth and uHealth*. Advance online publication. DOI: 10.2196/50745 PMID: 39401131

Ong, E. T., Pang, Y. J., Talib, C. A., Setiawan, R., Ng, J. H., & Por, F. P. (2023). Industrial Revolution (IR) and exemplary AR/ VR-based technological tools in preventive health education: The past, present, and future. *Immersive Virtual and Augmented Reality in Healthcare: An IoT and Blockchain Perspective*, 1–27. DOI: 10.1201/9781003340133-1

Ongena, D. (2024). *4 foundational ways that AI is transforming government. Global Government Lead*. Microsoft.

Onuoha, F. R. (2012). Library in the Clouds: OCLC Systems and Services. *International Digital Library Perspectives*, 29, 762–776.

Oprunenco, A., & Akmeemana, C. (2018). *Using blockchain to make land registry more reliable in India*. LSE Business Review.

Oriazowan, C. (2024). Edo State Government Holds Workshop on E-Government Challenges and Sustainability. Benin City: ICTA Projects and Events, News. Retrieved fromhttps://icta.edostate.gov.ng/2024/05/10/edo-state-government-holds -workshop-on-e- government-challenges-and-sustainability/

Osborne, S. P., & Brown, L. (2011). Innovation, public policy and public services delivery in the UK. The word that would be king? *Public Administration*, 89(4), 1335–1350. DOI: 10.1111/j.1467-9299.2011.01932.x

Ossai-Ugbah, M. S. (2012). A social cognitive theory of internet use and gratifications: Towards a new model of media attendance. *Journal of Broadcasting & Electronic Media*, 48, 358–377.

Overton, M., Larson, S., Carlson, L. J., & Kleinschmit, S. (2022). Public data primacy: The changing landscape of public service delivery as big data gets bigger. *Global Public Policy and Governance*, 2(4), 381–399. DOI: 10.1007/s43508-022-00052-z

Oyekan, A. (2007). The usage of intranet and its impact on organizational knowledge sharing: an explanatory investigation of a public hospital. Retrieved from Express Library: http://epress.lib.uts.edu.au/research/bitstream/handle/10453/20028/02Whole.df?sequence

Ozair, F. F., Jamshed, N., Sharma, A., & Aggarwal, P. (2015). Ethical issues in electronic health records: A general overview. *Perspectives in Clinical Research*, 6(2), 73. DOI: 10.4103/2229-3485.153997 PMID: 25878950

Ozkan-Okay, M., Akin, E., Aslan, Ö., Kosunalp, S., Iliev, T., Stoyanov, I., & Beloev, I. (2024). A Comprehensive Survey: Evaluating the Efficiency of Artificial Intelligence and Machine Learning Techniques on Cyber Security Solutions. *IEEE Access : Practical Innovations, Open Solutions*, 12, 12229–12256. DOI: 10.1109/ACCESS.2024.3355547

Panganiban, G. G. F. (2019). E-governance in agriculture: Digital tools enabling Filipino farmers. *Journal of Asian Public Policy*, 12(1), 51–70. DOI: 10.1080/17516234.2018.1499479

Pani, S. K., Lau, S. L., & Liu, X. (2021). *Blockchain and AI Technology in the Industrial Internet of Things*. Springer. DOI: 10.4018/978-1-7998-6694-7

Pansotra, E., & Singh, S. P. (2015). Cloud Security Algorithms. *International Journal of Security and Its Applications.*, 9(10), 353–360. DOI: 10.14257/ijsia.2015.9.10.32

Papadouli, D. J. V. (2022). *Transparency in Artificial Intelligence: A Legal Perspective. 4.*

Papenfuß, U., & Schmidt, C. A. (2021). Understanding self-regulation for political control and policymaking: Effects of governance mechanisms on accountability. *Governance: An International Journal of Policy, Administration and Institutions*, 34(4), 1115–1141. DOI: 10.1111/gove.12549

Papoutsi, C., Reed, J. E., Marston, C., Lewis, R., Majeed, A., & Bell, D. (2015). Patient and public views about the security and privacy of Electronic Health Records (EHRs) in the UK: Results from a mixed methods study. *BMC Medical Informatics and Decision Making*, 15(1), 1–15. DOI: 10.1186/s12911-015-0202-2 PMID: 26466787

Papyshev, G., & Yarime, M. (2023). The state's role in governing artificial intelligence: Development, control, and promotion through national strategies. *Policy Design and Practice*, 6(1), 79–102. DOI: 10.1080/25741292.2022.2162252

Parviainen, P., Tihinen, M., Kääriäinen, J., & Teppola, S. (2017). Tackling the digitalization challenge: how to benefit from digitalization in practice. *International journal of information systems and project management, 5*(1), 63-77.

Parycek, P., Schmid, V., & Novak, A.-S. (2024). Artificial Intelligence (AI) and Automation in Administrative Procedures: Potentials, Limitations, and Framework Conditions. *Journal of the Knowledge Economy*, 15(2), 8390–8415. DOI: 10.1007/s13132-023-01433-3

Patel, K. (2024). The Importance of Data-Driven Decision-Making in Public Health. *International Journal of Computer Trends and Technology*, 72(5), 27–32. https://doi.org/https://doi.org/10.14445/22312803/IJCTT-V72I5P103. DOI: 10.14445/22312803/IJCTT-V72I5P103

Patel, V. (2019). A framework for secure and decentralized sharing of medical imaging data via blockchain consensus. *Health Informatics Journal*, 25(4), 1398–1411. DOI: 10.1177/1460458218769699 PMID: 29692204

Paul, P. B. Karn, R. Rajesh (2015) Cloud Computing and its Deployment Model: International Journal of Applied Science and Engineering DOI:DOI: 10.5958/2322-0465.2015.00005.2

Pavithra, S., Ramya, S., & Prathibha, S. (2019, February). A survey on cloud security issues and blockchain. In *2019 3rd International Conference on Computing and Communications Technologies (ICCCT)* (pp. 136-140). IEEE.

Pearce, C., & Haikerwal, M. C. (2010). E-health in Australia: Time to plunge into the 21st century. *The Medical Journal of Australia*, 193(7), 397–398. DOI: 10.5694/j.1326-5377.2010.tb03967.x PMID: 20919969

Peeters, P. M., Gössling, S., Klijs, J., Milano, C., Novelli, M., Dijkmans, C. H. S., & Mitas, O. (2018). Research for TRAN Committee-Overtourism: Impact and possible policy responses. European Parliament, Directorate General for Internal Policies, Policy Department B: Structural and Cohesion Policies, Transport and Tourism. *European Union.*

Pencarelli, T. (2020). The digital revolution in the travel and tourism industry. *Information Technology & Tourism*, 22(3), 455–476. DOI: 10.1007/s40558-019-00160-3

Peng, Z., Namyalo, P. K., Chen, X., Lv, M., & Coyte, P. C. (2023). What Motivates Individuals to Share Information With Governments When Adopting Health Technologies During the COVID-19 Pandemic? *BMC Public Health*, 23(1), 2527. Advance online publication. DOI: 10.1186/s12889-023-17437-2 PMID: 38110945

Pereira, G. V., Parycek, P., Falco, E., & Kleinhans, R. (2018). Smart governance in the context of smart cities: A literature review. In *Information Polity* (Vol. 23, Issue 2, pp. 143–162). IOS Press. DOI: 10.3233/IP-170067

Pereira, A., Singh, P., & Kim, J. (2023). Integrating AI, blockchain, and cloud computing for improved public administration: Synergies and impacts. *Public Sector Technology Review*, 20(1), 34–50. DOI: 10.1080/14664505.2023.2141549

Peter, M. K., Wuersch, L., Neher, A., Lindeque, J. P., & Mändli Lerch, K. (2024). The Workplace of the Future: The COVID-19 Pandemic And working From Home In Swiss small Businesses. *Journal of Strategy and Management*, 17(4), 707–729. Advance online publication. DOI: 10.1108/JSMA-09-2023-0248

Petersen, S. A., Pourzolfaghar, Z., Alloush, I., Ahlers, D., Krogstie, J., & Helfert, M. (2019). Value-Added Services, Virtual Enterprises and Data Spaces Inspired Enterprise Architecture for Smart Cities. *IFIP Advances in Information and Communication Technology*, 568, 393–402. Advance online publication. DOI: 10.1007/978-3-030-28464-0_34

Phung, S., Richards, A. C., & Mohammadzadeh, M. (2022). Smart Cities in the Pacific Rim: A mapping of urban evolution in the Pacific. In *The Routledge Handbook of Sustainable Cities and Landscapes in the Pacific Rim* (pp. 670–686). Taylor and Francis. DOI: 10.4324/9781003033530-58

Pietropaoli, I. (2023). *Use of Artificial Intelligence in Legal Practice*. https://www.biicl.org/documents/170_use_of_artificial_intelligence_in_legal_practice_final.pdf

Pilares, Iris Cathrina Abacan, et al. "Addressing the challenges of electronic health records using blockchain and ipfs." *Sensors* 22.11 (2022): 4032.

Pilkington, M. (2016). Blockchain technology: principles and applications. In *Research handbook on digital transformations* (pp. 225–253). Edward Elgar Publishing. DOI: 10.4337/9781784717766.00019

Pourzolfaghar, Z., Bezbradica, M., & Helfert, M. (2016). Types of IT Architectures in Smart Cities – A review from a Business Model and Enterprise Architecture Perspective. *AIS Pre-ICIS Workshop on "IoT & Smart City Challenges and Applications" – ISCA 2016, 1*(1987).

Pratt, B., Parker, M., & Bull, S. (2022). Equitable Design and Use of Digital Surveillance Technologies During COVID-19: Norms and Concerns. *Journal of Empirical Research on Human Research Ethics; JERHRE*, 17(5), 573–586. DOI: 10.1177/15562646221118127 PMID: 36069118

Praveenadevi, D., & Velusamy, C. M., S. K., Gogula, R., Suryadevara, S., & Soans, S. V. (2024). Artificial Intelligence in E-Commerce: Protecting Data and Privacy. In P. K. Goel (Ed.), *Strategies for E-Commerce Data Security: Cloud, Blockchain, AI, and Machine Learning* (pp. 83–112). IGI Global. DOI: 10.4018/979-8-3693-6557-1.ch004

Praveen, G., Singh, P. K., & Ranjan, P. (2024). A Blockchain Integrated IPFS-based System. *International Journal of Intelligent Systems and Applications in Engineering*, 12(13s), 288–301.

Preeti, C., & Vinod, S. (2016, June). Cloud Computing a Survey Report. *International Journal of Recent Research Aspects*, 3, 139–142.

Proskurovska, A., & Dörry, S. (2018). Is a Blockchain-based conveyance system the next step in the financialisation of housing?: The case of Sweden. *The Case of Sweden (September 2018). Luxembourg Institute of Socio-Economic Research (LISER) Working Paper Series, 17.*

Prunkl, C. (2024). Human Autonomy at Risk? An Analysis of the Challenges from AI. *Minds and Machines*, 34(3), 26. DOI: 10.1007/s11023-024-09665-1

Punongbayan, J. (2019). *[ANALYSIS] Dismal PISA rankings: A wake-up call for Filipinos*. Rappler. https://www.rappler.com/voices/thought-leaders/analysis-dismal-programme-international-student-assessment-rankings-wake-up-call-filipinos

Puriwat, W., & Tripopsakul, S. (2021a). Explaining an Adoption and Continuance Intention to Use Contactless Payment Technologies: During the COVID-19 Pandemic. *Emerging Science Journal*, 5(1), 85–95. Advance online publication. DOI: 10.28991/esj-2021-01260

Puriwat, W., & Tripopsakul, S. (2021b). Understanding Food Delivery Mobile Application Technology Adoption: A UTAUT Model Integrating Perceived Fear of COVID-19. *Emerging Science Journal*, 5, 94–104. Advance online publication. DOI: 10.28991/esj-2021-SPER-08

Purves, D. (2022). Fairness in Algorithmic Policing. *Journal of the American Philosophical Association*, 8(4), 741–761. DOI: 10.1017/apa.2021.39

PWC. (2021). *Estonia – the Digital Republic Secured by Blockchain*. Retrieved from https://www.pwc.com/gx/en/services/legal/tech/assets/estonia-the-digital-republic-secured-by-blockchain.pdf

Qin, H., & Li, Z. (2024). *A Study on Enhancing Government Efficiency and Public Trust: The Transformative Role of Artificial Intelligence and Large Language Models*. DOI: 10.5281/ZENODO.12619360

Qualitative Report-Nova Education, 8(4), 2013. Retrieved from http://www.nova.edu/ssss/QR/QR8-4/golafshani.pdf

Quddusi, S. U. H. (2014).. . *Document Management and Cloud Computing: the TQM Journal*, 26(2), 102–108.

Rafi, M., Suswanta, S., Handoko, T., & Effendi, G. N. (2022). Transformation of Public Services through Digital Services in the Covid-19 Era: Efforts Towards Good Governance in Indonesia. International Conference on Public Organization (ICONPO 2021), 209(Iconpo 2021), 168–176. https://doi.org/DOI: 10.2991/AEBMR.K.220209.022

Rai, B. K., Kumar, G., & Balyan, V. (2023). *AI and Blockchain in Healthcare*. SpringerLink., DOI: 10.1007/978-981-99-0377-1

Rajasegar, R. S., Gouthaman, P., Ponnusamy, V., Arivazhagan, N., & Nallarasan, V. (2024). Data Privacy and Ethics in Data Analytics. *Studies in Big Data*, 145, 195–213. DOI: 10.1007/978-981-97-0448-4_10

Ralison Avotra, A. A., Ye, C., Sandra Marcelline, T. R., Ali, A., & Yingfei, Y. (2021). Examining the Impact of E-Government on Corporate Social Responsibility Performance: The Mediating Effect of Mandatory Corporate Social Responsibility Policy, Corruption, and Information and Communication Technologies Development During the COVID Era. *Frontiers in Psychology*, 12, 737100. Advance online publication. DOI: 10.3389/fpsyg.2021.737100 PMID: 34712183

Ramirez, M., Lans-Vargas, L., & Montes, H. M. (2022). Government influence on e-government adoption by citizens in Colombia. Latin America Journal, 25-45. doi:DOI: 10.1371/journal.pone.0264495

Rana, R. (2010). The future of cloud computing. *Analysis*, 1(1), 1–26.

Rani, M. (2024). Impacts and ethics of using Artificial Intelligence (AI) by the Indian Police. *Public Administration and Policy*, 27(2), 182–192. DOI: 10.1108/PAP-06-2023-0081

Rashed, H., Al, S., & Safei, S. (2023). Artificial Intelligence Adoption in Predictive Policing to Predict Crime Mitigation Performance. *International Journal of Sustainable Construction Engineering and Technology*, 14(3), 289–298.

Raskar, R., Nadeau, G., Werner, J., Barbar, R., Mehra, A., Harp, G., Leopoldseder, M., Wilson, B., Flakoll, D., Vepakomma, P., Pahwa, D., Beaudry, R., Flores, E., Popielarz, M., Bhatia, A., Nuzzo, A., Gee, M., Summet, J., Surati, R., & Louisy, K. (2020). COVID-19 Contact-Tracing Mobile Apps: Evaluation and Assessment for Decision Makers. https://arxiv.org/abs/2006.05812v1

Rastogi, (2010) A Model based approach to Implement Cloud Computing in E-Governance," Int. J. Comput. Appl., vol. 9, no. 7, pp. 15–18.

Rawashdeh, A. (2023). The consequences of artificial intelligence: An investigation into the impact of AI on job displacement in accounting. *Journal of Science and Technology Policy Management*. DOI: 10.1108/JSTPM-02-2023-0030

Reamer, F. G. (2023). Artificial Intelligence in Social Work: Emerging Ethical Issues. *International Journal of Social Work Values and Ethics*, 20(2), 52–71. https://doi.org/https://doi.org/10.55521/10-020-205. DOI: 10.55521/10-020-205

Redmiles, E. M. (2020). *User Concerns \&Amp; Tradeoffs in Technology-Facilitated COVID-19 Response*. Digital Government Research and Practice., DOI: 10.1145/3428093

Reen, G. S., Mohandas, M., & Venkatesan, S. (2019, December). *Decentralized patient centric e-health record management system using blockchain and IPFS. In 2019 IEEE conference on information and communication technology*. IEEE.

Reid, S. (2007). Communication channels and adoption of web-based courses by university

Reifels, L., & Murray, V. (2022). Digital Health Emergency Management—Pandemics and Beyond. *JAMA Network Open*, 5(2), e220218–e220218. DOI: 10.1001/jamanetworkopen.2022.0218 PMID: 35195700

Renn, O., Beier, G., & Schweizer, P. J. (2021). The opportunities and risks of digitalisation for sustainable development: a systemic perspective. GAIA - Ecological Perspectives for Science and Society, 30(1), 23–28. https://doi.org/DOI: 10.14512/gaia.30.1.6

Rerung, R. R., & Wahvuni, A., Rinasari, & Susrini, I. (2020). Blueprint of Smart Campus System Using TOGAF ADM. *6th International Conference on Computing, Engineering, and Design, ICCED 2020*. DOI: 10.1109/ICCED51276.2020.9415824

Riemer, K., Ciriello, R., Peter, S., Schlagwein, D., Ågerfalk, P., Conboy, K., & Myers, M. (2020). Digital contact-tracing adoption in the COVID-19 pandemic: IT governance for collective action at the societal level. *European Journal of Information Systems*, 29(6), 731–745. DOI: 10.1080/0960085X.2020.1819898

Rigano, C. (2018). *Using Artificial Intelligence to Address Criminal Justice Needs*. https://nij.ojp.gov/topics/articles/using-artificial-intelligence-address-criminal-justice-needs

Ristenpart, T., Eran, T., Hovav, S., & Stefan, S. (2009). Hey You Get of My Cloud: exploring information leakage in third-party computer clouds retrieved 2019 www.cloud.riste.tech.cornell.edu/papers/clouds.pdf pp.1-14 preofessors. Journal of Interactive Online Learning, 6, 142-158.

Robert, A., Valerie, J., Vincent, L., Filippos, P., Ieva, R., & Lara, V. (2021). The digital economy and the Euro area. *Economic Bulletin Articles, European Central Bank*, 8. https://www.ecb.europa.eu/press/economic bulletin/articles/2021/html/ecb.ebart202008_03~da0f5f792a.en.html#:~:text=Most%20euro%20area%20countries%20have,States%20(see%20Chart%201)

Roberts, K., Lee, T., & Martinez, R. (2024). Ethical and governance issues in AI, blockchain, and cloud computing for public administration. *Ethics and Governance Journal*, 22(2), 145–159. DOI: 10.1007/s12198-024-00123-4

Robertson, C., & Ridge-Newman, A. (2022). The Potential of Artificial Intelligence to Rejuvenate Public Trust in Journalism. In Manninen, V. J. E., Niemi, M. K., & Ridge-Newman, A. (Eds.), *Futures of Journalism* (pp. 127–142). Springer International Publishing., DOI: 10.1007/978-3-030-95073-6_9

Robles, P., & Mallinson, D. J. (2023). Artificial intelligence technology, public trust, and effective governance. *Review of Policy Research*, ropr.12555. DOI: 10.1111/ropr.12555

Rohde, F., Wagner, J., Meyer, A., Reinhard, P., Voss, M., Petschow, U., & Mollen, A. (2024). Broadening the perspective for sustainable artificial intelligence: Sustainability criteria and indicators for Artificial Intelligence systems. *Current Opinion in Environmental Sustainability*, 66, 101411. DOI: 10.1016/j.cosust.2023.101411

Roscoe, R. D., Salehi, S., Nixon, N., Worsley, M., Piech, C., & Luckin, R. (2022). Inclusion and Equity as a Paradigm Shift for Artificial Intelligence in Education. In *Artificial Intelligence in STEM Education*. CRC Press. DOI: 10.1201/9781003181187-28

Rowe, F. (2020). Contact tracing apps and values dilemmas: A privacy paradox in a neo-liberal world. *International Journal of Information Management*, 55, 102178. DOI: 10.1016/j.ijinfomgt.2020.102178 PMID: 32836636

Ruiz-Real, J. L., Uribe-Toril, J., Torres, J. A., & Pablo, J. D. (2021). Artificial intelligence in business and economics research: Trends and future. *Journal of Business Economics and Management*, 22(1), 1. Advance online publication. DOI: 10.3846/jbem.2020.13641

Saberi, M. A., Adda, M., & Mcheick, H. (2022). Break-Glass Conceptual Model for Distributed EHR management system based on Blockchain, IPFS and ABAC. *Procedia Computer Science*, 198, 185–192. DOI: 10.1016/j.procs.2021.12.227

Sabiti, M. Sarika Meher & Bulu, Maharana (2015). Awareness and usage of Cloud Computing Application among LIS Professionals: A case study of 17 Indian University Libraries. Library Philosophy and Practice. Retrieved from http://digitalcommons.unl. edu/cgi/viewcontent.cgi? article=3431& context=libphilprac.

Sadiq, M. S., & Singh, I. P., M., A. M., & A., I. M. (. (2023). Identification of the Leading Economic Sectors of Nigeria: A Typology Juxtapose of Nigerian Economy Vis-À-Vis African Economies. *Jordan Journal of Economic Sciences*, 10(2), 101–115. DOI: 10.35516/jjes.v10i2.1396

Saeed, H., Malik, H., Bashir, U., Ahmad, A., Riaz, S., Ilyas, M., Bukhari, W. A., & Khan, M. I. A. (2022). Blockchain technology in healthcare: A systematic review. *PLoS One*, 17(4), e0266462. Advance online publication. DOI: 10.1371/journal.pone.0266462 PMID: 35404955

Saggi, M. K., & Jain, S. (2018). A survey towards an integration of big data analytics to big insights for value-creation. *Information Processing & Management*, 54(5), 758–790. DOI: 10.1016/j.ipm.2018.01.010

Sahama, T., Simpson, L., & Lane, B. (2013, October). Security and Privacy in eHealth: Is it possible? In *2013 IEEE 15th International Conference on e-Health Networking, Applications and Services (Healthcom 2013)* (pp. 249-253). IEEE.

Saini, K., Roy, A., Chelliah, P. R., & Patel, T. (2021). Blockchain 2.O: A Smart Contract. *2021 International Conference on Computational Performance Evaluation,* ComPE 2021, 524–528. DOI: 10.1109/ComPE53109.2021.9752021

Saluky, S. (2017). Development of Enterprise Architecture Model for Smart City. [Information Technology Engineering Journals]. *ITE Journal*, 2(2), 12–18. Advance online publication. DOI: 10.24235/itej.v2i2.17

Samimi, A. J., Sadeghi, S., & Sadeghi, S. (2011). Tourism and economic growth in developing countries: P-VAR approach. *Middle East Journal of Scientific Research,* 10(1), 28–32. https://www.idosi.org/mejsr/mejsr10(1)11/5.pdf

Saranya, A., & Subhashini, R. (2023). A systematic review of Explainable Artificial Intelligence models and applications: Recent developments and future trends. *Decision analytics journal, 7,* 100230

Sarker, I. H., Kayes, A. S. M., Badsha, S., Alqahtani, H., Watters, P., & Ng, A. (2020). Cybersecurity data science: An overview from machine learning perspective. *Journal of Big Data*, 7(1), 41. DOI: 10.1186/s40537-020-00318-5

Sarzaeim, P., Mahmoud, Q. H., Azim, A., Bauer, G., & Bowles, I. (2023). A Systematic Review of Using Machine Learning and Natural Language Processing in Smart Policing. *Computers*, 12(12), 12. Advance online publication. DOI: 10.3390/computers12120255

Saura, J. R., Ribeiro-Soriano, D., & Palacios-Marqués, D. (2022). Assessing behavioral data science privacy issues in government artificial intelligence deployment. *Government Information Quarterly*, 39(4), 101679. DOI: 10.1016/j.giq.2022.101679

Savin, G. V. (2020). Quality indicator of the smart city transportation and logistics system. *Economic Analysis: Theory and Practice*, 19(11), 2116–2135. DOI: 10.24891/ea.19.11.2116

Savoldelli, A., Misuraca, G., & Codagnone, C. (2013). Measuring the Public value of e-Government: The eGEP2. 0 model. *Electronic Journal of E-Government,* 11(1), 373–388.

Scanlan, O., Siraj, N., Ritchil, P., & Mankin, S. (2024). Is "pro-poor land administration" a realistic proposition? How a land survey in Bangladesh reproduced and reconfigured gendered and racialised poverty. *Land Use Policy*, 138, 107016. DOI: 10.1016/j.landusepol.2023.107016

Schleicher, A. (2019). *PISA 2018: Insights and Interpretations*. https://www.oecd.org/content/dam/oecd/en/about/programmes/edu/pisa/publications/national-reports/pisa-2018/PISA 2018 Insights and Interpretations FINAL PDF.pdf

Scholl, H. J., & Scholl, M. C. (2014). *Smart Governance: A Roadmap for Research and Practice*. DOI: 10.9776/14060

Schöpper, H., Schnelle, J., Kersten, W. (2023) COVID-19: A Catalyst for Digitalization and Transparency?. Industry 4.0 Science, 39. Jg.,Nr. 1, S.72-79. https://doi.org/DOI: 10.30844/I4SE.23.1.72

Sekhari, A., Chatterjee, R., Dwivedi, R., Negi, R., & Shukla, S. (2019). Entangled blockchains in land registry management. *BW3, India, 356*.

Selimi, N., Sadiku, M., & Sadiku, L. (2017). The impact of tourism on economic growth in the Western Balkan countries: An empirical analysis. *International Journal of Business and Economic Sciences Applied Research*, 10(2), 19–25. DOI: 10.25103/ijbesar.102.02

Senadheera, S., Yigitcanlar, T., Desouza, K. C., Mossberger, K., Corchado, J., Mehmood, R., Li, R. Y. M., & Cheong, P. H. (2024). Understanding Chatbot Adoption in Local Governments: A Review and Framework. *Journal of Urban Technology*, •••, 1–35. DOI: 10.1080/10630732.2023.2297665

Sendor, J., Lehmann, Y., Serme, G., & de Oliveira, A. S. (2014, March). Platform-level support for authorization in cloud services with OAuth 2. In *2014 IEEE International Conference on Cloud Engineering* (pp. 458-465). IEEE.

Seymour, T., Frantsvog, D., & Graeber, T. (2012). Electronic Health Records (EHR). [AJHS]. *American Journal of Health Sciences*, 3(3), 201–210. DOI: 10.19030/ajhs.v3i3.7139

Shafritz, J. M., Russell, E. W., Borick, C. P., & Hyde, A. C. (2022). *Introducing Public Administration* (10th Editi). Routledge.

Shah, I. A., Wassan, S., & Usmani, M. H. (2022). E-Government Security and Privacy Issues: Challenges and Preventive Approaches. Https://Services.Igi-Global.Com/Resolvedoi/Resolve.Aspx?Doi=10.4018/978-1-7998-9624-1.Ch004, 61–76. https://doi.org/DOI: 10.4018/978-1-7998-9624-1.ch004

Shang, Q., & Price, A. (2019). A blockchain-based land titling project in the republic of georgia: Rebuilding public trust and lessons for future pilot projects. *Innovations: Technology, Governance, Globalization*, 12(3-4), 72–78. DOI: 10.1162/inov_a_00276

Shan, Y., Ji, M., Xie, W., Lam, K.-Y., & Chow, C.-Y. (2022). Public Trust in Artificial Intelligence Applications in Mental Health Care: Topic Modeling Analysis. *JMIR Human Factors*, 9(4), e38799. DOI: 10.2196/38799 PMID: 36459412

Sharma, A., & Rathod, N. S. (2024). Central Bank Digital Currency: Assessment of Digital Financing Approach Towards Safe Cashless Economy in India. In *Digital Currency Assets and Challenges to Financial System Stability* (pp. 37-51). IGI Global.

Sharma, G. K., Bhardwaj, A., Arya, S., & Singhal, M. (2023). Blockchain in healthcare: Some use cases. *Immersive Virtual and Augmented Reality in Healthcare: An IoT and Blockchain Perspective*, 206–220. DOI: 10.1201/9781003340133-11

Sharma, N. (2018). Tourism led growth hypothesis: Empirical evidence from India. *African Journal of Hospitality, Tourism and Leisure*, 7(2), 1–11. https://www.ajhtl.com/uploads/7/1/6/3/7163688/article_7_vol_7__2__2018.pdf

Sharphathy, M. N., & Sumalatha, V. (2024, March). A Secure Multi Factor Authentication Framework in Cloud Computing. In *2024 5th International Conference on Intelligent Communication Technologies and Virtual Mobile Networks (ICICV)* (pp. 761-767). IEEE.

Shaygan, M., Meese, C., Li, W., Zhao, X. G., & Nejad, M. (2022). Traffic prediction using artificial intelligence: Review of recent advances and emerging opportunities. *Transportation Research Part C, Emerging Technologies*, 145, 103921. DOI: 10.1016/j.trc.2022.103921

Shelfer, D., & Zhang, Y. (2024). A Social Network Analysis of Chronic Violent Offenders. *American Journal of Criminal Justice*, 49(5), 700–722. Advance online publication. DOI: 10.1007/s12103-024-09768-6

Shiji, O. (2016). Economic impact of tourism in India. *The International Journal of Social Sciences (Islamabad)*, 5(1), 35–46. https://ndpublisher.in/admin/issues/IJSSV5N1f.pdf. DOI: 10.5958/2321-5771.2016.00013.2

Shinde, N. K., Seth, A., & Kadam, P. (2023). Exploring the Synergies: A Comprehensive Survey of Blockchain Integration with Artificial Intelligence, Machine Learning, and IoT for Diverse Applications. In Shastri, A. S., Shaw, K., & Singh, M. (Eds.), *Machine Learning and Optimization for Engineering Design* (pp. 1–27). Springer. DOI: 10.1007/978-981-99-7456-6_7

Shin, L. (2016). Republic of Georgia to pilot land titling on blockchain with economist Hernando De Soto, BitFury. *Forbes*, (April), 21.

Shkarlet, S., Oliychenko, I., Dubyna, M., Ditkovska, M., & Zhovtok, V. (2020). Comparative analysis of best practices in E-government implementation and use of this experience by developing countries. *Administratie Si Management Public*, 2020(34), 118–136. DOI: 10.24818/amp/2020.34-07

Shoilekova, K., Ivanova, B., & Andreeva, M. (2024). The Meaning of Business and Software Architecture in the Enterprise Architecture. *Lecture Notes in Networks and Systems, 935 LNNS*. DOI: 10.1007/978-3-031-54820-8_28

Shuaib, M., Alam, S., Ahmed, R., Qamar, S., Nasir, M. S., & Alam, M. S. (2022). Current status, requirements, and challenges of blockchain application in land registry. [IJIRR]. *International Journal of Information Retrieval Research*, 12(2), 1–20. DOI: 10.4018/IJIRR.299934

Sihotang, D. M., Andriqa, M. R., Alfahmi, F. N., Wahyudi, A. S., Herdin Besila, M. A., Yulianang, M. A., Diana, E., & Hidayanto, A. N. (2023). The Moderating Role of Trust in Government Adoption E-Service During Covid-19 Pandemic: Health Belief Model Perspective. *International Journal of Information Technology : an Official Journal of Bharati Vidyapeeth's Institute of Computer Applications and Management*, 15(3), 1545–1553. Advance online publication. DOI: 10.1007/s41870-023-01203-z PMID: 37056795

Singh, A. K., & Jyoti, B. (2023a). Empirical evidence from different income group countries on the interdependency between digitalization and economic development. In Patricia Ordóñez de Pablos and Xi Zhang (Eds.), 5G, Artificial Intelligence, and Next Generation Internet of Things: Digital Innovation for Green and Sustainable Economies, (pp. 44-85). IGI Global. DOI: DOI: 10.4018/978-1-6684-8634-4.ch003

Singh, N. P., Srivastava, S. K., Sharma, S., Anand, Bh., Singh, S., & Ranjith, C. P. (2020). Dynamics of socio-economic factors affecting climate vulnerability and technology adoption: Evidence from Jodhpur district of Rajasthan. *Indian Journal of Traditional Knowledge*, 19(1), 192-196. http://op.niscpr.res.in/index.php/IJTK/article/view/30867/465477393

Singh, A. K. (2025). Causality of digitalization with social sustainability in selected countries. In Siyal, S. (Ed.), *Impact of Digitalization on Education and Social Sustainability* (pp. 39–78). IGI Global., DOI: 10.4018/979-8-3693-1854-6.ch002

Singh, A. K., & Jyoti, B. (2023b). Does digitalization have a bi-directional causal relationship with the entrepreneurship ecosystem? Evidence from a country-wise panel data analysis. In Yanamandra, R., & Indiran, L. (Eds.), *Handbook of Research on Designing Sustainable Strategies to Develop Entrepreneurial Intention* (pp. 178–172). IGI Global., DOI: 10.4018/978-1-6684-8781-5.ch007

Singh, A. K., & Jyoti, B. (2023c). Impact of digitalization on global sustainable development across countries. *Green and Low-carbon Economy*, 4(2), 1–20. DOI: 10.47852/bonviewGLCE32021482

Singh, A. K., & Jyoti, B. (2023d). Empirical investigation for assessing the causality of entrepreneurship ecosystem with entrepreneurial behavior and attitudes across countries. In Abe, E., & Abe, I. (Eds.), *Cases on the Interplay Between Family, Society, and Entrepreneurship* (pp. 315–353). IGI Global., DOI: 10.4018/978-1-6684-8748-8.ch012

Singh, A. K., & Kumar, S. (2022). Factors influencing entrepreneurship ecosystem and economic development: Evidence from cross-sectional country-wise imbalanced panel data analysis. *The IUP Journal of Entrepreneurship Development*, 19(3), 24–47.

Singh, A. K., Kumar, S., & Gupta, M. (2024e). Relationship between digitalization and environmental sustainability in selected countries. In Yıldırım, S., Yıldırım, D., Demirtaş, I., & Kandpal, V. (Eds.), *Green Transition Impacts on the Economy, Society, and Environment* (pp. 83–107). IGI Global., DOI: 10.4018/979-8-3693-3985-5.ch006

Singh, A. K., Kumar, S., & Jyoti, B. (2023). Does entrepreneurship ecosystem have a causal relationship with economic development? A country-wise imbalanced panel data investigation. In Magd, H., Khan, S. A., Nte, N. D., & Sarim, M. (Eds.), *Entrepreneurship and Economic Sustainability* (pp. 1–15)., https://www.researchgate.net/publication/366353165_Does_Entrepreneurship_Ecosystem_have_a_Causal_Relationship_with_Economic_Development_A_Country-wise_Imbalanced_Panel_Data_Investigation

Singh, A. K., Singh, R., & Singh, R. (2024a). Impact of digitalization on sustainable development in G20 countries. In Ahmed, E. (Ed.), *Developing Digital Inclusion Through Globalization and Digitalization* (pp. 287–335). IGI Global., DOI: 10.4018/979-8-3693-4111-7.ch013

Singh, A. K., Singh, S., & Gupta, M. (2024c). A literature review for the association of social media with micro and small enterprises in India. In Hossain, S. (Ed.), *Cases on Social Media and Entrepreneurship* (pp. 38–62). IGI Global., DOI: 10.4018/979-8-3693-1781-5.ch003

Singh, A. K., Singh, S., & Sankaranarayanan, K. G. S. (2024b). A comparative performance of green technology, green growth, social, and economic development in India and China. In Ordóñez de Pablos, P. (Ed.), *Digital Technologies for a Resource Efficient Economy* (pp. 107–141). IGI Global., DOI: 10.4018/979-8-3693-2750-0.ch006

Singh, A., & Gupta, S. (2023). Security and privacy in cloud computing for public administration. *Journal of Cloud Computing and Security*, 11(4), 265–280. DOI: 10.1016/j.jcc.2023.108794

Singhal, A., Neveditsin, N., Tanveer, H., & Mago, V. (2024). Toward Fairness, Accountability, Transparency, and Ethics in AI for Social Media and Health Care: Scoping Review. *JMIR Medical Informatics*, 12, e50048. DOI: 10.2196/50048 PMID: 38568737

Singh, N. P., Bhawna, A., Surendra, S., & Arshad, Kh. (2019). Mainstreaming climate adaptation in Indian rural developmental agenda: A micro-macro convergence. *Climate Risk Management*, 29(1), 30–41. https://www.sciencedirect.com/science/article/pii/S221209631830130X. DOI: 10.1016/j.crm.2019.04.003

Singh, S. (2020). Farmers' perception of climate change and adaptation decisions: A micro-level evidence from Bundelkhand Region, India. *Ecological Indicators*, 116(1), 1–10. https://www.sciencedirect.com/science/article/abs/pii/S1470160X2030412X. DOI: 10.1016/j.ecolind.2020.106475

Sipahi, E. B., & Saayi, Z. (2024). The world s first Smart Nation vision: the case of Singapore. *Smart Cities and Regional Development Journal, 8*(1), 41–58. https://doi.org/http://dx.doi.org/10.25019/dvm98x09

Sivakumar, P., NandhaKumar, M., Jayaraj, R., & Kumaran, A. S. (2019, March). Securing data and reducing the time traffic using AES encryption with dual cloud. In *2019 IEEE International Conference on System, Computation, Automation and Networking (ICSCAN)* (pp. 1-5). IEEE.

Siyal, A. A., Junejo, A. Z., Zawish, M., Ahmed, K., Khalil, A., & Soursou, G. (2019). Applications of blockchain technology in medicine and healthcare: Challenges and future perspectives. *Cryptography*, 3(1), 1–16. DOI: 10.3390/cryptography3010003

Smidt, H. J., & Jokonya, O. (2021). The challenge of privacy and security when using technology to track people in times of COVID-19 pandemic. *Procedia Computer Science*, 181, 1018–1026. DOI: 10.1016/j.procs.2021.01.281 PMID: 33643498

Snowdon, J. L., Kassler, W., Karunakaram, H., Dixon, B. E., & Rhee, K. (2021). Leveraging Informatics and Technology to Support Public Health Response: Framework and Illustrations Using COVID-19. *Online Journal of Public Health Informatics*, 13(1). Advance online publication. DOI: 10.5210/ojphi.v13i1.11072 PMID: 33936521

Soh, S., Ho, S. H., Seah, A., Ong, J., Dickens, B. S., Tan, K. W., Koo, J. R., Cook, A. R., Tan, K. B., Sim, S., Ng, L. C., & Lim, J. T. (2021). Economic impact of dengue in Singapore from 2010 to 2020 and the cost-effectiveness of Wolbachia interventions. *PLOS Global Public Health*, 1(10), e0000024. DOI: 10.1371/journal.pgph.0000024 PMID: 36962069

Solove, D. J. (2006). The digital person and the future of privacy. In Strandburg, K. J., & Raicu, D. S. (Eds.), *Privacy and Technologies of Identity*. Springer., DOI: 10.1007/0-387-28222-X_1

Soner, S., Litoriya, R., & Pandey, P. (2021). Exploring blockchain and smart contract technology for reliable and secure land registration and record management. *Wireless Personal Communications*, 121(4), 2495–2509. DOI: 10.1007/s11277-021-08833-1

Song, J. (2021). Ethical adaptation and legal regulation of modern technology. *Cultura e Scuola*, 4(3), 169–178. DOI: 10.1177/20966083211053085

Spacey, A. (2013). Library services in electronic environment:Changes, challenges issues and strtegies. Kaveri. doi:doi=10.1.1460.5639_pdf.

Spain, I. D. C. (2023). *IDC FutureScape: Worldwide Government 2023 Predictions*. Retrieved from https://www.idc.com/getdoc.jsp?containerId=prES48722621

Sposato, M. (2024a). Are leaders born or made? Asking the right question. *Development and Learning in Organizations*, 38(3), 1–3. DOI: 10.1108/DLO-05-2023-0123

Sposato, M. (2024b). Leadership training and development in the age of artificial intelligence. *Development and Learning in Organizations*, 38(4), 4–7. DOI: 10.1108/DLO-12-2023-0256

Sposato, M. (2025). Developing Digital Leadership Skills for AI-Driven Research Environments. In *Impacts of Generative AI on the Future of Research and Education* (pp. 235–254). IGI Global., DOI: 10.4018/979-8-3693-0884-4.ch010

Srivastava, R. K., Gupta, A., & Sharma, G. (2023). Forecasting Crime Rate Using Artificial Intelligence Applications. *2023 International Conference on Sustainable Communication Networks and Application (ICSCNA)*, 1222–1226. DOI: 10.1109/ICSCNA58489.2023.10370364

Stecyk, A., & Miciuła, I. (2023). Harnessing the Power of Artificial Intelligence for Collaborative Energy Optimization Platforms. *Energies*, 16(13), 5210. DOI: 10.3390/en16135210

Steiner, C. (2006). Tourism, poverty reduction and the political economy: Egyptian perspectives on tourism's economic benefits in a semi-rentier state. *Tourism and Hospitality Planning & Development*, 3(3), 161–177. DOI: 10.1080/14790530601132286

Stephany, F. (2020). It's Not Only Size That Matters: Determinants of Estonia's E-Governance Success. *Electronic Government, an International Journal, 16*(1), 1. DOI: 10.1504/EG.2020.10028669

Stephen Tochukwu, N., Methodius Ugwu, C., & Oluchukwu Wogu, J. (2021). Digital Learning in Post COVID-19 Era: Policy Options and Prospects for Quality Education in Nigeria. Library Philosophy and Practice, 1–18, 1–18. https://digitalcommons.unl.edu/libphilprac

Stoll, M., & Laner, D. (2014). *Performance improvement in public administrations by organizational learning*. Springer., DOI: 10.1007/978-3-319-06773-5_1

Sucgang, D. C., Villanueva, J. T., Macawile, N. C. C., Antivo, R. C., & Tipay, I. P. R. (2015). iSERVE-An Android Based Artificial Intelligence Emergency CP(Crime Prevention) Response System Using GPS Tracker. *International Journal of Conceptions on Computing and Information Technology*, 3(3), 105–108. https://studyres.com/doc/7934797/iserve--an-android-based-artificial-intelligence-emergenc

Suciu, G. (2013). Study on advantages and disadvantages of Cloud Computing: the advantages of telemetry applications in cloud. https://www.mobcomm.pub.ro/wp - content/uploads/2016/04/GeorgeSuciu_PhD-Thesis-Summary_v7.pdf

Sujan, M. S. H., Tasnim, R., Islam, M. S., Ferdous, M. Z., Haghighathoseini, A., Koly, K. N., & Pardhan, S. (2022). Financial hardship and mental health conditions in people with underlying health conditions during the COVID-19 pandemic in Bangladesh. *Heliyon*, 8(9), e10499. Advance online publication. DOI: 10.1016/j.heliyon.2022.e10499 PMID: 36060462

Sukmono, F. G., & Surya Kencana, A. P. (2023). *Pola Baru Pengelolaan Media Digital Dalam Instagram @Humasjogja. Mediator*. Jurnal Komunikasi., DOI: 10.29313/mediator.v15i2.10705

Sun, Y., Zhang, R., Wang, X., Gao, K., & Liu, L. (2018). A decentralizing attribute-based signature for healthcare blockchain. *Proceedings - International Conference on Computer Communications and Networks, ICCCN, 2018-July*. DOI: 10.1109/ICCCN.2018.8487349

Sun, T. Q., & Medaglia, R. (2019). Mapping the challenges of Artificial Intelligence in the public sector: Evidence from public healthcare. *Government Information Quarterly*, 36(2), 368–383. DOI: 10.1016/j.giq.2018.09.008

Surden, H. (2019). Artificial Intelligence and Law : An Overview. *Georgia State University Law Review*, 35(4), 1305–1337.

Swan, M. (2015). *Blockchain: Blueprint for a new economy*. O'Reilly Media, Inc.

Swapna G & Biradar B. S (2017). Application of Cloud Computing Technology in Libraries: International Journal of library and information studies,7(1);52-61

Swapna, G. & Biradar (2007). Application of Cloud Computing Technology in Libraries, International Journal of Library & Information Science https://ijlis.org

Swapna, G., & Birader, B. S. (2017). *Information literacy model for higher education institutions in India*. International Journal of Digital Library Service.

Syed Aun, M. (2021). *Naqvi, Tahir Alyas, Nadia Tabassum, Abdallah Namoun, H. H. N.* Post Pandemic World and Challenges for E-Governance Framework. International Journal of Advanced Trends in Computer Science and Engineering., DOI: 10.30534/ijatcse/2021/1571032021

Ta, A. W. A., Goh, H. L., Ang, C., Koh, L. Y., Poon, K., & Miller, S. M. (2022). Two Singapore public healthcare AI applications for national screening programs and other examples. *Health Care Science*, 1(2), 41–57. DOI: 10.1002/hcs2.10 PMID: 38938890

Tabuga, A. D., Domingo, S. N., Diokno-Sicat, C. J., Ulep, V., & Gilbert, T. (2020). Innovating governance: Building resilience against COVID-19 pandemic and other risks. Philippine Institute for Development Studies (PIDS), Quezon City. https://www.econstor.eu/handle/10419/241012

Takagi, H., Esteban, M., Mikami, T., & Fujii, D. (2016). Projection of coastal floods in 2050 Jakarta. *Urban Climate*, 17, 135–145. DOI: 10.1016/j.uclim.2016.05.003

Tamm, T., Seddon, P. B., Shanks, G., & Reynolds, P. (2011). How does enterprise architecture add value to organisations? *Communications of the Association for Information Systems*, 28(1). Advance online publication. DOI: 10.17705/1CAIS.02810

Tang, R. (2023). Digital economy drives tourism development—Empirical evidence based on the UK. *Ekonomska Istrazivanja*, 36(1), 2003–2020. DOI: 10.1080/1331677X.2022.2094443

Team, E. M. B. (2024). *Cloud Computing in E-Government Services*. Home Technology Cloud Computing in E-Government Services.

Tee, M. K. (2024). Malaysia's smart tourism framework. In Kumar, S., Talukder, M. B., & Pego, A. (Eds.), *Utilizing Smart Technology and AI in Hybrid Tourism and Hospitality* (pp. 51–78). IGI Global., DOI: 10.4018/979-8-3693-1978-9.ch003

Thakur, V., Doja, M. N., Dwivedi, Y. K., Ahmad, T., & Khadanga, G. (2020). Land records on blockchain for implementation of land titling in India. *International Journal of Information Management*, 52, 101940. DOI: 10.1016/j.ijinfomgt.2019.04.013

The Joanna Briggs Institute. (2015). The Joanna Briggs Institute Reviewers' Manual 2015 Methodology for JBI Scoping Reviews. Retrieved May 6, 2024, from The Joanna Briggs Institute website: https://reben.com.br/revista/wp-content/uploads/2020/10/Scoping.pdf

The Open Group. (2022). The Open Group Standard The TOGAF® Standard, Version 10. In *The TOGAF® Standard, Version 10.*

The State Council of The People's Republic of China. (2017, July 20). China issues guideline on artificial intelligence development. [English translation]. english.gov.cn. Retrieved from http://www.english.gov.cn/policies/latest_releases/2017/07/20/content_281474.htm

The World Bank. (2024). *Transformative technologies (AI) challenges and principles of regulation*. Digital Regulation Platform. https://digitalregulation.org/3004297-2/

Theophilus, O. C. (2013). Information communication technology support for an e-learning environment at university of Lagos. Library Philosophy and Practice (e-journal). Retrieved from http://epress.lib.uts.edu.au/research/bitstream/handle/10453/20028/02Whole.pdf?sequenc e e=2.

Thiyagarajan, B., & Kamalakannan, R. (2014, February). Data integrity and security in cloud environment using AES algorithm. In *International Conference on Information Communication and Embedded Systems (ICICES2014)* (pp. 1-5). IEEE.

ThomsonReuters.com. (2023). *e-Estonia: The Power and Potential of Digital Identity*. Retrieved from https://www.thomsonreuters.com/en-us/posts/news-and-media/e-estonia-power-potential-digital-identity/

Tian, C. (2017). Ukrainian Government to Start Blockchain Land Registry Trial in October. *CoinDesk News*, 23, 2017.

Tian, N., Zheng, J.-X., Li, L.-H., Xue, J.-B., Xia, S., Lv, S., & Zhou, X.-N. (2024). Precision Prediction for Dengue Fever in Singapore: A Machine Learning Approach Incorporating Meteorological Data. *Tropical Medicine and Infectious Disease*, 9(4), 4. Advance online publication. DOI: 10.3390/tropicalmed9040072 PMID: 38668533

Tirumala, S. S., Sathu, H., & Naidu, V. (2015, December). Analysis and prevention of account hijacking based incidents in cloud environment. In *2015 international Conference on Information Technology (ICIT)* (pp. 124-129). IEEE.

Tiwari, R. (2023). The Impact of AI and Machine Learning on Job Displacement and Employment Opportunities. *INTERANTIONAL JOURNAL OF SCIENTIFIC RESEARCH IN ENGINEERING AND MANAGEMENT*, 07(01). Advance online publication. DOI: 10.55041/IJSREM17506

Torfing, J., & Ansell, C. (2017). Strengthening political leadership and policy innovation through the expansion of collaborative forms of governance. *Public Management Review*, 19(1), 37–54. DOI: 10.1080/14719037.2016.1200662

Toufaily, E., Zalan, T., & Dhaou, S. B. (2021). A framework of blockchain technology adoption: An investigation of challenges and expected value. *Information & Management*, 58(3), 103444. DOI: 10.1016/j.im.2021.103444

Tran, G. A., Ketron, S., Tran, T. P., & Fabrize, R. (2023). Personalization, value co-creation, and brand loyalty in branded apps: An application of TAM theory. *Journal of Strategic Marketing*, •••, 1–20.

Tricco, A. C., Lillie, E., Zarin, W., O'Brien, K. K., Colquhoun, H., Levac, D., Moher, D., Peters, M. D. J., Horsley, T., Weeks, L., Hempel, S., Akl, E. A., Chang, C., McGowan, J., Stewart, L., Hartling, L., Aldcroft, A., Wilson, M. G., Garritty, C., & Straus, S. E. (2018). PRISMA Extension for Scoping Reviews (PRISMA-ScR): Checklist and Explanation. *Annals of Internal Medicine*, 169(7), 467–473. DOI: 10.7326/M18-0850 PMID: 30178033

Truc Nguyen, T. T. (2023). Citizens' Intentions to Use E-Government During the COVID-19 Pandemic: Integrating the Technology Acceptance Model and Perceived Risk Theory. *Kybernetes*, 52(7), 2329–2346. Advance online publication. DOI: 10.1108/K-07-2022-1023

Tsolakis, N., Schumacher, R., Dora, M., & Kumar, M. (2023). Artificial intelligence and blockchain implementation in supply chains: A pathway to sustainability and data monetisation? *Annals of Operations Research*, 327(1), 157–210. DOI: 10.1007/s10479-022-04785-2 PMID: 35755830

Tugendhat, T. (2023, October 31). Fraud and AI. [Speech delivered at the AI Safety Summit]. GOV.UK. https://www.gov.uk/government/speeches/security-minister-speech-on-fraud-and-ai

Tyma, B., Dhillon, R., Sivabalan, P., & Wieder, B. (2022). Understanding accountability in blockchain systems. *Accounting, Auditing & Accountability Journal*, 35(7), 1625–1655. DOI: 10.1108/AAAJ-07-2020-4713

UAE Ministry of State for Artificial Intelligence. (2018, February). UAE National Strategy for Artificial Intelligence 2031 [PDF]. Retrieved from https://www.aicouncil.ae/media/publications/4177/uae-national-strategy-for-artificial-intelligence-2031.pdf

Uche, D. B., Osuagwu, O. B., Nwosu, S. N., & Otika, U. S. (2021). Integrating trust into technology acceptance model (TAM), the conceptual framework for e-payment platform acceptance. *British Journal of Management and Marketing Studies*, 4(4), 34–56.

Uhrig, R. E. (n.d.). Introduction to artificial neural networks. *Proceedings of IECON '95 - 21st Annual Conference on IEEE Industrial Electronics, 1*, 33–37. DOI: 10.1109/IECON.1995.483329

Ullah, A., Pinglu, C., Ullah, S., Abbas, H. S. M., & Khan, S. (2021). The Role of E-Governance in Combating COVID-19 and Promoting Sustainable Development: A Comparative Study of China and Pakistan. *Chinese Political Science Review*, 6(1), 86–118. DOI: 10.1007/s41111-020-00167-w

Ullah, S., Khan, F. U., Trifan, V. A., Spînu, A. E., & Sanda, G. (2022). Modeling Key Strategies for Reducing Socio-Economic and Health Crisis: Perspective From COVID-19 Pandemic. *International Journal of Environmental Research and Public Health*, 19(21), 14127. Advance online publication. DOI: 10.3390/ijerph192114127 PMID: 36361010

Ulmanen, S., Hirvonen, M., Tattersall, P., Ristikari, T., Kuo, V., Virta, P., Jurvonen, T., & Niemelä, M. (2024). Description of crowdsourcing and AI-based tool for knowledge management and systems change in public services. *International Journal on Management of Innovation & Technology*, 21(04), 2450027. DOI: 10.1142/S0219877024500275

Um, S., & Crompton, J. L. (1990). Attitude determinations in tourism destination choice. *Annals of Tourism Research*, 17(1), 432–448. DOI: 10.1016/0160-7383(90)90008-F

United Nations Children's Fund and Southeast Asian Ministers of Education Organization. (2020). *SEA-PLM 2019 Main Regional Report, Children's learning in 6 Southeast Asian countries*. https://www.seaplm.org/PUBLICATIONS/regional results/SEA-PLM 2019 Main Regional Report.pdf

University of the Philippines. (2023). *Principles for Responsible and Trustworthy Artificial Intelligence*. https://up.edu.ph/up-principles-for-responsible-artificial-intelligence/

UP Media and Public Relations Office. (2020). *UP Resilience Institute introduces COVID chatbot*. https://up.edu.ph/up-resilience-institute-introduces-covid-chatbot/

Upadhyaya, A., & Bansal, M. (2015, March). Deployment of secure sharing: Authenticity and authorization using cryptography in cloud environment. In *2015 International Conference on Advances in Computer Engineering and Applications* (pp. 852-855). IEEE.

Uwizeyimana, T., Hashim, H. T., Kabakambira, J. D., Mujyarugamba, J. C., Dushime, J., Ntacyabukura, B., Ndayizeye, R., Adebisi, Y. A., & Lucero-Prisno, D. E.III. (2021). Drug Supply Situation in Rwanda During COVID-19: Issues, Efforts and Challenges. *Journal of Pharmaceutical Policy and Practice*, 14(1), 12. Advance online publication. DOI: 10.1186/s40545-021-00301-2 PMID: 33472702

Uwizeyimana, T., Manirambona, E., Musa, S. S., Uwiringiyimana, E., Bazimya, D., & Mathewos, K. (2023). Achieving COVID-19 Herd Immunity in Rwanda, Africa. *Public Health Challenges*, 2(1), e75. Advance online publication. DOI: 10.1002/puh2.75

Uzoma, J., Falana, O., Obunadike, C., Oloyede, K., & Obunadike, E. (2023). Using artificial intelligence for automated incidence response in cybersecurity. [IJIT]. *International Journal of Information Technology : an Official Journal of Bharati Vidyapeeth's Institute of Computer Applications and Management*, 1(4).

Valle-Cruz, D., Alejandro Ruvalcaba-Gomez, E., Sandoval-Almazan, R., & Ignacio Criado, J. (2019). A Review of Artificial Intelligence in Government and its Potential from a Public Policy Perspective. *Proceedings of the 20th Annual International Conference on Digital Government Research*, 91–99. DOI: 10.1145/3325112.3325242

Valle-Cruz, D., Criado, J. I., Sandoval-Almazán, R., & Ruvalcaba-Gómez, E. A. (2021). Assessing the public policy-cycle framework in the age of artificial intelligence: From agenda-setting to policy evaluation. *Government Information Quarterly*, 37(4), 101509. DOI: 10.1016/j.giq.2020.101509

Valle-Cruz, D., & García-Contreras, R. (2023). Towards AI-driven transformation and smart data management: Emerging technological change in the public sector value chain. *Public Policy and Administration*, 09520767231188401, 09520767231188401. Advance online publication. DOI: 10.1177/09520767231188401

Valle-Cruz, D., García-Contreras, R., & Gil-Garcia, J. R. (2024). Exploring the negative impacts of artificial intelligence in government: The dark side of intelligent algorithms and cognitive machines. *International Review of Administrative Sciences*, 90(2), 353–368. https://doi-org.sheffield.idm.oclc.org/10.1177/00208523231187051. DOI: 10.1177/00208523231187051 van Noordt, C., & Misuraca, G. (2022). Artificial intelligence for the public sector: Results of landscaping the use of AI in government across the European Union. *Government Information Quarterly*, 39(3), 101714. https://doi.org/https://doi.org/10.1016/j.giq.2022.101714. DOI: 10.1016/j.giq.2022.101714

van Wynsberghe, A. (2021). Sustainable AI: AI for sustainability and the sustainability of AI. *AI and Ethics*, 1(3), 213–218. DOI: 10.1007/s43681-021-00043-6

Vardavas, C., Odani, S., Nikitara, K., El Banhawi, H., Kyriakos, C., Taylor, L., & Becuwe, N. (2021). Public perspective on the governmental response, communication and trust in the governmental decisions in mitigating COVID-19 early in the pandemic across the G7 countries. *Preventive Medicine Reports*, 21, 101252. DOI: 10.1016/j.pmedr.2020.101252 PMID: 33364149

Varona, D., & Suárez, J. L. (2022). Discrimination, Bias, Fairness, and Trustworthy AI. *Applied Sciences (Basel, Switzerland)*, 12(12), 5826. DOI: 10.3390/app12125826

Varsha, R., Nair, S. M., Tyagi, A. K., Aswathy, S. U., & RadhaKrishnan, R. (2021). The Future with Advanced Analytics: A Sequential Analysis of the Disruptive Technology's Scope. In A. Abraham, T. Hanne, O. Castillo, N. Gandhi, T. Nogueira Rios, & T.-P. Hong (Eds.), *Hybrid Intelligent Systems* (pp. 565–579). Springer International Publishing. DOI: 10.1007/978-3-030-73050-5_56

Vasylieva, T. A., Kryklii, O. A., & Petrushenko, Y. M. (2021). Digital inclusion of population: economic, social, educational determinants in the COVID-19 era. Centre of Sociological Research. https://essuir.sumdu.edu.ua/handle/123456789/86161

Veale, M., & Brass, I. (2019). Administration by algorithm? Public management meets public sector machine learning. In Yeung, K., & Lodge, M. (Eds.), *Algorithmic Regulation* (pp. 121–149). Oxford University Press. DOI: 10.1093/oso/9780198838494.003.0006

Venkatesh, M., & Raj, D. J. (2016). Impact of tourism in India. *International Journal of Scientific Engineering and Applied Science*, 2(1), 167–184. https://ijseas.com/volume2/v2i1/ijseas20160119.pdf

Verma, V. (2021) Role of e-governance and digital India in empowering Indian citizens https://blog.ipleaders.in/role-e-governance-digital-india-empowering-indian-citizens

Verma, V., Kumar, P., Verma, R. K., & Priya, S. (2021). *"A Novel Approach for Security in Cloud Data Storage Using AES-DES-RSA Hybrid Cryptography," 2021 Emerging Trends in Industry 4.0 (ETI 4.0)*. Raigarh., DOI: 10.1109/ETI4.051663.2021.9619274

Vila, N. A., Cardoso, L., Archi, Y. E., & Brea, J. A. F. (2024). The role of digital technology and sustainable practices in tourists' decision making. In El Archi, Y., Benbba, B., Dávid, L. D., & Cardoso, L. (Eds.), *Promoting Responsible Tourism with Digital Platforms* (pp. 1–19). IGI Global., DOI: 10.4018/979-8-3693-3286-3.ch003

Villarica, M. V., Balahadia, F. F., Asor, J. R., & Catedrilla, G. M. B. (2022). Development of crime reporting system to identify patterns of crime in laguna. *International Journal of Computing Sciences Research*, 6. Advance online publication. DOI: 10.25147/ijcsr.2017.001.1.110

Villegas-Ch, W., & García-Ortiz, J. (2023). Toward a Comprehensive Framework for Ensuring Security and Privacy in Artificial Intelligence. In *Electronics* (Vol. 12, Issue 18). DOI: 10.3390/electronics12183786

Vimalachandran, P., Wang, H., Zhang, Y., & Zhuo, G. (2017). The Australian PCEHR system: ensuring privacy and security through an improved access control mechanism. *arXiv preprint arXiv:1710.07778.*

Vlahovic, N., & Vracic, T. (2015). An Overview of E-Government 3.0 Implementation. *In Encyclopedia of Information Science and Technology, Third Edition (p,* 2700–2708. Zhang, Z., Chen, Z., & Xu, L. (2022). Artificial intelligence and moral dilemmas: Perception of ethical decision-making in AI. *Journal of Experimental Social Psychology, 101*, 104327. DOI: 10.1016/j.jesp.2022.104327

Wada, I. (2014). Cloud Computing Implementation in Libraries: A Synergy for Library Services Optimization. *International Journal of Library and Information Science*, 10(2), 17–27.

Walden, I., & Michels, J. D. (2024). Getting Critical: Making Sense of the EU Cybersecurity Framework for Cloud Providers. In Carneiro Pacheco de Andrade, F. A., Fernandes Freitas, P. M., & de Sousa Covelo de Abreu, J. R. (Eds.), *Legal Developments on Cybersecurity and Related Fields. Law, Governance and Technology Series* (Vol. 60). Springer., DOI: 10.1007/978-3-031-41820-4_2

Wang, C., Han, B., Patel, B., & Rudin, C. (2023). In pursuit of interpretable, fair and accurate machine learning for criminal recidivism prediction. *Journal of Quantitative Criminology*, 39(2), 519–581. DOI: 10.1007/s10940-022-09545-w

Wang, C., Teo, T. S. H., & Janssen, M. (2021). Public and private value creation using artificial intelligence: An empirical study of AI voice robot users in Chinese public sector. *International Journal of Information Management*, 61, 102401. DOI: 10.1016/j.ijinfomgt.2021.102401

Wang, L., Jin, J. L., Yang, D., & Zhou, K. Z. (2020). Inter-partner control, trust, and radical innovation of IJVs in China: A contingent governance perspective. *Industrial Marketing Management*, 88, 70–83. DOI: 10.1016/j.indmarman.2020.04.018

Wang, Q., & Guan, Z. (2023). Can Sunlight Disperse Mistrust? A Meta-Analysis of the Effect of Transparency on Citizens' Trust in Government. *Journal of Public Administration: Research and Theory*, 33(3), 453–467. DOI: 10.1093/jopart/muac040

Wang, Q., & Huang, R. (2021). The impact of COVID-19 pandemic on sustainable development goals – A survey. *Environmental Research*, 202, 111637. DOI: 10.1016/j.envres.2021.111637 PMID: 34233155

Wang, Q., & Qin, S. (2021). A hyperledger fabric-based system framework for healthcare data management. *Applied Sciences (Basel, Switzerland)*, 11(24), 11693. Advance online publication. DOI: 10.3390/app112411693

Wang, Q., Su, M., Zhang, M., & Li, R. (2021). Integrating Digital Technologies and Public Health to Fight Covid-19 Pandemic: Key Technologies, Applications, Challenges and Outlook of Digital Healthcare. *International Journal of Environmental Research and Public Health*, 18(11), 6053. Advance online publication. DOI: 10.3390/ijerph18116053 PMID: 34199831

Wang, X., Weng, Z., Liu, L., & Liu, J. (2024). Factors That Facilitated the Development of Blockchain Technology in the AEC Industry: Study Based on System Dynamics. *Journal of Management Engineering*, 40(6), 04024049. DOI: 10.1061/JMENEA.MEENG-6137

Wanjiru, I. R., & Xiaoguang, L. (2021). Evaluating University–Community Engagement Through a Community-Based Lens: What Indicators Are Suitable? *Journal of Higher Education Outreach & Engagement*, 25(4), 133–146.

Warsono, H., Hanani, R., & Rahman, A. Z. (2023). *Local Governments' Financial Accountability Responses in Critical Time: Reflection From Intergovernmental Management in Indonesia During the Early Covid-19 Pandemic*. Academic Journal of Interdisciplinary Studies., DOI: 10.36941/ajis-2023-0025

Wescott, C. G. (2023). *E-government and the applications of technology to. working paper of Pacific Basin Research Center, and chapter in Dennis A. Rondinelli*. Pacific Region., https://www.unapcict.org/sites/default/files/2019-01/e-Government%20and%20the%20Applications%20of%20Technology%20to%20Government%20Services.pdf

Whig, P., Kouser, S., Sharma, A., Bhatia, A. B., & Nadikattu, R. R. (2023). AR/VR revolutions in future healthcare. *Immersive Virtual and Augmented Reality in Healthcare: An IoT and Blockchain Perspective*, 96–118. DOI: 10.1201/9781003340133-6

Wibowo, A. (2023). Enhancing Digital Transformation through Digital Innovation in the Context of Economic Advancement in the Era of Economic Society 5.0. Proceeding of Applied Science. *Educational Technology*, 1(1), 1–13. https://conferences.unusa.ac.id/index.php/paset/article/view/1313

Widodo, J. S., Kristiawanto, K., & Chandra, T. Y. (2021). *The Study of Implementation Effectiveness in the Various Criminal Law Policies During the Covid-19 Pandemic*. Kanun Jurnal Ilmu Hukum., DOI: 10.24815/kanun.v23i3.21912

Willem, L., Abrams, S., Libin, P. J. K., Coletti, P., Kuylen, E., Petrof, O., Møgelmose, S., Wambua, J., Herzog, S. A., Faes, C., Beutels, P., & Hens, N. (2021). The impact of contact tracing and household bubbles on deconfinement strategies for COVID-19. Nature Communications 2021 12:1, 12(1), 1–9. https://doi.org/DOI: 10.1038/s41467-021-21747-7

Wilson, A., & Tewdwr-Jones, M. (2021). Digital participatory planning: Citizen engagement, democracy, and design. Digital Participatory Planning: Citizen Engagement, Democracy, and Design, 1–292. https://doi.org/DOI: 10.4324/9781003190639/DIGITAL-PARTICIPATORY-PLANNING-ALEXANDER-WILSON-MARK-TEWDWR-JONES

Wirtz, B. W., Weyerer, J. C., & Geyer, C. (2019). Artificial Intelligence and the Public Sector—Applications and Challenges. *International Journal of Public Administration*, 42(7), 596–615. DOI: 10.1080/01900692.2018.1498103

Wirtz, B. W., Weyerer, J. C., & Sturm, B. J. (2020). The Dark Sides of Artificial Intelligence: An Integrated AI Governance Framework for Public Administration. *International Journal of Public Administration*, 43(9), 818–829. DOI: 10.1080/01900692.2020.1749851

World Economic Forum. (2020). *The Future of Jobs Report*. https://www3.weforum.org/docs/WEF_Future_of_Jobs_2020.pdf

World Economic Forum. (2024). Global Cybersecurity Outlook 2024. Retrieved from https://www3.weforum.org/docs/WEF_Global_Cybersecurity_Outlook_2024.pdf

World Economic Forum. (2024). World Economic Forum Global Risks Report 2024. Retrieved from https://www3.weforum.org/docs/WEF_The_Global_Risks_Report_2024.pdf

Wouda, H. P., & Opdenakker, R. (2019). Blockchain technology in commercial real estate transactions. *Journal of Property Investment & Finance*, 37(6), 570–579. DOI: 10.1108/JPIF-06-2019-0085

Wu, Q., Zhang, L., & Zhou, F. (2022). Cloud computing in the public sector: Benefits and challenges. *Journal of Public Sector Information Technology*, 14(1), 47–60. DOI: 10.1177/0193841X2090987

Xiang, Z., & Fesenmaier, D. R. (2017). Big data analytics, tourism design and smart tourism. In D. R. Xiang, Zheng, Fesenmaier (Eds.), *Analytics in Smart Tourism Design, Concepts and Methods*, pp. 299–307. Springer International Publishing Switzerland. DOI: 10.1007/978-3-319-44263-1_17

Xiao, M., Luo, S., & Yang, S. (2024). Synergizing technology and tradition: A pathway to intelligent village governance and sustainable rural development. *Journal of the Knowledge Economy*. Advance online publication. DOI: 10.1007/s13132-024-01937-6

Xia, Q. I., Sifah, E. B., Asamoah, K. O., Gao, J., Du, X., & Guizani, M. (2017). MeDShare: Trust-less medical data sharing among cloud service providers via blockchain. *IEEE Access : Practical Innovations, Open Solutions*, 5, 14757–14767. DOI: 10.1109/ACCESS.2017.2730843

Xu, J., Gao, X., Sorwar, G., & Croll, P. (2013). Implementation of e-health record systems in Australia. *The International Technology Management Review*, 3(2), 92–104. DOI: 10.2991/itmr.2013.3.2.3

Xu, X., Weber, I., & Staples, M. (2019). *Architecture for blockchain applications*. Springer. DOI: 10.1007/978-3-030-03035-3

Yaga, D., Mell, P., Roby, N., & Scarfone, K. (2019). Blockchain technology overview. *arXiv preprint arXiv:1906.11078*.

Yaiprasert, C., & Hidayanto, A. N. (2024). AI-powered ensemble machine learning to optimize cost strategies in logistics business. *International Journal of Information Management Data Insights*, 4(1), 100209. https://doi.org/https://doi.org/10.1016/j.jjimei.2023.100209. DOI: 10.1016/j.jjimei.2023.100209

Yallop, C. A., & Aliasghar, O. (2020). No business as usual: A case for data ethics and data governance in the age of coronavirus. *Online Information Review*, 44(6), 1217–1221. DOI: 10.1108/OIR-06-2020-0257

Yang, J., Kwon, Y., & Kim, D. (2021). Regional Smart City Development Focus: The South Korean National Strategic Smart City Program. *IEEE Access : Practical Innovations, Open Solutions*, 9, 7193–7210. DOI: 10.1109/ACCESS.2020.3047139

Yaqub, M. Z., & Alsabban, A. (2023). Industry-4.0-Enabled digital transformation: Prospects, instruments, challenges, and implications for business strategies. *Sustainability (Basel)*, 15(11), 8553. DOI: 10.3390/su15118553

Yen, C.-P., & Hung, T.-W. (2021). Achieving Equity with Predictive Policing Algorithms: A Social Safety Net Perspective. *Science and Engineering Ethics*, 27(3), 36. DOI: 10.1007/s11948-021-00312-x PMID: 34075448

Yu, L., & Li, Y. (2022). Artificial Intelligence Decision-Making Transparency and Employees' Trust: The Parallel Multiple Mediating Effect of Effectiveness and Discomfort. In *Behavioral Sciences* (Vol. 12, Issue 5). DOI: 10.3390/bs12050127

Yu, T.-C., Parng, I.-M., Yeh, J.-S., Cao, G.-W., & Wang, F.-C. (2023). A Digital Certificate System That Complies with International Standards: Taiwan Digital COVID-19 Certificate. *Standards 2023, Vol. 3, Pages 341-355, 3*(4), 341–355. DOI: 10.3390/standards3040024

Yun, J. Y., Sim, J. A., Lee, S., & Yun, Y. H. (2022). Stronger association of perceived health with socio-economic inequality during COVID-19 pandemic than pre-pandemic era. *BMC Public Health*, 22(1), 1–13. DOI: 10.1186/s12889-022-14176-8 PMID: 36114525

Yuvaraj, T. (2013). Modern Information Technologies: Their impact on Library Services. *Journal of Management Information Systems*, 11, 87–114.

Yuwono, E. I., Tjondronegoro, D., Riverola, C., & Loy, J. (2024). Co-creation in action: Bridging the knowledge gap in artificial intelligence among innovation champions. *Computers and Education: Artificial Intelligence*, 7(May), 100272. DOI: 10.1016/j.caeai.2024.100272

Yu, Z., Liang, Z., & Wu, P. (2021). How data shape actor relations in artificial intelligence innovation systems: An empirical observation from China. *Industrial and Corporate Change*, 30(1), 251–267. DOI: 10.1093/icc/dtaa063

Zajko, M. (2022). Artificial intelligence, algorithms, and social inequality: Sociological contributions to contemporary debates. *Sociology Compass*, 16(3), e12962. DOI: 10.1111/soc4.12962

Zandieh, S. O., Yoon-Flannery, K., Kuperman, G. J., Langsam, D. J., Hyman, D., & Kaushal, R. (2008). Challenges to EHR implementation in electronic-versus paper-based office practices. *Journal of General Internal Medicine*, 23(6), 755–761. DOI: 10.1007/s11606-008-0573-5 PMID: 18369679

Zeng, D., Cao, Z., & Neill, D. B. (2021). Artificial intelligence–enabled public health surveillance—from local detection to global epidemic monitoring and control. In *Artificial intelligence in medicine* (pp. 437–453). Academic Press. DOI: 10.1016/B978-0-12-821259-2.00022-3

Zevenbergen, J., De Vries, W., & Bennett, R. M. (Eds.). (2015). *Advances in responsible land administration*. CRC Press.

Zhang, P., Walker, M. A., White, J., Schmidt, D. C., & Lenz, G. (2017). Metrics for assessing blockchain-based healthcare decentralized apps. *2017 IEEE 19th International Conference on E-Health Networking, Applications and Services, Healthcom 2017, 2017-December*, 1–4. DOI: 10.1109/HealthCom.2017.8210842

Zhang, C., & Lu, Y. (2021). Study on artificial intelligence: The state of the art and future prospects. *Journal of Industrial Information Integration*, 23, 100224. DOI: 10.1016/j.jii.2021.100224

Zhang, P., Schmidt, D. C., White, J., & Lenz, G. (2018). Blockchain Technology Use Cases in Healthcare. *Advances in Computers*, 111, 1–41. DOI: 10.1016/bs.adcom.2018.03.006

Zhang, P., White, J., Schmidt, D. C., Lenz, G., & Rosenbloom, S. T. (2018). FHIRChain: Applying blockchain to securely and scalably share clinical data. *Computational and Structural Biotechnology Journal*, 16, 267–278. DOI: 10.1016/j.csbj.2018.07.004 PMID: 30108685

Zhang, S., Sun, Z., Fan, Z., & Weng, S. (2023). Transforming talent development: A reflective analysis of the innovative government-school cooperation model under the paradigm of knowledge innovation. *Journal of the Knowledge Economy*, 15(3), 15176–15201. Advance online publication. DOI: 10.1007/s13132-023-01677-z

Zhao, W., Yin, C., Hua, T., Meadows, M. E., Li, Y., Liu, Y., Cherubini, F., Pereira, P., & Fu, B. (2022). Achieving the Sustainable Development Goals in the Post-Pandemic Era. *Humanities & Social Sciences Communications*, 9(1), 258. Advance online publication. DOI: 10.1057/s41599-022-01283-5 PMID: 35967482

Zheng, Z., Xie, S., Dai, H., Chen, X., & Wang, H. (2017, June). *An overview of blockchain technology: Architecture, consensus, and future trends. In 2017 IEEE international congress on big data (BigData congress).* Ieee.

Zhong, W., Hu, Q., & Kapucu, N. (2022). Robust Crisis Communication in Turbulent Times: Conceptualization and Empirical Evidence From the United States. *Public Administration*. Advance online publication. DOI: 10.1111/padm.12855

Zhou, K. Z., & Li, C. B. (2012). How knowledge affects radical innovation: Knowledge base, market knowledge acquisition, and internal knowledge sharing. *Strategic Management Journal*, 33(9), 1090–1102. DOI: 10.1002/smj.1959

Zuiderwijk, A., Chen, Y. C., & Salem, F. (2021). Implications of the use of artificial intelligence in public governance: A systematic literature review and a research agenda. *Government Information Quarterly*, 38(3), 101577. DOI: 10.1016/j.giq.2021.101577

Zuo, B., & Huang, S. (2018). Revisiting the tourism-led economic growth hypothesis: The case of China. *Journal of Travel Research*, 57(2), 151–163. DOI: 10.1177/0047287516686725

About the Contributors

Miltiadis Lytras is a world-class expert in the fields of cognitive computing, information systems, digital transformation and smart cities, computers in human behavior, and knowledge management. He is an expert in advanced computer science and management, editor, lecturer, and research consultant, with extensive experience in academia and the business sector in Europe and Asia. He served as the Editor in Chief of the International Journal in Semantic Web and Information Systems. He has co-edited more than 110 high impact factor special issues in ISI/Scopus indexed journals and co-Edited/Authored more than 80 books in international publishers including Elsevier, Emerald, IGI-Global, Springer, etc. Dr Lytras has co-authored more than 120 high impact factor papers in Q1 and Q2, Web of Science and Scopus indexed Journals such as: ; Future Generation Computer Systems; Journal of Business Research; International Journal of Information Management; Journal of Innovation and Knowledge; Technological forecasting and Social Change, Computers in Human Behavior; Studies in Higher Education; Telematics and Informatics; Information Systems Management, IEEE Transactions on Knowledge and Data Engineering; IEEE Internet Computing; IEEE Transactions on Education; IEEE Access Journal of Ambient Technology and Humanized Computing; World Wide Web Journal;; IJ of Engineering Education; Journal of Universal Computer Science; Journal of Knowledge Management; British Journal on Education Technology; Interactive Learning Environment; Educational Technology and Society; Behavior and Information Technology, etc. Dr. Lytras has a 25 years' experience on Research and Development projects and grants with significant skills and competencies to the successful conceptualization, financing and implementation of R&D projects with extensive experience in Europe, Middle East, and Far East. He has involved in more than 70 R&D projects overtime.

Afnan Alkhaldi, the Acting Assistant Dean for the Arab Open University, is a distinguished academic and consultant with a profound impact on the development of Smart Cities and Information Systems. Her expertise is showcased through her significant role in consulting for Kuwait Economic Cities, particularly in the pioneering smart city project, Al-Hareer City. With a Ph.D. in operation and information management, she brings nearly a decade of experience to her field, emphasizing eGovernance and operational efficiencies. Dr. Afnan's innovative approach, coupled with her ability to effectively communicate and collaborate across diverse environments, positions her as a key figure in driving forward Kuwait's smart city initiatives.

Patricia Ordóñez de Pablos is a professor in the Department of Business Administration in the Faculty of Business and Economics at The University of Oviedo, Spain. She completed her education in The London School of Economics, UK. Her teaching and research interests focus on the areas of strategic management, knowledge management, organizational learning, intellectual capital and information technologies, with special interest in Asia (Bhutan, China, Myanmar). She is Editor-in-Chief of the International Journal of Learning and Intellectual Capital (IJLIC) and International Journal of Asian Business and Information Management (IJABIM), respectively. She has edited books for IGI Global, Elsevier, Routledge, and Springer. In 2021, 2022 and 2023, she earned placement on Stanford University's "Ranking of the World Scientists: World's Top 2% Scientists" list. Additionally she is listed in World Top Scientists of Research.com in the Areas of Social Science and Humanities in Spain and Engineering and Technology in Spain.

* * *

Bedour Alboloushi is an Assistant Professor of Business Management at Kuwait College of Science and Technology. She holds a PhD in Information Studies from the University of Sheffield, UK, and a Master's in Business Administration (MBA). Her research focuses on information systems, knowledge, and innovation management. She teaches a range of courses related to information systems and project management. She has considerable expertise in project management and is certified as a Project Management Professional (PMP) by the Project Management Institute.

Mohammad Albous is a highly motivated PhD candidate in Innovation Management at Arabian Gulf University. He specializes in innovation policy and has extensive experience in qualitative research methods, particularly grounded theory. His dissertation focuses on public sector innovation in Kuwait during and after crises, using grounded theory to explore the development of adaptability for future challenges. He also has research experience in the Kuwaiti banking sector and artificial intelligence (AI).

Shri Shubha Dattatreya Bahinipati is working as an officer of Odisha Administrative Service (OAS) cadre in Govt of Odisha. He is managing the operational aspect of various eGovernment initiatives of Revenue & DM Department. He worked as a software developer in few prestigious IT companies for 9 years before joining the Govt. Currently he is persuing PhD from Siksha 'O' Anusandhan Deemed to be University, Bhubaneswar, Odisha. He has done MTech in Computer Science & Engineering and MBA in Human Resource Management from BPUT, Odisha. His field of research interests are Artificial Intelligence, Blockchain and Cyber Security. He is associated with formulation of various data driven public policy.

Francis F. Balahadia is a Professor and the Dean of the College of Computer Studies at Laguna State Polytechnic University (LSPU). He serves as the ICT Cluster Representative for LSPU in STAARRDEC and is the Focal Person for the DOST SEI Scholarship at LSPU. He holds a Doctor of Information Technology from the University of the East-Manila. Dr. Balahadia has authored around 60 research papers, with nearly 30 published in refereed journals, 30 indexed in Scopus, and one ISI-indexed. He also chairs the committee responsible for establishing the LSPU Publication Office and its journal, the Journal of Interdisciplinary Science and Innovation Research (JISIR).

Mohammed Ali Berawi is a professor at the Department of Civil Engineering, Faculty of Engineering, Universitas Indonesia.

Eduardo Carlos Dittmar is an economist with a Ph.D. in Economic and Business Sciences. He has extensive teaching experience at both undergraduate and graduate levels and has presented his work at conferences worldwide. His research spans both foundational and applied studies, contributing over 40 indexed publications and book chapters to the field. He has been an active member of various research groups and has served on editorial committees for multiple academic journals. His academic interests include New Technologies, Strategic and Operational Marketing, Corporate Social Responsibility, and Business Ethics.

Meenakshi Gupta is working as an Associate Professor in the School of Economics, at Shri Mata Vaishno Devi University, Katra. She has teaching and research experience of almost 16 years. She has been a part of many academic and non- academic committees of the university since 2007. Her main areas of interest are Agricultural Economics, Environmental Economics and Development Economics. Her research work has been published in various national and international journals.

She has contributed to various books also. She has also presented various articles at National and International Conferences. She is also awarded with many prestigious national and international awards. She is a life Member of Indian Economic Association, Indian Society of Agri- business and Management, Indian Society of Agricultural Economics, TIES, AERA, etc.

MaryEbele Idahosa is a senior librarian in Benson Idahosa University Benin City and also a charter librarian (CLN). She has PhD in Library and Information Science, BSc in Accounting and OND in banking and Finance with others certifications. She is happily married with four children.

Vishal Jain is presently working as an Associate Professor at Department of Computer Science and Engineering, School of Engineering and Technology, Sharda University, Greater Noida, U. P. India. Before that, he has worked for several years as an Associate Professor at Bharati Vidyapeeth's Institute of Computer Applications and Management (BVICAM), New Delhi. He has more than 14 years of experience in the academics. He obtained Ph.D (CSE), M.Tech (CSE), MBA (HR), MCA, MCP and CCNA. He has authored more than 90 research papers in reputed conferences and journals, including Web of Science and Scopus. He has authored and edited more than 30 books with various reputed publishers, including Elsevier, Springer, Apple Academic Press, CRC, Taylor and Francis Group, Scrivener, Wiley, Emerald, NOVA Science and IGI-Global. His research areas include information retrieval, semantic web, ontology engineering, data mining, ad hoc networks, and sensor networks. He received a Young Active Member Award for the year 2012–13 from the Computer Society of India, Best Faculty Award for the year 2017 and Best Researcher Award for the year 2019 from BVICAM, New Delhi.

Ivan G. Liwanag has his Master's degree in Guidance and Counseling with a good background in psychology, group dynamics, and training for organizations. A strong teaching background has been developed while he teaches at the Don Honorio Ventura State University; he headed initiations on community services, leadership development, and interdisciplinary projects to focus on practical applications in social and industrial psychology. His technical experience includes psychometric testing, emergency response training, and gender equality and safety programs, reflecting his care for making the learning places safe, inclusive, and supportive.

David López Jiménez obtained his Law degree from the Complutense University of Madrid. He obtained one PhD (with European mention) from the Seville University and another PhD from the Rey Juan Carlos University. He has an Extraordinary Doctoral Award. He has leaded research stays in different European countries. He is the author of several monographs, some of them published by the prestigious publisher Thomson Reuters and Marcial Pons, as well as more than 200 publications in various scientific journals, book chapters, book reviews, and comments about national and international law.

Andréia de Bem Machado has a PhD in Engineering and Knowledge Management. Postdoctoral fellow at the Federal University of Santa Catarina. Evaluator of the National Institute of Educational Studies and Research Anísio Teixeira (Ministry of Education Brazil). She is an Ad Hoc evaluator of National and International Journals. Evaluator in the PNLD Infantile Education program. Consultant in the production of low vision UNESCO teaching material. She has been working in the educational field for over 25 years. She is part of the scientific committee of national and international journals. Currently the areas of study are: innovation, innovation in the public sector, entrepreneurship, smart cities, education, special education and digital pedagogical model. She likes to innovate in the art of researching and disseminating knowledge.

Jayson Magat is a dedicated public servant and entrepreneur with a passion for making a positive impact in his community. Balancing his professional commitments with a love for exploration, Jayson frequently embarks on travels to discover new places and cultures. His diverse experiences in both public service and business drive his commitment to innovation, leadership, and personal growth.

John Paul Miranda is an associate professor at Don Honorio Ventura State University. He is currently the international linkages and partnerships project head for the office for the international partnerships and programs of his university.

Morenikeji Abel Oke is a lecturer and researcher in the Department of Biological Sciences, Bamidele Olumilua University of Education, Science and Technology, Ikere-Ekiti, Ekiti State, Nigeria. His primary research cuts across Medical, Environmental, and Pharmaceutical Microbiology, Biotechnology, Nanotechnology and Nano-Oncology. He has published in reputable peer-reviewed journals and academic books. He has one registered accession of microbes with NCBI (USA). Oke is a Fellow of the Ife Institute of Advanced Studies (IIAS).

Muftau Kolawole Oladunmoye is a professor of pharmaceutical microbiology. His research focus is novel drug discovery and the characterisation of bioactive metabolites from plant and microorganism sources.

Busayo Olowe is a lecturer and researcher in the Department of Biological Sciences, Bamidele Olumilua University of Education Science and Technology,

Ikere Ekiti, Her research areas include water, environmental microbiology, and metagenomics.

Kehinde Adewole Oyeniran is a lecturer in the Department of Biological Sciences, Bamidele Olumilua University of Education Science and Technology, Ikere-Ekiti, and presently a postdoctoral fellow with the plant systems biology group, ICGEB Cape Town, South Africa. His multidisciplinary research combines bioinformatics and gold-standard wet-lab approaches to gain insights into the molecular mechanisms underlying pathogen emergence.

Olubukola Helen Oyeniran is a lecturer in the Department of Biochemistry, Federal University Oye-Ekti. Her research focus is on the use of plants as functional foods for management of degenerative diseases, using Drosophila melanogaster and Rattus norvegicus as study models.

Binod Kumar Pattanayak completed his M. S. in Computer Engineering in the year 1992 from NTU Kharkov Polytechnical Institute, Kharkov, USSR, Ph. D. in Computer Science and Engineering in the year 2011 from Siksha 'O' Anusandhan University, Bhubaneswar, India. He is currently working as a Professor in the Department of Computer Science and Engineering, Institute of Technical Education and Research, Siksha 'O' Anusandhan Deemed to be University, Bhubaneswar, India. His research interests include Internet of Things (IoT), Artificial Intelligence, Big Data Analytics and Cloud Computing. There are 238 research publications in journals and conferences of international repute to his credit. As many as 22 research scholars have been awarded with Ph. D. degree and 9 scholars are continuing their Ph. D. research work under his supervision. He has visited Build Bright University, Phnompenh, Cambodia and Universite des Mascareignes, Mauritius as a visiting professor. He belongs to the editorial boards of various reputed peer-reviewed international journals. He has edited one Springer Book. He has acted as General Chair, Program chair in various international conferences.

Nur Hairani Abd Rahman is a Senior Lecturer in Public Policy and Administration, contributing her expertise to Universiti Malaya since 2017. Armed with a Ph.D. in Public Policy from Universiti Sains Malaysia, a Master of Public Administration from Universiti Malaya, and a Bachelor of Social Science (Honours) from Universiti Kebangsaan Malaysia, Dr. Nur Hairani is a recognized authority in the intricate domains of social policy, encompassing social care, governance, social inclusion/exclusion, inequality, and wellbeing. Her influence goes beyond the classroom; she holds pivotal roles in academic editorial positions, currently serving as the Associate Editor for the Journal of Public Administration and Governance and as an Editorial Board Member for the Malaysian Journal of Social Sciences and

Humanities. As an esteemed member of the Social Policy Association in the United Kingdom, Dr. Nur Hairani's impact reverberates on an international scale. In addition to her academic role, Dr. Nur Hairani plays a significant part in administrative functions, including positions such as the Outbound Mobility Program Coordinator and Master of Public Administration Program Coordinator. Actively participating in various committees at both faculty and university levels, she contributes to policy development and implementation. At the national level, Dr. Nur Hairani is appointed as a Field Expert of the Malaysian Research and Development Classification System (MRDCS) by the Ministry of Science, Technology, and Innovation (MOSTI). Her expertise extends to consultancy roles for projects focused on poverty eradication, funded by the Economic Planning Unit of the Government of Malaysia. Her international experience includes a stint as a Visiting Scholar at the University of Messina, Sicily, Italy. In recognition of her outstanding contributions, Dr. Nur Hairani was honored with the Fulbright Scholar Program award in 2023, securing a position as a Visiting Scholar at the University of California, Berkeley, United States. Dr. Nur Hairani's dedication and excellence have earned her accolades such as the Excellent Service Award (2022) and the Certificate of Excellent Service (2021) from Universiti Malaya. Her impact in academia is underscored by the Best Presenter Award at the Asian Universities Alliance & Universitas Indonesia (2021). Recent publications in esteemed journals indexed in Web of Science and Scopus, including Public Policy and Administration and Ageing International, further highlight Dr. Nur Hairani's significant contributions to her field. For those seeking a highly accomplished professional with a proven track record, Dr. Nur Hairani Abd Rahman stands as an eminent figure in Public Policy and Administration. Connect with her via email at nurhairani@um.edu.my to discover the transformative possibilities she brings to academia.

Dharm Raj is currently working as Assistant Professor in CSE Department of Sharda University. He is gentle adept with technology and has integrated technology tools in the academic co-creation. He had successfully completed his various Academic Administration engagements in multiple roles at various organizations. He has institutionalized innovative system and process w.r.t. Academic Matters, Curriculum design, Examinations activities, Learner Affairs, Student Support in various capacities. He played Lead role played is policy creation, rules documentation along with ensuring statutory compliance. Dharm Raj has published/ presented 30 plus papers in various international and national journals/ conferences. He is senior member of IEEE, Life Member of CSI, ACM and other professional societies; contributing to the research communities by various volunteer activities.

Manmohan Rauthan is working as Head of the department and professor in HNB Garhwal University in computer science and engineering department with 30 years of teaching experience. He has done M.Tech in 1987 from Roorkee University and has done his Ph.D. from Kumaon University in 2013. He has written a several research paper as well as 5 books in computer science. He is a core member of research committees, visiting committees.

Cailvin Reyes is assistant professor at the Don Honorio Ventura State University where he teaches English specialized subjects and research subjects in teacher education programs. He earned his PhD in English Language Studies from the Bulacan State University. He has presented his research outputs to various national and international conferences. In addition, he has published research articles in the field of language education and preservice teaching in various international journals including scopus-indexed journals. In addition to his recent accomplishments, he was awarded the Foreign Language Teaching Assistant (FLTA) program of Fulbright Commission which will allow him to immerse himself in international foreign language teaching practices and explore U.S. society and culture at the Gonzaga University in Washington, USA from August 2024 to May 2025.

Mustika Sari is a lecturer at the Department of Civil Engineering, Faculty of Engineering, Universitas Indonesia. She is a senior researcher at the Center for Sustainable Infrastructure Development in Universitas Indonesia.

Gunawan Saroji is a senior researcher at the Center for Sustainable Infrastructure Development, Faculty of Engineering, Universitas Indonesia. He is a associate professor at the Department of Civil Engineering, Politeknik Negeri Bengkalis, Indonesia.

Ajay K. Singh is working as an Associate Professor (Research) in the Department of Humanities and Social Science, Graphic Era (Deemed to be University) Dehradun. He has worked as Assistant Professor (Economics) in the School of Liberal Arts & Management, DIT University Dehradun for 6 years. He did Post-Doctorate Research with EDI of India, Ahmedabad, Gujarat (India). He received MPhil (Economics) from DAVV Indore (India), and PhD (Economics) from IIT Indore (India. He has published several research papers in the diversified area such as climate change, agricultural productivity, assessment of food security; estimation of GFSI, development of environmental sustainability index (ESI) and its association with socio-economic indicators; measurement and determinants of entrepreneurship ecosystem, and dimension of sustainable development and its interlinkages with economic development.

Marlon Tayag is currently working at Holy Angel University, Angeles City as an Associate Professor-III. Teaching post-graduate and under-graduate studies. Has extensive experience in application development including desktop, web and mobile application (Android and iOS) multi platform environment. Work as the MIS Director for Systems Plus College Foundation in-charge of managing the day to day operation of the MIS Department and the school IT infrastructure. Had the pleasure of teaching at different colleges / universities that includes The Future University at Khartoum Sudan, University of the Assumption, Systems Plus College Foundation, Baliwag University and Angeles University Foundation as part-time instructor for under-graduate and guest lecturer for their post-graduate studies program.

Mobolaji Tenibiaje is a lecturer and researcher in the Department of Computing and Information Science, Bamidele Olumilua University of Education Science and Technology, Ikere-Ekiti. His research focus is the internet of things, big data, and machine learning.

Jenny Patricia Vargas Portillo is a PhD with the highest qualification, three master's degrees, an Advanced Studies Diploma and numerous specialization courses. The research carried out involves both basic and applied exploration. The lines she has been working involves, among others, Consumer Behavior, Marketing and New Technologies (Interactive Advertising and Electronic Commerce). She has been teaching and doing research in different countries of the world. She has been a professor at undergraduate and graduate levels. Likewise, she has directed a significant number of Bachelor and Master theses.

Jaymark A. Yambao is a dedicated educator with more than nine (9) years of experience in teaching Information Technology (IT) Education at various Universities and Colleges in Pampanga, Philippines. He finished his Master's degree at the age of 30 in System Plus College Foundation Main Campus in Angeles City on April 30, 2020, and is currently pursuing his Doctoral degree at the same school. He is passionate about advancing knowledge and innovation in IT education focusing on Software Engineering and Data Science.

Index

A

B

C

D

E

G

H

I

K

L

M

N

P

R

S

T

U

www.ingramcontent.com/pod-product-compliance
Lightning Source LLC
LaVergne TN
LVHW080356011026
849161LV00009B/2319